Odessa

Black Sea

VAKIA

UNGARY

• Budapest

RUMANIA

Bucharest •

Danube R.

Belgrade •

YUGOSLAVIA

Sofia •
BULGARIA

Istanbul
(Constantinople)

Ankara •

T U R K E Y

Adana •

• Aleppo

Sea

ALBANIA

GREECE

Aegean

Smyrna •

SYRIA

Athens •

CYPRUS

LEBANON
Beirut •

Sea

RHODES

ISRAEL

SICILY

CRETE

Jerusalem

MALTA

The Mediterranean

SUEZ
CANAL

Alexandria •

*Red
Sea*

oli

Benghazi •

Cairo •

UNITED ARAB
REPUBLIC
(EGYPT)

Nile R.

L I B Y A

A

R

A

A

THE MEDITERRANEAN

SUDAN

Mediterranean

Other books by Ernle Bradford

A Wind from the North
The Wind Off the Island
The Great Siege
Ulysses Found
The Wind Commands Me
The Sultan's Admiral

Ernle Bradford

MEDITERRANEAN
PORTRAIT OF A SEA

HARCOURT BRACE JOVANOVICH, INC.
New York

First American edition

ACKNOWLEDGMENTS

"The God Abandons Antony" by C. P. Cavafy is reprinted by permission of Deborah Rogers Ltd., London, on behalf of the Estate of Constantine Cavafy and Mrs. Singopoulo. The extracts by Denys Hay, William Culican, and Cyril Mango from *The Dawn of European Civilization: The Dark Ages* edited by David Talbot Rice, copyright Thames and Hudson 1965, are used with permission of McGraw-Hill Book Company, New York, and Thames and Hudson Ltd., London. The extracts from *A History of Europe* by H. A. L. Fisher, published by Houghton Mifflin Company, Boston, and Edward Arnold Publishers Ltd., London, are used by permission of Curtis Brown Ltd., London. The lines from "The Cuirassiers of the Frontier" by Robert Graves are from *Collected Poems 1955,* published by Doubleday & Company, Inc., New York, © 1955 by Robert Graves, and are reprinted by permission of Mr. Robert Graves and Collins-Knowlton-Wing, Inc., New York. The extracts from *The Greek View of Life* by G. L. Dickinson, published by Methuen & Co., Ltd., London, are reprinted by permission of A. B. P. International, London. The lines from Part IV "Death by Water" are from *The Waste Land* in *Collected Poems 1909-1962* by T. S. Eliot, copyright 1936, by Harcourt, Brace & World, Inc.; copyright, © 1963, 1964 by T. S. Eliot. Reprinted by permission of Harcourt Brace Jovanovich, Inc., New York, and Faber and Faber Ltd., London. The extracts from *The Mediterranean Lands,* by Marion I. Newbigin, published by Christophers, London, are used by permission of Chatto & Windus Ltd., London, and Alfred A. Knopf, Inc., New York. The extracts from Homer: *The Odyssey* translated by E. V. Rieu, published by Penguin Books Ltd., Harmondsworth, Middlesex, © E. V. Rieu 1946, and Herodotus: *The Histories* translated by Aubrey de Sélincourt, published by Penguin Books Ltd., © the Estate of Aubrey de Sélincourt 1954, are used by permission of Penguin Books Ltd. The extracts from *The Haven-Finding Art* by E. G. R. Taylor, published by Hollis & Carter Ltd., London, and American Elsevier Publishing Company, Inc., New York, are used by permission of the publishers. The extracts from *Nelson's Battles* by Oliver Warner, published by B. T. Batsford Ltd., London, © Oliver Warner 1965, are used by permission of B. T. Batsford Ltd. The extracts from *The Battle of Navarino* by C. M. Woodhouse, published by Dufour Editions, Inc., Chester Springs, Pa., and by Hodder and Stoughton Ltd., London, © C. M. Woodhouse 1965 are used by permission of Dufour Editions, Inc. and Hodder and Stoughton Ltd.

ISBN 0-15-158584-9
Library of Congress Catalog Card Number: 70-153682
Printed in the United States of America
A B C D E

Et dès lors, je me suis baigné dans le Poème
De la Mer, infusé d'astres, et lactescent,
Dévorant les azurs verts; où, flottaison blême
Et ravie, un noyé pensif parfois descend. . . .

And from then on I bathed in the Poem of the Sea,
Steeped with stars and foamy as milk,
Gorging myself on the green and blue; where,
Pallid and ruined flotsam,
A drowned and thoughtful man sometimes goes down. . . .

– ARTHUR RIMBAUD, *Le Bateau Ivre*

Preface

The conception of this book occurred several years ago, when I was talking with some students of the Royal University of Malta, one of whom complained that he could find few general works embracing the history of the Mediterranean. True enough, there were many thousands of volumes on every aspect of the nations, arts, and cultures that had arisen around this sea basin. There were also detailed treatises on everything from the rigging of Roman ships to the Etruscan art of granulation; but an overall portrait did not seem to exist. I have attempted here to fill this gap.

A portrait, of course, can never completely reveal the sitter and, indeed, is often as revelatory of the nature of the painter as of his subject. If one examines, for instance, the delineations of any famous historical character who sat to many artists, one finds that while all of them may combine to give a general idea of the appearance and even of the nature of the sitter, yet individually each reflects the bias of the painter – his particular interests perhaps, or his feelings towards his subject. It will therefore become evident that it is the sea and its ships, and the exercise of sea power in the long history of the Mediterranean, that occupy a large part of my foreground. At the same time I have tried to keep the broad sweep of historical events in perspective, as well as to show how cultures, races, and religions were affected by and related to one another. That the marine world is depicted in some detail is hardly surprising, since I have spent many years of my life wandering about these waters: firstly, under the compulsion of the Second World War; and secondly, in yachts and other small vessels, under the compulsion of love. To speak of love in the context of a particular sea is not irrational, for no one denies that love of country or of home are prime movers of mankind.

I saw the sea first at the age of nineteen from the foredeck of H.M.S. *Glenroy*, as we breasted out from the mouth of the Suez Canal into a long northerly swell, produced (though I did not know it then) by the prevailing midsummer wind in that part of the world. I was to spend most of the next four years here, first as a sailor and then as an officer. During that time I grew to know all the North African coast and much of the Aegean; as well as Malta, Sicily, and the coastlines of Italy, Corsica, and Sardinia. For a year I was the navigator of a destroyer – a lucky appointment, since it meant that I had to familiarize myself with innumerable charts of islands, coastlines, ports, and harbours; many of which I was to see years later under happier circumstances. But, even if the war had not brought me to the Mediterranean, I had long ago determined to come here at the first opportunity. A classical education, coupled with a youthful ambition to be either a painter or an archaeologist, had long centred my ambitions upon this area of the world.

Years spent in ships based on Alexandria – at that time a most cosmopolitan city – gave me an acquaintanceship with the harsh face of the world. So, too, did the war, but that seemed contained in its own special iron box, which had little or no relation to real life. Alexandria, however, was real enough; and life as it was lived there among the poor was a revelation to a young man who had been brought up in a secure home in the comfortable nursery-land of England. Under the vivid Egyptian sky, a far remove from the half-tones of my own country, the human condition was seen as a stark contrast of black and white. I saw, for instance, a man fall dead in a street, and the robed crowd pass him with indifference and leave him where he lay. In a side alley off the Rue Ras El Tin I saw a woman assisted by an old crone giving birth in the shadow of a mouldering doorway. On another occasion in the same area, I came across a dead donkey lying in the street. A butcher was cutting it up where it lay, his bare arms bright with blood, and his two-foot-long knife shining as he plunged it into the carcass. Neither the beginnings, nor the ends, nor the sustenance of life were concealed here under a discreet mask. The sun revealed everything. It was as if misty veils – similar to those that so often hide the English countryside – had suddenly lifted from my eyes. The marble sculptures that I had seen at the British Museum, with their honey-coloured reticence, were a far remove from this world. Now I understood, for the first time, why the Greeks had painted their statues and temples in bright primary colours. The air, the light, the sky, and the sea itself all demanded a violent radiance and even an element of visual vulgarity that would have been out of place in the North.

To compensate, as it were, for a certain fear that the city inspired, it had architectural graces; as well as colours, lights, and an immense clashing vitality that was unlike anything I had ever known. (I was to find out in later years that many Mediterranean cities from Barcelona to Istanbul were similar in these characteristics.) It had, too, bougain-villaeas plunging over dazzling white walls, the scent of gardenias in the evening (when the heat of the day had faded and a damp air was breathing off Lake Mareotis), and in summer the rustle of the wind from the north that made life supportable in the ancient city. Walking back one dawn after a night ashore, the sky tinged with apricot, the smells of the city erased by the dewfall, I heard the voice of the muezzin praising the perfection of God, "The One, The Forever Existing, The Almighty." I had then one of those moments of revelation which can sometimes change a life. I knew that I had "come home": not just to this city or this country, but to the whole of this sea. Since those days I have travelled and worked in many other seas and lands, but all my absences from the Mediterranean have been exiles. "The grand object of all travel," in Dr. Johnson's words, "is to see the shores of the Mediterranean," and he also concluded that "the man is little to be envied whose patriotism would not gain force upon the plain of Marathon, or whose piety would not grow warmer among the ruins of Ionia."

There is no other area of the world to equal this for the number of cultures and civilizations that have sprung from its shores, and that have moved across its almost tideless waters to cross-fertilize one another. Its richness stems largely from the fact that the sea is almost totally enclosed by three continents, which has led to a constant inter-action between the races inhabiting them. There have, indeed, been long centuries when it has been dormant, like a field left fallow, but these have always been succeeded by periods of great activity. As I write, the area is once again stirring uneasily as violence flares in the Near East, and as the fleets of the two major world powers, America and Russia, dispute for influence over the inhabitants of this ever-disputed basin. But, quite apart from the conflict between nations which has characterized this sea, the Mediterranean also celebrates the continuity of man. Although a transistor radio now keeps him com-pany, the fisherman who squats on the remains of a mediaeval quay still makes his delicate cane fish-traps just as they have been made since the fleets of Rome and Carthage struggled here for the mastery of the world.

It only remains to thank innumerable friends and acquaintances over the years who have helped me with their knowledge and enthusiasm. I owe a debt of thanks to the London Library, the Royal Malta Library, and Malta University Library; and also to Mr. Stewart Perowne and Mr. A. R. Burn, who were kind enough to read the book in manuscript form. The emendations and improvements are theirs, the errors and omissions remain mine. Finally, I dedicate it to the memory of Mrs. Freda MacIver-Reitsma – traveller. It was she who, many years ago, first inspired in a small boy the desire to sail this sea and to know these lands.

Kalkara, Malta   E.B.
1970

Contents

Maps

by Vaughn Gray

Illustrations

BOOK I

Καὶ τότε κοινὸν περὶ τὴν ἁλιείαν ἔχοντες ἔργον ἐν λόγοις ἦσαν, θαυμάζοντες τῆς θαλάσσης τὴν εὐφυΐαν καὶ τῶν χωρίων τὴν κατασκευήν.

And so now, as they were busy together with their fishing, they conversed, expressing their admiration of the richness of the sea and the character of the adjacent lands.

– Plutarch, *Lives: Timoleon*

ONE

An Island

It lifts abruptly out of the sea. It is unimportant in the world, unknown even to many of the inhabitants of Sicily, only seven miles to the east across the wind-freckled strait. Its name is Levanzo, and it is one of the small Aegadian group (three islands, several islets, and uninhabited rocks) which lies off the western coast of Sicily.

There is nothing about Levanzo to arouse much interest or curiosity. Its bald head, covered in spring and autumn with thin grass, moss, and lichen, is just over nine hundred feet high. Fringed with cliffs on almost all sides, Levanzo is pear-shaped; the tip of the fruit points to the north. It is largely barren, but in some sheltered folds of ground the vine is cultivated. There are also a few citrus trees. Other than these, only a rare and hardy olive hangs like a muscled wrestler to a shoulder of bare land, or a carob tree casts its dense evergreen shade. The prickly pear springs wild all over the harsh slopes of the island. Prickly pears, the "figs of India" as they are called, are comparatively new to the island. They reached the Mediterranean after Columbus' discovery of America, when they, as well as other more useful plants and vegetables, were brought back to Europe by the seamen and merchants who pioneered the early voyages of exploration.

Levanzo is only two miles long by one and a half miles at its widest point. This is the base of the pear, where its single village hides under the protective spine of the limestone hill that forms the island's peak. There are about three hundred inhabitants. They live off the sea – as well as the land. Often in winter they are cut off from the ports of Trapani and Marsala across the strait. They speak a broad dialect of Italian, and their way of life can have changed little since the first Phoenician and Greek traders came this way and used the two small anchorages as ports of call.

These are called Cala Fredda and Cala Dogana, the Cold Harbour and the Customs Harbour. The words explain a great deal, for *cala* is Arabic for an inlet or harbour, and *fredda* means cold in Sicilian. The Cold Harbour is where a strong current sets in throughout the winter months. This, then, is an old name – a fisherman's name that may well go back through all the vicissitudes of language for two thousand years. There are good lobsters in Cala Fredda, and always plenty of grey mullet and rock fish. Cala Dogana is the place where the customs officers live, in a small house overlooking the only village. The name is of comparatively modern origin. It is probably no older than the nineteenth century, dating from the post-Garibaldi period, when the reunification of Italy enabled a northern Italian bureaucracy to settle its agents as far afield as this remote island. On the other hand, it is possible that in the settled days of the Roman Empire one or two lonely customs officers would have been found living in Cala Dogana. In any case, in the names of these coves exists the evidence of a marriage between two worlds, the East and the West, the Arabic and the Latin. The Mediterranean is the sea where two worlds meet.

The village at Cala Dogana has three small stores. In one of them there is a bar. There is also a Catholic church and a small graveyard. Nearly all the population of the island lives in the village, and like the island itself, it is a microcosm of the whole world.

The island, with its silver slopes, its wind-washed ridges, its vines, olives, sparse soil, and well-fished shores, also mirrors the Mediterranean. In the blood of its few inhabitants run many strains: Phoenician, Greek, Roman, Arabic, Norman. Other passing sailors and travellers have no doubt added their share.

The island has no history. That is, unless one remembers that it belongs to this small group known as Aegadian – a word which stems from the Greek name Aegates, Goat Islands. Odysseus came this way on his long wandering back from the Trojan War. Driven westwards across the Mediterranean, while trying to double Cape Matapan and make his way home to Ithaca, he touched first at Djerba off the Tunisian coast. Then he made his way north, following the steady gleam of Polaris, the North Star, one of the few navigational aids known in his time. By sheer accident he came across the Goat Islands.

" 'Some god must have guided us through the murky night, for it

was impossible to see ahead. The ships were in a thick fog, and overhead not a gleam of light came through from the moon, which was
obscured by clouds. In these circumstances not a man among us caught
sight of the island nor did we even see the long rollers beating up to the
coast, before our good ships ran aground.' "

The island where Odysseus and his squadron found themselves was
almost certainly Favignana, three miles south of Levanzo. Out of the
three Aegadian islands, this is the only one where limestone ledges and
sandy beaches lie on the southern shore, and Odysseus was approaching
from the south. Both Marettimo and Levanzo are steep and precipitous, presenting an iron-bound coast for the careless mariner.

Looking almost due east from Levanzo, the massive bulk of Mount
Erice swells up from the Sicilian shores like a giant – grey in the early
morning, when the sun rises behind the mountain, and golden and
purple in the evening. The land of the Cyclops! Mount Erice, the
ancient Eryx, standing two and a half thousand feet out of the fertile
plains of western Sicily, dominates the whole of this corner of the world.
The people of Levanzo use it as their barometer, they know from the
way clouds fly across it, or hide its head, or huddle round its feet, what
kind of weather the day will bring. The fishermen use it as their landmark when working away from the island. No doubt, Odysseus, too,
like countless other mariners in later centuries, found Erice's peak a
guide and a comfort when sailing round these shores.

There are no temples, no Greek or Roman buildings on Levanzo, no
evidence that the classical world ever existed. Sometimes the fishermen
come in with amphorae in their nets, and occasionally a farmer clearing
the ground brings up a broken potsherd, but in the Mediterranean these
slender evidences of antiquity are hardly important. Yet Erice, glower-
ing and proud across the strait, is an ever-present reminder that, long
before the twentieth century, there were other centuries, other men,
and other cultures. Looking across from Levanzo shortly after sunrise
one can see, etched like dark fangs, the outline of the crenellated walls
that show the Normans once held this mountaintop as part of their
Sicilian fortress system. But long before the Normans, Erice's giant
Cyclopean walls were built by those early Sicilians who were in possession of these heights even before Odysseus came sailing this sea. There
the Phoenicians built a temple to Astarte, goddess of love, and there –

inspired by this giant breast of the earth – the Greeks built their temple to Aphrodite and the Romans their shrine to Venus. Now, in the Norman cathedral that fronts the blue strait and the offshore islands, the Madonna, Star of the Sea, comforts Her worshippers. Descendants of the sacred doves of a more sensual goddess than the Virgin rise in startled flights over the ancient walls and circle the cathedral towers whenever the bell rings for Angelus.

In the shimmering strait between Levanzo and Mount Erice lie the Formica, Porcelli, and Asinelli rocks – all that remains, as the locals will tell you, of the giant boulders which the blinded Cyclops, Polyphemus, tore from the mountain and hurled at Odysseus. And who can blame Polyphemus? The arrogance of Odysseus was one of his least attractive features. " 'Cyclops, if anyone ever asks you how you came by your unsightly blindness, tell him your eye was put out by Odysseus, Sacker of Cities, the son of Laertes, who lives in Ithaca.' "

Larger than Levanzo, but even more remote and inaccessible, is the third island in the Aegadian group, Marettimo. Here there are no harbours, coves, or any inlets at all. Only one small landing place on the northern coast permits the visitor, in clement weather, to make the shore. The Greeks called Marettimo "Holy Island", perhaps because on the long voyage westwards to Gibraltar it was their last stopping place after leaving Sicily. Furthermore, the Greeks had an intuitive genius for the "feel" of a place, and this westernmost of the Aegadian Islands has that cool and pure quality which man has always associated with holiness. The Phoenicians came here before the Greeks, as the rock-cut tombs in Mount Falcone bear witness. Like similar rock tombs in Malta and other Mediterranean islands, these silent hollows of darkness are a memorial to those early navigators who did not complete their voyages. In Tyre and Sidon, and in Carthage, wives and children waited for the merchants and mariners who never returned.

The small fishing boats in Levanzo still bear upon their bows the *Oculus*, or Eye of Horus. This, too, is a Phoenician legacy, for they first brought out of the East this device which they themselves had copied from the Egyptians. Long before the Phoenicians, even, had learned to venture upon this sea, the great Nile barges of the Upper and Lower Kingdoms of Egypt had swung down the lazy current of their parent river with the eye of the Hawk God to guard and guide them on their way. In Malta, once a Phoenician colony, they still paint eyes upon their small fishing boats: but no fisherman can tell you why.

Even remote, small, and unimportant Levanzo has its secret. On the west coast of the island, where the cliffs fall almost sheer into the sea, there are several caves. One of them, large enough for Polyphemus, is claimed by the locals as having been the giant's home; they dismiss Erice across the strait with ill-concealed scorn. But this vast cave, home of innumerable bats and used sometimes as a store by farmers, has little to command the world's attention. Further round the coast, inaccessible unless one approaches it by boat, lies Levanzo's real claim to fame.

In 1949 an Italian lady holidaying on the island heard a confused story about a haunted cave – "truly a cave of ghosts". It had long been spoken of, but only recently a man had rediscovered it when his dog had chased a rabbit into the cave's inconspicuous mouth. (Rabbits are the largest wild animals to be found on Levanzo, whose barren slopes can scarcely support even the hardy Mediterranean goat.) Intrigued by the story, the visitor found the man and arranged for him to take her to this mysterious cave.

Her discoveries there gave back to the world a lost treasure. The entrance to the cave is beneath a low ledge, so that it is necessary to get down on all fours to creep in under the glowing fangs of stalactites. Inside all is silence and darkness, until the torch's beam reveals the lines of bats hanging from the roof, rustling uneasily like dry leaves as the light plays over them. Deeper and deeper into the cave, and then the light uncovers the "ghosts". There on the stained limestone walls flicker figures of men and beasts. Deer run in herds, bulls arch their crested, muscular necks, and the men pursue with their spears or lie in wait with their nets.

The cave paintings of Levanzo are similar to those at Lascaux and Altamira. The hunters are all conspicuously male; pictured, most of them, as if they had three legs. There are also a number of figures which seem more like idols (though they may be priests), and these too are as ithyphallic as any Garden God of the classical world. One mysterious female figure in the recesses of the cave, painted with what appears to be white clay, seems to foreshadow the White Goddess, or perhaps that mighty Earth Mother whose worship was later to dominate the Mediterranean basin. She gives the cave of Levanzo an unusual distinction, for female figures are rare in prehistoric art. Some of the figures of men and beasts are painted, and some are incised in the limestone walls. And with what magnificent nonchalance did the artists, totally secure in their grasp of a bull's outline or the action of a running deer, scratch at one sweep these lines that catch the animal's totality!

Peering out from the cave's narrow mouth, down over the harsh incline to the wrinkled Mediterranean, the real impact of the drawings strikes home. If Levanzo is so small that it can now support only rabbits, whence comes all this portraiture of bulls and deer?

The mouth of the cave, lodged almost on the peak of the island, was once the summit of a lofty mountain that rose out of rich lowlands. The ancestor of Mediterranean man, who used this cave-shrine for his hunting and fertility magic, looked down from here not on the sea but on endless acres of fertile land running all the way south to Africa. Levanzo was then joined to Sicily, and Sicily to Italy. Down there, in that immense plain, ran the wild herds upon which man the hunter preyed.

The peak of Levanzo, under which the cave is sited, is 912 feet above sea level. The strait between the island and Sicily has an average depth of about 20 fathoms, or 120 feet. On that side, the mountain, like the other two Aegadian islands, formed part of the foothills to Mount Erice. But on the western side, and to the south of the islands, the sea plunges down rapidly to 600 feet or more. The cave painters who caused their magic to flower on these walls looked down from a height of 1500 feet on the lowlands, where, invisible to the men making their pictured dreams of death and fertility, the beasts roamed freely between Africa and Europe.

In spring the island still has its magic. For a brief month, all the scarred slopes and even the bare head of the ancient mountain are carpeted with wild flowers. Daisies enamel the thin grass, and wild orchids and marigolds, white, purple, and pale blue thistles, the blue anchusa, and the minute wild iris grow everywhere. The Mediterranean spring is beautiful but brief. Soon comes the season of *la grande chaleur*, the hot cloudless days, tempered occasionally by the summer north-westerlies; but often unbroken by anything except errant drifts of land and sea breezes for days on end. The fruit ripens on the fig trees, whose rock-splitting roots dive deeper and deeper for moisture. All over the island the dark red, orange, and yellow "figs of India" glow on the fleshy fans of the prickly pear.

The autumn is heralded by dark nimbus clouds swaggering over the head of Mount Erice. The first rain for many months begins to fall just about the time of the vintage. Even Levanzo makes its own wine, and on the farm that lies above a miniature valley they are carrying baskets of grapes on their heads. The women pick and carry, but the mystery of Dionysus is nowadays a male rite. A young man springs into a huge cask and begins treading the grapes. He is joined by two others. They wear nothing except their drawers, and soon these and the men's bodies are stained purple by the bubbling must. In another corner of the barn a scientific device as old as Archimedes is being employed: a large hand-operated press that has replaced the jumping feet of men. Every now and then, one of the treaders lifts himself clear of the vat, runs across the floor, and stands while a hose is played over him. The water not only cleans off the stain, the sweat, and the grape skins, but it clears his head from the rising fumes.

The pure grape juice spurts from a spigot at the base of the barrel and runs down a stone channel into a vat beneath the floor. It tastes delicious, all the sun and the earth and the sea wind in its clean astringency, but even a single glassful is a remarkable aperient. Tomorrow the men will begin adding the pure cane sugar to the vat of grape juice, and the process of fermentation will begin. Nowadays the men cross themselves before beginning the grape-treading. The Blessed Virgin is invoked, where once it was the long-locked Dionysus. But he, too, came out of the East.

Outside the barn a few idlers rest in the shade of a carob tree. It is one of the few trees in this part of the world to give shade all summer long. Its dark, shining evergreen leaves are a blessing to the traveller, while its leathery, brown pods feed both cattle and the very poor. These are the "husks" that the prodigal son was glad to eat, and are most probably the "locusts" that sustained John the Baptist. (It is also known as the locust bean.) From the fruit of the carob tree is derived the jeweller's weight, a "carat". Keration, as the ancient Greeks called it, was the weight of one-third of an obol: that small coin which closed the eyelids of the dead and provided the fee for Charon, the ferryman. The carob is one of the oldest trees in the world. The sole survivor throughout the ice ages from Tertiary times, it comes from very ancient stock. It is the unique species in the genus *Caratonia*.

The autumn in Levanzo is also a busy time for the fishermen, who must now make all the catches they can before the hostility of winter gales forces them to drag their small boats ashore. The sea around the island, and between it and Sicily, has been overfished for centuries, and catches are often sparse. But no legislation can prevent men who need to eat and who have families to support from using undersized mesh in their nets, or from tossing occasional cigarette tins stuffed with dynamite over the sides of their boats or off a rock. The water shudders as these primitive depth charges explode, and the stunned fish float belly upwards to the surface.

Generally speaking, though – and the *carabinieri* from their vantage points round the islands help to enforce a respect for the regulations – the fishermen work hard and honestly for their daily bread. In the autumn, the lobster pots with their bobbing cork floats are laid in the coves. Almost as delicate as lace, the beehive-shaped Mediterranean pots will not stand up to the storms of winter, so now, in the fall of the year, the last of the crustaceans must be gathered in.

The *Unione*, a small, open power boat, capable of operating a simple side-trawl, is busy around Levanzo. Other smaller boats are out line-fishing. In some of the coves they are setting seine nets, the floats bobbing on the surface, the nets hanging down vertically in the water, while the men haul in the constricting semicircle to trap any fish that the inlet contains. Youths dive for octopus, offering their arms and legs as moving bait to the gently waving tentacles that brush out from underwater holes in the rocks. Unworried by the clamping arms that slide like snakes over their bodies, they bring the octopus to the surface. With a quick twist of their wrists they turn the octopus-hood inside out, exposing its parrotlike beak, and fling it into a basket lined with seaweed, before diving again. Later in the evening, they can be seen beating octopus against a rock or pummelling the tentacles and body with a stone to tenderize the flesh.

In winter the straits between here and Sicily can rage with broken water. The soft and humid sirocco which prevails in the autumn months, bringing all the dampness of the summer-heated sea on its furnace-mouth from Africa, is displaced by westerlies and roaring northerlies. While the fishermen stay idle at home or sit over glasses of wine (or coffee with two or three drops of anise), the farmers are busy. Soon after the first rains of autumn the land comes alive again, and in the few cultivated areas wheat and barley are sown. Unlike winter in northern lands, winter in the Mediterranean is an active time for the farmer. The summer, with its "Lion Sun", is the time when the land goes to rest and the farmer sits part idle. August, with its blazing heat, is as useless to him as are the frost and snows of February to the northern farmer.

Even in winter the fishermen will sometimes find it worthwhile to launch their boats. Occasionally, for a period of ten days or more between January and March, the sea will become misted with calm – and the fish are still there, as at all times of the year. Three times a week, the ferry calls in from Sicily. Manufactured goods, items of clothing, sweetmeats, meat itself, vegetables, and minor luxuries such as chestnuts are landed at the small jetty. But when the sea booms fiercely through the narrow strait, the islanders are cut off entirely from the outside world. The police transmitting station is available to send out emergency calls, but the gravely ill and women soon due to give birth are sent across to Trapani in advance of winter. Bottled gas has replaced the old charcoal or brush-fired stoves which, until recent years, were the islanders' only means of baking bread, grilling fish, or roasting meat. Canned goods have provided a useful standby against the rigours of the brief winter. Meanwhile, transistor radios play the music of the world beyond the water.

TWO

The Sea and the Land

The Mediterranean Sea, which is bounded on the north by Europe, on the south by Africa, and to the east by Asia, occupies a deep trench between the continents. From Gibraltar to Syria the maximum length is about 2200 miles. The maximum width, from north to south, between France and Algeria, is 488 miles. Shaped somewhat like a horizontal sea-horse, the Mediterranean has at its north-eastern extremity the oyster-shaped appendage of the Black Sea. Including the latter, its total area is 1,158,300 square miles. Small compared to the great oceans of the world, it contains a greater range of peoples, cultures, and meteorological and geographical differences than any other comparable area.

It is the largest existing fragment of the immense ocean which geologists call Tethys. Tethys in Greek mythology was the daughter of the sky and the earth. She was married to Oceanus, the mighty ocean god who was believed to encircle the whole earth. In geological terms, Tethys was an ocean which covered the whole area of the ancient world, or nearly half the globe, from late Carboniferous to early Tertiary times. Standing on the lava-darkened slopes of Mount Etna, over two thousand feet above the modern Mediterranean, one can pick up fossil shells to prove that even this land, which has now soared to become the highest active volcano in Europe, was once below the deep waters of Tethys. The lands of the Mediterranean have struggled upwards with the crumpling of the earth's crust, and in many places they are still volcanic.

The sea has many faces. Within its comparatively small area it can boast as great a range of character as the cultures which have arisen on the shores that bound it. It is in more senses than one a Janus, a two-faced god, for it falls geographically into two main sections: the western and the eastern basins. The western Mediterranean, the area from Gibraltar to Malta and Sicily, is separated from the eastern by a submerged ridge on which the Maltese islands stand. This now hidden land once joined Europe to North Africa, and on either side of it – long after the ocean Tethys had receded – there probably lay two great lakes. The skeletons of miniature elephants found in Ghar Dalam (Cave of Darkness) in Malta certainly suggest that the two continents were once united. J. D. Evans, in *Malta*, a study of the island in prehistoric times, writes: "Three species of elephants have been distinguished according to size, the smallest being only 3 feet high. . . . Similar, though not identical, dwarf elephants have been found in deposits in other islands of the Mediterranean, such as Sicily, Sardinia, Crete and Cyprus. In some stratified sites it can be demonstrated that the smaller ones are later than the larger ones, because they are found higher up in the deposits. A plausible explanation of this is that a number of beasts of normal size were trapped on the newly formed islands and that their descendants decreased in size owing to a scarcity of fodder and worsening conditions generally. This hypothesis also has the merit of explaining why species of dwarf animals found on different islands are not identical, since they would have developed in isolation from each other, though along roughly parallel lines."

At some unknown point in time (but one which has persisted in man's memory), the land bridge which connected Africa with Spain at the Strait of Gibraltar was broken through and the ocean roared in, flooding first the western lake, then overrunning the land between Sicily and North Africa (marooning small islands like Levanzo, Malta, and Gozo), and finally uniting the western lake with the eastern to form what is now the Mediterranean Sea. This event, so momentous to the human race, is remembered in the Greek legend of Deucalion and possibly in the story of Noah in the Bible: "All the fountains of the great deep were broken up, and the windows of heaven were opened."

The Strait of Gibraltar was known to the Romans as the Pillars of Hercules because, in Greek legend, it was supposedly the hero Hercules who forced the continents apart. Afterwards he set up his two "pillars", the rock of Gibraltar to the north and the rock of Ceuta to the south.

This one-time land bridge, then, between Europe and Africa forms the basic dividing line of the Mediterranean Sea. The eastern basin, or more correctly the south-eastern, is all that area from Syria to Sicily and Malta. The biographer of Saint Paul, who was shipwrecked on the island of Malta, was geographically accurate when he wrote in The Acts of the Apostles, "And falling into a place where two seas met, they ran the ship aground. . . ." The Apostle was shipwrecked at the north-eastern end of Malta near the Malta-Gozo Channel and this is the place where the "two seas", the eastern and the western Mediterranean, do indeed meet.

The great Viennese geologist Eduard Suess in his book *The Face of the Earth*, in a definition of the Mediterranean, divides it into four distinct physical regions. Apart from the western basin, the other three are: the Adriatic; the area from Crete and Cyprus northwards through the Aegean and including the Black Sea; and the coastal region of North Africa westwards from Syria including the Gulf of Sirte.

To the mariner, the Mediterranean is divided into a number of minor "seas". There is the Balearic, between the Balearic Islands and the coast of Spain; and the Ligurian, between the Balearics and Corsica, bounded on the north by the coasts of France and Italy. Then there is the triangular Tyrrhenian, bounded by the northern coast of Sicily, the eastern coasts of Sardinia and Corsica, and the western coasts of Italy. Between Italy and Yugoslavia there lies the Adriatic. Between Sicily, southern Italy, and western Greece there is the Ionian; and between Greece and Turkey there is the island-studded Aegean.

Geographers may make their precise and scientific definitions, but sailors know by the palms of their hands the feel and the quality of these individual seas. Each region of the Mediterranean does indeed have a distinctive character of its own, one being more prone to violence, one more tranquil, one reliable but occasionally subject to fits of passion, and yet another being a dangerous schizophrenic. The Gulf of Lions and the Adriatic, for example, are both dangerous and violent areas when the north wind assails them. In the Gulf of Lions, this is the roaring mistral, the north-westerly gale-force wind that screams down from the Rhône valley and splinters the whole sea southwards as far as the Balearics. Even large modern vessels can be endangered by a heavy mistral. The scourge of the Adriatic is the bora, a cold dry wind from the north-east which can reach hurricane force – sometimes with gusts of over 110 knots. When the bora blows full force, the authorities are forced to erect life-lines in the city of Trieste, so that the inhabitants can get about the streets without being bowled over.

A more tranquil sea is the Ionian, which, in the summer months at any rate, is often varnished with calm for weeks on end. It was this fact that enabled the Greeks to expand their civilization so easily from the mainland of Greece to Sicily and Magna Graecia (Great Greece, or southern Italy). Only in winter does the Ionian burst into fury. Then the savage north-easter, the gregale, or Greek wind, leaps down from the mountains of Greece and Yugoslavia and piles up the seas all the way to the island of Djerba and the North African coast.

"Reliable but subject to fits of passion" is a description that might well be applied to the Aegean Sea. This is the only area in the Mediterranean where the sailor can be sure of regular winds throughout the summer months. These are always from the north, and are known as the etesian winds (Greek *etos*, a year, meaning reliable every year). Colloquially they are called the meltemi (possibly a corruption of the Venetian *bel tempo*, the time of good weather).

Henry Denham, an experienced navigator in these seas, makes this comment in his book *The Aegean*: "It may be expected to start each day towards noon, reaching a velocity of force 5 to 6 and sometimes 7 by afternoon, and falling off towards evening. Quite often, without warning, it blows all night without diminishing in strength." Usually, however, the small-boat sailor can be confident that it will decline after sunset, although a heavy swell will still keep rolling down from the north.

The meltemi blows all the way down the Aegean and south of Crete as far as Alexandria. This was the wind that nourished Greek navigation – giving the merchants a favourable beam wind between Greece and Asia and a happy stern wind when running down the Aegean. As their trade expanded, it also enabled them to sail easily to Egypt in the summer. They then waited at Alexandria or in the Nile mouth until spring, when, with sail and oar, they were able to return again to Greece and its islands. The Aegean, however, although reliable for its summer wind, can also be "subject to fits of passion". On the lee side of the islands, where the sailor ignorant of local conditions might well expect to find some shelter for his boat, the wind, instead of passing harmlessly overhead, leaps down in terrific squalls. Black squalls, those associated with passing thunderstorms, are easy enough to avoid, for the indigo cloud looming up over an island can be seen at once; at the same time there is lightning and the air tingles with ozone. But the white squalls are more dangerous, for there is no indication of their approach. They are called "white" because only by their scurrying feet can the sailor see them coming. They scream out of a clear and cloudless sky, where the meltemi has sheered up over an island, and then drop with savage violence on the unsuspecting sailor.

Quite unlike the comparatively stable Aegean, however, is that "dangerous schizophrenic" area of sea along the coast of Algeria and Tunisia. From Gibraltar to Cape Bon and the end of the western Mediterranean, the North African coastline has been the graveyard of innumerable ships and even of whole fleets. When a depression moves eastwards through the Strait of Gibraltar, or across southern Spain, it causes strong gales from west or north-west along this whole section of the African coast. The mariner caught out at sea finds himself on an implacably hostile lee shore. As the cold front of the depression passes over the Algerian coastline the westerly increases to gale force and then, as the front passes, switches to north-westerly. Often, with the approach of a secondary cold front, the whole process will be repeated. This is why these shores are littered with the bones of sunk ships from classical times right up to the present day. In the sixteenth century, the Spaniards lost several fleets under these conditions during their conflict with the Moslem state of Algeria. In 1541 a large Spanish invasion fleet was almost entirely destroyed in one of the worst maritime disasters in history, when it was caught off Algiers under just these weather conditions. Many galleys, 150 sailing galleons carrying eight thousand troops, together with the flower of the Spanish nobility, perished in this famous gale – referred to ever afterwards by the Algerian Turks as "Charles' Gale". The Emperor Charles V, contemplating the ruin of his fleet and army, is said to have bowed his head and cried, "Thy will be done!"

A sea, then, of many moods and a wide variety of weather conditions, the Mediterranean even meteorologically cannot be summed up easily. In some of the shallow areas, such as the Sicily–Malta Channel, which is only forty-five miles wide and nowhere deeper than one hundred fathoms, even a comparatively short blow from the north can raise a dangerous breaking sea. Although rare after May, such brief gales sometimes occur in summer. It was one of these which very nearly ruined the Allied invasion of Sicily during the Second World War in June 1943.

As opposed to such shallow areas, the Mediterranean has in places immense depths. One of the deepest trenches in the world occurs west of Crete, where soundings show 2400 fathoms, or 14,400 feet – nearly 4000 feet deeper than the height of Mount Etna above sea level. In the western basin of the sea the greatest depth known is a little over 1700 fathoms (10,200 feet), west of Cape Sandalo in southern Sardinia. In the southern part of the Tyrrhenian Sea, between Sicily and Naples, similar deep "pot-holes" are found, while the little island of Ustica, which is the peak of an extinct volcano, lifts its craggy head out of depths of over 1000 fathoms.

Two factors in particular distinguish the Mediterranean from the oceans of the world. The first and most important of these is the comparative absence of tides throughout the sea. Even in the few areas where tides do occur, they are so small as to be of little concern to the navigator. In the Strait of Gibraltar, for instance, the spring, or maximum range of tides, is rarely more than two feet. Further along the North African coast, at Djidjelli, it may sometimes be as much as five feet. But throughout the central and eastern areas of the sea the tidal range is so small as to be almost imperceptible. This absence of tides, combined with the long calm summers, undoubtedly helped Man the Navigator in his early days. Later, of course, it proved of the greatest benefit to the first civilizations as they emerged, enabling them to make contact with one another. The steady interchange of peoples and cultures between one area of the Mediterranean and another since man first learned to venture upon what Homer called the "fish-infested sea" can largely be traced to its freedom from tides.

Although of far less importance to man, the second characteristic which distinguishes this sea from the oceans is its salinity. Were it not for the fact that the Mediterranean is fed from the Atlantic through the Strait of Gibraltar, it would comparatively quickly turn into two large salt lakes, divided by the Sicily–North Africa land bridge. At its narrowest point, the Strait of Gibraltar is only nine miles wide – thus permitting the Atlantic to invade the Mediterranean on a very small front. The hot summers throughout the sea basin lead inevitably to considerable evaporation from the surface. Since this evaporation is a great deal more than can be replaced by rainfall, or by the rivers that discharge into it, it is not surprising to find that the specific gravity of the Mediterranean (1·028 in the west to 1·03 in the Levant) is higher than the Atlantic on the west (1·026) and the Black Sea in the east (1·012).

The Black Sea, with its large river supply, pours relatively fresh water into the Mediterranean through the Dardanelles. But at the other end, the Pillars of Hercules, the Mediterranean is replenished by an influx of colder, less saline, Atlantic water which runs in on the surface. Underneath it, the denser and more saline Mediterranean water runs out into the Atlantic. There is, then, a constant exchange in process between the inland sea and the ocean beyond. In parts of the Levant, it has been calculated that the salinity is as high as 39 per cent, while in the Strait of Gibraltar it is only 37 per cent. The visitor from non-Mediterranean lands discovers for himself, without the aid of scientific instruments, the evidence of this high salinity the minute he steps into the sea. On this warm, buoyant water he can float with scarcely any effort. In Greek legend, the poet Arion is said to have been borne back to his native city of Corinth by a friendly dolphin, but the Mediterranean itself is like a dolphin to any swimmer.

The temperature of the surface waters may occasionally reach 90° Fahrenheit, but is usually much less, the mean of the winter months being between 53° and 57°. Generally the temperature of the surface is higher than that of the air, especially in winter, but in some of the summer months the reverse is the case. There are indeed times around the shores of some islands when the air temperature in July or August may be in the 80s, but the sea can be as high as 90°. After the sea becomes stirred up by the first gales of winter, however, there is quite a sharp temperature drop. Although foreign visitors may still enjoy bathing as late as the end of November, few natives will consider it clement between mid-September and late May. "One should enter the sea," remarked a Greek islander, "only when there is no shock to the body." Told that in England and some other northern countries there exist bands of enthusiasts who bathe right through the winter (even when this entails breaking the ice of their frozen lakes or ponds), he merely shrugged as if to divest himself from the stupidity of some elements of mankind. Despite all his failures to achieve it, Mediterranean man, of whatever country, race, or religion, retains a feeling that true happiness lies in moderation. "Nothing in excess", that ancient Greek maxim (and upon their inability to live up to it the city-states foundered), is still cherished as an ideal concept.

At any time in the year the surface temperature is always highest towards the Levant in the south-eastern corner of the sea, and lowest in the Gulf of Lions, the northern Aegean, and in the north of the Adriatic. Throughout the whole area, at a little below a hundred fathoms there is an almost constant temperature of 54° to 56° Fahrenheit, the difference of temperatures again being between the western and eastern basins. This "layering" of the sea into two basic structures was made use of by submarines in the Second World War, which found that occasional pockets of the "cold water layer" enabled them to escape from the probing sonar beams of destroyers overhead.

The deep waters are subject to only slight annual variation, this being dependent upon the temperatures of the previous winter. The deeps of the Mediterranean, in fact, bear little life compared with those of the open oceans. Below two hundred fathoms hardly anything lives, and it seems that, in the deepest pockets of all, only sterile silence reigns. Although not completely enclosed, the Mediterranean resembles other totally enclosed seas in this fact: too high a salt content (and the denser saline water inevitably sinks beneath the fresher) is inimical to life. Man, like all mammals, came out of the shallow waters; like all mammals he must have salt in his diet; but not even deep-sea fish or organisms can survive where there is too much salt.

As an extension of this, the Black Sea, that strange appendage of the Mediterranean, has no organic life of any kind from about five hundred feet to its maximum depth of over seven thousand feet. This is because it receives the inflow of so many rivers – among them the Danube, the Dnieper, and the Don, via the Sea of Azov – that its surface water contains very little salt indeed. While this relatively salt-free water flows out through the Dardanelles to join the Mediterranean, a deep underwater current of salt water flows into the Black Sea. The sea is thus composed of virtually two layers; since the lower salty area makes no contact with the atmosphere, it receives no oxygen and therefore cannot support life.

People familiar with the indolent, salty Mediterranean can easily prove the difference between the Black Sea and its larger fellow. However hot the air outside, however much Istanbul may waver with heat, the Bosporus is cold. Not only is it cold; it is also less saline than the Mediterranean. In places it tastes little more than brackish; the current sweeps down at several knots; and the swimmer soon finds that this water does not bear him up.

At the other end of the Mediterranean, where the Atlantic feeds the inland sea, the volume of water entering is controlled not only by the narrowness of the Strait of Gibraltar, but also by a submarine ledge linking the two continents. Since, at its deepest, it is little more than a thousand feet, and in places a great deal shallower, the strait can admit only a relatively small volume of water. Were the strait wider, and were there no ledge between Africa and Europe, the character of the Mediterranean would change, since the cold waters of the Atlantic would flow freely back and forth. As it is, the Atlantic provides a saline drip-feed to the landlocked sea, while the Black Sea counterbalances this with its flow of comparatively fresh water.

The basic sea-surface circulation throughout the Mediterranean is anticlockwise. Running in by the Strait of Gibraltar, the flow goes along the coast of North Africa, turning north by Syria and going round the island of Cyprus, up the Turkish coast, anticlockwise round the Black Sea, round the coast of Greece, up the Adriatic, and back round Italy and the southern shores of France and Spain. The main variation on this simple pattern occurs in the Gulf of Sirte, where the current strikes on the bald, out-jutting head of Cyrenaica and is deflected backwards towards the Gulf of Gabes and the eastern shores of Tunisia. Sailors should not take this description of the Mediterranean current system as any more than a general picture. *The Admiralty Pilot* cautions: "The general circulation is not experienced as a steady flow in all parts of the sea, at the same time; the actual currents are variable. The currents, at any time, are largely affected by the wind, and local drift currents of a temporary nature, but of sufficient strength to mask the general circulation, are set up when the wind has been strong and continuous from any one quarter. It is thus possible, in any part of the

Mediterranean, to find a current setting towards any point of the compass. . . ." The sea is feminine, and the sailor will find her correspondingly capricious.

The comparative absence of any tide means that the wind has a far greater effect upon this sea than upon an ocean. Not only are the surface currents largely derived from whatever winds may have been blowing, but the absence of tidal range, which would nullify the effect of the wind, means that a breaking sea can be kicked up in a comparatively short space of time. A sudden electric storm, lasting no more than half an hour, can change the previous pattern of the sea's surface, leaving behind it a swell that will continue for some time.

Within a day's sailing the whole surface of the sea may change several times. In midsummer in the central Mediterranean, if the prevailing north-westerlies have been blowing gently for several days, at the beginning of the day the sailor will find that there is a perceptible swell from the north-west. He will know then that his vessel is being set all the time slightly to the south-east. Near an island he may encounter a thunderstorm racing out to sea, and this, in its turn, will leave behind a swell running in whatever direction the storm was heading. In the afternoon, near the mouth of a bay, he may find a strong sea breeze, purely local in character, completely overriding the prevailing north-westerly and imposing yet another pattern on the sea's surface. By nightfall it is probable that he will be left with a flat calm – and three conflicting swells riding at cross-purposes over the face of the water.

If the sea is unpredictable, the Mediterranean climate compensates for this by being generally stable and falling into a relatively simple pattern. Throughout the whole region the summer is hot, while the winter, though often cool, is brief and enlivened by much sunshine. One attempt at an empirical formula for the Mediterranean climate is given in the form of M/R: with R equalling the total millimetres of rain in the summer months of June, July, and August, while M equals the mean maximum temperature Centigrade of the hottest month. Using this formula, regions with a true Mediterranean climate are said to have a quotient of under seven.

The presence of the olive tree is a certain indication that one is in a Mediterranean area. It is true that the olive was probably not indigenous, but was imported from the East, yet its distribution throughout the

Mediterranean is now so wide that, wherever it is found, the area may be said to enjoy a true Mediterranean climate. The holm oak and the Aleppo pine are two other reliable climatic plant indicators. The olive is also a guarantee that ground frost is very rare, for the tree cannot endure a temperature much below 38° Fahrenheit.

The annual rainfall is moderate throughout the Mediterranean, with a mean average of about 24 inches. But whereas Corfu may have as much as 45 inches, Oran may have as little as 15 inches. In the Maltese archipelago, where accurate statistics have been kept since 1870, the mean average is about 20 inches, but in one or two exceptional years this has risen as high as 39 inches, and even sunk as low as 10 inches. Although the average figures are not so different from those of south-eastern England, rainfall in the Mediterranean tends to be mainly confined to the autumn, and even then the majority of days are free from cloud. The precipitation, clearly, is fierce when it comes. Records show that on one October day in Malta 11 inches of rain fell, while as much as 8 inches a day has been recorded in Gibraltar. One thing that the whole area is ignorant of are the long grey days of light-falling drizzle such as occur in the North. Several inches may fall in twenty-four hours, but then the sky will clear, the nimbus clouds fly over, and the sunshine comes back again.

In most areas the rainy season begins in September and is ushered in by heavy thunderstorms. After the first rains of autumn there is often a comparatively rainless period through November and December until the second period of rain in January and February. In most areas July and August are totally without rain, and in some places June, too, can be rainless. This is the period when, as Oleg Polunin and Anthony Huxley remark in *Flowers of the Mediterranean*, "the average sunshine is over 10 hours per day. . . . This hot season is ideal for ripening fruits of all kinds for which the Mediterranean region is justly famous.

"Most plant growth ceases during this hot period and only begins again when the first rains arrive. . . . Some species flower during late autumn and early winter, and some never stop active growth at all during the winter. Early spring is the time when most Mediterranean perennials flower, and the flowering period rises to its peak towards the end of April when in addition a rich variety of annual plants carpet the plains and hillsides. By June they have died down and many have shed their seeds, and only the thistles and members of the Mint family (*Labiatae*) are likely to be found in flower."

The mean August temperature is between 75° and 80°, but during daytime it is often up to 90°. The situation of a port or city can make a great difference to the summer temperature, which is largely controlled by the degree to which a place is exposed to the sea breeze. Tunis, for instance, which is relatively sheltered, has temperatures well over 90°. But other places on the North African coast that feel the sea wind rarely rise above 85°. During the summer months, the temperature at night in the western area usually falls to between 60° and 70°, but in parts of the central and eastern areas it is quite common for it not to fall below 75°.

While tourists and visitors from other regions of the world throng to the Mediterranean during July and August, most natives of this area actively dislike the two hottest months. Their pattern of living is disrupted; appetites fail; children grow listless and irritable; and flies, mosquitoes, and heat spoil the night's sleep. Those who can afford it often head north for the lands which the summer visitors have just left. Except in modern buildings transformed by air-conditioning, the siesta is a necessity and not a luxury. Most shops, offices, and other businesses now open early in the morning, in the cool bright hours before the sun has sapped vitality. They close at noon and then reopen from about four in the afternoon until seven or eight in the evening. Although the day is broken by the siesta, the hours worked are as long as at other times of the year. But both employers and employees are aware that the quantity and quality of work achieved in midsummer is below average. In Palermo and other cities, social life starts at about eight o'clock in the evening, when a cocktail party may be followed by a dinner party at ten-thirty, and a visit to a cinema at midnight. During midsummer, the best hours for work are between sunrise and ten in the morning, when the heat begins to bounce off sea and rocks. These cool, quiet hours, when the tired land still has a breath of the night's dampness and when the colours on earth, sea, and buildings are clear and vibrant (they will be burned shadowless at noon), are when Mediterranean man gets his best work done. The foreign visitor, who will later see him lying asleep in the shade of a carob tree (with some wine near by and a handkerchief containing bread, olives, garlic, and a tomato or half a cucumber), may well feel envious of such an apparently lazy life, compared to his own hustle in the North. He will be unaware that the slumbering labourer has probably risen before four in the morning, walked for an hour or more out to his fields, and has put in four hours' work before the visitor has even drunk a breakfast cup of coffee.

The modern traveller to Mediterranean lands must bear in mind that hardly anywhere is he seeing what the ancients saw. As a simple instance of this, the agaves, cacti, citrus, eucalyptus, loquat, and palm trees – all accepted nowadays as typical Mediterranean vegetation – are imported foreigners: some from China and the East and others from America. Similarly, the face of the land itself has changed. Islands that as late as the seventeenth century were thickly forested are now barren skeletons. Rich lands once rustling with wheat have become desert, and whole areas have changed through volcanic and seismic action. It is this alteration in the face of the earth that makes the problem of the scholar or historian so difficult when he tries to reconstruct the sites of ancient battlefields or to discover harbours mentioned by classical authors. On the one hand, the land has been altered in many places by the activities of man. On the other, there is the fact that the Mediterranean is a comparatively new part of the earth and is still in the process of change. Although the natural tendency of Western man is to think of the Mediterranean area as "old", it is, geologically speaking, fairly young.

The process by which the land itself develops, and then is altered by the arrival of man, falls into several stages. First of all, wild plants begin to colonize a hitherto barren area of the earth's surface. These are brought to the land either in birds' droppings or by the wind. Humus, that dark brown substance, renewer of life and product of the decomposition of organic matter, gradually develops from the decay of plants. This is aided, and the land further fertilized, by the guano of birds. As the soil deepens and becomes enriched, it attracts animals, who in their turn manure the ground and leave their fertilizing bodies and bones behind them. Man himself is one of these animals. What ecologists call a "climax" – a comparatively stable community of plants – is finally reached. In the Mediterranean this was when forest trees began to spread over the area. In this part of the world, the trees which flourish happily are the evergreens, whose leathery leaves can resist the fierce heat of summer and whose deep, water-searching roots can preserve the tree until the winter rains.

The first important stage in the Mediterranean was the spread of evergreen forests over the region. If man had not arrived upon the scene, this primeval forest would have remained. But man changes everything. Once he moves in as a hunter – long before he becomes an agriculturalist – he attacks the trees, burning them down to make open clearings. Later, as agriculture develops, this activity increases; the trees, which have previously sheltered the animals upon which he preys, are a hindrance to his husbandry. (Until comparatively recently the remains of a primeval forest were to be found in the region of Mount Circe in western Italy.)

With the clearance of the forest trees, the whole aspect of the landscape alters. Man with his tools and his animals (particularly the goat, which browses on saplings) soon sets in motion a process that, unless it is arrested, leads to desert land. After the evergreen forest has disappeared, there is left the maquis. This is a term for that typical Mediterranean plant-growth familiar to all who have visited Corsica. Maquis consists of thickets of shrubs, sometimes as high as five or six feet – largely broom and cistus. Myrtle, tree heather, holm oak, and Aleppo pine are also found in what is defined as "high" maquis. In "low" maquis there are no trees at all, only a tangled growth of herbs such as rosemary and sage, as well as other small bushes, none of which grow more than three feet high.

A third stage in the destruction of a forest area is reached when even the maquis has been cleared (used by man for charcoal, resin, and fibres) and there emerges another characteristic type of landscape, the garigue. The term means waste land, but the land has not yet become total desert. Amid its stony and dried-out ground it bears many small scattered bushes which cling tenaciously to hill-sides and rocky plateaux. Like the maquis, the garigue is redolent with aromatic plants. It is the parent of almost every culinary herb. Rosemary, lavender, thyme, sage, savory, garlic, and rue all inhabit this stony waste land where their scent, "mixing memory and desire", seems heightened by the sterility of the land around them. In the spring, the garigue bursts into flower, for dozens of bulbous and tuberous ornamental plants grow on these stony uplands.

If the garigue gives the European most of his herbs, it also produces the wild ancestors of the tulip, iris, crocus, and hyacinth. In spring the Star of Bethlehem shines, miniature irises and fritillaries nod in the wind, and the wild garlic unfurls its round white flowers. But the blaze is short-lived. Within a few weeks the parched soil looks as though it could never hold any life, let alone such a brilliance as early enamelled its harsh surface.

All areas of the Mediterranean show examples of the garigue, and it is typical of many islands where over centuries man's ignorance has laid bare the soil, leaving it so thin that only these hardy perennials can survive. Beyond the garigue, at the far end of the scale, comes the steppe – land where the soil has been almost totally destroyed, and only plants with deep root systems can survive. Some types of thistles and grasses, perennials such as anemones and irises, and a few bulbous plants inhabit the steppe. On the impoverished uplands of islands like Sicily, Malta, and Gozo, one of the most distinctive types of steppe can be seen, where nothing but the asphodel with its huge swollen tubers still remains. Perhaps it was not only the funereal pallor of the asphodel's flowers that made the ancient Greeks connect the plant with the underworld. Homer's description of the great "meadow of asphodels" which the dead inhabited may well have been prompted by the poet's recollection of some barren steppe, where all was desolation except for the trembling heads of the asphodels standing up like so many corpses in their shrouds.

The pattern of the Mediterranean landscape from evergreen forest to desert can be reversed by intelligent use of the soil, or by man, for one reason or another, being forced to leave the area. Once the process has gone too far, however, only intensive efforts at rebuilding the soil can return the landscape to anything like its original condition, and in many places nothing can be done to restore the force of the earth. The gaunt, bare islands which have become totally identified with modern man's image of Greece were once forested and thick with hardy plants that held the soil against the winter rains. In vain may one look for springs and streams mentioned by classical writers. True, they were there once, but with the deforestation and the disappearance of the soil the springs have dried up and the streams have vanished. The trailing nimbus clouds of autumn which once would have loitered over the holm or kermes oak forests now move on briskly downwind, sending no more than a sudden deluge over the barren limestone slopes.

If the face of the land has altered, the sailor looking ahead at dawn – when the sea begins to change from gun-metal to pewter to polished silver – can reflect that he looks upon the same world as millions of other seamen before him. He uses the same stars for navigation, breathes the same salt wind as a Phoenician, and is subject to the same weather. Yet even the sea has changed: no longer as "fish-infested" as in Homer's time, it has, like the land, been over-harvested.

From almost every corner of the basin, trawlers spread out to comb the sea. Every cove and creek and minute island discharges its day-fishermen, trawling or lining, and at night the islands are encircled by necklaces of light as carbide and gas flares lure the fish towards the nets. The swelling population of the Mediterranean lands must be fed, and if the land in many places is poor for crops or indifferent for grazing, then the sea must make up the balance. Yet, despite the fact that this sea is being largely depopulated through both the ignorance and the necessity of man, it still manages to provide a large part of the diet of the countries surrounding it.

Tunny, largest fish of the mackerel family, sometimes reaching a length of ten feet and weighing up to one thousand pounds, is a very important catch of the Mediterranean fisheries. Fresh or canned, it plays a large part in the economy of the fishermen in Sicily and other islands. Similarly, the swordfish, found north of the Strait of Messina, and hand-harpooned from special boats whose sole purpose is swordfish catching, is another delicacy – but one that few working men can afford to eat.

The methods used for catching tunny and swordfish in the Mediterranean are so unusual that both deserve a brief description. The Sicilians probably learned their particular tunny-catching technique during the Arab occupation of their island in the ninth and tenth centuries A.D. But it may be even earlier than the Arabic conquest, for it is on record that the Phoenicians established a tunny fishery on the coast of Spain, and the tunny is to be seen on Phoenician medals of Cadiz and Carteia. At a later date, salted tunny was a favoured dish of the Romans, who called it *saltamentum sardicum*.

Based on the knowledge that at certain points along the coast the tunny come close inshore to spawn, the fishermen spread out from the shore a long net that reaches down to the sea bed. The tunny, encountering this obstacle, turns seawards to go round it, and, in doing so, enters the first of the "chambers". This is a square boxlike construction of netting, supported on all four sides at the surface by wooden barges. Having entered this first net, and finding itself still enclosed, the tunny makes for the only opening to seaward, which leads inexorably into the second net. Again, another opening beckons the giant fish towards the freedom of the sea, and it enters the third and last net, the *camera della morte*. The "chamber of death" is similar to the previous square arrangements of net, with the exception that it has a strong net bottom. Totally confused by this time, the tunny swims aimlessly round and round in its prison. Since its instinct is always to turn away from the coast and towards the sea it does not double back on its tracks and escape to freedom the way it has come.

Every day during the tunny season, the *rais* (an Arabic word for foreman which has passed into the Sicilian dialect) inspects the catch through a glass-bottomed bucket from one of the barges that holds up the *camera della morte*. When he is satisfied that there are enough fish in the net, the *mattanza* (slaughter) is proclaimed. The word reveals yet another part of Sicily's history – the long centuries when Spanish influence predominated in the island. Gangs of fishermen are now ferried out to the four barges supporting the third net. Usually in the early morning (to avoid the harsh heat of the day), they begin to haul up the four-sided net – and with it the net at the bottom. Soon the fish feel their watery world beginning to constrict. They circle mindlessly; then panic takes hold, and they thrash round the enclosing square at increasing speed. Not only tunny have been trapped; sometimes a giant manta ray will leap like a black nightmare from the sea, to fall back in a fountain of spray. Sharks are there, too, and many other smaller fish that have unwittingly followed the kings of the sea to their doom. When the bottom of the net is only a few feet beneath the surface, the men turn up the main ropes that support the "chamber" round bollards on the barges. At a signal from the *rais*, the *mattanza* begins. This is described in my book *The Journeying Moon*: "Row after row, black against the sunlit water, the men poised themselves for a brief second and then – as if with one accord – struck downward. I

44

can see them still on that bright morning: the gaffs rising and falling; the huge floundering fish spouting blood and the men hauling them up the barges' sides and turning them with a twist of the gaff so that they fell into the holds. As the great tunny came over the side of a barge one of the men would place his hand over its eyes – it struggles less when blind. Sometimes, and the gesture had a curious touch of pity about it, they would give the fish a gentle pat on its shining side as they threw it down to die in the hold. . . ."

Swordfishing also has its own special techniques. The swordfishing boats of Sicily are unique. Nowadays they are all diesel-engined, yet only twenty-five years ago most of them were lateen-rigged sailboats. What distinguishes them from any other fishing boats in the world are their immense bowsprits and their towering spindly masts, at the top of which is the conning position. A boat with a hull length of about forty feet will have a bowsprit of sixty feet, and a mast of eighty feet. In the old days masts and bowsprits were not so long because they were made of wood, but nowadays they are made of aluminium lattices, which has permitted an even greater extension. The controls to the tiller and to the engine are led up to the top of the mast, where the captain and a look-out con the boat and direct it after the swordfish. From their great height they can see down into the water well ahead of their vessel. When a school of swordfish is sighted, the harpoonist runs to the end of the bowsprit while the captain manoeuvres the boat into position. Sometimes the harpoonist will catch sight of his target only a few seconds before he throws his harpoon; on other occasions he may well fire blind on instructions shouted by the captain.

To watch the boats working along the shores between Sicily and Italy in the Messina Strait is to witness a pattern of fishing that is almost as old as this sea. No records exist to indicate at what period in time this method of harpooning swordfish was evolved, but it may well go back to the ancient world. Homer certainly knew the fishing activities in the Messina Strait. When describing the dangers of the area – the whirlpool Charybdis and the monster Scylla – he tells how Scylla fishes, "scouting around the rock for any dolphin or swordfish she may catch, or any larger monsters which . . . find their living in the roaring seas."

Quite apart from the fact that Charybdis (which still exists) definitely localizes this passage in the *Odyssey*, the reference to Scylla's fishing activities is significant. The Messina Strait is one of the only places in the Mediterranean where swordfish are found in any great quantity. The interchange of water at this point between the Ionian and Tyrrhenian seas, the tidal activities in the strait, and the constant movement of the water attract swordfish to this part of the Mediterranean and make it their favoured spawning ground. As the boats zigzag up and down the strait on a sparkling June morning they are merely repeating – only with the advantage of engine power – the ancient pattern. The fishermen from Ganzirri, the Sicilian village opposite the whirlpool Charybdis, and their rivals from Scilla, the village on the Italian coast named after Homer's monster, can lay claim to belonging to one of the oldest fishing communities in the world. On a grey winter day, when the wind is from the north and the current in the strait is running against it, one can still hear Scylla's "yelp" as the wind and sea boom and cry in the caves round the base of the rock.

Unlike the coastal areas off Sicily, large parts of the Mediterranean, such as the central Ionian and the sea to the west of Corsica and Sardinia, are still little fished. As distinct from the English Channel, where a narrow sleeve of water separates two countries with large modern fishing fleets, the Mediterranean is bordered in many places by countries whose fishing activities are mainly confined to small boats operating in coastal waters. This fact ensures (though for how long no one can say) that, although certain areas are overfished, the sea as a whole is still capable of replacing its losses.

The "Careless Gallant's Song" recalls one virtue of fish, particularly shell-fish, which has (even if scientifically inaccurate) been widely credited for thousands of years:

> Fish dinners will make a man spring like a flea,
> Dame Venus, love's Lady, was born of the Sea;
> With her and with Bacchus we'll tickle the sense
> For we shall be past it a hundred years hence.

This anonymous English poet might have found even further inspiration in the names of some of the fish, aphrodisiac or otherwise, that haunt the island-dappled shallow waters or hide deep in the long dark acres of the main basins. A guide to the fishes of the central Mediterranean lists over nine hundred varieties in this area alone – some indication of the richness of this ancient sea.

Albacore, amberjack, angel fish, angler fish (also called St. Peter's fish), the armed gurnard and the Atlantic bonito begin the roll-call. But Poseidon is also fond of strange and dangerous creatures; the harmless basking shark is followed by the beaumaris shark with its long teeth and sharp cutting edges. (It is a fiction of hotel managers and tourist offices that no sharks are to be found in this sea.) Then come the black-bellied skate, the tompot blenny, the blue damsel-fish, the brown wrasse, and the buck mackerel. Cramp ray, which can give a severe electric shock, is followed by the deep-nosed pipe-fish, the devil fish, the friendly dolphin, and the dorade. Eyed dogfish, ugly and no good to eat, flat-headed mullet and the graceful, playful, shimmering flying fish (whose bright arching leap ends often in the frying pan) have strange companions such as the freckled goby and the frigate mackerel. The gapemouth, or king of mullets, wanders into the net, followed by the jadeboned garfish, as well as that Old Man of the Sea, the greater fork-beard. Hammerhead sharks and the delicate hippocampus, or sea-horse, have hounds (rough or smooth) to run behind them as the striped wrasse appears, together with the kingfish and the lamprey, or stone sucker, into whose primitive jaws fastidious Romans are reputed to have cast the occasional slave. The learned wrasse and the long-snouted skate, the manta ray, known as the devil fish for its sinister horns and whiplash tail, the voracious monk fish, the needle fish, and the nursehound, the old wife, and the parrot fish, which feeds around coral, couch's polyprion, pompilus, the poor cod, porbeagle, and the pout, all come willy-nilly into net or on to line – some to be discarded and others to be thrown gasping into the seaweed-lined hold or the stained duckboards of an open boat. The whip-tailed sting ray is given a wide berth by the wise, but not so the red bream, gurnard, or mullet, all of which can add flavour to a *zuppa di pesce* in Naples and further south. Rose-coloured apogon, sail fish, sapparine gurnard, gilt sardine, black-bellied skate, whiskered sole, and the bimaculated sucker have even more curious neighbours in the thick-lipped mullet and the three-bearded rockling. Toadfish, who live deep among weeds and stones, tompot, two-spotted sucker, weever, whistle fish, wide gab, Turkish wrasse, wreck fish, and yellow fish bring this abbreviated roll-call to an end.

In the Mediterranean the widest variety of fish, as well as the best, are to be found in the three most important "Sea Gates". These are the Strait of Gibraltar, the Messina Strait, and the Bosporus. Off Gibraltar, the meeting place of the inland sea and the Atlantic, are found not only a great number of species, but also firmer-fleshed fish, because of the inflow of cold Atlantic waters. Similarly, at the point where the Black Sea pours down its cold and relatively saltless water into the Mediterranean, there are better quality fish than in the luke-warm, tideless, and saline eastern basin. But the Messina Strait is another case altogether, and it is also exceptional for being the only area which has two distinct semi-diurnal tides. That is to say, each lunar day there are two high waters and two low waters.

The Admiralty Pilot describes how this effect functions in the narrow Strait of Messina: "Off Capo Peloro, at the northern entrance to the strait, the tide behaves like that of the Tyrrhenian sea; from Punta Pezzo southward it behaves like that of the Ionian sea. Though these two tides are of the same type, the times at which the high and low waters occur differ at the strait by about six hours; hence when it is high water at Capo Peloro it is low water at Villa San Giovanni, only three miles further southward, and vice versa. Hence twice each lunar day the water level has a maximum slope northward through the strait, and twice each lunar day a slope southward. Though the difference of level is small, amounting to less than a foot at springs, it is concentrated into such a short distance that streams with a rate of 4 knots at springs are generated by it."

Another characteristic of this strait is that, since the waters of the Ionian Sea are colder and saltier than those of the Tyrrhenian Sea to the north, the difference in density sets up a double current, one of which flows southwards through the strait on the surface, while the other flows northwards at a depth a little below fifteen fathoms. These two currents, combined with a submarine shelf connecting Sicily with the toe of Italy, give rise to the whirlpools for which the strait has been notorious ever since Homer described how "great Charybdis sucks down the dark waters." Because of a change in the structure of the sea bed after a great earthquake in 1783, Charybdis is no longer as formidable as it undoubtedly was in classical times. Yet, as late as 1824, Admiral William Henry Smyth writes, in *Sicily and Its Islands*, that "even in the present day, small craft are sometimes endangered by it, and I have seen several men-of-war, and even a seventy-four-gun ship, whirled round on its surface."

Quite apart from its tides and its currents, the strait is distinguished by the extraordinary number of unusual fish and maritime creatures which inhabit the area, many of which are never seen by man except if caught in a deep-sea trawl. Because of the submarine shelf connecting the island with the continent, deep-water currents strike this barrier and are deflected upwards, often bringing with them fish and organisms that normally do not see the light of day. In an article in *The National Geographic Magazine*, November 1953, Paul Zahl describes how, twice a month, during the spring tides, "the surface waters in the Strait of Messina abound with living or half-living creatures whose habitat is normally down where all is black and still. . . . After a strong onshore wind I have seen beaches along the Strait of Messina littered with thousands of tiny dead or dying creatures whose appearance would make even the artist Dali wince."

Another sea feature peculiar to Sicily, but sometimes felt in the Maltese archipelago, is the *marrobbio*. This consists of waves or surges, isolated or in series, which may raise the water level by as much as four feet. There is no forewarning of the *marrobbio*'s approach, and a vessel lying in harbour may suddenly find itself lifted up against the quayside with straining mooring-ropes. This change in water level is most frequently experienced in the harbours of south-western Sicily. Trapani, Marsala, and the fishing port of Mazara del Vallo are all prone to the *marrobbio*, which may occur at any period of the year during undisturbed weather.

The origin of this freak range of sea level has been disputed; some authorities associate it with a long period of prevailing winds in either the eastern or the western basin, others with sudden changes in the meteorological conditions prevailing over the whole sea. The latter theory seems to have the backing of more recent research. The reason that the *marrobbio* is experienced mainly in southern Sicily and the Maltese islands is probably due to the fact that a marked change in barometric pressure in either the eastern or western Mediterranean basins can cause a surge of water to pass between one section of the sea and the other. This is most distinctly felt at the point where the waters are shallow, and where the submerged land bridge connects Sicily with North Africa.

It is not only the sea that suddenly and mysteriously moves without warning. The land itself is prone to divide, split, rise, fall, and shudder in giant labour pains. Messina has twice been destroyed by earthquakes, once in 1783 and again in 1908. The Algerian coast is also subject to earthquakes; in 1716 one continued almost uninterrupted for a whole month. From Naples, where the active volcano Vesuvius puffs against the blue skies, southwards through the Lipari Islands, where Stromboli looms tremendous, down to Mount Etna in Sicily, runs a huge "fault" in the earth's crust.

At Etna this fault branches eastwards and sweeps through the Ionian Islands, making Levkas, Ithaca, and Zante prone to earthquake damage. Yugoslavia, the Greek mainland, and large parts of Turkey are areas of seismic disturbance. Islands such as Ustica, north of Sicily, Pantelleria to the south, and Santorin in the Aegean are volcanoes which have risen from the sea bed. While the first two are dead or dormant, Santorin is still active. In the centre of its great bay a new volcanic island smokes and fumes, discharging molten lava that turns to pumice in the blue waters.

Poseidon, Greek god of the sea, was also known as the "Earth-shaker". The trident with which he is usually depicted is the same as the one Greek fishermen still use for spearing flatfish in the shallows. But when the god took his trident ashore and stuck it in the earth, then he was rightly feared as the splitter of mountains and the destroyer of cities. As a corollary of the violence of the sea, the Greeks recognized the dangerous instability of the land they inhabited. Even at the peak of their colonial expansion – when they had spread into North Africa, Sicily, southern Italy, and that part of Asia Minor that is now Turkey but was then called Ionia – they never knew a land that was not subject to the sudden rages of the Earth-shaker.

Vesuvius, largest active volcano on the continent of Europe, seems to have been dormant – at least historically – until A.D. 63. The great Greek geographer Strabo had observed in 30 B.C. that the mountain was undoubtedly of volcanic origin, for he commented that it was "cindery and as if eaten by fire". But the real nature of the mountain did not become apparent to the people of Naples or of the many villages and towns around its foot until A.D. 79. It was then that there occurred the immense eruption which completely buried Pompeii and Herculaneum, as well as badly damaging the city of Stabiae, where Pliny the Elder, Roman author and admiral, lost his life.

His nephew, Pliny the Younger, in a letter to the historian Tacitus, graphically describes how his uncle met his death. "He was at that time with the fleet under his command at Misenum. On the 24th of August, about one in the afternoon, my mother desired him to observe a cloud which had appeared of a very unusual size and shape. He had just taken a turn in the sun, and after bathing himself in cold water, and making a light luncheon, gone back to his books; he immediately arose and went out upon a rising ground from whence he might get a better sight of this very uncommon appearance. A cloud, from which mountain was uncertain at this distance, was ascending, the form of which I cannot give you a more exact description of than by likening it to that of a pine tree, for it shot up to a great height in the form of a very tall trunk, which spread out at the top into a sort of branches; occasioned, I imagine, either by a sudden gust of air that impelled it, the force of which decreased as it advanced upwards, or the cloud itself being pressed backwards by its own weight, expanded in the manner I have mentioned; it appeared sometimes bright and sometimes dark and spotted, according as it was either more or less impregnated with earth and cinders. This phenomenon seemed to a man of such learning and research as my uncle extraordinary, and worth further looking into.

"He ordered a light vessel to be got ready, and gave me leave if I liked, to accompany him. I said I would rather get on with my work; and it so happened he had himself given me something to write out. As he was coming out of the house, he received a note from Rectina, the wife of Bassus, who was in the utmost alarm at the imminent danger which threatened her; for, from her villa lying at the foot of Mount Vesuvius, there was no way of escape except by sea; she earnestly entreated him therefore to come to her assistance. He accordingly changed his first intention, and what he had begun from a philosophical, he now carried out in a noble and generous spirit. He ordered the galleys to put to sea, and went himself on board with an intention of assisting not only Rectina, but the several other towns which lay thickly strewn along the beautiful coast. Hastening then to the place from whence others fled with the utmost terror, he steered his course direct to the point of danger, and with so much calmness and presence of mind as to be able to make and dictate his observations upon the motion and all the phenomena of that dreadful scene.

"He was now so close to the mountain that the cinders, which grew thicker and hotter the nearer he approached, fell into the ships, together with pumice stones, and black pieces of burning rocks; they were in danger too not only of being aground by the sudden retreat of the sea, but also from the vast fragments which rolled down from the mountain, and obstructed all the shore. Here he stopped to consider whether he should turn back again; to which the pilot advising him, 'Fortune,' said he, 'favours the brave; steer to where Pomponianus is.'

"Pomponianus was then at Stabiae [now Castellamare], separated by a bay, which the sea, after several insensible windings, forms with the shore. He had already sent his baggage on board; for though at that time he was not in actual danger, yet being within sight of it, and indeed extremely near, if it should in the least increase, he was determined to put to sea as soon as the wind, which was blowing dead inshore, should go down. It was favourable, however, for carrying my uncle to Pomponianus, whom he found in the greatest consternation; he embraced him tenderly, encouraging and urging him to keep up his spirits, and the more effectually to soothe his fears by seeming unconcerned himself, ordered a bath to be got ready, and then, after having bathed, sat down to supper with great cheerfulness, or at least (which is just as heroic) with every appearance of it.

"Meanwhile broad flames shone out in several places from Mount Vesuvius, which the darkness of the night continued to render still brighter and clearer. But my uncle, in order to soothe the apprehensions of his friend, assured him it was only the burning of the villages, which the country people had abandoned to the flames: after this he retired to rest, and it is most certain that he was so little disquieted as to fall into a sound sleep: for his breathing which, on account of his corpulence, was rather heavy and sonorous, was heard by the attendants outside. The court which led to his apartment being now almost filled with ashes and stones, if he had continued there any longer, it would have been impossible for him to have made his way out. So he was awoke and got up, and went to Pomponianus and the rest of his company, who were feeling too anxious to think of going to bed. They consulted together whether it would be most prudent to trust to the houses, which now rocked from side to side with frequent and violent concussions as though shaken from their very foundations: or to fly to the open fields, where the calcined stones and cinders, though light indeed, yet fell in large showers and threatened destruction. In this choice of dangers they resolved for the fields: a resolution which, while the rest of the company were hurried into by their fears, my uncle embraced upon cool and deliberate consideration. They went out then, having pillows tied upon their heads with napkins; and this was their whole defence against the storm of stones that fell round them.

"It was now day everywhere else, but there a deeper darkness prevailed than in the thickest night; which however was in some degree alleviated by torches and other lights of various kinds. They thought proper to go farther down upon the shore to see if they might safely put to sea, but found the waves still running extremely high and boisterous. There my uncle, laying himself down upon a sail cloth, which was spread for him, called twice for some cold water, which he drank, when immediately the flames, preceded by a strong whiff of sulphur, dispersed the rest of the party, and obliged him to rise. He raised himself up with the assistance of two of his servants, and instantly fell dead; suffocated, as I conjecture, by some gross and noxious vapour, having always had a weak throat, which was often inflamed. As soon as it was light again, which was not till the third day after this melancholy accident, his body was found entire, and without any marks of violence upon it, in the dress in which he fell, and looking more like a man asleep than dead. . . ."

The Younger Pliny's writings on this famous eruption of Vesuvius may well be considered the beginning of modern scientific vulcanology. His description of the cloud above Vesuvius resembling a pine tree has passed into the language of science, and this type of volcanic eruption is described today as a *pino* (the Italian word for pine). It is unlikely, however, that his uncle died from "noxious vapour", since the rest of the party managed to escape to safety. The reference to his corpulence gives us a clue. It is more likely that he died from a heart attack. He had bathed and dined well, and was then compelled to walk some distance; all this, combined with the difficulty of breathing because of the gas, most probably set in train a fatal coronary.

The most recent large-scale eruption of Vesuvius took place in 1944, when it was widely rumoured in Naples that the Allies had deliberately dropped a bomb into the crater in order to frighten the Germans! However, as the Allied forces were – with the co-operation of the Italian Government – already firmly in occupation of the city, this story must be dismissed along with many other legends that attach themselves to the subject of volcanoes. The eruption was particularly spectacular and, although few lives were lost, large areas of rich vine-lands were desolated. It will certainly never be forgotten by anyone who saw it. The smoke on the first day quickly assumed Pliny's classic pine shape, and then billowed over to form a giant umbrella of dust and ash. Through the looming shade of this, huge fragments of rock and pumice could be seen flying into the air. Both by night and by day a violent electric storm played around in the huge cloud. It was made even more ominous during the dark hours by the ribands of molten lava pouring down the sides. This eruption completely changed the face of Vesuvius by removing its clean domelike peak. Its effects were felt uncomfortably as far away as Capri, for a prevailing north-easterly wind drove the ashes and cinders over that island, until many of the narrow streets that now delight visitors were feet-deep under the cindery dust.

Why men go back century after century to inhabit the dangerous slopes below volcanoes is a question that teases many a foreigner. The reason is, simply, that at a certain stage, when it has broken down into usable earth, the volcanic soil is extremely rich and, above all, indulgent to vines. On this black or deep brown powdery earth the grape-vine thrives, producing from the slopes of Vesuvius and Etna some of the finest wines to be found in the Mediterranean area. Nitrates are plentiful in this volcanic earth, and few farmers can resist the promised yield.

About 140 miles south from Naples the volcanic Lipari Islands are strung across the sea: Alicudi on the west, Stromboli in the north, and Vulcano to the south. Vulcano, named by the Romans after Vulcan, the god of fire and metal-working, has given its name to "volcanoes" all over the world. From ancient times right up to the late nineteenth century, Vulcano was indeed the most active volcano in the Mediterranean. But Vulcan has been silent since 1890, his energies transferred to Stromboli. The Lipari Islands present numerous other volcanic phenomena such as hot springs, geysers, and sulphur blow-holes, as well as submarine springs and lava discharges.

Professor Judd in an article on the Lipari Islands describes the volcanic cone of Campo Bianco on Lipari itself in the following terms, which, though poetic for a scientist, are no exaggeration: "Lofty cinder cones of snowy white pumice, their vast craters breached by lava streams of solid glass, their surface coated with a reddish brown crust, arise amid the blue waters of the Mediterranean, and displaying in that clearness of outline and that vividness of coloring which only the brilliancy of an almost tropical sky can impart, they constitute scenery of startling novelty and wondrous beauty – the impression produced by it is as hopeless as it is impossible to forget. . . ."

Certainly there can be small doubt that it was this region of the Mediterranean which the much-travelled Odysseus was cautioned against by Circe when she gave him his "sailing directions" to get home to Greece. Dispute can reasonably exist as to which of the volcanic islands is referred to, but the reference is probably to one of the Liparis. Here, in Circe's words, " 'blue eyed Amphitrite sends her great breakers thundering in, and the very birds cannot fly by in safety. Even from the shy doves that bring ambrosia to Father Zeus the beetling rock takes toll each time they pass, and the Father has to send one more to make their numbering up; while for such sailors as bring their ship to the spot, there is no escape whatever. They end as flotsam on the sea, timbers and corpses tossed in confusion by the waves or licked up by tempestuous and destroying flames.' "

Vulcano or Stromboli would have equally fitted this description of an area where even the birds cannot fly in safety. Both islands are distinctive from Vesuvius or Etna in their volcanic nature. They are unusual for their violent explosive activity, in which great bombs of ash and fragments of lava are hurled violently into the air. The fiery streams that pour down the sides into the sea easily explain Homer's reference to the flames that devour both ships and men alike. Stromboli was known to the mariners of the classical world as the "Lighthouse of the Mediterranean". The description is still accurate, for the intermittent pulsating glow over the peak at night does indeed resemble an enormous lighthouse – sometimes occulting, sometimes flashing. Even in the twentieth century, with all the modern navigational aids that are available, few navigators will fail to take compass bearings off this ancient "signpost of the sea". It very probably guided Odysseus southwards to the Messina Strait.

The seventh or eighth century B.C. book of Judaic law, Deuteronomy, contains a description of a volcano which matches that of Homer: "And ye came near and stood under the mountain; and the mountain burned with fire unto the midst of heaven, with darkness, clouds, and thick darkness." The words could well be applied to Mount Etna on the eastern coast of Sicily. For Etna is, above all, a "mountain". It is distinguished from its fellows in the rugged hinterland of Sicily by its height, which at one time was over 10,700 feet, and by its classic proportions as it swells up from the coastal plain of Catania to dominate all this area of land and sea. Like all volcanoes its height has varied considerably over the centuries. After an eruption in 1950, it lost part of its central cone and was reduced to little more than 9000 feet.

The name Etna comes from the Greek word "to burn", and the mountain seems to have been active from the days of Greek colonization in Sicily. Greek legends differ, but according to Pindar and Aeschylus, the giant Typhon was believed to have been imprisoned there by Zeus. Later Latin authors transfer this tale to yet another giant, Enceladus. In any case, both are supposed to have belonged to the children of Earth and Underworld, who had the temerity to make war upon the gods. Defeated, they were buried by the triumphant immortals under mountains in various parts of the earth.

The Greek philosopher Empedocles, who held that four primal forces constituted the universe – fire, air, water, and earth – was traditionally supposed to have cast himself into the crater of Mount Etna, so that his sudden and inexplicable disappearance would cause his fellow citizens to reverence him ever afterwards as having been of divine origin. The crater, however, cast back his sandals – to indicate that he was no more than a man.

One of Matthew Arnold's poems, "Empedocles on Etna", describes the philosopher setting out for his self-sought death:

> I have seen many cities in my time
> Till mine eyes ache with the long spectacle,
> And I shall doubtless see them all again;
> Thou know'st me for a wanderer from of old.

(Empedocles was a believer in reincarnation.) Later, before he plunges to his death, he embodies his hopes, perhaps, as much as his philosophy in the words:

> Oh that I could glow like this mountain!
> Oh that my heart bounded with the swell of the sea!
> Oh that my soul were full of light as the stars!
> Oh that it brooded over the world like air!

Even today, when one approaches these lonely slopes, whether from the fishing port of Riposto or from the international artificiality of Taormina, the mountain casts the splendour of its spell. In spring or early summer, when the high snows still shine against the washed blue of the sky, and the pale liquid green of young vines and plants is tender against the land, Etna inspires a feeling of reverence. If a lazy cloud smokes from the peak, trailing seawards on the wind, even the most prosaic may come to understand the poetry that the mountain has inspired.

In the lowlands along the mountain's coastal roots, the chocolate brown earth is rich with olives and mulberry trees, acacias, holm oak, date palms, and the slender bushes of wine grapes. Cypresses stand out like dark spears from this land that is a tribute to the earth's fertility as well as to the work of man. Prickly pears hold out their yellow flowers like candles, and all along the roadside – which is walled with dark volcanic stone – the geraniums grow in dense clusters. Michaelmas daisies run riot, and the purple flowers of bougainvillaea tremble in the sunshine. Here, where earth and sun conspire together, plants which in other lands have to be tended carefully to ensure their survival grow riotously like weeds. Here it is only the vine that requires meticulous attention – spraying, pruning, and careful walling – to protect it against the briny breath of onshore winds.

Higher up the mountain the pattern begins to change: a more austere world is revealed. The friable volcanic earth gives way to unbroken masses of lava. In one place, a huge frozen river of black basalt dating from a seventeenth-century eruption overhangs the road. In this dark landscape, only the yellow broom retains a foothold, its flowers vivid against the Stygian surroundings. The broom, accompanied by a few hardy weeds, has already begun the process which will one day break down even this intractable land into earth where the vine will flourish.

Above the tree-line the traveller enters a world of desolation. But even here the twisted sinews of old lava streams possess austere beauty. Secondary cones, or craters, lying along the fractures of lateral eruptions, add their rounded patterns, while occasionally the brave flower of the broom shines out against the lunar landscape. Snow illuminates all the higher slopes, and the winding trails of skiers reveal modern man taking his pleasure where his ancestors would never willingly have ventured. It is possible in late spring to spend a morning skiing high up on Etna, and in the afternoon to swim and sunbathe in the sea at its feet.

"Mongibello" the locals call the great mountain, a name which may have derived from *monte bello*, beautiful mountain. A more prosaic explanation is that the word is no more than *monte* (Italian) and *jebel* (Arabic), both words meaning mountain, and run together.

The Arabic influence in Sicily should never be underestimated. Those long centuries of occupation have left their mark upon the racial type of the island, and the Sicilian dialect abounds with old Arabic words. The careful agricultural techniques which make the lower slopes of Etna a garden, together with the widespread use of elaborate irrigation systems, are a tribute to the Arabs as much as to the native Siculo-Italians.

Periodically, even if Etna is technically quiescent, it will put on a lavish firework display from its active crater: no longer at the summit, but lower down on a side vent. Then, at night, lightning will flicker in the dust cloud and fiery streams of lava will burn on the barren heights. Such reminders of its latent strength last perhaps a day or two, and then the mountain reverts to its peaceful role, with only a gentle trail of smoke to show that the banked-up fires are still there.

Eastwards across the Ionian, Ithaca and Zante were heavily shaken by earthquakes in 1952, and many houses were destroyed. The waterfront at Port Vathi completely lost its old Venetian appearance. Further east in the Aegean, the island of Santorin provides one of the most interesting examples of a *caldera* volcano anywhere in the world. *Caldera* (Portuguese for a cauldron or kettle) is a term derived from the bowl-shaped depressions found in the Portuguese Canary Islands. In the formation of a classic *caldera*, such as at Santorin, a volcano gradually elevates itself from the sea bed. Sometimes the mountain thus formed will subside, and, in doing so, fill up its crater. The solidified rock and stones then begin to seal up the vent out of which the hot *magma* rises from the earth. The effect of this, after a certain length of time, is to produce immense pressure under the old crater, which can lead to an explosion blowing apart the whole centre of the island. After the explosion and consequent subsidence, the sea rushes in to form an immense interior bay.

This was almost certainly the pattern of events in Santorin. It has been conjectured by some geologists and scholars that the explosion of Santorin in pre-classical times may well have had some connection with the sudden collapse of Knossos and the overwhelming of the Minoan civilization. When a *cratera* of these dimensions is formed – as happened when Krakatoa in the Sunda Strait between Java and Sumatra exploded in 1883 – a vast tidal wave is generated. (One gigantic wave from Krakatoa reached Cape Horn – 7818 sea miles away.) Santorin is only about sixty miles north of Crete, and an explosion of this magnitude would not only have thrown down almost every building on that island, but also would have drowned every harbour and port.

Once the collapsed bowl of a *cratera* has been flooded by the sea, over centuries the central core lifts itself again above sea level. This has happened at Santorin, where the small islands in the middle of the dazzle-blue bay (Palaea-, Mikra-, and Nea-Kaïmene – Old-, Little-, and New-Burnt Islands) are all part of the uprising of a new cone. In historic times, Strabo records a major eruption at Santorin in 196 B.C. Mikra-Kaïmene appeared during a violent disturbance in 1570, and Nea-Kaïmene in 1707. The land is still changing, and in recent years a violent earthquake threw down a large part of Thera, the modern capital of Santorin.

The Mediterranean is, at least in much of its central and eastern sections, a part of the world that is still in the process of change. Time and man, each in their different ways, have accounted for much of the erosion and alteration of the lands around the inland sea. But other vast structural changes have been caused by natural forces. The operation of these is, to a considerable extent, understood today, but it is hardly surprising that in the legends and history of this sea volcanoes and volcanic disturbances loom large. That the Greeks and Romans and other Mediterranean peoples should have attributed these fiery cones, these sudden terrifying tremors, these devastating explosions to superhuman forces is hardly surprising. At a time when, as A. K. Thomson writes in *Studies in the Odyssey*,"the limits of human and superhuman, material and immaterial, were but dimly realised," islands like Vulcano and Stromboli and mountains like Vesuvius and Etna were inevitably considered to be the dwelling places, if not of gods, at least of violent and destructive giants. When, to quote A. K. Thomson again, "Every stream and oak and mountain was the habitation of a spiritual being whose nature was on the borderland between the human and the divine and partook of both," man paid his tribute to these manifestations of the gods by prayers and sacrifice.

To this day, the small wayside chapels on the slopes of Etna and Vesuvius are filled with *ex votos* recording thankful deliverance from the violence of the mountain. The Madonna and Her Son now receive the candles and the incense, where once other deities – prehistoric, Phoenician, Greek, Roman – gazed down through the wavering smoke on the prostrate figures of their worshippers. The Pacific may have the most changeless ageless aspect of any ocean, but the Mediterranean Sea celebrates the continuity of man.

THREE

Early Mariners

Man had crossed certain parts of the Mediterranean by boat in pre-historic times. A type of pottery, decorated with patterns impressed into the clay before it was baked – "impressed ware" – has been found at very early levels in south-eastern Turkey, Greece, Italy, and Sicily. But similar pottery has also been found in Malta, proving that, even in the fourth millennium B.C., man had crossed the sixty miles of sea separating the Maltese archipelago from Sicily.

J. D. Evans comments in his archaeological history of the island: "The colonization of the Maltese islands from Sicily was certainly not accidental. . . . From Cape Passero, at the south-eastern corner of the triangular island of Sicily, Malta and Gozo can be discerned on a clear day lying far out to sea. The land-hungry peasants who first crossed the straits to them knew exactly what they were about, and must have planned their expedition thoroughly. As well as themselves and their families, they had to transport their domestic animals and supplies of seed for cultivation. For this they must obviously have had boats of some kind, though not necessarily more elaborate than some form of raft or dug-out canoe. We know nothing more about their boats, however, than inference will tell us, since no remains of such boats or pictures of them have been found, and pictures of more or less contemporary East Mediterranean craft, such as have been found scratched on potsherds in Greece and the Cyclades, are no help, since the boats of the more primitive peoples of the Western Mediterranean were probably much cruder and simpler."

The earliest representations of vessels bearing a definite relation to those which for centuries dominated the inland sea are to be found in Egypt. Some of these, dating from about 3000 B.C., show craft designed solely for the Nile, while others are clearly intended for the Red Sea.

Cattle are the chief cargo. Both types of vessel foreshadow the classical galley in being propelled by sail and oar. Two features are immediately apparent: paddling rather than rowing was the earlier practice; and the first masts were made in two pieces, stepped apart and then lashed together at the top. Similar types of mast are still to be found in some native craft in the Far East, where large bamboos take the place of the single "tree" mast of the Western world. Egypt was a land where trees were scarce. It was for this reason that the Egyptians, despite all their technological and cultural achievements, were slow to venture out upon the Mediterranean.

Twenty or more rowers are shown in some of the bas-reliefs, and it is noticeable that the men all face the bows. They are, in fact, paddling and not rowing. The oars themselves are paddle-shaped, rather similar in appearance to the leaves of the areca palm tree, from which they were possibly copied. Paddling is an earlier method of propelling a boat than rowing – for it is natural for men to wish to look towards the bows of their craft and see in which direction they are heading.

In parts of Asia and the Pacific, to this day, the paddle rather than the oar is generally used. The paddle is the simple, natural, and first implement with which man propels himself upon the face of the waters. The rowing oar is a sophisticated development. It requires that the men who provide the motive power of the vessel are prepared to accept orders from a superior and be no more than "muscle machinery", driving themselves towards an objective they cannot see. An early Egyptian hieroglyph portrays two arms grasping a paddle in the attitude of paddling – and hieroglyphs predate by many centuries other pictorial representations of sea-going ships.

At a later date in Egyptian history one finds pictures of vessels being both paddled and rowed. Later still, all the crew are facing aft. They are rowing blindly, accepting the orders of their officers in the stern.

Cecil Torr remarks in his monograph *Ancient Ships*: "That practice [paddling] may really have ceased before 2500 B.C., despite the testimony of monuments of that date; for in monuments dating from about 1250 B.C., crews are represented unmistakably rowing, with their faces towards the stern and yet grasping their oars in the attitude of paddling. . . ." It is clear that both methods continued to coexist. But when men came to the open sea – and therefore to the necessity for larger vessels – they found that the paddle did not exert enough leverage to drive their boats effectively through the water.

Egyptian reliefs show as many as twenty men working at oars or paddles on Nile boats, while the Red Sea ships seem to have required at least thirty men. However, this may not be an accurate representation, for the artist, then as now, was inclined to adjust his details according to the size of his painting or to his aesthetic feeling for balance. Nevertheless, a very good idea of the type of craft with which men were later to embark upon the Mediterranean can be gained from these early pictures.

The boats appear to be what a modern sailor would call "double-ended". That is to say, there is practically no difference between the shape of their bows and their sterns. The distinction, such as it is, occurs in the stern, where a platform has been constructed for the helmsman and officers who are navigating the ship. This platform has, inevitably, forced the boatbuilder to widen and thicken the stern. The stem is often curved back towards the centre line of the vessel. It is shaped in the form of the sacred lotus. In Egypt this was the water-lily, *Nymphaea lotus*, as opposed to the Homeric *Zizyphus lotus*, a bush with a sloelike fruit that could be used for making a kind of bread as well as a fermented drink.

Some of the vessels, with fragile stems and sterns and long delicate overhangs, are obviously not designed for the open sea. Although the Red Sea ships were certainly fathered by the river-dwellers, they were structurally much heavier. More often than not, the mast is now shown as a single trunk, supported at its base and belayed into the hull of the vessel by heavy twisted rope-strands. The mast is comparatively short – about half the vessel's length – but the single square sail it carries is attached to upper and lower yards which, when lowered, are almost the ship's length. With this type of square sail there could have been no chance of doing anything except run before a favourable wind. This was possible in the Red Sea, where the north–south prevailing winds were reliable. In the more contradictory Mediterranean conditions, this huge low-cut square sail would have been useless, particularly for the Egyptians, whose prevailing wind came "dead in the teeth" of the Nile Delta, out of Crete and the North.

A solution to the problem of how to keep a long vessel from "hogging", or sinking in the centre because her keel was not strong enough to maintain her weight, was evolved by these early Egyptian shipbuilders. They took a long, heavy cable of rope and bowsed it round stem and stern, usually about the point where the ends of the boat ran up from the water, where the "overhangs" begin. This large cable was then led right down the centre of the vessel and kept up taut from the deck, above head height, by strong supports which terminated in a Y-shaped fork through which the cable passed. The effect was rather like a giant clothes-line held up on props. By this means an equal tension was maintained between bow and stern, and much of the strain was taken off the long keel section.

In all these early sea-going vessels the steering was done from a raised platform aft, by means of a paddle (or paddles) hung over the side and fastened by thongs at a pivotal point on deck. The sterns of early vessels precluded the use of a centre-line rudder. It is a curious fact that even in the days of the Roman Empire, when large sailing vessels were regularly using the Mediterranean routes, the steering was still by means of paddles. The axled, hinged, centre-line rudder did not come into general use until the fourteenth century. In the Mediterranean, twin steering paddles were the accepted method of steering throughout the classical period. Later, in northern Europe, the long-boats of the early Norse seafarers adopted the convention of having the steering paddle on the right-hand side of the vessel; hence the "steerboard", or starboard, side.

The cultivation of flax and the techniques of spinning the fibres and weaving them into linen were first developed in the Nile Delta. It is probable that the Egyptians were also the first in this part of the world to make large and efficient sails. There are many references in classical literature to the excellence of Egyptian linen, both as a clothing material and for ships' canvas. A high proportion of the sails that drove the war galleys and the merchant ships of the ancient world were woven in Egypt.

In the early square sails, the sail itself was held between upper and lower yards. The lower yard seems to have been in use from very early times, for it figures in the Egyptian hieroglyph *nef*. But by about 1000 B.C., to judge from a famous relief of the Egyptian navy winning a sea battle over some Asiatic enemies, the lower yard had been discarded.

The bottom corners of the sails are now controlled by ropes, and the sail can be gathered to the upper yard by brailing-ropes, suspended at regular intervals along the yard. In battle, when the war galleys were propelled by oarsmen, the sails were always brailed up to the yards to keep them out of the way. In some types of war galley, the master of the vessel stood in a barrel-shaped crow's nest at the top of the mast. From this vantage-point he conned the vessel, indicating by hand signals to the helmsman in which direction to steer.

Since a vessel was primarily dependent upon oars for propulsion in the summer Mediterranean, it inevitably followed that nations seeking dominance at sea attempted to get as many oarsmen as possible into a ship. But, since a ship cannot be indefinitely lengthened to accommodate an increasing number of rowers, the logical step was to begin to arrange the oars in two or three banks, one above the other. There is no certainty who first evolved the two-banked warship, but it was probably the Phoenicians.

The Assyrians, who were an inland people, familiar only with navigation on their two great rivers, the Tigris and the Euphrates, conquered the area inhabited by the Phoenicians in the ninth century B.C. From this moment on there are representations of Phoenician ships in Assyrian sculpture. Phoenician warships with two banks of oars are depicted on a relief of about 700 B.C., but there is little doubt that this type of vessel had been in use for several centuries before this date.

The Phoenicians, master mariners who left their impress upon the Mediterranean, deserve a more important place in the history of the world than is normally accorded to them. Unfortunately, although it is to the Phoenicians that we owe our alphabet, their own literature has entirely disappeared. It is only from the Greeks and the Romans, both of whom came into conflict with this remarkable people, that we have any record of them, and the portrait of an enemy is nearly always distorted.

The Greek historian Plutarch, writing in the first century A.D., some two centuries after the fall of Carthage, describes the Phoenicians as "a bitter and surly people, submissive to rulers, but tyrannical to those they rule, abject when fearful, but fierce when provoked, unshakeable in resolution, but dour and alien to all humour and kindness." The

Alexandrian historian Appian, writing a century later than this, says that they were cruel and overbearing and "only humble in adversity". On the other hand, the Roman geographer Pomponius Mela, writing at about the same time as Plutarch, is more charitable, and perhaps more accurate, when he remarks: "The Phoenicians were a clever nation, who prospered both in war and in peace. They excelled in the arts, and in writing and literature, as well as in naval warfare and administering an empire."

The name "Phoenicians", *Phoinikes*, was bestowed upon them by the Greeks and it is probably derived from the Greek word *phoinos*, meaning blood-red. This may be an allusion to the famous Phoenician purple dye, which led to their being described as the "purple men", that is, traders in purple. Another Greek word, *phoinix*, from which some derive the origin of the name, means a palm tree, and the Phoenicians are generally credited with having introduced the date-palm into the Mediterranean basin.

They were a people of Semitic stock. They came from the Canaanite branch, and sometimes referred to themselves as *Chanani*, Canaanites. In the Old Testament they are called Sidonians after their major city, Sidon. Originating from either Arabia or the Persian Gulf, they settled along the Syrian coast. Hemmed in at their back by the great mountains of the Lebanon range, it was inevitable that such a people should have looked seawards to find an outlet for their products.

Our knowledge of the Phoenicians really begins in the sixteenth century B.C., when the Egyptians conquered Syria. From that moment on there are a number of references in Egyptian records to the two great cities of Tyre and Sidon, to their artificers and their artifacts. The Hebrew Prophet Ezekiel, in his prophetic lamentation for the fall of Tyre, gives a graphic picture of the city, its commerce, and its marine activities: "Thy borders are in the midst of the seas, thy builders have perfected thy beauty. They have made all thy ship boards of fir trees of Senir: they have taken cedars from Lebanon to make masts for thee. Of the oaks of Bashan have they made thine oars; the company of the Ashurites have made thy benches of ivory, brought out of the isles of Chittim. Fine linen with broidered work from Egypt was that which thou spreadest forth to be thy sail; blue and purple from the isles of Elisha was that which covered thee. The inhabitants of Zidon and

Arvad were thy mariners: thy wise men, O Tyrus, that were in thee, were thy pilots. . . .''

There follows a list of the cities and nations which traded with Tyre, and from which the city derived her wealth. Ezekiel mentions her trade in silver, iron, tin, lead, and horses; ebony and ivory, linen, Tyrian purple, coral, honey, spices, oil, and precious stones. "These were thy merchants in all sorts of things," the prophet concludes, "in blue clothes, and broidered work, and in chests of rich apparel, bound with cords, and made of cedar, among thy merchandise. The ships of Tärshish did sing of thee in thy market: and thou wast replenished, and made very glorious in the midst of the seas. Thy rowers have brought thee into great waters. . . .''

Quite apart from their geographical position on the Syrian coast, the Phoenicians were aided in their ambitions by the magnificent forests of the mountains of Lebanon. The cedars of Lebanon are justly famous, but the Phoenicians also had more common but equally practical woods in the pines, firs, and cypresses with which their land abounded.

The "oaks of Bashan" to which Ezekiel refers were used for the keels of warships rather than for oars. Warships had to be hauled ashore at regular intervals to keep them clean of rot and worm and free from weed, for speed was all-important for a fighting vessel; whereas merchant ships of necessity often had to be long months away from dockyard repairs. Hard oak keels, then, were essential for a warship. The merchant ship more often than not had a keel of pine, since this was cheaper; but even this was often given a false keel of oak to preserve the softer pine when the vessel was slipped. At a later date, in Greek and Roman times, merchant ships which regularly had to use the shipway that ran across the isthmus of Corinth were invariably fitted with these oak false keels. Although the Phoenicians had a plentiful supply of cedar, it was too precious a wood to be used much in shipbuilding. Certainly they did not use it for their masts (as Ezekiel says), for which it would have been unsuitable. The masts in Phoenician warships and merchantmen were most probably of fir or pine, as were the oars.

Byblos (modern Jebel) was one of the earliest Phoenician settlements. Traditionally it was said to be the first city built when the Phoenicians came to their new land. There is some likelihood that this may have been so, for even in historical times Byblos was celebrated for the cult of the fertility and corn god whom the Greeks called Adonis. A corn god is inevitably an important figure in the pantheon of an agricultural people. His cult at Byblos suggests, therefore, that the city was founded at a time when trade and seafaring had not become the Phoenicians' main source of income.

Four other cities are indissolubly linked with the memory of Phoenicia. These cities are Arvad, Tyre, Sidon, and Tripoli. (The last is a Greek name; the Phoenician name is unknown.) All four cities are sited on the coast, and only one of them, Sidon, is on the mainland proper. The others are on islets or on promontories more or less divorced from the shore. Arvad is on an islet, its original area being little more than eight hundred yards in length and slightly less in breadth. Marion I. Newbigin, in *The Mediterranean Lands*, writes: "In point of fact Arvad seems to have been literally a refuge, a magnified 'peel tower', such as one finds on the old border between England and Scotland. The people of Arvad had, on the mainland, lands and settlements, lands which could be cultivated, settlements where markets could be held, arts and crafts carried on. But if their customers suddenly showed a preference for raiding as against bartering, they could betake themselves to their island fortress and wait for better times. . . ."

Enlarging upon an account of Arvad given by the Greek geographer Strabo, Marion I. Newbigin describes the island's unique water supply: "Off the limestone coasts of the Mediterranean Sea it is very common to find that the water which sinks in through the porous rock in the hills fails to find an exit on land, and bubbles up as a powerful submarine spring. The hydraulic pressure ensures that mixing with the surrounding sea-water does not occur immediately. Such a spring occurs between Arvad and the mainland. A hemisphere of lead was placed over this spring, thus confining the fresh water, and to the hemisphere a leather pipe was attached. The force of the water ensured its rise through the pipe, which was placed in a cistern contained in a boat moored over the spot. The device, involving as it does observation, ingenuity and fairly advanced technique, helps us to realize the degree of civilization to which the Phoenicians had attained."

Tyre was a slightly larger island than Arvad, about one mile in length and separated from the coast by less than half a mile of shallow water. The modern city is situated upon a promontory. Alexander the

Great built a causeway out to the island when he sacked Tyre in 332 B.C., and since then the silt of centuries has enlarged this, so that the ancient island is now joined to the shore. As at Arvad, the water-supply system demonstrated Phoenician technology. There were no springs on Tyre, so a source of water was tapped on the mainland and led out by a submarine aqueduct beneath the narrow channel and into the centre of the island. Here, as in the other chief Phoenician cities, it is apparent that this mercantile, sea-going people were always in danger from their mainland neighbours. They were not soldiers. They found their only security in their ships – and in their wits.

The city of Sidon, known as "Sidon the Great, the Mother of Arvad and of Tyre", was on the mainland. But its situation was determined by the fact that a string of rocks and a small islet ran out just off the coast, forming sheltered roadsteads to north and to south. Tripoli was sited upon a promontory and again a chain of rocks and reefs to sea-wards provided two separate anchorages.

Donald Harden comments in *The Phoenicians*: "When they set out later on their colonial ventures the Phoenicians always sought similar sites, and planted colonies at some of the best and most famous fortress and harbour sites in the Mediterranean such as Cadiz in Spain, Valletta in Malta, Bizerta in Tunisia, Cagliari in Sardinia and Palermo in Sicily."

From their four principal cities the Phoenicians gradually built other similar trading posts and towns all along the coastline of what is now Syria, Lebanon, and Israel. From Tarsus in the north via Antioch, Byblos, Beirut, and Jaffa to Gaza in the south, these traders and sea-farers consolidated their hold upon the sea. In a sense they were never a nation, as the word is generally understood. They had no real "country". Although they spoke and wrote a similar language, their only interest in common was trade. A Phoenician was a citizen of Tyre, Sidon, or whatever place it might be, long before he had any conception of belonging to a specific homeland. Kingdoms and prin-cipalities might rise and fall, cultures develop or decline, but the market for the wares and the skills of the Phoenicians always remained.

It was probably this detachment from the vicissitudes of history that led to the dislike shown for the Phoenicians by so many writers of antiquity. From Ezekiel in the sixth century B.C. to Plutarch in the first century A.D., the complaint seems to be much the same: "These people care about nothing except material gain." Indeed, even after their great offspring, Carthage, was destroyed by the Romans, there seems little reason to doubt that the trader of Phoenician descent merely carried on with his business. The Phoenicians were survivors – and many of their descendants still people the inland sea.

Although the Phoenician may have been a merchant, a craftsman, or even a farmer, he was unusual if he grew up far removed from the sea. Whether born in one of the fortified promontories or islets, or on a strip of coast off-fringed by rocks, his whole nature was early conditioned by that element upon which he must either venture himself or entrust the merchandise he handled or the goods he made. It is not surprising that they were among the pioneers of navigation. The Cretans and the Mycenaeans had in many cases preceded the Phoenicians. Indeed, it may well have been a leavening of Mycenaean sailors and traders (dispossessed of the Aegean world by the new Greek invaders) that first started the Phoenician expansion westwards.

Herodotus, writing in the fifth century B.C., describes Phoenician trading methods when dealing with a primitive people, probably the inhabitants of what is now Morocco: "They trade with a race of men who live in a part of Libya beyond the Pillars of Heracles. On reaching this country, they unload their goods, arrange them tidily along the beach, and then, returning to their boats, raise a smoke. Seeing the smoke, the natives come down to the beach, place on the ground a certain quantity of gold in exchange for the goods, and go off again to a distance. The Carthaginians then come ashore and take a look at the gold; and if they think it represents a fair price for their wares, they collect it and go away; if, on the other hand, it seems too little, they go back aboard and wait, and the natives come and add to the gold until they are satisfied. There is perfect honesty on both sides; the Carthaginians never touch the gold until it equals in value what they have offered for sale, and the natives never touch the goods until the gold has been taken away. . . ."

A Greek *Periplus*, or Sailor's Guide, of the fourth century B.C. describes Phoenician visits to an island which many modern authorities consider to have been off the mouth of the Senegal. Here the Phoenician merchants exchanged glass vessels (they were skilled glass-makers), Greek pottery, and unguents for native wine, animal skins, and ivory.

It was possibly the fact that so much of the Phoenician trade was with primitive native countries, where money was useless and only barter understood, that slowed the development of Phoenician coinage. Although in sixth-century B.C. Persia and Greece money was regularly used in trade, the earliest Phoenician coinage that has been found was minted at Tyre in the mid-fifth century B.C. Appropriately enough, a number of the coins subsequently struck at Phoenician cities show on their obverse a war galley ploughing the waves.

The evidence that Phoenician traders were active as far afield as the west coast of Africa (not to be discovered by Europeans until the fifteenth century A.D.) is proof in itself of the seaworthiness of their ships and their navigational skills. By the time they had established their trading posts all over the Mediterranean, from the Levant to Malta and Sicily, Carthage, the Balearic Islands, and the coast of Spain, they seem to have been using two basic types of vessel. These were the "round ship" used for commerce and the "long ship" used for war and for trade protection. The merchant ships depicted on reliefs have convex bows and sterns and appear to be almost symmetrical, only the steering oar at one end indicating which is the stern. As well as a mast with a single square sail they also have double banks of oars. The war galleys are easily distinguished by the long pointed ram at the bows. Soldiers' shields are hung along the deck above the oarsmen, and the vessels are of the bireme type. It was with ships like these that the Phoenician navigators traded with West Africa and, in the reign of the Pharaoh Necho (609–593 B.C.), circumnavigated the whole continent.

Herodotus, who recounts the story of how they took nearly three years on the voyage, going ashore every autumn to plant corn, and then waiting for the next year's harvest, accepts the fact that "Africa is washed on all sides by the sea, except where it is joined to Asia." However, he refuses to believe the very fact that confirms the truth of the Phoenician account. The sailors maintained that as they sailed on a westerly course round the southern shore of Africa, they found the sun on their right, that is, to the north of them. As they were well south of the Equator, this is exactly what they would have observed. Herodotus, a Mediterranean man, could not believe it.

It is scarcely surprising that a people who were capable of circumnavigating Africa in the sixth century B.C. were familiar with every corner of the Mediterranean. Sailors who could venture north through the Bay of Biscay and who even discovered the Azores (as some coins found in the island of Corvo in the eighteenth century revealed) were unlikely to leave any part of the inland sea unexplored. Their colony at Gades (Cadiz) was traditionally founded in the twelfth century B.C., while Malta and Sardinia both seem to have had Phoenician settlements by the ninth century. Carthage itself was founded about 750 B.C. As Carthage rose to become the leading city of the Phoenician world, the establishment of colonies, rather than simple trading centres, became a deliberate point of policy.

Like the British in later centuries, the Phoenicians started out as traders and merchants and then found that in order to look after their trading posts they needed a standing army and navy as well as administrators. Unlike the Romans, who ultimately defeated them, they became an imperial power by accident. Trade drove the Carthaginians to embark upon the imperial role. The Romans, essentially a non-seafaring people, moved out by an extension of land conquest, until they found that they, too, must become mariners in order to control the trade routes of the Mediterranean Sea.

The Phoenician knowledge of navigation must undoubtedly have stemmed from their neighbours in Assyria, Persia, and Egypt – countries where the science of astronomy had been highly developed. The Phoenicians were an essentially practical people, with little real genius for the sciences or the arts. Whereas the astronomer is a man who deals in abstractions that seem to have little relevance to everyday life, the navigator is a practical seaman who makes use of astronomical data and concepts, often with little knowledge of how they are arrived at. The considerable navigational abilities of the Phoenicians must be seen as stemming from the astronomical knowledge of the non-seafaring nations by whom they were surrounded. These were the astronomers; the Phoenicians were the sailors who put their knowledge to practical use.

E. G. R. Taylor in her history of navigation, *The Haven-Finding Art*, sums up the Phoenician achievement in this sphere: "In Homer's own day, which was long after the destruction of the Cretan sea-power, the most able and active seafarers known to history were the Phoenicians. . . . Among them the men of Sidon were reckoned the most highly skilled,

Sidonian pilots being selected for difficult or important enterprises. Greek writers speak of the Phoenicians as their masters in maritime affairs, and in particular as teaching them the better way to distinguish the north by means of the Lesser Bear in place of the great Wain or Plough. As Strabo puts it, the smaller constellation 'did not become known as such to the Greeks until the Phoenicians so designated it for the purpose of navigation.' And here he is echoing the poet Aratus, who in describing the heavens in his *Phaenomena*, composed about 276–274 B.C., writes as follows: 'On either side the axis ends in two poles: but thereof one is not seen, whereas the other faces us in the north, high above the ocean. Encompassing it two bears wheel together. . . . One men call by the name Cynosura, and the other Helice. It is by Helice that the Achaeans [Greeks] on the sea divine which way to steer their ships, but in the other the Phoenicians put their trust when they cross the sea. But Helice appearing large at earliest night is bright and easy to mark, while the other is smaller, yet better for sailors, for in a smaller orbit wheel all her stars. By her guidance, then, the men of Sidon steer the straightest course.' "

Apart from their astronomical knowledge, the Phoenician seafarers brought to their voyaging that intuitive quality found in those who are born and bred by the sea. They knew their native winds and weather, could tell – as thousands of Mediterranean fishermen do to this day – by the humidity on a sail or a rope, if the south wind was going to blow. They knew by the crisp feeling in their hair and on their foreheads when the prevailing north-westerly of the central Mediterranean in summer months was beginning.

A fifteenth-century German monk, Felix Faber, who made a voyage to Egypt, describes pilotage methods with which the Phoenicians, the Mycenaeans, and the Greeks and Romans would have been completely familiar, for circumstances at sea and navigational techniques had changed little in two thousand years. "Besides the pilot, there were other learned men, astrologers and watchers of omens who considered the signs of the stars and sky, judged the winds, and gave directions to the pilot himself. And they were all of them expert in the art of judging from the sky whether the weather would be stormy or tranquil, taking into account besides such signs as the colour of the sea, the movements of dolphins and of fish, the smoke from the fire, and the scintillations when the oars were dipped into the water. At night they knew the time by an inspection of the stars."

Although these early navigators were capable of making extremely long voyages, their journeys were mostly coastal. Whenever possible the pilot navigated from cape to cape, keeping within sight of the land. In the comparatively confined waters of the Mediterranean, this coastwise navigating was practical for many of the trading routes; although even in the Mediterranean there were times when a vessel would have to be out of sight of land for several days on end. As all navigators know, in a sound ship the open sea is a safe place; it is the shore that wrecks ships. As the ancient pilot neared land he had one important navigational instrument – the oldest in the world – to assist him in conning his vessel safely into harbour. This was the lead and line, which may well have originated in Egypt, and must certainly have been used both by the Mycenaeans and the Phoenicians. An Egyptian wall painting of the second millennium B.C. shows some surveyors using a knotted cord for measuring, while the plumb-line, brother to the sailor's lead and line, was in constant use by Egyptian architects.

Herodotus describes how, when he visited Egypt, the lead and line was used to ascertain the depth of water. "If you take a cast of the lead a day's sail off-shore, you will get eleven fathoms, muddy bottom – which shows how far out the silt from the river extends." It is clear from this that navigators, then as now, not only used the lead and line to find depth, but also to find out the nature of the bottom. The lead was hollowed out in the foot and a small piece of tallow was inserted which picked up mud, sand, or gravel when it touched the sea bed.

Just as Noah released the dove to spy out land, so it was also the custom to keep pigeons or other birds aboard and let one out near any anticipated landfall, watching to see in which direction it headed. This practice is still used by some Polynesian sailors.

Another ancient instrument, for use only in shallow waters, was the measuring rod, or quant. This, too, is shown in early Egyptian paintings. One of these, from about 1500 B.C., depicts an Egyptian Red Sea merchant ship approaching land, with the pilot standing in the bows with his measuring rod in one hand. He is conning the ship by directing the helmsman with hand signals. Behind him sailors stand at the sheets of the square sail, ready to haul in, veer, or let the sheets fly at his command. There is also a reference in the *Odyssey* to the "long pole" carried aboard Odysseus' ship.

There were, in these early days, no charts and no means of calculating a ship's speed. The speed, however, was not so important, for, by constant familiarity with his ship, the seaman knew what distance she would cover during daylight hours under oars or under sail. A reference in the *Odyssey* tells us what was considered a good day's run for a Homeric war galley. Odysseus, who is pretending to be a Cretan sea-rover, describes an imaginary passage which he made from southern Crete to the mouth of the Nile: " '. . . we embarked . . . and sailed off with a fresh and favourable wind from the north, which made our going as easy as though we were sailing down stream. . . . On the fifth day we reached the great River of Egypt. . . .' " Presuming that it was probably Messara Bay in southern Crete, the distance from there to the mouth of the Nile is about three hundred miles. If Odysseus, then, made the run under favourable conditions in five days, his distance made good per day was a little over sixty miles or a speed of about three knots. His ship, of course, was comparatively simple compared to the large biremes of the Phoenicians, but it is doubtful whether these would have made more than six knots, even with a fair stern wind.

In the Aegean, once the prevailing northerly meltemi of summer had started to blow, the merchant ships would take advantage of these "favourable winds" to run down the archipelago to Crete, or on beyond Crete to Egypt. Once in Egypt they would have to wait for their return to Greece until a steady southerly, the hot khamsin of that land, began to blow off the desert and the delta. Then, taking this strong and sweltering wind under their stern, they would scud home for Crete and the North.

One of the few remaining evidences of the careful study given to the Mediterranean winds is the so-called Tower of the Winds, built in the first century B.C. in Athens. The knowledge implied in it is certainly not unique to the Greeks, nor to the century in which it was built. It is important to remember, when considering this building alone, that in the days before the magnetic compass, "direction", as we now understand it, meant a wind direction. True, there was the direction given by the rising and the setting sun, which varied in the Mediterranean between the winter and the summer solstice. But other than this the only sense of direction available to the mariner during daylight hours was provided by the winds. Hence, in areas such as the Aegean, where a steady wind prevailed throughout the summer months, it was comparatively easy to locate each island by the knowledge, say, that to sail from Paros to Naxos the wind would be on the port beam, since Naxos lies practically due east of Paros. Pliny the Elder, writing in the first century A.D., says of the island of Rhodes that "it lies fifty miles with the aid of Africus from Carpathos." That is, a sailor from the island of Carpathos in the southern Aegean wishing to reach Rhodes would have to take the "African wind" and sail fifty miles with it before he reached his destination. The "African wind" was the southerly that comes up across the sea from the Libyan Desert, and this would certainly boost his vessel in the required east-north-easterly direction from Carpathos to Rhodes.

The Athenian Tower of the Winds was constructed by the Greek astronomer Andronicus. It is octagonal in shape, and each of its eight faces is distinguished at the top by a personification of the wind coming from that direction. Thus, Boreas, the cold northerly, is shown in a heavy cloak, while Notus, the south wind, has a languid aspect. These two points of the wind were the most important for the classical sailor engaged in trade between Europe and Africa. They dominated the wind-compass; but there were other winds – east and west, for instance – which were important to voyagers working between one end of the Mediterranean and the other. Then again, it had been observed that there was a difference in the feel and texture of the north-west from the north-east wind, and similarly between the south-west and the south-east. These, too, had their names and served to define directions. Basically it seems that throughout the whole classical period the eight points of the wind served most sailors for their navigational purposes. But there were always some who insisted on further and finer definitions. A twelvefold system was evolved and at a later date the finesse of "rhumbs", the thirty-two points that covered the 360-degree circle of the heavens. On the roof of the Tower of the Winds, a bronze Triton, with a rod in his hand, turned and pointed in the direction from which the wind blew. This Triton was, in fact, the ancestor of all the world's weathercocks.

To have dealt chronologically with the history of man in the Mediterranean would have meant starting the account of his maritime activities with the Minoans. But, since the skills and crafts which enabled man to voyage upon the water seem to have come largely out of the East, it seemed reasonable to consider something of the Phoenician contribution first of all. Until comparatively recently, little was known about the earlier activities of the Cretan seafarers. The Minoans, to use the name given them by Sir Arthur Evans, whose excavations in Crete first revealed the existence of this early, pre-classical Greek culture, were great traders and mariners. But although the secret of the Linear B script has been unlocked by the late Michael Ventris, we still know little or nothing about the Minoan ships. The navigational methods and the lives of these Cretan seamen, who ventured into many areas of the Mediterranean centuries before the Phoenicians, are unrecorded.

Even before the rise of Cretan sea power, archaeological finds have shown that men from the eastern Mediterranean – islanders from the Cyclades – were trading from one end of the Mediterranean to the other. A. R. Burn, in his *History of Greece*, puts the date of these Cycladic traders as early as 2500 B.C.: "As in later ages, prospectors for metals made voyages of astonishing length and daring; especially after the discovery of the importance of tin, the Cycladic islanders seem to have made coasting voyages that would have taken many weeks. 'The way of a ship in the sea' proverbially leaves no track, and overnight camps ashore scarcely more; but it actually seems likely that they fared as far as Spain. In Almeria, in Professor Piggott's words, 'small defended settlements with bastioned walls follow the details of planning of town-ships in the Cyclades, and styles in pottery and dress-pins again link the two ends of the Mediterranean at a date which radio-carbon readings show to be soon after 2500 B.C.' "

In Crete and in Mycenae on the Greek mainland, there came into being for the first time a civilization that had grown up around the sea – a sea empire, or thalassocracy. It is now known from archaeological findings that Cretan goods were reaching Syria and Egypt during the reign of Amenemhat (1929–1895 B.C.). At a somewhat similar date, Cretan pottery was being shipped as far afield as the Lipari Islands and Ischia in the Bay of Naples.

After the collapse of this great Cretan civilization, Mycenae on the mainland of Greece became the dominant influence throughout the

Aegean. Later still, at about the time of the Phoenician expansion into the western Mediterranean, the arrival of the Achaeans in Greece led to a breakdown of peaceful sea trading. An inscription of Rameses III on the temple walls of Medinet Habu records that "The isles were restless, disturbed among themselves. . . ." During this predominantly warlike period, Greek trade with the western Mediterranean practically ceased, which helped the Phoenicians to establish trading ports at the other end of the sea, in the Balearic Islands and Spain.

Our first real knowledge of the Greeks as seamen comes from the two great poems of Homer, the *Iliad* and the *Odyssey*, written some time in the eighth century B.C. One thing is immediately apparent: the war galleys of these future conquerors of the Mediterranean are a far remove from the sophisticated Phoenician biremes. The nearest parallel to these Homeric ships seems to be the Viking long-boat of the North, some fifteen hundred years later. Epithets which the poet applies to these galleys range from "hollow", that is, open, to "swift", "well-balanced", and "black". "Black" almost certainly refers to the fact that they were tarred as a protection against rot and the voracious teredo worm, endemic in the Mediterranean.

Cecil Torr, in *Ancient Ships*, comments: "The whole of the outer planking was protected with a coat of tar or wax or both together. The wax had to be melted over a fire until it was soft enough to be laid on with a brush; and usually some paint was melted with the wax, so that the ship received a coat of colour in encaustic." This probably explains why the ship of Odysseus is sometimes described as "blue". At a much later date, Pliny recorded as many as seven different colours being used for painting ships. But the early Homeric craft seem to have been basically black, with sometimes a blue encaustic paint decorating the bows.

A great deal smaller than the Phoenician biremes, the war galleys of the Homeric Greeks had only one bank of oars. It is likely that they had no more than twenty oars, ten on each side. They probably carried a double complement of men, fifty or so for a twenty-oared vessel. All the sailors were free-born Greeks; the slave-powered galley is not found until much later. Again, the nearest comparison to the ships, the men, and the type of life described by Homer is to be found in the Norse sagas. The Greeks themselves were a northern people by origin.

In contemplating why their contribution to world culture was so much greater than that of the Scandinavian sea-raiders, credit must be given not only to their native qualities, but also to the beauty of the land they occupied and to the propitious climate of the Mediterranean.

Although we know that the Phoenicians, and no doubt the Minoans and Mycenaeans, had been using the stars for navigation long before the Greeks arrived upon the scene, the first man in recorded history to use the stars for this purpose is Odysseus. Homer describes in the *Odyssey* how the hero, after leaving Calypso's island, steers homewards to Greece on the sailing raft that he has built himself. "It was with a happy heart that the good Odysseus spread his sail to catch the wind and used his seamanship to keep his boat straight with the steering-oar. There he sat and never closed his eyes in sleep, but kept them on the Pleiads, or watched Boötes slowly set, or the Great Bear, nicknamed the Wain, which always wheels round in the same place and looks across at Orion the Hunter with a wary eye. It was this constellation, the only one which never bathes in Ocean's Stream, that the wise goddess Calypso had told him to keep on his left hand as he made across the sea."

The fact that Odysseus steered to keep the Pole on his left hand in order to get back to Greece, proves that he was steering east. Calypso's island, therefore, was somewhere well west of Ithaca. It may possibly be identified with one or other of the Maltese islands.

Further evidence that the ships of the Homeric Greeks were primitive compared to the great galleys of the Phoenicians occurs when Homer describes Odysseus' arrival in the "land of the Phaeacians". The Phaeacians and their ships are depicted in terms which suggest that the poet had either heard of the Minoan ships of antiquity or had in mind the superior skills and boatbuilding techniques of the Phoenicians.

At the time Homer was writing, the cities of Tyre and Sidon were prosperous and powerful. Indeed, the capital of the Phaeacians sounds very much like a Phoenician city. It is a great seaport, built on an island, and it is connected with the main shore by a causeway. On either side of the causeway there are two harbours – the usual Phoenician plan for their ports – where the shipowners have their own private slipways. The vessels themselves are far in advance of anything known to the Greeks, and are handled by seamen and navigators whose skills appear almost supernatural. The ship in which Odysseus is transported back to his homeland has fifty-two oars – something that Homer, familiar with the much smaller Greek galleys, clearly finds hard to believe. But a Phoenician bireme of this period would indeed have had twenty-six oars on each side, in two banks of thirteen. The Phaeacians' superior skill in navigation is also indicated in the passage where King Alcinous boasts: "Our ships know by instinct what their crews are thinking. . . . They know every city, every fertile land."

The specific references to the Phoenicians in Homer are, however, nearly always unflattering. They are greedy and grasping, sea-rovers who cannot be trusted, and as liable to steal as to trade. But when the poet was writing, the Greeks had already begun to come into conflict with the Phoenicians in the Aegean and Levantine trading routes. The Greeks were a hardy, warlike race, prompted to expand from their mountainous peninsula and rocky islands. The Phoenicians, on the other hand, were not a warlike people. Even in the great days of Carthage, their armies were largely composed of mercenaries. When the Greeks, in the eighth century B.C., began to challenge the Phoenician trading supremacy in the eastern Mediterranean, the Phoenicians more and more began to develop their trade and establish their colonies in the western end of the sea, which the Greeks had scarcely begun to penetrate.

It is already possible to see a pattern in Mediterranean history – one which was frequently repeated in the centuries to come. First of all, in one area or another, some new cultural or technological advance is made – in this case, navigation and shipbuilding. Then, after a certain length of time, nations from other parts of the inland sea profit by their neighbours' discoveries, improve on them, and begin to challenge them. Trade, which knits people together, leads also to conflict. At the same time, the meeting and mingling of people in the course of trade leads to an interchange of knowledge. During the eighth century B.C., the Phoenician alphabet, used principally by its originators for trade alone, was adapted by the Greeks. It spread rapidly throughout the islands and the mainland. But the Greeks, who may originally have seized upon it merely as a means to facilitate commerce, were, with its aid, to create some of the most imperishable literature in the world.

Just as a general surface current sweeps steadily round the sea itself, so the conflict of nations produces a current through the dissemination of trade, ideas, and cultures. The Phoenicians, who had started out as an inland, agricultural people, were first of all driven either by population pressure or by hostile neighbours to make their home on the Syrian seaboard. From there they began to colonize and trade throughout the Levant. The arrival of the seafaring, warlike Greeks then drove them towards the West – an area into which they had already ventured in their need for metals from Spain. Over the centuries this Greek pressure increased, and the Phoenicians, who by now had made Carthage in North Africa their principal city, were driven further west and also north. Sicily, which for a time was their undisputed trading ground, then began to be planted with Greek colonies along its eastern seaboard. So the Phoenicians retreated again – to Lilybaeum and Motya in the extreme west of Sicily, lying in the shadow of Mount Erice. In due course, their involvement in the western basin of the Mediterranean, which had been largely induced by Greek pressure in the east, was to lead to the giant conflict between Carthage and Rome.

Matthew Arnold in "The Scholar Gipsy" envisaged how

> . . . some grave Tyrian trader, from the sea,
>   Descried at sunrise an emerging prow
> Lifting the cool-haired creepers stealthily,
>   The fringes of a southward-facing brow
>   Among the Aegean isles;
> And saw the merry Grecian coaster come,
>   Freighted with amber grapes, and Chian wine,
>   Green, bursting figs, and tunnies steeped in brine;
> And knew the intruders on his ancient home. . . .

At the point where the western and eastern basins of the Mediterranean meet, the great promontory of Cape Bon stands out from the African coast. From there, the island of Sicily lies only about eighty miles away. The peninsula commands the whole east–west trade route of the sea. It affords a good starting point for ships bound not only for Sicily but also for Italy, Sardinia, and Corsica. It is an excellent half-way house for vessels bound for Spain in the far West. Little wonder, then, that the Phoenician merchants and sailors, as they drove their ships round this cape, moored them in the first suitable natural anchorage they found. Deep within the sheltering bay, formed by the horns of

Cape Farina on the west and Cape Bon on the east, there lay exactly the harbour they needed.

According to tradition, Elissa, or Dido as she became known to the Romans, set out with a company of Tyrian aristocrats and young women, and bargained with the local Libyans for the area which later became one of the greatest cities of the ancient world. Tradition has it also that they agreed to buy only as much land as an ox hide would cover. By cutting the hide into ribbonlike strips they managed to lay it round a large enough area of land to found a city and enclose a port. Carthage was born.

FOUR

Etruscans and Greeks

The Etruscans were yet another people to leave an imprint upon the history of this sea. There has been speculation about their origin for centuries, ever since Herodotus described how they emigrated from Lydia in Asia Minor. He recorded that there had been a famine in the land which lasted for eighteen years: ". . . so the King divided the population into two groups and determined by drawing lots which should emigrate and which should remain at home. He appointed himself to rule the section whose lot determined that they should remain, and his son Tyrrhenus to command the emigrants. The lots were drawn, and one section went down to the coast at Smyrna, where they built vessels, put aboard all their household effects and sailed in search of a livelihood elsewhere. They passed many countries and finally reached Umbria in the north of Italy, where they settled and still live to this day. Here they changed their name from Lydians to Tyrrhenians, after the King's son Tyrrhenus, who was their leader." The Tyrrhenian Sea takes its name from this legendary prince.

For a long time Herodotus' account of the origin of this mysterious people was taken as accurate. But then the Greek historian Dionysius of Halicarnassus, in the first century B.C., writing a twenty-volume history of the Roman people, attacked his predecessor's version. He maintained that the Etruscans, far from being immigrants, were autochthonous inhabitants of Italy. Dionysius' theory still has its followers but, as D. Randall-MacIver points out in an article on the Etruscans in the *Encyclopaedia Britannica:* "The insuperable difficulty is the language. Had the Etruscans really been indigenous, they would surely have spoken a language related in some degree to one or other of the dialects which were still being used in the days of Augustus [when Dionysius

83

wrote his history], by the descendants of the really native Italians, that
is to say, of the peoples of the Stone and Bronze ages. And yet, as
Dionysius himself says, their language was something entirely unique
and peculiar; a statement fully endorsed by modern philologists.
Dionysius' theory may contain a slight amount of truth. For the conclusion to which archaeologists are now beginning to rally is that
whereas the Etruscans themselves were immigrants, a very small ruling
hierarchy, the backbone of their power was in the native races which
they subdued: their citizens, agriculturists, workmen, soldiers, artisans
were almost all Italians.''

The fact that all the earliest Etruscan settlements are along the coast
of north-western Italy indicates a people who came by sea, subduing
first the coastal tribes and then moving on to settle the hinterland.
This is confirmed by archaeology, for all the inland towns and settlements have been shown to be of later date than those on the coast.
Vetulonia, one of the earliest settlements, appears to have been founded
about 800 B.C.

Modern research has in one respect confirmed Herodotus' story that
the Etruscans were an Oriental or semi-Oriental people, for the character
of their early art and their forms of religious worship clearly derived
from the East. It is fairly certain that they came from somewhere
between Syria and the Hellespont and that they were among the earliest
mariners of antiquity to settle on the west coast of Italy. They were
certainly not Phoenicians, although they borrowed their alphabet –
either from the Greeks or directly from the Phoenicians – a little before
700 B.C. The legend of Aeneas, the Trojan hero, as told by Vergil in
his *Aeneid*, may not be so very far from the truth after all – that the
founder of Rome, or at any rate of a civilized kingdom on the mainland
of Italy, came as a refugee from Asia Minor, possibly even from the
vicinity of Troy.

By the seventh century B.C. the Etruscans were in control of most of
northern Italy down as far as Campania and the area of Naples and
Salerno. At Cerveteri, Volterra, Terracina, Tarquinia, their cities
thrived and flourished. Skilled metal-workers, they were fortunate in
having all the iron they needed. This was mined in the island of Elba, a
few miles off the coastline where many of their towns were situated.
The woods of Elba (which exist no more) fed their furnaces. When

these were exhausted, they turned to the forests of the Campigliese hills on the mainland for fuel for their iron foundries at Populonia.

There can be little doubt that their techniques and skills were brought with them out of the East. Certainly, even if there had been native ironworkers in the area before the Etruscans arrived, they could not have equalled the sophisticated art and craft of the newcomers. The Etruscans were unsurpassed as jewellers and even to this day the delicacy of their filigree gold-work remains unequalled. The process known as "granulation", whereby patterns of silver or gold grains are soldered to the surface of an article, was a technique in which the Etruscans excelled.

There is further evidence that they had learned this craft in the East, for examples of granulation are found in Egyptian ornaments and jewellery. Herbert Maryon and H. J. Plenderleith in their article, "Fine Metal-Work", in *A History of Technology*, describe the granulation on an Etruscan bowl: "There are more than 860 linear inches in the pattern, and over 137,000 grains were used. . . . The arrangement of the grains and the soldering of such small masses, without flooding or clogging them with solder, required very skilful manipulation." So skilful indeed that, although great efforts were made to rediscover and revive this lost art in nineteenth-century Italy, the sheer technical excellence of the Etruscan gold-work was never equalled.

Robert Browning in *The Ring and the Book* echoes something of this desire to emulate Etruscan gold-work:

> Do you see this Ring?
>   'Tis Rome-work, made to match
> (By Castellani's imitative craft)
> Etrurian circlets found, some happy morn,
> After a dropping April; found alive
> Spark-like 'mid unearthed slope-side figtree-roots
> That roof old tombs at Chiusi: soft, you see,
> Yet crisp as jewel-cutting. . . .

Their art, too, reveals the quality of their life. D. H. Lawrence, in *Etruscan Places*, was carried away by his personal dream of the "good life", and no doubt he transferred a lot of his own dreams to the Etruscans. Yet the many figures of married couples who recline together upon their sarcophagi indicate that women in ancient Etruria occupied a higher and more civilized position than in either Greece or Phoenicia at that time. These husband-and-wife figures show a tenderness between man and woman rarely to be seen in Greek or Roman art.

The sixth century B.C. "Apollo of Veii," though his "archaic smile" may derive from Greek art and influence, is nevertheless far from Greek; the god is completely Etruscan. In the famous wall paintings in the tombs at Tarquinia there is a gaiety and a love of life that is peculiarly Etruscan: it could not be confused with the art of any other ancient nation. The Etruscans were to join the river of Rome, and to lose their own particular identity; yet, although their ships have long since gone under the sea, their art still remains to tantalize and arrest.

Lawrence writes: "There is a haunting quality in the Etruscan representations. Those leopards with their long tongues hanging out; those flowing hippocampi; those cringing spotted deer, struck in flank and neck; they get into the imagination, and will not go out. And we see the wavy edge of the sea, the dolphins curving over, the diver going down clean, the little man climbing up the rock after him so eagerly. Then the men with beards who recline on the banqueting beds: how they hold up the mysterious egg! And the women with the conical head-dress, how strangely they lean forward, with caresses we no longer know! The naked slaves joyfully stoop to the wine-jars. Their nakedness is its own clothing, more easy than drapery. The curves of their limbs show pure pleasure in life, a pleasure that goes deeper still in the limbs of the dancers, in the big, long hands thrown out and dancing to the very ends of the fingers, a dance that surges from within, like a current in the sea. It is as if the current of some strong different life swept through them, different from our shallow current to-day: as if they drew their vitality from different depths that we are denied."

It is hardly surprising that so skilled a race also produced excellent seamen. Seamanship was in their ancestry, and was needed to conduct their trade with the East and with Corsica and Sardinia. For several centuries, while the Greeks were occupied in the Aegean and while the Phoenicians were pushing westwards along the North African coast, the whole of this central area of sea was dominated by the war galleys and the trading ships of Etruria.

The Etruscans, like the Phoenicians, have suffered from the fact that the little we know about them comes from the Romans, who fought them for decades and ultimately conquered them. Lawrence sums up: "The Etruscans were vicious. We know it, because their enemies and exterminators said so. Just as we know the unspeakable depths of *our* enemies in the late war. Who isn't vicious to his enemy? To my detractors I am a very effigy of vice. . . .

"However, those pure, clean-living, sweet-souled Romans, who smashed nation after nation and crushed the free soul in people after people, and were ruled by Messalina and Heliogabalus and such-like snowdrops, they said that the Etruscans were vicious."

For about 150 years these gifted people seem to have lived undisturbed in one of the loveliest regions of Italy, filling their lives with exquisite artifacts in gold, silver, ivory, and bronze. Most of their cultural influences at this time were derived from the East, and they were certainly in regular contact with the Phoenicians. Then, towards the close of the seventh century B.C., the Greeks, sweeping into southern Italy and Sicily, began to make an impact upon the Etruscan world. Their influence is noticeable in the forms, the motifs, and the designs of Etruscan work of this period. Then the navies of the two powers came into conflict as the Etruscans strove to maintain their supremacy over western Italy and its bordering sea, while the Greeks, pushing up from the south, were gradually destroying the old-established power.

The soft Ionian Sea, providing a comparatively easy pathway from the Ionian Islands and western Greece to the mainland of Italy, had long beckoned the Greeks. From the northern tip of Corfu, touching at lonely little Fano Island, and then heading westwards across the narrow stretch where the Adriatic joins the Ionian, the sailor has at the most sixty miles of open water to cross, and only for a short time is he out of sight of land. A small harbour on the very heel of Italy, the modern Santa Maria di Leuca, provides a convenient resting place, and then he has all the southern coastline of Italy on his right hand. Even very unsophisticated boats could have made the journey, and the galleys of the Greeks, by the time their main westwards expansion began in the eighth century B.C., were efficient sea-going craft, manned by experienced sailors who had learned from their contacts with the East the elements of navigation as well as new shipbuilding techniques.

According to Herodotus, the first Greeks to make long voyages were the Phocaeans from the most northerly of the Ionian cities on the coast

of Asia Minor. They are said to have been the earliest Greeks to explore
the Adriatic coast and the Tyrrhenian Sea; they may even have been the
first to voyage as far as Spain, although this honour was disputed by
nearby Kyme in Ionia. A sea-captain of Kyme called Midacritos is
reputed to have brought tin from a "Tin Island" in the West, said to be
Spain, although it may have been Etruscan Elba.

It may seem strange that the first great Greek navigators should have
come from the Asia Minor coast, and not from Greece itself. But the
inhabitants of the Ionian cities were more often than not harassed by
hostile neighbours, which caused them to look outwards to the sea.
Also, their growing prosperity, coupled with a great acquaintance with
Easterners like the Phoenicians, possibly gave them some advantage
over the mainland Greeks. Similarly, Greeks from the long fish-shaped
island of Euboea were early to voyage into the western sea. Two towns
on Euboea, Chalkis and Eretria, formed a trading and colonial partner-
ship with the people of Kyme to set up a permanent headquarters and
trading post on the Bay of Naples. The colony, called Kyme after its
senior city, was founded about 750 B.C. It became better known under
its later Latin name, Cumae, and Vergil mentions it in the *Aeneid* as
having been the home of the earliest sibyl, or prophetess.

Cumae seems to have been deliberately planted not as a "colony" in
the later sense of the word, but as an advance trading post to enable the
Greeks to sell their goods and buy raw materials from their Etruscan
neighbours in the north. No doubt, initially, the Etruscans saw no harm
in this apparently convenient arrangement. At the time it probably
seemed of little importance to so prosperous a people, but they lived to
regret it.

The other Greek cities founded during the next thirty years or so
were colonies in the true sense of the word. The Greeks were becoming
land-hungry. As soon as the knowledge of the rich lands of southern
Italy and Sicily became widespread, there was a natural inclination for
cities to send out groups of men and women to establish new townships
and to take possession of the rich and untilled land surrounding them.
In just the same way, many centuries later, the European powers would
establish themselves throughout America from Boston to Buenos Aires.

Chalkis, one of the three pioneers involved in the Cumae settlement,
was prominent among the early Greek colonizing cities. The Chalci-

dians founded four important cities: Rhegion (modern Reggio), on the toe of Italy, in a superb position to command the trade route through those narrow and dangerous straits; Naxos, a little to the south on the Sicilian shore, not far from modern Taormina; Catane (modern Catania), couched in its favourable bay, with the fertile Catanian plain lying at its back; and Leontini, at the far end of the Catanian plain. All of this was logical and progressive colonization. It was made easier by the fact that the native Sicilians, who spoke a version of the Latin tongue and were primitive farmers of the Bronze Age, were no match for the armoured Greeks with their iron swords and their higher civilization. It is a sad fact that man's civilization, his culture even, marches hand in hand with his weaponry.

It was not long before that spirit of dissension, that inability to work together which bedevilled the Greek city-states throughout their history, led to a clash between Eretria and Chalkis, the two partners in colonization. During the ensuing conflict, in which various other Greek cities were involved, the rising power of Corinth became increasingly evident. The Corinthians were fine seamen; they inhabited a prosperous city; they were among the best Greek craftsmen (their pottery was already being exported to Etruria); and they were ideally situated on their gulf to open up trade and communications with the West. Leaving the gulfs of Corinth and Patras behind them, their war galleys and merchantmen had an easy route westwards; island-hopping up the Ionian via Cephalonia, Ithaca, Paxos, and Corcyra (modern Corfu). Corcyra they had long coveted, but the Eretrians had a settlement there. The war between Eretria and Chalkis provided the opportunity the Corinthians had been waiting for. They swept into fertile, prosperous Corcyra, overcame the Eretrian colonists, and made the island their own colony. They were now ready to progress westwards by easy stages.

In 734 B.C. the Corinthians founded a colony in Syracuse in Sicily. In so doing, they laid the foundations of what was to become the richest Greek city in Sicily; indeed, one of the richest cities in the ancient world. They chose their site well. Syracuse, even more than Catania or Naxos, is endowed with a splendid natural harbour, formed by the island of Ortygia (then unconnected with the mainland) and the great curving bay behind the island. Ortygia, Quail Island, was separated at its northern end from the mainland of Sicily by a very narrow gap. This was bridged at an early period in history and the city expanded inland.

The site had everything to commend it. Not only was there a freshwater spring on the island, the Fountain of Arethusa, but the River Anapus and its tributary the Cyane both flowed into the western side of the great bay. The island was easily fortifiable, and its unfailing spring ensured that in the event of siege the defenders would not be defeated by thirst. Nor were they likely to be starved out, for the countryside around could easily be made to harvest good crops.

Archaeological evidence shows that sailors from Chalkis had already been to the harbour, and no doubt the Chalcidians had had it in mind to make Syracuse one of their next colonies. But since they were occupied in their war with Eretria, the Corinthians, who had already profited from Eretria by seizing Corcyra, were also able to profit from Chalkis by colonizing Syracuse. A native Sicel settlement on the island of Ortygia was replaced by a new Greek town. The landward slopes to the north of Ortygia, below the heights of Epipolae, were settled with industrious farmers, while the ships of Corinth had two fine anchorages; one to the north of the island and one to the south in the great bay itself. Syracuse was destined by nature to become one of the most gracious cities in the world – and one whose history would be more bloodstained than most.

The Etruscans at first did nothing in the face of this steady Greek encroachment in southern Italy or Sicily. Their fertile lands, their rich iron-ore deposits, their skill, and their established dominance over the native Italians seemed to guarantee their security. They were not in conflict with the Phoenicians, whose interests lay mainly in Africa and the far West. They were as yet unaware of the threat that these colonizing Greeks posed to their sea trade.

FIVE

The Island Battlefield

Sicily, the ancient *Trinacria* (Three-cornered Land, so-called from its shape), is one of the largest islands in the Mediterranean. When the Greeks began to surge across the Ionian and plant their settlements, dispossessing the native islanders, Sicily was heavily wooded and had an extremely fertile soil. Its richness astounded the Greeks, used to their own harsh land, which even in those early days never boasted the quality of this "new-found land". At a later date, as E. H. Blakeney writes in his description of Sicily in *A Smaller Classical Dictionary*, the island "produced an immense quantity of wheat, on which the population of Rome relied to a great extent for their subsistence. So celebrated was it, even in early times, on account of its corn, that it was represented as sacred to Demeter, and as the favourite abode of this goddess. . . . Besides corn, the island produced excellent wine, saffron, honey, almonds, and the other southern fruits. The Phoenicians, at an early period, formed settlements, for the purposes of commerce, on all the coasts of Sicily."

The Phoenicians, in fact, were never much concerned with eastern Sicily and, in accordance with their general policy of avoiding conflict unless it was forced upon them, they withdrew before the advance of the Greek colonists. They maintained their principal towns and interests in the west. It was the western end of the island, in any case, that interested them, for it provided the ports and harbours useful for their ships bound to and from Spain. The western end was also closest to their largest and most important colony, Carthage.

The struggle for the possession of Sicily was to rage for nearly five hundred years, from about 700 B.C. until 212 B.C., when it was finally annexed as a province of Rome. Even stripped and denuded as it is today, it remains not only one of the richest, but also one of the most beautiful islands in this sea. The Sicily that the ancients knew was like a jewel. Through its flat fertile plains, its mountain valleys, its green coastal strips, and on every point, headland, and bay where man could beach a boat or build a town, the successive waves of conflict were to roll. Here, after driving the native Sicels inland, Phoenicians and Greeks would found their cities – and fall to war with each other. Here Greek city-state would turn upon neighbouring Greek city-state, in battles and massacres that were all the more bitter for being fought between fellow countrymen. Here, finally, the Romans would break the power of Carthage, subdue that of Greece, and impose that *Pax Romana* which, for all its virtues, was invariably founded upon the deaths of other peoples, cultures, and freedoms.

From its western coast, where the Phoenicians had their port and colony of Motya, to Catania in the east, the island is about 150 miles wide. From the Greek colony at Mylae, a little west of Messina, down to Cape Passero, the ancient Promontory of Pachynus, its greatest length is about a hundred miles. It is an island of extreme diversity, and must have presented an even more variegated pattern and appearance at the time the Greeks and Phoenicians were establishing their colonies. The bare inland mountains, which today dominate the lunar landscape of midsummer by sheer terror, were then thickly forested. There were more rivers than now exist, and valleys on the mountain flanks, today having only a thin, overworked topsoil, were once rich and fertile.

Since the history of the Phoenicians, Greeks, and Romans in Sicily is largely one of maritime endeavour and naval warfare, a sketch of the coastal outline may indicate the stage upon which the Sicilian drama took place. The northern coast of the island is rugged and impressively beautiful. Giant cliffs plunge into the sea, and behind them rise the serrated peaks of the Nebrodi and the Madonie ranges. There are a number of excellent harbours, the finest of which is Palermo. This was the ancient Panormus, one of the most important Carthaginian colonies in the land. Sheltered by the great peak of Mount Pellegrino on the west and Cape Zafferano on the east, the huge bay is protected from all except northerly winds. The Phoenicians had two harbours, one on either side of the town, which furnished all-year-round anchorages for their galleys. Behind the city rises a giant semicircle of mountains, in which nestles the fertile campagna of Palermo. This is the *Conca d'Oro*,

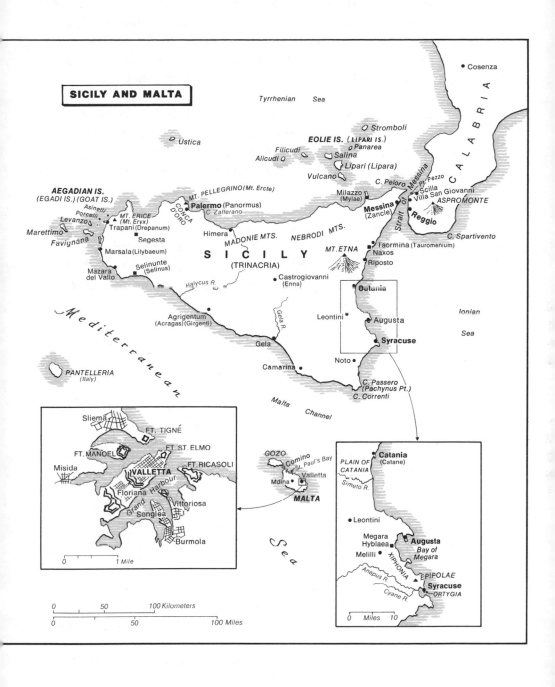

SICILY AND MALTA

or Golden Shell, one of the richest areas in the island. Westwards from Palermo along the northern coast was the land of the city-dwelling Elymi, perhaps old colonists from the Levant. Not that the Phoenicians colonized the land in the same way as the Greeks. Their sole interest was in ports and harbours where they could trade with the natives, rest, and repair their vessels.

The western coast of Sicily is dominated by the bulk of Mount Erice and ends in a point at Trapani, where the Aegadian Islands trail out to the open sea. Near by was the Phoenician trading post of Motya, later to become the main base from which Carthage prosecuted her Sicilian wars. It was set on a small circular island, itself sheltered from the sea by another long narrow island. A man-made causeway connected Motya to the mainland of Sicily. The lagoon between the island and the mainland provided a safe anchorage for most of the shipping, although the Phoenicians also constructed a small *cothon*, or artificial harbour, on Motya itself, for the repair and maintenance of their war galleys.

South-eastwards, the coast falls away into lower-lying land, where the Greeks later planted their colonies of Selinus, Acragas, Gela, and Camarina. If the south wind blows up hot from Africa, there are few sheltered harbours in this area, and only one river of any size, at Mazara, provides limited shelter in its mouth. The hills backing the southern coast are lower than those in the north and west, and recede further from the sea. The coastal strip is fertile.

Rounding the southernmost tip of the island at Pachynus, the sailor of ancient times saw ahead of him a rocky coast with little in the way of anchorages or harbours until he came to the great embracing bay of Syracuse. Not far north of here another large arm of sea inserted itself into the land, sheltered by the promontory Xiphonia. Too close to Syracuse to be of much importance in the classical world, the great Bay of Augusta nevertheless provided a welcome resting place on the voyage up the east coast of the island. Nearby, the Greek colony of Megara Hyblaea was established about 700 B.C. by emigrants from central Greece. From here on, the whole coastline was dominated by the swelling shoulders of Mount Etna, whose peak, streaming cloud or smoke, served as a beacon for mariners from miles away at sea.

Crossing the idle Ionian in high midsummer, the sailor's first sight of Sicily was this awe-inspiring peak, within which Hephaestus and his

Cyclopean minions forged the thunderbolts that Zeus hurled about so recklessly when the storms of autumn broke. Sheltered by the giant, the long plain of Catania spread its rich land to the south, watered by the Simeto River. The base of the mountain took up a total of four hundred square miles out of Sicily's 9800.

The vine, brought from Greece, soon established itself in the dark, friable volcanic earth, and various small farming settlements grew up on the mountain flanks. Catane lay to the south of the mountain, and Naxos slightly to the north. North again was the city of Zancle (modern Messina), a later foundation by the colonizers of Naxos. It guarded the Sicilian side of the Messina Strait, and provided a welcome haven for mariners bound north or south through those turbulent waters.

> O Singer of Persephone!
> In the dim meadows desolate
> Dost thou remember Sicily?

Out of the late Victorian Age, Oscar Wilde invokes the spirit of the island's greatest poet, Theocritus, who in the third century B.C. had written: "I, Theocritus, who wrote these songs, am of Syracuse, a man of the people. . . ." The creator of pastoral poetry, who disguised the harsh life of peasant and fisherman under a veil of grace and elegance, Theocritus still speaks for the island.

Beneath its harsh bones, its withered ribs of hills and mountains, its few streams, and its coastal plains, the Sicily that seemed like a place of magical richness to Greek, Phoenician, and Roman can still be discerned.

The olive and the vine, both of which the Greeks assiduously cultivated in their new colonies, are as emblematic of Sicily as they are of Greece itself. The importance of these two plants to the life of Mediterranean man, from the time the Greeks and the Phoenicians inhabited Sicily right up to the present day, can never be over-estimated. Marion I. Newbigin writes in *The Mediterranean Lands*: "Animal fat, especially in the form of butter, is difficult to get in typical Mediterranean Lands on account of the scarcity of summer pasturage. The olive oil obtained by pressing the fruit is an admirable substitute, especially when used with green salads, which contain substances in which the olive is deficient, though they are present in butter. A digestible fat like olive oil is especially necessary to Mediterranean man since his diet typically includes but little meat, especially butcher meat.

"Wine occupies a different but hardly less important place in the dietary. . . . The grapes swell with juice precisely at the period when the rainfall is minimal or altogether absent. But the drying up of the streams makes it difficult for man to get pure drinking water at the time when thirst is greatest. To express the juice from the grapes to get a drink is an obvious remedy, and suggests that fundamentally the vine is a kind of organic pump which brings water from the sub-soil to within man's reach. But, as we all know, the grape as plucked has a 'bloom' on its surface. In that waxy bloom lives a kind of yeast, which, if mingled with the juice by the crushing process, causes 'spontaneous' fermentation, turning sugar into alcohol. Wine-making in its origin is thus a purely natural process. Most Mediterranean wines are 'light', that is, have a small alcohol content, and such light wines, though not a food, are a valuable supplement to a diet so largely composed of vegetable matter as is that of Mediterranean man. Without it bread, beans, salad and oil do not give full satisfaction. Since also large quantities of fluid must be drunk, and in early days neither coffee nor tea was available, wine is a safer and pleasanter drink than tepid and probably impure water."

In Sicily, as in Greece, the foundation of a town or a port was totally dependent upon there being a natural source of water at hand. Syracuse, despite its good harbour, would never have arisen where it did but for the Fountain of Arethusa and the two streams which thread the land around. It is noticeable in Homer's *Odyssey* that every description of an anchorage where Odysseus and his men spend some time is distinguished by a remark about the water supply. At Goat Island, for instance, they find "at the head of the harbour there is a stream of fresh water, running out of a cave in a grove of poplar-trees." And in Circe's magic mountain, Odysseus makes a point of the fact that the great antlered stag, which he kills to make a meal for himself and his men, is brought down by the heat of the sun " 'from the forest pastures to drink at a stream, and as he came up from the water I caught him on the spine half-way down his back.' " Later, when Odysseus is alone (all his comrades having perished) and is detained by Calypso in her remote island west of Greece, he does not forget to mention that " 'Around the mouth of her cave a great vine surged with bunches of fine ripe grapes, and from

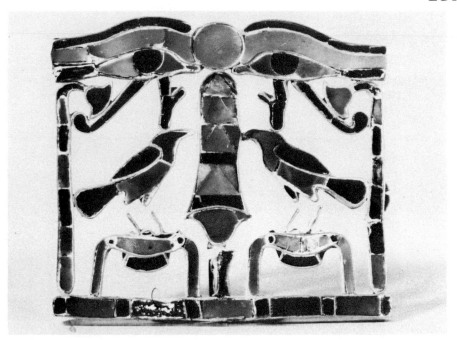

A jewelled pectoral from Riqqeh

A model reconstruction of an Egyptian ship of about 1300 B.C.

THE MOTHER GODDESS

In the Cyclades

In Crete

In Malta

four separate springs nearby four streams of crystal water were channelled throughout the land. . . .' "

Sicily had everything to commend it: good vine-growing country, land for pasturage and for agriculture, water, harbours, quarryable stone, trees for fuel and for boatbuilding, and craggy uplands where goats could pasture. Wherever the land could not support cereals or the vine, the hardy olive flourished. Before it was ravaged by thousands of years of occupation by man, Sicily was a Garden of Eden, floating on the water south of Italy and bridging the worlds of Europe and Africa. The men who came here first, seeing it rise at dawn or at sunse over the waves as they made their way westwards from Greece or northwards from Africa, must have felt their hearts lift.

The Phoenicians, in Sicily as elsewhere, sought sites that were easily defensible and provided good bases from which to trade with the interior. The Greeks made the same pragmatic demands on a site as their Phoenician rivals, but they could not be content if these needs alone were fulfilled. Motya, for instance, on its flat obscure islet, hemmed in from the sea by another islet and overlooking an unimpressive strip of coast, although practical, would not have satisfied the Greeks. It lacked situation; it lacked the necessary natural beauty. The Greeks had the ability to make use of hill shapes and land and sea vistas to create cities that were glorious as well as prosperous.

The great Roman orator and author Cicero, writing in the first century B.C., when Syracuse was no more than a town in the Roman province of Sicily, can still say of it: "Syracuse is the largest of all Greek cities, and the most beautiful of all cities. . . . It is both strong by its natural situation and striking to behold, from whatever side it is approached, whether by land or sea."

Not Syracuse alone, but all the major Greek cities planted in Sicily commanded sites that were not only defensible, but beautiful. The Greeks had a genius for "place", and they were fortunate in their time that they came upon the canvas of the Mediterranean world when it was still unspoiled. Not for them the modern architect's problem of having to establish a building or complex of buildings within a framework of previous architecture, roads, public utilities, and the disorganized rash left behind by speculative builders. Sicily, like southern Italy, was a virgin landscape. Zancle and Catane commanded lovely clean bays where there was no clutter and no detritus of the centuries. The city architect could decide exactly where the main square was going to be; where the principal temples and the treasury and the acropolis; where dockyards should be built and slips for the galleys laid out; and where the quarters of the boatbuilders and other craftsmen should lie.

Gela was planted on a low hill in southern Sicily overlooking the sea and the River Gela, surveying a rich coastal plain. Acragas, which was an offshoot of Gela, was also close to the sea, its acropolis two miles from the shore, but its main buildings were spread around its feet within a containing wall. The situation is breathtaking. So, too, is that of Selinus (modern Selinunte) whose ruins are still the most impressive of any Greek city in the island. It commanded a harbour (long since silted up), and its noble temples spreading northwards from the acropolis shone out against rich cultivated land. Hellenized Segesta, an Elymian foundation in the northwest corner of the island, though some distance from the sea, yet commands one of the finest situations of any Greek city. As backdrop there rise great flanks of land. Then, in the far distance, framed as if in the V-sight of a gun, there shines the long blue line of the Tyrrhenian Sea.

Upon this grand stage of Sicily, nature conspired to produce one of the most gracious environments in the Mediterranean. Here the genius of man embellished it with some of the finest planned cities in the world. And here the sad drama of jealousy, battle, and conquest was played out.

SIX

Greeks, Phoenicians, and Etruscans

The Greek expansion westwards did not by any means end at Sicily. The inhabitants of Phocaea, a seaport near Kyme in Asia Minor, were driven from their land by the Persians in the mid-sixth century B.C., and forced to find another home. They had already reached Spain and planted one of two colonies there, but their most famous achievement was to found, in about 600 B.C., the city of Marseilles. Herodotus says of them that they regularly travelled "not in merchant ships but in war galleys", and they were soon at loggerheads with both the Phoenicians and the Etruscans.

The westernmost Phocaean outpost of which we have certain knowledge was Emporiai, "Trading Posts", on the Costa Brava. They also established similar settlements in Corsica, but were ultimately driven out of these by the combined fleets of Carthage and Etruria about 535 B.C. By this time both Etruscans and Phoenicians had realized the growing danger of the Greek presence in the western Mediterranean, and had entered into a defensive alliance to keep out the newcomers. As A. R. Burn comments in his *History of Greece*: "The Greeks were certainly not innocent in the increasing hostility that developed in the west from this time on; and their enemies succeeded in limiting their advance."

The Greeks were far from "innocent". In fact, both the Etruscans and the Phoenicians would have been reasonably content to leave the Greeks secure of the Aegean, of most of southern Italy, and of eastern Sicily. But these territorial gains were not enough for the Greek city-states, driven both by prosperity and by population to increase their dominion in the central Mediterranean and the West. Prosperity, among other things, impelled cities like Corinth and, at a later date, Athens, to seek an expansion of trade routes and further sources of raw materials. Some city-states, on the other hand, were driven by foreign pressure to emigrate; and others by the poverty of their native land.

Talented, with a culture that was to become superior to any other in the Mediterranean, the Greeks were also an aggressive and warlike people. In later centuries, European scholars, poets, and historians have sometimes romanticized the Greeks. While giving full credit to them for their contributions in the arts, philosophy, mathematics, and social organization, it would be foolish to pretend that sheer aggression was not part of the rocketlike force that swept the Greeks all over the Mediterranean. This same urgent drive, no doubt, also fired their cultural achievements.

An important date in the history of the clash between the Greeks and the Phoenicians is the foundation of Carthage, traditionally 814 B.C. Quite quickly this new African colony came to assume the mantle of leadership in the Phoenician world. Admirably placed to command the westward trade to Spain and to the tin mines of Britain, Carthage was linked with her western colonies in Sicily and Sardinia by a short sea journey. By the sixth century B.C., it is the activities of Carthaginians that we hear about, not of Phoenicians. As is often the case, the mother country was eclipsed by her offspring.

About 580 B.C., a group of Greeks from Rhodes and Cnidus attempted to establish a colony at Lilybaeum. This was the westernmost promontory in Sicily, just south of the Carthaginian colony of Motya. Lilybaeum provided an excellent harbour (where the modern city of Marsala stands), and was the nearest point in Sicily to Cape Bon in North Africa and the city of Carthage. The Carthaginians could not permit such a threat to Motya and to their main trade route. They reacted swiftly. The Greek would-be colonists were driven out and were forced to take to their ships again. They made their way north, finally settling at Lipara, largest of the Lipari Islands.

The Phoenicians, whenever possible, followed their normal course of avoiding conflict. There is abundant evidence to show that their settlements and colonies throughout this period were trading with the Greeks and becoming partly Hellenized. The Phoenicians had little racial or religious prejudice and, provided that "business as usual" was the order of the day, were happy to coexist with the Greeks. It was only when they felt their trade routes seriously threatened that they resorted to arms.

In 600 B.C., Carthage attempted to prevent the Phocaeans from establishing themselves at Massilia (Marseilles). The reason they were concerned about a Greek presence on the French coast was simply a matter of trade, and that all-important metal, tin. John Boardman points out in his history of Greek colonization, *The Greeks Overseas*: "An alternative route from the tin islands of Britain to that which led to the south of Spain lay overland across France. On the southern route the East Greek traders – mainly Phocaeans, it seems – had to face the competition of the Phoenicians, and not even their island bases on Corsica, Sardinia, and the Balearics were safe. As long as Etruria was friendly, though, they could push up a safe coastline to France and to the other tin route where the Phoenicians did not operate, at least in strength. In accordance with their practice elsewhere, they safeguarded their trade by founding colonies."

The Phoenician attempt to keep the Greeks out of Marseilles was a failure. More and more, the "grave Tyrian trader" was forced to depend for his tin supplies upon Spain and the sea route through the Bay of Biscay to Britain.

Sixty-five years after the Carthaginians' failure to oust the Phocaean Greeks from Marseilles, the latter suffered an overwhelming defeat in a sea battle off Corsica. They had been settled in Corsica in a small way for some thirty years, but their piratical habits and their interference with the trade of both Etruria and Carthage at last provoked these two powers to form an alliance. In 535 B.C., the combined Etruscan and Carthaginian fleets fell upon the Phocaeans and defeated them. The small Greek colonies established in Corsica and Sardinia were forced to withdraw. The Etruscans and Carthaginians now defined their spheres of influence in this part of the sea – the Etruscans maintaining their hold over Corsica, and the Carthaginians over Sardinia.

The Greeks were now more or less barred from the western routes of the Mediterranean, and the existence of their colony at Marseilles became even more important to their economy. The importance of tin in the ancient world (for alloying with copper to make bronze) may in some ways be compared with that of fuel oil in the modern world. Tin routes, like oil routes today, were the Achilles' heel of a nation's economy. The need for tin was a major factor in driving nations into conflict.

Another group of Greek colonists, this time from Sparta, invaded Carthaginian territory in about 515 B.C., when they attempted to make a settlement on Mount Eryx, overlooking Motya and Lilybaeum. Once more the Carthaginians and their local allies, the Elymi, threw out the Greeks, maintaining their dominance over this corner of Sicily.

In Italy a few years earlier the Etruscans had realized the threat posed by the Greek colonies on the mainland and had attacked the settlement at Cumae in the Bay of Naples. But the attack failed and from this moment on the power of Etruria waned. The Greeks became increasingly active in the waters of the Tyrrhenian Sea; the Carthaginians held nearly all the trade routes to the west; and behind Etruria the shadow of Rome began to emerge.

Donald Harden writes in *The Phoenicians*: "Etruscan power was on the decline. Rome thrust out the Tarquin (Etruscan) kings in 510 and became an independent republic, and the very next year – and how surprising and significant this is – she made a treaty with Carthage defining mutual spheres of influence. Carthage no doubt saw that the new state was likely to prosper, though she cannot yet have suspected that serious rivalry for world power would break out between them in the future. Her real enemies were still the Greeks."

Alliances between nations, unlike friendships between individuals, are solely promoted by self-interest. Greeks were to be found in the ranks of the Latin alliance for defence against ancient Etruria. Similarly, in the conflict between Persia and Greece, it is hardly surprising to find that a large part of the Persian fleet was provided by the Phoenicians.

By 524 B.C., after the alliance of the Persians with Tyre, the whole of the Phoenician homeland was subject to Persia. This was one factor that led to the expansion of Carthage. But the real reason why the Phoenicians (quite apart from the fact that they were now subjects of the Persian Empire) so willingly provided their fleets for use against the Greeks was the struggle that still raged around Sicily for control of the central and western Mediterranean. "The duty of princes as to the obligation of keeping faith", about which Machiavelli wrote so convincingly in sixteenth-century Italy, was well understood in the sixth century B.C.: there is *no* obligation, provided that advantage may accrue.

A cynical outlook towards alliances is not a perverse modern product, but is as old as the history of man.

Just as in the choice of sites for their cities the Greeks had an empty and unspoiled canvas upon which to work, so they were clever experimenters in the manner in which these cities were operated and governed. Upon the new canvas of political thought they now tried out everything from dictatorship to democracy and even, in the Lipari Islands, a form of communism. During the Homeric period they had been led by kings or chieftains. Agamemnon, for instance, was King of Mycenae, and Odysseus was Leader of the confederation of Ithaca and the nearby Ionian Islands (more like a Scottish chief than a king).

This early pattern of sovereignty had begun to break down long before the age of Greek colonial expansion. G. Lowes Dickinson, in his study *The Greek View of Life*, indicates the main patterns into which Greek political experimentation fell: "The majority of the states in Greece were in a constant state of flux; revolution succeeded revolution with startling rapidity; and in place of a single fixed type what we really get is a constant transition from one variety to another."

This restlessness about political form is a trait which has never left the Greeks, as events in this century have amply demonstrated. Throughout their history they frequently discarded democracy in favour of oligarchy or even dictatorship – the rule of a "tyrant", not always synonymous with what the word has come to mean in English.

To quote G. Lowes Dickinson again: "Aristotle, whose work is based on an examination of all the existing states of Greece, recognises three main varieties [of government]: government by the one, government by the few, and government by the many; and each of these is subdivided into two forms, one good, where the government has regard to the well-being of the whole, the other bad, where it has regard only to the well-being of those who govern. The result is six forms, of which three are good, monarchy, aristocracy, and what he calls a 'polity' par excellence; three bad, tyranny, oligarchy, and democracy. Of all these forms we have examples in Greek history, and indeed can roughly trace a tendency of the state to evolve through the series of them. But by far the most important, in the historical period, are the two forms known as Oligarchy and Democracy; and the reason of their importance is that they corresponded roughly to government by the rich and government by the poor. 'Rich and poor,' says Aristotle, 'are the really antagonistic members of a state. The result is that the character of all existing polities is determined by the predominance of one or other of these classes, and it is the common opinion that there are two polities and two only, *viz.*, Democracy and Oligarchy.'. . . In other words, the social distinction between rich and poor was exaggerated in Greece into political antagonism. In every state there was an oligarchic and demo-cratic faction; and so fierce was the opposition between them, that we may almost say that every Greek city was in a chronic state of civil war, having become, as Plato puts it, not one city but two, 'one comprising the rich and the other the poor, who reside together on the same ground, and are always plotting against one another.' "

Throughout the struggle over Sicily, the Greek colonies themselves were in a constant state of ferment. It was not only that within one city oligarchy would be overthrown by a democracy, possibly to be over-thrown in its turn by a "tyrant"; cities were also at war with one another. It was only on rare occasions that a coalition could be formed strong enough to counter any Carthaginian threat. As Nathaniel Lee writes: "When Greeks joined Greeks, then was the tug of war."

In the long run, it was this inability to work together as one nation and one people that laid Greece and its colonies open to dominance by Rome. Then, as now, Greeks were individualists to a man. They would rather perish separately than agree together for any length of time or submit to the overall control of one city or state. Only on occasions of what were seen as "national emergencies" were the Greeks prepared to forget their private quarrels and combine, as happened during the Persian invasion of their homeland. Even then, there were some cities and islands prepared, for different reasons, to help the Persians rather than make common cause with their fellow Greeks. What the Greeks could achieve when they worked together in a unit larger than the city-state was demonstrated during the period of the Athenian Empire, and again, and more effectively, under the great Macedonian King Alexander.

The Phoenicians and the Carthaginians, on the other hand, seem to have had little interest in political theorizing. Their practical nature could find political content so long as business was not interfered with and prosperity reigned. In their early days they, like the Greeks, had

had kingships in their various cities, and even after hereditary royalty had disappeared from the old Phoenician cities it still seems to have held sway in Carthage. As late as the sixth and fifth centuries B.C., descendants of the Magon family such as the famous Hasdrubal and Hamilcar are referred to as "kings". Such a king was, perhaps, no more than *primus inter pares*, and the title may well have been only convention. In any case, the Carthaginians and their Phoenician ancestors had little use for the concept of democracy – something that they were all too familiar with from their Greek neighbours.

An oligarchy, whereby a few of the most powerful families held the chief reins of office, was the Carthaginian solution to man's political needs. This was in no way an unrestrained form of government, giving all power into the hands of a few who might well be irresponsible or incompetent. The Carthaginian form of oligarchy, which seems to have been derived from Tyre, was formed at the top by two magistrates who undertook the executive functions of the state. Known as Suffetes, they approximated to the modern conception of chief magistrates, and were elected annually. The main ruling body was a Senate of three hundred, appointed for life, all of rich and powerful families. Below them, or in conjunction with them (it is difficult to discover), came another lifetime group of 104 members, who were responsible for the safety of the state or city and the appointment of generals for national defence. It was to them that the leaders had to answer for their conduct of military and naval affairs. At the bottom of the Carthaginian system came the General Assembly of the people, whose opinion seems to have been consulted on matters of general moment, but whose advice was certainly ignored if it conflicted with that of the Senate. It is a system which has to some extent been copied in modern democracies, where the governing party, once safely elected, can more or less ignore the opinions of the people, but only until another election is in the offing. The Carthaginian Senate and the Committee of Public Safety, however, were fortunate in not having to submit to any electioneering. They never had to cultivate the masses with sweet promises in order to retain office.

Generally speaking, the real power in Carthage or in any of her colonial cities seems to have been exerted by the rich merchant class. Donald Harden remarks: "The choice of magistrates and entry to the senate seems to have been largely based on wealth rather than on hereditary qualifications, at least after the sixth century . . . neither in the east nor in the west do we hear of much internal unrest and rivalry amongst the citizens of various social grades – not nearly so much as we read of in Greek states or Rome."

In the battleground of Sicily and the Tyrrhenian, in the struggle between Carthaginian, Etruscan, and Greek, there was no conflict of religion or ideology. This occurred much later in the history of the Mediterranean; after Christianity had introduced the concept (incomprehensible to the ancients) that all other religions were false, and must be rooted out. Trade routes and land were the simple causes of the struggle between these three ancient peoples. Only in the Greek cities was there an internecine strife revolving round theories of government. More often than not, these theoretical considerations were no more than a smoke screen to obscure the real interests of individuals and parties concerned, as always, with power and wealth.

While this three-cornered struggle was going on around the three-cornered island, a new influence upon the history of this sea was beginning to make itself felt. While the Phoenicians were being driven ever westwards by the aggressive policies of the Greeks, the power of Persia was rising like a whirlwind over all the East and the Levant.

SEVEN

Persians and Greeks

"Behold, a people shall come from the north, and a great nation, and many kings shall be raised up from the coasts of the earth. They shall hold the bow and the lance: they are cruel, and will not show mercy: their voice shall roar like the sea, and they shall ride upon horses, every one put in array, like a man to the battle, against thee, O daughter of Babylon." The Jewish prophet Jeremiah foresaw the coming of the Medes and the Persians, and rejoiced because he envisaged Babylon, where the Jewish people were held captive, overthrown.

In 538 B.C., the great Cyrus at the head of his armies did indeed sweep into Babylonia from the north, bursting through the wall that Nebuchadnezzar had built between the rivers Tigris and Euphrates. Babylon fell to the all-conquering Persians. The proud city, so detested by its Jewish captives, was destined to become no more than the capital of a province in the immense Persian Empire. Cyrus' son, Cambyses, was now installed as King of Babylon. The voice of the great conqueror can be heard in the words inscribed in cuneiform script on what has become known as the "Cyrus Cylinder": "I am Cyrus, King of the World, the Great King, the legitimate King, King of Babylon, King of Sumer and Akkad, King of the four corners of the Earth, the descendant of men who have always been kings."

It was inevitable that the Persian Empire in its steady process of expansion should in due course come into conflict with the Greeks in Ionia. From there on, it was only a short step to mainland Greece itself. That so much is known about the Persian wars with Greece is due to one man, Herodotus of Halicarnassus. He was the first European historian, and is often called the "Father of History".

In the opening sentence of his great work, *The Histories*, still one of the keystones of all Western literature, and as entertaining as it is historically fascinating, Herodotus states his ambition: "In this book, the result of my inquiries into history, I hope to do two things: to preserve the memory of the past by putting on record the astonishing achievements both of our own and of the Asiatic peoples; secondly, and more particularly, to show how the two races came into conflict."

A. R. Burn, in his *Persia and the Greeks*, points out one of Herodotus' great strengths: although he may not have appreciated the economic and material causes which underlay the clash between Greece and Persia, he did sense the deep underlying conflict between West and East, which time and again in history has changed the whole pattern of life in the Mediterranean basin.

"On the causes of the Persian War he [Herodotus] does not, in fact, reveal any very profound thought; one of the chief points in which he himself is still primitive is that he does not probe for historical causes deeper than the desires of principal actors. But he does show . . . how in his time . . . there had arisen a conception of a deep cleavage between men living on opposite sides of the Mediterranean; a conception fraught with long-lasting and tragic consequences, even after the age-long union of the Mediterranean world under Rome."

The commercial rivalry between the Greeks and the Phoenicians in the Levant, which had led to this Semitic people being gradually driven from their home waters, was a prologue to the vast drama that was to be enacted upon the Mediterranean. Here first, the Herald had, as it were, announced the playwright's theme: The Conflict of East and West. Throughout this drama there would sometimes occur long periods of peace – which might be termed marriages – but these would invariably break down and another struggle would develop. At the same time, whether East and West were at variance or not, there would always be a steady process of cross-fertilization, which would immeasurably enrich the Mediterranean scene and the culture of the whole Western world.

Warfare, with its emphasis on improved arms, city defences, and warship construction, was not without its ultimate benefits, for the demands of war speed technology. In periods both of peace and of war, myths and religions, languages and cultures, were making an intricate warp and weft upon the web of the inland sea. Sometimes, like Penelope's robe, the day's work was undone overnight. But slowly over the centuries a tapestry was being evolved of amazing richness and splendour.

If the withdrawal of the Phoenicians before the Greek advance was the prologue, then the first part of Act One was the clash of Greeks, Phoenicians, and Etruscans in the central Mediterranean. This in its turn foreshadowed the next stage in the drama. While this struggle still continued in the background, the foreground was now occupied by the conflict between Persian and Greek, which was to have so momentous a bearing on Europe's future.

Many centuries later, when the Ottoman Turks advanced out of Asia upon the Byzantine Empire, the first Greek cities and colonies to fall were those on the Asian mainland. Foreshadowing this future pattern, the cities of ancient Ionia were the first to crumple under the Persian hammer. The interminable feuds and factions of the Greeks meant that on a number of occasions the Persians had no need to besiege or conquer the Greek cities. On the contrary, their inhabitants were often quite happy to come under Persian rule. Sometimes, too, a group of citizens would conspire with the Persians and hand over their city in return for being made its new leaders.

Even during the most desperate phases of the Greco-Persian struggle there were always Greeks to be found in the Persian camp – exiles seeking revenge on their fellow Greeks, or intentional defectors seeking power. As always in the history of power politics, both sides were willing to make use of renegades from the other camp; and traitors with grievances or imbued with the belief that the Persian cause was superior to the Greek were to be found in the King's court at Ecbatana. Some of them were his campaign advisers; others were in the army or aboard the ships that undertook the invasion of mainland Greece.

In 513 B.C., Darius I, having visited all his empire and extended its frontiers – except in the north-west, where the Asian mainland was nearest to Greece at the Bosporus and the Dardanelles – decided to complete the circuit and determine his northern frontiers. The important Greek island of Samos had by now come within the Persian orbit by the usual tale of intrigue, as in somewhat similar circumstances had the other principal eastern Aegean islands, Lesbos and Chios.

All the Ionian Greek allies of the Persian King had to put their ships at his disposal when Darius marched his army north to the narrows of the Bosporus. Here a skilled Greek engineer, Mandrocles of Samos, had constructed a bridge of boats across the strait. Without the delay that would have been caused by ferrying across so large an army, the troops simply marched over the sea into northern Thrace. Herodotus describes a picture which Mandrocles later had commissioned, paid for by part of the money Darius gave him for his bridge-building achievement. It showed "the whole process of the bridging of the strait, and Darius himself sitting on his throne, with the army crossing over".

Some indication of the naval power available to the Persians at this time can be judged by the fact that Herodotus states that six hundred ships now sailed into the Black Sea. Meanwhile Darius' army of allegedly 700,000 men marched through Thrace and northwards into the region known as Scythia.

Scythia at this time was considered to be roughly all that part of south-eastern Europe between the Carpathian Mountains and the River Tanais (the modern Don). Herodotus is a mine of stories, some accurate and some fanciful, about the life and habits of the Scythian nomads who roamed the steppes. Hardy and warlike, without any fortified towns, they lived in waggons in which whole families travelled whenever a tribe moved on. They fought from horseback with bows and arrows, despised agriculture, and moved with their great hordes of cattle as and where the grazing dictated.

"As regards war," says Herodotus, "the Scythian custom is for every soldier to drink the blood of the first man he kills. The heads of all enemies killed in battle are taken to the king; a head being a sort of ticket by which a soldier is admitted to his share of the loot – no head, no loot."

They scalped the dead, and then hung the scalps on the bridles of their horses, the greatest warrior being the one with the greatest number of scalps. A formidable people: "They have a special way of dealing with the actual skulls . . . they saw off the part below the eyebrows, and after cleaning out what remains stretch a piece of rawhide round it on the outside. If a man is poor, he is content with that, but a rich man goes further and gilds the inside of the skull as well. In either case the skull is then used to drink from."

It was hardly surprising that even Darius and his massive army nearly came to grief against such an enemy; an enemy, moreover, who well understood the tactics of guerrilla warfare and refused to stand and fight a conventional battle. The Scythians, like the Russians in later centuries, contented themselves with destroying their pastures and retreating deeper and deeper into the hinterland. Descending like cattle flies upon the slow-moving foot-soldiers, they harassed them continually, escaping on their hardy horses before they could be seriously engaged.

If Darius' campaign in Scythia was something of a failure, his expedition into Thrace was a resounding success. The whole southern part of the Balkans as far west as Macedonia was brought under Persian rule, and the King of Macedonia sent his tokens of formal submission to the Persian monarch. The way was now open for the inevitable clash between the Persians and the mainland Greeks.

Twelve years after Darius withdrew from Scythia and Thrace and made his way back to Persia, there was a great rebellion of the Ionian Greeks in Asia Minor, for not all Greeks willingly submitted to Persian domination. But, after a great naval victory in 494 B.C., the heart of Greek resistance in Ionia was broken. The Persian fleet, now dominant in the Levant and the eastern Aegean, completed a "mopping-up" operation among the islands. Miletus itself, Herodotus says, was "emptied of its inhabitants". In the mainland cities of Ionia and in the islands, "the best-looking boys were chosen for castration and made into eunuchs; the handsomest girls were . . . sent to Darius' court. Meanwhile the towns themselves . . . were burnt to the ground."

The first attempt to subdue mainland Greece was made in 491 B.C. It failed because one of those tempestuous storms that sweep down from the north caught the Persian fleet as it was rounding Mount Athos, and a large proportion of the invasion fleet was lost on the bony lee shore of the peninsula. Seemingly unperturbed by the disaster, Darius now set in action the whole machinery of his empire. Ionian Greeks and Phoenicians alike were given their orders: "Prepare the largest fleet that the world has ever seen! It is to undertake the transport of my army for the conquest of Greece."

The Phoenicians were probably delighted at the prospect of seeing the hated Greeks humbled, and willingly contributed their skills, their ships, and their seamen. Many of the Ionian Greeks, too, felt that they had been let down by their fellow Greeks in Athens, Sparta, and other cities. The feeling undoubtedly existed that, if the Ionian cities now paid tribute to Persia, Athens and other mainland Greek cities should not continue to enjoy their freedom. At this period of history a Greek was first and foremost a citizen of a particular city or small state; a "national" conception of Greece had not yet arisen.

In 491 B.C., the heralds of Darius went formally to all the islands of the Aegean and demanded their submission. There was an accepted ritual, in which the leading citizens, if they agreed to the demand, would hand over earth and water as a token that they were now subjects. As far as is known, all the islands of the Aegean, aware how ill-equipped they were to withstand the might of the Persians, submitted to Darius. So did many of the chief cities of mainland Greece. Prominent among those who refused the Persian King's demand were the two leaders of Greece, Athens and Sparta.

For the first time in history landing-craft vessels were used. They were specially designed to carry horses for the Persian army. Although Minoans, Phoenicians, and Greeks had long been carrying livestock in their ships, there is no previous record of specialized ships being built for this purpose. These horse-transports are first heard of in 490 B.C., when the Persian fleet set sail for the invasion of Greece. Herodotus states that they were requisitioned from the tributary states the year before. It seems likely they originated with the Phoenicians, who were still by far the most advanced shipbuilders and seamen of their time. Furthermore, the Phoenicians had a long history of distant voyages to the far ends of the Mediterranean, and it is probable that horses from Babylonia and Egypt were among the animals they carried to their colonies in the West.

The transport evolved for the operation was to differ little through thousands of years. In campaigns as far apart as those of the Romans, the Byzantines, and the mediaeval Crusaders, ships of similar type and dimensions were employed. These horse- and troop-carriers were not the long warship type, but more akin to the Phoenician "round ships" used for general cargo. They were not, however, dependent solely upon their sails (this would have been unthinkable, even in the summer Aegean), but had one bank of oars. Designed on the same principle as the double-banked bireme, the area which, in a bireme, would have accommodated the lower bank of oars and its rowers was devoted to horse-boxes. Such a vessel was about 120 feet long with a beam of

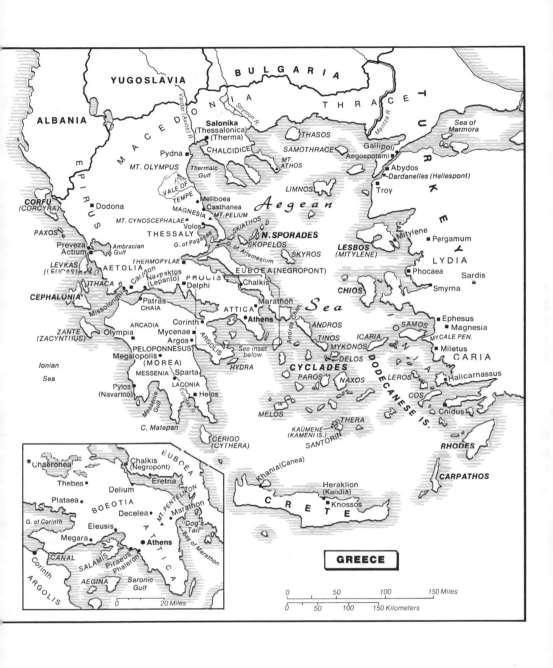

ALBANIA

YUGOSLAVIA

BULGARIA

THRACE

TURKEY

Sea of Marmora

Vardar (Axios) R.

M A C E D O N I A

Strymon R.

THASOS

SAMOTHRACE

Gallipoli
Aegospotami

Maritza R.

Salonika
(Thessalonica)
(Therma)

CHALCIDICE

MT.
ATHOS

Pydna

Thermaic
Gulf

MT. OLYMPUS

VALE OF
TEMPE

Aegean

Abydos
Dardanelles (Hellespont)

Troy

CORFU
(CORCYRA)

Dodona

Meliboea
Casthanea

MAGNESIA

MT. PELIUM

LIMNOS

Sea

E P I R U S

MT. CYNOSCEPHALAE

THESSALY

Volos

SKIATHOS

N. SPORADES

SKOPELOS

G. of Pagasae
G. of Artemesium

Mitylene

Pergamum

PAXOS

Preveza
Actium

Ambracian
Gulf

SKYROS

LESBOS
(MITYLENE)

LYDIA

LEVKAS
(LEUCAS)

AETOLIA

THERMOPYLAE

Calydon

Navpaktos
(Lepanto)

PHOCIS

Delphi

EUBOEA (NEGROPONT)

Chalkis

CHIOS

Phocaea

Sardis

ITHACA

Patras

CHAIA

ATTICA

Marathon

Athens

Sea

ANDROS

Smyrna

CEPHALONIA

Missolonghi

Andros Chan.

SAMOS

Ephesus
Magnesia

MYCALE PEN.

ARCADIA

Corinth

TINOS

ICARIA

Miletus

ZANTE
(ZACYNTHUS)

Olympia

PELOPONNESUS
(MOREA)

Mycenae

Argos

ARGOLIS

MYKONOS

DELOS

CYCLADES

CARIA

Ionian

Sea

Megalopolis

MESSENIA

Sparta

LACONIA

HYDRA

PAROS

NAXOS

LEROS

DODECANESE IS.

Halicarnassus

Pylos
(Navarino)

Messenia
Gulf

Eurotas R.

Helos

COS

Cnidus

MELOS

C. Matapan

CERIGO
(CYTHERA)

KAÜMENE
(KAMENI IS.)

THERA

SANTORINI

RHODES

CARPATHOS

Khania (Canea)

Heraklion
(Kandia)

C R E T E

Knossos

Inset map:

EUBOEA

Chaëronea

Chalkis
(Negropont)

Thebes

Eretria

Delium

MT. PENTELIKON

Plataea

BOEOTIA

Decelea

Marathon

"Dog's
Tail"

G. of Corinth

Eleusis

MT. PENTELIKON

ATTICA

Bay of Marathon

Megara

CANAL

SALAMIS

Piraeus
Phaleron

Athens

Corinth

ARGOLIS

AEGINA

Saronic
Gulf

0   20 Miles

GREECE

0   50   100   150 Miles

0   50   100   150 Kilometers

about a fifth of her length and a similar draught. True "round ships" had a breadth of more than a fourth of their length.

By 490 B.C., the preparations were complete, and the Persian army embarked from Cilicia on the Asian mainland, north of Cyprus, and sailed by easy stages via Samos across the Aegean. On their way they captured the rich island of Naxos, which had stood out against them a few years previously. Sacred Delos, birthplace of Apollo, the sun god, was spared out of Persian consideration for the god and his worship, since they equated him with their own god Ahura Mazda. All of the Cyclades, those islands that lie in a circle round Delos in the southern Aegean, now came under Persian control. The Grecian archipelago, the "Sea of the Kingdom", as it was called, was already little more than a Persian lake.

The whole operation took place in summer, for an invasion force consisting of an immense number of men and horses could not have been risked across the tricky Aegean at any other time of the year. But in the Aegean summer, the meltemi reach their maximum force. It was necessary, therefore, for the Persian commanders to find a safe area in which to harbour their fleet while the army was disembarking. They set their course for the island of Euboea, which lies close along the north-east coast of Attica. An anchorage in the lee of Euboea would serve the Persians well, for it was also conveniently close to one of their main enemies, Athens. Although both Sparta and Athens were resolved to defend the Greek mainland, the Persians realized that if Athens and her fleet were eliminated, the Aegean was securely theirs. Inland Sparta could be dealt with later, and at their leisure.

The Persian troops were put ashore in a sheltered bay in the south of Euboea, and soon they captured the neighbouring villages and laid siege to Eretria. Athenian colonists from nearby Chalkis were ordered to go to the city's assistance, for the Athenians themselves dared not denude their own territory of their troops. But the city had fallen before the relief could arrive, and all its people were enslaved and led captive to the invading fleet. So far, the strategy of Datis, the Persian commander, seemed to be working perfectly. He had established a safe anchorage for his ships and had cleared the territory behind him of any potential danger. Now he was ready for his next move – the swoop upon Athens.

Datis had no intention of landing his troops in the Saronic Gulf, where Athens itself is situated, for he knew well that he would meet with fierce resistance, and no intelligent commander wishes to put men ashore on a heavily defended beachhead. On his way north to Eretria he had no doubt noticed (if it had not, indeed, been brought to his attention by Athenian renegades among the high command) the well-sheltered Bay of Marathon. The bay was protected from north-easterly winds by a long narrow promontory called the "Dog's Tail", and behind it lay the open plain of Marathon. From Marathon itself, a coastal strip between the mountains and the sea runs southwards to Athens, only twenty-six miles away.

It was clearly Datis' intention to put all his troops ashore at this point. He could be reasonably confident of an unopposed landing, and he could then take the coastal route to the city. The narrow, flat coastal belt would suit his cavalry admirably. Since he had command of the sea, he had the initiative and could strike where it suited him. He could also be fairly sure that the Athenians would not dare leave their own city undefended, until it was quite clear that he had made his landing other than under the walls of Athens itself. By the time they realized this and set out to oppose him, Datis anticipated having his forces ashore and on their way to meet the Athenians.

In Athens, meanwhile, as the Persian fleet prepared to leave its anchorage off Euboea and coast down to Marathon, opinions were still divided as to the best method of meeting the enemy. There was no disagreement, however, about the first move. This was to send a message to Sparta, informing the Spartans that the Persians were about to invest Attica. A professional runner, Pheidippides, was immediately dispatched to ask them to honour the treaty between the two cities and send help. Running over the rough roads, goat tracks, and footpaths that separated the cities by some 140 miles, he reached Sparta the day after he had left – a good cross-country, or "Marathon", performance by any standards.

The Spartans immediately agreed to come to the help of their ally, but said they could not march until the moon was full. It was against their laws to take up arms during the festival of Apollo they were then celebrating. (This was in no way an excuse. The unrealistic conduct of many battles and campaigns in the ancient world must often be read in the light of religious ceremonies and observances then current.) But this refusal to march at once meant that the Spartans would not be able to assist the Athenians for a week. Although Herodotus says nothing about it, it is more than likely that the speed with which Datis moved his fleet was based upon knowledge that he had a clear week in which to overcome the Athenians without having to engage the Spartans as well. He had plenty of Greek advisers who knew that the Spartans would not take up arms at this time of the year.

Some of the Athenian leaders were now in favour of staying within the city walls and enduring a siege. They felt confident that they could hold out until the Spartans came up to take the Persians in the rear. Others, however, including a distinguished soldier, Miltiades, were against any such proposal. Miltiades was aware that there was a pro-Persian faction in the city, waiting to betray it. Fortunately for Greece, he and his followers carried the day, and it was resolved to move out in full force against the Persians as soon as news reached Athens of their landing.

Datis in the meantime had brought his fleet down to anchor in the lee of the Dog's Tail, and had started putting his troops ashore. Perhaps the technical and administrative difficulties of getting a large force established in a base camp took longer than he had anticipated. At any rate, instead of immediately securing the southern entrance to the plain, he delayed long enough to enable the Athenians to march north with ten thousand men and capture this bottleneck before him.

The Athenians had been alerted, almost within minutes of the Persian disembarkation, by a beacon fire lit on the peak of Mount Pentelikon, the mountain which broods over the plain of Marathon. They were now joined by a contingent from the little city of Plataea. This city lay just on the boundary of Attica, and had been under Athenian protection for some thirty years. The Plataeans sent their entire man power, about six hundred men – a gesture never forgotten by the Athenians even in the greatest days of their empire.

The Greeks now secured themselves in a good defensive position which denied the coast road to the Persians and commanded a small hill track leading back to Athens. Datis, either because of circumstances beyond his control or through over-confidence, had lost the tactical advantage. He probably thought that on the flat plain of Marathon his cavalry and his archers – for which the Persians were famous – would make short work of the Greek foot-soldiers with their cumbersome armour, spears, and swords.

A contemporary Greek estimate of the Persian numbers says they had 100,000 foot-soldiers and 10,000 horsemen. This is probably exaggerated, as are many such estimates in ancient history. The problems of transporting an invasion force of this magnitude were almost certainly beyond the capacity of the empire at the time of Darius. Nevertheless, if the most reasonable estimate is accepted, the Persians seem to have outnumbered the Greeks by four or five to one. They had, of course, been on a sea voyage – never the best tonic for soldiers, let alone cavalry. They were also in the position of all invading armies: far from home and, therefore, despite the expectations of loot and conquest, less determined than men whose wives and children were only a few miles behind their backs.

The Persians, encamped to the north of the six-mile-long plain, had their fleet and the sea on their left hand. At their back and on their right was a large marshy area. Having taken up positions facing one another, the two armies remained static for several days. They were somewhat like two boxers waiting for an opening: both commanders were far too experienced to lead with a flurry of blows that could lay them open to a devastating counter-punch.

It was the Persians who finally made the opening move. On the day after the full moon, when, as Datis probably knew, the Spartans would begin their march north to reinforce Athens, he embarked a section of his troops, among them, to quote A. R. Burn in *Persia and the Greeks,* "much of his comparatively small force of cavalry, destined for the dash up from Phaleron". Clearly his intention was to cut off the Athenians from their city by holding their army at Marathon while he made use of his sea power to effect a landing in their rear.

Faced with the sight of units of the Persian fleet moving south beyond their seaward flank, the Greeks had no option but to give battle at once. But, in order to cover the much longer Persian battle line, they had necessarily to extend their own line – and this meant weakening it either throughout all its length or at one specific point. Herodotus describes these preliminaries as if they were merely a matter of accident, which they may well have been. At the same time, in view of the known military efficiency of Miltiades and his fellow commanders, the credit may go to Greek intelligence. This is the account as Herodotus gives it:

"One result of the disposition of the Athenian troops before the battle was the weakening of their centre by the effort to extend the line sufficiently to cover the whole Persian front; the two wings were strong, but the line in the centre was only a few ranks deep. The dispositions made, and the preliminary sacrifice promising success, the word was given to move, and the Athenians advanced at a run towards the enemy, not less than a mile away. The Persians, seeing the attack developing at the double, prepared to meet it confidently enough, for it seemed to them suicidal madness for the Athenians to risk an assault with so small a force – at the double, too, and with no support from either cavalry or archers. Well, that was what they imagined; nevertheless, the Athenians came on, closed with the enemy all along the line, and fought in a way not to be forgotten. They were the first Greeks, so far as I know, to charge at a run, and the first who dared to look without flinching at Persian dress and the men who wore it; for until that day came, no Greek could hear even the word Persian without terror."

This weakening of the Greek line in the centre, if it was not a matter of deliberate policy, was an astounding stroke of fortune. If the Greeks had hardened their centre, leaving their flanks weak, they might indeed have burst through the middle of the Persian force. But, even if they had done so, they would then have been in the unenviable position of having the lighter-clad Persian archers, as well as the cavalry, closing in upon their flanks. Doubtless, they would have been cut to pieces. The Persians, furthermore, had their best native troops in the centre, since their standard tactic was to punch a hole clean through an enemy's advance. The wings of the Persian force were held by Persian subjects, including allies from formerly Greek Asia Minor; they were not likely to prove the best of soldiers against fellow Greeks.

What followed was exactly as might be expected. The Persian centre burst through the thin Greek line in the middle and poured after the fugitives, pursuing them inland, away from the sea. It was now that the Athenians on the one wing and the Plataeans on the other overpowered the opposing Persians and collapsed their wings. When they saw what had happened, the Persian troops in the centre gave up their pursuit and made a panic dash back towards the sea. The two Greek flanks now moved in diagonally towards one another, finally uniting in a solid line of armoured men. Their own centre, which had collapsed, was being driven back towards the Greek camp in the south, but between them and the amalgamated Greek wings now lay the Persian centre – cut off from both its flanks, which were in rapid and undisciplined retreat. The Greeks about-turned and began a slaughter of the Persians in their rear, and no doubt their own centre now rallied to give them support. The Persian army was cut in two.

By the end of that day, August 12, 490 B.C., the first Persian invasion of Greece was over. Not only were the Persians who had broken through the Greek centre cut to pieces but also a large part of their army was driven north to perish in the treacherous swamp. Some 6500 of the invaders were counted among the dead; less than two hundred Athenians were killed. There are no casualty figures for the Plataeans or for the slaves who had formed part of the Greek army. It was an outstanding victory, and a proof that disciplined courage and superior generalship are more than a match for sheer weight of numbers. A contingent of two thousand Spartans, probably an advance guard, reached Athens too late for the battle. Whatever their feelings, they were not Spartans for nothing, and they hastened to congratulate the Athenians and the Plataeans on so signal a victory.

Even to the last, the campaign might still have ended in defeat for the Greeks. Datis, as soon as he had embarked his remaining troops from the battlefield of Marathon, sailed south to attempt Athens from the sea. The victors had to hasten back by forced marches to Phaleron, the port of Athens. When the Persian fleet arrived offshore, it found the men who had just defeated them drawn up in battle-readiness on the olive-silvery slopes of their homeland. The invasion was over.

Pheidippides, the Athenian runner, while on his way south to Sparta with the news of the Persian invasion, later told how in the mountains of Arcadia he had encountered the god Pan. The latter called him by name and reproached him with the fact that the Athenians paid little or no worship to him – although he had always been their friend. When Pheidippides reported his meeting with the Arcadian god to the Athenians, they immediately built Pan a shrine on the Acropolis, and ever afterwards held an annual ceremony in his honour. Until this date this ancient earth god, who had been worshipped in Greece long before the Greeks settled there, had been no more than a very minor cult figure. From now on, Pan, who figures so largely in later Western literature as well as in myth, emerges as an important presence. He sends visions and dreams; rests at noon like any shepherd, and dislikes his siesta disturbed. According to a story which first circulated during the reign of the Roman Emperor Tiberius, Pan was the last of the old gods to die. Christians later said that his death occurred at the moment of Christ's birth.

So the year 490 B.C. ended with a Greek triumph over the hitherto invincible conqueror from the East. The story of Marathon became one of the pillars of Athenian history – comparable to Waterloo for the British in later centuries. It was a moment in time when it seemed that a spirit had been born which could give not only Athenians, but indeed all Greeks, the strength to declare their solidarity and assert the unique virtues of their race and culture. Unfortunately, within months the Greeks were at variance with one another. They had won a battle but not a war. The power of Persia was to test them yet again, within the lifetime of men who had themselves fought on the plain of Marathon.

EIGHT

Ships and the Men

The sea which had just witnessed the retreat of the largest fleet ever known was now startled by the appearance of a formidable new vessel. Walking on her triple banks of oars across the calm acres of summer the trireme comes upon the scene. An extension of the bireme evolved by the Phoenicians, this was the vessel that, for a time at least, gave the Greeks command of the Mediterranean.

Thucydides is the first writer to provide any information about the trireme and its origin. "The Corinthians are said first to have managed naval matters nearest to the modern fashion, and triremes were first built in Greece at Corinth." He goes on to say that "triremes in large numbers were first owned by the tyrants of Sicily and the men of Corcyra."

The period about which Thucydides is writing is the ten years between the Athenian victory of Marathon in 490 B.C. and the second Persian invasion of 480 B.C. Certainly there are no previous records of three-banked vessels. But in itself this means comparatively little, for there is hardly any literary evidence of specific types of ships at this stage in history. Poets and historians talk of "ships and transports"; they do not clutter up their narrative with descriptions of how these ships were built, or when and where. Furthermore, there is no visual record of them. The ships themselves, being built of wood, have disappeared as completely as the wooden furniture of the ancient world. Even in art we can find no reliable evidence as to the appearance of the trireme, for no detailed drawing or sculpture of this vessel is known.

Such evidence as we have of the construction and lay-out of triremes and other warships comes mainly from later classical authors, and has been pieced together by such specialists as Cecil Torr, Admiral Jurien de la Gravière, and contributors to *The Mariner's Mirror*. Even the matter of how its three banks of oars were managed is still a subject for dispute. Perhaps the comparatively new science of underwater archaeology may one of these days uncover enough of an ancient Greek trireme to clear up some of the points at issue. Unfortunately, the Mediterranean, with its teredo worm as well as the silt of the ages, is unlikely to yield anything so well preserved as the famous Gokstad ship of the Vikings.

One thing is clear: the years 490 to 480 B.C. witnessed a period of feverish shipbuilding throughout all of Greece and the Levant. The second great Persian invasion could never have been launched without a prodigious expenditure on shipbuilding, and the Athenian navy that was to resist it required an equally extravagant outlay on timber and materials. The deforestation of large parts of the eastern Mediterranean (too often blamed solely upon the ignorance of its Turkish masters nearly two thousand years later) had begun even before the golden days of classical Greece, before Periclean Athens, and long before the rise of the Roman Empire.

Mountains and islands that now present harsh limestone faces to the sailor as he coasts along their barren flanks were once dense and leafy with foliage. The forests pulled down the passing rain clouds, the humus at their feet grew rich, valleys were fed by streams now many centuries dry, and the whole natural scene wore a softer aspect before Man the boatbuilder, ignorant of his axe's power, began to change the face of the world. The forays which Athens was later to make into the great timber-bearing regions of Thrace, Macedonia, and the three-pronged peninsula of Chalcidice can only be explained by the city's need for wood. Then, as now, houses in Greece were largely built of stone, and the urgent hunger for wood was prompted by the insatiable jaws of the sea. Ships are not only lost in battles or on navigational hazards; the sea eats them remorselessly. Few seas are more avaricious than the Mediterranean, with its high salinity and humidity and its warm waters indulgent to the worm.

B. W. Bathe, in *Ship Models*, outlines a standard trireme of the type which dominated this sea for three hundred years. "[It] usually pulled 170 oars, arranged in three 'banks', of which the upper contained thirty-one oars a side while the middle and lower 'banks' each had twenty-seven oars a side. From an inventory found in the dockyard of the

Piraeus, no oars seem to have exceeded 14·2 ft in length, while, from the dimensions of the slipway still preserved in the harbour of Zea, it appears that a trireme must have been about 150 ft long, with a breadth of about 19 ft over the outriggers and a breadth of hull of about 16 ft."

Such a vessel, with so impoverished a beam, was clearly only designed for use in the clement summer season. Indeed, there were only about four and a half to five months of the year in which these war galleys could operate with any degree of safety. The limitation factor in ancient warfare was determined not only by the harvest season, when most of a nation's population was engaged in ensuring the bread supply, but also by the fact that armies could not be transported, garrisons maintained, or sea battles fought, except in calm weather.

Apart from its oars, the trireme could be propelled under favourable conditions (with a following wind) by a simple square sail set on a comparatively short mast. This sail would be used under cruising conditions, or whenever possible during a long sea passage. When it came to action, however, the first things sent ashore were the mast, sail, and the attendant rigging. The Greek trireme was, above all, a "powered warship". It was many centuries before Mediterranean man discovered enough about the use of sail to discard oars altogether.

The principal weapon of a warship of this period was the vessel itself. A trireme, or a bireme, or even a single-banked vessel was launched at its opponent like an arrow or sling-shot. The ultimate aim might well be to board an opponent and come to grips with the enemy with cold steel, but the ship itself was all-important. The great underwater ram in the bows was the equivalent of the firearms, cannon, and guns of later centuries.

To understand exactly how the ram was worked and how the ship had sufficient strength to contain the impact with another ship without itself sinking, the methods of ship construction used in a trireme of this period must be examined. The backbone of the hull, as in any ship, was the long keel, usually made of oak. On to the keel were grafted the ribs, which provided the strength in a lateral dimension for the planks forming the vessel's skin. These planks, usually of pine, were laid in carvel fashion: each plank was laid flush to its neighbour instead of overlapping each other. The average thickness of a trireme's planking seems to have been about three inches. The planks were fastened to the ribs by wooden dowels or metal nails, bronze being preferred for nails since it did not deteriorate, as iron did, with the action of sea-water.

So great was the length of the hull in proportion to the beam, that it was necessary to provide additional longitudinal strength by fastening heavy wooden wales (*zosteres*) outside the planks. Known in nautical terminology as waling-pieces, these heavy reinforcements extended from end to end on the outside of the vessel, their primary object being to prevent the bow and the stern from sagging. There might be as many as four waling-pieces running the length of a trireme, the lowest of which would serve yet another function. It was cut and fastened so as to dip down towards the bows, where it joined the forward projection of the keel. At this point it was firmly bolted right through, from side to side. Ahead of it stretched the great bronze ram. The lower waling-piece, therefore, provided extra strength for the whole of the forward area when the warship rammed an opponent.

Because of the immense structural shock incurred when ramming an enemy vessel, the hull was even further longitudinally strengthened by a set of cables, known as *hypozomata*. These heavy rope cables encircled the whole ship from stem to stern. There must have been some form of a windlass which could adjust the tension on them as required, for ropes would naturally contract with damp as well as expand when they dried out under the summer sun.

Quite apart from the shock of ramming, which necessitated these strengthening devices, it must be borne in mind that the sides of the hull were pierced with portholes for the two lower banks of oars, thus considerably weakening the planking.

The oars themselves were worked against wooden thole pins to which they were secured by leather or rope grommets – in exactly the same manner as Mediterranean rowing boats to this day. To stop the rowers in the two lower banks from being soaked with spray when the ship was labouring in a seaway, the entrance to the portholes was protected by a leather bag. Even so, in bad weather, triremes must still have shipped water, since Herodotus says that the oar-ports were large enough for a man to put his head through.

Since a trireme curved in at bow and stern, the lines of rowers could not follow the whole ship's length. They were seated in a rectangular boxlike structure, occupying about two-thirds of the ship's length.

The oarsmen were ranged on three tiers of seats, which ascended from the centre like steps. The rowers in the two lower banks had free play for the loom of their oar beneath the legs of the men above them. It was clearly no sinecure being an oarsman on the lower banks, and sometimes the lowest tier was unable to escape when the vessel was overwhelmed, because of the time taken to get up the gangway to the deck above. Aristophanes also jokes about how unpleasant it could be on the bottom tier if someone immediately above relieved himself.

The life of the oarsmen was unthinkably hard by modern standards, but they were not slaves. In the Athenian triremes they were all free-born citizens, and as much rivalry existed between the crew of one trireme and another as might exist today between two racing eights. Upon their ability to perform efficiently and to carry out swiftly the commands of the master in the stern depended the safety of their state and of their homes.

The triremes were ballasted by gravel and stones, contained in the bottom of the hold in wooden boxes, which had slats that could be removed so as to trim the ballast when necessary. A trireme when coming in to ram might need to depress her bows slightly or, if encountering heavy weather from ahead, to raise them. Below the ballast boxes, the hold itself slopped with bilge water, which had to be frequently baled out with leather buckets. At a later date, in merchant ships and other large vessels, it seems that an Archimedean screw, worked either by hand or by a treadmill, was used to lift the bilge water up and over the side.

Herodotus mentions one trireme as having a crew of 200 men, which sounds about right for a ship with, say, 170 oarsmen; leaving 30 for archers, men-at-arms, sailors concerned solely with mast, spars, and sail, and navigating officers. Judging from other accounts it seems that 200 men was the standard crew for a trireme throughout the classical period. It is probable that early triremes had no more than 150 oars, arranged in three tiers of 25 oars to each bank, and thus there were nearly 50 men to form the sailing and fighting crew.

In the early days, before the Greeks had properly learned the art of handling triremes in sea battles, they tended to carry a number of heavily armed soldiers, hoplites, to engage the enemy from the upper deck and act as boarding parties. In the Athenian fleet, when the techniques and tactics of using the ram had been thoroughly mastered, this out-of-place conception of using a warship to fight a land battle afloat was discontinued.

It was the forepart of the ship which dominated everything, for it was here that the lean underwater ram, designed to tear a hole in the enemy, swept out from its waling-pieces. It was usually made of bronze, laid in sheets over a wooden core. To judge from the prow depicted on the famous Victory of Samothrace (about 300 B.C.) it was sometimes formed in three parts like a trident; a Bithynian coin of about the same date also shows a three-pointed ram. On the stem itself, above the water, other projections served as additional rams to break up the enemy's side, once the main ram had penetrated her below water. In addition to all this, massive balks of timber, known as catheads, projected on either side of the bows far enough to provide some protection for the forward oars when the ram pierced the enemy. The catheads also served to tear away the upper works of an enemy vessel when the trireme swept along its side.

The three-pronged ram was probably only an elaboration. Representations of galleys of the sixth and seventh centuries B.C. show the ram as one simple long spur, projecting a considerable distance ahead of the vessel underwater. These single-pointed, long rams had the disadvantage of being liable to snap off in an enemy's side. As the ram tore away, it would, of course, "start" the timbers of the attacking vessel and probably open her up disastrously below the waterline.

Quite apart from the damage caused to the enemy's hull if a successful attack was launched (catching him broadside on), the bow could also be made to deliver a sweeping blow. It could be used to run right down the side of a ship, snapping off her oars like matchsticks. The looms of the oars would then leap back into the bodies of the unfortunate rowers, killing or maiming them. The trireme would then withdraw, leaving her opponent disabled. Having achieved this, the successful vessel could then back off and deliver the *coup de grâce* in a head-on attack square into her opponent's side. Galley warfare was no less terrible than any other method of combat at sea which the misplaced ingenuity of man has been able to devise.

Triremes were commissioned, bought, paid for, and manned by the citizens of a town, state, or country. Sometimes a rich man would pay for the equipment of a trireme out of his own pocket. Herodotus mentions one that was commissioned by Cleinias, son of Alcibiades, "who was serving in his own ship manned by two hundred men, all at his own personal expense".

When the Athenian fleet had to expand rapidly just before the second Persian invasion, the great soldier-statesman Themistocles put through a navy bill which designated a number of rich individuals who were each to be responsible for building a ship with loans from a providential rich "strike" at the state-owned silver mines near Sunium. These *trierarchs*, or masters and owners of triremes, often competed lavishly against one another to produce the best ship and the best crew. Competition was fierce, and the reward for those deemed to have achieved an unusual excellence was a simple wreath, or *stephanos*. Like medals in other times, these crowns, although of no intrinsic value, were considered marks of the highest distinction.

Throughout the central and eastern Mediterranean during the years 490–480 B.C. the shipyards resounded to the clunk of adzes, the clang of hammers on metal fastenings, and the shouts of men at work in rope-works and rigging shops, heating pitch for caulking and antifouling, and engaged in the hundred and one crafts attendant on shipbuilding. In Carthage the Carthaginians were enlarging their fleet to protect their remaining colonies in Sicily. In Syracuse, the greatest city in that disputed island, the tyrant Gelon, the most powerful individual in the Greek world, was supervising the construction of a fleet and the training of an army designed to make him master of all Sicily. Mainland Greece and the islands, the Ionian seaboard, the dockyards of Tyre and Sidon, all knew an activity far in excess of anything previous in history. Not for the first and certainly not for the last time, the inland sea was troubled by an impending conflict between East and West.

NINE

The Second Round

Soon after Marathon, Miltiades, who naturally enough was the hero of the hour, suggested that the logical policy for Athens was to win back the Cyclades. These islands, which had either willingly or unwillingly co-operated with the Persians, must be secured if the city was to feel safe. It was a sensible conclusion, for the Cyclades are like a shield or outer bulwark in the Aegean Sea, protective to the mainland coast of Attica and the Peloponnese.

For many reasons, among them an unwillingness to expend much money after what they had just endured, the Athenian Assembly was only half-heartedly behind the project. Miltiades, however, managed to raise an expeditionary force by promising that he would make the campaign pay its way. He had his eye on the prosperous and wealthy island of Paros. He felt confident that if he could bring this most important of the Cyclades to heel, he would be able to secure a large enough indemnity from the Parians to show Athens a profit and enable him to carry out the rest of the campaign. Unfortunately his attack on Paros failed, he himself was wounded, and upon his return to Athens he was held to blame for the expenses incurred. His wound became gangrenous, and he died shortly after being heavily fined by the Assembly. Athens, then as now, was a dangerous city in which to indulge in politics.

The man chosen to lead Greece against the second Persian invasion was Themistocles. He was an extremely able politician, a far-sighted realist who saw that the survival of Athens, as well as her ultimate expansion, lay on the sea. His great political opponent was Aristeides, who was known, because of his incorruptibility (rare in Greek politics), as "the Just". Aristeides was finally ostracized – that curious Athenian process whereby voters annually wrote on a piece of potsherd the name

A Late Minoan design featuring a squid

The Harvester Vase from Hagia Triada

Drawing of a wall-relief from the palace of Sennacherib at Nineveh, showing the flight from Tyre of Luli, King of Tyre and Sidon, in 701 B.C.

Bronze figurine of a Baal

of the man they felt the state could best do without; if there was a sufficiently high count of votes against one man he was exiled for ten years. The unfortunate Aristeides, it is recorded, wrote his own name on a piece of potsherd for an illiterate yokel, but could not help courteously asking the man why he wanted Aristeides banished. "Because I am sick and tired of hearing him called 'the Just', " was the unexpected, but very human, reply.

Themistocles and his party triumphed, and it was fortunate for Athens that they did. They were the "navy party"; and this was exactly what Athens, and indeed all Greece, was to need in the conflict that was coming.

"Themistokles," writes A. R. Burn in his *History of Greece*, "was for developing the navy, a policy more popular with the poor than with the rich, who would have to pay for it." In ancient Greece it was for this reason that the "navy party" usually represented the democratic element. The "army party", on the other hand, whose leaders were men of property like Aristeides, was usually the party of the rich. They provided their own armour and were unpaid; thus the profession of arms became considered part of the status of a "gentleman". The navy, which required the active co-operation of a high proportion of the poor and working classes to man, build, and maintain it, was clearly more of a "democratic" institution.

The success of Themistocles' party, coupled with a windfall in the shape of a rich new vein of silver discovered in the state silver mines, enabled Athens to produce her great trireme navy. This was to be that "wooden wall" which the Delphic oracle had counselled as being her best measure of defence, and which Themistocles had cannily interpreted as meaning ships. In the three years prior to the Persian invasion of 480 B.C., the Athenian navy had been increased to number two hundred triremes. The quality of the ships and the men must have been reduced by such a massive increase. Herodotus in his description of the new ships says that they were "heavier" (not an advantage) than those of the enemy, and that "the latter were better at sailing" – yet the dilution was not so great as to damage seriously their capability when it came to the test that lay ahead. The fact that the navy of Athens was built and manned by Athenians gave it an advantage over the composite fleet of the Persians, largely Phoenician built and manned by many subject races and allies.

Xerxes, eldest son of the great Darius, had succeeded his father to the throne of Persia in 486 B.C. Although Herodotus tells us that he had early decided on a campaign against Greece, he was not able to embark on it immediately. A serious revolt in subject Egypt (which he decisively crushed in the first year of his reign) detained him from the project. A little later, another revolt, this time in Babylonia, engaged his attention. Once again he extirpated it with merciless efficiency, leaving the ancient capital of Babylon bereft of its temples and its treasures. Despite these campaigns, however, he still managed to gear the Persian Empire for its war against the Greeks. Determined not to fail through insufficient preparation (which he and his advisers regarded as having been the cause for the defeat at Marathon), he turned all the resources of his empire to shipbuilding and to the preparation of the greatest invasion force the world had ever known.

For three whole years an occupying Persian army, aided by countless enslaved Greeks and others, was hard at work digging a canal across the isthmus of Mount Athos. Although this was widely regarded by the Greeks as a sign of megalomania, it was a very sensible operation. Xerxes had no intention of hazarding his ships in the area where the Persian fleet had come to grief ten years before. Great storage dumps were built along the route that the army was to follow, and stored with grain. "Mountains of salted meat", according to one Greek writer, were also piled up at points along the route. Although the army, when it did come, was to lay waste the land, living off it like a horde of locusts, yet provision had also been made for its victualling in an efficient manner.

The fact that the Greeks, including Herodotus, later regarded all these preparations as evidences of Xerxes' megalomania is little more than an indication of their own inability to understand the complexities of running a vast state and empire. Greek city-states tended to live somewhat hand-to-mouth. It was not until the rise of Macedonia and the conquests of Alexander the Great that the Greeks themselves had to face the organizational and bureaucratic problems which are part of running an empire.

The other great task, later derided by the Greeks but again eminently practical, was the famous "bridge of boats". This was, in fact, not one bridge but two; both constructed over the narrows of the Hellespont to permit the passage of the army. Herodotus, who tells us that 674 vessels were used to support the bridges, describes how "they were moored head-on to the current – and consequently at right angles to the actual bridges they supported – in order to lessen the strain on the cables. Specially heavy anchors were laid out both upstream and down-stream – those to the eastward to hold the vessels against winds blowing down the straits from the direction of the Black Sea, those on the other side, to the westward and towards the Aegean, to take the strain when it blew from the west and south. Gaps were left in three places to allow any boats that might wish to do so to pass in or out of the Black Sea."

There seems little reason to doubt that, apart from some Greek engineers from Asia Minor, the chief architects of this remarkable marine bridge were the Phoenicians. Even at this period of time, when the Greeks had already proved themselves upon the sea, the men from Tyre and Sidon had a more advanced knowledge of marine architecture and of rope and cable work than any other nation in the Mediterranean. Indeed, Herodotus remarked about the canal across the isthmus of Mount Athos that the workmen there all made the mistake of cutting the top of the canal the same width as the bottom. The result was that the sides kept falling in. The only people who did not make this mistake were the Phoenicians, who started at the top with a digging twice the required size of the base. As Herodotus observes, "the Phoenicians . . . in this – as in all other practical matters – gave a signal example of their skill." If the invasion of Greece was in the end to prove a failure, it was certainly not the fault of their ancient enemies.

By 481 B.C., not even the remotest Greek village in the mainland or the Peloponnese could have failed to have heard of the preparations that were afoot. The building of the fleet, the mustering of the army, the digging of the canal, and the construction of the amazing bridge across the Hellespont – the whole of the eastern Mediterranean was astir. The greatest empire known to man was girded for one object: the conquest and suppression of the Greeks.

From Sicily, the tyrant Gelon offered his services. He was willing, he said, to come to the aid of the homeland with 200 triremes (as many as the new Athenian fleet), 20,000 armoured infantrymen, 2000 cavalry, and an equal number of archers and slingers. In return for the provision of so large a force – and he coupled with it the offer to feed the Greek army with Sicilian grain for the duration of the campaign – Gelon asked for the leadership of all the forces. Neither Sparta nor Athens found this acceptable, which is hardly surprising. As ancient and distinguished cities, and the ones which must bear the brunt of the impending battle, they could hardly tolerate the thought of this colonial upstart assuming the high command. They may also have suspected that Gelon's motives were not entirely disinterested; if they prevailed against the Persians with his help, they might well find that they had an Old Man of the Sea upon their backs. To ancient Greece, Sicily, with its rich cornlands and forests, its metals and minerals, and its immense potential, was in a position somewhat analogous to that of the United States vis-à-vis Europe many centuries later. The offers of so rich a "country cousin", however well meant, were always open to the suspicion that the help might well prove to have too many strings attached to it. In any case, Gelon soon found that he had troubles enough on his own doorstep. While the Persians were arming and on the point of marching against Greece, Carthage had decided on a major strike in the West. The Greeks were, the Carthaginians reasonably assumed, about to be overwhelmed in their homeland, so it seemed a very good moment to strike against them in their principal colony, Sicily.

The year 480 B.C. was to be decisive for the future of Greece and her civilization. Although there is no evidence of an alliance between Persia and Carthage, it seems hardly coincidental that when Persia struck against Greece, the Carthaginians made a major attack on the Sicilian Greeks. The action of Carthage was probably taken on a purely opportunistic basis (rather like that of the Japanese against the Americans and British in the Far East during the Second World War). Despite the richness of his territory and of his capital, Syracuse, Gelon was forced to levy heavy war taxes. His Queen, Demarete, herself set a pattern that was to be followed by many royal ladies in other centuries, by giving her personal jewellery to the fund. Her name is commemorated in some of the finest and deservedly most famous ten-drachma pieces. These were minted at Syracuse after the war and were called *Demareteia*.

In the spring of 481 B.C., "Xerxes the King, King of Kings, King of all the lands, son of the King Darius" began to move his troops out of Persia. No one in the ancient world had ever seen an army of such size. Even allowing for the natural Greek tendency to talk in tens of thousands rather than in thousands, its number must have been almost unbelievable by comparison with the world population figures at that time. Twenty-nine divisional generals are named, each a commander of 6000 men. This in itself gives us a figure of 174,000, and we know from Herodotus and other sources that there were also some 80,000 cavalry, as well as charioteers from India and Libya, wild infantrymen from Ethiopia, and the elite division of the Persian Empire, the "Immortals". To quote Herodotus again: "There was not a nation in all Asia that he did not take with him against Greece; save for the great rivers there was not a stream his army drank from that was not drunk dry."

In the face of this apparently irresistible force it is hardly surprising that many of the smaller Greek cities were already preparing to accept the dominion of the Great King. One large Peloponnesian city, Argos, was unwilling to be involved, while Crete remained neutral throughout the campaign.

Even at this moment there were still bitter disagreements among the Greeks. Some of the naval states which came under the Spartan aegis were unwilling to serve under Athens. Themistocles, however, saw that unity was all that mattered. If unity meant putting the Athenian fleet under a Spartan admiral, then he would do so. He incurred much criticism at home for this, but his action was wise and statesmanlike. With the withdrawal of Gelon's offer of troops, the defence of Greece would rest upon Athens, Sparta, a handful of islands, and Sparta's allies in the Peloponnese. When Xerxes began to complete his preparations and muster his troops, the Greeks had about twelve months in which to settle their differences and complete their naval and military training.

It was in May 480 B.C. that the Great King gave the order for the army to march out of Sardis, the ancient city in Asia Minor where he had been wintering. Surrounded by his 10,000 Immortals, the flower of Persian nobility, among whom were his own brothers and cousins, Xerxes must have felt some confidence as to the outcome. Even if one takes the lowest acceptable estimate of his army, he had about 200,000 men, as well as the accompanying fleet. Herodotus (no doubt over-generously) estimates the fleet as having been manned by about half a million oarsmen, sailors, and marines. Stopping at the site of ancient Troy, the Great King sacrificed a thousand oxen to the Trojan Athene.

His intention, clearly, was to secure her assistance against the Greeks, who, centuries before, had laid waste her ancient city and scattered the Trojan race.

He reached the Hellespont at Abydos. "It now occurred to Xerxes that he would like to hold a review of his army. On a rise of ground near by, a throne of white marble had already been prepared for his use, and at his orders, by the people of Abydos; so the king took his seat upon it and, looking down over the shore, was able to see the whole of his army and navy at a single view. Suddenly as he watched them he was seized with the whim to witness a rowing-match. The match took place and was won by the Phoenicians of Sidon, to the great delight of Xerxes who was as pleased with the race as with his army. Still the king watched the spectacle below, and when he saw the whole Hellespont hidden by ships, and all the beaches of Abydos and all the open ground filled with men, he congratulated himself – and the moment after burst into tears. Artabanus his uncle, the man who in the first instance had spoken his mind so freely in trying to dissuade Xerxes from undertaking the campaign, was by his side; and when he saw how Xerxes wept, he said to him: 'My lord, surely there is a strange contradiction in what you do now and what you did a moment ago. Then you called yourself a lucky man – and now you weep.'

" 'I was thinking,' Xerxes replied; 'and it came into my mind how pitifully short human life is – for of all these thousands of men not one will be alive in a hundred years' time.' "

This anecdote is revealing in showing the human side of the Great King. Too often he is portrayed by Greek writers as a typical Oriental despot. It is Herodotus alone who reveals Xerxes' humanity; his ability to forgive his enemies, his open-handedness, and his love of natural beauty. Although the Greeks commonly referred to the Persians as "barbarians", the term *barbaros* meant no more than a man who did not speak Greek, and whose language was as incomprehensible as the "bar-bar" of a sheep. At this moment in their history the Persians were, in fact, possibly the most civilized nation in the world. They had a strong sense of honour and justice and were great lovers of nature and sport. If they had one main weakness it was their "gentlemanly code", which led them to despise merchants and artisans and commerce generally. The Greeks, on the other hand, were – as the English were later termed – "a nation of shopkeepers". Only the Spartans approximated in their society to the Persian idea of the way in which a gentleman should live; they were therefore held in respect by the Persians. Xerxes was certainly no barbarian. The Zoroastrian religion which he practised was far in advance of the Greek pantheon of amoral gods and goddesses.

After the troops had crossed the Hellespont by the bridge of boats, they marched steadily west through Thrace until they came to the great River Strymon, which had been bridged by the engineers. Persian ambassadors had already been sent to all the principal cities in Greece demanding the token of earth and water. A number of cities, particularly those in northern Greece, were willing to pay tribute. Athens and Sparta, however, received no ambassadors, for they had deliberately put themselves beyond the pale by killing the ambassadors who had been sent to them previously by Xerxes' father, Darius.

Even at this stage in history, it had long been recognized that the person of an ambassador was sacrosanct. The action of the Athenians and Spartans must, therefore, be read as a deliberate invitation to the Persians to come and attack them if they dare. (The Spartans had thrown the ambassadors down a well – saying that there was water and earth at the bottom if that was all they wanted.)

While the fleet sailed down to the canal across the isthmus of Mount Athos, and as ship after ship began to glide through the still waters in the lee of the sacred mountain, the army moved inexorably across the neck of the peninsula. Their route was designed to reach the sea at Therma, where the city of Thessalonica would one day stand, and it was in the Gulf of Therma that the fleet finally rendezvoused with the army. All was now set for the advance into Greece.

In accordance with the strategic policy of fighting as far forward as possible – denying the enemy entrance to their land in the far north – the Greeks had already sent a Spartan and Athenian contingent up to the coastal pass at Tempe. Themistocles himself led the Athenian division, and a Spartan officer the Peloponnesian troops.

The decision to hold the coastal pass at Tempe was sensible in theory, but in practice it proved to be impossible. The local Thessalians were eager to come to terms with Persia, while the southern Greeks discovered to their dismay that the Persians could by-pass the coastal route at Tempe by means of inland passes of which they had hitherto been ignorant. In view of the fact that the locals would happily "sell" these passes to the Persians, as well as the difficulty of remaining in territory where the inhabitants were hostile to them, the Athenians and Spartans decided to withdraw. They rejoined their ships and sailed south again.

Themistocles, who had probably never been in favour of the operation, was happy to be back with his new navy at Athens. The Spartans, however, as a military power, saw the conduct of the campaign against the Persians as being one that must principally be decided upon land. It was Themistocles who had the seaman's instinct that a great invading army, dependent upon ships for its return home, could best be beaten through the destruction of its fleet.

As the Persian army advanced, all of Greece was filled with gloom and despondency. Even the Delphic oracle (possibly susceptible to Persian gold) seems to have come out with general advice to the Greeks that the position was hopeless. From the various depressing responses that were accorded to the cities which sent to demand what they should do, of those that have survived only two seem to have had any relevance to the eventual outcome. One was the advice to the people of Delphi to "Pray to the Winds", and the other contained, among a number of obscure phrases, the statement that at "Divine Salamis, there should be a great destruction of men". Since the Bay of Salamis was where Themistocles and his friends had planned to defend their city, there was some consternation at these words. Assuming that the Delphic oracle was addressing itself to Greeks, many took it to mean that this "great destruction" referred to the Greek fleet. Themistocles, however, was an optimist. He was confident that his interpretation of the oracle was correct: the men who would be destroyed would not be the Greeks, but the Persians.

The most important point of the whole Greek position was the Strait of Artemisium, called after a small temple to the goddess Artemis, which stood on a headland at the northern end of the island of Euboea. This island, which had figured so prominently in the first Persian campaign of Darius, shielded Attica and the rest of Greece from an invasion from the north. Few naval commanders would be so rash as to risk their fleets down its exposed eastern side, especially when north winds were blowing. The obvious course was to come through the

Strait of Artemisium and sail down the narrow tongue of water dividing Euboea from Attica. As the ships would be under oars most of the time, it was easy to calculate that an invading fleet (restricted to a speed of perhaps one and a half knots) must always try to come under the lee of Euboea. The Strait of Artemisium, therefore, held the key to the whole naval situation. Two hundred Greek triremes, composed equally of Athenian and Peloponnesian ships, were set to guard the entrance to the strait.

Having been forced to withdraw from the pass at Tempe, the Greek position at Artemisium was now severely threatened from the north. There was one last position on the mainland of Greece where a military force could deny access to the invading Persian army. This was the narrow pass of Thermopylae, or Hot Springs, through which the Persians would have to move in order to overrun Attica and cut off the Greek fleet at Artemisium from its base.

It was once again, as during the previous invasion, the season of the full moon. But this time the Spartans recognized that the danger to all of Greece was too great to allow even this religious observance to detain them. Nevertheless, they were prepared to send only one of their Kings (Sparta had a dual monarchy), and only a limited number of men. Leaving his fellow monarch behind in Sparta, Leonidas, with a royal bodyguard of 300 Spartiates and about 2000 helots, or non-enfranchised lower-class members of the state, marched north. Leonidas also collected a further 2000 men from Arcadia, and about 700 men from Boeotia. It was with this force of approximately 4000 men that the Spartan King intended to hold the pass of Thermopylae.

Not long after the Spartans had reached the pass and taken up their positions, Xerxes, who had his spies all over the country, sent a horseman to see how many men awaited him in the pass, and what sort of disposition they had made. The man returned to tell the astonished monarch how small the force was, and that, far from trying to catch him, they had paid no attention to him at all. "Some of them," he said, "were stripped for exercise, and others were merely combing their hair!" Xerxes at first thought that the man must be either lying or joking: rash attitudes in the presence of an eastern potentate. A Greek renegade, Demaratus, hastened to assure him that such was typical Spartan behaviour.

"They have come," he said, "to deny us possession of the pass. They are preparing for the coming struggle. It is the normal practice of Spartans to attend to their hair when they are about to engage in battle."

Xerxes was still unable to believe what he was told. "So small a force will dare to engage my whole army?"

"Call me a liar, my lord," said Demaratus, "if they don't." It was on the basis of this famous incident that A. E. Housman wrote the lines:

> The King with half the East at heel is marched from lands
> of morning;
> Their fighters drink the rivers up, their shafts benight
> the air;
> And he that stands will die for nought, and home there's
> no returning.
> *The Spartans on the sea-wet rock sat down and combed*
> *their hair.*

While Xerxes' army moved down to assault the pass, his fleet sailed from its anchorage at Therma. It was now late August, a time when the Aegean is occasionally devastated by gales from the North. All the Mediterranean had by now been slowly heating up throughout the *grande chaleur* of midsummer. Only a slight change in barometric pressure is sufficient to produce an imbalance: then, the hot air suddenly rises over the sea like a great balloon and the cold air from the north roars down to replace it. "Pray to the Winds" the Delphic oracle had counselled – and the Greeks' prayers were to be answered.

A day's voyage out from Therma, the bulk of the Persian fleet was spread along the barren and inhospitable coast of Magnesia. Ahead of them lay Cape Sepias, over against which the island of Skiathos rides like a gull on the windy water. The area of sea between Skiathos and the neighbouring island of Skopelos is known to this day as the "Gate of the Winds".

Unable to round Cape Sepias before sunset, to gain the safety of the Artemisium Strait, the Persian captains were reluctantly compelled to anchor offshore. The leading ships were able to lie with their sterns made fast to the land, but the others, finding little suitable beach space, had to ride to their anchors.

"At dawn next day," says Herodotus, "the weather was clear and calm. . . ." It was that bright stillness which often precedes the onset of a north-easter. The *maistro*, the "master wind" as it is known, will often come raging out of a cloudless sky; with no banners of nimbus cloud to herald its approach, and no advance-guard of alto-stratus to forewarn the mariner. So it was on this day, as the Persian fleet prepared to move on down the coast. The wind came suddenly out of the north-east in gale-force fury, trapping hundreds of triremes and transports on a lee shore. "Those who realised in time that the blow was coming, and all who happened to be lying in a convenient position, managed to beach their vessels and to get them clear of the water before they were damaged, and thus saved their own lives as well; but the ships which were caught well off-shore were all lost; some were driven to the place called the Ovens at the foot of Mt Pelium, others on to the beach itself; a number came to grief on Sepias, and others, again, were smashed to pieces off the towns of Meliboea and Casthanea. . . . Four hundred ships, at the lowest estimate, are said to have been lost in this disaster, and the loss of life and of treasure was beyond reckoning."

The Athenians, according to Herodotus, had prayed to Boreas, god of the north wind, as soon as they observed from their station in the lee of Euboea that it was coming on to blow. The god obliged them. The gale lasted three days – somewhat unusual, since such August gales normally blow themselves out within about twenty-four hours. (After the war was over, the Athenians did not forget their debt to the god; they built him a shrine by the River Ilissus.)

Herodotus probably exaggerated the losses, just as he exaggerated the numbers of ships that formed the Persian fleet, but there seems little doubt that the Persians lost about a tenth of their fleet in this disaster. The Greek ships, for their part, weathered the gale, withdrawing under the lee of Euboea until it was over. The Greeks, however, were surprised, when they went north again to take up their station, to find how many hundreds of Persian ships had survived and were quietly heading into the safety of the Gulf of Pagasae, north of the entrance to the strait. They managed to cut out one squadron of fifteen ships, whose commander made the unhappy mistake of thinking that the Greek ships off Artemisium were part of the Persian fleet. A further detachment of the Persians later dispatched to the south, to round Euboea and hold the Andros Channel (thus cutting off the Greeks from their base), was caught by another storm and wrecked on the unfriendly flanks of Euboea. So far, at sea, at any rate, the gods seemed to be favouring the Greeks. But now the great test was to come by land.

The assault on the Greek position at Thermopylae was begun by Xerxes' Medean troops. The King was no doubt convinced that sheer weight of numbers would overpower the small force of men who held the narrow pass against him. What he, and possibly his generals, failed to understand was that, in so constricted an area as Thermopylae, the advantage would always lie with tough disciplined troops who had picked their defensive position with great care, as compared with a disorganized mass whose very numbers were a hindrance. After the onslaught of the Medean troops had proved a costly failure, the King's Immortals were sent in against the Greeks. Even they achieved no greater success.

Herodotus remarks on the superior training and weapons of the Spartans. He also describes one tactic by which the Spartans several times deceived the enemy: to turn and pretend to run away. At this sight the Persians at once came on "with great noise and shouting, supposing the battle won". But then the Spartans would suddenly wheel and face them, cutting them down with disciplined precision as they came on in their optimistic confusion. One weapon in particular which gave the Greeks a considerable advantage over the Persians was the formidable long spear; half again as long as those used by the enemy.

For two whole days the Persian army was thrown in relays at the Greek defensive line, and for two whole days they met with nothing but failure. The Greeks were not to be terrorized into submission by the sheer weight of the enemy. As evidence of the "laconic" Spartan approach to the vast numbers of the Persian army, Herodotus quotes a certain Dieneces. Warned before the battle by a man who had seen the Persians that they had so many archers that their arrows would darken the sun, Dieneces merely remarked: " 'This is pleasant news that the stranger . . . brings us: for if the Persians hide the sun, we shall have our battle in the shade.' " Against this spirit there could be no easy victory. Three times, it is said, during those first two days of battle, Xerxes leapt to his feet in horror at the losses being inflicted upon his army.

On the third day, in an attempt to take the pressure off the army and also in the hope that a naval victory might leave the Greeks ashore hopelessly outflanked, the entire Persian fleet was sent out from the Gulf of Pagasae. The Greek triremes at once engaged them, and a bitter, day-long struggle developed. At the end of this battle, called the Battle of Artemisium, both sides had taken a heavy mauling. The Athenians had lost nearly half of their ships, and the Persians had been so badly damaged that "both parties were glad when sunset ended the conflict". While this first major engagement was taking place at sea, the Spartans at Thermopylae were overwhelmed. In the phrase common now to almost every language, "the pass had been sold".

On the previous night a Greek traitor, Ephialtes, had come to the Persian monarch and had told him that he knew a track up the mountain. This path led to a long trough between the two main ridges of the peak. Once a body of troops had got up there, it was easy for them to out-flank the Greeks and come round behind them. The secret which Ephialtes promised to reveal was a narrow cliff path which would get the troops up to this trough. Xerxes and his advisers decided to send the Immortals, better-disciplined troops than any of the others; Persians to a man, and therefore used to mountain country. Leonidas, aware that there was always a possibility of his being outflanked, had posted one thousand of his Phocian allies to guard the mountain. But, as Herodotus tells the story, "The ascent of the Persians had been con-cealed by the oak-woods which cover this part of the mountain range, and it was only when they reached the top that the Phocians became aware of their approach; for there was not a breath of wind, and the marching feet made a loud swishing and rustling in the fallen leaves." Surprised and outnumbered, the Phocians withdrew under a hail of arrows to a higher point, and prepared to defend it to the last man. They presumed, quite incorrectly, that they were the object of the attack. The Persians, however, ignored them and pressed on down the descending track with all possible speed. By dawn they were at the coast and the Greek flank was turned.

Leonidas knew that the end had come. He sent back all his Pelopon-nesian allies, keeping with him, apart from his Spartiates and helots, only the men of Boeotia. Their land to the north was already lost, and they might reasonably be expected to stay and die with the Spartans. On this day, while the Persian and Greek fleets were locked together in their major battle at sea, the small force that remained ashore prepared to sell their lives dearly.

Leonidas and his fellow soldiers were all aware that, before the war had started, the Delphic oracle had proclaimed that a King of Sparta must die if their native land was not to be invaded. It is more than probable that Leonidas had this in mind as he willingly prepared for the last onslaught. In his company was a seer, Megistias, who by an inspection of ritually sacrificed animals had already descried that death waited for all the Greeks in the pass. Despite the fact that he was ordered back to safety by Leonidas, he preferred to stay with the King until the end.

As soon as the sun had risen, Xerxes poured a libation and prepared to send the army forward. He knew that it was only a matter of hours before the Immortals would come pouring down to take the Greeks in the rear. But Leonidas and his Spartans were not prepared to do no more than wait until they were crushed. They advanced out of the narrows of the pass and hurled themselves in a broad front upon the enemy.

Right up to the last the Persians were astonished at the conduct of these men, and even on this day of certain victory they were appalled at the casualties inflicted on their own forces. Company commanders were forced to drive on their troops with whips to withstand this last raging Greek advance. Thousands fell in the mêlée; the panic-stricken troops in front turning and trampling the men behind them underfoot as they strove to escape from the advancing wall of armoured Greeks. Others fell into the sea and were drowned. In the words of Herodotus, "No one could count the number of the dead."

In the end, inevitably, the Greeks were overwhelmed. Leonidas himself fell in the thick of the fray, and a violent battle developed over his body; the Greeks finally managing to drag it back with them to the place they had prepared for their final stand. This last defensive position was in the narrow neck of the pass, at a point where a wall crossed it, and it was here that the remnants of the Greeks gathered into a compact body. They fought to the bitter end, with swords after their spears were broken, then with rocks and stones, and then even with hands and teeth.

Thermopylae was a physical defeat, but a moral victory. Although at the time the news that a Spartan King and his Spartiate advance-guard had fallen in battle sent a shiver throughout Greece, at a later date it was seen how high a price the Persian monarch had paid for his victory. Furthermore, after the sea battle of Artemisium, although the Greeks had suffered severely, the Persian fleet, already depleted by its losses off Cape Sepias and along the eastern coast of Euboea, was in a far worse plight. The Greeks were able to make their way back from Artemisium through the Euboea Channel to Athens. They had friendly territory behind them, and time and facilities to make good their repairs. The Persians, on the other hand, were compelled to keep to the sea upon a hostile coast.

It was now the end of summer, and the provisioning of the great army, if it was to remain in Greece over the winter, presented immense problems. Xerxes and his commanders, as they laid waste the coastline of Phocis and Euboea, with the way into Greece apparently open to them, could congratulate themselves upon a victory. But they had won an expensive battle; they had not won the war.

Thermopylae passed into legend. It well deserved to do so; although upon analysis it seems that a wiser disposition of troops could have been made. Perhaps some Spartans should have been added to the Phocian flank-guard, for no trained Spartiate would have allowed his men to be surprised on night watch, nor would he have made the wrong assessment and allowed the Immortals to by-pass him so easily. A suitably un-emotional epitaph marked the burial ground of Leonidas and his men:

> Go tell the Spartans, you who read:
> We took their orders, and are dead.

Athens was now evacuated in haste, and only a garrison of volunteers was left behind on the Acropolis. Meanwhile the combined Greek fleets assembled in Salamis Sound. It was in this bay that the Persians must win a decisive victory if they were to occupy all Greece. A large army from the Peloponnese was now entrenched across the Isthmus of Corinth, ready to deny the enemy access to southern Greece. The latter would not dare land troops in the rear of this force so long as the Greek navy was still strong at sea. As so often in the history of the campaigns that have changed the face of the Mediterranean world, it was upon the sea itself, and the command of the sea, that everything hinged.

After a defence of the Acropolis that was every bit as heroic as the Spartan defence of Thermopylae, Athens was finally reduced. This resistance had delayed the Persian advance by several weeks, and allowed the Spartans and their allies to dig themselves in firmly across the Isthmus of Corinth. It also gave the naval forces a little time in which to make good their repairs, so as to be ready for the action that must inevitably follow.

This breathing space was important, for the Persian fleet, which had now moved down in force to Phaleron, had been at sea all the time, in hostile waters. It was without any of the facilities that the Athenians and their allies had for repairs, slipping, antifouling, and further training of the crews. Ancient fleets deteriorated rapidly, and the morale of their crews when long absent tended to deteriorate even more rapidly than the hulls and fabrics of their vessels. Furthermore, as wars throughout history have shown, the further invaders get from their homeland, the more they tend to lose that determination which inspires the invaded.

The island of Salamis, some ten miles long and ten miles wide, lies at the south of the Bay of Eleusis. It is about five miles east of Athens, and commands the whole of the Saronic Gulf southwards to the Peloponnese. It hangs like a shield across Eleusis Bay, protecting the narrow neck of the Corinthian isthmus. It was to this island, when Athens was abandoned, that the Athenian troops withdrew. With the retreating troops went the magistrates and other leading citizens of Athens. It was from Salamis, too, that the Athenians decided to carry on the war; much as, at a later date, Winston Churchill decided to carry on the war against the Germans in 1940 from Canada, if Britain itself fell to the enemy.

Salamis was the all-important objective for Xerxes, who quickly set his land forces to building an artificial promontory from the coast towards the island. His intention, no doubt, was to run out a bridge of boats from the promontory and invade the island, much as he had crossed the Hellespont. But time was against him. The winter was drawing on, and the Athenians had no intention of allowing Xerxes to push out the initial bridgehead without constant harassment from shipborne archers.

The battle seems to have been fought not off the eastern end of Salamis, but in the narrows between the island and the coast of Attica.

An old Venetian watch-tower on the headland overlooking the bay probably stands on the very site where Xerxes had his throne erected. Here, surrounded by secretaries and courtiers, he decided to watch, as upon some gigantic stage, the last act of the drama. He felt confident as to its outcome. The combined Greek fleet, composed principally of ships from Athens, Sparta, Megara, Corinth and the island of Aegina, consisted of probably no more than two hundred ships. Heavier than the ships of the enemy, possibly not so quick at manoeuvring, they needed to be handled in such a way that these potential disadvantages could be turned to assets.

But first, by a stroke of cunning, Themistocles inveigled Xerxes into a trap. The Greeks, even at this moment in their history, were still in their endemic state of dissension. Themistocles, for his part, was well aware that pro-Persian sympathizers in the Greek ranks were keeping the Great King well posted as to these internal troubles. There were some who held that the fleet should be withdrawn to fight further to the south, and others who maintained that the only reason the Athenians wanted to fight off Salamis was that this represented the "last ditch" for Athens. Themistocles himself was even taunted for being "a man without a city". He had to point out that, if he cared to withdraw the Athenian contingent, the others would have no hope at all. (He does, in fact, seem to have used a piece of simple blackmail by saying that unless he was supported in his intention to fight at Salamis, he would withdraw all the Athenian ships and troops, and sail over to Italy or Sicily and found a new Athens there.) Aware, then, that Xerxes knew how divided the Greeks were, Themistocles sent a messenger to the King saying that he and his Athenians were prepared to defect to the Persian side. The Greeks, he said, were all at sixes and sevens, and Xerxes' best course was to send part of his fleet to block off the western end of the strait – between Salamis and the mainland to prevent the Greeks escaping through it. At the same time he should advance boldly through the eastern end, past the mole that was under construction.

Xerxes fell for the bait. He divided his fleet, sending the Egyptian squadron, one of his best, round to the west of Salamis; the rest of his ships he dispatched through the narrow jaws of the strait. The battle took place under just the conditions that best suited the heavier Greek ships. Using the island of Salamis behind them like an anchor on which they slowly pivoted, the Greeks were able to present an impregnable front to the Persians. At the same time, having lured the enemy into entering the strait in full confidence that they would be meeting a divided, or already fleeing, opponent, Themistocles had the Persians caught between his own half-moon front of ships and the implacable shores of Attica.

Although the battle was fought at sea, and although it was the result of meticulous planning, the manner in which it took place much resembled the three-day battle at Thermopylae. Once again, the Persians were constricted by their numbers, and once again the superior discipline of the Greeks proved its value. From his throne above the narrows Xerxes watched the destruction of all his hopes. A west wind was blowing, and it was only with its aid that such of the shattered Persian fleet as escaped made its way back again to Phaleron Bay.

For the loss of some forty ships the Greeks had destroyed or captured two hundred of the enemy. Aeschylus, who, according to tradition, was present at both Artemisium and Salamis, gives a graphic account of the battle in his play *The Persians*. He concludes one passage with a description of how "the Greek ships, handled most skilfully, circled around us and kept striking in towards the centre until you could not see the sea itself for blood and broken ships. On every beach and every reef there lolled the bodies of the dead. All the ships of all our Persian fleet strove hard to get away. But still the Greeks, like men who circle round gaffing tunny or other great shoals of fish, stabbed and killed with oars and other lumps of wood, while cries and screams echoed across the sea – until the night came down."

The whole operation was in fact similar to a *mattanza*. The Greeks had, as it were, let the enemy into the *camera della morte* between the sland of Salamis and the mainland of Attica. Then they closed the net and killed the struggling enemy almost at their leisure.

With winter coming on, and the fleet decimated, the Persians had no chance of regaining the advantage. Xerxes took the advice of his general Mardonius and withdrew hurriedly to Persia. Mardonius himself, at his own suggestion, stayed on in Greece with a force of picked troops. He probably felt that, with the King out of the way, things would be easier to manage. Left with no more than a military campaign on his hands, he was confident that he could conquer the whole of Greece in the following year.

At the same time as the victory at Salamis – legend later said, on the very same day – the Greeks under Gelon in Sicily inflicted a major defeat upon the Carthaginians in the north of Sicily near the River Himera. Both in the West and in the East the Greek world was saved. The extraordinary flowering of art and culture in Athens during the next fifty years – that springtime of Western civilization – may perhaps be seen as rising from an earth that had been fructified by much blood and endeavour. It produced a crop that had been hardened by the frost of endurance.

In the spring of 479 B.C., Mardonius, having wintered his depleted army in Thessaly, returned to the attack – and failed. In the decisive Battle of Plataea the Persians were savagely defeated, and Mardonius himself was killed. This was the end of the great Persian invasion. Shortly after the victory at Plataea, a combined Athenian and Spartan fleet struck across the Aegean and freed the large island of Samos from the Persians, then caught up with the enemy fleet at Mycale on the Ionian mainland opposite Samos. Although less well recorded in history than any of the previous battles of this war, the action at Mycale, which resulted in the destruction of nearly all that remained of the Persian fleet, was of immense importance. It ensured, at any rate for the moment, the freedom of the Aegean for Greek shipping, and it helped trigger the revolt of the Ionian Greeks against their Persian over-lords.

By the end of the year 479 B.C., Greece was liberated from the threat of Persian domination. She had also very largely cleared her own sea, the Sea of the Kingdom, from the fleets of Persia and Persia's allies. Further west, in Sicily, by the great victory at Himera (which had been a formidable blow to Carthaginian power and prestige), Gelon of Syracuse had shattered Punic morale. Even in the great North African city itself there was a spate of rumours that the Greeks were about to invade their territory and possibly even come to the assault of Carthage. The repulse of the Carthaginians and the Etruscans (for the two nations threatened by the Greeks in Sicily had become allies for the occasion) was held to be – certainly by the Sicilian Greeks – as important as the Greek victory at Salamis.

Although almost the whole history of this war derives from Greek sources (with their natural anti-Persian bias), it would be difficult to maintain the view that a Persian victory would have furthered Mediterranean civilization. Persian government was, to judge by its results in the Near East, bureaucratic in the worst sense and not conducive to freedom of thought or the advancement of culture. It is just possible that a Persian conquest of Greece, followed by an inevitable expansion through Sicily and Italy, would have given the Western world the religion of Zoroaster in place of Greek and Latin paganism. It is also possible that, modified by centuries, this religion's sensitive and reasonably logical explanation of the universe would have become sophisticated into a creed that would have been adopted throughout the Mediterranean world.

TEN

After the War

The overwhelming defeat of the Carthaginians in Sicily left the Greek colonists in possession of nearly all the island, except the far west. Only at Panormus, and at Motya and Lilybaeum in the shadow of Mount Eryx, was there any trace of the Phoenicians. Their trading vessels and their once-triumphant biremes, moving between Carthage and Sardinia, kept carefully to the western harbours of Sicily, far away from the Greek sphere of influence.

The war between the Carthaginians and the Greeks continued in Sicily (in 408 B.C. the Carthaginians even recaptured Himera and destroyed the Greek city), but the strength of Carthage was ebbing. More and more she looked to the West, to the Pillars of Hercules, to the Atlantic trade routes, and to the interior of Africa itself. In these years, the Carthaginians began for the first time to expand outside the area of their city and to acquire a large inland territory in the fertile areas of Tunisia. Carthage now needed land to feed her growing population, and she also needed the natives of the interior as soldiers in her mercenary armies.

Carthage would not have developed as she did into a great imperial power had it not been for Greek pressure. The Carthaginians, like their ancestors the Phoenicians, would have been happy to continue without colonies, but with trading posts throughout the Mediterranean. Now, as in all their history, their main interest was international trade and no more; but Greek expansion had lost them many of their eastern, and now Sicilian, markets. It was the Greeks, then, who unwittingly compelled Carthage to become more than a great commercial and industrial city. They forced her to become an empire, backed by large land areas in North Africa.

The Etruscans, meanwhile, were to suffer further defeat at the hands of the Greeks. When the Syracusans relieved the Greek colony of Cumae on the Bay of Naples (which the Etruscans were besieging), they compelled the Etruscans to withdraw from all southern Italy. Their sphere of influence was rapidly being whittled down to their ancient mainland cities in Etruria and to Corsica and Elba and other off-lying ports and islands.

While Etruria was slowly dying (her independence was not finally extinguished until 309 B.C., when the whole land came under the rule of the Romans), the olive tree of Athens was already bearing the harvest that its deep roots had earned. Despite protests from Corinth and Sparta, who maintained that it was dangerous for the Athenians to rebuild the walls of their city (since it might be used by the Persians as a strongpoint if they came again), the Athenians refused to accept this specious advice. The "Themistoclean Walls", as they were called, after the great patriot, were to give Athens an inner shield. Behind them she could feel secure from any further Persian attacks and from the envy of her neighbours. Beyond them, she still had that outer defence, the "wooden wall" of ships which had helped to save Greece at Salamis.

After clearing the collaborators out of northern Greece, the Greeks were confronted with the Asia Minor problem; a problem that was not to be solved until the twentieth century. After their sea victory at Mycale, they had the whole coast at their mercy. Unfortunately the Spartan commander, Pausanias, soon lost the good will of the Ionians, who were ready enough by now to return to the Greek fold. The great problem was protection against the Persians should they decide to re-occupy the Greek mainland cities. This matter was never completely solved, and the inefficiency of Pausanias and his Spartans soon led to power in the Aegean being transferred to the hands of Athens. Themistocles, despite his good war record, did not recover his former position, but Athens was lucky in having to hand the formerly exiled Aristeides.

The uneasy wartime "League of the Hellenes" was dissolved three years after the war was over. Sparta had troubles at home in the Peloponnese and, in any case, Spartans rarely liked being far away from their own territory. So Athens became the overall leader of Greece and, together with her allies, she organized the Delian League. The son of Miltiades, who had served Athens so well in the first Persian war, became the general of this alliance. It was almost exclusively a naval one, with Athens providing the backbone of the ships, organizing the finances, and determining the policy. Like all alliances it was subject to many stresses and strains, particularly from those smaller territories and islands who felt they were being compelled to contribute to the greater glory of Athens, with very little benefit for themselves. Nevertheless, it was the nearest that Greece had yet come to any form of real unity based, as it were, on "Greekness".

The Delian League provided the cornerstone of power upon which Athens, during the next fifty years, was to erect that monument of civilization to which the whole world still pays tribute. Fifty years! It is a short enough space of time, and yet during it there was to flower in the arts, literature, philosophy, and mathematical speculation many of the forms, terms, and concepts, both intellectual and aesthetic, on which the Western world is based.

H. D. F. Kitto, in *The Greeks*, summarizes these years immediately after Salamis and Plataea: "In trade and industry, Athens was rapidly overhauling those other Greek cities who had had such a long start of her; the combination of Attic taste and intelligence with her central position, her excellent harbours, and her now overwhelming sea-power, was formidable indeed; and besides this, Athens, like London, enjoyed certain imponderable advantages derived from her probity and common-sense methods. Artistically, too, a new world was opening up. The long struggle with bronze and marble had brought architecture and sculpture to the verge of classical perfection, and it was to be the task of the Athenian artists . . . to combine Ionian elegance with Dorian strength. The Athenian potters and painters were approaching their greatest triumphs: the most Athenian art of all, tragic drama, was growing more assured and more exciting every year. . . ."

The withdrawal of Persia from the Aegean was a significant moment in Mediterranean history. As Eduard Meyer writes in the *Encyclopaedia Britannica*: "The disasters of Salamis and Plataea definitely shattered the offensive power of the empire. The centre of gravity in the world's history had shifted from Susa and Babylon to the Aegean Sea; and the Persians were conscious that in spite of all their courage they were henceforward in the presence of an enemy superior in arms as well as in intellect, whom they could not hope to subdue by their own strength."

Court intrigues, murderous internecine feuds, the insidious influence of harem politics (that bane of the East for centuries to come), all contributed to a decline in the power of Persia and in the quality of her civilization. Nevertheless the country still continued to produce brave and honourable men, and, as the Greeks were to find out to their cost, it did not pay to challenge them in military ventures, certainly not anywhere near their own soil. In a six-year war, from 460 B.C. to 454 B.C., the Athenians attempted to wrest Egypt from Persian control by means of their powerful fleet – and failed utterly. Some two hundred ships and all of their men were lost in this venture, and the Phoenicians, who still formed the backbone of the Persian navy, had something of a revenge for Salamis.

Persia continued to dominate the Near East until the arrival of Alexander the Great changed the whole face of that world. Herodotus closes his history with a story which shows clearly that he (and presumably many other intelligent Greeks) still retained a great respect for Persian qualities. He tells how one day a rich and influential Persian came to the great Cyrus and suggested that, since Persia was now the most powerful country in the world, it would be a good idea if the Persians were to migrate from their own poor mountainous country and occupy some rich and fertile lowland. "Cyrus did not think much of this suggestion; he replied that they might act upon it if they pleased, but added the warning that, if they did so, they must prepare themselves to rule no longer, but to be ruled by others. 'Soft countries,' he said, 'breed soft men. It is not the property of any one soil to produce fine fruits and good soldiers too.' The Persians had to admit that this was true and that Cyrus was wiser than they; so they left him, and chose rather to live in a rugged land and rule than to cultivate rich plains and be slaves."

The Persians ultimately forgot the virtues of frugality and manliness that Cyrus had counselled. So, too, at a later date, did the Spartans themselves. In the meantime, it was the Athenians who, with their love of life and acute visual receptivity, transformed the world. But in the end it was the Spartans who brought Athens to her knees. "Nothing in excess" was a Greek maxim for the ideal life – and it was one which they esteemed so greatly because it was so remote from their own passionate and excessive natures.

BOOK II

Quanta plura recentium, seu veterum revolvo, tanto ludibria rerum mortalium cunctis in negotiis observantur.

The more I think about the history of ancient or modern times, the more I see in everything the absurdity of all human activities.

– Tacitus, *Annals*, Book 3, 18

ONE

Goddess and Island

Her groves are in the high places, and her worship is the worship of life itself. She remains for all time the goddess of the Mediterranean peoples. The most ancient of deities, the fertility goddess originally dominated the whole sea. In the Near East and the Aegean her cult had long been paramount. In Crete, the Minoans had paid their tribute to her as a lunar and snake goddess, and also as mistress of the beasts, the Lady of Wild Things. She had been worshipped in the Maltese islands since the Neolithic period. Fecund and tranquil, her steatopygous images invited men to reproduce their kind, to cause their livestock to do the same, and to ensure that the fields grew fertile. She was a peaceful goddess. In the Maltese archipelago, during her uninterrupted reign of nearly one thousand years, there was no warfare between the agricultural settlements. No weapons of this period have been found and, even more significant, there are no signs of man-made destruction in any of the temples devoted to her cult.

The invasion of the Mediterranean by northern peoples, among them the ancestors of the Dorian and Ionian Greeks, had changed the pattern of life. The newcomers brought with them a belligerent sky god, with lightning in his hand. Before these invaders and their masculine-dominated pantheon of gods and goddesses, the ancient Mother Goddess, upheld by her simple Stone Age peoples, was powerless. She declined in influence, to be absorbed and to re-emerge in due course under many names and many forms. She was ultimately to triumph once again as the goddess of love, the Virgin goddess who bore the divine Son.

In western Sicily, high on the peak of Mount Eryx, the Phoenicians had built a temple to her during the early days of their occupation of the island. No doubt the site already housed a temple to the Mother

Goddess within the Cyclopean walls of the fortress built there by the native inhabitants. Now that they were confined almost entirely to the western corner of the island – and even here the Greeks were beginning to press them – these Phoenician or Carthaginian settlements acquired considerable importance. They lay on the trade route north from Carthage to Sardinia and Etruscan Corsica.

The temple of the goddess Astarte, overlooking the town of Motya and the Aegates Islands just offshore, served as a landmark for mariners along this rugged coast. The goddess herself, under one of her many aspects, was the guardian and patron of sailors. She was also, as Sir James Frazer observes in *The Golden Bough*, "identified with the planet Venus, and her changes from a morning to an evening star were carefully noted by the Babylonian astronomers, who drew omens from her alternate appearance and disappearance. Hence we may conjecture that the festival of Adonis was regularly timed to coincide with the appearance of Venus as the Morning or Evening Star."

Few sites more appropriate for her temple could have been found than the high peak of Mount Eryx. Standing aloof out of the western plains, the mountain clasps almost every cloud which passes over this corner of the sea; whether it be the towering alto-cumulus of late summer or the stratus brought by the sirocco with all the heat of the desert on its breath. The flanks of the mountain are thus nearly always hot and humid, forming a kind of open-air conservatory which nourishes one of the most diverse collections of wild flowers to be found anywhere in the Mediterranean.

It was fitting that the annual ritual of the death of the goddess's lover, Tammuz, or Adonis, should be celebrated here, where the wild daisies, orchids, marigolds, blue anchusa, purple thistles, and minute wild irises shone like scattered drops of the dead god's blood. As in all places devoted to the worship of Astarte, there was a sacred grove on the mountain where the doves of the goddess circled lazily against the sky.

Mountain shrines like this were the "high places" and the groves that the Hebrew prophets so abominated, and that King Josiah destroyed. "And the high places that were before Jerusalem, which were on the right hand of the mount of corruption, which Solomon the king of Israel had builded for Ashtoreth [Astarte] the abomination of the Zidonians, and for Chemosh [Tammuz] the abomination of the Moabites, and for Milcom [Melkarth] the abomination of the children of Ammon, did the king defile. And he brake in pieces the images, and cut down the groves, and filled their places with the bones of men. Moreover the altar that was at Bethel, and the high place . . . both that altar and the high place he brake down, and burned the high place, and stamped it small to powder, and burned the grove." The high place and the grove on Mount Eryx, however, were to endure for many centuries. The Phoenician worship of Astarte and her consort-lover persisted in this corner of Sicily for a thousand years, the Greeks worshipping her as Aphrodite, and the Romans later calling her Venus Erycina, mother of Aeneas, the founder of the Roman race.

The quiet islands lying offshore played no part in the dramatic history of the next two centuries. After the great Greek victory over the Persians in 480 B.C., coincidental with the Greek victory over the Carthaginians at Himera, the life of the Sicel inhabitants, poor farmers and fishermen, was relatively undisturbed by the travail of the world. The great years of Athens, the flowering of Greek genius, made no impression upon places so simple and remote. The war between the Greeks and Carthaginians, which flared up sporadically throughout the fifth and third centuries B.C., hardly affected the inhabitants of these islands. The galleys passed and repassed in the narrow strait to the east of them, where the shadow of Mount Eryx brooded over the water.

Sometimes, no doubt, rumours of burning towns and fleeing peoples were brought back by fishermen who had been across selling their catch on the mainland. Then, suddenly, in 398 B.C., even this remote corner of the world was shaken, when the ancient trading post and naval base of Phoenician Motya was sacked by Dionysius, the tyrant of Syracuse. One of the greatest Greek war leaders and one of the most powerful men of his age, Dionysius was intent on bringing the whole of Sicily under one rule.

Motya, the ancient Carthaginian foundation lying on its small round island just north of modern Marsala, had long been one of the linchpins in the trading route between its founding city and Sicily and the other islands to the north. Its loss was important, but did not prove disastrous, for the Carthaginians promptly transferred the remaining inhabitants to the fortified city of Lilybaeum on the nearby mainland.

Nevertheless, the fact that a Greek army and naval force could now strike as far west as this corner of the island was a grim reminder to Carthage that her hold over western Sicily was precarious. To the few inhabitants of the offshore islands the sight of Motya being razed must have been terrifying. They had known the city for generations, and had sold their fish and farm products there. Even the re-establishment of the Carthaginian colony at Lilybaeum immediately afterwards can hardly have eradicated the suspicion that the pattern of life was beginning to change in this part of the sea. Yet the centuries passed, and still the galleys of Carthage flaunted their colourful hulls between Levanzo and the mainland, while the smoke from the altar of Astarte rose from the distant blue peak of Eryx.

Dionysius was badly defeated in a later campaign (383–378 B.C.) against the Carthaginians. At this time the city of Himera, which had been saved from the Carthaginians in 480 B.C., was sacked by them and the Greek colonists were killed or enslaved. The beautiful city of Selinus, on the southern shores of the embattled island, was also totally destroyed by the Carthaginians and its Greek inhabitants were sold as slaves. The Sicilian Greeks were reluctantly forced to concede that all the territory west of the River Halycus (about a third of the island) came indisputably within the Cathaginian sphere of influence.

So, despite intermittent warfare throughout the third century B.C., the pendulum of power in the central Mediterranean remained uneasily balanced between Carthaginian and Greek. The beautiful but unhappy island of Sicily was the arena where East and West met in their almost continuous conflict.

The indigenous peoples of the island, meanwhile, continued to live in their remote hills. They came down to trade when necessary with Carthaginian and Greek, no doubt marvelling at the white cities which flaunted the power of these civilizations but which, often destroyed, reflected also the folly of man. The natives, however, were not exempt from human failings, for they, too, were prone to tribal wars. The defeated ended up being sold to Greeks or Carthaginians as slaves.

Vines and olives were grown not only on the fertile mainland but wherever possible on the three off-lying islands. Although Aegusa (modern Favignana) and Levanzo and Marettimo were basically "goat islands", inhabited largely during the summer months by goatherds who came across from Sicily, they also had a few permanent settlements. Aegusa, as described by Homer in the eighth century B.C., was "luxuriant . . . covered with woods, [and] is the home of innumerable goats. The goats are wild, for man has made no pathways that might frighten them off, nor do hunters visit the island with their hounds to rough it in the forests and to range the mountain tops. Used neither for grazing nor for ploughing, it lies for ever unsown and untilled; and this land where no man goes makes a happy pasture for the bleating goats." But Homer, or his sea-captain informant, also remarked that "it is by no means a poor country, but capable of yielding any crop in due season. Along the shore of the grey sea there are soft water-meadows where the vine would never wither; and there is plenty of land level enough for the plough, where they could count on cutting a deep crop at every harvest-time, for the soil below the surface is exceedingly rich "

Several centuries later this dream of the islands, transformed by agriculture, had become reality. In the secure northern harbour of Aegusa, and in the two bays of Levanzo, there could be found small fishing boats of the type known to the Greeks as *epaktra*. This was an open boat with four to eight oars, and an auxiliary sail that could be used whenever the wind set fair. In the long months of summer, when the sea was idle but the fishermen busy, these boats could be secured just offshore by a sleeping-stone – a large stone block with a hole bored through it to take a rope cable. Mostly, though, they were hauled up on the beach at night, safe from wind and weather. The men may have fished with iron hooks bought from their Carthaginian neighbours across the water, or laid out simple seine nets to close off the head of one of the small island bays. With reeds imported from the marshlands at the foot of Mount Eryx they made the same type of fish-traps which Mediterranean fishermen use to this day. These had a hole at the top large enough to admit fish as big as the horse mackerel, small dogfish, and mullet. Inside the trap were placed bits of gut and offal, sliced lug-worms, and pounded pieces of squid. Weighted down at the bottom with a few stones, the traps were taken out to the shallow, offshore fishing-grounds. Carefully buoyed with a piece of wood or an inflated pig's bladder, they were lowered to the sea bed on a line.

Ropes were sometimes made of thin strips of hide, but the Carthaginians introduced the flax, hemp, and papyrus cordage of their native East. Then, too, the islanders lured *palinurus vulgaris*, the clawless rock lobster or sea crayfish of the Mediterranean, into wickerwork creels or wooden-hooped lobster pots covered with netting.

There was an abundance of fish in those unpopulated and under-fished waters, on whose rocky sea margins only a handful of men and women had their homes. Mussels and other shell-fish clung to the sides of silent coves, while prickly sea-eggs, with their savoury orange roes, could be found clustering on every ledge in the shallows. Sardines abounded, and anchovies have always been a standard diet for the poor. Tobias Smollett remarked some two thousand years later: "The fishermen and mariners all along this coast [the South of France] have scarce any other food but dry bread, with a few pickled anchovies; and when the fish is eaten, they rub their crusts with the brine. Nothing can be more delicious than fresh anchovies fried in oil. . . ."

The vine, imported by the Phoenicians and the Greeks, had taken a firm hold. It yielded a deep-bodied, strong wine that many centuries later would be transformed into the sweet table wine known as Marsala. But these early inhabitants only tasted wine in a rough form, diluted most probably with spring water. The olives that clung tenaciously to the islands' hilly slopes provided not only the oil so essential for their diet, but also fed the simple pottery lamps that were the sole means of lighting their primitive stone houses. Similar lamps burned across the water in the shrine of Astarte, to honour both the goddess and the divine gift of the olive itself.

Scarcely affected, then, by the perturbations of the great world, where Greek and Carthaginian were locked in strife, and where the power of Etruria waned and the shadow of Rome lengthened over Italy, the islanders of the remote Aegates lived out their harsh and uncomplicated lives. Even so, they were more fortunate than peasants dwelling in colder and rainier lands. The indulgent sea and sky of the Mediterranean render a life of poverty far more tolerable than in the North. Fish and goat's meat could be dried by sun and wind to provide a larder to last through the comparatively brief winter. The rich soil, when enlivened by the rains of autumn, would raise enough cereal crops for their bread. Bread, oil, fish, and a little meat – although augmented nowadays by later importations such as tomatoes and citrus fruits – are still the basis of Mediterranean diet. The flour for their bread was no doubt made in the same way that Vergil describes in the *Georgics:* the grain first of all being toasted, and then crushed between stones or in a pestle and mortar. (*Nunc torrete igni fruges, nunc frangite saxo.*) The dough was most probably laid on a flat or convex-shaped stone; this was placed over a fire, and the dough covered with hot ashes. Bread of this type had been made since prehistoric times, and a very similar bread is still made in the Near East.

In primitive settlements the craft of fire-making must, even at this period in the world's history, have been important. The burning glass – a glass sphere filled with water – was a familiar object to the Greeks of the fifth century B.C., but it is unlikely that anything so sophisticated was known to the peasants of western Sicily. Making fire by percussion did not become a standard method until the Iron Age had advanced sufficiently for steel to be generally available. The inhabitants of Aegusa and Levanzo almost certainly used the age-old frictional method – either rubbing a stick back and forth along another piece of wood, or by rotating between the palms of the hands a vertical stick whose point rested in a wooden block on the ground. Mediterranean man was fortunate that his winters and his rainy seasons were short and that for about half the year he had no need of fire except for cooking.

Salt, that basic requirement of the human system, was easily obtained in such islands. Where the limestone rocks ran down to the sea in sloping shelves the inhabitants hollowed them into shallow trays or salt-pans. They filled these from the sea a few yards away, and allowed the evaporation of the summer sun to do the rest. More fortunate again than his fellows in the North, the Mediterranean peasant was not solely dependent upon the sun and the wind to dry his winter forage of food. He had ample salt with which to cure it, and hundreds of pieces of fish or meat could be rubbed with sea-salt and left on the rocks to be sun and salt cured within a few days. The soft limestone of Aegusa (though not the harder coralline) was easy to quarry and cut, and the few buildings of the islanders no doubt followed the traditional box-like structures of Motya and Lilybaeum on the mainland.

Life in these islands – as in many others throughout the Mediterranean, from the Balearics to the Dodecanese – changed imperceptibly over centuries. Then, as for hundreds of years to come, the greatest danger to the islanders came from wandering pirates, whose income largely derived from the capture and export of slaves to the great cities of the Mediterranean. Storms could usually be avoided by the coastal fishermen, and savage weather conditions only rarely disturbed the peasant farmer's routine. But the arrival of a lean-hulled "slaver", manned by armoured and iron-weaponed raiders, often meant the desolation of an island. The gods might shake the earth and bring great cities crashing to the ground; tempests might destroy whole fleets; disease might decimate crops and flocks; but man's worst enemy was always man.

Two Sides of a Greek Coin –
Athens and Sparta

The great Athenian achievement in the arts and the sciences, in philosophy and political experiment, which followed so shortly after the defeat of the Persians in 480 B.C., was triggered by an immense feeling of liberation. It was not only that men like Aeschylus had themselves fought in the battles of Marathon, Salamis, and Plataea (and could therefore re-create from personal experience the grandeur and the passion of those days), but also that every Athenian felt a new pride in belonging to the state which, more than all others, had overcome the greatest empire in the world. National pride, coupled with a sudden new access of wealth, and combined with the emergence of great artists and great art-forms, makes a heady mixture. The Athenians did not always use their new inheritance wisely. Yet at the same time, during what has been called the "Great Fifty Years", they did make a superb "break-through" in human culture. In any terms their achievement was outstanding, but even more so when one considers that it was made in so short a space of time.

H. D. F. Kitto, in *The Greeks*, points out that "There is some parallel between Athens of 480 and England of 1588: in whatever direction men looked they saw exciting possibilities – but the Athenian saw even more than the Englishman." It is true that there is a similarity between Elizabethan England after the defeat of the Spanish Armada and Athens after the defeat of Xerxes. But, whereas the English achievements were mainly in the fields of literature, exploration, and colonial expansion, the Athenians pushed forward the frontiers of man's knowledge and artistic experience in almost every direction.

Only in the area of religion do they seem to have made little advance, being interested in the speculation of philosophy rather than in the "revealed religion" of, for instance, the Jews. Centuries later, when Saint Paul came to Athens, he chided the citizens for being so superstitious that, despite the altars to innumerable gods throughout the city, he had come across one with the inscription "To the Unknown God". This had been erected to forestall the anger of any god who might possibly have been missed out of the immense pantheon adopted by the Greeks. Yet it would be true to say that the speculative nature of the Greeks, and particularly of the Athenians, was best served by their quest for the "Unknown God". As the Apostle himself remarked: "For all the Athenians and strangers which were there spent their time in nothing else, but either to tell, or to hear some new thing." But this was the source of their strength, and it was this spirit of eternal curiosity – like a child-genius confronted for the first time with all the mysteries and marvels of the world – that prompted the Athenian flowering of the fifth century B.C. If the Semitic acceptance of "revealed religion" had been part of their nature there might have been no Athenian achievement.

Great moments in time sometimes produce men to match them. These are not the men who create the national mood, but those who seize upon it. Such a man was Pericles, whose name is indissolubly linked with this period of Athenian history. H. A. L. Fisher writes in his *History of Europe*: "The conduct of Athenian affairs had from 462 B.C. onward fallen into the hands of a visionary of genius. Pericles was a democrat and an imperialist, and was therefore in full sympathy with the two main currents of political thought which prevailed in Athens at that time; but he appears to have had also what is a rare gift – a clear-cut ideal for his state, not only in its political and economic aspect, but also in relation to human conduct and character and artistic achievement. He wanted the influence of Athens to be widespread, and so planted out Athenian settlers far and wide from the shores of the inhospitable Euxine to the vine-clad hills of southern Italy; but it was also part of his philosophy that the mother city should occupy a position of commanding pre-eminence from the splendour and beauty of her public monuments. In a moment of inspiration he determined to restore the temples of Athens and Eleusis which had been destroyed by the Persians and to make of this act of restoration a demonstration, not merely of Athenian, but of Hellenic magnificence. A great architect and a great sculptor were at hand to serve his ambition. The famous statue of Athena has long since been destroyed, but the sculptured frieze of Pheidias may be seen in the British Museum, and we may still admire the genius of Ictinus, who contrived the exquisite proportions of the Parthenon."

The city that Pindar, a Theban, describes as "shining, violet-crowned, and famous in song" was not only an artistic triumph, but something of a political one. Although, like all Greek city-states of this period, it was partly based on a slave population, Athens was – for its enfranchised citizens, at least – a true democracy. This democracy is described by G. Lowes Dickinson in *The Greek View of Life*: "The citizenship was extended to every rank and calling; the poor man jostled the rich, the shopman the aristocrat, in the Assembly; cobblers, carpenters, smiths, farmers, merchants, and retail traders met together with the ancient landed gentry, to debate and conclude on national affairs; and it was from such varied elements as these that the lot impartially chose the officials of the law, the revenue, the police, the highways, the markets, and the ports, as well as the jurors at whose mercy stood reputation, fortune, and life. . . ."

The disadvantage of the system – as in all democracies that have since attempted to follow the Athenian pattern – was that the lower and middle classes (never so well educated as the aristocracy, and with less stake in the country) tended to exert the greatest influence on political power.

The "gift of the gab" became more important for a politician than a cool, appraising eye that could see what would really be of most benefit to the state. The demagogue, the specious, golden-tongued orator who could fasten upon the wants and prejudices of the majority, was always likely to outshine the reasoned argument of a man whose principles were set somewhat above the workaday strife of the market-place. Even in the different democracies that have evolved out of the Athenian original the problem still exists: how to make the voice of reason prevail over the voice of popular immediacy. It was a fortunate and rare occurrence that Pericles, who dominated Athenian politics during the formative years of the city's greatness, was an aristocrat who also knew how to appeal to the *demos*, or general public. Such men are rare. George Washington and William Pitt also had this quality.

Naturally, the intense rivalry between the democratic and aristocratic factions of Athens often led to bitterness and even violence. Aristophanes, greatest of all Greek comic playwrights, had little or no use for the pretensions of the demagogues. His greatest enemy – and their dislike was mutual – was the famous Cleon, originally a tanner by trade, who became the people's favourite after the death of Pericles. In Hookham Frere's translation of Aristophanes' *Knights* we hear the true voice of aristocratic Athens. Demosthenes, a well-born general, is addressing an ignorant sausage-seller.

Demosthenes. O happy man!
Unconscious of your glorious destiny,
Now mean and unregarded; but tomorrow,
The mightiest of the mighty, Lord of Athens.
S-Seller. Come master, what's the use of making game?
Why can't ye let me wash my guts and tripe,
And sell my sausages in peace and quiet?
Dem. O simple mortal, cast those thoughts aside!
Bid guts and tripe farewell! Look here! Behold!

(*pointing to the audience*)

The mighty assembled multitude before ye!
S-Seller (*with a grumble of indifference*).
I see 'em.
Dem. You shall be their lord and master,
The sovereign and ruler of them all,
Of the assemblies and tribunals, fleets and armies;
You shall trample down the Senate under foot,
Confound and crush the generals and commanders,
Arrest, imprison, and confine in irons,
And feast and fornicate in the Council House.
S-Seller. Are there any means of making a great man
Of a sausage-selling fellow such as I?
Dem. The very means you have, must make ye so,
Low breeding, vulgar birth, and impudence,
These, these, must make ye, what you're meant to be.

S-Seller. I can't imagine that I'm good for much.
Dem. Alas! But why do ye say so? What's the meaning
Of these misgivings? I discern within ye
A promise and an inward consciousness
Of greatness. Tell me truly: are ye allied
To the families of gentry?
S-Seller. Naugh, not I;
I'm come from a common ordinary kindred,
Of the lower order.
Dem. What a happiness!
What a footing will it give ye! What a groundwork
For confidence and favour at your outset!
S-Seller. But bless ye! only consider my education!
I can but barely read . . . in a kind of way.
Dem. That makes against ye! – the only thing against ye –
The being able to read, in any way:
For now no lead nor influence is allowed
To liberal arts or learned education,
But to the brutal, base, and underbred.

The greatest merit of Athenian social and political life is shown in the fact that his play could be produced at a time when Cleon was at the height of his power. It is true that Cleon, with all the resources of influence at his disposal, did his best to deprive Aristophanes of his civic rights and have him exiled, but he was never able to remove his sharp-tongued enemy from the Athenian scene.

Late in 431 B.C., when the tragic Peloponnesian War had already broken out between Athens and Sparta, the noblest panegyric of Athens was proclaimed by her greatest leader. Perhaps the words, like most wartime speeches, are evidence of aspirations rather than of actuality. Yet it is enough that such sentiments could have been expressed. They indicate, if not the true state of Athenian life at that moment, the desired ideal.

At the end of the first year of the war against Sparta, Pericles had been chosen to give the customary funeral oration over those who had died during the campaign. Such orations were traditionally devoted to extolling the bravery and nobility of the fallen and to reminding the other citizens of their obligation to the dead – not to fail them by want of courage in any further campaigns. Pericles, however, chose the occasion to remind the Athenians of the kind of people that they were (or were supposed to be), and of the way of life that they were defending.

Thucydides records the oration:

"Our form of government does not enter into rivalry with the institutions of others. We do not copy our neighbours, but are an example to them. It is true that we are called a democracy, for the administration is in the hands of the many and not of the few. But while the law secures equal justice to all alike in their private disputes, the claim of excellence is also recognised; and when a citizen is in any way distinguished, he is preferred to the public service, not as a matter of privilege, but as the reward of merit. Neither is poverty a bar, but a man may benefit his country whatever be the obscurity of his condition. There is no exclusiveness in our public life, and in our private intercourse we are not suspicious of one another, nor angry with our neighbour if he does what he likes; we do not put on sour looks at him, which, though harmless, are not pleasant. While we are thus unconstrained in our private intercourse, a spirit of reverence pervades our public acts; we are prevented from doing wrong by respect for authority and for the laws, having an especial regard for those which are ordained for the protection of the injured, as well as for those unwritten laws which bring upon the transgressor of them the reprobation of the general sentiment.

"And we have not forgotten to provide for our weary spirits many relaxations from toil; we have regular games and sacrifices throughout the year; at home the style of our life is refined; and the delight which we daily feel in all these things helps to banish melancholy. Because of the greatness of our city the fruits of the whole earth flow in upon us, so that we enjoy the goods of other countries as freely as of our own.

"Then, again, our military training is in many respects superior to that of our adversaries. Our city is thrown open to the world, and we never expel a foreigner or prevent him from seeing or learning anything of which the secret, if revealed, an enemy might profit from. We rely not upon management and trickery, but upon our own hearts and hands. And in the matter of education, whereas they from early youth are always undergoing laborious exercises which are to make them brave, we live at ease, and yet are ready to face the perils which they face.

"If, then, we prefer to meet danger with a light heart but without laborious training, and with a courage which is grained by habit and not enforced by law, are we not greatly the gainers? Since we do not anticipate the pain, although when the hour comes, we can be as brave as those who never allow themselves to rest; and thus too our city is equally admirable in peace and in war. For we are lovers of the beautiful, yet simple in our tastes, and we cultivate the mind without loss of manliness. Wealth we employ, not for talk and ostentation, but when there is a real use for it. To avow poverty with us is no disgrace; the true disgrace is in doing nothing to avoid it. An Athenian citizen does not neglect the state because he takes care of his own household; and even those of us who are engaged in business have a very fair idea of politics. We alone regard a man who takes no interest in public affairs, not as a harmless, but as a useless character; and if few of us are originators, we are all sound judges of a policy. The great impediment to action is, in our opinion, not discussion but the want of that knowledge which is gained by discussion preparatory to action. For we have a peculiar power of thinking before we act, and of acting too, whereas other men are courageous from ignorance but hesitate upon reflection. And they are surely to be esteemed the bravest spirits who have the clearest sense both of the pains and pleasures of life, but do not on that account shrink from danger.

"To sum up, I say that Athens is the school of Hellas, and that the individual Athenian in his own person seems to have the power of adapting himself to the most varied forms of action with the utmost versatility and grace. This is no passing and idle word, but truth and fact; and the assertion is verified by the position to which these qualities have raised the state. For in the hour of trial Athens alone among her contemporaries is superior to the report of her. No enemy who comes against her is indignant at the reverses which he sustains at the hands of such a city; no subject complains that his masters are unworthy of him. And we shall assuredly not be without witnesses; there are mighty monuments of our power which will make us the wonder of this and succeeding ages: we shall not need the praises of Homer or of any other panegyrist, whose poetry may please for the moment, although his representation of the facts will not bear the light of day. For we have compelled every land, every sea, to open a path for our valour, and have everywhere planted eternal memorials of our friendship and of our enmity."

Unfortunately such nobility and such a superb conception of a democracy in action could not be sustained. During the lifetime of Pericles, there is little doubt that he managed by his genius to infuse such a spirit into the whole nation. For, although Athens was a democracy, it was, as Thucydides himself commented, "a government administered by the first man".

When such a man was Pericles, then Athens was supreme in Greece. But others succeeded to the office who were little more than self-seeking demagogues. To quote Thucydides again, "those who came after Pericles, being men scarcely distinguished one from another in ability, were forced to devote not only their speeches, but even the measures they proposed, to the whims of the populace."

Cleon and others like him were in a comparatively short space of time to reduce the great Athenian dream to the paltry level of money-grubbing politics and pandering concessions to the people who elected them. Democracy, at least in its original form, only works when the people elect a man of ability and integrity to be, as it were, their self-imposed "tyrant". Such a system is excellent, so long as there are men of this quality available.

Within a century the democracy which Athens had gloried in during her age of greatness had become corrupted by vote-catching demagogues. That great orator and genuine democrat Demosthenes complains that "the public welfare is bandied away for a moment's popularity. . . . In former days the people had the courage to be soldiers, and so they controlled the statesmen and themselves disposed of all the offices of the state (as they thought best). Any man was happy to receive from the people his share of office, honour, or advantage. But now, on the other hand, it is the politicians who dispose of the offices and emoluments. It is through them that everything is done. Meanwhile you, the people, have become enervated. Stripped of treasure and of allies, you have become underlings and dependents of these men, happy if they condescend to give you tickets for the theatre or paltry presents of food. The saddest thing of all is that you are actually grateful for receiving what is no more than your own. . . ." This enfeebled type of democracy, so common in the Western world in the twentieth century, was ultimately to lay Athens at the feet of the undemocratic but manly Macedonians.

The second city that divided the hegemony of Greece was the unwalled city of Sparta, lying in the secluded valley of the River Eurotas – unwalled because, as her citizens were proud to boast, their swords and their courage were wall enough to keep out any invader. Sparta represents one extreme of political development in Greece, but one which, as G. Lowes Dickinson accurately comments, "approaches nearest, perhaps, to the characteristic Greek type." Democratic Athens was, in fact, unlike most Greek city-states, which, if they were not dominated by a "tyrant", tended to be ruled by a handful of rich citizens: aristocracy or oligarchy, therefore. The Spartan constitution evolved the way it did through necessity: a comparative handful of Spartans kept down a conquered populace.

A. R. Burn, in his *History of Greece*, remarks: "Sparta had not always been 'Spartan' in the sense of being austere and 'fascist'; but she was military from the beginning of her history. Dominating all Laconia, she ruled over many subject villages and townships, in some of which the people kept their personal freedom as *perioikoi* or neighbours, while in others, which had resisted too fiercely, they became serfs, attached to the soil (not slaves, who could be sold), called helots. The name was said to come from Helos, a town on the south coast, which was treated in this way." What had been imposed upon the Spartans by sheer necessity became in due course elaborated into a pattern of living for which their lawgiver Lycurgus was given the credit. The "Spartan Code", however, was an unwritten constitution, and there can be no doubt that it was added to and amended at various times after the eighth century B.C. (when Lycurgus is said to have lived).

Since the Spartans were surrounded by hostile and potentially rebellious subject peoples, they had to be eternally prepared for war. Fitness for warfare was made into the principal Spartan virtue, and everything else was subordinated to this end. Private luxury was forbidden, austerity in everything from food to clothing was enjoined as a virtue, and a form of secret police was used to watch the subject peoples and dominate them by terror – and by the murder of any who seemed to threaten Sparta's hegemony. Having indicated this unattractive aspect of Sparta, it would be unfair to deny that in many respects the Spartan system was the admiration of other Greek states. Many philosophers, Plato among them, could not withhold their respect for a state so well disciplined and well ordered.

G. Lowes Dickinson gives one of the best analyses of the Spartan system: "The production and rearing of children . . . instead of being left to the caprice of individuals, was controlled and regulated by the state. The women, in the first place, were trained by physical exercise for the healthy performance of the duties of motherhood; they were taught to run and wrestle naked, like the youths, to dance and sing in public, and to associate freely with men."

All this was regarded by most other Greeks, particularly the Athenians, as highly immodest, if not immoral. But in fact Sparta was the only state at that time where women can be said to have enjoyed anything approaching an equality with men. "Marriage was permitted only in the prime of life; and a free intercourse, outside its limits, between healthy men and women, was encouraged and approved by public opinion. Men who did not marry were subject to social and civic disabilities. The children, as soon as they were born, were submitted to the inspection of the elders of their tribe; if strong and well-formed, they were reared; if not, they were allowed to die."

By this rigorous system of selective breeding the Spartans deliberately and carefully produced that dream of so many other peoples over the centuries – "a master race". The male children were removed from their parents at the age of seven and were brought up in groups under the direction of older youths, the whole being supervised by a public official, a kind of "headmaster". To quote G. Lowes Dickinson again: "One garment served them for the whole year; they went without shoes, and slept on beds of rushes plucked with their own hands. Their food was simple, and often enough they had to go without it. Every moment of the day they were under inspection and supervision, for it was the privilege and duty of every citizen to admonish and punish not only his own but other people's children. At supper they waited at table on their elders, answered their questions and endured their jests. In the streets they were taught to walk in silence, their hands folded in their cloaks, their eyes cast down, their heads never turning to right or left."

Such discipline did indeed produce the Spartan type; men like those who died at Thermopylae. As Herodotus writes, "Fighting together they are the best soldiers in the world. They are free – yes – but not entirely free; for they have a master, and that master is Law, which they fear much more than your subjects fear you [the King of Persia]. Whatever this master commands, they do; and his command never varies: it is never to retreat in battle, however great the odds, but always to stand firm, and to conquer or die."

The Spartans lived all their lives in a military camp, yet this does not mean that the arts were entirely neglected. Choral songs and dances, poetry, and an appreciation of brief and pithy statements ("laconic"), to some extent made up for the lack of the visual and plastic arts in which the Athenians excelled. Athletics, hunting, and of course military training provided a healthy outdoor life that was further complemented by the necessity of looking after their helot-farmed estates. Except for the eternal emphasis on warlike activities, the life of these Spartan nobles was not so far removed from that of an English country squire in the eighteenth century. The chief difference was that the whole of the Spartan state was erected upon the labour of an oppressed and subject majority.

Unlike the Etruscans, who had originally occupied their section of Italy as foreign invaders and had then managed to secure the co-operation of the indigenous Latin people, the Spartans were forced to hold down their territory by fear and force of arms. Only at a later date in her history did Sparta manage to erect a series of strong alliances throughout the Peloponnese which gave her internal security.

One of the most instructive stories which illustrates the Spartan psychology is given by Plutarch in his life of the Spartan King Agesilaus. Sparta's allies had been complaining that during the war in which they and Sparta were at that time engaged it was they who provided the bulk of the army. Agesilaus, accordingly, called a council meeting at which all the Spartan allies sat down on one side and the Spartans on the other. He then told a herald to proclaim that all the potters among the allies and the Spartans should stand up. After this the herald called on the blacksmiths, the masons, and the carpenters to do likewise; and so he went on through all the crafts and trades. By the end of the recital nearly every man among the allies had risen to his feet. But not a Spartan had moved, for they were forbidden by their laws to indulge in any form of business. King Agesilaus laughed and, turning to the allies, remarked: "You see, my friends, how many more soldiers we send out than you do."

This aristocratic contempt for trades and crafts was the weakness, as well as the strength, of the Spartan system. If it meant that the Spartan was the finest soldier of his period, it also meant that at a later date, when he had acquired overseas power and come into contact with the wealth of the East, his moral fibre was quick to deteriorate. Also, having little or no understanding of finance or economics, in overseas ventures the Spartans were no match for the quick-witted Athenians. The latter were needle-sharp at business, and as devious as they were brilliant.

THREE

The Peloponnesian War

Corcyra was the island destined to be the apple of discord leading to the conflict which devastated Greece. Another island, Sicily, was the scene of disaster that led to the death of the Athenian Empire. But it would be misleading to suggest that Corcyra was in any way the real cause of the great war between Athens and Sparta. Given the different natures of these two great Greek powers, and their conflicting ambition, war between them was inevitable.

Corcyra, some forty miles long and little more than ten miles at its widest point, was green and fertile; a rich island for its size, rustling with olive and vine. The most prosperous of all the Greek islands in the Ionian Sea, it had been famed since Homeric saga as the land of the Phaeacians, those outstanding mariners whose King, Alcinous, welcomed the shipwrecked Odysseus and finally sent him back home to Ithaca in a Phaeacian ship. The sea god Poseidon, the story goes, was so enraged at this assistance given to his enemy that he turned the ship to stone just before it reached safety.

Historically, Corcyra became important soon after its colonization by the Corinthians. With its excellent harbours it was an important stepping-stone on the route to Sicily, and in particular to the Corinthian colony of Syracuse – a passage of only about 250 sea miles. Unlike most colonies, which, though independent, were usually respectful to their mother cities, Corcyra soon showed that it would not only dispense with Corinth, but even pursue policies hostile to the founding city. The result was that war broke out between Corinth and Corcyra, and both parties appealed to Athens to intervene in the dispute.

The Athenians probably had nothing in mind save the thought that, if Corinth was humiliated and her naval power cut down to size, they would be able to secure a far larger part of the important western market for their own trade and commerce. Thucydides also says that the Corcyran navy, second only to that of Athens, must be prevented from falling into hostile hands. They decided, accordingly, to assist the Corcyrans, and a naval action took place in the narrow strait between Corcyra and the Greek mainland, in the course of which the Athenians intervened against a combined force of Corinthian and other allied ships. Unfortunately, both Corinth and her ally Megara were members of the Spartan Confederacy. This engagement, therefore, between Athens and cities which were under Spartan protection inevitably brought the two great powers face to face.

The war that was now to involve the whole of the Greek world for twenty-seven years – broken only by a few brief intervals of peace – was essentially a conflict between Leviathan and Behemoth. Athens with her navies and her marine supremacy was Leviathan, while Sparta with her armies and her military supremacy was the land giant Behemoth. In this respect one can find a parallel between the Peloponnesian War and the Napoleonic Wars. Both wars scarified the Mediterranean world and both saw a predominantly naval power engaged against a predominantly land power.

"This war," as H. D. F. Kitto comments in *The Greeks*, "was the turning-point in the history of the Greek *polis*. . . . Fighting went on in almost every part of the Greek world – all over the Aegean, in and about Chalcidice, in Boeotia, around the coasts of the Peloponnese, in north-west Greece, in Sicily, where two powerful expeditionary forces of the Athenians were destroyed with scarcely a survivor: and Attica, all but the city and the Piraeus, which were enclosed by a single line of fortifications, was left open to the Spartan armies and systematically devastated."

Pericles withdrew all the population within the walls of Athens and refused to give battle to the Spartan armies. His policy was a wise one. He knew that Athens could not starve, for her fleet commanded the sea, and the grain supply from the Euxine was, therefore, secure. At the same time he used his naval power to harass the Spartans: he ordered attacks on undefended coastlines and raids on isolated fortresses and towns. The Spartans contented themselves, at least in the early stages, with little more than an annual expedition into Attica, in the course of which they carried off the harvest and laid waste the countryside. It was the fact that these two powers, warily circling round one another, were so dissimilar that ensured the continuance of this tragic war for so long a time.

From Thucydides' account it seems that Pericles himself considered that war between Athens and Sparta was inevitable. Consequently, he deliberately embarked upon a course of action that led the two states into conflict. Although the slanders of his opponents can be disclaimed – that he led Athens into war to safeguard his own political position – Pericles certainly bears a grave responsibility for the war. It seemed clear to him that if his policy was followed Athens would certainly emerge the victor, and this would lead to the union of all Greece, with Athens as its leader. Rare in any age, he was a great enough statesman to have had a vision of a united Greece. This was totally beyond the comprehension of most of his fellow Athenians, let alone of the Spartans, who had no clear war aim beyond the simple defeat of their enemy. Unfortunately for Pericles there were one or two factors that nobody could have foreseen.

In 430 B.C., when the Athenians were crowded within their long walls during the annual Peloponnesian invasion, a plague broke out in the city. This seems to have been brought from Egypt or Phoenicia by visiting merchant ships – certainly, it hardly affected the Peloponnese at all, for the Athenian blockade had isolated the Spartans and their allies from trade with the East. The plague was by far the greatest disaster to befall the Athenians during the first ten years of the war. It carried off innumerable citizens, particularly among the poor, decimating also the ranks of the rich and the prosperous. It has been calculated by various authorities that somewhere between a quarter and a third of the population was lost. Thucydides himself was a victim, but recovered and, thus immunized (as he remarks, "no man ever caught it twice"), assisted in nursing the sick. His description of the plague has provoked many arguments among the medical profession, but the general consensus seems to be that it was probably similar to the bubonic plague which ravaged Europe on several occasions in the centuries to come.

Thucydides concludes a detailed description of the disease: "Originally seated in the head, beginning from above, [it] passed throughout the whole body; and if any one survived its most fatal consequences, yet it marked him by laying hold of his extremities, for it settled on the pudenda, and fingers, and toes, and many escaped with the loss of these, while some also lost their eyes. Others, again, were seized on their first recovery with forgetfulness of every thing alike and did not know either themselves or their friends."

He ends with an analysis of the moral effect the plague had upon the citizens of Athens. "The plague was the origin of lawless conduct in the city.... For deeds which formerly men hid from view, so as not to do them just as they pleased, they now more readily ventured on; since they saw the change so sudden in the case of those who were prosperous and quickly perished, and of those who before had had nothing, and at once came into possession of the property of the dead. So they resolved to take their enjoyment quickly, and with a sole view to gratification; regarding their lives and their riches alike as things of a day."

The plague, Pericles himself sadly commented, "was the one thing I did not foresee." Neither could he have foreseen that he himself would catch it. Accused by his fellow citizens of having initiated the policy of concentrating all the people within the long walls (which gave the plague free rein among the thousands of people herded within a small space), he was suspended from office. He died from a constitution weakened by the disease, and saddened by the knowledge that his beloved Athens had suffered so terribly through an accident of fate.

Yet, despite this disaster, and despite having suffered a severe military defeat in 424 B.C., Athens recovered. Her fleet was never more powerful; her arts and sciences were in the full bloom of high summer, and life in the city showed a vigour and clarity that was unmatched in the Greek world. Throughout all the trials and vicissitudes of the war it is remarkable how few of Athens' allies defected. It was certainly not eagerness on their part to be free of the imperial bond that led to the city's defeat.

One famous occasion, when the island of Lesbos and its principal city, Mitylene, did indeed revolt, must be mentioned, since it produced a magnificent debate in the Assembly. The superiority of the Athenian system to the Spartan can be judged from the fact that, even in the middle of a life-and-death struggle, great issues could be intelligently discussed and both sides of an argument rationally presented. Some of the Assembly were in favour of punishing the people of Mitylene by wholesale slaughter, while others were for moderation and reason. Cleon, in the conclusion to his speech, put the first case in a nutshell: "Punish these men, I say, as they deserve; and give a striking example to the rest of your allies, that whoever revolts will pay the penalty for it with his life. For if they know this, you will less frequently have to neglect your enemies, while you are fighting with your own confederates." His attitude was harsh, but logical. The opposition case was put by a man called Diodotus, whose sole claim to fame is to have spoken one of the truly noble speeches of antiquity.

"I am not here," he said, "to defend the Mityleneans, nor indeed to accuse anyone else. It is not a question of their guilt, but of our interest. . . . The death penalty has been enacted in many cities and for various offences, yet men still commit them, driven to do so by the hope of success. No city has ever rebelled except that it believed there was a fair chance of success. Men by their nature are disposed to act wrongly, both in their public and private affairs, yet penalties however severe have never checked them. . . . I do not, any more than Cleon, wish you to be guided only by pity and moderation, but I do ask you to give a fair trial to the ringleaders and let the others go unpunished. This policy is not only advantageous, but it is also a strong one. For the party which deliberates wisely and carefully against its enemy is always more formidable than the one which acts with a reckless violence."

The voting was close, but Diodotus' arguments prevailed. The Athenians had already sent a trireme to Lesbos with orders to their occupation forces to kill the entire male population and enslave the women and children. After this debate, however, they dispatched another trireme to rescind the decree. So anxious were they to prevent the massacre that, as Thucydides records, the crew of the second vessel "ate and drank as they rowed, and slept in turns" so as to make sure of overtaking the other. The latter, for her part, "did not sail in any haste, being engaged on so distasteful a business." The result was that the second trireme arrived in the nick of time and prevented the massacre.

Unfortunately, as the war progressed, such reasoned argument became rarer and a calculated savagery began to prevail. One of the main points made by Thucydides is that, in the early stage of a war, men may still respect and even deal courteously with their opponents. But the longer war continues, the more hatred grows on either side, until in the end no quarter is given and brutish violence becomes an accepted fact. Again and again, in the long history of this sea, this tragic pattern has repeated itself.

In 421 B.C., a peace was concluded between Athens and Sparta which was substantially to the benefit of Athens. For a moment it looked as if that dream of Pericles, the Athenian Empire, was so securely founded that it would ultimately unite the whole of the Greek-speaking world. It was not to be. As H. A. L. Fisher remarks: "Had the peace mind really prevailed in Athens, it would have been an easy task to avoid giving fresh provocation to the principal enemy. But a new and dazzling star had risen above the political horizon in Athens. . . ."

This star was Alcibiades, beautiful, young, gifted, and dangerously ambitious. The protégé of Socrates (who had vainly tried to moderate his vanity and his insolent misuse of his gifts), Alcibiades was one of the principal engineers of the Sicilian expedition – that foreign adventure which led Athens to ruin.

The Sicilian expedition can only be understood in terms of the rivalry that existed between the various colonies of that unhappy island. Some of these had been planted by Dorian Greeks and others by Ionian Greeks, but the fact that their founders and their inhabitants were all Greeks had little bearing upon the matter. The same rivalry and dislike that was felt between Ionian Athens and Dorian Sparta had merely been transplanted to the soil of Sicily – a soil that has ever been productive of envy and hatred.

In 416 B.C., ambassadors arrived in Athens from the city of Segesta in Sicily with a request for assistance. Curiously enough, the city was a native, and not a Greek foundation. Over the years, however, it had become almost totally Hellenized. The citizens of Segesta had a number of disagreements with neighbouring Selinus – a Dorian founda-tion – and they implored mighty Athens to come with her fleet and settle matters in their favour. The arrival of these Segestan ambassadors in Athens – an event, on the surface, even less remarkable than the murder of the Austrian Archduke Francis Ferdinand in 1914 – was to set in train a series of events every whit as disastrous in Mediterranean and, indeed, world history as the First World War. The Athenians decided to embrace the cause of this Sicilian city and to dispatch an army and a navy for the purpose.

Their reason for so doing was not only that the humiliation of a Dorian colony would be helpful to the cause of Athens; they had other and more far-reaching designs. The real target was Syracuse. This city, founded by Corinth (and, after all, it was because of Corinth that Athens had engaged upon this long war), was now predominant in all the Greek-speaking world of the West. Syracuse was to the cities of Greece rather what New York was to become centuries later to the cities of Europe. Her wealth and her magnificence, combined with a certain harshness and violence that blows in the Sicilian air just as much as in that of America, exerted a profound attraction–repulsion upon the native Greeks. But Syracuse was not only rich, it was also a great cultural centre. In the fifth century B.C., the greatest of all Greek tragedians, Aeschylus, had stayed at the court of Hieron, ruler of Syracuse, as had the poet Simonides; while the lyric poetess Sappho was also reputed to have lived for a time in the city of the fountain nymph Arethusa.

Syracuse, as the head of all the Dorian forces and colonies in Sicily, was clearly the place to be attacked. Athenian policy had quickly become more grandiose, and the Athenians already envisaged themselves as becoming masters of the whole island. (The importance of Sicily's grain and wood to the Greek economy must not be forgotten, for wars and military expeditions were never undertaken for purely altruistic motives.) If "brave little Segesta" needed to be defended against overbearing Selinus, the Athenians could not help noticing that the island in which these city-states existed was a particularly rich one. They dreamed, perhaps, that the city of Syracuse might well become an "Athens of the West".

In the spring of 415 B.C., a large fleet of 100 ships, with over 5000 Athenian armoured troops aboard, together with many other allies and nearly 1500 archers and slingers, left Athens and headed across the Ionian for Sicily. In command of the whole expedition was Nicias, a brave but conservative upper-class Athenian. Nicias had all along tried to dissuade the people from the expedition, for he sensibly felt that the continuance of the war was a folly that would not benefit Athens. Since these were his known views, it might seem surprising that he was chosen to command the expedition. The fact was that his proven qualities of leadership, courage, and ability made him the best choice. With him as fellow generals – but under his command – went Alcibiades and another well-known soldier, Lamachus.

On the eve of the expedition an event took place in Athens which remains one of the great unsolved puzzles of history. There were throughout the city certain ancient statues known as Hermae. These were square pillars which bore at their top the head of Hermes, Messenger of the Gods, and the protector of traders and merchants. During the course of one night nearly all of these Hermae were broken or defaced by a person or persons unknown. Such an act of impiety to these ancient guardians of the city not unnaturally provoked anger, consternation, and even panic. Whether the crime was committed by someone intent on demoralizing the expedition before it started (not necessarily a Spartan sympathizer, but someone who disapproved of the whole idea of the expedition), or whether it was no more than a drunken prank, is immaterial. Suspicion immediately focused upon Alcibiades. He was known to be irreligious – he was said to have parodied the sacred Eleusinian Mysteries at a drinking party – and he was notorious as a loose-living freethinker.

Alcibiades at once denied the charge: and it seems unlikely that he would have so bedevilled his chances on the eve of the great expedition towards which his whole ambition prompted him. (In fact, the Hermae were so numerous and so widely scattered throughout the city that it would have been beyond the ability of any one man, even if sober, to have damaged them all in a night.) His detractors, however, refused him an immediate trial – probably because they wanted to conduct their investigation in the absence both of the accused and of his numerous friends in the army. The expedition, accordingly, sailed on time – with a serious charge hanging over the head of one of its generals. It was not a happy omen for the future.

Once arrived in Sicily, irresolution seized the leaders, who were divided in their aims and intentions. Alcibiades maintained that they should first of all see what allies they could find among the Greek Sicilian city-states; while Nicias said that they had come to deal only with Selinus. Lamachus, on the other hand, was in favour of striking immediately at Syracuse; a plan that, given the size of the Athenian forces and the unpreparedness of the Syracusans, would very likely have been successful. With the generals thus divided in their aims, they argued until Lamachus was finally induced by Alcibiades to side with him and outvote Nicias on the matter of policy. They then wasted time trying to win local allies.

Shortly afterwards, a vessel reached Sicily with orders from Athens for Alcibiades to return and face the charge of mutilating the Hermae and profaning the Mysteries. But he was not the kind of man to submit to being led like a lamb to the slaughter, for he knew how dangerously powerful were his enemies at home. He escaped and made his way to Sparta, where he spent the next three years devoting his abilities to encompassing his city's ruin. Found guilty in his absence, he was condemned to death. One thing is certain: whoever defaced the Hermae was – unwittingly perhaps – largely responsible for the downfall of Athens.

The absence of Alcibiades not only deprived the Athenians of his forceful abilities, it also left in charge of the fleet and expeditionary force a man who, whatever his courage, was opposed to the principle of being in Sicily at all. In the spring of the following year, unable to find any further excuse for delay, Nicias was forced to move against Syracuse. But the Syracusans had now had time to prepare their defences, and time also to steel their spirits for a siege.

While the Athenians were busy securing Epipolae, the high ground north of the city, Alcibiades back in Sparta was giving the Spartan high command the advice that was to ensure their success. First of all, they must send out a Spartan general to take charge of the Syracusan defence. Secondly, they must renew the war in Attica; he suggested that the best way of doing this would be to seize Decelea. This was a strongpoint in Attica itself, from which the Spartans would be able to cut off Athens from most of her native food supplies, as well as from her silver mines. The Spartans agreed to both of these suggestions and acted upon them.

Nicias, meanwhile, had driven the Syracusans back within their city and had set his troops to building an encircling wall designed to cut off Syracuse from the surrounding countryside. He might have done better to open an immediate attack upon the city, but this was not in his nature. His fellow general, Lamachus, who from the beginning had urged a swift assault on Syracuse, had been killed in action, so there was no one left to put any real fire into the conduct of the campaign. Meanwhile, a Spartan general, Gylippus, landed in western Sicily with a small company of men. He ignored rumours that Syracuse was completely encircled and marched east, gathering additional local forces en route. Nicias failed to prevent him from forcing an entrance into Syracuse – and from that moment on the fate of the expeditionary force was sealed. The Athenians lost their command of the heights of Epipolae. They now found to their consternation that it was they, in their base camp south of the great harbour, who were in danger of being cut off and besieged.

Nicias sent an urgent dispatch to Athens saying that there were only two courses of conduct. The Athenians must either recall the expedition (which he would all along have preferred) or reinforce it with as many men again. Athens responded like a committed gambler by a further throw upon the board. Seventy-three triremes and 5000 armoured men were sent to reinforce Nicias, and another general, Demosthenes, to replace the fallen Lamachus.

At first it seemed as if the Athenians must certainly succeed. Then one misfortune after another struck them. They were repulsed in an attempt to regain the heights of Epipolae (the possession of which was essential if they were to besiege the town), and sickness among the troops and the crews of their ships was weakening and demoralizing their whole force. Further reinforcements reached the besieged Syracusans, and, as is always the case on such occasions, there was an accession of morale far greater than the actual number of fresh troops justified.

The Athenians now decided that their only course was to withdraw. But Nicias was dilatory even in this, justifying the delay on account of an eclipse of the moon – always considered in those days an unpropitious time in which to engage upon any major action. An irreligious (or less superstitious) man like Alcibiades would not have hesitated to act, whatever the theoretical "will of the gods". This delay proved fatal, for by the time the Athenians began to move the Syracusans had got wind of their intentions. A classic sea battle took place in the harbour itself and the result was a severe Athenian defeat: a demoralizing blow to men who believed themselves invincible at sea.

Thucydides, in one of his grandest passages, describes the conflicting hopes and fears of the Athenians and Syracusans as they watched the dramatic battle: "The troops on shore, on both sides, when the sea-fight was equally balanced, suffered a great agony and conflict of feelings: those of the country being ambitious now of still greater honour, while their invaders were afraid of faring even worse than at present. For, since the Athenians' all was staked on their fleet, their fear for the future was like none that they had ever felt before; and from the unequal nature of the engagement they were also compelled to have an unequal view of it from the beach. For as the spectacle was near at hand, and as they did not all look at the same part at once, if any saw their own men victorious in any quarter, they would be encouraged and turn to calling on the gods not to deprive them of safety; while those who looked on the part that was being beaten, uttered lamentations at the same time as cries, and from the sight they had of what was going on, expressed their feelings more than those engaged in the action. Others again, looking on a doubtful point of the engagement, in consequence of the indecisive continuance of the conflict, in their excessive fear made gestures with their very bodies, corresponding with their thoughts. . . . And thus amongst the troops of the Athenians, as long as they were fighting at sea on equal terms, every sound might be heard at once, wailing, shouting, 'they conquer', 'they are conquered', and all the other various exclamations which a great armament in great peril would be constrained to utter – very much in the same way as their men on board their ships were affected – until at length, after the battle had continued for a long time, the Syracusans and their allies routed the Athenians, and pressing on them in a decisive manner, with much shouting and cheering on of each other, pursued them to the shore."

This disaster, on that very element where the Athenians felt themselves to be the appointed rulers, finally broke their spirit. Although they still had as many triremes left as the Syracusans, the Athenian sailors refused to embark in a last attempt to break through the barricade of ships which the Syracusans had lashed together across the narrow entrance to the harbour. There was nothing for it but to try to retreat into the interior of Sicily. Naturally enough, the Syracusans were not prepared to let their enemies escape so easily – possibly to regroup and come back to the assault at a later date. The Athenians now found that the passes leading out of the fertile plain around Syracuse were all held against them. They were even further demoralized by the onset of the rainy season, which was accompanied by the violent thunderstorms so typical of Sicily in the early autumn. They took these as a sign that even the gods were against them.

Harassed by the Syracusan cavalry, short of food and water, the Athenians were at last cut to pieces on the coast road south of Syracuse, while trying to ford a small river swollen by the recent rains. Nicias and Demosthenes surrendered. Despite the fact that Gylippus would have preferred to spare their lives and take them back in triumph to Sparta, they were both executed by the Syracusans. What was left of the great Athenian army and fleet – only about 7000 men – was now confined in the stone quarries, the Latomiae, which lie just to the north of the city. The Athenians had lost about 40,000 men and 175 triremes in their expedition to Sicily. It was a fatal wound; one from which the city (and the dream) of Pericles never recovered.

The fate of the few survivors is movingly told by Thucydides: "As for those in the quarries, the Syracusans treated them with cruelty during the first period of their captivity. For as they were in a hollow place, and many in a small compass, the sun, as well as the suffocating closeness, distressed them at first, in consequence of their not being under cover, and then, on the contrary, the nights coming on autumnal and cold, soon worked in them an alteration from health to disease, by means of the change. . . ."

What happened was that, after the sharp initial change of weather (often the case in this part of the Mediterranean), October and November were comparatively hot and still – an agony for men confined in the depths of the rock quarries. Then the advent of winter, when snow lies deep on all the inland mountains, brought a bone-chilling rigour to the half-starved, half-naked captives. "Since, too, in consequence of their want of room, they did everything in the same place; and the dead, moreover, were piled up one on another – such as died from their wounds, and from the change they had experienced, and such like – there were, besides, intolerable stenches: while at the same time they were tormented with hunger and thirst; for during eight months they gave each of them daily only a *cotyle* [a little over an English half pint] of water, and two of corn."

Such was the end of the flower of the Athenian army and fleet – cut to pieces ashore, drowned in the harbour of Syracuse, or dead from hunger and disease in the rock quarries of the city that they had set out to capture. Some of those who survived were sold as slaves, and a few were spared – not from any sentiment of mercy, but because they were educated men and capable of reciting poetry. The sophisticated Syracusans enjoyed hearing them recite long passages from Euripides, a dramatist for whom they had an inordinate passion.

Plutarch tells us that "the Greeks of Sicily were more fond of his poetry than any other Greeks who lived outside the homeland of Hellas. Even minute fragments of his verse were learned from strangers who set foot in the island and the Sicilian Greeks took great pleasure in passing on quotations from this poet between one another. It is said that a number of the Athenian soldiers who finally managed to reach their homeland made a point of visiting Euripides to thank him for the deliverance which they owed to their knowledge of his poetry."

Even after so great a disaster, the spirit and the resources of Athens were sufficient to keep her in the fight against Sparta and her allies for over eight years (412–404 B.C.). Despite the establishment of the Spartan fortress at Decelea, which deprived the city of much of her silver and agricultural produce, Athens struggled on. At times it even looked as if she was about to reverse the balance that had tilted against her so disastrously after the Sicilian expedition.

Alcibiades, by one of those mercurial changes of heart and of policy that are so innately Greek (it was probably one of the reasons his fellow citizens continued to love him), returned to Athens and was welcomed home in 408 B.C.

"They long for him, they hate him, yet they cannot do without him," as Aristophanes puts it, but he warns:

"It is preferable not to rear a lion within your city –
But if you do, then you must humour all his moods."

For a time it seemed as if the touch of the "Golden Boy" would change the whole balance of the war. A large Peloponnesian and Syracusan fleet which was trying to cut Athens' life-line to the corn belt and the Black Sea was decisively beaten. The rich island of Thasos and the important city of Byzantium – both of which had revolted – were successfully brought back into the fold. But all the time the running sore of Decelea (for which Alcibiades, above all, had been responsible) kept draining the city's strength. Then, in one of those fits of irrationality to which the Athenians became more and more prone as the war dragged on, Alcibiades was once again accused, this time of incompetence. He left the city never to return, and was murdered in Phrygia some years later.

The life of this gifted but unprincipled man reflects in some measure the history of the city which he both adorned and disgraced. It is certainly true that, if the first expulsion of Alcibiades was largely responsible for Athens' discomfiture in Sicily and at home, the second expulsion was fatal. There was no one to replace him, and the Spartans had by now found a tough and able war leader in Lysander.

An opportunity in 406 B.C. to make a peace that would have left the city with some dignity – if little of her empire – was turned down, and the miserable tragedy dragged on for a further year. Then, at the Battle of Aegospotami in the Hellespont, the Athenian fleet – the last of all those great fleets which she had poured out upon the seas for twenty-seven years – was totally destroyed by Lysander. Even at this late hour, Alcibiades had ridden down to warn his fellow countrymen of their perilous position at Aegospotami, but his only reward was to be met with insults. In the following year, 404 B.C., the city of Pericles tasted the bitterness of unconditional surrender. Her navy was gone, her empire was lost, and now her walls were razed. The victors imposed upon the Athenians an oligarchic government of their own persuasion, and "to the sound of the music of flute-girls the allies garlanded their ships with flowers."

"Men hailed that day," Plutarch writes, "as the beginning of freedom for Greece." Such optimism after the conclusion of a war was to be repeated throughout the centuries, usually with as little justification.

In the long and melancholy tale of man's folly, which only too often constitutes what is termed "history", it is easy to overlook those things which represent man at his best. Thus, in outlining the course of the Peloponnesian War, with its horrors, bloodshed, and tragic outcome, no mention has been made of the positive achievements of those years. While the long struggle with Sparta was continuing, Socrates was insisting on definition and precision in man's thinking and was laying the basis not only of moral but of metaphysical science. "Virtue is knowledge" was his belief. If there is one flaw in the thinking of Socrates (as we know it from his disciple Plato) it is that, as A. R. Burn points out in his *History of Greece*, "A man of iron self-control himself, he was unfamiliar with the Pauline predicament, 'The evil that I would not, that I do.' "

While Socrates and his followers were encouraging men to use their minds efficiently, one of the greatest poets of history, the rationalist Euripides, was describing man's predicament on earth in words that still sing off the page; in the second year of the war Herodotus completed his great history; and in the year that marked Athens' downfall, Euripides' masterpiece, the *Bacchae*, was being performed. Throughout these years, too, Athenians were recognizing and laughing at many of their own follies in the incisive and bawdy comedies of Aristophanes, and at the same time the other arts flourished. Outstanding pieces of sculpture, metal-work, jewellery, and ceramics were produced at this time.

The Spartans have left nothing of value behind them to record either their struggle or their ultimate victory – unless the story recorded by Plutarch is true. This at least goes to show that, even if they were not creators, the Spartans were still sensitive to the Greek genius. Shortly after the fall of Athens, it was proposed by some of the Peloponnesian allies that they should raze the whole city and sell all the Athenians into slavery. At that moment, someone in the company sang the opening chorus from Euripides' *Electra*. "Hearing this, all of those present were so moved that they felt it would be a horrendous crime to destroy so wonderful a city – and one which had produced such men of genius."

FOUR

Greece and the East

The Athenian orator Isocrates remarked that the curse of Hellenic politics during this period was the desire for empire, and there can be no doubt that he was right. One after another, Athens, Sparta, and Thebes attempted to dominate Greece; and one after another they failed. As soon as one power seemed to have established an ascendancy, its rivals were always prepared to forget their differences and form an alliance strong enough to check the more powerful state. This pattern was to be repeated throughout European history, up to and including the twentieth century. The machinations, rivalries, and wars of the small Greek city-states foreshadowed in microcosm the alliances and the giant wars that blazed across the Mediterranean basin for centuries.

But the unification of Greece was temporarily achieved in the mid-fourth century B.C. – though not by Athens or Sparta. The consolidated energy of the Greek people was then to be turned eastwards in one of the most dramatic episodes in history. "The solution of the Greek question," writes H. A. L. Fisher, "came from an unsuspected quarter. To the north of Thessaly, in the coastlands round the Thermaic Gulf, there was established a Greek people, rougher and less civilized than the inhabitants of Athens or Corinth, and regarded by the southern Greeks much as a Parisian views a provincial from Brittany or Langue-doc. These were the Macedonians, deep drinkers, lusty fighters, passionate in pursuit of the bear and the wolf through the forests and glens of their mountain home, and still living in the Homeric stage of civilization. . . ."

These rough highlanders, imbued with all the hardihood of the north, were welded into the most powerful state in Greece by a most remarkable and far-sighted King, Philip of Macedon (359–336 B.C.). Philip was a great deal more than a fine soldier; he was also an able statesman who laid the foundations of that immense empire which his son, Alexander the Great, was to carve out of the East. In order to achieve a unity in Greece that would leave his armies free for colonial expansion in Asia Minor and the Near East, Philip had first of all to silence all opposition within the Greek mainland. This he finally achieved in 338 B.C. on the battlefield of Chaeronea, where the combined forces of Athens and Thebes were defeated.

By a magnanimity towards the conquered rare in Greek history, and by a series of sagacious political manoeuvres, Philip managed to unite the touchy and divided Greek states in a union, or league, in which free and equal membership for all was to be the criterion. Even so, he might have failed in his aims if he had not been able to point overseas to Persia. "There," he said, "lies the eternal enemy of all Greeks; remember the atrocities of Xerxes; bear in mind that we Greeks will never be safe so long as Persia threatens us not only here at home, but also in the Ionian cities of Asia Minor."

He might also have added that there, across the island-studded Aegean, lay rich earth and fine potential farms, business for merchants, and innumerable administrative posts in the empire he meant to create. For the first time in their history the Greeks were able to envisage themselves not as a series of eternally divided city-states, but as a nation united by language, religion, and common customs. They realized that if they could only forget their mutually destructive rivalry, they would be able to conquer and administer all the riches of the East.

The dream was Philip's, but the execution of it was left to his son Alexander. In 336 B.C., on the eve of his departure for Asia Minor at the head of an allied Greek army, Philip of Macedon was murdered.

Alexander's immediate reaction was to remind all Greeks that "Nothing has changed – except the name of the King!" It was a proud boast, but in fact the early part of his reign was to be occupied in reasserting over Greece that supremacy which his father had achieved. The Greeks, as always, separated the moment they felt self-assertion might gain them or their cities the smallest advantage.

Having re-established a unified Greece behind him – a Greece, it might be added, that had accepted its unification only out of fear of the formidable arms and genius of Alexander – the young conqueror prepared to set out for the East. Shortly before this major event in world history took place, a small incident occurred in Corinth that deserves to be remembered. It reveals so clearly those two sides of the Greek nature – self-confident assertion and philosophic abnegation – which have become part of the whole Mediterranean heritage.

When he arrived in Corinth, the young general secured from the league of Greek states the acceptance of his position as supreme commander in the war against Persia and her empire. Alexander at this time was no more than twenty years old, "a young Apollo, golden-haired", on the eve of his most amazing adventure. Dignitaries from the states who recognized his supremacy, as well as many of the most famous men in other walks of life, were present in Corinth. They were there to confer upon him their acceptance of his leadership against the once-dreaded Persians. However, one of Corinth's most distinguished citizens, the famous "cynic" philosopher Diogenes, was conspicuous in failing to pay his respects to this young master of Greece.

Diogenes is described in the eleventh edition of the *Encyclopaedia Britannica*: "He inured himself to the vicissitudes of weather by living in a tub [probably one of the large pottery storage jars of the time, tipped up on its side] belonging to the temple of Cybele. The single wooden bowl he possessed he destroyed on seeing a peasant boy drink from the hollow of his hands. On a voyage to Aegina he was captured by pirates and sold as a slave in Crete to a Corinthian named Xeniades. Being asked his trade, he replied that he knew no trade but that of governing men, and that he wished to be sold to a man who needed a master. As tutor to the two sons of Xeniades, he lived in Corinth for the rest of his life, which he devoted entirely to preaching the doctrines of virtuous self-control. . . . Virtue, for him, consisted in the avoidance of all physical pleasure; [for him] pain and hunger were positively helpful in the pursuit of goodness; [and] . . . moralization implies a return to nature and simplicity."

Diogenes' teacher, Antisthenes, himself a pupil of Socrates, had held that virtue, not pleasure, was the whole aim of existence. As a corollary of this it was accepted by Diogenes and other philosophers that wealth, ambition, power, and popularity tended to corrupt and pervert the soul from its true pursuit of reason. Little wonder, then, that the old master in his tub was unwilling to bestir himself and pay court to

Alexander. But Alexander was sufficiently intrigued by this famous man – one who could not be bothered to join the crowd of his adulators and well-wishers – that he could not resist paying a call upon the aged (and possibly somewhat odoriferous) philosopher.

The conversation between them was short and to the point. Conquerors usually have little time for verbosity, and neither do philosophers of the cynic persuasion.

"I am Alexander the Great," said the youthful general, on being led in front of Diogenes' makeshift home.

"And I am Diogenes the philosopher," replied the other, not a whit deterred by the armour, the gold, and the scarlet of his visitor.

"Is there anything I can do for you?" the future conqueror of the East demanded – perhaps not without a shade of condescension.

"Yes, Alexander," replied Diogenes. "Would you and your friends kindly mind standing out of my sunlight?"

It says much for a proud, ambitious, and young man, that Alexander took no exception to this riposte. He accepted, perhaps, that the force which drove him to make his mark upon the exterior, physical world also impelled this lean ascetic who had renounced that world in order to pursue an interior quest.

"Were I not Alexander," he is said to have remarked later, "then I would be Diogenes." Both men died in the same year, 323 B.C.: Alexander at Babylon, master of nearly all the known world at the age of thirty-one; and Diogenes at Corinth, aged ninety. According to one tradition, the conqueror and the philosopher died on the same day as one another. Both were human beings of the rarest quality, and both were among the outstanding examples of the Greek genius.

As is not uncommon in Mediterranean history, the conqueror is better known to the world than the philosopher. Alexander's career influenced many men, including Hannibal, the Carthaginian; Julius Caesar, the Roman; Napoleon, the Corsican; and – ultimate degradation – Adolf Hitler, the Austrian. Alexander's dream of world conquest has not always had the most fortunate results. Yet it must be seen in the context of its time, for this was a period in human history when one man could indeed change the world. But it must always be remembered that Alexander's influence upon the East would have been less important if he had not brought with him the arts and the architecture, the culture and the philosophy, of men who were not warriors and conquerors; of men, in fact, like Diogenes and his masters.

The Mediterranean itself fades from view as Alexander pursues his dreams into the East. Having liberated Ionia, he swept into Syria, routed the Persian monarch Darius at the Battle of the Issus Valley, and swept on to invade Phoenicia. Since the Phoenicians were the backbone of the Persian fleet, it was essential for Alexander to eliminate this threat to his sea life-line before he invaded Persia itself.

Most of the year 332 B.C. was occupied with the siege of Tyre, which held out obstinately and courageously against him for seven months, but was finally taken by assault from the sea. The city became a Macedonian fortress, and Tyrian fleets were never again to challenge Greek supremacy on the sea. The capture of Tyre was possibly Alexander's greatest feat of arms. But great feats of arms often have an unpleasant aftermath. In the ancient world, where it was the legal right of the victor to sell the defeated into slavery, the sack and capture of a city resulted in thousands of men, women, and children being sent to the slave markets. The obverse of the medal Glory may show the youthful, golden head of the conqueror, but the reverse is a pyramid of skulls and slaves.

Arrian, in his *Life of Alexander the Great*, describes Alexander's next move. He subdued the ancient city of Gaza, and then "made for Egypt, which was the original object of his southerly march, and a week after leaving Gaza arrived at Pelusium [on the eastern mouth of the Nile], where the fleet which had accompanied him, sailing coastwise from Phoenicia, was already at anchor." Mazaces, the Persian governor of Egypt under Darius, had no native troops under his command, and this, added to the report of the battle of Issus and of Darius' ig-nominious scramble for safety, and the fact that Phoenicia, Syria, and most of Arabia were already in Macedonian hands, induced him to receive Alexander with a show of friendship and to offer no obstacle to his free entry into Egypt and its cities.

Having been formally accepted as Pharaoh of Egypt, Alexander's next move was to find a suitable site for a major port on the Egyptian coastline. Since Egypt was to become part of the Greek world, she must now look outwards – towards the Mediterranean – and not inwards as had been her habit for thousands of years. Near the western mouth of the Nile, between Lake Mareotis and the sea, he found the perfect site, at a point where a narrow rocky island and an outcrop of rock on the shore afforded an excellent basis for a sheltered deep-water harbour.

"Here was the very place," writes E. M. Forster, in *Alexandria*, "– a splendid harbour, a perfect climate, fresh water, limestone quarries, and easy access to the Nile. Here he would perpetuate all that was best in Hellenism, and would create a metropolis for that greater Greece that should consist not of city-states but of kingdoms, and should include the whole inhabited world.

"Alexandria was founded.

"Having given his orders, the young man hurried on. He never saw a single building rise. His next care was a visit to the temple of Ammon in the Siwan Oasis, where the priest saluted him as a god, and henceforward his Greek sympathies declined. He became an Oriental, a cosmopolitan almost, and though he fought Persia again, it was in a new spirit. He wanted to harmonise the world now, not to Hellenise it, and must have looked back on Alexandria as a creation of his immaturity. But he was after all to return to her. Eight years later, having conquered Persia, he died, and his body, after some vicissitudes, was brought to Memphis for burial. The High Priest refused to receive it there. 'Do not settle him here,' he cried, 'but at the city he has built at Rhakotis, for wherever this body must lie the city will be uneasy, disturbed with wars and battles.' So he descended the Nile again, wrapped in gold and enclosed in a coffin of glass, and he was buried at the centre of Alexandria, by her great cross roads, to be her civic hero and tutelary god."

Alexandria's subsequent history was certainly to justify the Egyptian priest's forebodings, for, both physically and intellectually, the city was a storm centre of the Mediterranean for centuries. Only during the long period of its Arabic occupation, from the seventh to the sixteenth centuries A.D., did it decline into a comparatively unimportant seaport – to decline even further under two centuries of Turkish rule, and to emerge again as a centre of strife in the twentieth century. The bones of the great conqueror have long since been lost. Only his uneasy spirit still haunts this meeting place of West and East, where the

Mosque of the Prophet Daniel now rises above what was the tomb of Alexander.

Whether it is true or not that Alexander "wanted to harmonise the world now, not to Hellenise it", the fact remains that the ultimate effect of his stormy and vivid life was to impose upon the Near East an image and a vision of the Greek genius. More intelligent even than the tutor of his youth, the sage Aristotle, he did not make the mistake of regarding the Orientals as an inferior race. Unlike the Athenians of an earlier time, he did not see the Persians as less civilized; he accepted that in many ways they were in advance of the Greeks. He was also helped towards an understanding of Easterners by the fact that, being a Macedonian warrior-king, he had an aristocratic conception of life rather than a democratic one. Emulators of Alexander in later centuries have sometimes been compelled to pretend that they listen to the "voice of the people"; that they are, in fact, no more than an embodiment of that voice. Such reasoning is usually specious: the great conqueror is never a democrat.

Persia conquered, India invaded, the coasts of Arabia explored, Alexander's spear-thrust into the East had made a great change in the Mediterranean world. Whereas before it had been the East which had invaded the West, it was now the arts and technological skills of the northern Greeks which were disseminated throughout the Aryan Persians and the Semitic peoples. Alexander's conquests were ultimately to pave the way for the great Roman Empire of the East.

He had never looked to the future and had never made sure of his dynastic succession. A mother-dominated youth, he was probably a homosexual; and his lack of interest in any future beyond his own life-span led inevitably to a collapse of coherent policy after his death. The great kingdoms that he had conquered became the disputed provinces of ambitious generals, whose very "Greekness" became modified – not always subtly – by the influences of the Orient. (Something very similar happened to the Christian Crusaders of the Middle Ages.)

"Alexander dead?" The Athenian orator Demades is reputed to have said. "Nonsense! The whole world would stink." Yet at the age of thirty-one he was indeed dead – of a fever, in the conquered city of Babylon. His legacy is difficult to define, for what he achieved in one sense far outran the capacity of his successors to administer. In terms of Mediterranean history, the principal effect of Alexander's meteoric career was to divert the Greek genius into Egypt and the Near East, and thus to make certain the rise and dominance of Rome in the central Mediterranean. A. R. Burn, in *Alexander the Great and the Hellenistic Empire*, puts this viewpoint: "If the Greek drive to the East had not happened to find a leader of such transcendent brilliance, and therefore to penetrate so far, the Greek offensive and defensive in the West would have had more weight behind it. What a blessing to humanity if the Greeks could have checked Rome, at least long enough to civilise her, before Italy became the centre of a unified Mediterranean world. The Romans took kindly enough to Greek art and thought in the end; but they (far more than any other barbarians) *first* broke the back of Greek civilisation, in the appalling last two centuries B.C. before, with Vergil and Augustus, they learned to spare as well as conquer."

On the other hand, such suppositions do not greatly help the study of history. Rome was triumphant, and Rome unified the Mediterranean. Knowing the inability of the Greeks to pursue a common cause for any length of time, it is doubtful whether they could have managed to equal the Roman achievement. Despite the brilliance of the Greek race, or perhaps because of it, they lacked that necessary hardness which makes an imperial people.

If Rome was in the end "civilised" by Greece – and her literature, her arts, and her science were all borrowed from the Greeks – there was a major legacy which she inherited from Alexander and the Hellenistic world. The Greeks themselves, prior to his lifetime, had never had to administer a vast empire. They had mocked, rather than marvelled at, the vast projects and logistic organization of Xerxes during his invasion of Greece. But now, with immense areas of Persia, Ionia, the Levant, and Egypt to administer, the heirs of Alexander were compelled to cope with statistics and organized bureaucracy. They found these essentials to administration ready to hand in Egypt, where, as H. A. L. Fisher points out, "exact knowledge, more particularly with regard to revenue, had long been regarded as a perquisite of government." The Macedonian Ptolemy dynasty of Egypt took over the bureaucracy that they found already functioning there. In due course, when Egypt became part of the Roman Empire, this provided a model for Rome and for all the Western world.

One of the other great consequences of the Greek expansion into the East was to bring the comparatively simple polytheism of the invaders into contact with the far more elaborate, and in many ways considerably more mystical, polytheism of Egypt. The somewhat austere monotheism of the Persians had little appeal to the Greek spirit, although its influence may possibly be discerned upon the later development of Jewish and Christian thought. The Greeks, however, found no difficulty in reconciling the myriad gods and goddesses of Egypt with their own pantheon. Foreign gods from Egypt, Phoenicia, and the Levant merely took Greek names. Thus, Melkarth, the chief god of Tyre, became transformed into the Greek Heracles and later the Roman Hercules.

One of the unexpected consequences of Alexander's irruption into Asia was to destroy the simple faith of the Greek masses in the Olympian gods, who had sufficed their needs ever since Homer had written of them. For the educated, the Olympians with their manifest irresponsibility and amorality had long since been little more than a joke. Philosophy had killed them. But philosophy provided little or no replacement for the uneducated masses, who needed, as throughout all history, some form of revealed religion – something that gave them hope with which to confront the harshness of everyday life. They needed also ritual and ceremony to help transcend the apparent hopelessness of the human condition.

Greece may have introduced Asia to science and philosophy, but it was Asia whose gods and whose mystery religions ultimately triumphed. As Sir William Tarn writes in *Hellenistic Civilisation*: "The conquest of Asia and Egypt . . . was a conquest by the sword alone, not the spirit." Out of the East came the religions that were to dominate the Mediterranean for centuries.

Once again it can be seen that every action in this sea provokes a reaction, or, rather, that fertilization from one source is speedily followed by a cross-fertilization. Apart from the field of religious thought, the influence of the East was also felt in luxury goods, woven cloths, Egyptian glassware, and purple Tyrian dye. Trade in such articles had been taking place for centuries, but the fact that the countries concerned now came within the Greek sphere of influence meant an immediate expansion of this trade. Similar effects were felt in everything from shipbuilding to sail-making. It is clear that the great merchant ships of the Hellenistic Age (later to be adopted by the Romans) stemmed from the *gaulos*, the round, tub-shaped merchantman of Phoenicia, in use from the sixth century B.C. onwards. Alexander's fabulous eastern adventure in some respects surpassed even his own dreams. It enriched the whole of life in this sea.

FIVE

Romans and Carthaginians

At the beginning of the third century B.C., the city of Carthage was the commercial capital of the Mediterranean. Its population has been estimated as about one million – an immense figure for the ancient world. Its trading activities, backed by its fleet, extended the length and breadth of the sea and to remote Britain, the Azores, and the west coast of Africa. From its North African hinterland the city drew its agricultural independence and stability, for this part of Tunisia contains some of the richest land in the Mediterranean basin.

The Carthaginians were not only able traders and master mariners, but also had inherited from their Semitic peasant forebears the accumulated agricultural knowledge of the East. A great work on husbandry by a Carthaginian named Mago was translated into Latin by order of the Roman Senate shortly after the final destruction of Carthage. Although the original treatise has long since disappeared, it is often quoted by Latin authors as the standard work on Mediterranean agriculture. It would not be untrue to say that, if the Romans borrowed their culture and their science from the Greeks, it was from the Carthaginians that they borrowed much of their knowledge of grafting, pruning, stock-breeding, cereal growing, and the other necessary skills of the farmer. As Donald Harden writes in *The Phoenicians*: "The forty or so extracts we have from Mago's lost treatise cover all types of husbandry and agriculture – cereals, vines, olives, stock-raising, apiculture. His treatise could not have been written if Punic farming had not been carefully systematized." Large estates were owned and farmed by wealthy Punic families, and the Carthaginians, making use of a considerable slave-labour force, seem to have been the first nation ever to industrialize agriculture.

The city's first line of defence was, of course, her navy. By the time that the great conflict broke out between Carthage and Rome, the trireme, which for centuries had been dominant in the inland sea, had been superseded by the quinquireme. Unlike the bireme, that two-banked fighting ship which the Phoenicians had themselves pioneered, the quinquireme, or five-banked vessel, most probably originated in Sicily. The Greek historian Diodorus, in his work *The Historical Library*, attributes its invention to the great Dionysius of Syracuse as early as 398 B.C. Inventories of the Athenian dockyards do not show even quadriremes as being built there until about sixty years later. The quinquireme was quickly adopted by the Carthaginians, and it was to be the supreme vessel in the forthcoming wars between Carthage and Rome.

Cecil Torr has the following comment in *Ancient Ships* regarding the crews needed to power these battleships of the period: "The five-banked ships in the Roman and Carthaginian fleets in 256 B.C. [the First Punic War] each carried three hundred rowers besides the combatants. [There were] fifty-four oars in the lowest bank and four more in each succeeding bank. A five-banked ship would have three hundred and ten oars in the banks, and therefore three hundred rowers approximately – or perhaps exactly, if . . . some of the banks were not fully manned. Subsequently the rowers in such five-banked ships were reckoned roughly at four hundred."

Since it is reasonable to expect that spare crew to replace men who were sick – were normally carried, it is likely that the figure of about four hundred was standard on a Carthaginian or Roman quinquireme of this period. The historian Polybius, who took part in the Third Punic War (which ended in the destruction of Carthage in 146 B.C.), states that in one of the early sea battles 330 Roman ships engaged 350 Carthaginian ships; all of them five-banked vessels. He calculated that on this occasion the Romans had 140,000 men afloat and the Carthaginians about 150,000. These early engagements between the quinquiremes of the two hostile powers were not insignificant scrambles between small groups of galleys. They were massive sea battles, involving considerable organization, elaborate signal systems, complicated supply problems, and, in fact, all the requirements of later and more familiar wars.

The military harbour of Carthage, known as the Cothon, was circular and had over 200 docks that could take at least 150 quinquiremes. Sited close to the shore, and near the protecting citadel of Carthage, the Cothon covered an area of about 22 acres. It was connected with the larger commercial harbour (60 acres) by a canal. In the centre of the Cothon was an artificial islet. This was the head-quarters of the Carthaginian admiral and his staff, from which he could at a glance inspect the whole of his fleet.

Immensely strong, the city of Carthage could be attacked from only two directions; down the neck of the peninsula upon which it stood; and across a sand bar. The latter was difficult to assault on account of the nature of the terrain, while the peninsula itself was sealed off across its neck by a massive triple wall, about 45 feet high and 33 feet wide.

Projecting into the sea like the head of a double-axe, the proud city was the richest and possibly the strongest in the Mediterranean world. Towers, four storeys high, were sited within the circuit of the wall at regular intervals so that they were able to give covering fire to one another. Their foundations went down more than 30 feet into the ground, and according to one authority there were stables in vaulted chambers below the walls for 300 elephants (the "heavy armour" of the Carthaginian land forces) and for 4000 horses. Between the walls there were barracks for 20,000 infantry and for at least 4000 cavalry. The whole of the wall-girded peninsula was not only a city but also a vast fortress with magazines and stores and immense underground cisterns. These were supplied by catchment rainfall as well as by an aqueduct running down from the mountains behind. There was also a fresh-water spring, the Fountain of the Thousand Amphorae, within the city limits. So long as Carthage commanded the sea she was virtually impregnable.

Byrsa, as the citadel was called, was a small eminence little more than two hundred feet high, rising out of the land to the north of the harbours. It was heavily fortified, and like the acropolis of Greek cities provided an ultimate defence point, should the city walls ever be breached. On its summit stood the temple of Eshmun, the Phoeni-cian god of health and healing, which served also as a meeting place for the Carthaginian Senate. Artificially raised above the mound of the Byrsa, the temple gave a pyramidal effect to the whole hill. This, possibly, was deliberately reminiscent of those artificial "hill temples" of the Middle East, such as that of Baal in Babylon.

At the foot of the citadel and to its south lay the forum, or public meeting place, whence three narrow streets of six-storied houses ran up to Byrsa itself. These houses formed an important defensive outwork to the citadel. When the Roman general Scipio captured Carthage, he found that he had to storm them house by house before he could reach the citadel's main wall. Around Byrsa and the forum lay the principal temples to the Sidonian gods, as well as the senate house and the tribunal. The pattern of the city was one that was to be followed in the Mediterranean for centuries; it was later copied throughout the New World. Straight streets were regularly disposed at right angles to one another, for Carthage was a deliberately planned city. It had not simply grown, with each generation of buildings evolving upon its predecessors. The area of the defensible peninsula had always imposed those restrictions upon the city.

Sacked and devastated by the Romans, and then built upon by successive waves of invaders over the centuries, it is difficult to "read" ancient Carthage in the few ruins that survive outside the sprawling weight of modern Tunis. It needs the reconstructive genius of Gustave Flaubert to envisage the city as it may have looked, at the dawn of a summer day, in the years of its power and glory. In *Salammbô* he writes: "They were on the terrace. A huge mass of shadow stretched before them, looking as though it contained vague accumulations, like the gigantic billows of a black and petrified ocean.

"But a luminous bar rose towards the East; far below, on the left, the canals of Megara were beginning to stripe the verdure of the gardens with their windings of white. The conical roofs of the heptagonal temples, the staircases, terraces, and ramparts were being carved by degrees upon the paleness of the dawn; and a girdle of white foam rocked around the Carthaginian peninsula, while the emerald sea looked as though it were curdled in the freshness of the morning. Then as the rosy sky grew larger, the lofty houses, bending over the sloping soil, reared and massed themselves like a herd of black goats coming down from the mountains. The deserted streets lengthened; the palm trees that topped the walls here and there were motionless; the brimming cisterns seemed like silver bucklers lost in the courts; the beacon on the promontory of Hermaeum was beginning to grow pale. The horses of Eschmoun, on the very summit of the Acropolis in the cypress wood, feeling that the light was coming, placed their hoofs on the marble parapet, and neighed towards the sun."

Against this great Semitic city and its empire, Rome waged a war that lasted for well over a hundred years (264–146 B.C.); a war that changed the whole face of the Mediterranean world. The outbreak of the First Punic War is one of the most important dates in history. It marked the beginning of the unification of this sea – the only unification that it has ever known.

Although the clash between Sparta and Athens might be seen (by hindsight) as having been inevitable, at first glance there seems comparatively little reason why Rome and Carthage should not have pursued their separate ways without coming into conflict. The Romans, a dour Italian people, far less civilized or sophisticated than their Etruscan neighbours (of whose dominion they had once formed a part), seem on the surface to have had little to recommend them as the future rulers of the Mediterranean world. One quality that they did possess – one which the Greeks so conspicuously lacked – was an aptitude for government. A disciplined and hardy people, they were also skilled at warfare; again, not with the brilliance of the Greeks, but with a dogged tenacity. In any comparison between the Greek and Roman tempers, Aesop's fable of the tortoise and the hare comes to mind.

By the third century B.C., through a process of slow political evolution and gradual military expansion, the Romans had made themselves masters of Italy. The Gauls to the north, the Greek cities to the south, the Etruscans, and the Samnite hill tribes had all yielded before the Roman sword – and the Roman sense of patriotism. Patriotism (that love of country coupled with a sense of belonging to a particular people felt to be superior to all others) was what differentiated the Roman from the Greek or the Carthaginian. The Greek might feel himself to be superior to all "barbarians", but even under the compelling genius of Alexander he remained an individualist, seeking the principal benefit for himself above any consideration for his fellow Greeks. The Carthaginian, on the other hand, was like his Phoenician ancestors – he was always prepared to avoid conflict, provided that he was left alone to trade in peace. If erratic brilliance was the hallmark of the Greek, industrious cupidity marked the Carthaginian. The Roman, however, had a peasant farmer's sharpness, coupled with a peasant's endurance.

Once again, the bone of contention in the Mediterranean was fertile, crop- and fruit-bearing Sicily, that island so geographically dominant and so important to the economy of the ancient world. This land, described by a latter-day Sicilian, Giuseppe di Lampedusa, in *The Leopard*, as "undulating to the horizon in hillock after hillock, comfortless and irrational, with no lines that the mind could grasp, conceived apparently in a delirious moment of creation", was once again to be disputed by the two dominant powers of the Mediterranean. Like a vast warm-fleshed woman, lying negligently in the middle of this sea, Sicily was to provoke yet another conflict as to who was to be her master.

The incident which led to war between the two major Mediterranean powers was similar to that which had brought Athens and Sparta face to face in Sicily. Then it had been the small city of Segesta which had appealed to Athens to intervene on her behalf against her neighbour Selinus. Now, in 264 B.C., it was an appeal to both Rome and Carthage from a band of Italian mercenaries who had seized the city of Messina for help against an invasion from Syracuse that brought the two rival powers into conflict. The Carthaginians arrived first upon the scene, occupied Messina and effected a reconciliation with the Syracusans. The Romans, unwilling to see the Carthaginians in control of the city that dominated the all-important strait between Sicily and Italy, put troops ashore and seized the Carthaginian admiral. The Carthaginians were now forced to withdraw, and the Romans no doubt felt that they had gained an important vantage-point; for they already had their eyes on the conquest of the whole island. In response to the Roman action, two former enemies, Greeks and Carthaginians, now made common cause against the newcomer upon the Sicilian scene. A treaty was signed between Syracuse and Carthage, and both cities declared war upon Rome.

The early years of this, the First Punic War (called "Punic" because the Romans always referred to the Carthaginians as *Poeni*, Phoenicians), were marked by Roman successes. They held Messina against Carthaginian attack, and at the same time wrested several cities away from their enemy. Two things clearly emerged from the opening phases of the war. The first was that the mercenary soldiers employed by Carthage were no match for the disciplined Roman infantrymen. The second was that Rome had no chance of defeating her rival so long as Carthage controlled the seas.

A captured Carthaginian quinquireme is said to have furnished the Romans with a model, and they immediately set about building a new fleet with their usual practical tenacity. The Romans evolved few things of their own. Their genius lay in taking ideas, concepts, and even practical inventions from other nations, adapting them, improving them, and then "mass-producing" them. There is some parallel here with the Japanese in later centuries.

No sooner had the Romans begun to build a fleet to challenge Carthage than they added their own improvement to the Carthaginian prototype. Aware that they would be unable to outmanoeuvre Carthaginian ships and admirals (who had centuries of experience in Mediterranean sea warfare), they determined to change the whole pattern of how that warfare should in future be conducted. If they must concede that the Carthaginians were better seamen and ship-handlers than themselves, then they would promote a type of naval engagement in which seamanship and ship-handling counted for the minimum. The Roman invention was the *corvus*. This was a bridge strong enough to permit the passage of foot-soldiers which was triced up to the mast until the Roman quinquireme was alongside its opponent. Hinged at the base, the *corvus* was rapidly lowered at the moment of impact. It swept down upon the deck of the enemy, and a strong iron spike held it firmly embedded. It was this which gave the bridge its name *corvus* (a raven), on account of its sharp beak. Once the bridge was down, the Roman soldiers could stream across and engage their opponents just as if they were fighting a land battle. Since their swords and javelins were more efficient, and since they were better soldiers than the Carthaginians, they thus managed to turn their inferiority as seamen into an advantage.

Unlike previous galley actions, where the ram had been the decisive factor, and the aim of a commander had been to ram his opponent and sink him, the Roman intention was to make sure that their ships were firmly secured alongside the enemy. This meant that they must be more strongly built, even if it meant throwing away the advantages of manoeuvrability. Central Italy was at that time thickly forested, and the tough oaks of the Campagna gave the Romans an excellent material for their new ships. These were designed to withstand the impact of the Carthaginian rams, as well as to provide a steady fighting platform for the Roman legionaries.

The first engagement in which the new invention and the new navy was fully tried out occurred in 260 B.C., off the promontory of Mylae (modern Milazzo) in north-eastern Sicily. The point is about twenty miles west of the Messina Strait, that eternally disputed area through which so much of the trade of the Mediterranean must necessarily pass between the Tyrrhenian and Ionian seas. The Roman admiral Duilius, true to the tactics which had been evolved, refused to be drawn into a conventional galley action. Using grapnels as well as his raven-bridges, he compelled the Carthaginians to fight a soldier-against-soldier battle. The result was an overwhelming victory for the Romans, and a demoralizing defeat for their opponents. The Carthaginians were, for the first time, compelled to acknowledge that there was a new power active in the Tyrrhenian Sea. This was the first major naval victory ever gained by the Romans and its memory was perpetuated by the *Columna Rostrata* erected in the forum at Rome. It was called the "Beaked Column" because it was adorned with all the rams, or "beaks", of the Carthaginian ships taken on that fateful day.

The effect of the victory was to give the Romans command of all the Mediterranean north of Sicily, thus enabling them to secure control of Corsica. The Carthaginians were to be expelled from that island in which, at one time, only they and the Etruscans had had any rights. Acting quickly upon their success, the Romans now transported a whole army to North Africa, landing it in the homeland of Carthage itself. This master-stroke at the very heart of their enemy failed only because the Romans did not give their general and his troops the necessary backing and reinforcements. The Carthaginians, aided by their strange new allies the Greeks – as well as by an able Greek general – were able to defeat the Romans on the field and compel them to withdraw. Even so, the Romans were capable of sending a fleet to Africa to evacuate their army, and this fleet managed to put the whole Carthaginian fleet to flight. The war in Sicily was now reopened, the Romans taking the important Carthaginian city of Panormus by seaborne assault. These hitherto predominantly land fighters had learned how to exercise sea power in a way that even their experienced adversary had not grasped.

The Romans may have invented little, but they had the capacity to learn and adapt, and this was to be the basis of their success. The Carthaginians, who had started the war with all the advantages of experience and of a well-equipped fleet behind them, failed to make proper use of these advantages. When they should have been harassing the long western seaboard of Italy – or even landing a sea-borne force to strike straight at Rome itself – they contented themselves with defensive actions upon the wind-riddled chessboard of the Mediterranean.

After the capture of Panormus, the Romans attempted to wrest the hitherto inviolable west of Sicily from the Carthaginian grasp. Lilybaeum was invested by sea, but the Romans had hardly looked for the stout-hearted defence that they met from the garrison and the citizens of this ancient Phoenician seaport. In 249 B.C. they were forced to withdraw their fleet after they had been heavily defeated during an attempted surprise attack on nearby Drepanum (Trapani). Those small offshore islands, the Aegates, so long happily secure from the invasion of historical events, were once more compelled to witness "clanging fights, and flaming towns, and sinking ships, and praying hands".

During the campaigns that followed in western Sicily, the most noteworthy feature was the emergence of a Carthaginian general of rare ability and courage. This was Hamilcar Barca, a statesman who foresaw that Carthage must ultimately either crush Rome or submit forever. He realized that these Latins were far more of a threat to his city than ever the Greeks had been.

Hamilcar conducted a successful campaign in Sicily, using as his base the sacred mountain of Eryx. Finally he seized Mount Ercte (Monte Pellegrino, near Palermo) and managed to carry his raids against the enemy as far as the mainland of southern Italy. His successes on the land were to be nullified, however. In 242 B.C. the Romans equipped an entirely new fleet to replace the one that had been lost in action and in storms off western Sicily, and returned to the investment of Lilybaeum. The Carthaginians hastily collected a relief force and sailed north to attempt to break the Roman blockade of this all-important post. On March 10, 241 B.C., in the narrow strait between the Aegates and Drepanum, they were brought to battle, and once again the Roman use of grapnels and raven-bridges turned the scales. The result was an appalling defeat for the Carthaginians; the sea between Sicily and the Aegates, it is said, was dyed red with their blood.

Despite Hamilcar's inspired guerrilla warfare in Sicily, nothing could now prevent a Roman conquest of the island, for the Romans had at last achieved the undisputed command of the sea. Carthage, weary of a war in which she had watched the flower of her youth and her navy destroyed, sued for peace. That spring battle off the lonely Goat Islands cost Carthage the last of her strongholds and trading centres in Sicily. All of these were now ceded to Rome, together with the Lipari Islands, which dominated the north–south trade route of the Tyrrhenian Sea. But Hamilcar and his troops were still in control of the Sicilian hinterland. The Romans, rather than carry on a guerrilla war that might have lasted for years, allowed them to leave the island for North Africa without even a token submission.

As if the loss of Sicily was not enough, the Carthaginians were now confronted with a terrible war that broke out on their own soil: the famous Revolt of the Mercenaries. Enemies of Hamilcar among the governing aristocracy of Carthage refused to pay the troops he brought back with him from Sicily, with the result that they broke out into open revolt and laid waste the country. (The war that followed forms the subject of Flaubert's novel *Salammbô*.) In the end, it was Hamilcar himself who crushed them, and from that moment on his control of Carthage was complete and he enjoyed a virtual dictatorship.

His prescience that Rome would not be content with Sicily alone was justified by events that took place during the three years in which he was occupied with the Revolt of the Mercenaries. Italian traders supplied the mutineers with food and arms, and a Roman force occupied Sardinia, the last Carthaginian island in the central Mediterranean. With all her markets in Sicily, Sardinia, and Corsica now lost, and with her ships virtually expelled from the Tyrrhenian Sea, Carthage was threatened with economic ruin.

Hamilcar looked west. Just as had occurred in the eastern Mediterranean, when the Greeks had deprived the Phoenicians of their former trade routes, the effect of the Roman occupation of the central basin of the sea was to cause the descendants of the Phoenicians to go even further west. For centuries they had had trading centres and even permanent settlements in Spain, but they had never sought to dominate the peninsula and make it a colony in the true sense of the word. But Hamilcar saw that if Carthage was to survive, she must now occupy a great territory in the West, where she could build up a second empire from which to strike at Rome. He had no illusions that the Romans were ever going to leave Carthage in peace. Now that Rome had established a naval supremacy over the northern and central Mediterranean, it was essential for Carthage to hold not only the western basin, but also the rich metal mines and farmland of Spain itself.

Spain, which until now had appeared in the history of the Mediterranean only as a source from which men had drawn tin and other metals since Mycenaean times, now began to exert an influence upon the pattern of this sea. Hamilcar, on his own responsibility, led an expedition to Spain; an expedition not like previous Carthaginian trading ventures, but designed to establish a new empire. He was not only a great soldier but also an able statesman. In a brief eight years, by diplomacy as well as by force of arms, he created in southern Spain a new state, a new army, and a source of wealth that more than compensated for his country's losses in the First Punic War. He died on the battlefield in 229 B.C., leaving behind a rich material legacy for Carthage, as well as a legacy of revenge.

During the twenty-three years of peace that followed the First Punic War, the Romans were also actively extending their territory. They now controlled Sicily, Sardinia, and Corsica, and they had extended their northern frontier right up to the Alps. With the whole of Italy secure behind them they began to look east, and in 229 B.C. made their first inroad into Greek territory. Concerned by the activities of the Illyrian pirates in the Adriatic, the Romans set themselves to eliminating this threat to their eastern trade routes. They dispatched an efficient naval force to the area and seized Corcyra, one of the main bases of the pirates. Although they retained it only as a naval station, making it nominally a "free state", the writing was on the wall for the Greeks. They would retain their independence from Rome only so long as Rome was preoccupied with the Carthaginians in the West.

When Hamilcar had set out for Spain on his imperial mission he had taken with him his nine-year-old son, Hannibal, after making the boy swear an oath of eternal hatred against the Romans. Hannibal grew up inspired by this notion of revenge and, when his father was killed in battle against one of the Spanish tribes, he felt that his life must be dedicated to completing the task that had been set him. As a young man he served in Spain under his brother-in-law Hasdrubal, and on Hasdrubal's death in 221 B.C. he automatically assumed control of the army and province of Spain. He was twenty-five years old.

The collision with Rome was now inevitable, for Hannibal was determined upon a war to the death with the Latin enemy. How much of this campaign was of his own choosing, and how much may have been inspired by his father, it is difficult to say, but within two years of taking over control of the army he had provoked a quarrel with Rome and the Second Punic War had begun. This was undoubtedly the greatest war in the whole history of ancient Rome, and it determined the future of the Mediterranean world.

The immediate cause of the war was an attack by Hannibal upon the city of Saguntum, which lay south of the River Ebro, and which was therefore technically within the Carthaginian sphere of influence. The Romans, however, had guaranteed Saguntum's security. Both ancient and modern writers have made much of the fact that Rome's action in concluding this treaty was itself in contravention of a previous agreement with Hasdrubal: that all of Spain south of the Ebro should be regarded as Carthaginian territory. This is true, but there can be little doubt that even if the Romans had not reacted over Saguntum, Hannibal would soon have moved across the Ebro into the Roman sphere.

Hannibal's plans were carefully laid, and he had every intention of provoking a major war. Gaetano de Sanctis writes in an article on the great Carthaginian in the *Encyclopaedia Britannica*: "Politically it is clear that by attacking Saguntum Hannibal accepted responsibility for the war and all its consequences. He did so because he thought it necessary in order to uphold the position of Carthage as a great power, and at the same time he thought that he could win – not realizing the granite solidity of the Italic confederation centred in Rome, which he hoped to dismember by the hammer blows of his army. Thus Hannibal's whole action was based on a grave and fatal error of valuation ... [also] he failed to realize with sufficient clearness the absolute necessity of naval supremacy for a definitive victory in the great duel with Rome, and, taking the view that the predominance gained by the Romans in the First Punic War was unalterable, he made no serious attempt at preparing to dispute it. Thus he lessened the efficiency of his conduct of the war; for there is no doubt that the ultimate victory of Rome in the Second Punic War was essentially due to the fact that her naval supremacy was maintained throughout."

Hannibal, in fact, was a great general, but he had little or no understanding of the uses of sea power. Rare for a Carthaginian, he had been trained almost entirely as a soldier by his father and his brother-in-law, and he seems to have ignored the fact that what had made Carthage great in the first place was her navy. The lesson of the First Punic War – that it was naval supremacy which had made Rome victorious – seems to have escaped him.

Hannibal accepted, then, the dominance of Rome in the Mediterranean, and it was this acceptance which determined his astounding march through Spain and Gaul and over the Alps into Italy itself. Despite the fact that his army never numbered more than thirty thousand, and that many of the famous elephants he took with him perished in the Alpine passes, Hannibal's arrival in the plain of the River Po sent a tremor of fear through the heart of Rome.

"In the ruses and stratagems of war," H. A. L. Fisher writes, "in the handling of cavalry as well as in the moral gift of leadership which inspires the devoted loyalty of troops, Hannibal was supreme. A magical aura seemed to surround him. Though he had no siege train and could never have taken Rome by force, he created in his adversaries a paralyzing sense of their inferiority." Like Alexander, he was one of those inspired leaders who seem to shine with an almost superhuman radiance. Unlike Alexander, however, he was destined for tragedy and failure. Despite the amazing successes of two battles – at Lake Trasimene in 217 B.C. and at Cannae in the following year – he could not break the Roman spirit. Their armies he did break – it has been estimated that the Romans lost forty thousand men at Lake Trasimene, and almost double this number at Cannae. But what Hannibal had been hoping for failed to materialize. Although much of southern Italy seceded after the Battle of Cannae, the important Latin colonies and Greek cities still remained faithful; although the Gauls, on whose support he had certainly been counting, regained their independence, and thousands of them joined Hannibal's army. The Romans themselves, moreover (unlike the Greeks of the past when similar disasters befell them), did not collapse into splinter groups. Quarrels between nobles and commons, which had previously prevented unanimity on policy, were healed in the face of the Carthaginian threat. A dour determination "to strive . . . and not to yield" united the Roman Republic as never before in its history.

Although Hannibal managed to maintain himself for years in Italy – from 217 to 203 B.C., an astounding achievement – his venture failed. He was defeated in the long run not on the battlefield, but by lack of support from home and by the careful guerrilla tactics of an able Roman general, Quintus Fabius. Fabius, who became known to the Romans as "Cunctator", the Lingerer, took care never to give Hannibal the opportunity of forcing upon him a "set-piece" battle. Instead, he dogged the Carthaginian army right down through Italy without taking on the invader in a major engagement; by this means he prevented the Carthaginians from acquiring a secure and permanent base.

Hannibal's brother, Hasdrubal, who was sent out with a fresh invading force from Spain, and who marched overland in Hannibal's tracks in 209–208 B.C., was beaten on the banks of the Metaurus River in northern Italy by a fresh Roman army, raised despite all their losses. From that moment, Hannibal was doomed. Although he and his own troops still continued to occupy Calabria in the south, the failure of his brother to effect the long-dreamed-of thrust at Rome meant the end of his hopes.

The Romans in the meantime had discovered a brilliant general in Cornelius Scipio. While Hannibal was moving almost unrestricted throughout Italy, Scipio struck at the new source of Carthaginian power – Spain itself. By the end of 206 B.C., he had stormed the principal Carthaginian city, Carthago Nova, or New Carthage (modern Cartagena), and had driven the last of the Carthaginian forces from Spain. Although many centuries later Spain fell under North African (Moslem) domination for several hundred years, the Latin mould of Spain, which endures to this day, was cast by Scipio. When he evicted the Carthaginians, he set the hitherto little-known peninsula on the road to becoming part of what would one day be the immense Roman Empire.

It was not until 203 B.C. that Italian soil was finally cleared of Carthaginian troops, and then only because Hannibal, on orders from Carthage, sailed for home. Scipio, who had destroyed the Carthaginian Empire in Spain, now invaded Africa itself. A year later, in the Battle of Zama, on the borders of Carthaginian territory, Hannibal suffered the only major defeat of his career, at the hands of Scipio. The Second Punic War was over.

In 201 B.C. a peace was concluded in which Carthage ceded Spain and the few Mediterranean islands still in her hands to victorious Rome. The Carthaginians agreed to pay an immense financial indemnity within the next fifty years, and all their navy, with the exception of a few triremes, was burned. They were forbidden to conduct any foreign policy without the consent of Rome, and – final indignity – they must apply to Rome if they wished to conduct any campaign within their own North African territory.

Max Cary sums up the outcome of this war in the *Encyclopaedia Britannica*: "The failure of Hannibal's brilliant endeavour . . . was not due to any strategical mistakes on his part. It was caused by the indomitable strength of will of the Romans, whose character during this period appears at its best, and to the compactness of their Italian confederacy, which no shock of defeat or strain of war could entirely disintegrate. It is this spectacle of individual genius overborne by corporate and persevering effort which lends to the Second Punic War its peculiar interest."

The battle at that obscure and geographically still-disputed place known as Zama decided the fate of the West. Yet the commercial resilience of Carthage was such that, despite the crippling terms imposed upon her, she was able within a comparatively short time to pay in full the heavy war indemnity that Rome had exacted. This recovery was largely due to the administrative ability of Hannibal himself, who, despite his defeat, had been placed at the head of the government by the Carthaginians. He quickly showed that he was as good at administration as he was at warfare.

It was hardly surprising that the Romans took note of the startlingly quick recovery of their late enemy – a recovery largely due to the man who had almost brought them to their knees. Hannibal was accused of conspiring against the peace and was forced to flee from the city and the land to which he had devoted his life. He died in Asia Minor in 183 B.C., having spent most of the intervening years engaged in one way or another on the side of Rome's enemies in the East. Even though little is known of his character, Hannibal emerges as one of the ablest generals in history – a man who deserves the often misapplied word "genius". In the final analysis, he was defeated not on the battlefield of Zama, but by the character of the Roman people.

The scars of the war were never forgotten by the Romans. For centuries it was remembered as the time of their greatest trial – as well as of their ultimate triumph. Many of Rome's most influential families, among them the Scipios, owed their later position to the achievements of their ancestors during the Second Punic War. During the great days of the Roman Empire, a statesman, writer, or orator who wished to remind the Roman people of their duty would expatiate upon the men, the virtues, and the resolution that had finally defeated Carthage.

Yet even after the disastrous losses of the war, the great North African city was not entirely crushed. Hannibal's conduct of home affairs and trade had set her on the road to recovery, and able Carthaginian merchants were still active throughout North Africa and the western Mediterranean. The commercial rivalry of Roman businessmen, traders, and sea-captains was soon excited by the Carthaginian ability to regain markets that they had hoped to make their own. They noted, too, how the city drew its strength from its fertile African farmlands, and how, despite the loss of Spain as a colony, Carthaginian trade still continued in that region, as well as further afield, beyond the mysterious Pillars of Hercules, into the great Atlantic itself.

By the mid-second century B.C., despite the fact that the political power of Carthage was insignificant, there were many in Rome who feared that her mercantile revival threatened their security. In somewhat similar fashion to Western Germany after the Second World War, Carthage had achieved an "economic miracle", and there were those in Rome who feared that this might be followed by a political or military one. Primarily, however, the causes of the Third Punic War were no more than Roman jealousy and greed. Roman politicians, among them Cato the Elder, who concluded his speeches with the words "Carthage must be destroyed", found it easy to play upon these deep-seated feelings.

If the Carthaginians, led by Hamilcar and Hannibal, had deliberately set in motion the second great war, the third, and last, was entirely initiated by Rome. Masinissa, a prominent Libyan leader, who had sided with Rome during the Second Punic War, increasingly harassed the Carthaginians and encroached upon their territory. Undoubtedly, even if Rome did not actively help him, it was not without a smile of satisfaction that many Roman senators watched his actions – and waited for the Carthaginian response. In 150 B.C., tried beyond all endurance, Carthage took action against Masinissa and, in the campaign that followed, was decisively defeated. The Romans were not content with seeing their ancient enemy humbled once more. As B. L. Hallward writes in "The Fall of Carthage" in *The Cambridge Ancient History*: "The balance of power in North Africa had broken down. Numidia threatened to absorb Carthage into a strong North African kingdom with an interest in the Mediterranean. A powerful Numidian ruling in Carthage might be a new Hannibal. The danger from Carthage was not that she was too strong, but that she had become too weak, and that her weakness might make Masinissa too strong."

Political and strategic considerations were now happily allied with cupidity, and the Roman Senate could no longer resist the temptation to intervene. The Carthaginians, it was maintained, had, in defiance of the Treaty of Zama, acted on their own account and made war in Africa. (The fact that they had lost did not mitigate their offence in the eyes of Cato and his party.) Rome must therefore dispatch an army and bring the city to heel; unless, of course, the Carthaginians were themselves prepared to destroy and then vacate their city. It was among the more cynical demands of history.

The despairing Carthaginians, beset by Masinissa in their homeland, and now threatened by the might of Rome and her army and navy, realized that they had reached the end of a long road – from imperial power to degradation. They had no option but to refuse the Roman demand. If they abandoned Carthage, where had they to go? The East was long since closed to them; Spain was under Roman control; and all nearby Africa was now held by a Roman protégé. The Roman offer was refused, and the Carthaginians, in a last surge of courage and ability, raised a new army and prepared themselves for siege. To quote B. L. Hallward again: "The whole city became a workshop and the population toiled feverishly day and night to forge new weapons of war, while the hair which made the best strings for catapults was freely offered by the noblest and the poorest of the women."

The siege of Carthage was opened in 149 B.C., and for two whole years the ancient city held out against every device that the Romans could bring against it. Blockaded by sea, cut off from the hinterland by the Roman army, the Carthaginians still refused to yield – while the losses of the Roman troops encamped in the unhealthy marshlands around the city mounted steadily from disease and sickness. But the end of Carthage was foreshadowed by the arrival upon the scene of a Scipio: Scipio Aemilianus, adoptive grandson of the famous "African" Scipio, former conqueror of the city. The young general intensified the blockade, walling off the whole isthmus, beyond the walls of the city itself, so that nobody could get in from the country. At the same time he stepped up the naval blockade to the point where no vessels, except an occasional indomitable small boat, could creep into the city even by night. The Carthaginians, seeing the noose growing steadily tighter about their necks, contrived one last and desperate surprise – one in keeping with their ancient history. Within the inner harbour they secretly contrived to build a whole new fleet of fifty ships; at a given moment they sallied out to give battle. The Romans were caught entirely unaware, and if the Carthaginians had pressed home their attack they might even at this last moment have saved their city. Unfortunately they delayed a whole day, and the Romans – a people never long inclined to remain in a state of shock – returned to the engagement and won what was in effect the decisive battle of the war.

The fate of Carthage was sealed. Scipio Aemilianus completed a mole which completely prevented the access of any shipping to the doomed city; he then attacked the citadel of Byrsa itself. The Romans captured the market-place first, but they still had to fight every inch of the way up to the citadel. The Carthaginians, often enough in their history, were not sufficiently aggressive to cope with the harsh combat of the world; they were traders who preferred to retreat in order to trade elsewhere rather than meet a determined enemy face to face. But in their last years, months, days, and even hours, they put up a resistance that the Spartans of Thermopylae would have respected. They were now starving; their numbers were reduced from 500,000 to about 50,000; the last of all the Carthaginian fleets was gone; yet still, street by street, house by house, and even room by room, they resisted the incoming Roman tide.

But once Scipio had breached the citadel walls, there was no hope. While the old men, women, and children streamed out to be killed, raped, or sold into slavery, the last of the defenders shut themselves up in the Temple of Eshmun, to perish in its flames. It is said that Scipio himself wept as he watched Carthage burning. He wept because he had a prophetic vision that one day the same thing would happen to Rome.

The ancient enemy was no more. Temples, buildings, and walls were razed, and the whole area was symbolically put under the plough – to signify that the city should return to the earth itself, but not to be fruitful, for even the furrows were sown with sea-salt. Outside the harbour, the victorious Roman galleys puffed their sails under the African wind, while the devastated ruins burned for seventeen days and nights. Rome, that city and empire founded upon the ruins of a thousand and one other cities and empires, was *Roma Victrix*, Rome the Conqueror.

All the territory of Carthage was proclaimed a new Roman province under the name "Africa". The Kingdom of Numidia, ruled by the sons of Masinissa, became an allied state under Roman protection, and also served as a useful buffer to protect the new province against the raids of the warlike desert tribes. The great Punic city, which for seven centuries had dominated the sea-lanes of the Mediterranean, was erased from the map as if it had never been. Even the activities of modern archaeologists have managed to recover only a vestige of that lost civilization, so thorough was the Roman destruction. Yet the site itself, its geographical situation and advantages, could not be ignored and, only a hundred years after the fall of Carthage, a new town arose upon the site. But this was a Roman city, a provincial capital in the vast Roman Empire, and no longer the heart of a great Semitic power.

SIX

Romans and Greeks

The massive struggle, which had culminated in Rome becoming supreme throughout all the central and western Mediterranean, was to be paralleled by a similar expansion in the East. The Greeks, who had watched this battle of giants from the sidelines, were mostly eager to see their ancient enemy, Carthage, defeated. Polybius, the Greek historian who is the principal source for the history of these times, does not disguise his admiration for the Roman virtues of courage and endurance, never more in evidence than during the period of the Punic Wars.

There were, however, two friends of Carthage among the Greek rulers of this period, Antiochus III of Syria and Philip V of Macedon. Both saw Rome as the principal threat to their dominions, and both attempted to profit by the Roman involvement in the West. Although Roman policy during the Punic Wars was necessarily to avoid having to fight on two fronts – peace in the East was their hope and aim – yet Antiochus and Philip offered threats that could not be ignored. Once again, the Roman legionary proved himself the finest fighting man in the Mediterranean world. Philip was routed in his home territory at the Battle of Cynoscephalae in 197 B.C., and Antiochus seven years later, at Magnesia, in Asia Minor. Rome, whether she had wished it or not, was inevitably to be involved in the affairs of the eastern Mediterranean and the countries bordering upon it.

The Greeks, who had long cried out for independence from Macedonian rule, should, in theory at least, have been content with the home rule which they had now achieved. But discontent is an integral part of the Greek nature. As they had been in the past, so – true to their national character – they remained during these years when the shadow of Rome steadily lengthened over Greece itself, over Asia Minor, and over all the Near East. "Divide and rule", even though it was never said by a Roman, may have been the maxim of the later Roman Empire, but in acquiring their empire in the East the Romans did not need to practise it. The Greeks did the "dividing" for them.

The climax came when the Macedonians, under a King who bore the ancient name of Perseus, once more posed a threat to Roman interests. At the Battle of Pydna in 168 B.C., the Macedonian power was finally extinguished. The country itself was divided into four republics, and the Macedonian leaders, together with their most important friends in other Greek states, were carried off into captivity in Italy.

The Greeks still failed to see that their only hope of common salvation was to accept the fact that Rome was the dominant Mediterranean power, and that their interests would best be served by this acceptance – which would permit them to continue to enjoy their liberty and independence. A further conflict flared up, and the Romans, inflamed at last against the permanent dissidence and disaffection of Greece, stamped it out with brutal thoroughness. The city of Corinth was treated in exactly the same way – and in the same year, 146 B.C. – as the city of Carthage. The ancient rival of Athens, the home of philosophers and of the most gifted craftsmen and artists, was razed. Its men were killed, its women and children sold into slavery, and all the art treasures which had accumulated for centuries in this rich and cultured city were transported to Rome. With true Roman canniness, the victorious Roman consul, Lucius Mummius, insisted that the shippers of these looted art treasures should put the usual clause in the contract (as if the goods were cattle or bags of wheat) that, if any of them were lost in transit, they must be replaced by others of equal value. As he stands astride the smoking ruins of Corinth, Mummius is recognizable as a figure to become only too familiar in later centuries – the victorious parvenu.

Few empires have been the result of deliberate policy. Exceptions are those of Alexander the Great and of Napoleon Bonaparte and Adolf Hitler. The only factor that is held in common by these three very different creations is the brevity of their life-span. Long-lived empires, it seems, grow like oak trees. They are the result not of planned expansion, but of slow and, more often than not, unintended accretions. The Roman Empire was no exception to this: it grew outwards very gradually, starting with the small seedling state of Rome. It was unlike the British Empire, which resembled the Carthaginian more nearly in that it evolved through a desire to protect trading posts. The Roman Empire, on the other hand, grew out of a desire to protect first its own state and then, when that was secure, of maintaining peace on the boundaries of that state. The Roman involvement with the Greeks and in the East is a clear instance of this.

Spain became a Roman province because the Romans had to conquer it in order to protect themselves against this new Carthaginian power in the West. The Carthaginian territories in North Africa became Roman because Hannibal had forced the issue upon the Roman people – war to the death. Greece and its dependencies in Asia Minor became Roman because the Greeks were always at variance with one another, and because Greek instability threatened the whole of Rome's trade with the East. The Roman Empire grew not so much out of greed – though this was a factor, as with all empires – but because, having started with the necessity of preserving their own frontiers, the Romans found that each preservation provoked a new necessity.

After the destruction of Corinth, Greece became a Roman protectorate, administered from Macedonia. As Sir William Tarn writes in *Hellenistic Civilisation*: "Greece had no more wars or foreign politics, except boundary disputes. Timocracies – governments of the wealthy – were set up in many cities, and attempts to alter the constitution prohibited. Antigonus I had once claimed, in certain cities, to 'reprehend and punish' those who proposed laws which he considered inexpedient, but Rome now made 'new laws' punishable by death, an illustration of the difference between Roman and Macedonian rule. Nevertheless in Greece, if anywhere, the Roman Republic for a time justified itself; it gave peace and prosperity, even if enforced." The Greeks, in fact, had lost their freedom, but had gained in return the stability that had long eluded them.

The line of the Roman poet Horace, "Captive Greece made captive her rude conqueror," was indeed true. Long before Rome had actually imposed her rule upon Greece, she had been greatly influenced by the Greek cities and settlements scattered throughout southern Italy and Sicily. From Naples to Syracuse, Greek influence was predominant. It was, for instance, from the most ancient Greek colony in Italy, the town of Cumae on the Bay of Naples, that the Romans had first acquired the alphabet. A knowledge of the Greek language, its poetry, philosophy, history, and scientific theory, became the *sine qua non* of the Roman gentleman. So much was this so, that Romans of the calibre of the elder Cato – conservatives who believed above all in the ancient virtues of modesty, temperance, and frugal living – found an affront to the dignity of Rome in the "new wave" of Greek culture. Like their successors throughout the centuries, these Roman puritans re-coiled before what they felt was the enervating effect of Greek art and literature, and, even more, of Greek morals. Homosexuality had long been an accepted fact in Greek life and was an integral part of it. Socrates did not blush to confess the love he felt for Alcibiades, and the whole of his pupil Plato's work is coloured by a sympathetic attitude towards homosexual love. The comparatively lowly position held by women in Greece had no doubt contributed towards the celebration of homo-sexual love between men, which was common even in military states such as Sparta. But it was not only Greek morals that affronted the Catos of Rome. They felt that the very statues, the pottery, the jewel-lery, and the fabrics of Greece and the Hellenistic world were corrupt-ing, since they developed a taste for luxury and ease.

The Greeks who lived in the countryside had always been (as they are today) a frugal people, counting a handful of olives, a piece of bread, a fish, and a glass of rough wine as quite sufficient for the needs of the day. But Alexander's conquest of the East had introduced a new element altogether. The luxurious habits of Persian, Syrian, and Egyptian rulers and nobles had been quickly adopted by the rulers of the Greek kingdoms that evolved out of Alexander's empire.

M. I. Finley writes in *The Ancient Greeks*: "The gradual conquest of the Hellenistic world flooded Rome and Italy with Greek ideas, Greek works of art and Greek-speaking slaves. Thereafter, in most fields of endeavour (with the notable exceptions of law, the army, and political administration) it is impossible to discuss Roman ideas apart from their Greek models or inspiration. The eastern part of the Empire, indeed, was in many ways still Greek – Hellenistic Greek – to the end." The Roman conservatives, the preachers and practisers of the ancient virtues, never managed to stem the Greek tide and, more especially, that com-bination of Greek and Near Eastern culture known as Hellenism.

Quite apart from the more obvious influences of art and literature, the most significant Greek contribution to the Roman world was probably in philosophy. R. D. Hicks writes in the *Encyclopaedia Britannica*: "The introduction of Stoicism at Rome was the most momentous of the many changes that it saw. After the first sharp collision with the jealousy of the national authorities it found a ready acceptance, and made rapid progress amongst the noblest families. It has been well said that the old heroes of the republic were unconscious Stoics, fitted by their narrowness, their stern simplicity and devotion to duty for the almost Semitic earnestness of the new doctrine. In Greece its insensibility to art and the cultivation of life was a fatal defect; not so with the shrewd men of the world, desirous of qualifying as advocates or jurists."

The austerity of Stoicism appealed to something in the Roman character while, at the religious level, it provided satisfaction for the deepest cravings of the human spirit. The magnificent *Hymn to Zeus* by the third-century Greek Stoic Cleanthes foreshadows the Semitic monotheism which was ultimately to triumph in the Roman world.

"Most glorious of immortals, O Zeus of many names, almighty and everlasting, sovereign of nature, directing all in accordance with law ... Thee all this universe, as it rolls circling round the earth, obeys wheresoever thou dost guide, and gladly owns thy sway. ... No work upon earth is wrought apart from thee, lord, nor through the divine ethereal sphere, nor upon the sea; save only whatsoever deeds wicked men do in their own foolishness. ... Deliver men from fell ignorance. Banish it, father, from their soul, and grant them to obtain wisdom, whereupon relying thou rulest all things with justice."

The Greeks, for their part, seem at first to have benefited by the stability of Roman rule, but they ultimately suffered from their annexation more deeply than any of the other peoples conquered by Rome. The Romans, however, derived almost nothing but benefit from Greece and her culture. Much as it would be impossible to write a history of the United States without referring to the European origins of its culture, or of Russia without pointing to the influence of Byzantine Greece, so the whole city, state, and empire of Rome must be considered – at least in its ideas and art-forms – as largely an extension of Greece. At a much later date, when the latest of the eastern mystery religions,

Christianity, arrived upon the Roman scene, it was in Greek dress. It was preached first to Greeks and to Hellenized Jews and peoples of the Near East in Greek, and framed in the conventions of Greek rhetoric. The Old Testament had been translated into Greek as early as the third century B.C., and it was this version – not the original Hebrew, which few outside Palestine could read – that became familiar to the Christians of the Roman Empire. Even more important, perhaps, was the fact that all Christian theology was framed by men who had absorbed Greek philosophy, and who cast this theology from a mould of ideas and concepts derived from Plato, the Stoics, and other Greek philosophers.

The tragedy of the later impact of Rome upon Greece was occasioned largely by the rapacity of Roman governors in Greece and Asia Minor. After the defeat of Carthage and the destruction of Corinth, Rome was left unchallenged in the Mediterranean. The city that had evolved on the basis of a community of industrious peasant farmers suddenly found itself the most powerful and the richest city in the Mediterranean. The old frugal virtues that Cato the Elder had preached could no more withstand the impact of this sudden luxury than could the primitive culture of Rome withstand the influence of Greece and Hellenism. Rich senators now vied with one another in ostentatious gladiatoral shows, as well as in vote-catching largesse and in outright bribery. For all of this expenditure money was the necessary life-blood, and money could best be extracted from the eastern territories.

Roman trade now extended the length and breadth of the Mediterranean, and these early Roman traders were as unscrupulous as any profiteers of later wars. A. R. Burn, in his *History of Greece*, describes how "Italian trade also extended beyond the frontiers [of the Roman provinces]; and, moreover, in her own supposed interests, Rome set herself to weaken independent states; the resulting chaos then repeatedly made annexation necessary." What had begun by accident was later continued as a matter of deliberate policy. Empires, like big business concerns, often become uncontrollable in the rate of their growth.

In the first century there opened the last phase of a struggle in Asia Minor that was to result in the degradation and devastation of Greece. A remarkable leader, Mithridates, King of Pontus in north-eastern Asia Minor, taking advantage of a civil war in Italy, managed to over-

Tomb fresco showing musicians in a garden

Tombs at Cerveteri, near Rome

Odysseus tied
to the mast
of his galley,
against the
blandishments
of the Sirens

Sixth-century cargo ship (*left*) and warship

run all ancient Ionia and Lydia – the area which had now become the Roman Province of Asia. All the hatred felt for Rome by the Greeks and other inhabitants of Asia Minor and the Aegean now crystallized around the figure of Mithridates.

The Greeks who had suffered at the hands of Roman governors, tax-gatherers, and unscrupulous merchants felt that here at last was a chance to be free once more. True, Rhodes and some other cities honoured their obligations to the Romans, but the majority of the Greek cities rose in open revolt and joined the forces of Mithridates. In Asia Minor alone, it is said that eighty thousand Italian men, women, and children were massacred in one day. In the Aegean islands at least twenty thousand more perished in a wave of hatred which suddenly engulfed the whole of Greece and the eastern Mediterranean. Even Athens, a city which had been traditionally respected and well treated by the Romans, and which had not engaged in any war for generations, joined the rebellion. Delos – sacred Delos which had for some time become little more than a Roman slave-market, was sacked and devastated by the fleet of Mithridates as his army crossed over to Greece to oust the Romans and give the Greeks back their liberty. His armies, chiefly led by Greeks, now occupied Athens, which had risen to receive him, as well as most of the area to the north of Attica. With Asia Minor lost to Rome, and with the threat of all Greece breaking free, it looked for a moment as if once again the empire of Alexander the Great might rise from its ashes.

But the Romans, as they had shown during the Second Punic War, were never better than in adversity. It brought out in them those old qualities of dogged endurance and determination which had first made their imprint felt upon the Mediterranean world. A distinguished general, Sulla, hastened over to Greece. Athens was besieged and stormed (it was never fully to recover from this devastation inflicted by the Roman legionaries), and Mithridates was defeated. Greece was ravaged by the conflicting armies as they struggled together, Delphi being sacked by the one and Olympia by the other. Meanwhile the anarchic state prevailing in the Aegean provided an ideal opportunity for pirates, who plundered its islands and cities remorselessly caring little whether their allegiance was to Mithridates or to Rome.

Mithridates finally sued for peace in 84 B.C., and it was granted him by the victorious Romans. Soon afterwards, however, a second war broke out in Asia Minor. Greece was now secured for Rome, and the battleground was transferred across the Aegean. The struggle did not end until 63 B.C., when Mithridates committed suicide. During his reign of nearly sixty years he had given the Romans more cause for alarm than any man since Hannibal. Indeed, there was something about his character that brings to mind the great Carthaginian. More than a simple war-lord, he was a man of enormous energy and ability (he was said to have mastered twenty-five languages), and he was an able strategist. At one moment in his long campaigns against Rome, he even conceived the dream of Hannibal in reverse. This was to march north of the Euxine, through the wild tribes of Russia – calling upon them to rise and join him against Rome – and invade Italy over the Alps.

After the war was over, Sulla's exactions throughout Greece and Asia Minor were such that the ancient "glory that was Greece" was almost entirely extinguished. Little was left in the land but ruined towns and a war-worn and depressed people. The Greeks would never again rise in rebellion against imperial Rome. But, although they now relinquished their liberties in exchange for peace, they suffered even further during the civil wars which broke out between the Romans themselves.

Whereas it was the Greeks who had once devastated Sicily in their struggle to establish which of their two leading cities was to dominate the Greek world, it was Greece itself which now became the battlefield in the struggle between Pompey and Caesar as to who was to become master of the Mediterranean. Three times the land was despoiled and plundered as the contesting armies tore at each other in the contest for the dominion of the world. Greece suffered as not even Sicily had formerly suffered: so much so that, in 45 B.C., a friend of Cicero's could write to the great Roman orator, "As I was returning from Asia, I looked at the coastlines round about me. The island of Aegina lay astern, and Megara before me. On my right was Piraeus, and on my left was Corinth. These were all once prosperous, highly populated cities – but now they lay before my eyes ruined and devastated. . . ."

At no time in her subsequent history has Greece recovered from that century (130–30 B.C.) when she became the cockpit of the Mediterranean world. The cities and temples that appear to many travellers to be ruined through the inexorable action of time were indeed ruined when the Romans passed through them nineteen hundred years ago. Many of the statues and buildings whose losses we deplore had been broken or looted before the birth of Christ. Columns may have fallen in earthquakes, but many more were overturned by marauding armies.

To quote Sir William Tarn: "Whole districts were half depopulated; Thebes became a village, Megalopolis a desert, Megara, Aegina, Piraeus heaps of stones; in Laconia and Euboea individuals owned large tracts, perhaps worked only by a few herdsmen; Aetolia, like Epirus, was ruined for ever."

The Roman Empire was founded upon a desert of bones – and nowhere was this truer than in Greece.

SEVEN

The Roman Sea

From Carthage to Sicily and Greece, and eastwards to Asia Minor and the Levant, the centuries of Roman expansion had been marked by the steadily increasing number of ships that carried the men, the horses, and the weapons of war that enabled Rome to become dominant. The sea was not only often the battlefield itself, but sometimes the life-line that carried the armies to other battlefields.

The Romans had first learned from the Carthaginians how to build an efficient bireme; had then improved upon the Punic design; and had subsequently adopted the quinquireme, which had probably originated in Sicily. In the long harsh century when Greece was being devastated by warring armies, and when Asia Minor was also a main centre of conflict, the sea-routes from Italy to the East became increasingly important. The vessels inevitably underwent those alterations and modifications that result from increasing use and experience; at the same time the Romans applied their native building talents to the construction of great harbours and the improvement of sheltered roadsteads along their lines of communications. The Greeks, and the Carthaginians before them, had carefully utilized the natural resources of a coastline, and had built efficient dockyards and harbours for their war galleys and merchantmen. But they had not been faced with quite the same problems the Romans had to deal with when the entire commerce and administration of the inland sea became their preserve.

The Romans tackled the issue of their expanding sea empire with their usual tenacious efficiency. The Greeks may have taught the Romans the refinements of architecture, but these north Italians – as they were to prove during the centuries of their dominance – were among the master-builders of all time. Their genius lay in the practical: in the roads which still sweep throughout Europe, from Britain in the

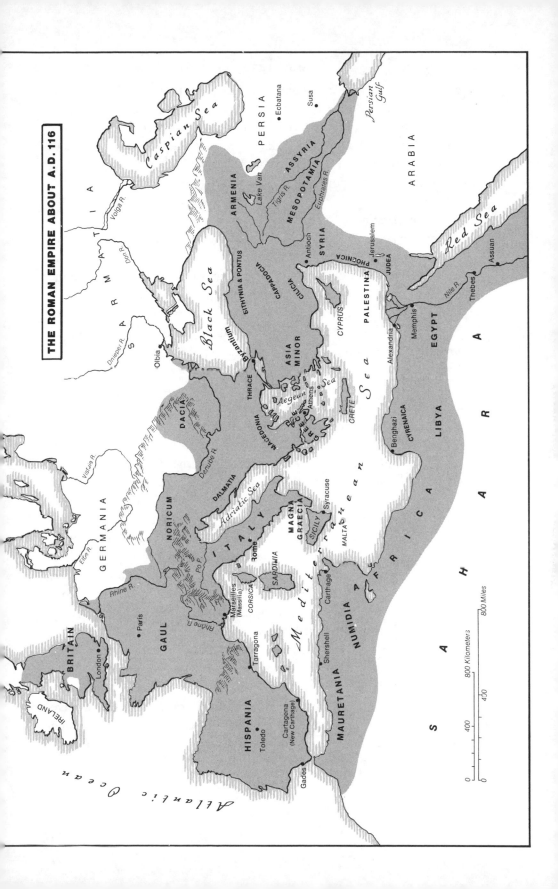

THE ROMAN EMPIRE ABOUT A.D. 116

far North, across the continent, down through Italy itself, and then re-emerge all over North Africa, Asia Minor, and the Near East. At the end of every road that led to a Mediterranean seaport, whether it was Marseilles or Alexandria, lay the departure point for the far side of the Mediterranean. Here the Romans completed their road by creating the most efficient port and harbour systems that this sea had ever known.

The unification of the Mediterranean basin which was achieved during the period of the Roman Empire was in no small measure due to the building abilities of its founders. They built more efficiently than man had ever built before – not only upon the land, but also upon the shores of the sea. If a Roman legion had to be transshipped, within a minimum of time, from Spain to Italy, North Africa, or Egypt to suppress a revolt, it was not enough that the legion should be able to proceed efficiently to its port of embarkation. Once there, it had to find barracks and storage sheds, arsenals and granaries all ready and waiting. There, too, efficient quays must provide shelter whether the cold north wind or the humid sirocco blew; quays where the great transports and their escorting galleys could lie secure no matter what the weather.

Unlike the Greeks, whose trade and whose internecine wars had been regularly limited by the onset of the winter, the Romans, when they came to administer an empire covering the whole Mediterranean basin, had more complex problems. The Carthaginians, like the Greeks, had always called a halt to the season's sailings, and recommenced them only when the fair spring weather set in. The Romans, on the other hand, while still limited by the weather, often had to operate ships in inclement seasons. A revolt might occur in Palestine at a time when Italy itself lay under the heavy hand of winter – but still the legions must sail. Quite apart from material activities, the complex feeding problems that arose as cities grew larger and populations increased meant that the merchant ships must also be able to operate at times which would have been unthinkable in earlier centuries.

It is a curious fact that the Romans exercised sea power almost despite themselves. They had little or no natural affinity to the sea, and there are few instances in Latin literature which describe the sea in anything but unsympathetic terms. It is true that, even in Homer, the Greeks also tend to describe sea life as something to be avoided if possible, but in Greek literature the sea is real and the descriptions of it carry actuality. These men, one knows, have been across the Ionian or the Aegean; they know what a storm is like; and how welcome it is to find a safe harbour with fresh water near to hand. Homer clearly understands a mariner's requirements: " 'Also it has a safe harbour, in which there is no occasion to tie up at all. You need neither cast the anchor nor make fast with hawsers: all your crew have to do is to beach their boat and wait till the spirit moves them and the right wind blows. Finally, at the head of the harbour there is a stream of fresh water, running out of a cave in a grove of poplar-trees.' "

The Roman view of the sea, as J. H. Thiel points out in his *History of Roman Sea-Power*, is almost exclusively the bather's sea. In Ovid, Vergil, Catullus, and others, the sea is regarded as something that can be enjoyed by the bather or the holiday-maker on the shore. But if one is unwise enough, or forced, for some reason, to embark on a ship, then due libations and sacrifices must be made to Neptune, both before and after the voyage. One of the most tender references to the sea to be found in Latin literature is in a poem attributed to Petronius:

"O shore dearer to me than life! O Sea! How happy am I with leave to come into these lands of mine. How beautiful the day! Here once upon a time I used to swim, disturbing Naiads with my every stroke! And here's the fountain's heart, and there the seaweed waves. This is the haven of my quiet desire."

Professor Thiel observes: "The sea as a sentimental frame, as a sounding-board for the sensations of the lonely human being on the beach is found in the poems of Catullus and others. . . . And yet, however delicately and sensitively these things may have been worded and voiced by many a Roman poet, the fact remains that their effusions are utterances of the observer on the beach, who is lonely perhaps, but at heart feels safe and comfortable, and not of the man who has conquered the sea or rather who, in a continuous fearful struggle, shares his life with her."

The Roman (not unlike the modern Italian) regarded the sea and everything to do with it with some distaste. Yet it was the Roman who first of all imposed upon the whole Mediterranean an organized discipline: ports and harbours, customs' officials, marine insurance, lighterage, harbour dues, wharfage and warehousing rates; in fact, a commercial and bureaucratic network similar to that of the modern marine world.

Gibbon remarked: "To the Romans, the ocean remained an object of terror rather than of curiosity," and it was probably this which caused them to treat it as something to be dominated rather than lived with and loved. It was this attitude, perhaps, which enabled them to impose upon the inland sea an efficient commercial system. The action which had first brought them into Greek waters – their determination to extirpate the pirates of the Adriatic – is evidence of their practical approach towards maritime affairs. In their attitude towards this sea, the Carthaginians were entrepreneur traders, the Greeks cavaliers, but the Romans were peasant farmers, who took to the sea only because of necessity.

Here, from the *Satyricon* of Petronius, is the *nouveau riche* Trimalchio describing how he made his first fortune: "I got a passion for trade. I won't keep you long – I built five ships, put a cargo of wine in – wine was worth its weight in gold at the time – and set off for Rome. You might think I'd fixed the whole thing. Every ship was wrecked; a fact, I'm not romancing. Neptune swallowed up thirty million in one day. But do you think I was downhearted? Heavens, no, I no more kept the taste of the loss in my system than if it had never happened. I built another fleet, bigger, better, with a larger layout. No one could say I didn't have pluck. You know, a big ship has got a big sort of strength about it. I put in another cargo of wine, bacon, beans, perfumes, slaves. And here's where Fortunata [his wife] showed the stuff she's made of. She sold all her jewellery, all her clothes, and put a hundred gold pieces in my hand. That was the leaven that made my fortune rise. When the gods give a push, things happen quick. I turned in a cool ten million from the one trip. Straight-off I bought all the estates that had been my master's. I built a mansion and bought slaves and cattle. Whatever I touched, grew like honeycomb. When I came to have more than all the revenues of the land of my birth, I dropped speculation. Retired from direct trade and went in for financing freedmen. . . . If I could only extend my estates as far as Apulia, I'd have gone far enough for this life."

Petronius, in satirizing the new class of rich freedmen, gives us at the same time a convincing portrait of the type of man who in the days of the empire was at the heart of Roman trade throughout this sea. But what of the sailors themselves? From where did the Romans draw the crews who manned their imperial navies? The answers are largely to be found in the phrase that occurs over and over again in Latin literature, *socii navales*, "naval allies". In contradistinction to Carthage, where the native citizens formed the major part of the crews of the warships while the army was largely mercenary, Roman citizens formed their army while they relied upon foreign allies for the navy. The phrase *socii navales* became so stereotyped that it was commonly used for the crew of any ship, whether referring to oarsmen or sailors. Rhodes and Pergamum, allies of Rome and important naval states, regularly provided a large part of the Roman navy during the later days of the republic as well as during the empire.

As Professor Thiel points out, service in the army, that is, legionary service, was considered "a point of honour for the citizen, naval service on the contrary as a necessary evil. . . ." In Greece and Carthage, on the other hand, naval service had long been regarded as part of the duties of a native-born citizen (although it is true that in Greece it was always better to be a cavalry officer). In Rome, too, the *equites*, or "knights", were the upper-class citizens, for it is axiomatic throughout the ages that what costs money – horses, armour, and private weapons – are marks of distinction that set a man above the generality, who can afford only boots and a sword, or to tug at the loom of an oar. The fact that Rome was based on a farming culture, and on sturdy, independent-minded smallholders, was a prime reason why her civilization regarded service in the army as a natural duty, but the sea as an alien element.

Yet, although the Romans were not seamen by nature, a large part of their mercantile marine was supplied from the homeland. The Greeks, who had been in southern Italy so long before the rise of Rome, helped to make good the complement of Italian ships. So, too, did the natives of Etruria, those other non-Italian people, who had dominated the coastal trade of western Italy before even the Carthaginian fleet came sweeping up the Tyrrhenian Sea.

It was the Greeks, and even such defeated Semitic peoples as the Carthaginians, who very largely helped to man the ships of Rome. To quote Professor Thiel: "Up to the age of Caracalla you will find among the naval personnel . . . no Roman citizens, no Italians, and during the whole imperial age naval service was regarded as inferior to service in the land army, exactly as had been the case in republican times." What is particularly interesting about this is that the two main Roman fleets, one at Misenum, on the Bay of Naples, and the other at Ravenna, on the Adriatic coast, both safeguarding the Roman homeland, were largely foreign-manned. It is difficult to imagine any other great imperial power – Britain, say, in the nineteenth century – having its principal fleets manned by foreigners. Yet such was the case with Rome.

The crewmen themselves fell into two categories (categories which had arisen centuries before in Phoenician and Greek times): sailors and oarsmen. The general term *nautae* (sailors) which occurs constantly in Latin is used so loosely as to cover almost every man aboard a ship, from the humblest deck-hand to the master. On closer investigation, however, it usually means the sailors who worked the sails, the ropes, and the rest of the deck-gear. The steersman, an important figure in any ship, is always given his proper title of *gubernator* – from which the English word "governor" derives.

When on passage between one port and another, the sailors worked a four-part watch system; presumably two parts resting, one part stand-by, and the duty part attending to the sails and providing look-outs. Greek and Roman merchant ships also seem to have regularly towed behind them a *scapha*, or skiff; a large all-purpose boat used for taking mooring-ropes when entering harbour, as well as for transporting passengers and goods. One of the duty watch was always stationed in the skiff, presumably to keep an eye upon the tow. A second class of sailors is sometimes referred to – *mesonautae*, literally "half-sailors". These are always shown as being of lower rank than the true *nautae*. They were probably the equivalent of an "ordinary" seaman as opposed to an able seaman.

The oarsmen were of inferior rank to any upper-deck sailors. In the war galleys, of course, they provided the main motive power. But oarsmen were also carried aboard the large sailing merchantmen that evolved during the Roman Empire. Their function was to man the large skiff whenever the vessel needed a tow; on entering or leaving harbour, for instance, or, in flat calm, to pluck her into an area where there was some wind. Apart from the large skiff, which was towed astern, other smaller skiffs were carried on board. All of these could be used, if necessary, to give the vessel a tow out of harbour, handle lines, pick up pilots, and embark or disembark passengers and gear.

Philostratus, in his life of the philosopher Apollonius of Tyana, gives us a graphic picture of a vessel leaving port. Apollonius was trying to reconcile the inhabitants of Smyrna (who were in the habitual Greek dispute as to how their city should best be run), and used the behaviour of the crew aboard the ship as an illustration of how men should work together in a city. A three-masted vessel was just leaving the harbour, the crew busy about their several tasks, and Apollonius drew the attention of the quarrelling citizens to the spectacle. "Just look at the crew of that ship," he said. "Do you see how some are embarked in the skiffs ready to take her towing ropes? Look, too, how some are hoisting the anchors and securing them inboard, while others are readying the sails to spread them before the wind, and at the same time another lot go about their duties on poop and prow. If a single member of the crew failed to do his own particular task, or did it in an inefficient and unseamanlike manner, all would have a bad passage and they would themselves be their own tempest. But if there is a healthy rivalry between them, and if each one strives to be as efficient as his neighbour, then the ship will make a good landfall, the weather will be good and their navigation serene. . . ."

Cecil Torr and others have enumerated over thirty different types of vessels used in the ancient world, and known under specific names to designate their different functions. Some of these – such as specialized river craft and barges – belong to the history of the land rather than of the sea, but an idea of the complexity of ancient shipping can be gauged by the following brief list.

Barides were almost invariably ships hailing from Egypt; more often than not they were grain ships. The term did not denote size or tonnage, but only that, to the Romans, they were foreign vessels. *Camarae* were small open rowing boats, usually holding about twenty-five men, and used mainly on the Black Sea. *Celoces* were fast cutters originating in Greece; they were used as dispatch boats for communications in a fleet or for taking senior officers from place to place. *Cercuri* (possibly first built in Corcyra) were oared vessels that had enough beam and draught to be used either as merchantmen or as war galleys. *Corbitae* were the great Roman merchant ships which began to dominate the trade lanes of this sea from the first century B.C. onwards. These, above all, were sailing ships, and according to the accounts some of them exceeded one thousand tons. A vessel of this type, which brought the Apostle Paul to Rome in A.D. 60, had 276 passengers and crew aboard. Another is on record as having carried as many as six hundred passengers. The ancestors of these great passenger- and cargo-carriers were the *gauloi* of the Phoenicians. Then there were the *lembi* of the Adriatic pirates, small warships without rams that could carry a number of men and a few horses. *Phaseli* were sailing ships, designed for passenger-carrying. *Speculatoriae*, "spies" or "scouts", were light, fast vessels used like *celoces* as dispatch boats. By the fourth century A.D. they had become a distinct type of their own – somewhat similar in purpose to the frigates of the Napoleonic Wars, and largely used for shadowing the enemy and acting as guards on the flanks of a fleet. Flavius Vegetius, the Roman author of a treatise on warfare written in the fourth century, describes how they were carefully painted so as to be difficult to pick out against the horizon. "Their sails and ropes are dyed blue, the colour of sea-water; and even the wax with which the ships' hulls are painted is similarly coloured, while the soldiers and sailors aboard them likewise dye their clothes." This is possibly the first example of warship camouflage in history. Finally, and somewhat similar to *phaseli*, were *vectoriae*, "carriers". These were passenger ships, although they were sometimes used as troop transports. Julius Caesar refers to them in this connection in his *Gallic Wars*.

The size of some of these ancient ships is surprising, and after the fall of the Roman Empire it would be many centuries before the Mediterranean would again see vessels of such dimensions. One, for instance, launched in the reign of the Emperor Caligula, had a cargo capacity of 1335 tons and transported an Egyptian obelisk to Rome. It is true that ships of this size, and even larger, had been built centuries before. The *Syracosia*, built in the third century B.C. for Hiero II, the ruler of Syracuse, is said to have had a load capacity of over four thousand tons. It sounds improbable, and in any case she proved something of a white elephant. By the second century A.D., however, ships of one thousand tons and over were common all over the Mediterranean, from the ports of Spain to Alexandria and the Levant.

A standard type of merchantman during the period of the Roman

Empire had a load of about 250 tons, and was about 90 feet long overall. Reliefs found at Ostia, Porto, and on the Syrian coast have provided enough information for fairly accurate models to be constructed, while several ancient writers provide details that enable the picture to be filled in. Most of these vessels seemed to have stepped two masts, the main-mast setting a square sail with a triangular topsail above it, while a small forward mast was stepped at an angle of about 45 degrees from the vertical – resembling a heavily raked bowsprit. This small foremast, called the *artemon*, carried a spritsail, or small square sail laced to a head-yard. It was invaluable for manoeuvring and for assisting in the steering of the ship. After the fall of the Roman Empire, the *artemon* entirely disappeared. It did not appear again until the end of the fifteenth century, when it had been transformed into a bowsprit.

The topsail, which had come into use by the first century A.D. (when it was described by Seneca), was an important innovation. It had been observed over the centuries that the higher a sail was carried, the more a ship's sailing efficiency was improved. It had long been the custom to have a hoist on the main-yard by which, under suitable conditions, the mainsail itself could be raised almost to the masthead. But with the introduction of the triangular sail, placed above the main-yard and secured to it at the foot, it was possible to get a large addition of canvas without making the vessel unstable; and without putting too great a strain on the top of the mast. On some large vessels there was also a third mast aft; a small mizzen which set a sail similar to the spritsail on the *artemon*. Not until the fifteenth century were European or Mediter-ranean waters to see again such efficient large cargo-carriers as these which regularly traversed the sea from one great port to another in the heyday of the Roman Empire.

The mainmast was supported by shrouds that were sloped slightly aft. Since the square sail was only efficient with a wind from astern, it necessarily exerted a pressure that pulled the mast forwards. One large fore-stay was considered sufficient to hold the mast upright against the backwards pull of these shrouds. It was a strong and efficient rigging system, but it had one great defect. If the wind switched suddenly (as it often does in thunderstorms) and came from ahead, the fore-stay, large though it was, was often not able to take the pressure of wind on the backed sail. Since the shrouds exerted a pull towards the stern, the fore-stay had only to break and the mast inevitably collapsed on to the poop. Even as early as Homer's *Odyssey*, there is a description of this happening. The fore-stay of Odysseus' vessel snaps and as "the mast fell aft, all the rigging fell into the bilge, and the mast itself, reaching the stern, struck the helmsman on the head and smashed in all the bones of his skull."

The yard that held the mainsail aloft was restrained by ropes which were led aft to the poop. The mainsail itself could be brailed up to the yard by ropes passed through rings on the fore side of the sail, and then led up to tackles on the yard. From the yard itself, these ropes were carried aft to the stern, so that the sail could be swiftly brailed up on the orders of captain or helmsman. When tacking, half the sail was brailed up to the yard, which was then swung round in the required direction. Thus, temporarily, a square sail was transformed into a triangular sail – effective when working to windwards. The tublike hull shapes, however, suggest that even under the most favourable circumstances these Roman merchantmen possessed poor sailing qualities, except with a wind from abaft the beam, and preferably from almost dead astern.

Vergil describes in the *Aeneid* how Aeneas got his fleet under way after a storm: "He ordered all the masts to be swiftly erected, and the yard-arms to be spread with sails. Then together they made fast the sheets [the ropes controlling the sails], and together they eased out their canvas now on the port and now on the starboard side. In unison they moved and moved again the high yard-arms. Perfect and favourable breezes now sent the fleet on its way." Vergil is writing of a voyage that was supposed to have taken place after the Trojan War, but he is, of course, thinking of the handling of ships such as he himself was familiar with in the late first century B.C.

Sails, as they had been for many centuries past, were made of flax and other fibres. The edges of the sails were strengthened with rope (bolt-rope), but in earlier days they had been fastened with hide. Sailors, then as always, had their curious superstitions, and the skins of seals and hyenas were particularly in demand for edging sails, since it was believed that these kept off lightning. The sails of *speculatoriae* were dyed blue to render them less conspicuous; admirals or emperors, on the other hand, would display purple or vermilion as a distinguishing mark. Generally speaking, sails seem to have been left their natural colour, although striped or patchwork coloured sails – somewhat similar in appearance to the spinnakers of modern yachts – were not uncommon.

Decorative devices were applied to the sails. This added to the rich appearance of large vessels, whose stern posts were often curved into swans' necks, and whose poops were ornamented with elaborate carvings. A stone relief found at Porto, near the Tiber's mouth, depicts a merchantman which in decorative elaboration would have rivalled any vessel of Renaissance Europe. Her stem is carved with human figures; Romulus and Remus being suckled by the she-wolf adorn her mainsail; on the masthead there is a figure blowing a musical instrument; behind the helmsman rises a large swan's neck; another figure surmounts the stern post; while the whole of the stern itself is a mass of complicated carving. Only the fact that a large steering oar projects on the starboard side distinguishes this Roman merchantman from one that a seventeenth-century European monarch would have been proud to call his flagship.

The trireme and its successor, the quinquireme, with which the great naval battles of the Punic Wars had been fought, were found after long experience to be less efficient than the earlier bireme. To quote Edward Gibbon, in his *Decline and Fall of the Roman Empire*: "Experience seems at length to have convinced the ancients, that as soon as their galleys exceeded two, or at the most three, ranks of oars, they were suited rather for vain pomp than for real service. . . ." The Liburnians, who inhabited the Adriatic coast of Illyria (modern Yugoslavia), had long been famous for the speed and seaworthiness of their ships, and they built them with only two banks of oars. The Romans profited from their contact with the Liburnians when stamping out piracy in the Adriatic; with their usual perspicacity, they adopted the enemy's design. The term *liburna* soon became standard in the Roman world for a two-banked ship, and in due course it acquired such a casual familiarity that it was applied indiscriminately to almost any type of oared vessel. Although the Romans continued to use some triremes and even quinquiremes in their fleet, it was the bireme which provided the backbone of their navy throughout the centuries of their rule in the Mediterranean.

The poet Lucan, writing in the first century A.D. during the reign of

Nero, describes, in his *Pharsalia*, a shipboard scene which gives some evidence as to the use of stars for navigation. The shipmaster is explaining to a passenger what stars he uses to steer by: "We do not follow any of the errant stars that move in the sky, for they are deceivers of poor sailors. We follow only the never-setting Axis, the brightest star in the twin Bears. It is this that guides the ships. When this rises high above me and stands in the yards, then we are looking towards the Bosphorous and the Black Sea, where it curves round the Scythian shores. But when Arcturus descends from the masthead, and the Lesser Bear gets nearer to the horizon, then the ship is approaching a Syrian port."

Lucan, like most poets, was not a navigator, but the sense of this passage is quite clear. The principal star for navigation is still (as in Homer's day and indeed in the twentieth century) the Pole Star. When the ship is headed north, it will clearly be pointing towards the Pole Star – so this will be seen above the long yard-arm on the mainmast. Conversely, when the ship is going to Syria, the Pole Star will decline "nearer to the horizon". The reference to Arcturus, however, is a poetic blunder, for when heading south for Syria at this period in history, Arcturus would have *risen* rather than descended in relation to the mast. But the main point is that, then as now, the helmsman roughly measured star altitudes relative to his mast and yards. Even in a modern sailing boat, once having established a compass course, it is quite common to note how the Pole Star stands relative to a part of the rigging, and to steer so as to keep it in that position.

The Greek astronomer and geographer Eratosthenes had fixed the value of a degree as early as the second century B.C. Once this knowledge was available, as Gordon Childe remarks in *What Happened in History*, "Angular measurements on the elevation of the Pole Star and on meridian transits gave a much more accurate idea of distances north and south than any calculations from marching or sailing times. By correlating such observations the positions of places could be plotted on a terrestrial sphere divided up, like the sky, into parallels of latitude, numbered 0 to 90 to indicate the angular distance from the Equator. Latitude just means 'width', and so the word reveals how the system started with sailors' observations in crossing the long Mediterranean."

Since the Mediterranean is comparatively narrow from north to south, passages involving calculations of latitude were fairly easy. Calculations of longitude – distances *along* the Mediterranean – were far more difficult. Indeed, not until the invention of an efficient chronometer as late as the eighteenth century were sailors ever quite sure about their longitude. By the second century A.D., Ptolemy, the celebrated mathematician and geographer of Alexandria, had managed to construct a map on a framework of both latitude and longitude, and there can be little doubt that charts of the Mediterranean were in use by sea-captains long before this period.

E. G. R. Taylor comments in *The Haven-Finding Art*: "That no Greek or Latin map or chart has survived of any that may have been drawn more than two thousand years ago is hardly to be wondered at. And since after the destruction of the Roman Empire it was Christian monks who preserved what we now possess of classical literature and learning, it cannot be expected that they would have interested themselves in the technical equipment of sailors, or made copies of their sailing directions."

What we do possess, however, are a few examples of the ancient *Periplus*. These reveal how, once the precise unit of a mile had been established, sailing directions were given in terms of mileage and of the relevant favourable wind. Ancient charts were marked with a wind-rose, in the same way that modern charts carry a compass-rose. But, even without a chart, a seaman can gauge the cardinal points of the compass by the Pole Star at night and by the sun during the day. A basic east and west is provided by the sunrise and sunset, and the ancients discriminated between winter east and west and summer east and west. At noon, in Mediterranean latitudes, the sun is south, so it is never difficult at the peak of the day to calculate roughly the direction in which a vessel is sailing. It is interesting to notice that in an ancient language like Maltese (which probably has some Phoenician roots in it) the word for noon is *nofs-in-nhar*, which is also the word for south.

For measuring distance over the sea, much depended upon the captain's knowledge of his ship. The term "a day's sail" occurs frequently, but this can have no meaning unless the sailing master knows his ship well enough to make distinctions between a slow, medium, or fast day's sail. Such knowledge of a vessel's capabilities, then as now, is quite commonplace, and he would be a poor sailor who could not say of his own boat, "I reckon we are making five knots" and not be right. Although there are no references to it in ancient literature, it seems likely that early seamen used the simple method of recording speed through the water known as the "Dutchman's Log" (a contemptuous English reference presumably dating from the Anglo-Dutch wars). A fixed length is paced out on the upper deck – say, sixty feet – and a piece of wood is thrown over the bows. When the wood passes the first point a sand-glass is inverted, and when it passes the second point a note is taken of the time elapsed. A comparatively accurate calculation of the vessel's speed through the water is thus obtainable. Hour-glasses, minute-glasses, and even quite complicated water-clocks were commonplace in the Roman world.

The log and line for measuring a ship's speed was the first English contribution to navigation, and did not come into use for many centuries, but the mechanical log had been invented in classical times. Vitruvius, author of a work on architecture in the first century B.C., describes how distance could be measured at sea by a device that was not to be met with again until the "impeller log" of the twentieth century. The mechanics of this piece of engineering involved the use of two small paddle-wheels, fitted on either side of the ship. The whole device was probably an Alexandrian invention, since the Alexandrians were foremost in their knowledge of the applications of water power. In theory, as the ship advanced, so these paddle-wheels turned; at the same time, by means of a series of cogs, a stone was dropped into a bronze pan at every four-hundredth revolution of the wheels. There is no indication as to whether these "logs" were fitted in sailing or oared vessels, or both. If in sailing vessels, however, then the reason for having two paddle-wheels is clear enough – if the vessel was at all heeled, one of the wheels would become inoperative. Indeed, even in a vessel propelled by oars, a strong beam wind would be sufficient to render the windwards paddle practically useless. But in a large sailing ship, running before the wind on an even keel – say from Crete to Egypt during the summer months – this mechanical log might have been quite effective. In an oared vessel in the calm Mediterranean summer, there seems little reason to doubt that such a form of recording distance may have worked quite well.

The sailors of the Roman Mediterranean, like the Greeks and

Phoenicians who had preceded them, had, apart from their charts, their limited number of mechanical devices, and their technical knowledge, an intimate acquaintanceship with the areas which they navigated. In many parts of the world to this day, skippers of coastal traders and fishing boats have little or no need of charts. They have acquired by experience (and have been taught by their fathers) the shapes of headlands and the outlines of coasts. They carry their charts in their heads, and no doubt in the past many rhymed mnemonics helped sailors to recognize their landfalls. Modern "literate" man often forgets that those who have never learned how to read and write (a condition of many of these early seamen) possess far more retentive memories than the literate. The visual memory is more highly developed in men who have never had to tax their brains with the printed word, and the senses are also equally sharpened in those who live a simple life close to the elements.

Anyone who has ever lived for some length of time in a small boat knows that, even when asleep, the body recognizes that the wind has changed or the swell in a harbour altered. The sailor will awake at once to an alteration of rhythm that the city-dweller would almost certainly not notice. Similarly, a working knowledge of meteorology is common to many peasants and fishermen to this day – without the use of modern instruments. A Sicilian fisherman known to the Author could "taste" the wind and tell with considerable accuracy whether it was going to change, and from what direction the new wind would come. Similarly, a Maltese peasant farmer gave an accurate long-range forecast of the next three months' weather by observing that a particular sequence of winds had set in with the full moon. All this inherited, man-acquired knowledge of the Mediterranean Sea was available to the shipmasters and navigators of the Roman period. At the same time they had the benefit of a few improved technical devices.

Throughout its history, and particularly during times when there has been no strong naval control of the trade routes, the Mediterranean has always proved a haunt of piracy. The innumerable islands of the Aegean, the long indented coast of Greece and Illyria, the North African coast from lotus-eating Djerba to the Pillars of Hercules, wild Sardinia and Corsica, the Balearic Islands, all these have at one time or another provided havens for renegades who preyed on the shipping routes.

Piracy had long been endemic in the Aegean, and whenever Greece was divided in one of her interminable internecine wars, the lean hulls of the raiders had been active about the islands.

In 67 B.C., driven to desperation by the activities of the pirates, the Senate entrusted the task of "cleaning up" the Mediterranean to Pompey the Great. This remarkable man, whose conflict with Julius Caesar was later to set the Roman world afire, justified his appointment by a series of successful campaigns against the pirates. So bad had the situation become at this time that the corn supplies of Rome were seriously endangered through the constant loss of the great corn ships coming from Egypt; and the cost of provisions in the capital had become exorbitant. In an organized sweep, starting at Gibraltar, Pompey completed the task (which, it had been estimated, would take him three years) in about nine months. Over one thousand vessels are said to have been destroyed in this campaign, several hundred brought back in triumph to Rome, and thousands of the pirates either killed or resettled on generous terms in Asia Minor.

Before the year was out, the price of corn in Rome had stabilized and the life-blood of trade was moving securely throughout the sea. This police action was probably the greatest sea-triumph in the history of Rome. Although at later periods of stress the pirates were to raise their heads again, Pompey had done much to cure a disease that had long been troubling the Mediterranean. The sea was now divided into a number of provinces, each apportioned to a land province, the governor of which was henceforth to be responsible for the maritime security of his area.

During the centuries of the empire, the trade routes became increasingly standardized. Small vessels or "coasters" formed the myriad veins of commerce, but the main arteries are comparatively easy to trace. In the far West, outside the Pillars of Hercules, there was the large port and trading centre of Gades. Inside the Mediterranean, on the east coast of Spain, there was the Carthaginian foundation Carthago Nova. To the north, at the head of the Gulf of Lions, was Narbo (Narbonne), and on the other side of the gulf the ancient Greek foundation Massilia – main port and industrial and communications centre for all France and the North. Moving eastwards the route ran directly to Ostia, the port of Rome, whence another route ran down to re-established Carthage.

From Carthage and from Ostia, two all-important routes ran east to Alexandria, where all the northern and eastern shipping converged. From Alexandria the shipping routes spread out to the Levant and Asia Minor, northwards to the ports of Greece, to Thessalonica, and to increasingly important Byzantium – the recipient via Sinope of all the corn trade and raw materials from the lands around the Black Sea. To Alexandria, too, came the overland caravans, bringing spices and luxuries from Arabia and Mesopotamia, as well as the commerce of India, which was landed at the Red Sea ports of Arsinoë and Berenice.

It can be seen, then, that the commerce of the Mediterranean had two main hearts. If all roads – and all shipping routes – ultimately led to Rome, the world's greatest market, it was the eastern heart of Alexandria which provided the major source of supply. Here were united the raw materials of Asia and the North with the sophisticated and luxury products of the East. With the acquisition of their eastern empire, the interests of Rome became increasingly directed towards the East. The impact of the ancient civilizations, religions, luxuries, and cultures of the eastern world was to have as marked an effect upon the Romans as it had had upon the Macedonians.

EIGHT

Portrait of a City

Lying between the sheltering arms of its eastern and western harbours, the city of Alexandria at the beginning of the first century B.C. was the acknowledged queen of the eastern Mediterranean. Here Euclid had systematized geometry in the time of the first Ptolemy (323–285 B.C.) and founded the Alexandrian mathematical school. It was in reply to Ptolemy's question whether geometry could not be made easier that Euclid had answered: "There is no royal road." It was here, too, that Aristarchus of Samos, mathematician and astronomer, some time between 280–265 B.C., had evolved the theory that the sun, and not the earth, was the centre of the universe – a concept that was to be disregarded (and then lost) for centuries. It was in Alexandria, too, during the same century, that Eratosthenes had successfully measured the circumference of the earth. He had been told that in Assuan on midsummer day the sun shone right to the bottom of a dry well; that is, that it was vertically overhead (indicating that Assuan was on the tropic). He then measured the shadow cast by a vertical pole at Alexandria, also at the summer solstice, and thus found the angle subtended by the distance between the two cities, which corresponded to one-fiftieth of a great circle. From this he calculated the circumference of the earth. Even with such primitive instruments, he made no more than a 10-percent error. A man of extensive learning, Eratosthenes was an example of the type of scholar and scientist who thrived in the culture of Alexandria. He wrote on almost every branch of knowledge – astronomy, geometry, geography, history, philosophy, and grammar. The word "encyclopaedia" (instruction in the whole circle of learning) probably originated in this great Hellenistic city on the Nile Delta.

Alexandria was the Mediterranean city par excellence. Here East and West met and interfused, to produce a unique amalgam. It was a combination of elements, however, that had the disadvantage of often proving unstable. Gibbon's description of Alexandria, in his *Decline and Fall of the Roman Empire*, conveys both sides of the Alexandrian coin: "The beautiful and regular form of that great city, second only to Rome itself, comprehended a circumference of fifteen miles; it was peopled by three hundred thousand free inhabitants, besides at least an equal number of slaves. The lucrative trade of Arabia and India flowed through the port of Alexandria to the capital and provinces of the empire. Idleness was unknown. Some were employed in blowing of glass, others in weaving of linen, others again manufacturing the papyrus. Either sex, and every age, was engaged in the pursuits of industry, nor did even the blind or the lame want occupation. . . . But the people of Alexandria, a various mixture of nations, united the vanity and inconstancy of the Greeks with the superstition and obstinacy of the Egyptians. The most trifling occasion, a transient scarcity of flesh or lentils, the neglect of an accustomed salutation, a mistake of precedency in the public baths, or even a religious dispute, were at any time sufficient to kindle a sedition among that vast multitude, whose resentments were furious and implacable. . . ." The prophecy of the High Priest at Memphis that, wherever Alexander's body lay, the city would be uneasy and disturbed with wars and battles, proved true enough. Alexandria was always a city of schism.

The two great institutions founded by the Ptolemies in Alexandria were the Palace and the Mouseion (from which our word "museum" derives). The Palace of these Greek Pharaohs was surrounded by gardens and was, in the words of Sir William Tarn, most probably "a cluster of juxtaposed halls and living rooms". Standing on the southern promontory of the eastern harbour, remote from the main commercial harbour, it was directly connected with the Mouseion. E. M. Forster comments in *Alexandria*: "It was in this area, among gardens and colonnades, that the culture of Alexandria came into being. The Palace provided the finances and called the tune: the Mouseion responded with imagination or knowledge. . . ." The Ptolemies were nothing if not responsive towards the arts, and their main claim to fame lies in the culture that they encouraged, and the artists, scientists, and others that they helped by their patronage.

The Palace controlled all – and this was the weakness as well as the strength of the Mouseion. The artists, poets, mathematicians, and others in the Mouseion were pensioners of the Palace – and they felt called upon to respond accordingly. To quote E. M. Forster again: "Victory odes, Funeral dirges, Marriage-hymns, genealogical trees, medical prescriptions, mechanical toys, maps, engines of war: whatever the Palace required it had only to inform the Mouseion, and the subsidised staff set to work at once."

Inevitably, such a system tended to produce more second-rate than first-rate work, for the artists and savants felt constrained to operate within the framework that suited their patrons in the Palace. Nevertheless, the products of the Alexandrian school, particularly in the sphere of literary scholarship, made a permanent contribution to Mediterranean culture. In the great library, the librarians classified the literature of Greece, emended manuscripts, and assisted the Ptolemies in their desire to own a copy of every single important work that had ever been written in Greek. It was these librarians, too, who first divided the works of classical literature into definite "books"; the division being determined by the length of a papyrus roll.

As might be expected, the literature that grew up in such an atmosphere of royal patronage was graceful rather than original, epigrammatic rather than epic. It is true that we have one epic poem, *Argonautica*, by Apollonius, but this, as one might expect, while derivative from Homer, possesses none of his robust genius. Love was the dominant theme of the Alexandrian poets, an elegant Eros contained within the silken net of courtly convention. Only one great poet is known to us as having worked in the Mouseion; this was Theocritus, a native of Syracuse. He had spent much of his life in Sicily, and he brought into the cloistered atmosphere of the Mouseion and the overheated air of the Nile Delta something of a Sicilian freshness and a real feeling for the countryside. It was, perhaps, this very fact – for Greeks living in Alexandria often tended to pine for the simplicities of island life – that gave Theocritus such an immediate success. His pastoral poems, celebrating the loves of shepherds and shepherdesses, set a fashion that was to be copied in Europe over and over again, right up to the pastoral masquerades of Versailles. His is, indeed, a Fragonard-and-Watteau kind of world, but it is one through which there blows a genuine Sicilian wind.

His Fifteenth Idyll is unusual in dealing with Alexandria itself. In it can be heard an authentic voice out of the past – an Alexandrian one that until quite recently might have been heard in many a Greek drawing room perched in the suburbs above the uneasy, teeming streets of Egypt.

A lady called Gorgo enters a house and asks: "Is Praxinoe at home?"

Praxinoe. "Oh my dear Gorgo, it's ages since you were here. She *is* at home. The wonder is that you've come even now. (Calls to the maid.) Eunoe, give her a chair and put a cushion on it."

Gorgo. "Oh it does beautifully as it is."

Praxinoe. "Sit down!"

Gorgo. "My nerves are all to bits – Praxinoe, I only just got here alive. . . . What with the crowd, what with the carriages . . . soldiers' boots – soldiers' great-coats, and the street's endless – you really live too far."

Praxinoe. "That's my insane husband. We took this hut – one can't call it a house – at the ends of the earth so that we shouldn't have neighbours. Mere jealousy. As usual."

Gorgo. "But, dear, don't talk about your husband when the little boy's here – he's staring at you. (To the little boy) Sweet pet – that's all right – she isn't talking about papa."

Praxinoe. "Good heavens, the child understands."

Gorgo. "Pretty papa!"

Praxinoe. "The other day, papa – we seem to call every day the other day – the other day he went to get some soda at the Baccal and brought back salt by mistake – the great overgrown lout."

Gorgo. "Mine's exactly the same. . . ."

Another, more typical, Alexandrian poet was Callimachus, who may have become head of the library. He is principally remembered for one poem and for the aphorism "A big book is a bad thing" – an idea echoed centuries later by an American poet, Edgar Allan Poe, who felt that the only true poem was a short one. Callimachus is best remembered by English readers for his poem on hearing of the death of his friend Heraclitus. This was translated by William Cory, and scholars have complained that Cory expands the brevity of the Greek – six lines in all – and infuses it with Victorian sentiment. Yet, like Fitzgerald's translation of the *Rubáiyát* of Omar Khayyám, it will probably live longer than the more accurate versions:

> They told me, Heraclitus, they told me you were dead;
> They brought me bitter news to hear and bitter tears to shed.
> I wept, as I remembered, how often you and I
> Had tired the sun with talking and sent him down the sky.
> And now that thou art lying, my dear old Carian guest,
> A handful of grey ashes, long long ago at rest,
> Still are thy pleasant voices, thy Nightingales, awake,
> For Death, he taketh all away, but them he cannot take.

Unfortunately, the "nightingales" of Heraclitus – the poems which his friend hoped would give him immortality – have long ago been lost. Only this tribute preserves his memory and his name.

But it is in the sciences, particularly in astronomy and mathematics, that the main Alexandrian achievement is to be found, for in science no Ptolemy's feelings of dignity could be offended. Under royal or state patronage, science can flourish – its application being left in the hands of the rulers. The arts, on the other hand, demand a free air in which to breathe, and they are, as often as not, critical of the existing system. (In the twentieth century the rulers of Russia cultivate science, but not the arts.) This accounts for the fact that they were only "decorative" in Alexandria. Philosophy, of course, was also a victim of the Palace/Mouseion relationship. Freedom of thought was not encouraged under the Ptolemies, and it was not until much later that the great "mystical" school of Alexandrian philosophers developed.

As always, these cultural activities could only exist where there was a ground well-nourished by the mundane activities of the trader, manufacturer, and merchant. Alexandria was a rich city under the Ptolemies, and could afford to indulge in the luxuries that are only made possible once the subsistence level has been passed. The city which had inherited the trade of Tyre, and which had become the connecting link between the new Roman Europe and the ancient lands of the East, benefited also from the destruction of Carthage. All the trade that had for centuries been carried in Phoenician or Carthaginian ships, all the warehousing, shipping, and mercantile insurance, became part of the heritage of the Alexandrians. In less than a century it became a city larger than Carthage at its prime; it was rivalled in population and prosperity only by Rome itself. Alexandria was not only a centre of the entrepôt trade but also an important manufacturing city. H. I. Bell writes in *The Cambridge Ancient History*: "Alexandria was a manufacturing as well as a commercial centre, and a large proportion of the export-goods of Egypt must have been produced there. . . . Egypt produced, besides emeralds, several kinds of stone, particularly porphyry and granite, which were valued abroad. . . . The exports of Egypt were indeed greater than the imports, according to Strabo, who remarks that ocular demonstration of the fact might be got from a comparison between the lading of the ships entering and those leaving the port of Alexandria."

One complete monopoly which Egypt, and therefore Alexandria, possessed was the manufacture of papyrus. Cultivated in the Nile Delta, the paper reed, *cyperus papyrus*, was the principal writing material of the ancient world – and without it the poets and the authors and the bureaucrats would have ceased to exist. During the reign of the Emperor Tiberius, the Egyptian papyrus harvest failed and the giant Roman Empire – in administrative and bureaucratic terms – almost ground to a halt. The plant was ubiquitous in its usage, and practically nothing of it was lost. The stem of the papyrus made writing paper and sails, mats, cloth, and cordage; river boats were constructed of it, while Herodotus mentions that the pith was used as a common article of food and that priests' sandals were also made of papyrus. Pliny enumerates the various classes of writing materials that could be made from the plant, and he describes the methods and processes whereby it was converted into the "woven" layers that formed the paper of the ancient world.

Another major Alexandrian product was glass. Egyptian glass-workers had long been famous for the quality of their work, for rich beds of vitreous sand had made the Egyptians among the first people in the world to turn glass-making into a highly developed craft. In the days of the Roman Empire glass from Alexandria was particularly prized. Not all of this glassware was of an artistic quality, and a great deal of it was no more than cheap, mass-produced, commercial glass designed to satisfy the requirements of the vast markets in Rome and the other principal Mediterranean cities.

The city of Alexandria also ranked as one of the major centres for jewels (emeralds, amethysts, topaz, and onyx), and for medicinal drugs and commercial dyes. The textile trade – much of it inherited from ancient Tyre – was a further support of the Alexandrian economy. This was yet another sphere in which the quick-witted Alexandrians had anticipated the mass-production of modern times. The tastes of individual nations were carefully catered for, and, as F. Oertel points out, "Barbarian cloth was specially made for Axum, the Sabaeans, and the natives of the Somaliland coast, while a particular type of ready-made sleeved garment was worked up at Arsinoe (near Suez). . . ." In the high-quality market there were the much-prized Egyptian linens and fabrics, which were woven out of cotton from India and silk from China.

The city which "rose thus so strangely beside the waters, is expressive of what in the ways of a thousand years men had to come to desire. . . ." Hellenistic Alexandria, and later Roman Alexandria, was indeed the unique Janus-faced Mediterranean city, looking both to the East and to the West, which most completely embodied the history of this sea. Rome was always Italian, Athens Greek, and Carthage a North African-Semitic trading emporium. But Alexandria, alone of the many city-foundations of the great conqueror, united East and West and, in the interreaction between them, later inspired some of the most exalted flights of religious thought.

One of the first great "planned" cities of the ancient world, Alexandria was rigidly geometrical. Its main street, the Canopic, running east and west, was crossed by the street of the Soma (Alexander's burial place), while all the other streets ran parallel to one of these two thoroughfares. It had not grown or evolved as had Athens and Rome, but had been laid down by Alexander's architect, Deinocrates, on practically virgin soil. Like New York, it was imposing but somewhat heartless; even the streets were designated by no more than the letters of the Greek alphabet. At the same time, it had a grandeur uncommon to most ancient cities; the great dyke Heptastadion, which connected the island of Pharos with the mainland, was one of its most impressive features. The dyke has subsequently silted up, to become the neck of land which connects the modern city with the area of land now known as Ras-el-Tin (Headland of Figs). It was, above all, a city dedicated to the gods of water. On either side of Heptastadion were the two great harbours, the soft arms of the Mediterranean, while just to the south lay Lake Mareotis. Today the lake is largely silted up and of little importance, but in classical times it was one of the main reasons for Alexandria's existence. Between Lake Mareotis and the Nile a canal had been cut, capable of taking the large cargo-carrying Nile boats. These then proceeded down the Nile itself until, at Memphis, they entered another canal which connected with the Red Sea. Alexandria was not only the finest deep-water harbour on all this long inhospitable coast, it was also in direct communication with the traffic of Arabia, India, and the Far East. A centre not only of Hellenism, but also of Semitism, it was to become the greatest Jewish city in the world.

One of the wonders of the world, the Pharos Lighthouse, stood on the eastern arm of the island. So much has the Pharos become identified with all Mediterranean lighthouses that in French the word for a lighthouse is *phare*, and in Italian *faro*. This masterpiece of engineering was over four hundred feet high (possibly five hundred), and was designed by a Greek architect, Sostratus, during the reign of Ptolemy Philadelphus in the third century b.c. Standing in a colonnaded court, it was four storeys high and contained every known mechanical device for the protection of shipping and the prognostication of the weather. One statue on the top (if we are to believe the Arabs who later conquered the city, but were unable to maintain either it or the Pharos) indicated the passage of the sun. Another turned and pointed in the direction of the wind, another called out the hours of the day, and yet another shouted the alarm if a hostile fleet was sighted. There is nothing improbable in this account, for the Alexandrians were enamoured of mechanical toys, and the scientists of the Mouseion were fully capable of making such ingenious automata.

The crew of the Pharos were housed in the square bottom storey, which is said to have contained three hundred rooms. Hydraulic machinery lifted the wood fuel up to the great beacon at the top. The cupola was supported on eight columns, beneath which there burned a huge fire of resinous wood. From the various, but somewhat confusing, accounts it seems that the light of the fire was intensified and reflected by mirrors, possibly of glass although more probably of polished metal. One account even suggests that the Alexandrians had invented the telescope, for it refers to a man sitting beneath a mysterious glass mirror with the aid of which he is able to see ships out at sea that were invisible to the naked eye. It is conceivable that the mathematicians and skilled glass-workers of Alexandria had indeed discovered the lens, but, if so, all trace of this knowledge was lost when the lantern collapsed not long after the Arab conquest of Alexandria in A.D. 641.

When Cleopatra came to the throne in 51 B.C., she was a young woman of seventeen. Her father, Ptolemy XIII, had died practically bankrupt. He had been driven from Egypt and then restored by the Romans, but for this restoration they had made a hard bargain, and Ptolemy was forced to cripple Egypt with taxation in order to pay his Roman creditors. Egypt, in any case, had long been under Roman influence and, as Rome absorbed all the rest of Alexander's empire in the East, it seemed clearly only a matter of time before Egypt also would become a Roman province. Cleopatra, who was as clever and unscrupulous as she was attractive, undoubtedly hoped that Rome would rend herself to pieces before this annexation could occur. On the far side of the Mediterranean the savage struggle was taking place between Caesar and Pompey for the rulership of the whole Roman world, and it may well have seemed to the watchers on the sidelines that Rome would destroy herself in the process. Cleopatra, as was the custom with the Greek Ptolemies (who had adopted the sacred incest of the Egyptian Pharaohs along with their throne and kingdom), was married to her younger brother Ptolemy XIV, with whom she jointly ruled Egypt. A born intriguer, she conspired against her brother–husband and was banished by him to Syria. It was at this moment that Pompey, vanquished by Caesar, fled to Egypt, hoping for protection from the Ptolemies, whose guardian he was. He was treacherously murdered upon arrival, probably at the instigation of his wards, who cared little for honour or indeed for anything except their own survival. Next arrival upon the Alexandrian scene was Julius Caesar, fresh from his triumphs and master of the world. He was instantly captivated by Cleopatra. In the clash that followed when the Egyptians rose against the Romans, it was Cleopatra who sided with the Romans, and Ptolemy XIV who led the Egyptian national uprising. Defeated by Caesar in a battle near the Canopic mouth of the Nile, Ptolemy was drowned and his army destroyed. Egypt and Cleopatra were Caesar's.

Although Cleopatra now married another younger brother, she soon rid herself of him by poison. Following Caesar to Rome, she lived with him openly as his mistress and bore him a son, Caesarion. To the Romans she was the embodiment of everything that they mistrusted about the sybaritic and immoral East and, after Caesar's murder, Cleopatra was astute enough to remove herself swiftly to Egypt. Whatever her real feelings for Caesar may have been, she did not allow any grief to deter her from pursuing whatever policy best suited Egypt – and, of course, herself. Once more in Alexandria, she watched the next Roman duel take place: the conflict between Mark Antony and the murderers of Caesar. It might have been expected that in such a contest she would automatically side with Antony, but she contented herself with remaining neutral. Alexandrian to the core, the product of three centuries of Hellenistic subtlety and sophistication, one may suspect that she found all Romans gross and boorish; but she had no weapons except her body with which to intrigue them and, if possible, defeat them.

In the division of the Mediterranean world between Octavian (the future Augustus) and Mark Antony, the latter received the whole of the eastern empire. He had already met Cleopatra and had fallen as instant a victim to her charms as had the dead Caesar. During the years in which she, although only his mistress and never his wife (at least by Roman law), was to rule over the eastern empire with her protector, Alexandria became their capital. Cleopatra bore Antony three children, while her son by Julius Caesar was crowned as Ptolemy XVI. There seems no reason to doubt that this period of their lives was both happy and tranquil. In the voluptuous air of Alexandria, Antony, that simple "Son of Mars", began perhaps to lose something of his mental, as well as his muscular, tone. Cleopatra had Antony deified and built a temple to him; it was ornamented with those two famous obelisks, Cleopatra's Needles. The wine of adulation is heady stuff, and Antony was suffering from a surfeit of it when he visited Athens in 39 B.C., where he behaved, according to one commentator, "in a most extravagant manner, assuming the attributes of the god Dionysus".

Octavian, meanwhile, with his cold and logical brain, was preparing for the day when the Roman world should once again be united under one ruler. Antony, seduced by Cleopatra and by the whole atmosphere of the Alexandrian world, disposed of kingdoms and provinces in his

mistress's favour, and thus gradually alienated his supporters in Rome.
Octavian watched and waited. In 32 B.C., when the Senate decided to
deprive Antony of his powers, Octavian declared war upon Cleopatra.
The outcome was the Battle of Actium, on September 2, 31 B.C.
Actium was a promontory in western Greece at the entrance to the
Ambracian Gulf, and it was here that some two hundred galleys supporting Octavian met an equal number of galleys belonging to Antony
and Cleopatra. At the decisive moment of the battle, for reasons which
will never be clearly known, Cleopatra fled with her Egyptian squadron
of sixty ships. Antony's morale, debilitated by enervating years in the
East, collapsed, and he followed his mistress to disgrace and ruin.

Shakespeare puts it in the mouth of Antony's friend Scarus:

> She once being loofed,
> The noble ruin of her magic, Antony,
> Claps on his sea wing, and like a doting mallard,
> Leaving the fight in height, flies after her.
> I never saw an action of such shame.
> Experience, manhood, honour, ne'er before
> Did violate so itself.

Escaped to Egypt and established once more in Alexandria, the two
seem to have made no preparations to ward off the pursuing Octavian.
Instead, they sank back under the drug of love into the sybaritic life of
Alexandria, after concluding a mutual suicide pact should the avenging
Octavian descend upon Egypt. It is said that it was during this period
of their lives that Antony heard the god Hercules, who had hitherto
loved him and protected him, leaving Alexandria to the sound of flutes
and wonderful singing. This incident was to inspire one of the finest
poems of the twentieth-century Alexandrian Greek poet C. P. Cavafy,
"The God Abandons Antony".

When at the hour of midnight
an invisible choir is suddenly heard passing
with exquisite music, with voices –
Do not lament your fortune that at last subsides,
your life's work that has failed, your schemes that have proved illusions.
But like a man prepared, like a brave man,

Fragment of the Parthenon frieze showing the battle
of the Lapiths and Centaurs

The lions of Delos

Greek temple at Segesta

Mount Etna from the air

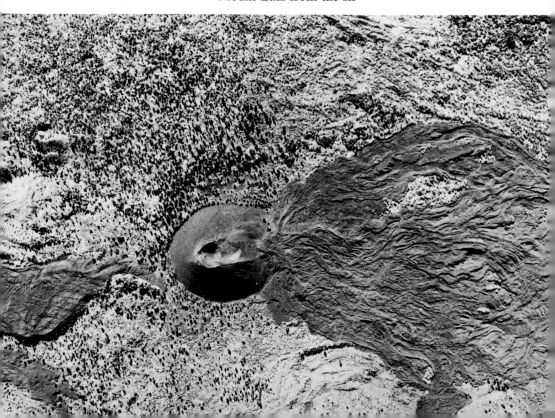

bid farewell to her, to Alexandria who is departing.
Above all, do not delude yourself, do not say that it is a dream,
that your ear was mistaken.
Do not condescend to such empty hopes.
Like a man for long prepared, like a brave man,
like to the man who was worthy of such a city,
go to the window firmly,
and listen with emotion,
but not with the prayers and complaints of the coward
(Ah! supreme rapture!)
listen to the notes, to the exquisite instruments of the mystic choir,
and bid farewell to her, to Alexandria whom you are losing.

Almost a year after his victory at Actium, Octavian arrived in Egypt. It seems likely that he and Cleopatra had already been in correspondence, for whatever love she may have felt for Antony she loved herself and Egypt more. The last of the Macedonian Pharaohs, the last Greek Queen of Egypt, she respected power and success above all things. She had gambled first on Caesar and on becoming Empress of the whole Roman world; after Caesar's death she had fallen back upon Antony, gambling that he in his turn would become master of the Mediterranean. With Antony's eclipse and decline, it would not have been out of character for her to try once again to exercise her intelligence and her physical charms upon the new ruler of the Roman world.

Antony roused himself from his despairing lethargy, but only to make an ineffective resistance to the triumphant Octavian outside the Canopic Gate of Alexandria. His troops deserted in the face of Octavian's battle-hardened legions – and the world was lost for Antony. Under the impression that Cleopatra had honoured their suicide pact, he retreated into the city and fell on his sword.

Even at this late hour Cleopatra felt that she might be able to save something from the ruins. She had enchanted Caesar when she had had herself smuggled into his presence in a carpet. She had bewitched Antony when she had first come to meet him in her gilded barge – perhaps Octavian, too, was susceptible? Hoping to touch his compassion rather than arouse his senses, she had herself carried to his quarters in, as E. M. Forster puts it, "the seductive negligence of grief".

But Octavian was far too cool a customer to feel anything but shocked disapproval of this woman who, to his censorious nature, was nothing more than an adulterous courtesan – the embodiment of everything that he disliked about the languorous East.

Cleopatra realized at last that all was over and that, if she lived, it would be only to walk in Octavian's triumph through Rome, mocked and jeered at by that crowd which had long ago shown its dislike of her. On August 29, 30 B.C., according to tradition by applying an asp to her bosom, Cleopatra committed suicide. She was buried next to Antony in the tomb they had prepared for themselves. Thus ended Royal Alexandria, a unique Greek creation from the moment of its foundation by the great conqueror to its final loss by the queen who, whatever her morals, in her fearlessness and ambition was not unworthy of Alexander himself.

Octavian was now, in his own words, "master of all things". A prefect from the imperial household was put in charge of Alexandria. Egypt joined all the many other ancient kingdoms in becoming a province of Rome. Yet as a provincial capital, as a seaport and trading centre, and as a major granary of Rome, Alexandria quickly recovered its importance. Its population (not counting an immense number of slaves) was estimated as 300,000 during the Augustan Age, and it remained the second greatest city in the Mediterranean. Its principal achievements were now to come in philosophy and religion. In A.D. 45, Christianity was introduced into Alexandria, possibly by Saint Mark. The sea- and desert-bound foundation of Alexander, the city where Mark Antony had been deified and from which the god Hercules had finally departed, was to become one of the fountainheads of Christian doctrine.

NINE

Romans, Jews, and Christians

It was inevitable that the Romans in their eastwards expansion – during the course of which they were absorbing the *disjecta membra* of Alexander's Macedonian Empire – should come into collision with the Jews. A race which stubbornly believed that it alone was chosen of God, and that all other religions were false, was bound to invite persecution. The liberal attitude of the ancient world towards another man's gods – or towards another nation's pantheon – was not shared by this remarkable Semitic people. In the end, as is well enough demonstrated in history, one intolerance always breeds another – and the second will often prove more fearsome than the first.

For a long time the Romans tried to avoid a head-on collision with this small subject nation. But it was not to be. The wars with Rome, so well chronicled by the Jewish historian Josephus, were provoked not only by Jewish intransigence, but also by the venality of a succession of more than usually inefficient Roman governors. The growing disorder of the province of Judaea was not typical in the Roman Empire of this period, and finally the Romans were forced to take action. On May 10, A.D. 70, Titus, son of the Emperor Vespasian, laid siege to the city of Jerusalem itself. The siege was stubborn and protracted. James Parkes writes, in *A History of the Jewish People*, "The Jews had so many secret tunnels and exits through the limestone cliffs on which the city is built that they were constantly able to burn or destroy the machines of the attackers, or bring in food from outside. But finally Titus stood before the walls of the temple itself, and made a last appeal to the defenders to surrender. It was rejected, but, even so, he tried to save the actual shrine from destruction. It was, after all, the most famous building in the eastern half of his father's empire. But his effort was in vain, and on 29 August it caught fire and was gutted. Resistance still went on in pockets throughout the ruins, and it was not until 26 September, after a siege lasting 139 days, that the Roman army possessed the whole city."

The subsequent melancholy history of the Jewish people forms part of the history of the world as much as that of the Mediterranean. Enslaved in their thousands, the Jews were sold off throughout the empire – a deliberate policy to prevent their reunification as a people. But even after this, the Jews of Babylon and those who were still left within the area of their ancient country continued to provoke the Romans by continual unrest, insurrections, and outright revolt. The end came in the reign of the Emperor Hadrian (who had outraged the Jews by proposing to build a shrine to Jupiter on the site of their ancient temple). Bar-Cochba, one of the many Messiahs who arose during this turbulent century, led the Jews in their last desperate resistance to the Roman master. The conflict raged for three years, but Jerusalem fell yet again, in A.D. 135, together with the last Jewish stronghold of Bethar, to the south-west of the city.

The Romans had long come to the conclusion that the total destruction of the enemy was the only solution. The name of Jerusalem was erased from the Latin language, and the city, suffering the same fate as Carthage, was wiped off the face of the earth – to arise again as a new Roman city called Aelia Capitolina. The country of Judaea itself was renamed Palestina, and a second and more or less conclusive dispersion of the Jews took place. Upon the site of the temple – the projected defilement of which had provoked the final uprising – the Romans erected a shrine to Hadrian. Temples were also dedicated to Bacchus, Venus, and the Egyptian Serapis, and the new city of Aelia Capitolina was declared an area into which no Jew might ever enter. As a final indignity, the sign of the victorious Tenth Legion – a boar – was placed over the southern gate of the city.

It is significant that Christians (by this time a numerous sect), who had not sided with the Jews in the recent uprising, were permitted entry to the new city. Since the impact of Christianity upon the Roman world marks an all-important change in the religious climate of the Mediterranean, some account of the origins of their triumph over the old pagan world is necessary. Gibbon, despite his hostility concealed under irony, aptly records some of the reasons why this offshoot of orthodox Judaism succeeded where its parent failed.

"The promise of divine favour, instead of being partially confined to the posterity of Abraham, was universally proposed to the freeman and the slave, to the Greek and to the barbarian, to the Jew and to the Gentile. Every privilege that could raise the proselyte from earth to heaven, that could exalt his devotion, secure his happiness, or even gratify that secret pride, which, under the semblance of devotion, insinuates itself into the human heart, was still reserved for the members of the Christian church; but, at the same time, all mankind was permitted, and even solicited, to accept the glorious distinction, which was not only proffered as a favour, but imposed as an obligation. It became the most sacred duty of a new convert to diffuse among his friends and relations the inestimable blessing which he had received, and to warn them against a refusal that would be severely punished as a criminal disobedience to the will of a benevolent but all-powerful Deity. . . ."

Christianity, in fact, unlike Judaism – and, indeed, unlike the innumerable pagan cults of the ancient world – was a proselytizing religion. Saint Paul in his work and travels had shown the way, and had opened the path to Jew and Gentile alike. His life had proclaimed "Christianity is for all." It was this fact which, above all else, led to its gradual permeation throughout the whole of the Mediterranean world. Christianity spread at the roots. It was for the poor, and for slaves, and for all those for whom life held little prospect or hope.

If the Romans were markedly tolerant in religious matters, why did Christianity suffer so greatly at their hands? The answer is that the Romans granted tolerance provided that the religious group concerned exercised tolerance in its turn. The Christians did not. Whereas the Jews were convinced that their race and the practice of their religion marked them alone as God's chosen people, the Christians were determined to convert all whom they could, to save them from the spiritual death of paganism.

There were others factors, too, as R. H. Barrow, in *The Romans*, points out: "In the first place, Christianity was particularly vulnerable to misinterpretation: secondly, Christians often deliberately invited persecution. To the Roman of the time Christians appeared to hate the human race. They looked forward to the early return of Christ when all but themselves would be destroyed by fire as being evil; and in this disaster to 'Eternal Rome' and to the hopes of mankind they seemed to glory. In the second century and onwards this attitude of mind expressed itself in a different way; Christians went out of their way to provoke enmity that they might win a crown of martyrdom. Christians came from the lower orders of society, and their teachings seemed to aim at special revolution."

The fact that they did not hold their prayer meetings in public inevitably laid them open to charges of curious immoral practices, even of cannibalism. What could a sophisticated Roman make of this passage in Saint John?

"Then Jesus said unto them, Verily, verily, I say unto you, Except ye eat the flesh of the Son of man, and drink his blood, ye have no life in you. Whoso eateth my flesh, and drinketh my blood, hath eternal life; and I will raise him up at the last day."

Iconoclasts, slaves who refused to co-operate in many household duties, citizens who would not serve in the army – what was any civilized Roman to make of such a people? They seemed to him to be a threat to the state, and to everything that Rome stood for. And there can be no doubt that in many ways the early Christian did represent a threat to the state and the Roman way of life. Jesus had said "Render unto Caesar the things that are Caesar's," but his followers would not even render the token homage to Rome and the Emperor which all the other religious sects were quite prepared to do. The Jews, it is worth noting, did render an annual sacrifice on behalf of the Emperor in the temple at Jerusalem.

The breach between Christianity and Judaism was almost complete when Jerusalem fell for the second time. The fact that the Christians had not assisted the Jews in their national struggle against Rome increased the bitterness and the division between them. For some considerable time conversions from Judaism had practically ceased, and Christian efforts at proselytizing had been directed almost entirely towards the Gentile world. While Judaism was preserved by the rabbis, who formed a centre for the conservation of their ancient traditions in a small town called Jamnia, the Jews themselves were dispersed throughout the empire.

One of their main settlements was at Alexandria, where a great centre of religious philosophy sprang up. James Parkes writes, "This Jewish philosophy is inevitably associated with the name of Philo, a contemporary of Jesus of Nazareth. . . . His essential contribution was to set *revelation* beside *reason* as a basis for a system of human thought. He was quite prepared to use allegory and symbolism in his interpretation of the Torah, but he insisted that it was *reasonable* to accept its divine authority, because its content gave a firm foundation to a universal philosophy. It was thus compatible with the deepest understanding which Greek philosophers could offer of the nature of life and of the world we live in."

The Christians of Alexandria profited by Philo's work and built upon his foundation – as did the Moslems at a later date. Alexandria, where the Bible had first been translated into Greek, became one of the great Christian centres, and it was from here that the early Church's influence was disseminated along the sea routes of the Mediterranean. Sailors, because of the hazardous nature of their lives, have always been not only superstitious but also religious-minded men. The early symbol of Christianity, the Fish, must certainly have appealed to them. (It was derived from the Greek letters IXΘΥΣ – meaning "fish" – which embodied the first letters of the Greek words that stood for Jesus Christ, Son of God, Saviour.) There is much, too, in the New Testament that is readily attractive to sailors. The many references to fishing and the sea, the storm on Lake Galilee, Christ walking upon the waters, the miraculous draught of fishes, above all, the fact that Peter was himself a fisherman must have attracted men who knew the hardships of the sea life. Along with the many cargoes, then, that Alexandria dispatched to Rome, it is certain that a large consignment of Christianity was to be found among the crews and the steerage passengers.

It is surprising, perhaps, that it was Christianity which ultimately triumphed over all the other religions of the ancient world, for it was far from being the only Oriental mystery religion. One rival which might well have triumphed, and which showed a remarkable kinship with Christianity, was Mithraism. The cult of the sun god Mithras had originated in Persia and had first been transmitted to the Roman world in the first century B.C. Like Christianity it throve particularly among the poorer classes. It was also extremely popular in the Roman army.

Mithras was conceived of as a youth of divine origin who, by slaying a sacred bull, had first created life upon earth. His worshippers, *sacrati*, passed through seven grades of initiation – somewhat similar to those of

Freemasonry. The third grade, *Miles* (Soldier), was, as it were, the watershed between those who were not fully in communion and those in the higher orders. The mystics in the advanced grades partook communion with bread, water, and wine (symbolic of the sacred bull's blood).

The highest grade, *Pater* (Father), was a title also to be adopted by Christianity for its priests. The *Pater* was a mystic who was responsible for the direction of the cult for the rest of his life. Saint Jerome states in one of his letters that Mithraism, again like Christianity, had its celibate degrees, and that it offered immortality in union with the Godhead in return for pure and noble lives. Certainly the worship of Mithras seems to have demanded of its followers a high moral standard, and the *Miles* was akin in conception to the later "Warrior of Christ". It was this idea of being a soldier in the forces of good against those of evil that undoubtedly endeared it to the Roman legionaries.

The worship of Mithras appealed to the Stoic in the soldier's nature. Disillusioned he might well be with the civilization that he protected, but at the same time he could find in the company of his fellows, and in the virtues of courage and endurance, a way of life that made sense and that was lent hope by the practice of his religion.

Robert Graves, in his poem "The Cuirassiers of the Frontier", has perfectly captured this aspect of the soldier's mood:

"Here is the frontier, here our camp and place –
Beans for the pot, fodder for horses,
And Roman arms. Enough. He who among us
At full gallop, the bowstring to his ear,
Lets drive his heavy arrows, to sink
Stinging through Persian corslets damascened,
Then follows with the lance – he has our love. . . .
We, not the City, are the Empire's soul:
A rotten tree lives only in its rind."

Evidences of the cult of Mithras are found throughout the length and breadth of the Roman Empire – from London in the far North, all over France, Spain, and Italy to Asia Minor and North Africa. Mithras, the soldier's god, travelled with the legions. It was, perhaps, the fact that this religion tended to be somewhat exclusive to the military that prevented its wider dissemination. Civilians of whatever country might well find something to admire in the virtues of the soldiers who protected their frontiers – but admiration is not the same as love. As in later empires, such as the British, the colonized may indeed recognize that the colonizing and protecting power possesses qualities, even a religion, superior to their own. In the long run, however, in order to preserve their self-respect, they are almost certain to reject either the qualities or the religion, or both.

There were other reasons why the cult of Mithras ultimately yielded before Christianity. Mithraism, although it had many of the ingredients of a universal religion, suffered from the weakness that its central figure was a mythical, and not an historical, personage. In common with many of the other mystery religions it inculcated the virtuous life and offered the hope of immortality, but at its core was myth and not fact. Jesus may have become semi-mythological (with accretions like the Virgin Birth, and his physical ascent into Heaven), but at the core there was the historical fact that he had indeed existed. Another weakness of Mithraism was that there was no place in it for women, who seem to have been totally excluded from its rites. Christianity, on the other hand, was suffused with the influence of women: from the Virgin Mary Herself, right through the Gospel story, and throughout the early history of the Church.

A religion that excludes women will never have an attraction for the inhabitants of the Mediterranean world. Too deeply sunk in the core of their natures is the memory of the Mother Goddess. Even the masculine Zeus/Jupiter and the rest of the Greek and Roman pantheon had to allocate a large place to female deities. A further weakness in Mithraism was the fact that it compromised with polytheism. The totally uncompromising nature of Christianity, on the other hand, was a great source of strength. The Roman Emperors, for their part, favoured Mithraism because it was their army's favourite religion. It also upheld (in the Persian style) the divine right of kings and monarchs. Mithraism, however, began to wilt in the contest with Christianity during the late third century A.D. Its death knell was sounded in the fourth century when the Emperor Constantine the Great became Christian. Soon afterwards Christianity became the state religion of the empire.

TEN

Rome and Constantinople – the Pendulum Swings East

Rome, the capital of the ancient world, the heart of the vast Roman Empire, remained to the end of its days an essentially inland city. Seventeen miles north-east of the Tiber's mouth, it turned its back upon the sea. This foundation of Etruscan princes and indigenous peasant farmers was never in the true sense a Mediterranean city as were Naples and Athens, Syracuse and Alexandria. It was the centre of a world power, and that power was a Mediterranean one, but the city itself, with its temples, palaces, aqueducts, baths, amphitheatres, and noble monuments, stood at the heart of what was essentially a land empire. All sailing routes had led to Carthage, but all *roads* led to Rome.

The first two centuries A.D., that "golden age" of the Antonines to which Edward Gibbon looked back with nostalgia, was the period when the armies, the technical skills, and the Greco-Roman culture of Italy Romanized western Europe. At the end of the first century A.D., under the Emperor Trajan, the empire was at its greatest extent. Gibbon's famous opening to *The Decline and Fall of the Roman Empire* evokes something of the mood of the Mediterranean at that time: "In the second century of the Christian era, the empire of Rome comprehended the fairest part of the earth, and the most civilized portion of mankind. The frontiers of that extensive monarchy were guarded by ancient renown and disciplined valour. The gentle but powerful influence of laws and manners, had gradually cemented the union of the provinces. Their peaceful inhabitants enjoyed and abused the advantages of wealth and luxury. The image of a free constitution was preserved with decent reverence: the Roman senate appeared to possess the sovereign author-ity, and devolved on the emperors all the executive powers of government. During a happy period of more than fourscore years, the public administration was conducted by the virtues and abilities of Nerva, Trajan, Hadrian, and the two Antonines."

But even during this period there were ominous symptoms of impending disease in the whole imperial structure. The empire had outgrown its strength, and its real strength lay in the native peoples of Italy. As early as the time of Augustus the birth rate in Italy had been falling. The requirements of empire now meant that more and more soldiers had to be recruited from non-Roman peoples – from the very tribes who had until recently been the enemies of Rome.

"The wastage of almost incessant warfare," writes H. A. L. Fisher, "the practice of infanticide, the growth of luxury and self-indulgence, the inability of science, as then conceived, to cope with the sanitary problems of large towns, were among the causes which contributed to the depletion of the man power in the two leading countries in the Mediterranean [Italy and Greece]." The conditions, in fact, which led to the split between the Roman Empire of the East and that of the West were attributable to a number of causes. But certainly an important one was the enlargement of the frontiers which necessitated a permanent standing army that was far too large to be manned by native Italians.

One result of having armies in different provinces composed of natives of those lands was to introduce a competitive rivalry between the armies themselves. Their devotion was more to their local general than to some Emperor thousands of miles away in the imperial city. Out of this feeling there arose the tragic situation which was to squander the wealth and power of Rome: generals fought generals throughout the Mediterranean lands, and individual armies made and unmade Emperors.

The third century A.D. was a sad contrast to its predecessor. Quite apart from the blood-letting that took place between rival Roman armies, another grave threat to the whole structure made itself increasingly felt. From the middle of the third century onwards the Goths had begun to hang like a dark thundercloud over the northern borders of the empire. This Teutonic people, who seem to have emigrated originally from the eastern borders of Scandinavia, began a lemminglike movement towards the sun, the sea, and the south. The whole of Europe as far south as the lower Danube was constantly ravaged by them, and ultimately the province of Dacia (modern Rumania) had to be abandoned. In A.D. 251, the Emperor Decius was defeated and killed, after driving them back from the Balkans. Within a year of his death, the Goths were raiding the Black Sea area, and about ten years later, in 263, they attacked and sacked Athens, Corinth, and Sparta. The famous temple of Artemis at Ephesus in Asia Minor was burned to the ground, and over all the eastern empire there hung the shadow of dissolution. It was little wonder, then, that as the East became more and more a matter of concern, the centre of gravity of the Roman world began to shift.

Even in view of this increasing preoccupation with the East, the Roman Empire would possibly not have divided as sharply as it did if there had not been trouble also in its western provinces. But in this century it seemed as if the whole of Europe was on the move. The German Alemanni, for instance, were continually invading Roman dominions and on one occasion even thrust right into Italy, nearly reaching the walls of Rome. Meanwhile another German tribe streamed into Spain and sacked Tarragona on the north-east coast of the Iberian peninsula. "It is not to be wondered, therefore," comments R. H. Barrow in *The Romans*, "that separate parts of the Empire took independent steps to save themselves, setting up states and armies of their own and defying the central government." In A.D. 285 Carausius, the Roman commander of the British fleet, proclaimed himself an independent Emperor of Britain. In view of the turbulent and self-destructive situation, the Emperor Diocletian finally reorganized the whole empire into two sections, the western and the eastern.

If the Senate, as in Republican days, had really held the reins of power, then indeed Rome might have remained the focal centre of that power. But, since the executive was entrusted to the Emperor, it followed that wherever he was, there was Rome – or that aspect of Rome which represented everything except the city itself.

The Rome that Juvenal had satirized many years before remained:

> "So farewell Rome, I leave you
> To sanitary engineers and municipal architects, men
> Who by swearing black is white land all the juicy contracts
> Just like that – a new temple, swamp-drainage, harbour-works,

River-clearance, undertaking, the lot – then pocket the cash
And fraudulently file their petition in bankruptcy. . . .
                . . . The waggons thundering past
Through those narrow twisting streets, the oaths of draymen
Caught in a traffic jam – these alone would suffice
To jolt the doziest sea-cow of an Emperor into
Permanent wakefulness. If a business appointment
Summons the tycoon, *he* gets there fast, by litter,
Tacking above the crowd. There's plenty of room inside:
He can read, or take notes, or snooze as he jogs along –
Those drawn blinds are most soporific. . . .
Look around the arcades, try to pick out a woman
Who's worthy of your devotion. Check every tier of seats
At all the theatres in town: will they yield one single
Candidate you could love without a qualm? When pansy
Bathyllus dances Leda, all *fouettés* and *entrechats*,
Just watch the women. One can't control her bladder,
Another suddenly moans in drawn-out ecstasy
As though she was coming. Your country girl's all rapt
Attention, she's learning fast. . . .
Rich ladies send out to hire their own tame Phrygian
Prophet, they skim off the cream of the star-gazers, or
Pick one of those wise old parties who neutralize thunderbolts:
The Circus and the Embankment preside over more
Plebeian destinies. Here, by the dolphin-columns
And the public stands, old whores in their off-shoulder
Dresses and thin gold neck-chains come for advice –
Should they ditch the tavern-keeper? marry the rag-and-bone man?"

This Rome, which Juvenal (who knew it) etched in acid, this Rome which Gibbon (from a safe distance) described as the period and the place where "the condition of the human race was most happy and prosperous", would continue for several centuries. It was not until A.D. 476, that Romulus Augustulus would be deposed by a barbarian king, and the Emperor at Constantinople would be informed that there was no longer a Roman Empire of the West.

But Rome, long before its fall, had ceased to be the heart of Roman power. Even before the division of the empire, the Emperor had been more often east of the Adriatic than in Italy or the western Mediterranean. Constantine, who had himself been born at Naissus (Nish, in modern Yugoslavia), had early in his career thought of removing the imperial capital to his birthplace. But what prompted the ultimate choice of Byzantium and the foundation there of a new capital was that, during the struggle between Constantine and his brother-in-law Licinius for the control of the empire, Licinius had used Byzantium as his main base. Constantine had observed that upon this city, and the control of it, the whole of the eastern empire of Rome pivoted. After the defeat of Licinius, when Constantine assumed the mantle of Emperor of both East and West, he decided that the new Rome should be formed upon the nucleus of Byzantium.

Apart from political and military reasons, Constantine's decision to found a new capital was prompted not only by human pride, but also by religious considerations. He had been converted to Christianity by a conspicuous miracle – the "Vision of the Flaming Cross" – which had appeared to him one day at noon, accompanied by the words "In this sign, conquer." Constantine had conquered, and he had become a Christian. As a token of his new faith he wished to erect a Christian capital for the Roman Empire, whose state religion would be Christianity.

Byzantium had been an ancient Dorian colony, founded about 650 B.C. by Greek traders who had early appreciated its superb position at the southern extremity of the Bosporus. It was sited upon a hilly promontory which ran out from the European side of the strait towards the Asiatic bank. To the south of it lay the Sea of Marmora, while to the north that huge inlet of the Bosporus, the Golden Horn, provided a deep-water harbour nearly seven miles long. Quite apart from its superb harbour facilities, the site was a natural fortress. It was, as Alexander van Millingen describes in the *Encyclopaedia Britannica*, "difficult to approach or to invest, and an almost impregnable refuge in the hour of defeat, within which broken forces might rally to retrieve disaster. To surround it, an enemy required to be strong upon both land and sea. Foes advancing through Asia Minor would have their march arrested, and their blows kept beyond striking distance, by the moat which the waters of the Bosporus, the Sea of Marmora and the

Dardanelles combine to form. The narrow straits in which the water-way connecting the Mediterranean with the Black Sea contracts, both to the north and to the south of the city, could be rendered impassable to hostile fleets approaching from either direction, while on the landward side the line of defence was so short that it could be strongly fortified, and held against large numbers by a comparatively small force. Nature, indeed, cannot relieve men of their duty to be wise and brave, but, in the marvellous configuration of land and sea about Constantinople, nature has done her utmost to enable human skill and courage to establish there the splendid and stable throne of a great empire."

The original Greek colonists had early appreciated the fact that its position meant that whoever held it could dominate the Euxine grain trade. In the ancient world this was one of the main sources of grain, and bread, then as now, was a basic constituent of the Mediterranean diet. There was another geographical factor which played a large part in determining the foundation of a great city at this point. The narrows of the Bosporus formed the main crossing-point between Europe and Asia for the overland caravan routes. The city stood not only at the gate to the Black Sea and the all-important Russian grain trade, but it was also the meeting point of Europe, Asia, and the Far East – ideally situated to become an immense commercial, manufacturing, and trading emporium.

It might seem surprising that, in view of all its natural and geographical advantages, Byzantium had played a comparatively small role in ancient history until Licinius used it as his military base and Constantine decided to make it his capital. But it had – until the threat to the Roman world devolved from North and East – the disadvantages of its northerly situation. Byzantium was outside the mainstream of Mediterranean life. It was this geographical fact that was always to give the city a curious quality, as if it did not really belong to the Mediterranean world at all.

Situated on the latitude of 41 degrees north and the longitude of approximately 29 degrees east, the city suffered from an unenviable climate. In summer there was a lethargic humidity rising from the three seas that hemmed it in, and in winter and spring the northern winds from frozen Russia blasted the city with their icy breath. At hardly any season of the year could the climate be called truly congenial, and Mediterranean man, who enjoys one of the pleasantest climates in the world, was unlikely to choose Byzantium as a place to settle. Sea-captains, grain merchants, traders in furs and skins and Baltic amber, all these might find the northern city congenial for business, but it could hardly be expected that the rich and sophisticated would settle there for preference – even though the Golden Horn and the shores of the Bosporus present in summer some of the most agreeable scenery to be found anywhere. The adjective "Byzantine" (in its later pejorative sense) might well be applied to the city's double-faced weather, which is governed by the north and south winds – neither of which, being humid, are refreshing.

The foundation of the New Rome marked a new era in the history of the Mediterranean. From this moment on the two halves of the Roman Empire moved further and further apart. While the western half ultimately collapsed under the weight of successive Germanic invasions, the eastern half survived into the thirteenth century as the repository of all that Rome had once meant, and as the inheritor of the Greco-Roman culture which had once dominated the whole Mediterranean. In the West, on the other hand, all that was salvaged from the wreck was salvaged by the Church – which inevitably transmuted the flotsam of imperial Rome in its own fashion.

"In November 324," writes N. H. Baynes, in *The Cambridge Ancient History*, "the transformation of Byzantium into the City of Constantine was begun. It has been objected that it is an error to speak of Constantine's foundation as a Christian city: it is true that the pagan temples were not destroyed, that just as Rome had her Tyche – her Fortune – so naturally must the Eastern capital have her Tyche, her presiding spirit: this is traditional form; true also that pagan statues were collected from every side and housed in Constantinople as an adornment for the city, but when all this – and more – is admitted, the fact remains that the essential act in pagan worship was sacrifice, and pagan sacrifice, it is acknowledged, was banished from Constantine's city. That is the crucial fact, and because of that fact Constantinople stood as a *Christian* Rome. From the first its destiny was determined." Constantine, it might be added, was perspicacious enough to realize that to persecute paganism would only be to give it a new vigour. (It had already been proved that persecution had not harmed Christianity, but hardened it to endure.) For himself, he remained tolerant towards pagan practices, and his indulgent scorn probably did more to kill them than anything else could ever have done.

The legend goes that it was Christ Himself who had ordained the circuit of the walls. When the Emperor, spear in hand, was tracing out the lines to be taken by his new capital, a courtier asked him, "How much further, my Lord, do you intend to go?" To which Constantine replied: "Until He tarries who now goes before me." Certainly the area enclosed by the new city walls far exceeded that of the Greek trading port of Byzantium. According to one ancient authority, the line of the landward walls was erected two miles west of the limits of the old town. Even so, within eighty years of its foundation, the city was too small for its growing population, and it had to be yet further enlarged and another defensive wall erected to take in an even larger area of land.

To adorn the new city, the ancient shrines and towns of Greece, which had suffered so severely during the struggle between Pompey and Caesar, were looted once again. To quote Philip Sherrard, in *Constantinople*: "The Artemision at Ephesus; the Athenaion at Lindos in Rhodes; the temple of Zeus at Dodona; Castor and Pollux; the Delphic Apollo; the Muses of Helicon; the Cyzicene Rhea; the Genius of Rome; the four horses of Lysippus (further displaced to the façade of the church of San Marco at Venice where, after an interlude on the Arc de Triomphe, they still survive); the bronze eagle and Calydonian boar; the bronze triple pillar from Delphi on which were written the names of the thirty-one Greek states that took part in the victory at Plataea over the armies of the Persian Xerxes in 479 B.C.: these were some of the sanctuaries and some of the works on which Constantine drew for the decoration of his new capital." Constantine was nothing if not eclectic in his tastes. At the entrance to the imperial palace there was an encaustic painting of the Emperor with his head surmounted by a cross and a serpent (signifying evil) under his feet. On the other hand, in the great forum of the city – called the Forum of Constantine – it did not seem unsuitable to have his statue erected, on top of a huge porphyry pillar, in the guise of Apollo.

Constantinople was founded upon the dual tradition of Rome and

Christ, and this strange blend of West and East – of military power and of ascetic spiritual abnegation – set the seal upon the city from its foundation to its end. The city was adorned not only with the statues of pagan antiquity, but also with innumerable Christian relics which the superstitious faithful had already begun to collect in somewhat improbable numbers. As well as the crosses of the two thieves crucified with Christ, there was the adze with which Noah had hewn the ark and crumbs from the bread with which Christ had fed the five thousand. Not forgotten, however, was the Palladium – that antique image of Pallas Athene which Aeneas was supposed to have taken from Troy to Italy – and which now came back from Rome to this new site not so far removed from its ancient home in Asia Minor.

So Constantinople arose on the banks of the Bosporus, a city – like Alexandria – deliberately planned by a great conqueror to enshrine his fame and to be the centre of government and of military and naval power. Unlike Rome, the new capital was above all a sea city, a vast port, and the harbour for a great fleet. The resources and the abilities of the seafaring Greeks were now to be efficiently harnessed to the imperial Byzantine navy.

One curious fact which the Emperor could not have foreseen was that the New Rome would ultimately be dominated by the Greek language; it would, in fact, become the capital of a Greek, rather than a Latin, empire. *Romaioi*, Romans, the Byzantines would call themselves to the end, but they were largely of Greek blood, and the tongue they spoke was Greek. Rome, on the other hand, which had been bereft of its supremacy partly because of its pagan associations, was, by a supreme irony, finally to emerge as the capital of the Christian world.

ELEVEN

The Navel of the Sea

Islands, even more than cities, sometimes serve as a microcosm of history. The Maltese archipelago situated at the strategic cross-roads of the Mediterranean is a case in point. This small group of islands, consisting of Malta, Gozo, Comino, and two uninhabited islets, has a total area of little more than 120 square miles. But territorial insignificance does not always imply cultural, political, or strategic insignificance – for this is largely determined by geographic position. Delos, in the Aegean, for instance, had no natural resources.

Seventy miles south of Sicily, and almost equidistant between Cyprus at the one end and Gibraltar at the other, the Maltese islands commanded the north–south trading routes between Sicily, Italy, and North Africa, as well as a large part of the east–west routes. They were thus from early times, and throughout a large part of Mediterranean history right up to the twentieth century, to exercise an influence quite out of proportion to their size. Since almost every power that dominated, or attempted to dominate, the Mediterranean made use of Malta's magnificent natural harbours, it follows that the history of Malta in many respects epitomizes the history of this sea.

In A.D. 330, when Constantine was founding his new capital on the banks of the Bosporus, Malta was a prosperous municipality of the Roman Empire. The remains of villas, baths, and artifacts show that this small island and its even smaller sister Gozo were comfortable under the rule of Rome. This had not always been so. In the first century B.C., the notorious Verres, then governor of Sicily and the adjacent islands, had looted all the works of art that he could find in Malta, in particular its famous temples (dating from Greek and Phoenician days), which were a treasure-house of votive offerings from sailors. Later, the islands had been sensibly and carefully administered, and the principal harbour of Malta, Grand Harbour, had become an important depot, mart, and repair centre for merchant ships and war galleys working the area of the central Mediterranean. The value of Malta as a naval base had been established during the Punic Wars, but the islands had played their part in Mediterranean history thousands of years before that particular conflict had – for a few centuries, at least – decided the balance of the inland sea.

The islands were first colonized at some time during the fourth millennium. Until comparatively recently it was believed that man did not reach the archipelago until about 2500 B.C., but recent carbon 14 analyses have established the fact that man was present in the island about 3800 B.C. These first inhabitants most probably crossed from nearby Sicily, either in wooden canoes or hide-covered coracles. Malta and Gozo are so close to Sicily that on a clear bright day, looking from the foothills of southern Sicily, it is possible to see the islands lying out in the sea like pale autumn leaves. The land-hungry settlers who first came across the strait found an area – small though it was – which was fertile, well wooded, and with sufficient water for their needs. The Neolithic men settled in the islands, and seem to have brought with them a fertility cult and a worship of the maternal principle. It is possible that, as with other primitive races, they were completely ignorant of the part played by the male in conception. This may well have led to the emergence of the Mother Goddess, the mysterious female "source of all life", to whom the great Maltese temples were later dedicated.

Some six hundred years later, further immigrants of the more advanced Copper Age civilization arrived in Malta and Gozo. It was during this period of nearly one thousand years (c. 3000–2000 B.C.) that the great temples formed of the island's native limestone began to arise in an almost bewildering profusion considering the small number of people that the islands could have supported in those days. Brian Blouet, in *The Story of Malta*, has estimated that "the islands could have fed a population of approximately 5,000 persons, in the Copper Age, if the greatest part of the available land was brought within the system of cultivation. . . ."

Some have surmised that during this thousand years the Maltese islands may have become a kind of Lourdes of the ancient world, but little evidence exists to show that visitors came to the archipelago from other parts of the Mediterranean during this period. It seems more likely that this small group of people on these fertile islands was able to enjoy the luxuries of a sophisticated architecture and an elaborate religious ritual. Under the benevolent aegis of the Mother Goddess, the islanders developed a peaceful and refined culture of their own. They seem to have been cut off from all the tribal movements taking place in Europe, and there is no evidence to show that they ever made war upon one another.

The great temple culture died out. Shortly before 1800 B.C. the temple builders vanished as if by magic. Their sudden disappearance may have been due to the fact that the population outgrew the natural resources of the islands or was decimated by some disease; or possibly a change of climatic conditions (which may well have occurred after 2500 B.C.) drove them away. The islands, if not left desolate, were at any rate left very sparsely populated, until a further invasion from a Bronze Age people from Sicily reoccupied them. A poorer culture than its predecessor, it lasted, with the addition of later Bronze Age invaders, for a further thousand years.

Carthage was destroyed in 146 B.C. Romulus Augustulus, last Roman Emperor of the West, was deposed by the barbarians in A.D. 476 – a period of little more than six hundred years. The great age of Athens from 478 B.C. had lasted barely fifty years. Time is relative. If the Madonna is substituted for the ancient Mother Goddess, the life of many Maltese peasant farmers is still little different from that of those earlier tillers of the island soil, for whom generation succeeded generation in simple tranquillity.

Malta emerges into history proper with the arrival of the Phoenicians about 1000 B.C. It is possible that the Mycenaeans in their westward voyages had reached the archipelago even before this, for stylistic changes occur in the second millennium B.C. in some of the temple decorations which strongly suggest a Mycenaean influence. But if these earliest of the great Mediterranean seamen did indeed reach Malta, they seem to have left no other evidence of their visits. From about 1000 B.C. onwards, however, there is plenty of evidence of a Phoenician presence. The newcomers seem to have made use of the great southern harbour of Marsaxlokk rather than Grand Harbour. Even if they had berthed their ships and built ashore around Grand Harbour, as they certainly did at a later date, the evidence would now be far down under the accumulated buildings of the centuries. In any case, Marsaxlokk was the first harbour that a sailor would encounter on a voyage northwards from Africa. These early Phoenician seamen most probably did not attempt to colonize the island, but used it in their customary fashion; as a trading post and a haven in which to rest and refit their vessels.

After the foundation of Carthage, the little archipelago on the route between North Africa and Sicily assumed a considerable importance, and a permanent Punic settlement grew up. D. H. Trump, in *Malta's Archaeology*, writes: "Other influences too are visible. Trade brings a few objects from Egypt and Greece, though the islands were never occupied by these people." A terra-cotta sarcophagus confirms the Egyptian influence, while Greek vessels in some of the Phoenician tombs, an attractive Rhodian "bird bowl" of the mid-seventh century, and a Corinthian or Cycladic cup have been found. Malta, in fact, records part of the process that took place all over the Mediterranean from 1000 B.C. onwards. Man the Boatbuilder arrived, and cross-fertilized the cultures of the inland sea. The long isolation of the Maltese archipelago, which had produced in its temples a unique contribution to architecture, was at an end. Like other islands, Malta became involved in Mediterranean history – in the struggles between different groups and nations to dominate the whole of the basin.

The name Malta stems from the Phoenician word *malat*, a harbour, haven, or place of refuge. This it must certainly have seemed to these early navigators, who came across it lonely in the middle of the sea, standing at the cross-roads of the trade routes, on the dividing line between the eastern and western basins. Its sister island Gozo they called "Gaulos". The word in Phoenician meant a "tub" or any round receptacle – hence its application to their round-shaped merchantmen as well as to Gozo, which is almost circular and which, from the sea, does somewhat resemble an inverted tub.

As elsewhere throughout the Mediterranean in the seventh century B.C., hard on the heels of the Phoenicians came their commercial rivals, the Greeks. In Malta, Greeks and Phoenicians seem to have coexisted without strife. At Marsaxlokk, where the Phoenicians had erected a temple to their god Melkarth, two pillars describing its dedication bear inscriptions in both Greek and Phoenician. (It was the discovery of these pillars in the seventeenth century that enabled a French Orientalist to decipher Phoenician writing, that parent of all European alphabets.) The reason why Greeks and Phoenicians do not seem to have clashed in Malta was probably that the island was very much a Carthaginian colony before the Greeks arrived. Punic culture had put down deep roots, and the Greeks were in no position to challenge their rivals' supremacy.

The Greeks, for their part, referred to the island as "Melita", a word derived from the Greek *meli*, honey, for which the island was famous in ancient times. It is probable, however, that this was no more than a corruption of the Phoenician *malat*, which the Greeks associated with the word most similar to it in their own language.

The first reference in Greek literature to this small archipelago may possibly be found in Homer's *Odyssey*. At one point in the hero's wanderings he is shipwrecked on a mysterious island ruled by a goddess called Calypso, whose home is described as "the navel of the sea". This is an extremely apt description of Malta, and indeed could hardly apply to any other place in the Mediterranean. Malta had been for thousands of years the centre of a goddess-worship, and there is no reason to imagine that it had disappeared by the eighth century B.C., when Homer was writing. The hero's seven-year sojourn with the "goddess" is perhaps no more than a reference to a seven-year rule as the "sacred king" to the priestess who represented the goddess. A further clue that Homer may have been referring to Malta is contained in the name of the goddess herself. Calypso in Greek means "hidden" or "hider", and the Homeric words for Calypso's island, *Neesos Kalupsous*, can best be translated into English as the "Island of the Hiding Place". This is, in effect, no more than a Greek translation of the Phoenician name for the island.

If Greeks and Phoenicians managed to coexist in Malta, the same was not to apply to Carthaginians and Romans. During the Punic Wars, when the whole of the central Mediterranean was embattled with Carthaginian and Roman fleets, it was inevitable that the once-peaceful island should become involved in the struggle. The Carthaginians, like other nations in other centuries, used its superb harbours for their fleets and war galleys. During the First Punic War Malta was a Carthaginian naval base, and the Romans, realizing its importance, invaded and captured it. The island seems to have changed hands several times during this first war between the two rival powers. After the peace concluded by Hamilcar in 241 B.C., although Sicily was ceded to Rome, Malta remained a colony of Carthage. The Romans no doubt felt that if they owned the great central island of the Mediterranean they could afford to leave this small archipelago to the defeated. In the Second Punic War, however, they realized their mistake. In 218 B.C., the island's eight hundred years of Phoenician control ended when the consul Sempronius captured Malta and Gozo and brought them under Roman rule.

Phoenician, Greek, and now Roman, the little archipelago reflected the fate of many large cities and states. But the long centuries of Phoenician and Carthaginian influence had left their mark, and the language of the people and their culture showed little change during the next seven centuries of Roman dominion. When they were mounting their great invasion force for the destruction of Carthage in 146 B.C., the Romans used the Maltese harbours. The Maltese inhabitants were treated as allies and at a later date both Malta and Gozo were created municipalities and enjoyed a certain measure of home rule. There seems no reason to doubt that during the Roman period the islands once again enjoyed both peace and prosperity. Malta at that time was still green and fertile. Although during the previous two thousand years there must have been considerable deforestation, with its consequent soil erosion, yet the poet Ovid, writing in the first century B.C., could still describe it as "the fruitful isle of Malta, against which there breaks the wave of the Libyan sea". The loss of its trees (leading to its later barren and desertlike appearance) occurred at some period between the end of Roman rule and the arrival of the Knights of Saint John in the early sixteenth century. So much had it changed during this thousand years that the knights' commissioners, who inspected the island, described it as "no more than a rock of sandstone, the surface of which is barely covered with three or four feet of earth, also very stony, and quite unfit to grow corn or other grain".

In the Maltese islands, remains of the Roman period indicate that the agricultural system was largely based on grain production and olive growing. Malta was also renowned for its famous honey and for its textiles. It is more than likely that the Phoenicians, who were among the foremost clothmakers of the ancient world, had established the industry during the days of their ascendancy. While the ports and harbours continued to flourish during the great trading days of the "Roman Sea", the administrative capital was sited in the centre of the island, on a rocky eminence commanding a view of almost the whole terrain. Here the remains of Christian catacombs serve as a reminder that Malta was one of the first places in this sea to become Christianized.

It was in A.D. 58 that Saint Paul and Saint Luke, on their way to Rome, were shipwrecked in Malta by the tempestuous wind Euro-clydon. This was almost certainly the gregale, the north-east wind which still harasses the islands in winter. The description of the events is given in The Acts of the Apostles, Chapters 27 and 28.

"And when it was day, they knew not the land: but they discovered a certain creek with a shore, into which they were minded, if it were possible, to thrust in the ship. And when they had taken up the anchors, they committed themselves unto the sea, and loosed the rudder bands, and hoisted up the mainsail to the wind, and made toward shore. And falling into a place where two seas met, they ran the ship aground; and the forepart stuck fast, and remained unmoveable, but the hinder part was broken with the violence of the waves. . . . And when they were escaped, then they knew that the island was called Melita. And the barbarous people shewed us no little kindness: for they kindled a fire, and received us every one, because of the present rain, and because of the cold."

The inhabitants of Malta are called by the Greek word *barbaroi* because they spoke neither the Latin nor the Greek of Paul and his fellow passengers. Almost certainly they were still speaking some dialect of Phoenician, acquired during their centuries of Punic colonization. Despite more than two hundred years of Roman occupation, there seems little doubt that the Latin tongue made small headway among the conservative peasant population. Indeed, the Greek historian Diodorus Siculus described Malta and Gozo as "Phoenician colonies" at a time when they had long been part of the Roman Empire.

The traditional site of Saint Paul's shipwreck is an islet off the north-east coast of Malta, at the entrance to the bay which is still called after the Apostle. During the three months that the two saints stayed in the capital of Malta, Paul is credited (among other miracles) with having cured the sick father of Publius, the leading citizen of the island. Undoubtedly, the Gospel was preached to the natives during this period.

Even the tradition that Publius was converted to Christianity, to become the first Bishop of Malta, seems likely. The Maltese islands thus became one of the earliest centres of Christianity in the Roman Mediterranean. It is possible that, even at this early stage, a tinge of Mariolatry – so strong a feature of the island's religious history in later centuries – may have existed. The feminine principle, for thousands of years dominant in these islanders' religion, was unlikely to disappear entirely. The Earth Mother, who in so many parts of the Mediterranean had merely transmuted herself into goddesses under other names, was still capable of other – and equally elaborate – transformations.

At the time when Constantine was founding his new capital in the East, Malta was enjoying a comfortable tranquillity. The archipelago's history had accurately reflected for many centuries the history of this sea. It had been occupied by peoples of a northern European stock in the third millennium, and had subsequently been occupied and re-occupied by the conflicting races of the Mediterranean basin. In the blood of its people there was a mixture of Semitic, Latin, and Greek, as well as other seafaring peoples. Its tongue was Semitic, but its laws and customs were largely Roman, while its religion was Semitic in origin, yet transmuted by Greco-Roman civilization into that blend of philosophy and revealed religion which we know as Christianity. In Malta, as in the whole of the Mediterranean, East and West had interfused to produce that unique creation later to be known as European civilization.

In A.D. 330, as the new Christian capital of the Roman Empire began to arise on the banks of the Bosporus, the Mediterranean world was superficially tranquil. It was united in its laws, on the sea the ships passed "upon their lawful occasions", and one religion was beginning to unite its various races and nations. In many places – in the small Maltese archipelago, for instance – it might have seemed that a reconciliation was being achieved between the material and the spiritual, between eastern mysticism and northern practicality, and between the various bloodstreams of the inland sea. All was to change. The mysterious pendulum of human affairs was about to swing. The conquerors would become the conquered; the conquered the conquerors; and the arts, sciences, languages, and cultures would be once more redistributed. The current that swings eternally around this sea was to commingle all its waters yet again.

BOOK III

"I feel as if the heaven lay close upon the earth and I between the two, breathing through the eye of a needle."

— 'Amr, Arab conqueror of Egypt,
upon his death-bed, A.D. 664

ONE

The Troubled Sea

During the fifth century A.D., Germanic invasions of the countries bordering the Mediterranean attained the dimensions of an immense tidal wave. Outstanding among the many warrior leaders who now began to strip the fabric of empire from Rome was Alaric the Bold. This remarkable Teutonic chieftain struck first at the eastern empire, but, deterred by the seeming impregnability of Constantinople, turned back westwards. Having ravaged all of Greece, he besieged Rome three times, finally capturing and sacking the city in A.D. 410.

Meanwhile a steady pressure of other Teutonic tribes was constantly making itself felt upon the western province of Gaul. The legions were withdrawn from outflanked Britain. Alans and Vandals went south of the Pyrenees into Spain, and Attila and the Huns for a brief period controlled the whole of the area from the Rhine to the Urals. The monarchies of both Rome and Constantinople were for a time little more than puppets, paying their tribute to these primitive but powerful chieftains and their savage fighting men. In the process, many of the invaders became Romanized and even converted to Christianity. Their respect for the superiority of Greco-Roman culture meant that – like so many other races during the long history of the Roman Empire – they often became allies, or federates within what remained of its structure.

H. A. L. Fisher comments: "By this time the Roman world had become so familiar with the German soldier in the legions, the German adventurers at court, and the German immigrant in the fields, that the true drift of the events of the fifth century went unperceived." The "true drift of the events" was that these constant invasions – coupled with the division of the western empire into what no longer amounted to provinces, but to countries occupied by Gothic, Visigothic, and other Nordic tribes – were completely destroying the imperial structure. A century before, when Constantine had founded his New Rome on the Bosporus, the Mediterranean world still had a unity. It was fast disappearing.

Ravenna, which Augustus had made one of the main bases of the Roman fleet, now became the working capital of the West. In A.D. 404 the Emperor Honorius, alarmed by the progress of Alaric in the north of Italy, transferred his court and administration to this city on the sea. Two hundred and fifty ships, it was said, could ride at anchor in its bay, while a branch of the River Po had been diverted through the centre of the city so that small-boat traffic could come right within the shelter of its walls. An aqueduct nearly twenty miles long brought in fresh water, and the city throve on the export of timber from the Alps. The great pine-woods to the east of Ravenna provided good shipbuilding material, for in these late days the last Roman rulers had discovered that it was only at sea, or in a city based upon the sea, that they could maintain any semblance of power or stable government. From 404 to the fall of the western empire in 476, Ravenna was for all practical purposes the capital of the West.

The same canal which poured through the centre of Ravenna was also diverted into innumerable ditches and sub-canals, while vast, water-filled dykes ringed the city about on the landwards side. Communication was almost entirely by boat or by bridge, and the main causeway connecting the city with the hinterland – through an almost impenetrable morass – could itself be destroyed if the northern invaders attempted the town. Nothing quite like fifth-century Ravenna had been seen upon the Mediterranean – or would be seen again until, centuries later, Venice rose in splendour on the waters of the same Adriatic. Even the houses of the western capital were built upon stilts. In its defensibility and choice of situation, it was perhaps the safest Roman city of this period, with the sole exception of Constantinople.

So long as the invaders of the western empire remained landsmen – sword-bearing Teutonic warriors or horse-riding Huns – there was a chance that, around the fringes of the sea, the remains of the Roman Empire could stay in communication. If control of the sea itself could be retained, there was always the possibility that the successive waves of invaders would eventually be absorbed – and Romanized to such an extent that the empire could enjoy a second summer.

In the East, the "God-defended" walls of Constantinople still ensured that the capital remained a real and pervasive power. Even though
the Emperors often had to pay tribute to Teutonic or Mongol invaders,
the fact that their navy controlled the adjacent sea meant that trade
could continue with the lands around the Black Sea and south to the
important granary of Egypt. Ravenna, on the other hand, although in
a good defensive position, was separated by the land-mass of Italy from
the western basin. Its fleet might maintain the security of the Adriatic,
but it was wrongly situated for safeguarding the corn route from Africa
or for protecting the western coast of Italy or Sicily; let alone for
patrolling the long lines of sea-communications to the Balearic Islands
and Spain. In the days of the Augustan empire, this had been the duty
of the western fleet, stationed at Misenum, on the Bay of Naples, and at
Frejus, in Provence. But the western fleet had by now practically ceased
to exist.

It was during the fifth century A.D., a period which had been aptly
termed the "Wandering of the Nations", that the greatest blow fell,
with the arrival in the Mediterranean of the Vandals. Far from being
a seafaring people, they were a race of horsemen, stemming from the
plains of Hungary. In company with two other tribes, the Suevis and
the Alans, they had fought their way into Spain early in the century.
After a period of bloody conflict with the Visigoths, who had preceded
them, the Vandals and their allies made themselves masters of the
Iberian peninsula. By 425 they were in control of nearly all Spain, and
their dominance was complete when Cartagena and Seville fell into
their hands. These were the last two bulwarks of Roman power in
southern Spain; and the whole of this rich and important province was
now lost to the western empire. If the Vandals had been content to
settle, they might ultimately have been absorbed within the structure
of the empire. But in the course of their capture of Cartagena and other
ports they had also acquired a fleet. The horsemen from the plains
turned themselves into sailors.

The Mediterranean coast of Spain which they occupied was served
by ships bringing trade from eastern ports such as Alexandria, and these
merchantmen were seized as they unwittingly ran into harbours occupied by the Vandals. The Vandals then extended the area of their
conquests; they sailed across the Strait of Gibraltar and attacked the

rich Roman province of Mauretania (modern Morocco and western Algeria). With nearly all of Spain for their territory, it might have been thought that they would settle there happily, but these nomadic horsemen were no farmers. Once they had committed themselves to their great onrush into western Europe, they knew no other mode of existence except plunder and loot. Like the Turks in later centuries, theirs was a power based solely upon an ever-extending conquest.

In the year 428, the redoubtable Gaiseric came to the Vandal throne, and a new chapter in the history of the Mediterranean had begun. Gaiseric was one of the most remarkable men to emerge in this turbulent age. He was about twenty-eight when he became King, lame from a fall off a horse, and of small stature. Jordanes, a sixth-century historian who wrote a history of the Gothic nations, does not paint an agreeable picture of this most famous of all Vandals. He was, we learn, "deep in his designs, taciturn, averse to pleasure, subject to transports of fury, greedy of conquest, and cunning in sowing the seeds of discord among nations, and exciting them against each other." He was also ruthless and cruel, a master strategist and tactician. It was he who more than any other changed the face of the western Mediterranean.

Not content with harrying the province of Mauretania, Gaiseric determined to cross over into North Africa and occupy it. Only a year after his accession, in 429, he embarked his people – according to one account about eighty thousand in all – and sailed for Africa. The western Roman fleet, which should have been guarding Mauretania and Numidia (eastern Algeria), had almost ceased to exist. The Moors were in open revolt against the rule of Rome, and the military governor of Africa (modern Tunisia and Libya) was in conflict with the Emperor at Ravenna. It has even been suggested that it was this governor, Bonifacius, who invited the Vandals into North Africa. The story, however, was almost certainly invented later by the court at Ravenna to discredit him, for in fact he did everything he could to save the province. But the initial landing of the Vandals was totally unopposed, and they stormed along the coastline of Mauretania. Spain was already lost to the empire, and Italy's most important source of corn was now being overrun by these locustlike invaders. The following year, 430, as the Vandals swept into Numidia, Bonifacius summoned what troops he could and attempted to oppose them. The result was a sweeping victory for

Gaiseric, and the whole of the open countryside now lay at his mercy.

Only a few of the walled cities, Constantine and Carthage among them, were left in the hands of the Romans and of the imperial government. In one of these cities, Hippo Regius (modern Bône), a port on the North African coastline due south of Sardinia, there was living an aged bishop, Aurelius Augustinus, now known to the world as Saint Augustine. Shortly after the sack of Rome by Alaric the Goth in 410, Augustine had begun work on one of the greatest pieces of Christian writing, De Civitate Dei (The City of God). Shaken by the disaster that had overwhelmed Rome, the city which for centuries had been regarded as the centre of all human authority and which was considered the spiritual capital of the world, Augustine had striven to show that only in the "Eternal City" of God could man find salvation. In 430, twenty years after Rome itself had been sacked, the city of Hippo Regius suffered the same fate as Gaiseric and his Vandals laid siege to it and breached the walls. Saint Augustine died during the siege, praying that God would help his Church, but grant himself a release from the miseries of this mortal life.

The Mediterranean world that was now evolving was to be divided almost as much by religious strife as by barbaric conflict. Gaiseric himself was no pagan. He was an ardent member of the Arian branch of the Christian Church, and the fury with which he persecuted other Christians must be attributed to his fanaticism as well as to his greed for plunder.

The Arian heresy, called after its propagator, Arius (an obscure Alexandrian deacon of the early fourth century), maintained that the Son, Jesus Christ, was not co-equal or co-eternal with the Father, but only the first and highest of all finite beings. At the Council of Nicaea, convoked by the Emperor Constantine in 325, Arianism had been condemned, and the absolute unity and equality of the three persons of the Trinity had been proclaimed as integral to the Christian faith. Nevertheless, the heresy continued to exercise considerable influence in parts of the empire. Alexandria itself, a hotbed of religious sects, was one of the main centres of the heresy. It flourished as an almost "national" brand of religion among the Germanic tribes, and the Vandals were as fanatically anti-Catholic as any Lutherans in later centuries. It is told of Gaiseric that when he was embarking on a piratical expedition, the pilot asked him where he was going. "Against all who have incurred the wrath of God," he replied.

After a brief period, when Gaiseric and his Vandals were accepted as allies by the emperor at Ravenna (and nominally included in the service of what remained of the western empire), the urge to become absolute master of North Africa on his own account drove Gaiseric to attack the last important Roman city on the coast – the ancient foundation of Carthage. In 439, without any resistance, it fell to the Vandal King. The third largest city in the empire, Carthage now became the capital of this implacable enemy of the Romans. For ninety-five years the Vandal kingdom set up by Gaiseric was to disrupt the trade of the Mediterranean and to deprive Italy of a major part of its African corn supply.

Aware that the imperial government at Ravenna would do all that it could to try to expel the invaders from this rich province, Gaiseric immediately fitted out a large fleet at Carthage, wisely regarding attack as the best method of defence. Within a year of his capture of the city, he was in control of the sea-lanes of the central Mediterranean. He landed almost unopposed in Sicily, and once again that unhappy island was the scene of looting and rapine as the Vandals swept almost un-opposed throughout its length and breadth. From now on, it was the Vandal fleet which ruled the western and central Mediterranean, raiding Sardinia and Corsica and cutting off nearly all supplies from the Italian mainland. It was the fleet of the eastern Emperor which finally attempted to set the situation to rights by challenging the Vandal supremacy at sea. But, after an ineffectual appearance off Sicily, the Byzantines had to withdraw because the Persians and the Huns were threatening their eastern and northern borders. From now on, there was no disputing the fact that Gaiseric was master of nearly all the Mediterranean.

The horsemen from the Hungarian plains had indeed turned them-selves into seamen, and had inflicted an incurable wound upon western Rome. There was nothing for the ineffectual Emperor at Ravenna to do but make his peace with the conqueror and endeavour to get as good terms as possible. In 442 Gaiseric was acknowledged the independent ruler of the wealthiest part of North Africa. The Catholic clergy were driven from their churches – as were the bishops of Carthage and Hippo Regius – and Arian priests were installed in their place. The Strait of Gibraltar remained in Vandal hands, and all effective control of the central and western Mediterranean now belonged to the Vandals. Even Alexandria felt itself menaced, and only in the Aegean, where the Byzantine fleet still retained its mastery, was there any relief from a reign of piracy that was to last for nearly one hundred years. The year 445 probably marked the peak of Gaiseric's career. It was then that he landed on the Italian coast near Rome and swept into the city that had once been the undisputed capital of the world. He was met at the gates by the Pope, Leo I, who is said to have persuaded Gaiseric to refrain from fire and slaughter, and only to permit his troops to plunder. To quote Ludwig Schmidt, in *The Cambridge Medieval History*: "The Vandals stayed a fortnight (June 455) in Rome, long enough to take all the treasures which had been left by the Visigoths in the year 410 or restored since. First of all the imperial palace was fallen upon, all that was there was brought to the ships to adorn the royal residence in Carthage, among other things the insignia of imperial dignity. The same fate befell the Temple of Jupiter Capitolinus, of which even half of the gilded roof was taken away. Among the plundered treasure the vessels of Solomon's Temple, formerly brought to Rome by Titus, took a conspicuous place." It might be said that this was the moment when the sad prevision of Scipio Aemilianus, sacker of Carthage, became actuality. Rome was not burned to the ground as Carthage had been, but it was stripped of nearly all its imperial grandeur, and its treasures vanished as if a host of driver-ants had passed through it. Carthage, after some six centuries, finally had its revenge upon Rome.

As a security against reprisals upon his own kingdom, Gaiseric carried off the widowed Roman Empress Eudoxia and her two daughters. These were valuable hostages (he had Eudoxia married to his eldest son), and until his death in 477 Gaiseric was undoubtedly the most important figure upon the Mediterranean scene. He had conclusively proved something that no Mediterranean ruler can ever afford to forget: any kingdom bordering upon this basin is totally insecure unless it has control of the sea. The Mycenaeans, the Phoenicians, the Greeks, the Carthaginians, and the Romans had all, in their turn, found out that only naval supremacy could secure their countries and their trade. It was now the Vandals who gazed out from the prows of their war galleys upon the subjugated sea and knew that all the lands bordering upon it, with the exception of the Byzantine Empire, were theirs to raid and plunder.

Although the name "Vandal" has become synonymous with wanton and savage destruction, there is no reason to affix the opprobrium solely upon this particular people. During this unhappy century Huns, Visigoths, and Goths were equally ruthless as they surged around the Mediterranean basin. "Vandal", in a pejorative sense, owed its origin largely to the fact that the Vandals, being Arian Christians, were always on bad terms with, if not active persecutors of, Catholic Christians – and it is largely from Catholic writers that we have any accounts of this warrior nation. It is true that they seem to have left very little behind them culturally; there are no recognizably "Vandal" churches or works of art or crafts. Some of the jewellery found in Africa and ascribed to Vandal workmanship has a curious crude charm. But a great deal of it was probably plunder from other races, and cannot be safely attributed to these horsemen-sailors.

The kingdom which Gaiseric founded, and which he dated from the day of his capture of Carthage, lasted until 533. In that year, Belisarius, the greatest general of the Byzantine Emperor Justinian, overthrew both the Vandal kingdom in Africa and also the Gothic kingdom which had been established in Italy. Leaving little but their name behind them, the Vandals vanished from the Mediterranean scene. They had done more than any other race to destroy the unity which Rome had once imposed upon the countries bordering upon this sea. But the triumph of Belisarius was not to prove the supreme benefit which it seemed at the time. The Vandals, whatever their faults, had been Christians and had become largely Romanized. The Vandal language, for instance, was used only in popular speech, and all legislation and diplomatic exchanges were conducted in Latin. In the later years of the Vandal kingdom in North Africa there was even a renaissance of Roman poetry and a minor architectural revival. But once the Vandals had been overthrown, all the southern shores of the Mediterranean were left in something akin to a state of vacuum. It was a vacuum that would ultimately be filled by the Arab invasion from the East.

TWO

Byzantium and the Sea

The city that Constantine had founded, and which was to preserve Roman civilization in the East for over a thousand years, was not only protected by its unique defensive situation and its great landward and seaward walls. Byzantine civilization, despite the fact that it was always threatened and usually under attack, was only enabled to survive because the New Rome of Constantinople maintained control of its adjacent sea areas. Gaiseric completely disrupted the pattern of the western Mediterranean and even threatened parts of the eastern basin, but he never posed a serious threat to the city that was situated between the Black Sea and the Aegean. The Byzantine navy, then, played a salient part in the history of the Mediterranean, particularly during that period termed the Dark Ages (largely because of our ignorance of so many of the events), which lasted for some five hundred years.

In the science of navigation itself, the Byzantine contribution seems to have been negligible. E. G. R. Taylor summarizes, in *The Haven-Finding Art*, the reasons why in a theocratic society the mathematical arts failed to develop, remained stagnant, or even languished: "It is not surprising that when education first fell almost entirely into the hands of the clergy, at monastic and cathedral schools, its scope was narrowly restricted to the preparation of boys for office either in the Church or in administration and stewardship. All the mathematics they needed was sufficient arithmetic to keep household and estate accounts, and sufficient astronomy for the computation of the calendar. . . . Even in the Greek Byzantine Empire, where a man like Cosmas Indicopleustes could cite familiarly the great Alexandrine astronomer Ptolemy, the pursuit of science and mathematics was left largely to the Syrians. Great churchmen decried the old pagan learning, but the Syrians had become Nestorian heretics, and perhaps this (and their ancient Phoenician tradition) accounts for the fact that they translated the more important Greek texts into Syriac, and that we owe to one of them the oldest treatise on the astrolabe [possibly the earliest instrument used for taking the altitudes of the planets and the stars]." The Arabs – a people with a mental aptitude for mathematics – overran Syria early in the seventh century and "captured" the Greek knowledge which had lain locked up in that country. It was from the Arabs that the first major progress in the science of navigation was to come. It is doubtful, indeed, whether the Byzantines had as accurate a knowledge of this sea as Roman sea-captains had possessed in the days of the Augustan empire.

In shipbuilding, however, the inhabitants of Constantinople had all the mental resources of their Greek forebears to draw upon, as well as the thickly forested areas of Thrace in northern Greece. The vessels that formed a large proportion of their navy were an adaptation of the classical bireme. The *dromon* ("racer" – the Byzantine generic term for warships) is clearly described in a treatise attributed to the Emperor Leo VI in the ninth century. There is no reason to suppose that there was any important difference between the vessels of his period and those of several hundred years earlier. The *dromon* was a direct descendant of the Roman *liburna* of the first century B.C., which the Romans had themselves adapted from the handy and practical vessels of the Liburnian pirates in the Adriatic.

The Byzantine *dromons*, which so largely secured the city's and the empire's safety, fell into two categories. The larger (which might be termed battleships) carried two hundred to three hundred men, some fifty or more of whom were sailors and soldiers. In battle, it seems that the upper bank of oars was abandoned as soon as the *dromon* closed with the enemy; the oarsmen of this bank transforming themselves into fighting men for the action of boarding. These large *dromons* usually had a hundred oars – fifty a side in two banks, each oar being worked by one man. The smaller *dromons* seem to have had a crew of about one hundred men, and to have approximated in their duties to the modern cruiser or heavy destroyer. Contrary to modern practice, the Byzantine admiral flew his flag aboard one of these small *dromons*. They were more easily manoeuvrable, and, at a time when naval signalling was primitive, it was essential for the admiral to be able to move rapidly from place to place to ensure that his orders were executed.

Dispatch vessels, or scouts, were single-banked and were termed *galea*. With fifty or sixty oarsmen, they were not used in general actions – at least in the early days of the Byzantine navy. At a later period, the term *galea* (the European "galley") was to be applied to all single-banked ships. But by then improved mechanical systems gave a single-banked vessel all the speed and thrusting power of the *dromon* or bireme. In the early galleys of the eastern empire each oar was manned by only one oarsman. In the later galleys, however, the oars were made of different lengths inboard. The oarsmen were now arranged in several lines, each oar requiring several men – sometimes as many as five or six.

The Byzantine war cry "The Cross has conquered!" was one of the only things that distinguished this navy of the fifth and sixth centuries A.D. from the navy of Themistocles a thousand years before. The manoeuvrability of the Byzantine *dromons* (greater than that of earlier triremes and biremes) meant that the ram was retained well into the late Middle Ages. But one immense advantage that the Byzantines had over all who had preceded them was their renowned "Greek Fire".

Liquid fire had been used in warfare for hundreds of years. At the siege of Delium, in 424 B.C., it is recorded by Thucydides that a cauldron containing pitch, sulphur, and burning charcoal was placed against the walls of the city and whipped into flame by a bellows, the blast of the fire being conveyed through a hollow tree trunk. In the next century there occurs a description of a sea battle in which wooden barrels packed with pitch, sulphur, charcoal, and tow were lighted and thrown upon the enemy's decks. In the fourth century A.D. Vegetius, in his treatise on the military arts, gives a number of formulae for Greek Fire in which, in addition to the previous ingredients, he mentions naphtha. Other later formulae add saltpetre and turpentine, as well as resin, sulphur, and tallow.

The true Greek Fire of the Byzantines, however (used not only aboard their ships but also to defend the walls of Constantinople), seems to have been the invention of a Greek Syrian architect, Callinicus, in the seventh century A.D. The important addition that Callinicus made to the previous formulae was to introduce quicklime – which becomes extremely hot when brought into contact with water. There is an early reference to the fire "being driven out by siphons" and there is no doubt – as manuscript illustrations and literary references show –

that the Byzantines projected the fire by means of bellows through metal tubes. In the city of Constantinople itself, these tubes were sited along the seaward walls, looking to the inexperienced eye like drain-pipes for rain water. On one occasion, a Russian fleet under Prince Igor was rash enough to attack the great Marmora sea-walls of the city. The Russian chronicler records that his fleet was put to flight when "liquid fire shot out upon our ships from long tubes placed in the parapets. . . . The Greeks have a fire like lightning from the skies. They cast it against us and burned us so that we could not conquer them."

In the fleet, on the other hand, it seems that two different types of Greek Fire were used. The first was akin to the earlier mixtures, and was either hurled by catapults at the approaching enemy or – in the closing stages of the attack – was thrown by hand, packed into pots which broke and exploded upon impact (the ancestor of the hand grenade). The parent of the modern flame-thrower, however, was the metal pipe in the bows of the Byzantine *dromon*, through which a mixture of quicklime, petroleum, and sulphur was pumped out. The effect of this upon the morale of Russians, Arabs, and others who sought to engage the Byzantine navy was probably almost as great as its physical effect. In later centuries – during the struggle with the Arabs – the security of the whole Byzantine Empire often hinged upon its use.

The exact mixture of this Greek Fire was a closely guarded secret, and the formula which was used in sea warfare was commonly referred to as "wet" or "sea" fire. A fourteenth-century manuscript depicts a Byzantine *dromon* repelling an enemy vessel by shooting fire out of a tube in the bows. It is noticeable that the liquid has ignited at the mouth of the tube before it has touched the sea. Byzantine mech-anics were quite capable of having combined a bellows, which pumped out the mixture, with the hose of a water engine at the breach of the siphon – so that it roared out from the tube already ignited. At a much later date (during the period of the Crusades) a Pisan fleet which had been looting some of the Greek islands was put to flight by a Byzantine admiral whose ships "had at their prow the head of a lion or other land animal, made of brass or iron, with the mouth open, and all gilded so that the very aspect was terrifying. The fire which he directed against the enemy was passed through tubes set in the mouths of these beasts, so that it seemed as if the lions and other monsters were vomiting fire. . . ."

Although different dispositions were made as occasion warranted, the Byzantine navy was mainly based at Constantinople, with subdivisions operating from Asia Minor and the Dodecanese, and a western division from the well-wooded, deep-harboured island of Cephalonia. At various times, of course, depending upon which enemy was threatening the eastern empire, the disposition of the fleet was changed. Crete, when it was being raided by the Arabs, became an important base, while the Aegean island of Samos also became a haven for the fleet after the Seljuk Turks made heavy inroads into Asia Minor in the eleventh century.

The navy was largely manned by Greeks from the coasts of Asia Minor and from the islands of the Aegean. These seamen-fishermen, who had played so large a part in the fleets of ancient Greece and had later been the mainstay of the navy of imperial Rome, were once more in demand. Now, and for many centuries to come, they held together the navies of eastern Rome by their qualities of endurance, self-reliance, and inherited ability. Fifteen hundred years and more after the *Odyssey* had been written, the Greeks still showed that they were the foremost seamen in the Mediterranean. If Constantinople and its empire lasted longer than that of Rome, some of the credit for this must be accorded to the Greek sailor.

THREE

West and East

With the collapse of the western empire, and in face of continuous threats from the East, Constantinople and the lands it controlled had all its energies engaged in the battle for survival. There came a moment, however, in the sixth century A.D., when the two divergent halves of the Roman Empire nearly reunited. This occurred in the reign of the Emperor Justinian, who ascended the throne in 527. He was in his forty-fifth year, a Macedonian peasant by origin, owing his election to the fact that his uncle, the previous Emperor (also from the same part of northern Greece), had died childless.

Justinian, unlike most of the Byzantine rulers, was a "Roman-minded" Emperor. It was said of him that he spoke Greek with a barbarous accent. Certainly his whole temperament was Latin – and his interests were equally inclined towards the West. A man of immense ambition, he deserves an important place in the history of the Mediterranean, not only for what he achieved, but also for what he attempted.

Justinian's desire to restore the western area of the Mediterranean and to bring it and the western Church under the rule of one emperor was understandable enough; it was indeed praiseworthy. However, it would not have been possible but for the fact that, in the year 432, he managed to secure peace at home and peace with the Persians, with whom an inconclusive struggle had been dragging on for some years. Peace at home was never easy in strife-ridden Constantinople, where every variety of Christian dispute was likely to be coupled with every variety of human greed and ambition – the whole seasoned by the confused mixture of races which inhabited the eastern capital. In 532 the city had been almost reduced to the ground in the Nika riots, which initially arose out of the quarrel between the two rival groups at the Hippodrome – the Blues and the Greens. Justinian, his courage reinforced by his eminent general, Belisarius, as well as by his wife, Theodora, had dealt with the situation in a rough-handed way that left the two factions (and the city itself) stunned into fear and silence. Theodora, a Cypriot courtesan by origin but a clever Empress, seems on this occasion to have shown far more courage than her husband, who was at one moment prepared to flee the city.

"I hold," she said, "that now, if ever, flight is inexpedient – even if it brings safety. When a man has once been born into the light it is inevitable that he should also meet death. But for an Emperor to become a fugitive is not a thing to be endured. . . . Royalty makes a fine winding sheet." Emboldened by her words, Justinian acted with a decisive violence that left many thousands dead in the city, but which secured peace in Constantinople for a sufficient number of years for him to engage upon his major projects in the West. In this same year the Persian ruler Chosroes agreed to a truce – thus securing the eastern frontiers of the empire – and Justinian was enabled to focus his attention upon the area which, in his view, most merited it.

There have been many arguments as to the wisdom of this sixth-century Byzantine Emperor in having turned away from the problems that confronted him in Asia and the East to engage in grandiose projects in the ruins of the western empire. The merits and demerits of his policy will long be debated; they are put succinctly by Cyril Mango, writing in *The Dark Ages*: "It is customary to censure Justinian for having dissipated the resources of the Empire for the sake of his own colossal ambition; and for having neglected the real interests of the state, which lay in the East, by embarking on the reconquest of the West, a reconquest that was bound to prove ephemeral. There is no denying that Justinian had a very exalted idea of his own mission; but to censure him in this fashion is to require from him a degree of prescience that no political figure has ever possessed. Actually, when we look into the political situation of the West in the early 6th century, we must grant that Justinian judged it rather shrewdly. In the West all was chaos; and Justinian probably saw what modern historians have come to realise, namely that those Vandals who ruled North Africa, those Ostrogoths who ruled Italy, those Visigoths who ruled Spain, even perhaps the Franks who had conquered Gaul, were simply squatting on the ruins of the Roman civilization. . . ."

To this might well be added that it is easy, with hindsight, to say that Justinian should have concentrated on his eastern frontiers and forgotten about the West, and that he should have realized he could never retain what he reclaimed. But there is no reason to suppose that, in Justinian's lifetime, it did not seem perfectly possible to reintroduce law and order, and even restore the ancient western capital and hold the whole Mediterranean once again under the rule of one monarch. Indeed, the very ease of his first successes against the barbarians must have encouraged Justinian in this belief, for, if the territories were so easy to recover, they should be equally easy to maintain.

Belisarius, under whom so much of the West was recaptured, had already proved his worth in suppressing the Nika riots and in the Persian campaign. Sent to Africa to evict the Vandals, he had achieved complete success by 534, capturing Carthage and transferring the whole area to Byzantine rule. Unfortunately, the Moors and Berbers, who had already tested the Vandals to their utmost capacity, were not so easy to control.

In the long run the whole of North Africa was once again to fall away from the imperial administration. But for the moment there was nothing to deter Justinian from his other projects: clearing Sicily and Italy of their Gothic invaders. Sicily fell to Belisarius and his Byzantine soldiers and cavalry almost without a struggle. Italy was another matter. Although this great general appeared at first to achieve complete success – so much so that within six years of his capture of Carthage he had entered Rome – several years of conflict followed. Byzantine lines of communications were overstrained, and the advent of an exceptionally able Gothic leader, Totila, meant that war once again broke out. In the year 540, however, it looked as if Justinian's dream had come true. Most of Africa had come under Byzantine rule, the south of Spain had even been restored to the empire, and Belisarius and his army were established in Rome. The Byzantine fleet was now in almost complete control of the Mediterranean. For the first time since Gaiseric had stormed into North Africa nearly one hundred years before, it was possible for normal trade to be resumed throughout the whole sea. Even if Justinian's ambitions were in excess of what the empire could afford, it must be admitted by all except the most biased that his was an amazing achievement.

Justinian's two other major contributions to the Mediterranean world were his codification of Roman law, and the building of the great Cathedral of Santa Sophia in Constantinople. This cathedral has provided the inspiration for many other buildings throughout Europe and the East. In Justinian's lifetime, however, it was his rearrangement and simplification of the innumerable laws that had grown up over the centuries which earned him his most deserved fame.

But the immense expenditure for Justinian's western expeditions led to so great an increase in taxation that the Byzantine tax collector became a detested figure throughout the eastern empire. This was particularly the case in the West, where so much of the animosity that arose towards the Emperor and Byzantium was due to the immense burden of taxation now laid upon Sicilians and Italians. The fact that the peoples of these ancient Roman areas did not at a later date fight wholeheartedly with the Byzantines against the Lombards – that last great wave of Teutonic invaders who ultimately subdued most of Italy – may to some extent be blamed on the Byzantine tax-man or, rather, on the Emperor and officials who sent him. As later centuries have shown, an overtaxed people, whose incentive for personal enrichment and advancement has been removed, is likely to become hostile to its government and passive towards foreign encroachment.

The Church of the Holy Wisdom, Santa Sophia, is one of the achievements of Justinian's reign which still stands to delight the eye and the mind, and to serve as a reminder of this Emperor who, even if mistaken in his territorial ambitions, was nevertheless one of the most remarkable men of his time. The church which had formerly stood on this site in Constantinople had been reduced to a heap of ashes during the Nika riots, and Justinian determined, both for his own self-aggrandizement and to set the seal of peace upon the recently strife-torn city, that the new cathedral should surpass all others in Christendom. The Byzantine historian Procopius relates how, "the Emperor then, regardless of expense, pressed on with the building, gathering artisans from everywhere. And Anthemius of Tralles, most skilled in the builder's art not only among the living, but also of those who had been before him, served the Emperor's eagerness. . . . With him was another master-builder, Isidorus, a Milesian. . . ." Santa Sophia was six years in the building and then, "the great door of the new-built temple groaned on its opening hinges, inviting Emperor and people to enter; and when the inner part was seen sorrow fled from the hearts of all, as the sun lit the glories of the temple." Justinian is said to have raised his hands to heaven and cried out: "Glory be to God, who has thought me worthy to finish this work. Solomon, I have outdone thee!"

Justinian died at the age of eighty-three in 565. He had attempted what in fact proved impossible – to reunite the whole Mediterranean world within one framework. If it was an over-ambitious dream, it was at least a noble one. But within a few years of his death, the Byzantines were again at war with Persia. Despite some early Byzantine successes, Persian armies later ravaged the ancient provinces of the empire as far north as Anatolia. Meanwhile a warlike nomadic tribe, the Avars, had swept south to establish themselves in the plains of Hungary, with the result that successive Emperors were compelled to pay them tribute to leave the imperial territories alone.

Justinian's temporary achievements in Italy were nullified when the Lombards, dispossessed from their former territories by the Avars, invaded Italy. By the end of the sixth century they were in possession of over half the peninsula. Backwards and forwards the seesaw swayed – sometimes Persia triumphing in the East, and sometimes the Byzantines regaining great areas like Egypt, Syria, and parts of Asia Minor that had been lost. On more than one occasion the whole fate of Constantinople and the empire rested solely upon the fleet. In 626, the city itself was threatened by a combination of Avars, Slavs, and Bulgars, while a Persian army was in occupation of Chalcedon, just across the Bosporus. Only the marked superiority of the imperial fleet, its better ships, seamanship, and its "secret weapon", Greek Fire, prevented this formidable alliance from destroying once and for all the Roman Empire of the East.

Shortly after the great Persian and Avar attack on the city of Constantinople – one of the most dangerous moments in its long and ever-threatened history – the Emperor Heraclius reversed the tables and secured for some time the eastern frontiers of the empire. Advancing deep into the heart of Persia, he wiped out the Persian army in a battle fought near the ancient capital of Nineveh. In the following year, 628, the Great King of Persia was murdered, the Sassanian Empire collapsed, and Heraclius could justifiably feel that he had restored and secured the

Byzantine Empire to a degree that had not been known since the reign
of Justinian. All the losses of previous years were made good by his
successes. Asia Minor, Egypt, and Syria were all freed from the Persians
and returned to the Byzantine Empire. The liberation of Jerusalem, and
the return to its ancient home of that most precious of all relics, the Holy
Cross, made it seem as if the Christian empire of New Rome had finally
stabilized the whole position in the eastern Mediterranean.

When Heraclius returned to the "God-guarded city" on the Bosporus
to a well-deserved triumph in 629, it did indeed look as if the dream of
Constantine was still attainable. Although all the West had long since
fallen away in ruin and barbarism, here at the far end of the Mediterranean a consolidated eastern Roman Empire still stood in all its power
and glory – defying the Asiatics, the Avars, and the tribesmen of
primitive Russia. When all the lamps were lit in Santa Sophia, the
Cathedral of the Holy Wisdom, and the people had assembled to pay
thanks to God for their Emperor's success on the battlefield, it seemed as
if Paul the Silentiary's poem in praise of the building almost paled before
the actuality: "Thus through the spaces of the great church come rays of
light, expelling clouds of care, and filling the mind with joy. The
sacred light cheers all: even the sailor guiding his bark on the waves,
leaving behind him the unfriendly billows of the raging Pontus, and
winding a sinuous course amidst creeks and rocks, with heart fearful at
the dangers of his nightly wanderings – perhaps he has left the Aegean
and guides his ship against adverse currents in the Hellespont; awaiting
with taut forestay the onslaught of a storm from Africa – does not guide
his laden vessel by the light of Cynosure, or the circling Bear, but by
the divine light of the Church itself. Yet not only does it guide the
merchant at night, like the rays from the Pharos on the coast of Africa,
but it also shows the way to the living God."

The hopes aroused by Heraclius' success and by the triumph of
Byzantine arms in the East were destined to be extinguished. The
power of Persia had finally been broken, and, in the last of all the great
conflicts over the centuries between Persians and Greeks, it was the
Greeks who had won. But a new and even more deadly enemy to
Constantinople, to Roman rule, and to the whole of Christian Europe
was now spurring out of the lonely heartland of the Arabian peninsula.

While the struggle between Persia and the Byzantines had been swaying back and forth during the years between 614 and Heraclius' victory in 627, one of the earth-shaking figures of history had been growing to maturity. Born in Mecca in 570 – five years after the death of Justinian – Mohammed had fled from Mecca in 622 after his dispute with its citizens over their idolatrous practices. This was the year when Heraclius was just setting out on his Persian campaigns. It is better known in history, however, as the year of the Hejira (Arabic *hijrah*, flight), and it marked the beginning of a new era. Later distinguished by the initials A.H. (*Anno Hegirae*), it was a year from which millions throughout the world would henceforth date all events. The challenge to the Christian calendar – "Before Christ" or "In the Year of Our Lord" – was nothing compared to the massive military challenge that now completely changed the face of the countries surrounding the Mediterranean basin.

FOUR

Invasion of the Arabs

Many different circumstances – not least the religion preached by Mohammed – combined to give the Arabic expansion a rocketlike impetus that can hardly have been equalled in history. In a brief fifty years, between 630 and 680, the Arabs occupied a vast area of the earth and transformed the pattern of life in the Middle East, the Levant, and North Africa. In the Levant and the Middle East, the desperate rivalry between Byzantium and Persia had weakened both sides, and, although the issue was finally resolved by a Byzantine victory, the Byzantines were never able to hold their eastern territories against a really efficient and ambitious enemy. In Persia itself, the collapse of the Sassanian power left a dangerous vacuum that was soon to be filled.

At first glance it is difficult to see why the barren and agriculturally unimportant peninsula of Arabia should ever have acquired any import-ance in the world – even if the Arabs had not suddenly swept out of it in their astonishing warlike expansion. Geography, however, as in the case of Delos or the small Maltese archipelago, often compensates for lack of material or mineral riches. Sir John Glubb points out, in *The Great Arab Conquests*, that "then, as now, the influence and importance of Arabia was largely due to its geographical position, separating the Indian Ocean and Southern Asia from the Mediterranean and Europe. The eastern trade was as important to the Byzantine Empire in the sixth and seventh centuries as it is to Western Europe in the twentieth, and this trade could be facilitated or impeded by whatever power exercised influence in Arabia and the Red Sea.

"The secret of the monsoons had been discovered in A.D. 45 by the Greek pilot Hippalus and thereafter an active trade had been maintained between India and the Roman Empire, ships sailing directly from Bombay or even from the coasts of Southern India. . . ."

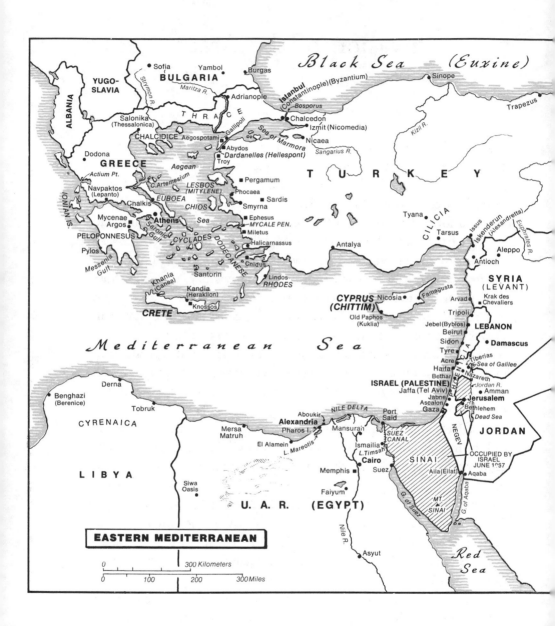

EASTERN MEDITERRANEAN

Black Sea (Euxine)

YUGO-SLAVIA
ALBANIA
BULGARIA
Sofia
Yambol
Burgas
Sinope
Trapezus
Salonika (Thessalonica)
Adrianople
Istanbul Constantinople (Byzantium)
Bosporus
Chalcedon
THRACE
Izmit (Nicomedia)
Maritza R.
Strymon R.
Gallipoli
Sea of Marmora
Nicaea
Sangarius R.
Kizil R.
TURKEY
CHALCIDICE
Aegospotami
Abydos
Dardanelles (Hellespont)
Troy
Dodona
GREECE
Aegean
Pergamum
Sardis
Smyrna
Phocaea
Tyana
CILICIA
Tarsus
Issus
Aleppo
Iskenderun (Alexandretta)
Euphrates R.
C. Artemesium
Actium Pt.
Navpaktos (Lepanto)
LESBOS (MITYLENE)
Chalkis
EUBOEA
CHIOS
IONIAN IS.
Athens
Sea
Ephesus
MYCALE PEN.
Miletus
Mycenae
Argos
PELOPONNESUS
Saronic Gulf
CYCLADES
DODECANESE
Halicarnassus
Antalya
Antioch
SYRIA (LEVANT)
Pylos
Messenia Gulf
Cnidus
Lindos
RHODES
Krak des Chevaliers
Arvad
Tripoli
Khania (Canea)
Santorin
Kandia (Heraklion)
Knossos
CRETE
CYPRUS (CHITTIM)
Nicosia
Famagusta
Old Paphos (Kuklia)
Jebel (Byblos)
Beirut
Sidon
Tyre
LEBANON
Damascus

Mediterranean Sea

Derna
Benghazi (Berenice)
Tobruk
CYRENAICA
Acre
Tiberias
Sea of Galilee
Haifa
Nazareth
Bethar
ISRAEL (PALESTINE)
Jaffa (Tel Aviv)
Jordan R.
Amman
Jerusalem
Jabne
Ascalon
Bethlehem
Gaza
Dead Sea

LIBYA
Mersa Matruh
El Alamein
L. Mareotis
Aboukir
NILE DELTA
Mansurah
Port Said
Alexandria
Pharos I.
SUEZ CANAL
Ismailia
L. Timsah
NEGEV
JORDAN
OCCUPIED BY ISRAEL JUNE 1967
Siwa Oasis
Memphis
Cairo
Suez
SINAI
Aila (Eilat)
Aqaba
U. A. R.   (EGYPT)
Faiyum
G. of Suez
MT. SINAI
G. of Aqaba
Nile R.
Asyut

Red Sea

| 0 | | 300 Kilometers |
| 0 | 100 | 200 | 300 Miles |

Since the waters of the Red Sea were notoriously infested with pirates, as well as navigationally dangerous owing to their numerous offshore reefs, it followed that the bulk of this eastern trade was off-loaded either at Aden or on the Yemen coast. It was then transported overland up the Red Sea coast of Arabia to its main distribution point at Eilath. It was this overland caravan route that gave Arabia its particular importance to the Mediterranean world, for the routes fanned out from Eilath to Egypt and to Syria. Alexandria was the principal port for the inland sea's eastern merchandise. From Damascus the goods went either to Gaza and other ports on the coast or overland to Chalcedon – and thus to Constantinople. In the twentieth century it is the oil routes from Arabia and the Persian Gulf which are salient to the economy of Europe and the Mediterranean, but at this period in history it was the merchandise from India and the East. A hostile power standing astride Arabia could sever nearly all communications with the trade of the Orient.

When Mohammed died in 632, his authority hardly extended beyond the Hejaz (roughly from Eilath in the north to Hali Point on the Red Sea coast, south of Mecca). But the fire that he had lit in the hearts of the desert-men was to burn for decades, and to change not only the religious beliefs of millions but also the whole structure of the southern and eastern Mediterranean. The new faith, Islam (Arabic, "submission" to God), was not entirely revolutionary in itself. It combined elements of Judaism and Christianity, together with features of the old polytheism previously practised in Arabia. At the same time, it made the claim that these conflicting ingredients had been completely changed and purified by their absorption into the Prophet's message. In much the same way that the Christian Church had made use of Greek philosophy and other Oriental mystery religions as well as incorporating certain pagan festivals into its calendar, so the religion proclaimed by the Prophet did not entirely reject what had existed before. It transmuted these beliefs, or claimed to have done so. Where it differed from Christianity and Judaism was in being a religion for warriors. Conceived in the desert, the words that Mohammed claimed had been given him by the Archangel Gabriel were, in their fiery simplicity, acceptable to a society of nomad Bedouins who were still in the tribal stage of development. They understood the exhortations of the Koran: "Fight in the way of Allah against those who fight against you. . . . Kill them wherever you find them and drive them out from where they drove you out. . . . It is incumbent upon you to fight although you may dislike it. And perhaps you dislike a thing and it is good for you, or perhaps you like a thing and it is evil for you. Allah knows, but you know nothing."

At the same time, Islam was not essentially a proselytizing religion. It was not with the aim of making converts that the Arabs swept out of their homeland. Indeed, in the countries they conquered they showed a marked degree of tolerance towards the religious practices of both Jews and Christians. Economic conditions in Arabia, as much as anything else, seem to have driven these hardy horsemen into a series of plundering raids upon the eastern territories of Byzantium. One important thing, however, that the new faith had given them was a unity among themselves. Whereas one tribe had fought another for centuries throughout the desertlands, they were now held together by this ardent new monotheistic religion.

In the latter years of his reign, the successes of the Byzantine Emperor Heraclius against the Persians were totally nullified. In 636 he was defeated by the Arab armies, and Syria was lost to the empire. Mesopotamia fell to the invaders in the following year, and in 639 the Arabs were at the borders of Egypt. Alexandria, that unique creation of the great conqueror which had mirrored the confusions, the theological conflicts, and the finesse of so much Christian thought for close to six hundred years, fell to the Arabic conqueror 'Amr in 642. With the departure of the Byzantines from Egypt, the great city of the Pharos fell into a decline that was to last for a millennium.

There was one important difference between the religion preached by Mohammed and the Christianity that had evolved in cities like Alexandria and Byzantium. The question which had troubled innumerable Christians and had been largely responsible for their division into variant sects was "How can the human be linked to the divine?" It was this problem of how to establish through Christ, and then to a lesser degree through the Saints, this "ladder between Earth and Heaven" that had caused so many of the passionate divisions in the old Christian communities. E. M. Forster points out in *Alexandria*: "It may be argued that this question must be asked by all who have the religious sense, and that there is nothing specifically Alexandrian about it. But no; it need not be asked; it was never asked by Islam, by the faith that swept the city physically and spiritually into the sea. 'There is no God but God, and Mohammed is the Prophet of God,' says Islam, proclaiming the needlessness of a mediator; the man Mohammed has been chosen to tell us what God is like and what he wishes, and there all machinery ends, leaving us to face our Creator."

To this day the Moslem – be he Turk, Algerian, Arab, or Pakistani – needs no mediating priest to intercede for him. He does not even need a mosque in which to celebrate his regard for the Creator; a prayer mat in the desert, or the earth of a hut, or the floor of a tenement in a city is sufficient for his needs. Allah, God of Mohammed, is a god of power and not of love. He may temper his inexorable justice with mercy, but he is not "loving" in the Christian sense. His link with his worshippers is not one of love, but of a required obedience from them. To quote E. M. Forster again: "Islam, strong through its abjuration of Love, was the one system that the city [Alexandria] could not handle. It gave no opening to her manipulations. Her logoi, her emanations and aeons, her various Christs, orthodox, Arian, Monophysite, or Monothelite – it threw them all down as unnecessary lumber that do but distract the true believer from his God."

The religion of the Prophet accepted the harshness of life and never laid any claim that this could be altered – or that a code of conduct based on love would change the inexorable pattern of the world. It was a simpler and more pragmatic religion than Christianity, and in this lay much of its strength. Of its founder, Edward A. Freeman writes, in *The History and Conquests of the Saracens*: "Call him Prophet, Reformer, or Impostor, as we will, the camel-driver of Mecca, the conqueror of Medina, soars above every other man recorded in the history of the East. Nowhere in the history of the world can we directly trace such mighty effects to the personal agency of a single mortal."

A desert people, the Arabs had no natural inclination for the sea. At first, after their conquests of coastal areas and towns, they seem to have regarded the whole environment with invincible suspicion. As 'Amr, conqueror of Alexandria, remarked, when it was suggested that he should build a fleet: "If a ship lies still, it rends the heart; if it moves it terrifies the imagination. Upon it a man's power ever diminishes and calamity increases. Those within it are like worms in a log, and if it rolls over they are drowned." Despite this dislike, this actual hostility to the sea, the Arabs – like the Vandals, that other race of horsemen – were ultimately to take to the sea and to become proficient navigators.

Just as the Romans had used the naval resources and aptitudes of the Greeks to further their imperial expansion, so the Arabs found a race of seamen ready to their hand in Egypt and in Syria. They also acquired a fleet of merchant ships and war galleys, as well as dockyards; and a maritime administrative system that was inherited from the Byzantines and the Romans. Within a comparatively short space of time the naval supremacy of Byzantium was challenged by a formidable Arabic sea power. Using the captured islands of Cyprus and Rhodes as advance bases from which to harass the trade of the Aegean, the Arabs dominated large areas of the sea.

Constantinople was saved on several occasions only by the skill of its fleet and the use of Greek Fire. The disruption of commerce in the eastern Mediterranean, coupled with the loss of the important province of Egypt, meant that the empire was now permanently on the defensive. N. H. Baynes and H. St. L. B. Moss, in *Byzantium*, write, "Under the pressure of invasion the Byzantine Empire took on its medieval, and final, form. The days of New Rome as a great land-power were now over. Apart from Asia Minor and the immediate hinterland of the capital, Byzantine territory was reduced practically to the fringes of the northern Mediterranean coast. During the course of the seventh century her Spanish outposts had been ceded to the Visigoths, and north-west Africa fell at length to the Saracens. Sicily and south Italy, the Magna Graecia of classical times, still owed allegiance to their Greek-speaking rulers; Naples, Venice, and Istria were still in Byzantine hands, and by her hold on the districts of Rome and Ravenna, joined by a narrow corridor, New Rome had succeeded in preventing the complete Lombard conquest of Italy. . . ."

Nevertheless, Constantinople and the Empire were henceforth to be permanently, if not in a state of siege, at any rate dominated by the siege mentality. Invading Slav tribes had succeeded in establishing themselves in the Balkan peninsula, and the Roman and Greek populace was driven to the islets and defensible cities of the Adriatic coast. Thus, between New Rome in the East and Italy, the overland artery of communications had been severed. It was only Byzantine sea power that enabled the two broken halves of the empire to remain in communication. Soon this, too, would be threatened, as the Arabic invaders learned to master the unfamiliar element.

An additional threat to Constantinople arose towards the end of the seventh century when an Asiatic people, the Bulgars, swarmed over the Danube and began to make forays into the area that now bears their name. Menaced, embattled, and constantly under threat (if not under direct attack), Constantinople – despite internal conflict and the reigns of many indifferent Emperors – survived for many centuries. But, in order to survive, the whole administration had to be put on a defensive war footing. The various provinces in Asia Minor, Greece, the islands, Italy, and Sicily, termed *Themes*, were administered by military governors who also combined the duties of the civil executive. The army, constantly needed to maintain the land boundaries of Asia Minor and northern Thrace, was mainly recruited from the sturdy peasantry of Anatolia. The navy, as throughout its long history, was manned by mainland Greeks and the islanders of the Aegean. The loss of Cyprus and Rhodes was a severe blow to the Byzantine fortunes, depriving the capital not only of these two important islands, but also of their experienced seamen. One major result of the gradual severance of the two halves of the empire was that the Latin element in Constantinople gradually declined. New Rome, the foundation of Constantine the Great, became more and more a Greek city. The Greeks, whose culture had "civilized" ancient Rome, were, by an irony of fate, to be the last to maintain the laws and the imperial conceptions of ancient Rome by force of arms in Asia Minor and the Aegean.

It is quite possible that the Byzantine Empire would have collapsed before the Arab invaders if the Moslem world itself had not become split into two deep divisions. In the second half of the seventh century, a dispute arose as to the succession in the leadership of the Mohammedan world. Ultimately to develop into that deep rift (which still exists) between the Shiite and Sunnite sects, this division quickly cleft the thinkers, the politicians, and the peoples into two venomously irreconcilable factions. While Syria and Egypt became predominantly Sunnite, Iraq and Arabia itself were Shiite. It was not until the close of the century, in 692, that the Caliphs of the Umayyad house, whose capital was Damascus, managed to establish their supremacy over the Moslem world and to reunite it. But the civil war between the two factions had given Byzantium a breathing space. When the Moslem world became reintegrated, the power-centre moved eastwards – ultimately to Baghdad – which undoubtedly did much to enable Christian Europe to survive. Had Constantinople been captured, it is extremely likely that Islam would have spread rapidly throughout the Bulgars and the Slavs. The whole pattern of Mediterranean civilization in the north of the sea would then have been irrevocably changed.

The greatest Arab threat to the Mediterranean world occurred early in the eighth century, when the full weight of the Umayyad Empire was hurled at Constantinople. The city and the empire were fortunate in having for once, during these lean and desperate years, an Emperor of a calibre that had not been known in Byzantine history since Heraclius. This was Leo III from Isauria in northern Syria, known as Leo the Isaurian and founder of the dynasty that bears this name. Of Asiatic origin, and alleged to have been a fluent Arabic speaker, Leo had seized the throne of Constantinople from a weak predecessor at one of the gravest moments in the city's history. The Arab leader Maslama with eighty-thousand men had crossed over from Asia Minor and had marched through Thrace to besiege the city. The Arab army encamped beneath the walls, prepared for a lengthy siege. They even brought their grain seed with them and ploughed up the land, prepared if necessary to wait right through a year until next harvest-time. While their army watched and waited, the Arab fleet tried to storm the city walls. They failed to enter the Golden Horn, for the Byzantines had sealed it off with a huge chain strung between the city and the northern banks of Pera. Driven back from the walls by liquid fire spurting from those metal tubes, the Arab fleet was in complete disarray when it was set upon by the Byzantines. At a given moment, the chain securing the entrance to the Horn was lowered. The Greek fleet rowed out at full speed and fell upon the enemy. Once again Greek Fire demoralized the attackers and completed their ruin.

The first battle of this great siege was convincingly won by Leo, by the superior ships of the Byzantines, and by their superior technology. Sir John Glubb, in *The Empire of the Arabs*, writes: "The second was won by General Winter. By a piece of singular ill fortune for the Arabs, the winter of 716–717 was peculiarly severe and deep snow covered their camp for more than three months. . . ." The invaders suffered severely, not least because the destruction of their fleet prevented food and reinforcements reaching them from Syria and Egypt. In the spring, however, their morale revived, and they began a serious investment of the city. But they were still badly hampered by the fact that the Byzantines retained command of the sea, and were thus able to bring in all the stores and reinforcements that they needed. Meanwhile Leo III, by a clever piece of diplomacy, managed to persuade the Bulgars to sweep down from their settlements along the Danube and attack the Arab army from the rear. As well as being compelled to fight on two fronts, the Arabs were now cut off from the countryside upon which they had hoped to forage for their supplies, and their army began to disintegrate.

By 718, the great Arab invasion was over, and Maslama had withdrawn what remained of his troops and returned in dejection to Syria. Byzantium had met the full force of the Arab empire at the moment of its greatest power and expansion – and had emerged victorious. Had the city fallen, there can be no doubt that Arab armies and the Moslem faith would have swept through eastern Europe.

While Byzantium had held the gate in the eastern Mediterranean, and had successfully checked the advance of Arab power throughout that area, all of North Africa was now in Arab hands. The Berbers, hardy warriors as they had proved themselves against Carthaginians, Romans, Vandals, and Byzantines, had ultimately been tamed, and only isolated groups in the mountains held out against the forces of Islam. Spain had long since yielded to the onrush of the warriors from the East. In 718, Moslem forces had broken through the Pyrenees and advanced into France as far as Carcassonne and Narbonne. In 732, the high-water mark of Arab expansion was determined on the battlefield of Poitiers, when the Frankish sovereign, Charles Martel, defeated a great Arab army under Abdul Rahman. It was exactly one century after the death of Mohammed – one of the most astonishing centuries in Mediterranean history, and one which so changed the face of this sea and the lands and cultures surrounding it that it has never been the same since.

Moslem faith and Arabic culture still dominate the whole North African littoral, penetrating far into the hinterland of the continent. The eastern basin and the Levant are still largely marked by the impress of the great Arabic invasions, while the whole art and architecture of Spain have been deeply coloured by the centuries under the Moslems. It was one of the greatest cross-fertilization processes that this sea has ever known. Now that it can be looked at dispassionately, and not just from the standpoint of a threatened Christian world, its benefits can be more justly assessed.

As William Culican writes, in *The Dark Ages*: "The Islamic invasion gave Spain a new importance in the history of Europe. . . . Although Christianity was now on the defensive, Islamic Spain not only tolerated it but contributed largely to the art and culture of Christian Europe. In science, mathematics, medicine and astronomy, Islam had much more to teach than to learn and Muslim craftsmen brought into Europe arts of weaving, metal-founding, inlaying and engraving that had been formerly known only as imports from the Sasanian orient. Spain itself made enormous advances under Muslim rule: the fertility of land was greatly increased, especially in Andalusia, by the methods of irrigation introduced from the Near East. Trade with North Africa, Egypt, and Syria flourished, much of it in the control of Jews, now unfettered of Christian repression and taxation. Wealth and war brought new industries: Toledo produced fine weapons, Cordoba became the centre of silk weaving and leatherwork, and Almeria, long dependent on export of esparto grass, became the centre of glazed-pottery making and one of the wealthiest towns in the Mediterranean."

The peculiar fascination of the seventh and eighth centuries in the history of the Mediterranean arises largely from the fact that two apparently contradictory forces are seen at work. In the north-eastern hemisphere and in the Aegean Sea, the ancient Greco-Roman culture is being preserved against the steady invasions of Persians, Asiatics, Slavs, and the various northern tribes. The religion, the architecture, and the arts of the Byzantines are exercising a great effect upon these barbarians and semi-barbarians who are constantly threatening them. At the same time, in the far West of the sea, it is the culture and religion of the Arabs that is making the greatest impression. Out of the East has come a new leaven to make the whole sea rise again. Knowledge locked away in Syria since Hellenistic days, knowledge from Alexandria, and knowledge from mathematicians and astronomers of Persia and ancient Babylonia has been fired by the gunpowder of the Moslem faith in a trajectory that curves along North Africa – ultimately to burst upon the Spanish peninsula.

The Mediterranean, which had, in a sense, been growing stagnant after the collapse of the western Roman Empire, had been stirred up by a gale from the East. When the storm subsided and the sand-fevered sea put on its blue again, it would be seen that many previously familiar landmarks had gone for ever. Cities and cultures that had withstood the mute erosion of time were transformed by the great Arab invasions.

FIVE

Arabs and Vikings

The Arab conquest of Syria, which resulted in the translation of so many Greek works out of either Syriac or the original Greek, can be seen as the foundation stone of the Arabs' subsequent maritime advances. Mathematics appealed to the Arabic temperament, and it was not long before their aptitude for making mathematical instruments became allied to a passion for astronomy. There seems little doubt that it was the Arabs who first introduced into the Mediterranean the use of the lodestone, or magnetic compass. The credit for the discovery of the compass is still disputed, but it certainly came from the Far East – either India or China being its first home. The Arabs undoubtedly came across its use during their monsoon voyages across the Indian Ocean.

An Arabic manuscript of the late thirteenth century refers to the use of the lodestone. "Sea-captains of Syria, when the night is dark and they cannot see the stars which show them the four cardinal points, take a vessel of water which they shelter from the wind by going below. They take a needle which they thrust into a [piece of] acacia or straw so that it forms a cross. They throw it into the water. The captains then take a lodestone of a size to fill the hand or smaller. They bring it to-wards the surface of the water and make a circular movement from the right with the hand: the needle follows it round. Then they abruptly withdraw it, and the needle turns to stand in the north-south line. This operation I saw myself on a voyage from Tripoli in Syria to Alexandria in 1242–3."

It is appropriate enough that one of the first reports we possess of the use of the magnetic compass should come from a passenger out of Syrian Tripoli – that ancient city and harbour of the great Phoenician navigators. It is clear from a number of early references that the needle was suspended on water in a small piece of stick or straw in the early

primitive compass. Curiously enough, the first written description of
the compass comes in the work of a twelfth-century English monk,
Alexander of Neckam, although England is not one of the countries
that has ever laid claim to having originated this all-important piece of
navigational equipment. He writes: "Mariners at sea, when, through
cloudy weather in the day which hides the sun, or through the darkness
of the night, they lose the knowledge of the quarter of the world to
which they are sailing, touch a needle with the magnet, which will turn
round till, on its motion ceasing, its point will be directed towards the
north."

In the Mediterranean, the seaport of Amalfi was later to lay claim to
having "invented" the compass. The Italian poet Panormita commented: "Amalphi first gave to sailors the use of the magnet." But
this, like many other similar claims, can be safely disregarded. Amalfi
by the thirteenth century had become an important trading post with
the East and, out of a reviving Italy, was in constant sea-communication
with Alexandria and the great Arabic ports in the Levant.

The Arabic geographer Edrisi, who lived about 1100, refers somewhat confusingly to a magnetic compass. There are no earlier European
references, and it is quite clear that throughout the whole classical
period the compass was totally unknown. The Arabic names given to
it – and still in use to this day in the Red Sea – were *dairah* and *beit el-
ibrah* (the circle, and house of the needle).

The pivoted compass may well have been a European improvement,
for the first known mention of it occurs in *A Book about the Magnet*,
written by Peregrinus de Maricourt in 1269. He describes how a needle
is thrust through a pivoted axis, which is placed in a box with a transparent cover. It is not until the fourteenth century – and this indeed may
have been an Amalfian improvement – that we find references to a
compass "card", mounted upon the magnet and revolving with it.
Until this date, it would seem that the magnet was used in conjunction
with the old "wind-rose" which gave the eight principal winds – such
as had been delineated upon the Tower of the Winds in Athens
centuries before.

To the Arabs, then, credit must be given for the first introduction of
the magnetic needle into the inland sea. It was from the East that there
came the first major navigational advance since the discovery of the

comparative fixity of the Pole Star in pre-classical times – and that, too, was very likely derived from the astronomical knowledge of the Babylonians. The West had, over the centuries, introduced many improvements in shipbuilding and in the organization of rowing and sailing techniques. But almost all mathematical and scientific advances in Mediterranean navigation seem to have stemmed from the eastern end of the basin. Another advance in taming the sea was the *kamal*. Whereas the mariner's compass soon became an essential part of equipment aboard vessels in the Mediterranean trade, the seaman voyaging south of the Red Sea to India and the Far East needed not only to know the direction of his heading, but also his latitude. In the Mediterranean itself, latitude did not count for very much, because of its comparatively constricted area. The Pole Star, somewhat vaguely "fixed" relative to the mast and rigging, had sufficed the mariner's needs until the advent of the compass. In the great expanse of the Indian Ocean, however, a knowledge of latitude was very important indeed. While navigation in the western Mediterranean and in the European countries facing upon the North Sea or the Atlantic Ocean was still largely determined by wind directions, in the East the first ancestor of the sextant had made its appearance.

The *kamal* (still in use in sailing dhows in the Red Sea) was the first known simple instrument by which star altitudes could be determined. It works, to quote E. G. R. Taylor, "upon the familiar principle that an object of fixed length will measure the height of any heavenly body above the horizon according to the distance at which it is held from the eye." A small wooden tablet, which was all that the basic *kamal* consisted of, was pierced through the centre and a knotted string subtended from this point. The observer held the end of the string in his mouth, the string itself being knotted at various points along its length to correspond with known star altitudes for various ports. The error of parallax undoubtedly existed, for the string should really have gone to the centre of the observer's eye in order to make his observations accurate. The navigator, with the end of the string in his mouth, held up the tablet so as to cover the line of the horizon and whatever star he was using. According to the length of the string subtended from his mouth, and marked at regular intervals by knots (known as *isbas* and corresponding to $1° 36'$), he could calculate a star's altitude. On the Red

Sea route, where the difference in star altitudes between one port and another had long been calculated, it was possible to use a simple *kamal* that merely had knots along its length for the latitude of these specific ports. Such a method, primitive though it was, and even allowing for the fact that the Pole Star is not constant at the pole but revolves, was undoubtedly accurate enough for the navigator in the Red Sea, who was automatically on a more or less north-south passage. Similarly, in the Mediterranean, where men had been navigating for centuries without any such mechanical benefit, it must have greatly improved the landfall of ships bound between the southern (Arab-dominated) areas and the northern shores of the sea.

The Arabs, then, had the help of the compass for their expeditions into the sea that had hitherto been dominated by the Byzantines. They had also (though from quite what date we do not know) the *kamal* for obtaining a star altitude. Like all other Mediterranean navigators throughout the centuries, they also benefited from the fact that the sea was tideless. In the north of Europe, Scandinavian, English, French, and Dutch navigators always found their main problems were concerned with tides and tidal streams. The Arab sailor, so newly come to the sea, could concentrate solely upon course and wind direction without having to bother about his vessel being offset in one direction or another by tides.

The Arabic invasion of the sea was even given a blessing by the Prophet himself. He had written in the Koran: "Allah himself hath appointed for you the stars, so that you can guide yourselves in the darkness of the land or the sea. The signs have been made clear for those people who have the necessary knowledge." This knowledge the Arabs quickly obtained, and the result was that their fleets were soon active throughout the whole sea. Only in the Aegean, and north of Constantinople in the remote Black Sea, were the waters still dominated by the imperial fleet of Byzantium.

Quite apart from navigational advances, another major Arabic contribution to the science of sailing was the lateen sail. Although "lateen" means "Latin" – as if the sail was of this origin – it was, like so many other things, a specifically eastern contribution to the mariner's world. Again, there will always be some doubt as to its exact source of origin. It may have been an Arabic invention, or the Arabs may have derived it from India. Certainly the Mediterranean can lay no claim to its evolution. There is no hint of anything like a lateen sail in the ships of classical antiquity.

Whether the lateen sail was Indian or Arabic, the fact remains that it was the Arabs who first introduced it into the Mediterranean. It was the most efficient type of sail ever known until the introduction of the fore-and-aft rig in northern countries many centuries later. The great advantage of the lateen sail was that, unlike the square sail, which is inefficient except with a wind from abaft the beam, the lateen could be used quite efficiently to tack to windwards. In essence, it consists of a triangular sail, the leading edge of which is laced to a long spar. The heel of this spar is secured by block and tackle to the deck forward of the mast to provide a pivotal point. The mast that supports the sail and spar is quite short, but the high spar lifts the sail well above the head of the mast, thus providing a good driving surface for windwards work. The sail can be hauled in to set fore-and-aft almost as taut as in the much later gaff and Bermudan rigs. Indeed, until their advent, the lateen sail was the most efficient in the world for windwards work. On the Arabic dhows, similar to those which still operate on the Nile, in the Red Sea, and in the Indian Ocean, a comparatively small crew could operate a large sail area. In the larger vessels, which stepped two masts, the rig was equally efficient for running before the wind. The two great sails were boomed out on opposite sides, and the vessel then sailed "goose-winged".

A legacy from the Arabic occupation of the Maltese islands is the "Gozo boat". Although their hull shape owes much to the European galleys of the sixteenth to eighteenth centuries, their sailing rig is almost identical with the Arab dhows. Two lateen sails are set on a foremast and a mainmast, the foremast being slightly shorter than the main. These large lateens, known as "settees", are hoisted with the yard of the fore-sail to part of the foremast, and the main-yard hoisted to starboard of the mainmast. In this way, when they are boomed out in opposite directions, they give a balanced pull to the boat. At the same time, when beating to windwards, one or other of the sails is always working at maximum efficiency, no matter which tack the vessel is on. In the single-masted vessels, on the other hand, in order to keep the leading edge of the sail working efficiently, it was – and still is – customary to shift the foot of the lateen yard from one side of the mast to the other when going about.

One reason for believing that the lateen sail was an Arabic contribution to the Mediterranean world is the fact that it has long been recognized as typical of Red Sea craft, and is still in use in that area. The Red Sea, unlike the Mediterranean, has marked prevailing winds. In the northern part they blow from north and north-west, while the middle region has variable winds. In the southern region, south-east and east winds prevail. In summer, however, from June through August, the north-west wind dominates the whole area. For a sailor, then, the Red Sea is an area in which he can easily run down from north to south, but in which he is forced to tack and tack again – beating to windwards – when he wants to get back to the ports at the head of the sea. It would seem logical, therefore, to assume that it was here that Arab seamen first evolved a sailing rig that would work efficiently when the wind was adverse. In the Mediterranean, on the other hand, the square sail was used whenever a steady wind set in for a required direction. But in that sea of contradictory winds and long summer calms, the main motive power had always remained the long oars of the galleys and the strength of the oarsmen.

The Arabs adopted the Mediterranean galley hull but added to it the lateen rig. It was this combination of oared vessel coupled with lateen sails that was to dominate the sea right up to the seventeenth century. The fact that the first areas of Arabic conquest were in the eastern Mediterranean promoted the use of the new rig. From the Aegean down to Alexandria and over all the Levant as far east as Cyprus, the prevailing etesian winds give, throughout the summer months at any rate, a sailing condition not so very different from that obtaining in the Red Sea. The fact that the Arabs were in occupation of Rhodes and other islands so early in the period of their expansion may be partly ascribed to the efficiency of the vessels which formed their navy. No doubt the lateen sail had been known in Alexandria for many centuries – but mostly, it would seem, in terms of Nile and canal trade. It was not until the new conquerors learned to cure their dislike of water and take to the sea that the lateen sail is found scudding over the length and breadth of the Mediterranean.

While the history of this sea was to be eternally affected by the great

Arabic conquests and by the wave of new knowledge and culture that spilled out of the East, an unusual presence suddenly made itself felt in the ninth century. From the far north of Europe, a race of men native to the sea, as hardy as the Arabs, and through whose whole literature breathes a quite unusual love of battle – *berserksgangr*, "the berserk's way" – began to swoop into the Mediterranean from two very dissimilar routes. Although the Vikings, or Norsemen, have left little trace upon the culture of this sea, and although the period of their influence may seem relatively unimportant compared to that of the Arabs, they cannot pass without mention. They are the first men from the North, except for the Vandals, to have left the imprint of their long scudding keels upon its surface. Unlike the Vandals, the ships and the culture they brought with them were entirely their own. They were the forerunners of a long line of warriors, sea-captains, and merchants from northern Europe who would, in the next ten centuries, look south towards the delectable Mediterranean lands and try to occupy them.

Upon Ireland, England, and France the Vikings had long left their mark. In the late ninth century, Ermentarius of Noirmoutier could go so far as to say: "The number of ships grows: the endless stream of Vikings never ceases to increase. Everywhere the Christians are victims of massacres, burnings, plunderings: the Vikings conquer all in their path, and no one resists them: they seize Bordeaux, Périgueux, Limoges, Angoulême and Toulouse. Angers, Tours and Orléans are annihilated and an innumerable fleet sails up the Seine and the evil grows in the whole region. Rouen is laid waste, plundered and burnt: Paris, Beauvais and Meaux taken, Melun's strong fortress levelled to the ground, Chartres occupied, Evreux and Bayeux plundered, and every town besieged. Scarcely a town, scarcely a monastery is spared: all the people fly, and few are those who dare to say, 'Stay and fight, for our land, children, homes!' In their trance, preoccupied with rivalry, they ransom for tribute what they ought to defend with the sword, and allow the kingdom of the Christians to perish."

It is little wonder that in some of the litanies of the West a special prayer was inserted: *A furore Normannorum libera nos, Domine,* "From the fury of the Norsemen deliver us, O Lord!" But it was not only northern and western Europe that was to feel the wind of the Vikings' swords and grow to dread the sound of their horns as they sailed up

rivers or ran their long-ships aground on the beaches. The Mediterranean, too, was to know the "fury of the Norsemen" as they swept in,
during the summer months, past the Pillars of Hercules to batter at the
gates of Arabic Spain.

For the first time in the history of this sea, there arrived sailor-
warriors who had a genuine passion for the sea itself. Mediterranean
man, generally speaking, throughout all the centuries, had only taken
to the sea of necessity. Even the Greeks regarded seafaring as a necessary evil – a means of trade and overseas colonization – while the
Romans had actively disliked the watery element. In Homer's *Odyssey*,
which has been called "the greatest epic of the sea", there is not even
one line that would persuade a volunteer to ship before the mast. The
sea, the azure Mediterranean, is nearly always described as grey and
inhospitable. Lines such as "we struck the grey sea-water with our
oars and sailed on with heavy hearts" abound. The newcomers from
the North, however, had that genuine love of seafaring which is
characteristically Nordic, and which has never been felt by the inhabitants of the Mediterranean littoral.

In the Anglo-Saxon epic *Beowulf*, written in the eighth century, a
voice is heard that could never have come out of the South. It was to be
heard over and over again in the centuries to come; as first the Norsemen, then the Normans, and later the English descended to fight or trade
in this ancient home of navigation. "A man cunning in knowledge of
the sea led them to the shore. Time passed on; the ship was on the
waves, the boat beneath the cliff. The warriors eagerly embarked. The
currents turned the sea against the sand. Men bore bright ornaments,
splendid war-trappings to the bosom of the ship. The men, the heroes
on their willing venture, shoved out the well-timbered ship. The
foamy-necked floater like a bird went then over the wave-filled sea,
sped by the wind, till after due time on the next day the boat with
twisted prow had gone so far that the voyagers saw land, the sea-cliffs
shining, the steep headlands, the broad sea-capes."

The ships in which the Vikings ranged the sea routes of the world
from Greenland and Iceland to Spain, Sicily, and Italy were in many
respects similar to the early vessels of the Homeric Greeks. One major
difference in their construction was that the longitudinal planks forming
the sides were laid so as to overlap one another – "clinker built" – as

323

opposed to the Mediterranean carvel building, or edge-to-edge planking. (To this day the only clinker-built wooden vessels to be seen in the Mediterranean have come from the North, carvel building still being the regional style.) The long-boats stepped one mainmast on which a simple square sail was set – again similar to the early Greek vessels – and, depending upon their size, pulled between ten to thirty oars a side. The biremes and triremes of the classical period would have been totally unsuitable for the Vikings' navigations. They were dependent mainly upon the wind to wing them over dangerous areas like the tumbled North Sea and the cold North Atlantic. In every respect, these long-boats of the Norsemen were the finest vessels of their type that had yet been devised.

Holger Arbman, in *The Vikings*, analyses the famous Gokstad ship, which is the basis for much of our knowledge about Viking craft. It must be borne in mind, however, that the Gokstad ship was not typical of the vessels in which the Norsemen did their long sea crossings; it was designed more as an oared craft than as a sailing vessel. "The Gokstad ship is 76½ feet overall, with a beam of 17 feet, a hull draught of under 3 feet (the rudder projected below this) and a freeboard amidships of 3 feet 9 inches. . . . The oars are by no means the heavy sweeps with a long and ponderous stroke that some have imagined. They are only 16 feet long (though at bow and stern, where the bulwark was higher above the waterline, they were longer in compensation), no longer than modern lifeboat oars, and are light and very narrow-bladed. . . ."

An important feature of the Gokstad ship, and one which was certainly to be found in the larger sailing ships, was that the keel was a foot deeper amidships than at the ends. The Vikings were aware that, to enable a vessel to tack with ease, it is necessary to concentrate its lateral resistance at this point. Their vessels set a square sail, but a considerably more efficient one than that of the early Mediterranean craft. The Viking shipmasters extended the foot of the otherwise loose-footed mainsail by means of a wooden spar, the *beiti-ass*. In the bulwarks on either side, just forward of the mast, a heavy wooden beam was inserted, with two holes set upwards at slightly different angles. Depending upon which tack the vessel was on, the *beiti-ass* was set into one of these holes. It was thus possible to set up the leading edge of the sail taut enough to be able to sail to windwards. It was not as efficient as the Arabic lateen rig, but it was at least a great improvement on the old basic square sail.

The traditional "day's sailing", as given in the old sagas, is one hundred miles, or just over four knots. This was clearly an average figure, for a copy made of the Gokstad ship in 1893 had no difficulty in averaging eleven knots over a twenty-four-hour run – a speed which would be very good by modern racing-yacht standards. The magnetic compass was unknown to these northern seafarers, but all the evidence seems to suggest that they had some kind of instrument (possibly similar to the Arabic *kamal*) for establishing sun and star altitudes. Perforated boards, resembling the mediaeval traverse board, have also been excavated. These suggest that the Viking navigators kept a record of the various directions and distances made good during the day's run.

Between the mid-ninth century and the late tenth century there were numerous Viking raids in the Mediterranean. Naturally enough, it was the lands at the western end which suffered most from their depredations. In 844 the Vikings stormed Seville and destroyed its ancient Roman walls. While the inhabitants of northern Europe may have prayed to be spared from these Norsemen, it was now the Arabs who felt their steel and who in their turn cried out, "May Allah curse them!" The Moors of Spain seem to have referred to them as *al-majus* (wizard or heathen), presumably for much the same reason that Anglo-Saxon writers called them "the pagans".

A Viking expedition which left the Loire area in 859 raided North Africa and Italy. To quote Holger Arbman: "It is presumably not coincidence when we hear of black slaves being sold in Ireland soon after this expedition." The following year they raided Pisa and seem to have penetrated into the eastern Mediterranean, possibly even reaching Alexandria. The efficient resistance put up by the Spanish Moors, however, who had built themselves a formidable fighting fleet under the Emir of Seville, seems to have deterred the Norsemen from many more sallies into the Mediterranean via the Strait of Gibraltar. Northern Spain and the coastline of modern Portugal were constantly harried by the Vikings throughout the following century. Meanwhile, out of the bases which they had established in the south of France (in places like the Camargue in the Rhône Delta), they continued to sally forth and add to the general insecurity of the western and central areas of the sea.

In the East, too, the Vikings made an unexpected appearance. They came this time, not over the open sea, but down the long river routes via the Volga and Dnieper. These Vikings – the word is a generic one applied, at one time or other, to all the Scandinavian races – came mainly from the area now known as Sweden. Unlike their Norwegian and Danish cousins, the Swedes, instead of heading out for the open seas to the north, went inland. They followed the great rivers of Russia and Europe southwards until, through the Dnieper, they reached the port of Olbia, and through the Volga, they reached the Caspian. They possibly also made use of the Don, to sail and row through Russia down to the Black Sea. These Swedish adventurers pursued a very different course – in both senses of the word – from the other Nordic emigrants. They came principally in search of trade. Their own resources consisted of skins, furs, and amber, which they were eager to exchange for the goods of the East. Since, of necessity, they had to travel through thousands of miles of territory inhabited by primitive Slavonic tribes, they proceeded rather in the manner of the ancient Carthaginians. They set up trading posts, tried not to provoke the natives, and acted as far as possible like peaceful merchants. That they were fine warriors, however, is borne out by the fact that the Emperors of Byzantium were eager to employ them as mercenaries. By the eleventh century, they formed the imperial bodyguard in Constantinople. The first known mention of the "Waring" or Varangian Guard occurs in 1034. From this period onwards there are frequent references to the activities of the Swedes along all the trade routes leading out of Russia. Because of their exceptional fighting ability and their unswerving loyalty, the Emperors were pleased to have these stalwart northern warriors as their personal bodyguard. Their main weapon was the axe and their commander was known as the Acolyte, "Leader of the Axe-bearing Guard". Reorganized into a special corps by the Emperor Romanus IV in the mid-eleventh century, they were to play a colourful and important part in Byzantine history until well into the thirteenth century. The axe was a typical Nordic weapon; one which had been little seen in the Mediterranean until the appearance of the Vikings and the "Warings". The racial origins of the Waring Guard are made clear by the Byzantine historian Leo the Deacon: "They have flaxen or reddish hair and blue eyes. Their hair is worn long on either side of the face. They are bearded and have large moustaches. They will never be taken in battle, and will kill themselves rather than surrender." Such was the *corps d'élite*, then, that for several centuries was to guard the rulers of Byzantium – a northern exotic in the Greek-speaking court, helping to guard the last territories and dignity of what had once been the mighty Roman Empire.

Thus, while the North African coast, Spain, Sicily, and the central areas of the Mediterranean had come (or were about to come) under the rule of the Arabs, the Vikings made a sudden appearance in the East and the West. While Goths, Visigoths, Huns, and Vandals had already made their impact upon the Mediterranean basin, this was the first time that peoples from the far north of Europe had to any real extent influenced this sea. The extent of their contact with the eastern end of the Mediterranean can be gauged by the fact that, in Sweden alone, more than twenty thousand Moslem coins have been found. A marble lion bearing a Runic inscription, carved by a member of the Waring Guard in Athens, is now to be seen in Venice. A seventh-century Kashmir statue of the Buddha has been found at Helgo in Sweden.

In the western basin, the Norse invaders came mainly as raiders and plunderers, but at the far north-eastern end, in Byzantium and the Aegean, they came as traders. Although a number stayed to serve the Byzantine Emperors, it was principally in their capacity as carriers of merchandise through the great rivers of Russia and northern Europe that they first made contact with the Levant and the eastern Mediterranean. The culture and the religion of this sea, until now almost entirely remote from northern Europe, began to be disseminated throughout those distant lands. Philosophers, religious leaders, scientists, artists, and craftsmen may create cultures. But raiders, as well as traders, help to cross-fertilize the different regions of the world.

SIX

The Arabic Centuries

The new-found Arab ability in seamanship and navigation was not long in making itself felt. In 823 the Arabs invaded and conquered Crete. This was a bitter blow to the Byzantines, for the great island lying at the foot of the Aegean Sea now became a drawn scimitar shutting them off from the southern Mediterranean. The loss of the island had been clearly foreshadowed during the reign of the famous Harun-al-Rashid, who had swept through Asia Minor, driving as far north as the Byzantine city of Heraclea on the Black Sea. The reason for this invasion was that the Emperor Nicephorus had been rash enough to write to the Caliph informing him that he did not intend any more to pay the tribute that had formerly secured peace on his southern boundaries. Harun-al-Rashid's reply to the Emperor's letter displays all the self-confident grandeur of the Moslem world at the peak of its power: "In the name of the most merciful God, Harun-al-Rashid, Commander of the Faithful, to Nicephorus, the Roman dog. I have read thy letter, O thou son of an unbelieving mother. Thou shalt not hear, thou shalt behold, my reply."

The storm of violence unleashed over the eastern province of Byzantium reminded the Emperor that in future it would be better to be more circumspect in his dealings with the Caliph. It was during the caliphate of Harun-al-Rashid's son that this further blow – the loss of Crete – weakened Byzantine power in the Aegean and Asia Minor. From Crete, for a century and a half (when the island was recaptured by the Byzantines), Arab sea-rovers sacked and pillaged cities and islands that had hitherto been protected by the imperial navy. Crete became not only a nest of pirates but also one of the largest slave markets in the Mediterranean, whence luckless Greek mainlanders and islanders were shipped to the palaces and harems of Baghdad and Alexandria.

If the loss of Crete was a severe blow to Byzantium, worse was to come. Only a year later, a seditious Greek officer invited the Aghlabid dynasty in Africa to dispatch an army for the conquest of Sicily. Sicily, that eternal battlefield, was to see enacted over its plains, valleys, and mountain passes a repetition of the drama that had taken place so many centuries before. Once again the island was to be disputed between Europe and Africa. The cities that had known the conflict of Greek and Carthaginian and of Carthaginian and Roman became unhappy testators to the fact that their founders had indeed built them on the most important sites of the island.

The Arab fleet bearing the invasion force sailed from Sousse and reached Sicily without incident. The essential requirement for the conqueror was again shown to be control of the sea. Mazara, in the south of the island, a small port sited on one of Sicily's few rivers, was captured and made the Arab headquarters. Curiously enough, it was the southern and western parts of the island – that old terrain of the Carthaginians – which first came under the new Semitic rule. Syracuse, although besieged early in the campaign, was to survive as a Christian bastion in Sicily for a further fifty years. In 832 the invaders secured their first major success with the capture of Palermo. The city was destined to become for them, as it had been for the Carthaginians, the capital of the island. Messina fell eleven years later, and the road into Italy lay open.

Had it not been for dissensions between the Moslems themselves, the whole of Sicily would have fallen into their hands much more quickly. But the Moslem conquest was slowed down by recurring differences between the invaders from Africa and others who had crossed over from Spain. Nevertheless, the fact that as yet they had not conquered the whole island did not prevent them from invading Italy. As Sir John Glubb writes in *The Empire of the Arabs*: "In August 846, they took Ostia and appeared before the walls of Rome itself. They withdrew without attacking the city but only after sacking the shrine of St. Peter's on the opposite bank of the Tiber. Bari was occupied by an Arab garrison, which held no less than twenty-four fortresses in the province of Apulia alone. The establishment of the Arabs in Sicily and Southern Italy, at a moment when the Abbasids were weakening, gave the Moslems in 850 more complete naval control of the Mediterranean than ever before. . . ."

During the second half of the ninth century the Arabs did not hesitate to use this power. Out of Spain they dominated the Gulf of Lions, setting up colonies all along the southern coast of France, and penetrating inland up the Rhône as far as Arles. The Balearic Islands became an easy prey for their ships operating out of Barcelona. In the central Mediterranean, Moslem corsairs from Africa terrorized and devastated large areas of Sardinia and Corsica. Few ports on the western coast of Italy and the southern coast of France were spared – Genoa and Civita Vecchia were sacked as well as Nice and Marseilles. The last vestiges of imperial sea power in the central and western Mediterranean disappeared. Only in parts of the Adriatic, in the northern Aegean, and in the Black Sea was there any evidence left of that Roman dominion which had once united the whole sea. For centuries to come, the conflict between East and West was to render the Mediterranean a battlefield. Sometimes for a generation or more some areas would be relatively trouble-free, but then in one form or another war would again break out. The move inland from the ancient coastal ports, which had begun as long ago as the onslaught of the Vandals, was to continue.

Palermo, now the seat of the emir, or lord, of Sicily, was to remain for 230 years a Moslem city. With the fall of Syracuse in 878, the island, for the first time in its long and troubled history, came totally under the sway of a Semitic power. Where the Carthaginians had failed, a combination of Moslems from the old Carthaginian area of Africa and Arabs and Moslem converts from Spain had succeeded.

Even after the fall of Syracuse there was still some resistance to the new masters of the "flowery island". Rametta, near Messina, and Tauromenium (Taormina), that ancient Greek foundation of the fourth century B.C., managed to hold out until nearly the end of the tenth century. "In 138 years," writes Edward Freeman, in the *Encyclopaedia Britannica*, "the Arab did what the Canaanite had never done. The whole island was a Semitic, that is, a Mohammedan possession. But its first and longest period lasted only 73 years. In 1038, George Maniaces, the first captain of his time, was sent back by the eastern emperor to win back the lost land. . . . Four years of Christian victory followed. . . . Town after town was delivered, first Messina, then Syracuse, then a crowd of others. The exact extent of the reconquest is uncertain;

Byzantine writers claim the deliverance of the whole island; but it is certain that the Saracens never lost Panormus. But court influence spoiled everything: Maniaces was recalled; under his successor Stephen, brother-in-law of the emperor Michael, the Saracens won back what they had lost. Messina alone held out, for how long a time is uncertain."

The loss of Sicily to the "Saracens", or Moslems, has often been considered a grave disaster by European historians. In the history of the Mediterranean, however (and perhaps ultimately in the history of Europe), it is possible to view the matter in a somewhat different light. Spain and Sicily, at the time of their conquest, were both depressed countries – one worn out beneath successive waves of barbarian northern invaders, and the other depressed by maladministration and the rapacious tax-gatherers of Byzantium. Moslem conquest was, in many respects, a revitalizing influence upon Spain, the western pillar of the Mediterranean, and upon the great central arch of Sicily. At the very moment when the heart of the Arab Empire was about to be shattered by the invasions of Tartars and Turks, Arabic culture was enabled to take root and flower in the far West and in the centre of the sea. "The gateways of Spain and Sicily," writes Sir John Glubb, "began slowly to open and the accumulated skill, learning and science of Arabia and the East, matured in Damascus and Baghdad and carried from thence to Qairawan and Cordova, poured into Europe at the very moment in which it was extinguished at its source."

Although Sicily was in the process of becoming a Mohammedan power, the treatment of the Greek, Latin, and other inhabitants does not seem to have been particularly harsh. More tolerance was shown by the Moslems to the members of other faiths than was to be shown to them in their turn when European Christians once again gained the upper hand. Many of the peasantry were enslaved, but it is doubtful whether their condition as Moslem serfs was much worse than it had been throughout the centuries of Byzantine, Roman, Greek, and Carthaginian rule. It is noticeable that when the Normans ultimately came in conflict with the Arabs for the possession of Sicily, those of the population who did not speak Arabic still spoke and wrote Greek, for no coercion had been used to enforce the Arabic tongue. More than that, no attempt had been made to eradicate Christianity. Churches and monasteries still existed, and they had been allowed, throughout the long period of Arab rule, to hold property and to conduct their own religion and way of life. The admirable agricultural and irrigation techniques of the Arabic peoples had improved large areas of the island, while Arab architecture (as many buildings in Palermo still bear witness) had brought a glory which almost rivalled the first springtime of the classical Greeks. Here, as in Spain, the Arabic conquest brought many benefits; benefits which, although difficult for Europeans to appreciate during the generations of conflict, are more evident to the spectator of the twentieth century.

The history of Sicily under the Arabs is a vast subject in itself. As in earlier stages of the ebb and flow of life in the Mediterranean, it is sometimes easier to trace the overall pattern of events by looking at a microcosm. The Maltese archipelago again provides a suitable small canvas for study. The islands which, like Sicily, had been part of the Byzantine Empire were captured by the Arabs in 870. As in Sicily, the Christian Church was permitted to survive – although there is some evidence that it became a minority religion. The Maltese, still speaking some version of a Semitic tongue inherited from the Phoenicians, must have swiftly adopted Arabic. Certainly, the greatest impress left upon these islands was the language, which still – though augmented by Italian, Spanish, French, and English – survives to this day. (In Sicily, too, even though the dialect is basically Italian, a great many Arabic words survive.)

As in the days of Carthaginian supremacy in the central area of the Mediterranean, Malta benefited by the fact that its harbours provided a fine staging-post for vessels bound north or south between the heartland of Africa and the great colony of Sicily. Other benefits which accrued during the centuries of Arabic occupation were considerable improvements in agriculture. Among these mechanical improvements was the animal-powered water-wheel (Maltese *sienja*) for lifting well-water for irrigating the land. Citrus fruits were also introduced from the East by the new rulers. Both the lemon and the orange were unknown to the ancient world. Both seem to have originated in India, and to have been introduced into Sicily and Malta – as well as into Spain – by the Arabs. Cotton, another importation from the East, was introduced into Malta by the Arabs, thrived in the climate, and in later centuries became a staple part of the small archipelago's economy. The Arabs also introduced that improved system of numerals now known as "Arabic", but which, again, probably originated in India. All these were benefits that the islands (and indeed the whole Mediterranean) received from their new owners. On the debit side, a European might maintain that the Christian Church declined. Again, however, it must be pointed out that the Church and the practice of Christianity were never deliberately suppressed. Although the convert to Islam undoubtedly received benefits from his Moslem masters, those who chose to adhere to their faith were never persecuted as Christians later persecuted Arabs and Jews. Although there is no evidence, it is likely that in Malta, as in Spain, Sicily, and the Balearic Islands, Jews played an important part in the community, for the Arabs respected and encouraged their intellectual abilities.

From 870 to 1091, more than two centuries of Arab rule, the islands seem to have prospered. An Arab chronicler (quoted by Brian Blouet in *The Story of Malta*) refers to Malta as follows: "Malitah . . . rich in everything that is good and in the blessing of God . . . well peopled, possessing towns and villages, trees and fruit." The same might well be said of Sicily and many other Arabic possessions during this period. But, as Heraclitus had observed in the sixth century B.C., "Everything flows." There is no constancy in nature or in human affairs. The flux which the Arabs had introduced into the Mediterranean basin was not to be allowed to settle.

A twelfth-century Arabic tombstone found in the Maltese island of Gozo recalls the death of Maimuna, daughter of Hassan, son of Ali from Sousse. It seems to echo the eternal voice of this sea:

"Ask thyself if there is anything everlasting, anything that can repel or cast a spell upon death.

"Alas, death has robbed me of my short life; neither my piety nor my modesty could save me from him. I was industrious in my work, and all that I did is reckoned and remains.

"Oh, thou who lookest upon this grave in which I am enclosed, dust has covered my eyelids and the corners of my eyes.

"On my couch and in my abode there is nought but tears; and what will happen when my Creator comes to me?"

The tombstone is broken. The inscription ends on this plaintive note of inquiry. The Arabic centuries would also be broken. But the contribution of the Arabs to the life and culture of this sea, and all the lands around it, would remain as delicately and deeply etched as is little Maimuna's tombstone.

SEVEN

Normans and Arabs

The Vikings had preceded them into the Mediterranean, it is true, but the first Scandinavian race to make a major impact upon the societies and civilization of this sea were the Normans. The name "Norman" in itself is no more than a softened form of the word "Northman", and it was for some time applied to all Scandinavians. Later, it became exclusively the name for those northern invaders who had settled in ancient Gaul and colonized "Normandy" – Land of the Northmen. They had, of course, intermarried with the Gallic inhabitants as well as with survivors from Germanic races who had settled there. They had adopted the French language and customs, and the Christian religion. They remained, nevertheless, a basically Scandinavian people, and the *furor Normannorum* – that northern aptitude for battle – was an essential trait in their character. It was not to be effaced by a few generations of settlement in the easier land of France.

The plundering raids of the Vikings, driving their long-ships up the Seine as far as Paris, had been the inception of the conquest by the Northmen of all the fertile delta-land of the Seine Valley. The somewhat dour climate of the area (not for nothing has Rouen, the capital of Normandy, been called *le pot-de-chambre de France*) suited the physical and temperamental characteristics of these Northmen. The driving urge in their blood, however, remained unassuaged by the rich farmland that they had conquered and, generation by generation, inherited and cultivated. They were still pulled towards the sea and further expansion; towards the whicker of swords and the sound of the surge on a long-ship's prow.

Edward Freeman, in the *Encyclopaedia Britannica*, quotes a contemporary historian, Geoffrey Malaterra, who analysed their character: "He sets the Normans before us as a race specially marked by cunning, despising their own inheritance in the hope of winning a greater, eager after both gain and dominion, given to imitation of all kinds, holding a certain mean between lavishness and greediness – i.e., perhaps uniting, as they certainly did, these two seemingly opposite qualities. Their chief men, he adds, were specially lavish through their desire of good report. They were, moreover, a race skilful in flattery, given to the study of eloquence, so that the very boys were orators, a race altogether unbridled unless held firmly down by the yoke of justice. They were enduring of toil, hunger and cold whenever fortune laid it on them, given to hunting and hawking, delighting in the pleasure of horses, and of all the weapons and garb of war. Love of imitation is marked. Little of original invention can be traced to any strictly Norman source; but no people were ever more eager to adopt from other nations, to take into their service and friendship from any quarter men of learning and skill and eminence of every kind. To this admirable quality is perhaps to be attributed the fact that a people who accomplished so much, who settled and conquered in so large a part of Europe, has practically vanished from the face of the earth."

The Normans were, temperamentally, not so dissimilar to the Arabs, with whom they soon came into conflict. They originated little – but they were wise enough to know how to assimilate. They were great fighting men. They were also respecters of justice, but they needed to be held down with a firm hand, and to be made conscious that justice was indeed being administered. Given these considerations, the Normans, as they were to prove, could go anywhere and achieve practically anything. Their strength lay in their adaptability as much as in anything else. The men who conquered England also plunged deep into the Mediterranean and conquered Sicily. Later, they or their descendants were to hold down a large part of the Near East.

Shortly after 1057 two Norman nobles, Robert Guiscard and his brother Roger, arrived in southern Italy and began a carefully planned attack upon the Moslem strongholds in the area. Encouraged by the Pope, who had promised them whatever territories they could recover, they made themselves masters of most of the area known as Calabria. Robert, by his capture of Reggio and Cosenza in 1060, established himself as ruler of nearly all southern Italy, and was confirmed in his possessions by Pope Nicholas II. Formally recognized as papal champions in the battle against the infidel, the two brothers and their Norman followers now began a systematic attack upon Moslem-dominated Sicily. The year after their success in Calabria, they crossed the narrow strait from Reggio to capture Messina. Once again, the importance of sea power was made clear. Had the Moslems retained their former naval supremacy, the invasion of Sicily would have been impossible.

The Normans were, therefore, as Edward Freeman writes, "crusaders before crusades were preached. Norman warriors had long before helped the Christians of Spain in their warfare with the Saracens of the Peninsula, and in Sicily it was from the same enemy that they won the great Mediterranean island." They sounded, in effect, the first warning note of the conflict that was to trouble the whole of this sea for centuries – the wars of religion. This was a new factor in the history of the Mediterranean, for hitherto wars had been conducted for the sake of material conquest and gain. The great Arabic conquests (although the Arab war cry proclaimed the supremacy of Allah and his Prophet) had not been undertaken for the sake of Islam as a religion. The wars between Byzantine and Arab had been largely over the security of frontiers. With the coming of the Normans (even though the religious aspect may sometimes have been employed as an excuse), religious differences, foreshadowing the ideological differences of the twentieth century, were now to be used as the *casus belli*.

The struggle for the possession of Sicily lasted for close on thirty years. After the capture of Messina, Catania was the next city to fall to the Normans. Taormina once again held out, although this time under a Moslem governor, and then, in 1071, Palermo was taken. Among the last cities to fall was Syracuse (in 1085), always, throughout its long history, to be the occasion of long and obdurate sieges because of its superbly defensible position. Only Girgenti, Castrogiovanni, Noto, and a few other cities in the south of the island remained to be captured, and when the last of these fell in 1090, the whole of the island became a Norman kingdom. This remarkable achievement of Robert and Roger Guiscard, with a comparatively small number of Norman followers, marked the opening of a new phase in the turbulent and blood-stained history of the island. Sicily was now to blossom into one of the most gracious and civilized powers in the whole Mediterranean. The legacy of the Arabs, combined with the astute qualities of its new Norman rulers, produced a remarkable effusion of architecture and cultural achievement that was uniquely Sicilian.

To quote Gibbon: "After a war of thirty years, Roger, with the title of great count, obtained the sovereignty of the largest and most fruitful island of the Mediterranean; and his administration displays a liberal and enlightened mind above the limits of his age and education. The Moslems were maintained in the free enjoyment of their religion and property; a philosopher and physician of Mazara, of the race of Mahomet, harangued the conqueror, and was invited to court: his geography of the seven climates was translated into Latin; and Roger, after a diligent perusal, preferred the work of the Arabian to the writings of the Grecian Ptolemy."

Unusual in that age, Roger the Norman was intelligent enough to allow both Arabs and Greeks in his new kingdom to pursue their own ways and to expand their own different civilizations. The result was that Sicily, under its Norman rulers, was united as it had never been before and as it has scarcely been since. Everywhere the Mohammedan religion was tolerated and Moslem troops willingly formed the backbone of the army. At the same time the Greeks continued their worship according to the ritual of the eastern Church, without any significant pressure being put upon them by the newly reinstated Catholic priesthood. A by-product of Roger's conquest of Sicily was his expedition to the Maltese islands, which he took without any opposition in 1090. He now held not only the richest island in the Mediterranean, but also the magnificent harbours of its dependency, Malta. The establishment of the Normans in the central Mediterranean meant that Moslem power was now threatened with the severance of its eastern from its western territories. Although it was to be several centuries before Spain would become European rather than Moslem, yet the Norman ascendancy in Italy and Sicily was the foreshadowing of this event.

Moslem power was indeed on the wane, and the tidal current was about to reverse itself throughout the basin, and begin to run from west to east. The brilliant addition that the Arabs had brought to Mediterranean and European culture, which scientifically and artistically injected so many new ideas and forms, was as important as almost anything that had happened in the sea's history. But in the East, as had happened so often before in the past, yet another new power was rising up like an anvil-headed thundercloud. It was a power that would shatter the old Arabic Empire to its foundations, and which would then storm at the gates of Europe just as the Persians had once done. A race of hardy, nomadic horsemen was riding out of the steppes of Turkestan.

Like so many nations before them, the Arabs had made use of other races to stiffen their own armies. The Romans had employed Franks and Huns, and the Byzantines had used Bulgars and Vikings. An older, weakening power always tends to buttress its decline by a bracing of warlike, if primitive, peoples. In the ninth century the Arabs had begun to do exactly the same. As Sir John Glubb writes in *The Empire of the Arabs*: "On 9th August, 833, in the army camp where Mamoon died, his brother Mutasim was proclaimed khalif. He was the eighth son of Haroon al Rasheed and the third of his sons to become khalif. . . . Seventy years had elapsed since Mansoor had founded Baghdad and had settled in it the Khurasan troops on whom he relied. But the Khurasanis, after the disastrous civil war between Ameen and Mamoon, had abandoned their traditional devotion to the Abbasids. Mutasim felt himself obliged to seek elsewhere for loyal troops. He seems to have disliked the Arabs and placed almost all his reliance on Turkish mercenaries. Many of these were already in service but Mutasim greatly increased their numbers. He imported as many as he could from beyond the Oxus until he had built up a bodyguard of ten thousand of them. He dressed them in splendid uniforms, some of them being entirely clad in silk, while their belts and weapons were inlaid with gold and silver. The recruitment of Turks was entirely different from the previous employment of Khurasanis, for the Persians and the Arabs were Muslims and possessors of high cultures. The Turks came from tribes of barbarians. . . ."

By the time that the Normans were beginning to drive southwards through Italy, the Turks had, like many mercenaries before them, become masters in their own right. The sons and followers of a certain Turkish chieftain named Seljuk had not only captured Khorasan and Persia, but in 1055, one of them, Togrul Beg, had been proclaimed Sultan in Baghdad. These "Seljuk" Turks became ready and passionate converts to Islam. Like the Arabs of the eighth century, they in their turn were inspired by the fiery monotheism of the Prophet. Culturally primitive, bred for hardihood and endurance, these Asiatic tribesmen changed the whole pattern of life in the eastern basin of the sea. Originating nothing, they inherited the cultural world of the Persians and Arabs, but added to it little more than their vast capacity for warfare.

During the years when Count Roger was slowly annexing Sicily, the Seljuk Turks in the East were laying the foundations of an empire. Unlike the empire of the Arabs, that of the Seljuk Turks and their successors, the Ottomans, was to make little contribution to Mediterranean civilization. It was, however, to have a formidable influence upon the peoples of this sea, and the Turks were to terrorize the European powers so thoroughly that on one or two occasions they very nearly united them. Ottoman power, therefore, did not augment the quality of life but acted, rather, as a catalyst. The growth of the empire of the Turks coincided largely with the growth of Norman dominion. Syria and Jerusalem (that magnet for the Christian pilgrims) were added to other Turkish conquests by 1076. The capture of Jerusalem was in itself to provoke a whole series of invasions from the West – the Crusades.

Five years after Jerusalem fell, the Turks struck a deadly blow against that remnant of the once universal Roman Empire which Byzantium had, for so many centuries, been safeguarding in the East. The Battle of Manzikert is not one which has passed into the common knowledge of history, but it was, nevertheless, one of the decisive battles of the world.

The province of Asia Minor had always been the mainstay of the eastern empire. It was from Asia Minor that Constantinople drew the sources of its wealth as well as its ablest soldiers and many of its finest intellects. At Manzikert, near Lake Van in Armenia, Asia Minor was, for the time being, lost to the West. The Byzantine Emperor, Romanus Diogenes, determined to remove the threat of the Seljuk Turks, had marched into Armenia with a force of about 60,000 men. It was at Manzikert that he encountered Alp Arslan, the Turkish Sultan of Baghdad, with an army of 100,000. The Turks, whose army consisted mainly of horsemen armed with bows, refused to engage the Byzantines and their allies in a "set-piece" battle. In some ways their tactics were rather similar to those with which William the Conqueror had defeated the Anglo-Saxons at Hastings a few years before. They poured an incessant hail of arrows upon the Byzantine forces, but refused to close with them in a general engagement until the latter were physically and morally weakened. Then, when the Byzantines rashly left the rear of their army uncovered, the Turkish cavalry swarmed in and cut the whole force to pieces – the Emperor himself being taken prisoner.

The Battle of Manzikert was a disaster for Byzantium. Although the empire was to struggle on in a much depleted form for a further four centuries, it was doomed from this moment. The whole of Asia Minor, the rich province of Anatolia, was now overrun by the Turks. Unlike the Moorish conquest of Spain, the Turkish conquest brought little but misery in its wake. Like driver-ants, the Turks annihilated and absorbed, leaving behind them little but the whiteness of a picked bone.

The eleventh century was a period when the Mediterranean was curiously divided. In the West, a cultured Moslem rule prevailed over the ancient province of southern Spain. In the centre a new and unusual northern element, the Normans, had broken through Italy to establish itself in Sicily. In the East, on the other hand, the Arabs were dominated by primitive Asiatics who – though espousing their religion – had nothing in common with either Arabic or Persian culture. The Turks had swarmed over the rich farmlands of Asia Minor and had occupied the eastern coastline of the Aegean Sea. Byzantium, which for centuries had been the shield guarding Europe from so many invasions from north and east, was threatened as never before in its history. But for its ships and its superior technology, it would undoubtedly have fallen.

EIGHT

Crusades

The Normans, those Vikings with a Latin background, had begun the renewed movement of northern Europeans into this southern sea. Following upon their ancestors in their long-boats, they had conquered and settled in Apulia, Calabria, and Sicily, thus laying a firm hand upon the Mediterranean's central basin. They had come into conflict with the Byzantines, not only in these territories but even in Greece itself. Fortunately for Byzantium at this moment in its history, menaced by the Turks in Asia Minor, under attack by Norman barons on the Dalmatian coast, and constantly harassed by barbarian invaders from the North, a brilliant Emperor ascended the throne in 1081.

Alexius Comnenus came from a family of distinguished soldiers, but he was also a subtle and sophisticated politician. He early realized that the only hope of survival for the empire was to avoid a war on two fronts, and that there was no chance of effecting any lasting treaty with the Turks. His hope, therefore, lay in persuading the western powers – particularly those able soldiers the Normans – to make common cause with him against the enemies of Christendom. Despite the fact that the eastern and western Churches were in dispute, it seemed reasonable to assume that, for the purposes of a Holy War, these differences might be put aside.

Constantinople claimed to be the true seat of the Christian faith – a claim which was as forcibly denied by the Popes of Rome. If the Byzantine Emperor conceived the idea of combining forces against the infidel Turks (primarily with the object of regaining his lost territories in Asia Minor), the driving force for the first of the Crusades came from the Pope. No Norman baron would have heeded the appeals of Byzantines, those Greek-speaking schismatics with whom their fellows were already in conflict in Dalmatia and southern Italy. But at the Council of Clermont in northern France in 1091, Pope Urban II, recognizing the brotherhood of all Christians, called upon them to forget their differences and to unite in driving Turks and Saracens alike out of the Holy Places. It was, above all, the loss of Jerusalem, to which Europeans had been making pilgrimages for so many centuries, that occasioned the preaching of what was later to be called the "People's Crusade". The interests of the Pope and the Norman French coincided with those of the Byzantine Emperor, but it is doubtful if either party conceived how great would be the response.

Pope Urban II said in his famous address: "Why fear death when you rejoice in the peace of sleep, the pattern of death? It is surely insanity to endanger one's soul through lust for a short space of living. Wherefore rather, my dearest brothers, if it is necessary, lay down your lives for your brothers. Rid the sanctuary of God of unbelievers, expel the thieves and lead back the faithful. Let no loyalty to kinsfolk hold you back; man's loyalty lies in the first place to God. No love of your native soil should delay you, for in one sense the whole world is exile for the Christian, and in another the whole world is his country. So exile is our fatherland and our fatherland exile."

His words set in train a sequence of events that had a profound effect upon the Mediterranean world. In themselves, viewed in a Mediterranean context, they are totally revolutionary. No one had ever suggested before that warlike expeditions should be inspired by religious motives. There had been occasions – the Norman conquest of Sicily, for instance – when religion had been called upon to bless what was in essence no more than a traditional exercise in land acquisition; but the idea of assembling armies to fight in the cause of a religious ideal had no precedent in history.

Mycenaeans, Phoenicians, Greeks, Persians, Carthaginians, Romans, and all the other races who had at one time or another attempted dominance in this sea basin had had basically material ends in view. Only the Jews, in their struggle against the Romans, had used religion as an inspiration for battle. The Crusades, however, were the first real "Wars of Religion". Implicit in them was the idea that, just as the Hebrews had regarded themselves as a people chosen of God, so the European Christian now saw himself in a similar light. Even if cynicism may have often prevailed among some of these early (and many of the later)

Crusaders, the fact remains that the attacks upon the Moslem world in the Levant were triggered by religious belief.

The Pope's speech at Clermont, writes Denys Hay in *The Dark Ages*, "provoked a massive response beyond the expectation of Urban, beyond the intention of the Byzantine Emperor, Alexius I, who had asked for western help in recovering his lost provinces in Asia Minor. Not only did large numbers of knights set out in great cavalcades, but the poor responded too. Was not poverty already linked with pilgrimage? Was not the Heavenly Jerusalem already confused with the real Jerusalem?"

This confusion of the ideal with the material – the essence of the "crusading spirit" – was remote from the thought-processes of the Mediterranean world. It is doubtful whether any of the Byzantines, who sometimes benefited (but ultimately suffered) from the Crusades, understood the mixed motives that drove these Franks through their land and into the East. The pilgrims and the Crusaders who now passed through Byzantine territories were probably equally disconcerted by what they regarded as the cynicism of these latter-day heirs of the Roman Empire.

Steven Runciman, in *A History of the Crusades*, describes how: "Throughout the eleventh century till its last two decades, an unending stream of travellers poured eastward, sometimes travelling in parties numbering thousands, men and women of every age and every class, ready, in that leisurely age, to spend a year or more on the voyage. They would pause at Constantinople to admire the huge city, ten times greater than any city that they knew in the West, and to pay reverence to the relics that it housed. . . . Thence they went on to Palestine, to Nazareth and Mount Tabor, to the Jordan and to Bethlehem, and to all the shrines of Jerusalem. . . . But the success of the pilgrimage depended on two conditions: first, that life in Palestine should be orderly enough for the defenceless traveller to move and worship in safety; and secondly, that the way should be kept open and cheap. The former necessitated peace and good government in the Moslem world, the latter the prosperity and benevolence of Byzantium."

The Battle of Manzikert, the most disastrous event in Byzantine history, shattered at one blow the economic stability of the empire; at the same time it deprived the West of its traditional pilgrim route to the

Holy Land. Normans and other Europeans saw in this decisive defeat of the Byzantines a moral and physical weakness that inspired their contempt; they also saw in it a justification for their interference in the affairs of the East. Pope Urban's appeal at the Council of Clermont was further augmented by the work of visionaries such as Peter the Hermit and Walter Sans-Avoir ("Have Nothing"), who between them assembled the strangest collection of religious and worldly, inspired and cynical, that had ever been gathered together in one expedition. It was not only feudal barons, knights, and men-at-arms who made their way eastwards, but thousands of peasants – men, women, and even children – struggled through Europe bound on the Crusade. There is no doubt that consternation seized the Emperor Alexius Comnenus when reports reached him not only of the numbers, but also of the mixed quality of the Crusaders who were bound for his territory.

In the summer of 1096 the two main bodies had arrived at the walls of Constantinople. Their progress throughout Europe had been chaotic, and marked by innumerable ugly incidents. They travelled somewhat like an army of ants – but without the discipline – and were unwelcome guests in most of the cities where they rested. Alexius, who had asked for assistance, but had expected efficient troops and not a rabble, was uncertain what to do with this People's Crusade. He did attempt, however, to fulfil his part of the bargain, and had provisions made available to the Crusaders, while the Greek people lent them food, horses, and even clothing. Nevertheless, inspired though many of the Crusaders may have been by a vision of Jerusalem the Golden, there were inevitably many scoundrels in their ranks.

Unable to tolerate their looting and plundering any longer, the Emperor had them transported by the Byzantine fleet across the Bosporus. He arranged for them to be accommodated at Cybotus on the Gulf of Nicomedia. Quarrels now broke out between the different racial groups which composed this sad, undisciplined army. Peter the Hermit went back to Constantinople to try to secure some further aid from the Emperor. Meanwhile, the Crusaders, having pillaged the country-side under Byzantine control, began to extend their activities into areas where the Turks were waiting for them. After a number of minor clashes, the whole army, numbering some twenty thousand men, marched out to give battle to the infidel. The result was a foregone conclusion. Despite many individual acts of bravery, the Crusaders were put to flight under a hail of arrows and cut down by the Turkish cavalry as they tried to escape. It was a total massacre, the Turks sparing neither men, women, nor children when they overran the Crusaders' camp. Only a few attractive boys and girls were saved for the houses and the harems of the conquerors. Three thousand survivors, who had managed to barricade themselves in a castle on the edge of the sea, were rescued by the Byzantine fleet and taken back to Constantinople. It was the end of the People's Crusade. If it served any purpose at all, it was to remind western Europeans that faith alone was not enough. The road to Jerusalem would be opened only by the sword, wielded in disciplined hands.

While the Crusades occupy the centre of the historical stage through-out this period, in terms of the Mediterranean itself the most important event was the changing pattern of sea power. In the north-east and in the Aegean the Byzantine navy still maintained its supremacy, and was to be part of the lifeline that enabled the next wave of Crusaders to achieve their goal. But the pattern in the central area of the sea had changed utterly. With the capture of Sicily and the establishment of the Normans there and in southern Italy, a strong defensive shield had arisen which enabled the seaports of Italy to revive. For centuries they had been relatively unimportant and, with the exception of Ravenna, had played little notable part since the collapse of the western empire. As well as the Norman dominance in the central basin, the fact that Crete on the eastern side of the Ionian Sea had been recaptured by the Byzantines in 960 added a further stability to the whole area. Venice, Genoa, and Pisa are the three names that now begin to emerge from relative obscurity and henceforth play an increasing part in the naval history of this sea.

The First Crusade (in the true sense of a properly organized military expedition) was that of 1097, when four main divisions set out to rendezvous in Constantinople. The first, commanded by Godfrey de Bouillon, came mainly from what is nowadays Belgium. The second, led by the eldest son of Robert Guiscard, the conqueror of southern Italy, was largely composed of Normans and Italians. The third, consisting of men from Provence, was commanded by the Count of Toulouse; and the fourth, which came from Normandy itself, was led by Robert, Duke of Normandy, the eldest son of William the Conqueror. Although Pope Urban stated that some three hundred thousand people had "taken the Cross" for this Crusade, the majority of these were noncombatant pilgrims. It is probable that fewer than thirty thousand were armed knights and trained foot-soldiers. Even so, it was an immense expedition that, late in 1096 and in the spring of the following year, began to assemble at Constantinople ready to be transported across to Asia Minor. The Emperor, eager though he had been to have the assistance of these Normans and Franks to reclaim the lost territories of Byzantium, may well have had second thoughts as to the wisdom of his appeal. He had invited into his house a rapacious guest, and a guest who was not always too friendly to the host. Although the fruits of the First Crusade may well have exceeded his expectations, Alexius had in fact saddled the empire with a problem that would one day lead to its downfall.

Ably convoyed across the strait by the Byzantine fleet, which, throughout the operations to follow, maintained regular supplies to the Crusaders and transported siege engines and other matériel, the army achieved its first major success with the capture of Nicaea. This famous old city was the capital of northern Asia Minor, and its loss was a blow to Turkish pride – quite apart from material considerations. The Crusaders had previously taken an oath to Alexius Comnenus that they would hand over to him, as their supreme commander, all their conquests. The capture of Nicaea must have seemed to the Emperor to justify his calling in the rude strength of the West to redress the balance in the East. More advantages to Byzantium followed. The army streamed southwards through Asia Minor and restored to the imperial control nearly all the coastal area and a large part of the hinterland. Nevertheless, the Turks, tough and efficient fighting men that they were, disputed every inch of the way. "Who," as the author of the *Gesta Francorum* writes, "is so wise that he can afford to decry the skill, the warlike gifts and the valour of the Turks? Indeed they claim that none but the Franks and themselves have the right to call themselves knights. Certainly if they kept the faith of Christ, they would have no equal in power, in courage and in the science of war."

The concept of the "Warrior of Christ" was alien to Byzantine thought. Warfare had never been considered by the Byzantines as noble; it had generally been regarded as something that the Christian should avoid if at all possible. They preferred to negotiate rather than to fight. Indeed, the capture of Nicaea was largely due to negotiations between the Byzantines and the Turks. When the Crusaders were about to storm the city walls they found the flags of Byzantium floating above them. The Turks had preferred to treat with their ancient enemies rather than submit to these foreigners.

Byzantine conceptions of strategy and politics had long been based on the concept that war was the result of political failure. The Normans with their resolutely simple approach and their innate northern love of battle always found the Greeks tortuous, over-subtle, and, in the final analysis, treacherous. The Byzantines, on the other hand, found these foreigners useful tools (or so they at first thought) to their hand, but considered them to be adherents of a corrupt church as well as being uncultured and uncouth. It is all very well for Gibbon to say of the Crusades, "A new spirit had arisen of religious chivalry and papal dominion; a nerve was touched of exquisite feeling; and the sensation vibrated to the heart of Europe." Up to a point this was correct, and the Crusades were indeed a unique phenomenon; but the Greek inheritors of the eastern empire of ancient Rome found them difficult to understand. True, their Emperor had implored these Franks to come to his aid and prevent the destruction of Christian civilization in the East, but they had envisaged the Crusaders as mercenaries (who would do their duty, be paid, and then go) rather than as what they turned out to be. For the Norman barons, once they had found themselves large tracts of territory in the East, aspired to become landowners in their own right. Adept as they were at warfare, their ultimate aim was to own a comfortable area of land and settle down. Unlike mercenaries of the past – although they did not consider themselves mercenaries – they had no intention of winning battles, receiving payment, and returning to their homelands.

There can be no doubt that the First Crusade was a resounding success. It was, however, a success that was not to be repeated. After driving southwards through Asia Minor, the Crusaders now entered upon the serious invasion of Syria and Palestine, which remained areas of conflict for centuries. But their conquest of the vital areas of Asia Minor was so complete that it was largely responsible for the survival of the Byzan-

tine Empire for a further three centuries. In this respect Alexius Comnenus had indeed proved himself to be one of the most able Emperors
in the long history of his city. At a moment of great humiliation, with
the coastline of the Bosporus opposite the city actually occupied by the
Turks, he had managed to recoup most of the losses occasioned by
Manzikert, and there were now Christian armies at the very gates of
Jerusalem. Antioch, the third greatest city of the mediaeval world,
fell to the Crusaders in 1098. The year after that, Jerusalem itself, the
Holy City, was recaptured from Islam.

Although the Crusaders' behaviour after the capture of the city and in
many other sieges and affrays has often – and rightly – been deplored,
it must be borne in mind that they were not only rough soldiers, but
also devout Christians to whom the Moslem enemy constituted the
anti-Christ and all the forces of evil. William of Tyre's description of
their behaviour when they first set eyes upon their goal, Jerusalem, is
not to be dismissed as fictitious: "When they heard the name Jerusalem
called out, they began to weep and fell on their knees, giving thanks to
Our Lord with many sighs for the great love which He had shown them
in allowing them to reach the goal of their pilgrimage, the Holy City
which He had loved so much that He wished there to save the world.
It was deeply moving to see the tears and hear the loud sobs of these
good folk. They ran forward until they had a clear view of all the
towers and the walls of the city. They then raised their hands in prayer
to Heaven and, taking off their shoes, bowed down to the ground and
kissed the earth."

One unlooked-for outcome of the First Crusade was the rapid enlargement of the Italian mercantile marine. For the first time for
centuries, the seaways between the ancient fatherland of Rome and the
Near East were bristling with European sails. Subsequent Crusades
were only to confirm the importance of the Italian seaports; and the
wealth and vigour of Genoa, Venice, and Pisa stemmed largely from
this renewed activity between central Europe and the East. Crusaders
and pilgrims needed to be transported to the Holy Land, and trade began
to flow between the new Christian territories in the Levant and their
homelands in Europe. Something that had been largely disrupted by
the great Arabic wave of conquest in the eighth and ninth centuries
began to be restored. The presence of northern Europeans in the Levant

started afresh a steady interchange of goods, men, and ideas between France, Italy, and the East.

The Christian kingdoms carved out under alien Levantine skies by tough Norman barons were not destined to last, but their impact upon the territories which came under their control has never been quite effaced. But it was Europe itself which in the long run may be said to have benefited most by the Crusaders' conquests. Just as in Spain and Sicily, improvements in agriculture and in the arts and crafts had resulted from the Arabic conquests, so now a steady stream of luxuries and works of art (beautiful glass objects such as had hardly been known for centuries) began to pour into the countries of northern Europe.

It is from the period of the Crusades onwards that we notice a change taking place in the furniture and interior decoration not only of England, but of all Europe. It is important to bear in mind that the Crusades were not, as romantic writers would often have us believe, spearheads of a superior culture against barbarians from the East. It was the reverse, in fact. It was from their hated enemies that the Crusaders first began to learn the refinements of silk hangings, the use of ornaments, and improvements in the techniques of metalcraft. All of this was inevitably reflected by the furnituremaker, and upholstery and cushions returned to a Europe from which they had almost been exiled since the collapse of the Roman Empire.

Although it is customary to speak of the Crusades in terms of the First, Second, Third, and so on, the fact is that these definitions only apply to the major movements of Europeans into the Near East. The Crusades were more of a continuous process that went on year after year for centuries. Those that were marked by great successes or great failures have been dignified by historians with numerical titles. But it is best to envisage the whole period, from the First Crusade of 1097 right up to the last Crusade of 1464, as one in which whole armies, private militant bands, and individual barons and knights were continually storming out of Europe into the Near East, there to fight against Moslem emirs and rulers. Some of the individuals carved out kingdoms and principalities for themselves – the kingdoms of Antioch and of Jerusalem, for example – while others set up small feudal courts in the ports of ancient Syria. The true monuments to the Crusaders, which still decorate the eastern Mediterranean lands, are the ruins of their superb fortresses surmounting the hills and frowning over the valleys of the Holy Land. Quentin Hughes writes in *Fortress*: "Because of the shortage of manpower, impregnable sites had to be chosen and exploited. Strong keeps built after the manner of French castles became a feature of these fortresses, and concentric rings of defences, built one inside the other and rising higher and higher, were constructed, so that those defending the outer walls were covered by fire from positions behind and above them."

If fortress architecture is the principal legacy that the Crusaders have left upon the Mediterranean scene, the Crusades themselves – together with the annual stream of pilgrims to the Holy shrines – led to an immense expansion in shipbuilding. The great ports of Italy flourished as they had not done since the prosperous years of the Roman Empire. Venice acquired trading rights, her own Venetian quarter, churches, and markets in many of the cities of the Levant. The foundation stone of her greatness, as indeed that of Genoa, was laid by the Crusades. In the strange marriage that took place between West and East during the crusading centuries, the whole Mediterranean was to benefit. The old shipping routes, which had been disrupted for centuries, resumed something like their ancient vigour. Ship design improved, and the typical Mediterranean galley, which was to dominate the sea until the seventeenth century, assumed its final and perfected shape.

NINE

Knights of Saint John

'Amr, the great Arab general who had conquered Egypt in the seventh century, was asked by a friend, as he lay upon his death-bed, "You have often said that you would like to find an intelligent man on the point of dying, and find out what his feelings were. Now I ask *you* that question." 'Amr replied, "I feel as if the heaven lay close upon the earth and I between the two, breathing through the eye of a needle."

His words seem to epitomize the whole history of the Mediterranean between the period of the great Arab conquests and the Renaissance in Europe. Between the Hejira of the Prophet in 622 and the mid-fifteenth century, the Mediterranean world was in the grip of a religious fever. Curiously enough, although the lands surrounding this basin have given birth to two of the principal world religions, the Mediterranean temperament is not in itself of a mystical bent. In the ancient world, with its plethora of gods and goddesses, the observance of ritual had been considered the main factor in religious worship. Men did not take arms against others because they maintained that Zeus was superior to Ammon, that Heracles was stronger than Melkarth, or that Aphrodite was more beautiful than Ishtar. They merely equated the qualities of their varying gods and goddesses and said with a shrug, as it were, "There is little or no difference. If I am in Athens I pay my respects to Heracles, and if in Tyre to Melkarth." The Romans despised the religious practices of the Carthaginians, but they did not make war upon them because they found the worship of Baal unattractive, or less efficacious than the worship of Jupiter. Religious intolerance came out of the East, a by-product of Judaism and Christianity. This intolerance of other religions was inherited by European Christians, along with so much else, from Judaism, but it was the Christians of western Europe who most actively promoted religious intolerance. The Eastern Orthodox

Church of Byzantium, although the Byzantine state was constantly in conflict with Moslems and barbarians, did not make the religious issue a driving force in that conflict. "The Cross has conquered!" was their cry, but they were always ready and willing to reach accommodation with the enemy. At a later date, Constantinople was conspicuous for its colony of Moslems. One of the many things that incensed visiting Christians of the Roman Church was that the Byzantines even tolerated the presence of a mosque in the city.

One of the most interesting growths occasioned by these centuries of religious warfare in the Near East was the formation of special *corps d'élite*, the Crusading Orders. In them, as in the microcosm of some islands, the basic constituents of the period are so firmly etched that they serve to epitomize a whole era. The Knights Templars, or "Poor Knights of Christ and of the Temple of Solomon"; the Teutonic Knights; and the Knights of the Order of Saint John of Jerusalem; these were the three great orders which sprang out of the Crusades and whose names are indissolubly linked with this period of history. In terms of the Mediterranean, however, the one which carries the deepest and longest association is the Order of Saint John. It is of particular interest since the knights attached to it ultimately became the finest fighting seamen of their time. They developed superb shipbuilding techniques as well as advanced navigational skills, and in two areas of the Mediterranean they made island-homes from which they exerted an influence disproportionate to their numbers.

In the history of the Knights of Saint John one can trace with some confidence the essential history of the next four hundred years, at least in terms of the conflict between West and East. In their relationship with the East, their lendings and their borrowings also reveal something of the mutual transactions of the era. They were unlike the Templars, who were a military order only (and who were suppressed for papal and political reasons early in the fourteenth century), and unlike the Teutonic Knights, who from the thirteenth century onwards were more occupied with the conquest and conversion of Prussia than with the Mediterranean. The Order of Saint John was conceived during the First Crusade, as were the other Mediterranean orders, but it remained part of the sea's history for over seven hundred years. To all intents and purposes it died there during the cataclysm of the Napoleonic Wars.

To understand something of the pattern of events from the period of the First Crusade onwards, the history of this remarkable "club" of warriors, Christians, hospitallers, and noblemen must be outlined.

They were hospitallers first and foremost. They had originated indirectly out of a hospice, or hospital, which was maintained in Jerusalem to look after sick pilgrims. During the First Crusade the head of this hospital was a certain Peter Gerard, who earned the gratitude of the Crusaders by his assistance to them during the course of the siege. After the city had been captured (amid most unchristian scenes of lust and violence) the hospital was showered with donations and privileges. Dedicated to Saint John the Baptist, and administered first by Benedictines and later by Augustinians, this hospital was the seed from which sprang the great, proud, and military order of the Knights of Saint John.

Gerard petitioned the Pope for the institution to become a recognized religious foundation. A number of knights who had been healed of wounds or who had otherwise joined the community lent weight to his entreaty, and in 1113 Pope Paschal II took the order and its possessions under his protection. His action was confirmed by his successor, and subsequently by other Popes. The hospital in Jerusalem had now acquired all the dignity of papal favour – no unimportant matter at that time, when the conquest of the Holy City by the Crusaders seemed to have set the seal of God's affection upon the Popes who had inspired this religious war.

Gerard, who must be considered the founder of the order, died in 1120, to be succeeded by Raymond du Puy, who was as statesmanlike as he was religious. It was he who really established this new and comparatively insignificant order upon a firm financial basis, and who set its course in a direction that was to last for centuries. Because many of his new members were more qualified to be soldiers than "nursing brothers", and in view of the fact that Saracen attacks were gaining strength upon the new Christian strongholds and routes through the Holy Land, Raymond du Puy suggested to the Pope that some of his serving brothers should become more than hospital attendants. The pilgrim routes needed defending and he had a number of men who, he felt, were suitable for that task. This was the inception of the military side of the order, and it was the military side that was ultimately to predominate. Nevertheless, throughout their history, the Hospitallers remained a nursing brotherhood and – even in the years when their military arm was most strongly developed – a large proportion of their revenue was spent upon nursing the sick and upon the advancement of surgery and medicine in general.

By the middle of the twelfth century the Order of Saint John had combined its functions, and had become a curious mixture of hospitallers and warriors. Roderick Cavaliero, in *The Last of the Crusaders*, writes: "Who were the Knights Hospitaller entitled to carry the eight-pointed cross emblazoned upon their person, the four arms signifying the Christian virtues of prudence, justice, fortitude and temperance, the eight points the beatitudes these virtues bestowed and its colour the incandescent whiteness of knightly purity? They were the younger brothers and second sons for, unless the Pope granted a dispensation, the wearer was a monk. But he was a monk with a difference. He had not abandoned the world; he was not a priest but a lay brother. He wore no distinguishing costume but the cross. He was free to move about the world but at the same time he had taken a vow of poverty, chastity and obedience. It was a strange and difficult vocation." In their early days there seems little doubt that the knights did to some extent manage to reconcile the contradictions in their calling. In later centuries their vows of chastity and poverty were often forgotten.

The Knights of Saint John played a large part in the Second Crusade of 1148, which failed disastrously before the walls of Damascus. This defeat was to some extent mitigated by the capture of Ascalon in 1153, in the course of which the Grand Master and his knights played a conspicuous part. As the century advanced, the order became more and more wealthy. Its income derived from a number of sources, including the fee paid by the new entrant, as well as the death-duties of the knights, which entailed all their possessions except a fifth (which they might privately will away) becoming the property of the order. In addition, the spoils of war, whenever a city was taken or a caravan of Moslems successfully surprised, went to swell the order's treasury. What had begun as a simple hospital in Jerusalem ended up as an immensely rich and powerful international organization, with hospitals spread along the pilgrim routes of Europe, and with huge estates in various European countries. Its composition was still mainly French, but the order gradually became internationalized into eight Langues, or Tongues, comprising the European countries who played a major part in crusading activities. These Langues were Auvergne, France, Provence, Aragon, Castile, England, Germany, and Italy. The knights thus became one of the first examples of an international army; owing their allegiance not to their countries of origin, but to their Grand Master and the order (to some extent foreshadowing, in this respect, the North Atlantic Treaty Organization which now protects Europe and the Mediterranean). The national division of the Langues served also to encourage a healthy spirit of rivalry, and to ensure that in battle each Langue would be inspired to try to fight better than the others.

Their history throughout the twelfth and thirteenth centuries reflects very nearly the history of the Crusaders in the East. Between 1162 and 1169 they shared in a series of abortive expeditions which attempted to wrest Egypt from the Moslems. The confusion prevailing in the Latin kingdom of Jerusalem was not helped by a series of scandalous disputes between the Templars and the Hospitallers, which prevented serious co-ordinated action against the common enemy. The early successes of the Christians had largely been made possible by the fact that they were campaigning against a number of emirs, none of whom were particularly powerful – and most of whom were at daggers drawn with each other. But when a great co-ordinating figure emerged upon the scene, it became clear that the European position in the Holy Land was precarious. Lines of communication were far too long, for the Crusaders depended for their reinforcements of men and matériel upon ships from Venice and Genoa. In those days of poor communications it might be weeks before the news got back to northern Europe that assistance was required.

In 1186 the distinguished Sultan of Egypt, Saladin, began a systematic reconquest of the Frankish kingdom. The Hospitallers were in the forefront of the battles against him, but suffered a disastrous defeat in 1187 at Tiberias, where the Grand Master himself, Gilbert des Moulins, fell under a hail of arrows. Worse was to follow in July of the same year. At the Battle of Hittin, Saladin completely routed the Crusaders, killing or capturing the bulk of their army. So greatly did the Sultan fear the fighting quality of the Templars and the Hospitallers that he gave instructions that none of them should be taken prisoner; any that were, were summarily executed. Then, in October 1187, the greatest blow of all fell. Saladin recaptured Jerusalem.

The Sultan's successes led to a reinvigoration of the crusading spirit in Europe. In the campaigns that followed (in which Richard Cœur de Lion played so conspicuous a part) the Hospitallers were always in the forefront. The important city of Acre was recaptured, and in the next few years nearly all the coastal area. But during the following decades the Hospitallers showed all the faults that beset the whole European cause in the Holy Land. They were constantly quarrelling with the Templars, and the relaxing climate, manners, and morals of the East sapped their fibre. It was a constant complaint of knights and others newly arrived in the Holy Land that those knights and knightly orders already established there had succumbed to the temptations of luxury and loose living. The old obligations of chastity and poverty were largely forgotten, and the knights long resident in the East adopted many Moslem habits and ways of thought. The young campaigner fresh from Europe was likely to be startled not only by their mode of living, but also by the fact that they even had cordial relations with Moslem neighbours and exchanged mutual visits. Not thus, felt the newcomer, had the Holy Places been restored to Christendom. The "old India Hands" (inevitably the comparison springs to mind of British India centuries later) felt, for their part, some contempt coupled with amused scorn at the inexperienced antics of the "fresh from Europe" brigade: "They don't understand the natives and they don't know the terrain."

The invasion of the Tatar Mongols took the dissident and divided Christians by surprise. Jerusalem fell yet again, Gaza was overwhelmed, and in 1247 the great Crusader fortress of Ascalon capitulated. Two years later, the Hospitallers shared in the disastrous expedition of Saint Louis of France, which culminated in the Battle of Mansourah in Egypt. Although the wave of Tatars had receded from the Holy Land, the Christians still could not reconcile their internal differences, and another spate of quarrelling between Hospitallers and Templars imperilled their whole position at the very moment when a truce had been arranged with the surrounding Moslem powers.

In 1260 Baybers, Sultan of Egypt, began a series of campaigns which achieved what even Saladin had failed to do. Having driven the

Tatars out of his kingdom, Baybers now proceeded to drive out the Franks as well. Antioch fell in 1268, and the superb Crusader fortress Krak des Chevaliers in 1271. Built at the beginning of the thirteenth century by the Order of Saint John on a mountain peak in Tripoli, north of the old kingdom of Jerusalem, its ruins still provide one of the most moving monuments to this period in Mediterranean history.

Further attempts to redeem the position in the Holy Land, notably by Prince Edward of England, failed to avert the ultimate fate of the Latin kingdom, and with it that of the Order of Saint John. When, in 1291, the last Christian stronghold of Acre fell to the Moslems, all was lost, and the order left the Holy Land for ever. Its members went first to Cyprus. Then, in 1309, at the instigation of the Pope and the Genoese, they captured the island of Rhodes from the Latin admiral of the Byzantine Empire. (How the Byzantine Empire had largely been taken over by the Latins is a story to be told in due course.)

It was in Rhodes that the knights perfected the final form of their order: one that was later to follow them to Malta, where it would endure until the close of the eighteenth century. The significant factor, however, which caused this band of crusading warriors to leave so lasting an imprint upon Mediterranean history, was the change in their whole status that the move to Rhodes occasioned. For nearly two centuries they had been hospitallers in the Holy Land and militant guardians of the pilgrim routes and of the Latin kingdom established there. In Rhodes their role was to undergo an immense change. From being hospitallers first and soldiers second, they became sailors first and hospitallers second. No longer able to prosecute their war against the Moslem on land, they became Christian corsairs, dedicated to raiding the enemy's shipping routes and fighting such of his warships that dared intrude upon the sea round their island. They were the outermost bastion of Christian Europe against the East, and the Pope had rightly seen that the position of Rhodes, just off the coastline of Asia Minor, was ideal for disrupting the traffic of the enemy. As the threat to Europe began to come more and more from the invading armies of Turks, so Rhodes increased in importance. It was a pestilential thorn in the side of subsequent Turkish Sultans long after the Ottoman Turks had made the whole of ancient Ionia their kingdom.

The beautiful and gracious island of Rhodes had somewhat faded from the pages of history since its days of greatness in the classical period, when the Rhodians had been one of the foremost naval states in the Aegean. Later, they had played a large part in the navy of imperial Rome, and the Byzantines had also made considerable use of their sailors and shipbuilding and navigational experience. Rhodes has a breadth of twenty miles at its widest point and is about forty-five miles long. It was big enough, therefore, to furnish the Knights of Saint John with most of their requirements (although, despite papal injunctions to the contrary, they still often traded with Turks and Moslems from the East). The island had an excellent harbour, the same from which the ancient galleys had swept the eastern seas.

It was on the site of the classical city that the knights began to build their new fortified port and home, from which, for over two centuries, they were to harass Moslem shipping and prove an implacable foe to the Turks. Rhodes was divided roughly on a north-east, south-west axis by a range of mountains which reached their highest peak at Mount Anavaro, almost in the centre of the island. On either side of this ridge lay the fertile plains and valleys which played so large a part in the island's economy. Both Byzantines and Saracens, during their varying periods of occupation, had improved the agriculture; the Saracens introducing efficient irrigation methods as well as citrus fruits. Olives abounded and the sea around was rich in fish.

The fortifications that the Knights of Saint John erected in Rhodes during their long tenancy remain one of the glories of the eastern Mediterranean. The knights lived in the northern part of the city, in an area known as the Collachium, or Citadel. It was here that the auberges of the individual Langues were sited, as well as the great hospital that they maintained, the arsenal, and the palace of the Grand Master. Near-by lay the small harbour, Mandraki, where the galleys that they were to make a byword in the Mediterranean were hauled ashore in winter or lay alongside in the summer months – ready to swoop out like hawks upon the fat migrant birds of eastern merchantmen. The Rhodians, with their inborn aptitude for the sea, provided their new rulers with fine ships and sailors, while the hitherto shore-based knights soon proved that their military prowess could swiftly accommodate itself to another element. They were to prove themselves among the finest fighting sailors that the Mediterranean had ever seen. Comparatively small though Rhodes was, and numerically insignificant though the numbers of the knights were, compared to their Turkish enemy, they were to act like a running sore on the Moslem world until their final expulsion from the island in the sixteenth century.

The galleys which they used in their naval warfare were an adaptation of the single-banked Byzantine galley. They were the product of all those centuries of development, from the biremes of Greece and Rome, but refined into the most efficient warships ever known until the great sailing galleon, armed with cannon, once again changed the balance of power at sea. Long and narrow, with little free-board and a shallow draught, these galleys were specialized greyhounds, designed for the summer sea, whose period of activity extended from May until September. Since most merchant shipping of the period (even the lateen-rigged Arabic merchantmen) confined their activities to the summer, their unsuitability to winter conditions was of little importance.

The Rhodian galleys were somewhat smaller than those developed in the sixteenth century, after the knights shifted their base to Malta, but they were little different in essence. They might attain an overall length of over 150 feet, but between perpendiculars were no more than 120 feet or less. Like all galleys they were mainly powered by the sinewy backs and arms of men. In the early phases of their operations out of Rhodes, the local Greeks themselves provided the oarsmen. At a later date, when Turkish slaves had become plentiful, the practice was introduced (soon to become common throughout the whole Mediterranean) of using the captured enemy at the looms of the oars. This, in its turn, necessitated the construction of slave quarters for housing the oarsmen during the winter months and other periods of inactivity. The use of slaves in galleys was a radical change from ancient Mediterranean practice, where the freemen of a state manned their own ships. The Vandals and the Vikings and other raiders of the Mediterranean had also been their own oarsmen and fighting men. The contest between Christian and Moslem gradually produced an alteration in this pattern. Not long after the Turks themselves had taken to the sea, both they and their European enemies manned their vessels very largely with their captives.

Efficient the galley certainly was, but life aboard was far from pleasant, even for its officers. At a much later date, a French naval officer, Barras de la Penne, wrote a first-hand description of galley life. It probably reflects fairly accurately the conditions aboard a galley of the Knights of Saint John during their last years in Rhodes. "Many of the galley-slaves had not room to sleep at full length, for they put seven men on one bench; that is to say, on a space about ten feet long by four broad; at the bows one sees some thirty sailors who have for their lodging the floor space of the *rambades* [the platform at the prow] which consists of a rectangular space ten feet long by eight wide. The captain and the officers who live on the poop are scarcely better lodged. . . . The creaking of the blocks and cordage, the loud cries of the sailors, the horrible maledictions of the galley slaves, and the groaning of the timbers are mingled with the clank of chains. Calm itself has its inconveniences [because of] the evil smells which arise from the galley. . . ."

The ram was still the principal weapon. Although the secret of Greek Fire had been captured from the Byzantine Greeks and was known by this time to both the knights and the Turks, it would seem that the Rhodian galleys still relied mainly upon the ancient technique of ramming. In the fourteenth century, after the use of gunpowder and firearms had become widespread, galleys mounted a bow cannon as well as small anti-personnel guns which discharged showers of scrap metal and stones. In the early days in Rhodes, the run-in approach towards the enemy was backed up by flights of arrows, followed by hand-to-hand combat once the opposing ships were firmly interlocked. The Knights' ardour for battle and the Rhodians' skill as sailors combined to make their small fleet far more efficient than that of their enemies.

"The Knights," wrote Gibbon caustically, but with some accuracy, "neglected to live, but were prepared to die, in the service of Christ." Nevertheless, Europe owed them some considerable debt of gratitude during their centuries first at Rhodes and later at Malta. They changed the faces of these two islands completely and forever; nobody can visit either of them today without being made immediately aware of the long shadow of the Order of Saint John. In their early history, during nearly two centuries in the Holy Land and the Near East, they had reflected the crusading spirit of that age which, quite apart from the ruins of its castles, left a lasting French connection with those Moslem countries. The visiting European is still often referred to as a "Frank", and the French language and culture, though disseminated largely in later centuries, still retains a strong hold upon the Levant. In their island fortress of Rhodes the Order of Saint John now began to leave an enduring architectural monument in the Greek Aegean.

It is difficult to leave the subject of the order and of its sojourn in the island of Rhodes without mentioning the Great Carrack of Rhodes: a vessel almost as extraordinary as the Colossus of Rhodes, which had been one of the wonders of the classical world. The Great Carrack was built not long before the knights were finally expelled from the island by the Turks in 1522. One of the most extraordinary vessels of the Middle Ages, it was the flagship of the order, and it was in her that the last Rhodian Grand Master, Villiers de l'Isle Adam, embarked with his knights after handing over the island to the victorious Sultan Suleiman I. If the galley had been the principal weapon of the knights in their long years of battle against their enemies, the Great Carrack foreshadowed the Age of Sail that was to prove the end of the galley's long reign in the inland sea.

J. Taafe, in his *History of the Order of Saint John of Jerusalem*, gives the following description of this vessel: "It rivalled with our lifeboats in this, that however pierced with multitudinous holes, no water could sink it. When the plague was at Nice [the Great Carrack was built at Nice], and the mortality so frightfully huge that the stench of the corrupted air made the birds of the sky drop down dead, not a man was ever sick aboard it, which is chiefly attributed to the great quantity of fires kept by the workmen to supply the requisite screws, nails, and other irons. . . . [It] had eight decks or floors, and such space for warehouses and stores, that it could keep at sea for six months without once having occasion to touch land for any sort of provisions, not even water; for it had a monstrous supply for all that time of water, the freshest and most limpid; nor did the crew eat biscuit, but excellent white bread, baked every day, the corn being ground by a multitude of handmills, and an oven so capacious that it baked two thousand large loaves at a time. The ship was sheathed with six several sheathings of metal, two of which underwater were lead with bronze screws (which do not consume the lead like iron screws), and with such consummate art was it built, that it could never sink, no human power could submerge it. Magnificent rooms, an armoury for five hundred men; but of the quantity of cannon of every kind, no need to say anything, save that fifty of them were of extraordinary dimensions; but what crowned all is that the enormous vessel was of incomparable swiftness and agility, and that its sails were astonishingly manageable; that it required little toil to reef or veer, and perform all nautical evolutions; not to speak of fighting people, but the mere mariners amounted to three hundred; as likewise two galleys of fifteen benches each, one galley lying in tow off the stern, and the other galley drawn aboard; not to mention various boats of divers sizes, also drawn aboard; and truly of such strength her sides, that though she had often been in action, and perforated by many cannon balls, not one of them ever went directly through her, or even passed her deadworks."

This prodigy in shipbuilding is a fitting note on which to leave the Order of Saint John and its knights. They had come a long way from their territories in France, Germany, Spain, Italy, and England to the hot skies of the Holy Land, to battles in Egypt, Syria, and Asia Minor, to conclude – as it seemed at the time – their unique record in the Aegean island of Rhodes. In one sense, "in their end was their beginning." Their name would become so indissolubly linked with their next island home that they would ever afterwards be known as the "Knights of Malta". For the moment, however, it is time to consider how they ever came to be occupying an island in the Aegean that should, by rights, have belonged to the Byzantine Empire.

TEN

The Fall of Byzantium

The reason why the island of Rhodes was, with the connivance of the Pope and the assistance of the Genoese, captured by the Knights of Saint John in 1309 was that the ancient Byzantine Empire had ceased to exist. Constantinople, New Rome, that imperial foundation of Constantine the Great which had maintained the eastern and northern borders of Europe for nearly nine hundred years, had been captured in 1204 by an army of Crusaders theoretically bound for Egypt and the Holy Land. This action, all-important in the history of the Mediterranean, constitutes one of the darkest stains on the conscience of western Europe.

The Fourth Crusade was launched in France in 1199, when a group of French knights, inspired by an itinerant preacher, decided to "take the Cross" and set out for the Holy Land. They sent an immediate notice of their intentions to Pope Innocent III. He had become Pope the year before and had proclaimed his desire for a new Crusade immediately he ascended the pontifical throne. At this period in history the old crusading spirit had largely evaporated, but it was Innocent's main aim throughout his life to revive it. At the same time, he wanted to re-establish papal control of the Crusades, which in later years had become largely secularized. He failed utterly to achieve this in the Fourth Crusade, for it soon became apparent that the French knights and barons had every intention of organizing matters in their own way – even as to their choice of objective. Their intention was to invade Egypt, mainstay of Arabic wealth and power, but now weakened by civil war and by drought, for the Nile had failed to inundate the delta for the past five years.

Owing to the sudden death of its chosen leader, the Crusade took some time to gather momentum, but by 1202 there was considerable activity all over Europe. Negotiations had been concluded with the great maritime republic of Venice for the transportation of the army. The old Crusader route via Constantinople, across the Bosporus, and down through Asia Minor to Syria had become more and more dangerous because of the increasing activity of the Turks, who in the Third Crusade had almost totally destroyed a great German army under Frederick I, Emperor of the West. To take the sea route was practical, then, especially since the objective was Egypt and the first target was to be Alexandria. With Alexandria captured, the leaders of the Crusade felt confident that they would have a perfect base for the maintenance of further men and supplies while they themselves stormed south into the Sultan's lands. They chose Venice to undertake their transport, since the Venetians had the best shipbuilding capability and offered them terms which at the time seemed acceptable.

The Doge of Venice was Enrico Dandolo, a shrewd and unscrupulous patrician. He cared more for his city than he did for any Crusade, and would have transported Moslems as willingly as Christians if it had led to increased trade and the aggrandizement of the Republic. Pope Innocent III was aware of this, and from the very first viewed the choice of Venice with grave suspicion. He feared that the Venetians would try in some way to use the Crusaders for their own purposes. He would have had ample grounds for his fears had he but known that even before the Crusaders had assembled in Venice to join the fleet, the Venetians were conducting trade talks with the Sultan of Egypt. The Sultan had offered the Venetians a large sum in cash, as well as promising them valuable trading concessions in Alexandria, if they saw to it that the Crusaders were diverted from his land. In view of what followed (although there is no documentary evidence to confirm that any agreement was signed), it seems almost certain that the Doge and the Council had decided to divert the Crusade even before it assembled on their soil.

During the years 1202 and 1203 the bulk of the crusading army made their way through Europe, over the Alps, and south through Lombardy to Venice. The agreement that had been made with the Republic was that the Venetians, for the sum of 86,000 marks, would transport 4000 knights, each with his horse, 9000 squires, and 20,000 foot-soldiers; and that they would, in addition, victual them for a year. But many of the Crusaders, unwilling to wait for the rest, had arranged for separate transport for themselves, and had sailed independently for Acre. Others failed to arrive. This loss in numbers meant that their leaders were now saddled with a sum far in excess of what they could hope to raise from their dwindled company. The Venetians, for their part, were adamant that the stipulated amount must be paid. As they pointed out, they had built the agreed number of galleys and merchantmen, including special transports for the horses, and it was not their fault if the crusading army did not need so large a fleet. They had spent their time, money, and materials on the preparation, and now they wanted their money back. The leaders of the Crusade, the Marquis of Montferrat, the Comte de Villehardouin, the Count of Saint Paul, and the Count of Flanders, were in a quandary. Many of the Crusaders had run out of funds, the leaders had already borrowed 5000 marks from Venetian money-lenders, and, even though their private plate and valuables were sent over to the Doge in lieu of money, they still lacked 34,000 marks of the agreed sum.

The Venetians were unwilling to have too many of these quarrelsome Franks in their gracious city, and anyway there was not enough room, so a large part of the knights and men-at-arms were encamped on the island of Saint Nicholas, about three miles from Venice. This suited the Doge very well. While they were on the island they could be supplied only by boat – and boats could run only at his convenience. He had the Crusaders in the palm of his hand, for they certainly could not return to their homes after having come all this way. Many of them, indeed, had no choice, for they had no money left and could only go forward in the anticipation of profitable loot in the sack of Alexandria. Dandolo now called a meeting of the Council. He carefully pointed out that Venice had fulfilled her side of the contract; if the Crusaders could not keep their part of the bargain, the city was fully entitled to retain the money they had already paid. He suggested that it would be more profitable to offer them terms: they should be made to work for the residual sum. At a later meeting with the leaders of the Crusade he was quite explicit: "From the moment that your ambassadors first made this proposition about the fleet, I have ensured that every aspect of business throughout my territories should be directed to the sole aim of furnishing your crusade. . . . But my people have now lost a great deal – and that's the reason why they, and I too, are determined that you shall pay us the money you owe. And if you don't, then let me tell you that you shall not move a foot from the island until we have been paid. Quite apart from which, you will not find anyone who'll bring you anything to eat or drink."

Shortly afterwards the Doge made his intentions plain. If the Crusaders were prepared to help him in the reduction of the great Adriatic seaport and city of Zara (which had been taken from him by the King of Hungary, and which now seriously threatened Venetian trade in the Adriatic), then he was confident that they would lay their hands on enough specie, plate, and other valuables to pay their debt. He would then, of course, fulfil his side of the bargain and transport them to Egypt.

Although many of the Crusaders were revolted by the idea of attacking the city of the Christian King of Hungary (some even left the expedition at this point), their leaders and the bulk of the army felt that they had no option but to accede to this request. So, in the late autumn of 1202, 480 ships left Venice with the army of the Fourth Crusade aboard, bound for the reduction of Zara. In the face of so large a fleet and army the city inevitably fell, amid scenes of murder and rapine and pillage; not even the churches of their fellow Christians were spared. On hearing the news, the Pope's immediate reaction was to pass sentence of excommunication upon the Venetians and Crusaders alike.

Excommunicated, compelled to pass a long hard winter on the Adriatic shore, and disappointed because the city had not yielded half as much as had been expected, the army became even further demoralized. There were many defections; some knights and men fought their way through to try to get back to their homes in the North; while those who stayed soon found that the cost of their keep was eating into what money and valuables they had stolen. The result was that by the spring of 1303 their position was in every way as desperate as it had been in Venice – if not worse. They were still short of the sum they owed the Venetians; they were cut off in a hostile country; and they had no way of leaving except with the assistance of the Venetian fleet. This was the moment that the Doge had been waiting for, and he was assisted in his machinations by one of the leaders of the Crusade, Boniface, Marquis of Montferrat.

There had been, as was not unusual in the labyrinthine intrigue of Byzantium, a recent change of rulers: the last Emperor, Isaac, had been dethroned by Alexius III. Alexius, however, had been inefficient enough to allow Isaac's son to escape. He had made his way to Germany, where he had proposed to the Marquis of Montferrat that the Crusaders should restore him to his father's throne. In return for this favour, he had promised a large sum of money and the assistance of the Byzantine fleet and army in the Crusade. This young man was to provide both the excuse and the instrument by means of which the Fourth Crusade was diverted from its expedition against Egypt.

Doge Dandolo, so a contemporary account tells us, "seeing that [the Crusaders] were disturbed by their predicament, called a meeting and addressed them: 'My Lords,' he said, 'there is in Greece a country that is rich, and well supplied with everything that you need. If we could only find a reasonable excuse to go there and take what we need to see us on our way, that would seem to me an ideal solution. In this way we could easily manage to get ourselves to the lands overseas.'"

The plotters had rehearsed their dialogue well. At this moment the Marquis of Montferrat rose to his feet. "'My Lords, I have been staying during Christmas in Germany, at the court of the Emperor. There I happened to meet a young man who is the brother of the Emperor's wife. This young man is the son of the Emperor Isaac of Constantinople, who was removed from the throne by the treason of one of his brothers. If we take this young man with us, we could justifiably enter the territory of Constantinople, and there secure our stores and provisions, for he is indeed the legitimate Emperor.'"

The stage was now set for one of the most despicable acts of history – the diversion of the Fourth Crusade from its legitimate expedition against Egypt to the conquest and subjection of Constantinople and the Byzantine Empire. Christians who had "taken the Cross" to fight against the Moslem and restore the security of the Holy Places were now to capture the citadel of eastern Christendom and destroy the bulwark of Byzantium – that shield behind which the countries of Europe had been enabled to survive and evolve.

The relationship between Byzantium and the West had rarely been friendly. From the time that the Normans had begun to move into the ancient territories of the eastern empire in southern Italy and Sicily, there had been many conflicts. At the end of the eleventh century, Alexius Comnenus thought he had found a convenient way in which to harness the rude fighting abilities of these northerners to his own ambitions when he had invited them to assist in the reclamation of the Holy Places. Little more than a century later it was to be seen that, although he had for a time helped to salvage a large part of the Byzantine Empire, he had inadvertently invited a guest who was to turn thief. Byzantine Greeks of the Orthodox Church and Latins of the Roman Church had never made easy bedfellows, in either religious, intellectual, moral, or military terms. Many of the Normans disliked a Byzantine more than a Moslem, conceding to the Moslem that he was, at least, a good fighter. (Other allies in later centuries have also ended up disliking each other almost more than the common enemy.)

The proposition of Doge Dandolo and the Marquis of Montferrat that the Crusaders should now invade the territories of Byzantium in order to secure enough provisions, property, and money to prosecute their journey was not distasteful to many of the knights. Certainly, a high proportion of the ordinary men-at-arms cannot have cared very much whom they were fighting against, provided that they earned a living and could put aside some small bonus of loot. Not without some dissentients, the Crusade was now diverted into Byzantine territories. Venice provided the fleet, and Doge Dandolo, over eighty years old though he was, went along too. Despite his age he had "taken the Cross" before the Crusaders had first left Venice. Like the Crusaders he had been excommunicated after the capture of Zara. But, whereas the Crusaders had now been forgiven by the Pope (who had learned the truth of how they had been blackmailed into the assault), the Doge and the Venetians remained under the papal interdict. It is unlikely that Enrico Dandolo was unduly troubled.

The army sailed from Zara in the spring of 1203. It stopped for a time in the green, high-pinnacled island of Corfu, which had once provided the bone of contention leading to the Peloponnesian War, and which was witnessing once again a great movement of ships and men inspired by ignorant rapacity. The Venetian fleet consisted of over 450 warships, merchantmen, and transports, and it must have made an awe-inspiring impression upon the citizens on the walls of Constantinople when, on July 5, it dropped anchor on the far side of the Bosporus. The

Comte de Villehardouin in his memoirs of the Crusade wrote that, "to the east the Straits seemed to blossom with the decorated warships, galleys, and merchantmen. It was something so beautiful as to remember all one's life."

During the reigns of a succession of weak and corrupt Emperors, the Byzantine fleet, upon which the safety of Constantinople and the security of the empire had always depended, had been allowed to run down until it was, at this moment, almost non-existent. Nicetas, the Greek historian of the Fourth Crusade, remarks of the Byzantine admiral, "He had sold the anchors, sails, and everything else belonging to the Byzantine navy which could possibly be turned into money." There can be no doubt that Doge Dandolo was aware of the condition of the fleet, for the Venetians maintained an excellent intelligence service through their merchants, and there was a whole Venetian colony in Constantinople. He certainly knew that he was unlikely to encounter much naval opposition, and this must have encouraged him in his plans. The city itself, secure behind its magnificent series of walls, could well have withstood the Crusaders, as it had withstood many other and larger armies. But once control of the sea had been lost, the fall of Constantinople was inevitable.

The entrance to the Golden Horn was still protected in time of siege by a vast chain, one end of which was secured at the city walls on the southern side, and the other to a windlass in a fortified tower, the Tower of Galata, on the northern side. The chain was normally lowered so that it was well below the water, providing no obstruction to vessels entering or leaving. But when the city was threatened, the chain was hauled up, presenting an impregnable front to any advancing warships. This form of protection had served well for centuries, and had kept out the Arabs and other invading fleets. But the designers of the tower and of the city walls had never considered that the Byzantine fleet would ever be too weak to provide opposition to a landing. Accordingly, the Tower of Galata had not been built to withstand a siege, and the city walls facing the Golden Horn were not as strong as the Marmora walls, for it had not been anticipated that any hostile ships would be able to pass the chain.

The army of the Fourth Crusade was ferried across the Bosporus by the Venetian fleet, landing practically unopposed near the Tower of

Galata on July 6, 1203. On the following day an ineffective force of Byzantine cavalry was put to flight by the heavily armoured knights, whose training, armour, and weapons were expressly designed for this kind of warfare. A brief struggle followed, and then the all-important tower was in the hands of the Crusaders and Venetians. The latter, familiar with such harbour defences as chains and windlasses, took but a matter of minutes to unshackle the great cable. As it slipped away from the tower to disappear at the bottom of the Golden Horn, the galleys of Venice, which had been waiting for this moment, swept into those waters where no hostile fleet had ever preceded them. The moribund Byzantine ships offered practically no resistance. "So they took the galleys of the Greeks and all the other vessels that were in the harbour."

This was the beginning of the end. Although plot and counterplot within the city and outside went on for a further nine months, the fate of Constantinople and its empire was decided in that moment when the Venetians breached the entrance to the Golden Horn. On April 12, 1204, the great city of Constantine fell to the army of the Fourth Crusade amid scenes of rapine and plunder that equalled, if they did not exceed, the behaviour of those earlier Crusaders in their capture of Jerusalem. The Byzantines, once their city wall was breached and the invaders within the gates, had laid down their arms, expecting that the normal rules of warfare would obtain and that, having submitted, they would be spared. They had never seen the berserker fury of a western army when let loose in a captured city. The Crusaders, for their part, had never had such a city to sack. As one of them wrote in his account of the entry into Constantinople: "One found there a vast wealth of richness, for there were the rich crowns which had belonged to previous emperors, and rich jewels of gold and rich garments of silk embroidered with gold, and rich imperial robes, and rich precious stones. Indeed there were so many rich things that one could hardly count the huge treasure of gold and silver to be found in the palace as well as in many other places in the city." At long last, the Venetians were to be paid, in full measure and running over.

In the sack of the city nothing was spared, not even the greatest church of Christendom, Santa Sophia itself. Even the altars were broken up for the sake of their gold and silver, and priceless ikons were ripped from their frames so that their precious stones could be extracted and the frames themselves melted down. For years to come western Europe was to be flooded with loot from Constantinople. Churches and private houses were to be enriched with jewellery, enamels, and works of art that had come from the great city on the Bosporus. Nicetas, writing in exile after the fall of Constantinople, states the crime of the Crusaders explicitly: "They had taken up the Cross and had sworn on it and on the Holy Gospels that they would pass over the lands of the Christians without shedding blood and without turning to the right hand or the left. They had told us that they had taken up arms against the Saracens only and that they would steep them in their blood alone. They had promised to keep themselves chaste while they bore the Cross as be-fitted soldiers of Christ. But instead of defending his tomb, they had outraged the faithful who are members of Him. They used Christians worse than the Arabs use Latins, for at least the Arabs respected women."

Now that the city and the empire were theirs, there was no more talk about the original object of the Crusade. Egypt, Syria, the Holy Land itself, all were forgotten in the haste to share out the territories of Byzantium between the victorious nobles and their partner, Venice. Pope Innocent III's dream of a great Crusade to recapture the East had been shattered by a nightmare of screams as the swords of western Christians cut down the Christians of the Orthodox Church. Any hope the Pope may have had that the horror of the sack of Constantinople might be redeemed by the union of the two Churches was to be equally vain. The manner in which Constantinople had been taken and the way in which the men who had taken it proceeded to divide up the Byzan-tine Empire between them induced such a loathing of the western Church among the Greeks that their dislike of Rome has continued into the twentieth century.

The Byzantine pretender to the throne, young Alexius, who had provided the pretext for the diversion of the Crusade, had been killed by the Byzantines in a counterplot during his brief reign. His successor was equally promptly killed by the Crusaders. It was inevitable, there-fore, that the next Emperor of East Rome would be a Latin, and Bald-win, Count of Flanders, was accordingly elected. Boniface, Marquis of Montferrat, the other leader of the expedition, carved out a large territory for himself in Salonika. Meanwhile small Latin feudal principalities were set up throughout the whole area of Greece. All that now remains to show they ever existed are Crusader castles, still to be found in many parts of Greece, dominating a silent valley or overhanging a high headland.

It was Venice which, above all, profited from the Fourth Crusade – just as Doge Dandolo had always intended. He demanded and got from the Crusaders what he was pleased to call "a half and a quarter of the whole Roman Empire". In fact, while Baldwin and Boniface acquired large areas of territory on the mainland, it was Venice which acquired the really useful spoils – all the main harbours and islands that furnished stepping-stones to the East. In this way Venice acquired the Ionian coast of Greece, together with the Ionian Islands, the ports on the northern side of the Sea of Marmora, whatever ports she required in the Greek Peloponnese, and the islands of Andros, Euboea, and Naxos, as well as Gallipoli and the great inland trading centre of Adrianople. At one blow Venice had destroyed Byzantium, long her greatest rival in the eastern trade, and had secured an invaluable lifeline that would ensure her predominance over other rivals like Genoa.

The real foundation of Venetian fortunes was laid by Doge Dandolo. In later centuries his countrymen acclaimed him as one of their greatest heroes. The historian of the Mediterranean must regard him, however, not so much as a great architect of Venetian power, but as a vandal who did incalculable damage to the whole structure of Europe and of Christendom. The Latin kingdom of Constantinople did not last long. Torn by dissension and surrounded by a hostile populace, it was destined to fall at the first concerted blow. The historian Gregorovius best pronounced its epitaph: "a creation of western European crusading knights, of the selfish trade-policy of the Venetians, and of the hierarchical idea of the papacy, it fell after a miserable existence . . . leaving behind it no other trace than destruction and anarchy. That deformed chivalrous state of the Latins belongs to the most worthless phenomena of history."

Only fifty-seven years after its conquest by the Crusaders, Constantinople was recaptured by the Greek ruler of Nicaea, Michael Palaeologus. A Greek dynasty was restored, the rite of the Roman Church was expunged, and a Greek Patriarch returned once more to Santa Sophia and the ancient city of Constantine. For nearly two hundred years more the shadowy relic of the eastern Roman Empire was to maintain an existence that, although always threatened, showed a remarkable revival in terms of art and culture. But so much of its territories had been lost – the Crusaders and the Venetians had done their work too well – that at the first major assault by a hostile power it was doomed to fall again. In 1453, the Ottoman Turks stormed the city and established their permanent presence in Europe. They were to make the kingdoms of the West bitterly regret that the Byzantine Empire was no longer there to protect them.

If there was one by-product of the Fourth Crusade which may be said to have benefited Europe as a whole, it was the unleashing of a flood of works of art, as well as emigrant artists, throughout Italy, Sicily, and other parts of the Mediterranean. The Renaissance, which it was once customary to date as beginning shortly after the capture of the city by the Turks in 1453, had begun long before that. As D. Talbot Rice remarks in *Art of the Byzantine Era*: "It was really as a result of the immense influx of Byzantine works of art brought after 1204 as loot accumulated by the Fourth Crusade that the imitation of Byzantine objects began on a really wide scale, and it was then that Venice became really active as a centre for the production of works in metal and enamel, and even stone, in a basically Byzantine style, so that it is sometimes hard to tell the Venetian copies from the Byzantine originals. . . ."

The presence of the Knights of Saint John in Rhodes is, as can now be seen, only a footnote to the fall of the Byzantine Empire. If the Venetians and the soldiers of the Fourth Crusade had not betrayed their cause and their faith in 1204, there would have been no Latin crusading order in the formerly Byzantine island of Rhodes. But it is reasonable to add that, if the Byzantines had maintained their first line of defence – their fleet – in proper order, there would not have been a Latin conquest of their city. The fact that it was the Pope and the Genoese who, in 1309, assisted the Order of Saint John in their conquest of Rhodes derives also from the events of 1204. After that date no Pope ever felt that he could trust Venice; and after that date Venice's great commercial rival, Genoa, would do anything to make sure that the Venetians acquired no further islands or trading posts in the Aegean. Religious differences may have been widely exploited during this period of Mediterranean history, but in the end cupidity governed all.

ELEVEN

The Maritime Republics

One of the principal results of the Fourth Crusade was to establish Venice as the dominant maritime power in the eastern Mediterranean. She consolidated her recent gains by buying Crete from the Marquis of Montferrat, who had little use for an island so remote from his mainland territory in Salonika. Crete, as far as the Venetians were concerned, gave them a controlling hold over the whole of the Aegean. The Moslems had found out before them that it could act like a sword laid across the throat of this northern section of the sea. It was also invaluable for their trade with Egypt and the Levant, having excellent harbours at Khania and Kandia (Heraklion) in the north, and Messara Bay and many other useful anchorages in the south.

Venice was now happily astride all the main routes to the trade of the East, having signed a very favourable agreement with the Sultan of Egypt in 1208 (four years after Dandolo's betrayal of the Fourth Crusade). This gave her markets and trading privileges in Alexandria far above those of any of her European rivals. Venice had made herself dominant throughout the Adriatic, the Ionian, the Grecian archipelago, the Sea of Marmora, and the Black Sea, as well as on the trade route between Constantinople and Europe. Now, established in Alexandria and Syria, she controlled most of the trade between the Near East and Europe. The "City of the Lagoons", whose *sposalizio del mar* (wedding of the sea) dated from the eleventh century, was indeed mistress of the eastern Mediterranean. As H. R. Forbes Brown writes in the *Encyclopaedia Britannica*: "She was raised at once to the position of a European power. In order to hold these possessions, she borrowed from the Franks the feudal system, and granted fiefs in the Greek islands to her more powerful families, on condition that they held the trade route open for her. The expansion of commerce which resulted from the Fourth Crusade soon made itself evident in the city by a rapid development in its architecture and by a decided strengthening of the commercial aristocracy, which eventually led to the great constitutional reform – the closing of the Maggior Consiglio in 1296, whereby Venice became a rigid oligarchy. Externally this rapid success awoke the implacable hatred of Genoa, and led to the long and exhausting Genoese wars. . . ."

Venice was the first great Mediterranean oligarchy for many centuries. The beauty that still confronts the modern traveller is a testimony to the fact that an oligarchy in the hands of cultured men can often achieve more than the free-for-all of democracy. The glory of Periclean Athens might be quoted in argument against this, but in the fifth century B.C. Athens was largely the product of an aristocratic dictatorship – in which the ordinary citizen was merely encouraged to feel that he was living in a democracy.

Venice, in the centuries of her greatness, was perhaps nearer to ancient Carthage than any other Mediterranean city before or since. She fought wars reluctantly, and only when her trade routes were imperilled. Her constitution was administered by great and powerful mercantile families, and, despite a few abortive attempts at revolution, most of her citizens grew to realize that they were better off under such guidance than under any more "popular" form of government. Trade was the great concern of Venice – not empire, politics, or religion. Like Carthage in the early phases of that city, Venice was not concerned with colonies, but with suitable anchorages and marts where her ships could rest and repair and her merchants buy and sell. True, Venice owned the great island of Crete as well as large areas of mainland Greece, but her interest rarely extended to the hinterland. Venetian citizens, the emigrant population derived from her increasing birth rate, were not to be found as inland farmers, but as shopkeepers, merchants, and craftsmen in seaports spread from the Adriatic to the Levant.

Some large part of Venice's success as a naval power during the latter part of the thirteenth century was due to her improvement on the basic Mediterranean galley form. The city also created a state galley system, rather on the lines of a modern nationalized industry. Venice did not make the mistake, however, of creating a monopoly out of her state

SWITZERLAND
AUSTRIA
HUNGARY

FRANCE

Trent
• Zagreb
RUMANIA
Timisoara
(Temesvar)

Milan
Turin •
Pavia
Cremona •
Trieste •
Venice
Chioggia

PIEDMONT
Marengo
Po R.
ISTRIA
Danube R.
Belgrade

Genoa
Bologna •
Ravenna •

Nice •
Florence •
SAN MARINO
Zara •
YUGOSLAVIA
Sarajevo •
Naissus
(Nish) •

Fréjus •
Toulon •
Pisa •
Livorno
(Leghorn)
Volterra •
Siena
Metaurus R.
Adriatic

MONACO
Portoferraio
Populonia •
Vetulonia •
Trasimene
Spalato •

Calvi •
Bastia •
ELBA
Tiber R.
Pescara •
Sea

CORSICA
(Fr.)
Porto •
Ajaccio •
Tarquinia •
Civita Vecchio
Cerveteri •
Rome

Ostia •
Anzio •
Terracina •
Cannae •
Bari •
ALBANIA

ITALY
Calvi •
Naples
Salerno •

SARDINIA
See inset below
Heraclea •
Taranto •

Cagliari •
Tyrrhenian Sea
Sybaris •
C. Santa Maria
di Leuca
GREECE

C. Spartivento
Cosenza •
CORFU
(CORCYRA)
Actium ■
LEUCAS

Med
Palermo
(Panormus)
Messina •
CEPHALONIA

Bône
(Hippo
Reglus) •
Bizerta •
C. Farina
Trapani
(Drepanum) •
Reggio •
ZANTE
(ZACYNTHUS)

Carthage
C. Bon
SICILY
(TRINACRIA)
Catania •
Ionian
Pylos •

Constantine •
Tunis •
Zama •
C. Passero
Syracuse •
Sea

Quairawan •
Sousse •
GOZO
MALTA

TUNISIA
Sfax •

Gabes •
DJERBA I.

Tripoli •
Gulf of Sirte
Benghazi •

ALGERIA

CENTRAL MEDITERRANEAN

L I B Y A

CAMPANIA
Kyme
(Cumae) •
Pozzuoli (Puteoli)
Naples
(Neapolis)
MT. VESUVIUS
Herculaneum
PROCIDA
Misenum •
Pompeii •
Torre
Annunziata
Castellammare
(Stabiae)
Salerno •
*ISLE OF
ISCHIA*
Gulf of Naples
Sorrento •
Amalfi •
ISLE OF CAPRI
0   *Miles*   20

0   200 Kilometers
0   100   200 Miles

galleys, or of outlawing private industry; she merely used them to implement the city's trade and to add greater lustre to its reputation abroad. The state galleys were, in fact, a spur to private ownership. Sometimes it would appear that these galleys were under state control, while at other times they were hired out to private contractors. By using the capital resources of the state purse, it was possible to make them a great deal larger, better built, and better equipped than most of the trading galleys then operating in the Mediterranean.

It must be stressed that these "Great Galleys", as they were called, were primarily merchant ships. They were quite capable of fighting if need be, but, unlike the war galleys of the Knights of Saint John, the state galleys of Venice were more like fast armed merchantmen. Because so much of the Republic's trade was in the spices of the East (a small expensive cargo needing swift transshipment), Venice developed the large galley rather than the even larger sailing carrack. The latter was the mainstay of the mercantile marine of Genoa. Genoese trade was principally in bulk cargoes like wool and grain, so it was natural for her to place more reliance upon slower, but larger, sailing ships.

From the last decade or so of the thirteenth century right through to the sixteenth century, the Great Galley was the most impressive vessel to be seen in the Mediterranean. Carracks might be larger and carry more tonnage, but for sheer splendour the Great Galley was supreme. Built wider in the beam than the long galley or warship, she would have an average length of nearly 140 feet, on a beam of 20 feet or slightly less, while her midships depth would be about 9 feet. She was not so fine fore and aft as a war galley, but had a softer and more rounded profile. The overhangs were not so extreme, with the result that she had greater carrying capacity. Although, like all galleys, she was an oared vessel, the Great Galley was primarily a sailing ship. Her oars were mainly used for taking her in or out of harbour, or in calms, or if the wind blew foul. She generally set two masts with lateen sails, although three masts were not unknown, and a drawing in a treatise on galley construction shows a Venetian Great Galley stepping three lateen-sailed masts. One great advantage that the galleys of the late Middle Ages and the Renaissance period had over their classical ancestors was that, by the fourteenth century, the centre-line, axled, hinged rudder had displaced the old steering paddles. The rudder, a northern development, had first been introduced into the Mediterranean on the sailing carracks, but it was quickly adopted by the galleys.

M. E. Mallett, in *The Florentine Galleys*, although writing of a somewhat later period, compares the complement of war galleys and Great Galleys: "The size of the crews in the two types of galley was in fact very similar. The great galley might require a few more sailors to handle its greater sail area, while the long galley would normally carry more fighting men. The Florentine great galleys carried between 200 and 220 men, of whom about 150 were oarsmen and ordinary sailors and the remaining 50–70 made up of officers, senior sailors, and marines. Venetian galleys of the same period also carried a crew of about 210, while the Genoese long galleys carried 176. Much of the fighting strength of a galley lay in its large crew, for in addition to the officers and marines, who were naturally armed, it was usual to provide arms for the sailors and sometimes for the oarsmen as well."

Unlike the vessels of the Knights of Saint John and their Turkish enemies, those of the Italian maritime states – at least at this period in their history – were still manned by freemen: professional sailors and oarsmen who came from the major ports, as well as the local fishing villages. At a later date, when the whole Mediterranean was torn by the wars between the Ottoman Turks and the European powers, it became increasingly the practice to fill the oar-benches with enslaved Moslems and civil criminals and debtors. But, so long as it was possible to man a Great Galley with free citizens, the ships of the Italian maritime republics were more efficient than those of their enemies.

Navigational methods were little changed from those of previous centuries. Generally speaking, in the Mediterranean, at any rate, it was the custom to "port-hop", cruising along the coast on runs of a set length between one harbour or anchorage and another. Quite apart from its navigational convenience, large crews needed a considerable quantity of stores, and there was little space for them when the galley was fully loaded with her cargo. Apart from the bread, dry biscuit, salt meat, and salt fish that formed their iron rations, it was customary to take aboard fresh stores at every new port of call.

The Great Galleys were far less tied to the coast than the war galleys and, since they relied largely on the wind rather than their oars, they often made direct open-sea passages. Again unlike the war galleys, which tended to follow much the same routine as all earlier warships in Mediterranean history (in harbour from autumn until spring), these large merchant galleys worked the sea day in, day out. Since they were later to be used regularly by Florence (among other cities) on the wool trade with England – which necessitated crossing the hazardous Bay of Biscay at almost all seasons of the year – it is quite clear that the galleys of the Italian maritime republics were more efficient than any that this sea had known before.

The Venetians were the first to employ Great Galleys in any numbers, after the enormous development of their trade with the East subsequent to 1204. By the end of the century they had a fleet of about a dozen running on regular schedules between Venice, Crete, Alexandria, and Syria, as well as north to Constantinople and the Black Sea. Venice exported woollens and silk clothes, as well as the numerous products of her rapidly increasing industries in glass and metalware. In return, she imported the spices so necessary for the preservation and titillation of European food and palates (some were also used medicinally), together with the silk and cotton of the East and furs and other raw materials from Constantinople and the Black Sea. Slaves were later to form a fairly constant item on the cargo lists of vessels returning from the East, and black slaves became a regular feature of the Venetian nobleman's house.

In the conflict that was to arise between the maritime republics, particularly between Venice and Genoa, it was the long war galley that, as always, was to play an all-important part. These were similar to the galleys of the Knights of Saint John, being often over 130 feet in length, on a beam of 15 feet, with the greatest depth amidships about 6 feet. It is doubtful whether, under oars, they made much more than four and a half knots – and even this only in short bursts, such as when going in to ram. Under sail, however, they could, with their great waterline length, have made two to three times this speed, provided that they had a fair wind.

The wars between Pisa, Genoa, Venice, and Florence were in many respects very similar in cause, effects, and in the method of their conduct to those which centuries before had bedevilled the city-states of Greece (to which the Italian maritime republics bore a remarkably close resemblance). If one changes the names to Athens, Corinth, Corcyra, and Syracuse, the following, by H. A. L. Fisher, might have been written about events of the fourth century B.C.: "Despite the fact that [Italy] was now fast securing for herself the leadership of the world in craftsmanship and international commerce, the warfare of city with city was almost perpetual. Cities would fight about diocesan boundaries and feudal rights, over tolls and markets, for the extension of their powers over the *contado* or surrounding country, or in pursuance of the long-inherited feuds within their walls.

"Mere contiguity was a potent cause of fiery and enduring hatreds. If Florence took one side in a quarrel, it was sufficient for Pisa, Siena, and Genoa to take the other; if Milan entered into an alliance with other cities, it would not at least be with Cremona and Pavia; and so long as the exploitation of Corsica and Sardinia was an open question between them, Genoa and Pisa were inveterate in rivalry."

After the decline of Pisa, which became subject to Florence in the fourteenth century, the great struggle that convulsed the sea was between Venice and Genoa. They had been rivals for the eastern trade ever since the period of the Crusades, when Venice had scored heavily over her rival in the misdirection of the Fourth Crusade. The Genoese, however, had seen how much of Venice's prosperity stemmed from her Byzantine success and turned the tables neatly on the Venetians in 1261, when to some extent they reversed the achievement of Doge Dandolo by assisting in the restoration of the Greek Emperor, Michael Palaeologus. This, of course, gave them a "most favoured nation" status in the revived Byzantine city. The Genoese received for their services the whole quarter of Pera, on the northern side of the Golden Horn – the area where had stood the fateful Tower of Galata. Genoa now succeeded in almost entirely ousting Venice from the vital Black Sea trade.

So long as Venice continued happy with her trade to Egypt and the Levant and the Genoese held the monopoly of the North, there was little reason for conflict. For a whole century the two cities managed to preserve some semblance of peace on the sea routes between Italy and the eastern Mediterranean. Their naval and mercantile fleets, though of somewhat different calibre, were almost equal, and both cities thrived and grew prosperous. Genoa the Superb and Venice the Serene Republic acquired during these years that atmosphere of aristocratic dignity and self-confident grandeur which still, despite the depredations of the centuries, remain theirs to this day. Both cities also might willingly have echoed the old Latin proverb "Let me be called the worst of mankind, so long as I am called rich."

The conflict which developed between the two republics centred, inevitably, around the eastern trade routes. During the late thirteenth and fourteenth centuries, Cyprus became a centre of dispute – much as Sicily had been in earlier centuries. After the fall of Acre and the collapse of the Latin kingdom, Cyprus automatically acquired a considerable importance in Latin eyes. Venetian and Genoese ships and armies fought back and forth over its gracious lands and ancient cities.

In 1373 the Genoese seized the superb old port of Famagusta. Its capture, together with their occupation of the important eastern Aegean island of Chios, centre of the mastic trade, greatly improved their position in the East. But it was in the western Mediterranean that the Genoese were at their strongest, for they had occupied Corsica and had their eyes on Sardinia. (Their interest in Sardinia was later to bring them into conflict with the Catalans of Aragon, who were to become the third naval power in the Mediterranean after Venice and Genoa.)

Once again, this time in the thirteenth century, the Aegadian Islands and the strait between them and Trapani in western Sicily were to witness a sea battle that, for a time at least, determined the maritime balance of power. The Venetian fleet caught the Genoese in the shadow of Mount Erice and the constricted waters of the Goat Islands, and defeated them so decisively that the Byzantine Emperor (who owed his throne to Genoa) callously abandoned them and took the Venetians back into favour. So, backwards and forwards over the sea, the conflict of trading interests, represented by the passage of the Great Galleys and carracks, resulted in the clash of arms, the sigh of arrows, and the splintering crash of timbers as the rams of the long galleys tore into one another's sides.

The main reason for the ultimate victory of the Venetians was probably the fact that their republic, safeguarded by the oligarchic Council of Ten, had a political stability that their rival lacked. While Venice's geographical position was nothing like as safe as that of Genoa (which fronted upon the sea and was backed by a ring of mountains), the

Venetians to some extent possessed that type of iron-bound certainty which had once helped to raise Rome out of the ruck of her other rivals. Venice's constitution, narrow and dictatorial though it was, was strong enough to withstand adversity – and small enough to be a guarantee of quick action. In some respects also, the Council of Ten resembled the Council of Elders at Carthage: senior members of the rich merchant class who, because they had the greatest investment in the state, were considered the most suitable men to wield the power of that state. Against the strength and stability of Venice, Genoa presented a very dissimilar picture. She was eternally divided between the four noble houses of Doria, Grimaldi, Fieschi, and Spinola, whose bitter feuding and in-fighting on more than one occasion nearly destroyed the whole structure of their city-state.

In 1339, in an attempt to emulate Venice, the Genoese elected a "Doge", or chief magistrate, and disqualified the nobility from holding any political office. But the nobles were far too rich and powerful to be deterred by this. All that happened was that they bought the interests of different plebeian families, with the result that the office of Doge in Genoa became something of a farce – the chief magistrate automatically becoming an adherent of whichever noble family supported him. Furthermore, the fact that the military and naval forces of Genoa were still commanded by the nobility meant that, outside of civil politics, they commanded the real power of the state. From time to time, the citizens of Genoa, anxious to secure some stability in their strife-torn city, would invite one of the greater powers – France or Milan, for instance – to take them under their protection. Even this voluntary sacrifice of their liberty (often regretted within a few months) did not give their prosperous city its necessary internal repose. Genoa's political weakness was, more than anything else, the cause of her ultimate decline.

The final conflict between the two states was sparked off by a palace revolution in Constantinople, in which the Venetians backed the Emperor, John Palaeologus, while the Genoese backed his son. War again broke out between Venice and Genoa, in which the Venetians at first gained the upper hand, defeating the Genoese fleet off Cape Antium in the Adriatic. But in the following year, 1379, the Venetian Admiral Vettor Pisani was totally defeated by Luciano Doria, and the

Genoese fleet captured the town of Chioggia at the head of one of the main entrances to the Venetian lagoons. They at once settled down to blockade Venice itself, and for a time it looked as if the final defeat of their ancient enemy was in the offing. The blockade was a mistake in policy, however (Venice might have failed had it been immediately assaulted), and Admiral Pisani was put in command of a new fleet.

Meanwhile the Venetian fleet of the Levant was hastily summoned back to the defence of the Republic. The besiegers became the besieged and Pisani drove the Genoese back to Chioggia, where they in their turn found themselves blockaded. The arrival of the Levant ships completed the ruin of Genoese hopes, and the whole of their force was compelled to surrender in June 1379. It was a blow from which the proud city never quite recovered. Although, for a long time to come, the Genoese mercantile marine, her galleys and carracks, continued to play a large part in western Mediterranean trade, she had now lost most of her interest and influence in the eastern basin. For the next century, forfeiting her independence first to one and then to the other, Genoa – politically, at least – served mainly as a bone of contention between France and Milan. Her greatest days were over.

The triumph of Venice, complete though it seemed at the time, was not to last for more than half a century. Even this period of prosperity was to be constantly threatened by the waxing power of the Turks in the East. During the period that the two great maritime republics had been engaged in their bitter duel for naval supremacy, they had inadvertently allowed the Ottomans to increase their power in the very area about which they were both contending. It was to their mutual interest to safeguard what remained of the eastern empire, but their self-destructive rivalry hastened what the Fourth Crusade had begun. The war between Venice and Genoa ended in the complete disintegration of European power in the East, and ultimately led to the conquest of Constantinople and its territories by the Ottoman Turks.

TWELVE

Triumphs in the East and West

By the fourteenth century, the Arab geographer Abulfeda could remark of Constantinople – for centuries the greatest capital in Europe, and renowned throughout the Middle Ages as the almost mythical "Micklegarth", The Mighty City – that it was dying. "There are sown fields within its walls and a great many ruined houses," he commented. Fifty years before its conquest by the Turks, another traveller, Gonzales de Clavijo, wrote that nearly all its great palaces and churches were desolate, adding, "it is clear, however, that at one time Constantinople must have been among the most noble cities of the world." To such a state had its conquest by the Crusaders brought this city which the Byzantine historian Ducas had once called the "heart of the four corners of the world, Paradise planted in the West."

In 1453 the final blow fell. Mohammed II, henceforth to be known throughout Europe as "the Conqueror", had long planned to make the ancient Byzantine capital his own. His father, Murad II, had already added Corinth, Patras, and the north of the Morea to the Turkish dominions, and it was Mohammed's ambition to complete his father's work by securing all of northern Greece. He had plans for an impressive Ottoman fleet, and he naturally envisaged the great harbour of the Golden Horn as its headquarters. The Turks had already come into conflict with the Venetians in the Morea, and Mohammed knew that in order to sweep this enemy out of the Aegean and the eastern seas, he must concentrate on the naval arm. The conquest of Constantinople was inspired partly by the desire to add so important a city to his dominions, and partly by long-term strategic considerations.

After many months of preparations, the siege of Constantinople began in the spring of 1453. At first the Turkish assault was repulsed, and a Genoese squadron of ships even managed to fight its way through the Ottoman fleet, to bring in supplies and reinforcements. But the defenders did not have enough troops to man the massive extent of the city's walls, and even these had fallen into disrepair during recent centuries. Furthermore, the defences had not been designed to withstand the impact of cannon shot, and the Sultan had had some large pieces of ordnance specially constructed for the siege. This was one of the first occasions when artillery was used in the assault on a European city. It foreshadowed a new age in warfare, and a complete reappraisal by military architects of all fortress and walled-city design.

The final assault was launched on May 29, when the dreaded Janissaries, those crack troops of the Ottoman Empire, stormed their way through a breach in the walls that had been made by the cannon. The last Emperor of Byzantium, called, by some irony of fate, Constantine, the name of the city's founder, was killed fighting in the breach. At long last, after twelve hundred years of astounding history and cultural achievement, the Byzantine Empire was finally destroyed. It had been a mere shadow of its former self ever since the Fourth Crusade, but even in its last two hundred years it had still helped to shield Europe from the Turks, and had produced many notable works of art and literature.

The Greeks had given the Mediterranean, Europe, and the world three civilizations: Classical Greece; Hellenistic Greece; and Byzantine Greece. Their last achievement was by no means their least. Behind the sheltering arm of the Byzantine Empire, Europe had been able to recover in some measure from the catastrophe of the fall of the western Roman Empire. The influence of Byzantium upon the arts and architecture of the Mediterranean was even now not at an end. Numerous artists and craftsmen joined all those others who had preceded them during the past two centuries to invigorate the expanding cities of Renaissance Italy. Those who stayed behind played an important part in influencing the development of Turkish arts and crafts. The vast dome of Santa Sophia itself was to be copied in many mosques throughout the city and in the widespread territories of the Ottoman Empire.

Meanwhile, as Steven Runciman writes in *The Fall of Constantinople, 1453*: "The Sultan himself entered the city in the late afternoon. Escorted by the finest of his Janissary Guards and followed by his ministers, he rode slowly through the streets to the Church of the Holy Wisdom. Before its gates he dismounted and bent down to pick a handful of earth which he poured over his turban, as an act of humility towards his God. He entered the church and stood silent for a moment. Then, as he walked towards the altar, he noticed a Turkish soldier trying to hack up a piece of the marble pavement. He turned on him angrily, and told him that permission to loot did not involve the destruction of buildings. Those he reserved for himself. There were still a few Greeks cowering in corners whom the Turks had not yet bound and taken away. He ordered that they should be allowed to go in peace to their homes. Next, a few priests came out from the secret passages behind the altar and begged him for mercy. Them too he sent away under his protection. But he insisted that the church should at once be transformed into a mosque. One of his *ulema* climbed into the pulpit and proclaimed that there was no God but Allah. He himself then mounted on to the altar slab and did obeisance to his victorious God."

The decline of the city that had occurred over the past two centuries was only too evident from the ruined state of many of the buildings. Huge columns stood lonely under the sky, where a roof had collapsed; and wild grasses grew through the cracks in ancient marble floors. The conqueror, moved by the giant melancholy of the capital, is said to have recited a verse from the Persian poet Sa'di:

> Now the spider weaves the curtains in the palace
> Of the Caesars,
> Now the owl calls the night watches in the
> Towers of Afrasiab.

The fall of Constantinople sent a wave of consternation throughout Europe. The Emperor had appealed for assistance long before the Sultan's attack but, involved as they were in their rivalries, feuds, and wars, the newly emergent nations of the continent had done little or nothing to help. Only the Catalans, the Genoese, and the Venetians, whose trade with the East was involved in the security of the ancient kingdom, had done what they could in terms of ships and men to fend off the Turkish attack. All were losers in the fall of Constantinople – all except the city itself. Mohammed II was a wise and far-sighted statesman and a great military leader, and he determined that his new capital should be justly and efficiently administered. Far from penalizing the Christians for their faith, he declared himself the protector of the Greek Church and had a new Patriarch installed. Although Santa Sophia became a mosque, many of the other churches were allowed to carry on as Christian centres of worship. By thus showing his liberal instincts and restoring the dignity (even if subservient to his own) of the Orthodox Church, Mohammed capitalized on the hatred felt by the Greeks for the Latin Church and its adherents.

Genoa and Venice, meanwhile, intent on their own commercial rivalry to the exclusion of almost all else, were quick to make terms with the conqueror. Both cities agreed to pay him tribute in return for being allowed their former trading privileges and the control of all territory still in their possession. Mohammed was willing enough to grant them their privileges – at least temporarily. His designs were far-reaching, and he looked not only towards the annexation of all Greece, but also ultimately to the conquest of eastern Europe.

The fall of Constantinople brought the Ottoman Turk in full force upon the sea-lanes of the Mediterranean as yet another race of horsemen transformed itself into a great naval power. Constantinople itself, for so long moribund, was given a new injection of life by becoming the principal city of the Sultans. Trade revived; art and industry flourished; and the victorious Turks dignified the ancient capital with many splendid mosques, as well as fine private houses, warehouses, workshops, palaces, and bazaars. From now on the Sublime Porte (as it became known to generations of Europeans) was the greatest city of the East – but it was lodged in Europe, and directed its designs like a dagger at the heart of the European Mediterranean.

Action provokes reaction. Long before the Turkish conquest of Constantinople, in the far West, beyond the Pillars of Hercules, a Portuguese prince of genius had set in train a series of events that would change the history of the world. Henry of Portugal, known as Henry the Navigator, was born in 1394, the third surviving son of John I, founder of the Portuguese dynasty of Aviz, and of Philippa, daughter of John of Gaunt of England. A dedicated Christian, of somewhat the same fibre as the Knights of Saint John but a genuine celibate and ascetic, he had early in his life "taken the Cross" and had determined to carry on the war against the Moslem wherever possible. The news of the Turkish successes at the other end of the Mediterranean basin only hardened Henry's resolve to see that the Moors never regained Portugal, and that their power was cut down in all that area of coast which lay nearest to his own country. His father had been victorious in his war against Spanish Castile, and had also successfully combated attempts by the Moors to return to the Portuguese kingdom from which they had been driven in the twelfth century.

The dream of Henry the Navigator was to find a route round Africa, so that his own country might trade with the East without being dependent upon the indirect routes controlled by the Genoese and the Venetians. But what may have begun as no more than an intelligent attempt to benefit his country was materially altered by the great Turkish advances during the latter part of Prince Henry's life. Henry, in his capacity as Crusader, and in his unusual (for a prince of that period) dedication to the science of navigation and exploration, was to have an immense effect upon Mediterranean history. The discoveries of his sea-captains were to open direct trade routes with the Orient, and were to result in the ancient sea becoming of considerably less importance to northern Europeans. (In future they would largely by-pass it as they sailed south down the lanes of the Atlantic bound for the New World, India, and the Far East.) But all this was in the unforeseen future at the time when Henry, Prince of Portugal, was preparing in company with his father to capture the city and trading-post of Ceuta in North Africa.

The capture of Ceuta in 1415 by the Portuguese fleet and army was an unusual event in Mediterranean history. It marked the first time that Portugal, as a separate country from Spain, made an incursion into territories that for centuries had been ruled by Moslems. Ceuta was the second of the Pillars of Hercules – it was the ancient Abyla and the complement to the Rock of Gibraltar, which loomed over the strait fourteen miles away. Although Gibraltar itself was still in Moorish hands, Ceuta was more important, for it was from this bold African headland that the Arabs had always launched their attacks upon the Spanish peninsula. That their power was now declining was clearly shown by the fact that a comparatively small European power could land an army on the Arabs' home territory and seize one of their major cities. Out of Ceuta, the Arab galleys had long preyed upon merchant shipping as it passed through the strait, and it was from here that Arab raiding parties were sent to Spain and the Balearic Islands, to Sardinia, and as far afield as Sicily. The Phoenicians, over two thousand years before, had established a trading post at Ceuta. They had identified this rocky outcrop of North Africa and the frowning mountain of Gibraltar with the two great pillars of the world. Ceuta and Gibraltar had reminded them of the pillars in the Tyrian temple of Melkarth. These two headlands throughout most of ancient history had marked the navigator's limits. Euripides had written: "[Here begins] the untraversed sea beyond the Pillars, the end of voyaging, where the Ruler of Ocean no longer permits mariners to travel on the purple sea."

With the capture of Ceuta the Portuguese were established on the North African shore of the Mediterranean at its far western extremity. It might have been expected, perhaps, that they would now attempt to carve out an empire in North Africa (and, indeed, they would probably have been happy to do so if they had possessed sufficient man power to take on their surrounding enemies). Their subsequent actions, owing so much to the genius of a single man, took them right out of the basin of the Mediterranean and opened up the ocean sea routes of the world. When, in the far north-east of the sea, a whole civilization had collapsed and a door to the East had closed for Europe, at the western mouth of the sea another door was opened.

The contemporary historian Azurara wrote of Prince Henry that "after the taking of Ceuta, the Prince had ships always at sea to do battle against the Infidel. . . . [also] he desired to know what lands there were beyond the Canary Isles and a cape called Bojador. For at that time there was no knowledge, either in writing or in the memory of any man, of what might lie beyond this cape." Cape Bojador, which lies a little south of the Canary Islands on the west coast of Africa, had long been considered the point of no return. It was true that the Phoenicians, centuries earlier, had circumnavigated the whole continent, but this knowledge had been lost. In any case, until the Ottoman Turks threatened to cut off mediaeval Europe from its trade and contacts with the East, there had been no driving force to compel men to try to find out what lay to the south, in the dangerous reaches of the great Atlantic Ocean. In order to prosecute his studies of the Atlantic and its navigation Prince Henry now moved himself, his advisers, and his circle of navigators to Cape Sagres, the southernmost point of Portugal.

It was here, surrounded by the surge and thunder of the ocean, that he spent most of his life.

At this period in history, the Arabs' knowledge of geography and astronomy was superior to that of their European enemies. Even as early as the twelfth century, King Roger of Sicily had commended the work of the Arabic geographer Edrisi as being far in advance of any equivalent European production. Edrisi, for instance, knew that beyond the apparently limitless expanse of the Sahara there lay a fertile land beginning at the Senegal River. It was called Bilad Ghana, "Land of Wealth", and was depicted on a map made for King Roger about 1150. The Arabs were also in contact with the interior of Africa by overland trade routes, and were under no illusions that the dark continent suddenly came to an end, and that men fell off the edge of the world. On the other hand, they had little knowledge of the Atlantic coasts of Africa, and it was this area that interested Prince Henry. He was unwilling to accept the statement of the traveller Ibn Said that the world ended in the Sea of Obscurity just south of Cape Bojador. His biographer Azurara says that Prince Henry spent a vast fortune on his ambitious projects of exploration because "no sailor or merchant would undertake it, for it is very sure that such men do not dream of navigating other than to places where they already know they can make a profit."

For forty years, aided by Jewish and Arabic geographers and cartographers, Prince Henry sent out expeditions from Portugal and gradually began to push back the boundaries of the ancient world. It is true that his dream was never fulfilled in his lifetime, but he laid the foundations for all the many subsequent voyages of exploration. In 1419, Porto Santo, the smaller of the two principal Madeira Islands, was discovered, and the following year Madeira itself. The Canaries had long been known to European navigators, but it was not until Prince Henry's ships began visiting and using them systematically that they were properly explored. Between 1431 and 1444 the Azores were also discovered and charted – or perhaps rediscovered, for it seems that the Phoenicians had once used them, though once again their knowledge had long since been lost. Capo Blanco, the "White Cape", opening into Arguim Bay, was rounded in 1441, and in 1446 the Portuguese happened upon the lonely and uninhabited Cape Verde Islands. From then on, Prince Henry had less difficulty in getting other Portuguese to follow in the wake of his ships: two lucrative commodities had been found on the west coast of Africa south of Capo Blanco – gold and slaves. Before he died in 1460 he had set in train the great age of discovery, from which his own country, then Spain, France, England, and Holland would soon reap the benefits. In his quest for a sea route to India and the East, he had also inadvertently set in motion two unlooked-for by-products of exploration: the slave trade and the colonization of remote countries by Europeans.

The vessels in which Henry's captains made their first voyages were of two types. They were both of Mediterranean origin: barks, or carracks; and *barinales*, a Portuguese adaptation of the Venetian galley. Neither of these vessels was particularly suitable for coastal work off West Africa, since the *barinal* had all the disadvantages of the galley, and the square-sailed bark had difficulty in returning to the Mediterranean against the prevailing north-easterlies. It was the fear of these north-easterly "trade winds" (as they were later to become known) that had previously prevented men from exploring Africa and the Atlantic. Mariners felt sure that if they were caught running before them in a square-rigged ship, they would never be able to return, but would drive ever onwards until one day they would reach the end of the world and plunge over into the Sea of Obscurity. What was needed for successful exploration of the Atlantic, and particularly of West Africa, was a light, shallow-draft vessel that could work well to windwards – so essential for her return passage. It was these requirements that led to the evolution of the Portuguese caravel.

The caravel (from which the English word "carvel" derives) owed its lateen rig to the Arabs and its general lines to the small offshore craft that Portuguese fishermen had been using on their Atlantic coast for generations. An early sixteenth-century Portuguese painting depicts a vessel that is probably very similar to those in which Henry's navigators made their voyages of discovery. She has a graceful stem, with a fair amount of overhang, while her stern rises up into a poop with an after-castle in which a mizzenmast is stepped. The mainmast is a little abaft the centre of the boat, and the vessel sets two lateen sails. Caravels were usually quite small, with shallow draft – very important amid the shifting sandbanks of the African coast – and the term "caravel" was generally applied to vessels of under one hundred tons. At a later date Columbus applied it exclusively to vessels of about forty tons. Built of pine planks on oak frames and keel, they were later to become widely used in the Mediterranean, particularly on the North African coast.

Although the first caravels were rarely more than one hundred tons, they quickly became more elaborate and increased in size. A typical caravel of the mid-fifteenth century might be sixty to ninety feet long, with a beam of twenty to thirty feet, and sometimes stepping a third and even a fourth mast. In this case the foremast would set a square sail, and the other masts would all be lateen-rigged. The large lateen mainsail was soon found to be unwieldy to handle – particularly in the long following seas of the Atlantic – and a square mainsail was substituted. It was the foremast that now set a lateen, in company with the mizzen. This type of caravel was to become particularly popular in the western Mediterranean, and to remain in use there for at least two centuries. A sixteenth-century tapestry in Madrid, showing the capture of Tunis by the Emperor Charles V in 1535, depicts a large caravel which, it has been estimated, would have been of about four hundred tons burden. Caravels with square-rigged mainmast and lateen-rigged foremast were usually known in the Mediterranean as xebecs (Spanish *xebeque*), and were employed as fighting ships as well as fast cargo-carriers.

But the greatest achievement of Henry the Navigator was to open a new door to the East at the very moment when Turkish successes at the other end of the Mediterranean had begun to deprive Europe of her traditional trade routes. In 1486, twenty-six years after Henry's death, Bartholomew Diaz rounded the Cape of Good Hope, and in 1498 Vasco Da Gama made a continuous voyage from Lisbon to Calcutta. The road was now open. Even before this, in 1492, Christopher Columbus, bound on the same quest, sailed to what he thought were the "West Indies" but in fact discovered the continent of America. It is significant, incidentally, that Columbus married the daughter of one of Henry's sea-captains, and that he inherited from his father-in-law all his charts, instruments, and log-books. The Spanish bishop Bartolomé de Las Casas records in his *History of the Indies* that Columbus had often sailed with the Portuguese, "as if he had been one of them", in order to learn their navigational methods. The hand of the dead Prince was thus instrumental in the discovery of America.

Prince Henry the Navigator died seven years after the fall of Constantinople. That Christian catastrophe had caused him the deepest grief, and he had even thought of leading a great Crusade against the Ottoman enemy in order to redeem its loss. But the Portuguese Prince had already set in motion a sequence of events that far outweighed the triumphs of the Ottomans. Azurara has best summed up his character: "How many times did the rising sun find him seated where it had left him the day before, waking all the hours of the night, without a moment of rest, surrounded by people of many nationalities. . . . Where will you find another human body capable of supporting, as his in battle, the fatigue from which he had so little rest in time of peace! I truly believe that if strength could be represented, its very form would be found in the countenance and body of this prince. It was not only in certain things that he showed himself to be strong, but in all. And what strength is there greater than that of the man who is conqueror of himself?"

The eighteenth-century Scottish poet William Mickle compared Henry the Navigator with another, more famous, conqueror: "What is Alexander crowned with trophies at the head of his army, compared with Henry contemplating the ocean from his window on the rock of Sagres?" He had opened the sea-lanes of the world. His caravels, which combined centuries of Mediterranean shipbuilding experience with the lateen rig of the Arabs, had inaugurated a new era in history.

THIRTEEN

The Turkish Sea

As the interests and activities of the European nations became more and more concentrated on America, India, and the Far East, the Mediterranean became something of a backwater. This change in its importance was to be permanent. Not even the Renaisssance in Italy, not even the many wars which have subsequently been fought upon its surface have ever quite effaced the effect of the European discovery of the Atlantic routes to the East. Not until the opening of the Suez Canal in the nineteenth century was the sea to recover something of its earlier vigour. The art of the navigator, the craft of the shipbuilder, and the myriad attendant trades of rope-making, iron-founding, canvas-making, victualling, marine insurance, and port and dockyard construction (which had largely originated in this sea) were now to be deployed throughout the whole watery world.

Quite apart from the effect produced by the navigational discoveries initiated by the Portuguese, the Mediterranean was about to undergo a vast change owing to the activities of the Turks. Although the Mediterranean during the sixteenth and seventeenth centuries has sometimes been referred to as the "Forsaken Ocean", this represents an exclusively European outlook. It was never "forsaken"; it was still carrying an immense volume of traffic – but a large part of that traffic belonged to the Ottoman Empire. Europeans may prefer to forget the time when they were partly driven from the cradle of their civilization by the hardy Turk, but in the history of this sea the Turks played almost as important a part as the Arab before him.

The great difference between the empire of the Ottoman Turks and that of the Arabs lay in the characters of the two nations. Whereas the Arab had learned much of his civilization from Persia, and had then added his own contribution – particularly in the mathematical sciences –

the Turk absorbed only as much as suited him and contributed very little. He remained a nomad at heart, totally alien to Europe, in which he had now acquired a sizable empire. Even his empire was primitive in conception. It has been described as "that military state *par excellence* . . . built upon an ever-extending conquest." Even the greatest Sultans and their most distinguished ministers seem to have had no idea of any real form of government. They merely saw the Turks as destined to be a military, slave-owning oligarchy, while the other countries in the Mediterranean were seen as providers of the necessary slaves. The Turks certainly possessed qualities which even the Europeans who suffered most under them could still respect. They were extremely courageous fighting men, as good as any in the world – perhaps better than most; they had considerable dignity coupled with a sense of humour; and they were also disciplined, steadfast, and enduring. But they remained at heart, to the end of their days as an imperial power, a race of nomad Asiatics who had stormed into Europe and the East, and who were just as likely to move on again at any moment.

Writing as late as the end of the nineteenth century, Sir Charles Eliot, in *Turkey in Europe*, describes the house of a Turkish gentleman – not a peasant – in the following terms: "The very aspect of a Turkish house seems to indicate that it is not intended as a permanent residence. The ground floor is generally occupied by stables and stores. From this a staircase, often merely a ladder, leads to an upper storey, usually consisting of a long passage, from which open several rooms, the entrances closed by curtains, and not by doors. There are probably holes in the planking of the passages and spiders' webs and swallows' nests in the rafters. The rooms themselves, however, are generally scrupulously clean, but bare and unfurnished. . . . The general impression left on a European is that a party of travellers have occupied an old barn and said, 'Let us make the place clean enough to live in; it's no use taking any more trouble about it. We shall probably be off again in a week.'" This description, only slightly modified, might still be applied to the homes of many quite prosperous Turks, whose only evidences of wealth or aesthetic interests are likely to be found in a number of fine carpets displayed on walls or on bare polished floors. And these, too, one reflects, could be rolled up tomorrow and secured to the back of a horse while the owner rode off into new territory.

Nomadic horsemen, as the Vandals and Arabs had shown before, often seem to have an affinity with the sea. Exchanging a horse for a boat is perhaps not so big a difference in the quality of life. Both require hardiness and endurance, and both appeal to the wanderlust in a certain type of temperament. Certainly the Turks, once they had acquired Constantinople, soon began to show that they had every intention of making themselves masters of the sea. As the ruler of Constantinople and most of the ancient kingdom of Byzantium, the Sultan was hardly likely to tolerate for long the presence of so many Italian enclaves in the archipelago. The Genoese and Venetians, furthermore, had been the backbone of the resistance against the Turks in 1453. Although he was temporarily prepared to grant them trading privileges and the retention of such islands as they owned in the Aegean, it could not be expected that he or his successors would continue this policy for ever.

There was another reason why the Sultan, within a few years of the Turkish conquest, began to occupy the Aegean islands. The collapse of the old Byzantine Empire, coupled with the almost total disintegration of its fleet in the past decades, had allowed the pirates to prosper and increase. It could not be expected that the Sultan of the Ottomans, the "Possessor of Men's Necks", would gladly suffer raids by Catalan, Sicilian, and Italian pirates upon his territories. Furthermore, these insolent Latins even had the effrontery to carry off Turkish citizens into slavery and to sell them in the marts of Genoa and Venice.

One of the first islands to feel the wind of his sword was prosperous and rich Lesbos, whose capital, Mitylene, and whose other harbours and anchorages (such as the beautiful Gulf of Kallioni) had become infested with European sea-rovers. In 1462 the island fell to the Turks, and, in accordance with his policy of rewarding deserving soldiers with the lands that they helped to conquer, the Sultan settled a number of Janissaries and others in the island. In the following year the Turks, who had already overrun Serbia, attacked Bosnia. Now Venice in her turn declared war upon the Ottomans. In retrospect it may seem to have been a brave and noble act on the part of the Republic to throw down the gage to this implacable foe. Up to a point it was, but Venice had little option in the matter. She was fighting for survival. Although she had appealed for assistance to other European powers, none was willing to become involved – any more than they had been on behalf of the Byzantine Empire. Furthermore the Venetians had established so rigid a monopoly in their trade with the East that they had incurred the enmity of most of Europe.

This first Turco-Venetian War lasted for fifteen years, and ended in Venice ceding the Negropont (ancient Euboea) to the Turks, as well as a number of trading posts in the Morea. She also had to agree to pay the Turks an annual tribute for trading rights in the East. It was during this period, engaged in a war with a powerful maritime state, that the Turks began to expand their navy and to acquire an added interest in the Aegean and its islands. In the ancient archipelago the Turks began to learn the arts of seamanship and navigation just as the Greeks themselves had done so many centuries before. It was from here that they would ultimately expand throughout the length and breadth of the Mediterranean, until there would not be a single seaport safe from them. The time would even come when the Pope himself could not go to sleep without fearing that he would awake to find a marauding band of Turkish soldiers and sailors storming through the streets of Rome.

The island of Lesbos was destined to play an important part (even if indirectly) in this subsequent expansion of Turkish naval power. It was here that Ya'Kub, one of the Sultan's resettled Janissaries, married the widow of a Greek priest, fathering six children, four boys and two girls. Two of the boys, Aruj and Khizr, were to be largely responsible for expanding Turkish power in the Mediterranean: the one laying the foundations of the kingdom of Algeria; the other becoming High Admiral of the Ottoman navy.

Their careers began, as did those of many islanders at that time, as coastal traders who indulged in a little piracy on the side. The Sultan was not concerned if his citizens cared to harass the trade of the Venetian and Genoese islands, which in any case he had already marked out for occupation as soon as it suited him. Aruj, the elder, on one of these ventures, was unfortunate enough to fall foul of a large galley belonging to the Knights of Saint John, who from their island-fortress of Rhodes still pursued their implacable war against all Moslems. Captured, enslaved, and chained to the oar-bench, he was later ransomed – possibly during an exchange of prisoners such as took place from time to time. The experience in no way broke his spirit, but, rather, tempered it into an inveterate hatred of all Christians. During the next few years, he and his brother Khizr acquired a reputation as fine seamen and rapacious pirates among the Latin-occupied islands of the Aegean. Some time between 1500 and 1504 both brothers set sail with two small galleys for North Africa. They came to a working arrangement with the Sultan of Tunis that they might operate from his port – in return for a tithe on the loot and slaves that they captured from Christian shipping in the central Mediterranean.

The circumstances in the North African kingdoms, a heterogeneous mixture of sultanates and sheikdoms dating from the Arabic conquests, were particularly favourable at this moment for the warlike activities of the Turks. In 1492, by the conquest and subjugation of Granada – the last surviving Moslem state in the Spanish peninsula – the sovereigns of Spain had achieved a victory that was widely hailed as a triumph for Christian arms. It had, however, repercussions which disturbed the waters of the western Mediterranean for centuries to come.

Stanley Lane-Poole comments in *The Barbary Corsairs*: "When the united wisdom of Ferdinand and Isabella resolved on the expatriation of the Spanish Moors, they forgot the risk of an exile's vengeance. No sooner was Granada fallen than thousands of desperate Moors left the land which for seven hundred years had been their home, and, disdaining to live under a Spanish yoke, crossed the strait to Africa, where they established themselves at various strong points, such as Shershel, Oran, and notably at Algiers, which till then had hardly been heard of. No sooner were the banished Moors fairly settled in their new seats than they did what anybody in their place would have done: they carried the war into their oppressors' country."

Prior to the arrival of these Moorish expatriates in North Africa, relationships between the various Moslem states along the littoral and the European powers had usually been well conducted and business-like. Treaties were signed and honoured, and a considerable volume of trade flowed back and forth between Spain, France, the Italian states, and the Moslem world. All this was to change with the arrival on these shores of an embittered Moorish populace, eager for revenge and, if possible, for a return to their ancient home in the kingdom of Granada. At the same moment, the vast expansion of Turkish power at the eastern end of the sea sent out young Turks like Aruj and Khizr in search of their fortunes in Africa. They were to exploit the feelings of the Moslems in North Africa, and to turn the whole central and western basin into a battlefield. From now on, a geographical name was born that was to haunt European merchants, sea-captains, coastal dwellers, fishermen, and even princes – the Barbary Coast.

During the years in which the two Turkish brothers were expanding their power and influence along the coastline from Tunis to Algiers, their attacks upon European shipping could not fail to go unremarked. In the year 1504 they achieved one of their earliest and most remarkable successes when in their two small Turkish galleots they captured two large Italian galleys, one of which was the papal flagship itself – about the largest and most powerful vessel operating in the Mediterranean. But this was only the beginning. Soon, aided by numerous other Turks, Moorish expatriates from Granada, and Christian renegades, they had turned the whole formerly pacific North African coastline into the most serious threat to the trade of this part of the sea since the Vandals. Not only the internal trade of the sea became insecure, but the external trade – that lifeline between the Americas and Spain which had only recently opened up – was also disrupted.

By the early sixteenth century the great galleons of Spain were already running regular passages between the new continent of America and their home ports on the Atlantic and Mediterranean coastlines of the peninsula. Laden with the wealth of a hitherto unexploited world, the "stately Spanish galleon" seemed a fat and natural prey for the revengeful Moors operating out of Morocco. Meanwhile, further east, south of the Balearics, Sardinia, and Sicily, the corsairs led by Aruj and Khizr were causing something akin to panic among the Italian maritime republics. Spain itself, with its long communications route to the Spanish forces in the kingdoms of Naples and Sicily, was seriously affected.

Although he was writing at a later date, some idea of the havoc wrought by the Barbary corsairs can be gauged by this quotation from the Spanish Abbot Diego de Haedo in his *History of Algiers*: "While the Christians with their galleys are at repose, sounding their trumpets in the harbours, and very much at their ease regaling themselves, passing the day and night in banqueting, cards, and dice, the Corsairs at pleasure

Coin portraits of Julius Caesar (*left*) and Mark Antony

Roman ships, from one of the reliefs at Ostia

Punic coin, with a horse and a palm tree on the reverse and what may
be a portrait of Hannibal on the obverse

A Roman version of the story of Odysseus and the Sirens, at Tunis

At left, Pompey's Pillar at Alexandria

IMPERIAL ROME

Portrait head of Augustus

The amphitheatre at Arles

are traversing the east and west seas, without the least fear or apprehension, as free and absolute sovereigns thereof. Nay, they roam them up and down no otherwise than do such as go in chase of hares for their diversion. They here snap up a ship laden with gold and silver from India, and there another richly fraught from Flanders; now they make prize of a vessel from England, then of another from Portugal. Here they board and lead away one from Venice, then one from Sicily, and a little further on they swoop down upon others from Naples, Livorno, or Genoa, all of them abundantly crammed with great and wonderful riches. And at other times carrying with them as guides renegadoes (of which there are in Algiers vast numbers of all Christian nations, nay, the generality of the Corsairs are no other than renegadoes, and all of them exceedingly well acquainted with the coasts of Christendom, and even with the land), they very deliberately, even at noon-day, or indeed just when they please, leap ashore, and walk on without the least dread, and advance into the country, ten, twelve, or fifteen leagues or more; and the poor Christians, thinking themselves secure, are surprised unawares; many towns, villages and farms sacked; and infinite numbers of souls, men, women, children, and infants at the breast dragged away into a wretched captivity. With these miserable ruined people loaded with their own valuable substance, they retreat leisurely, with eyes full of laughter and content, to their vessels. In this manner, as is too well known, they have utterly ruined and destroyed Sardinia, Corsica, Sicily, Calabria, the neighbourhoods of Naples, Rome, and Genoa, all the Balearic Islands, and the whole coast of Spain; in which last they feast it as they think fit, on account of the Moriscos who inhabit there; who being all more zealous Mohammedans than are the very Moors born in Barbary, they receive and caress the Corsairs, and give them notice of whatever they desire to be informed of. Insomuch that before these Corsairs have been absent from their abodes much longer than perhaps twenty or thirty days, they return home rich, with their vessels crowded with captives, and ready to sink with wealth; in one instant, and with scarce any trouble, reaping the fruits of all that the avaricious Mexican and greedy Peruvian have been digging from the bowels of the earth with such toil and sweat, and the thirsty merchant with such manifest perils has for so long been scraping together, and has been so many thousand leagues to fetch away, either from the east or west, with inexpressible danger and fatigue. Thus they have crammed most of the houses, the magazines, and all the shops of this Den of Thieves with gold, silver, pearls, amber, spices, drugs, silks, cloths, velvets & c., whereby they have rendered this city [Algiers] the most opulent in the world: insomuch that the Turks call it, not without reason, their India, their Mexico, their Peru."

But this was in the future; this was the end-product of the lives of Aruj and Khizr and their Turkish followers. Aruj himself was killed in 1518 when the Spaniards, determined to rid the coast of the corsair menace, dispatched an army to Algeria and destroyed a large part of the Turkish forces. They failed, however, to make proper use of their victory and plant Spanish garrisons along the whole length of the coast. The result was that Khizr, the younger brother, was able to re-establish Turkish control over nearly all the coastline within a short space of time.

Khizr, who was to become famous throughout the Mediterranean as Kheir-ed-Din (Protector of the Faith) to the Moslems and as Barbarossa (Red Beard) to his Christian foes, was a man of considerable stature. Master of seven languages, he was no ignorant pirate. As brave and hardy as his brother, he was also an excellent administrator, a superb naval tactician, and a statesman as able as any ruler of his period.

Between the years 1520 and 1529, Barbarossa, to give him the name which had now become a byword in Europe, managed to make himself master of nearly all the North African coast between the Strait of Gibraltar and the Gulf of Gabes. In 1529 his second-in-command, Aydin Rais, scored a notable triumph over the forces of Spain. In a battle off the Balearic Islands, his comparatively small force of light galleots completely routed eight of the largest war galleys of Spain – among them the flagship of the Spanish Mediterranean fleet. He returned in triumph to Algiers towing seven of his captured prizes. The Mediterranean Sea was to be a battlefield between the rival empires of Spain and Turkey for many years to come, but at this particular moment it was clear that the Turks were gaining the upper hand.

It was hardly surprising that the ruling Sultan, Suleiman I, was eager to enlist the services of his remarkable subject in the reconstruction of the dockyards of Constantinople and in improving the whole administration of the Ottoman navy. Suleiman, known to Europeans during his lifetime as "the Magnificent", and to the Ottomans as "the Lawgiver", was one of the most outstanding rulers ever produced by his country. It was during his lifetime that the Ottoman Empire attained the peak of its power. He had inherited from his father an efficient army, a well-organized country, and a full treasury, and he proceeded to make use of the many able men then available at the Sublime Porte. His choice of administrators, though sometimes hampered by the sinister influences of harem intrigue, was generally excellent. During the course of his sultanate he had added to the Ottoman dominions Aden, Algiers (by virtue of Barbarossa), Baghdad, Belgrade, Budapest, Nakhichevan, Rhodes, Rivan, Tabriz, and Temesvar. At this period of his life, however, although his armies were triumphant on the battlefields of the East as well as in Europe, he was dissatisfied with the state of his navy.

The distinguished Genoese admiral Andrea Doria, a member of the same noble family that had furnished the city with so many admirals, generals, and administrators, had recently joined forces with the Emperor Charles V. This meant that the Spanish naval arm was now augmented by twelve galleys belonging to Doria, as well as enjoying Doria's talents. In 1532, for instance, Doria had conducted a highly successful campaign against the Grecian outposts of the Sultan's empire. He had captured the important port and trading centre of Patras and had seized the two forts that commanded the entrance to the Gulf of Corinth. He had also captured the port of Coron, commanding the Gulf of Messenia in the southern Peloponnese, and had garrisoned it with Genoese and Spanish troops.

Suleiman's Grand Vizier, Ibrahim, had long had an eye upon Barbarossa, the man who had made himself ruler of Algiers, and who seemed to have made the western basin of the sea into his own native territory. He saw in him an antidote to Doria. It was at his suggestion that, in the spring of 1533, Barbarossa was summoned to Constantinople to present himself before Suleiman.

During the following year, Barbarossa, his lieutenants, and the advisers whom he brought with him from Algeria completely reorganized the dockyards of Constantinople. They improved the quality of the Turkish fleet in ship design, manning, training, and administration, and set a pattern that was to serve the Porte in good stead for many years to come. The Grand Vizier had not been wrong when, after his first meeting with this Turk from Algiers, he had written to the Sultan: " We have set our hand upon a veritable man of the sea. Have no hesitation in naming him Pasha, Member of the Divan, and Captain General of the Fleet." Jean Chesneau, who was the French Secretary at Constantinople during this period, reported to his master, Francis I of France, that "Before [Barbarossa] took charge, the Turks, with the exception of some corsairs, did not know anything about the seaman's art. When they wanted to find the crews for a fleet, they went into the mountains of Greece and Anatolia and brought in the shepherds . . . and put them to row in the galleys and to serve aboard the other ships. This was quite hopeless, for they knew neither how to row or be sailors, or even how to stand upright at sea. For this reason the Turks never made any showing at sea. But all at once Barbarossa changed the whole system." Admiral Jurien de la Gravière later comments: "He changed it so much that in a few years they acquired the reputation of being invincible."

It was probably during this period, when the new Ottoman fleet was in the process of construction, that Francis I, who was in conflict with the Emperor Charles V, decided on that famous realignment of French policy which was to make his Catholic country the ally of the Moslem Ottomans. If the Emperor would have the ships and skill of Andrea Doria to assist him against France, then he, for his part, would have the ships and the admiral of the Sultan. Barbarossa had himself pressed this idea upon Suleiman. He had pointed out that the greatest enemy of the Moslems – whether Moriscos, Arabs, Berbers, or Turks – was Charles V. During the winter of 1533, Barbarossa, "Inspiring his men with his own marvellous energy, laid out sixty-one galleys . . . and was able to take the sea with a fleet of eighty-four vessels in the spring. . . . He was continually in the arsenal, where he did both eat and drink [in order] to lose no time."

A great raid on the Spanish domains in southern Italy was Barbarossa's first stroke against the Emperor Charles V. Reggio, so often the scene of conflict (but a city which not even the great Hannibal had been able to capture) fell easily to the Turkish fleet. This was the beginning of a devastating raid, right up the west coast of Italy, in which cities and harbours were laid waste, and the inevitable train of human captives was sent back to the slave mart of Constantinople. Turning south in the late summer, Barbarossa swept into Tunis, the kingdom of an independent Arab Sultan, and captured it for the Sultan of the Ottomans. It was his intention to give Tunis to Suleiman, together with Algeria, as extensions of the Turkish Empire.

The events of the year 1534, in which the Turkish navy had shown itself supreme in the central area of the sea, were felt for a long time to come. Although Tunis was recaptured in the following year by the forces of Charles V, it was now clear that there were only two forces of any real weight in the Mediterranean: the Spaniards and the Ottomans. Not since the collapse of the Roman Empire had the Mediterranean world been in so few hands, for, apart from Venice and Genoa (both greatly declined), the south coast of France, and a few small Italian states, by the end of the sixteenth century the whole sea was almost equally divided between these two hostile powers. The summer of 1534, when the Turkish fleet rolled up the coast of Italy like a tidal wave, marked the beginning of this new era.

The news of these Turkish successes sent a quiver of apprehension throughout the courts and chancelleries of Europe. It was not only from the land that the Turkish threat was now making itself felt. Barbarossa's actions showed only too clearly that a pincers movement was developing via the sea from the south. In recent years the activities of the Moslem corsairs had raised mercantile insurance rates to a crippling level, and these rates were now being raised yet again. Venice, a shadow of its former self (since both Egypt and Syria were now part of the Sultan's domains, and her trade with the East was largely at a standstill), was compelled to raise additional taxes to revive her galley fleet. The Genoese, who up to now had been not too badly affected on their western trade routes, saw the writing on the wall. They, too, were forced to increase taxation in order to build more war galleys to protect their large trading carracks; they also had to construct watch-towers and coastal defences against the possibility of Turkish attack.

Many of the forts and towers which dot the coastlines of the sea date from this period of the sixteenth century. Strongpoints and refuge centres, they are scattered over the Maltese archipelago, all round Sicily, up and down the coasts of Italy, Sardinia, Corsica, and the Balearic Islands, and along the Mediterranean coast of Spain. Norman Douglas writes, in *Old Calabria*: "The ominous name '*Torre di Guardia*' (tower of outlook) – a cliff whence the sea was scanned for the appearance of Turkish vessels – survives all over the south. Barbarossa, too, has left his mark; many a hill, fountain or castle has been named after him. . . ." It was during this time that many coastal towns and fishing villages began to fall into disuse, as the inhabitants removed themselves to inland villages, high up on the peaks of mountains. Large areas of threatened coastline became underpopulated, and agriculture declined. Islands like Sicily, where coastal fishing had always played a large part in the economy, were heavily affected, since fishermen were naturally unwilling to hazard themselves upon waters where they were only too likely to end up on a Turkish oar-bench.

The age of the corsairs had begun, and for nearly two centuries the Mediterranean was a haven for pirates. It was not only the Turks and Moriscos of the Barbary Coast who caused this disruption of the trade routes of the sea, for their ranks were swelled by many Europeans. Some of these were self-exiled in order to avoid the justice of their own lands, while others had "turned Turk" and embraced the Moslem faith rather than remain as slaves. The Abbot Diego de Haedo commented that many of the sea-captains to be found in command of galleys ranging out of Morocco, Algeria, and Tunisia were Christian renegades. Barbarossa's right-hand man, Dragut, later to become his successor as the greatest Moslem seaman of his time, was born of Christian parents in Anatolia. Another prominent corsair was Sinan, a renegade Jew, nicknamed "the Jew of Smyrna", while Ochiali, an extremely able sea-captain, was an Italian from Calabria. Among well-known corsairs operating out of the North African coastline were Frenchmen, Venetians, Genoese, Sicilians, Neapolitans, Spaniards, Greeks, Corsicans, Albanians, and Hungarians – men, in fact, from all the nations bordering upon the Mediterranean.

The insecure state of the sea, coupled with the opening of the new Atlantic routes, led to a decline in nearly all the ancient ports. Only Algiers in the west and Constantinople in the far north-east enjoyed some considerable prosperity. Meanwhile, Spain, France, and Portugal, who possessed ports on the Atlantic as well as on the Mediterranean, tended to base the major part of their trading fleets, as well as their navies, upon their Atlantic coastlines. Those battles for power and trade supremacy, which had convulsed the inland sea for thousands of years, were now, at least in their major phases, transferred to the great oceans of the world.

FOURTEEN

Preveza – Malta – Lepanto

The naval power of the Ottoman Empire became evident to the nations of Europe in the spring of 1538. Barbarossa led out a fleet of more than one hundred galleys from Constantinople and moved south through the Aegean. Since Venice was now at war with the Turks, it could not be expected that the Sultan's admiral would spare any of the islands that came under Venetian control or protection. The first to feel the power of the new Ottoman fleet was Skiathos, lying just off the northern end of Euboea and commanding the entrance to the Gulf of Volos. The small fortified township had no chance of holding out against so many ships and men, and fell in less than a week. A garrison was left behind to secure the island for its new masters and the Turks moved on, having taken whatever loot and slaves they could find. The pattern of events in Skiathos was to be repeated often in the future, both during this particular spring sweep through the Aegean and in many others that were to follow all over the Mediterranean. The lifeline of islands that had been secured for Venice by Doge Dandolo's misdirection of the Fourth Crusade was destined to collapse over the following years. Those which were not of immediate strategic importance were left under their Italian rulers, in return for a payment of tribute to the Sultan. Thus, during this first major spring offensive, Barbarossa captured Skyros but left Andros to the south of it technically under Venetian protection, only exacting tribute from the ruling families. He next attempted Crete, but, finding that the walls of Kandia were too strong for the limited artillery of his ships, he moved on to lay waste all the coastal fishing villages and hamlets. Over eighty villages were made desolate in this campaign, and their young men were enslaved and condemned to the oar-benches.

While it is possible to admire Barbarossa as an administrator, admiral, and warrior – in all of which capacities he was supreme – yet he represents par excellence that aspect of the Ottoman Empire which was to make it one of the most barren edifices ever known to man. His campaigns in the Aegean, in western Italy, and elsewhere, while conducted with ruthless efficiency and considerable strategical ability, were basically no more than destructive. Neither he nor his successors destroyed in order to replace; the Turks were conquerors like the Vandals. They laid waste a land, enslaved the people, and then passed on, leaving only ruin and desolation behind them. It was not only in their capacity as warriors that they turned the eastern Mediterranean into a desert of bones. Their administrators had little or no care about the lands that were placed under their charge, provided that the taxes were paid and slaves (when required) were forthcoming. The Arabs had improved the agriculture of the lands that came under their domain, introducing advanced methods of farming and irrigation learnt from the East. The Turk, however, was no farmer and his sole contribution to Greece and the Aegean islands was to introduce in increasing numbers the ubiquitous goat, that murderer of saplings.

The decline of the Aegean islands had begun in classical times, when man, ignorant of the tree's function in nature, cut down the forests without replacement. But it was under the centuries of Turkish rule that the islands achieved their present condition of stark and barren poverty. Once introduced, the goat left a wilderness behind it, and, in doing so, made the islanders almost totally dependent upon it. Thus began that vicious circle which still exists today. Once the goat has become the basis of an island economy there is practically no hope of reafforesting in order to conserve what soil still remains. Islanders dependent upon the animal for meat, milk, and hair cannot afford to wait for decades while the trees grow, the soil improves, and the conditions for some limited agriculture return. The wind-picked skeletons of so many Aegean islands – victims of man's ignorance and folly – are symbolic of the triumphs of Barbarossa.

After his devastation of Crete in the spring of 1538 he learned that a large enemy fleet had been sighted in the Adriatic, heading south towards the Ionian Islands. Corfu, Ithaca, Zante, and the other islands in this group had played an important part in Venice's economy as forming stepping-stones to her eastern trade. Barbarossa was eager to secure them for the Sultan, and the news that it was a very large fleet that was now bound in his direction did not in any way deter him. Perhaps he had hoped that his activities would provoke this response, for he had already summoned a squadron of twenty galleys from Egypt to reinforce his own ships. There could be no doubt that his successes in the western Mediterranean and the news of what he was doing in the eastern basin had induced the warring European states to combine their forces for once.

Waiting to meet Barbarossa among the summer-misted islands of the Ionian was one of the largest fleets that this part of the world had seen since the Fourth Crusade had assembled at Corfu – or since Antony and Cleopatra had fled from the forces of Octavian in 31 B.C. It consisted of eighty-one galleys and sailing ships from Venice, a papal squadron of thirty-six galleys, and thirty galleys from Spain. This in itself outnumbered the fleet under Barbarossa, but it was soon to be joined by a further forty-nine galleys under the command of Andrea Doria, together with no less than fifty large sailing galleons. The Emperor Charles V was determined once and for all to drive the Turkish menace from the Mediterranean and restore the whole area of European rule. Had he done so, the sea's history might have been considerably more tranquil and prosperous.

The Battle of Preveza which followed was uniquely interesting for two reasons. First of all, the site itself was where the battle between the fleets of Octavian and of Antony and Cleopatra had taken place. Preveza itself was a Turkish village opposite Actium Point, situated at the mouth of the channel leading into the Gulf of Arta, known in classical times as the Ambracian Gulf. This is a giant inlet of the Ionian Sea, a few miles north of the Ionian island of Levkas. The Gulf of Arta is twenty-five miles wide from east to west, and ten miles deep from north to south. It can accommodate an immense fleet, and the admiral who stations himself within the gulf has complete command of the narrow and winding entrance. Barbarossa had headed swiftly north on receipt of the news that the allied fleet was bound down the Ionian, and had established himself inside the gulf before Doria and the other commanders had assembled at Corfu. Like an octopus, secure within a rocky cleft, Barbarossa could snap up what he wished; he had only to be aware that he did not fall for any obvious "bait" dangled outside the opening of his haven.

Doria tried just such a trick, and trailed a line of galleys across the opening to Preveza. Barbarossa ignored the lure, and Doria was compelled to move off to the south in order to dislodge his wily opponent. Barbarossa, for his part, could not afford to let so large an enemy force sail off in the direction of his master's Grecian territories, and ordered his ships to up anchor and give chase. The spectacle of this massive Ottoman fleet winding down the channel past Actium Point, where Octavian had made himself master of the world, was so vivid a repetition of those previous events that it seems as if fate had decided to revive an ancient drama.

The battle that followed, though less conclusive than the victory of Octavian, determined the course of events at sea for several decades to come. Despite Doria's great superiority in numbers, he was outmanoeuvred by Barbarossa, who refused to be drawn into a general engagement with the heavier (and far more heavily armed) sailing galleons. He contented himself with snapping up stragglers wherever possible; at the end of the day he had seven captured vessels to his credit. In the handling of his galleys against a far superior fleet, the Turk had shown himself the Italian's superior, and, had it not been for one particular phase of the action, Kheir-ed-Din would have achieved his victory without the loss of a single ship.

The one action in which the Ottoman admiral was nonplussed was that involving the huge "Galleon of Venice". This was a warship somewhat resembling the famous Great Carrack of the Knights of Saint John, a sailing vessel, but armed with a weight of cannon far greater than that carried by a squadron or more of galleys. Commanded by one of the greatest Venetian seamen of the time, Alessandro Condalmiero, this great galleon became becalmed and lingered far behind the rest of the fleet as Doria was hastening southwards. It was inevitable, therefore, that this was the first vessel which the Turks came across as they rowed in pursuit of the enemy. The heavily built, heavily gunned galleon soon showed that no galley, however manoeuvrable, could compete with the weight of metal that this new type of sailing vessel could discharge.

"So she lay there in the water, the great dark Galleon of Venice, with her gunners poised with their slow matches ready, and her upper-deck crew lying low beneath the bulwarks. Condalmiero had further ordered his gunners not to waste their shot by trying for individual targets, but to lay their guns in the line of the approaching vessels and use a ricochet effect against the galleys – rather like a boy skipping stones across the water. He had decided he was more likely to succeed by this method than by asking his gunners to try to drop individual cannon balls upon individual ships. His judgement proved sound. As the first wave of Barbarossa's galleys came within a few hundred yards of the motionless galleon, every gunport discharged a thunderstorm of flame and death. The new navy – the navy that was to triumph all over the world until the advent of steam, the navy of sail – showed in this first action of the Preveza campaign that it was the broadside with its solid weight of shot that now counted in warfare. Always, prior to this, it had been manoeuvrability and the ultimate act of boarding which gave one side or another the victory. This had been so since classical times. But the fact that sailing ships could now be built large enough to contain an armament about as heavy as that of a shore-based fortress was to change the whole aspect of naval warfare." (Quoted from *The Sultan's Admiral*, by Ernle Bradford.)

Despite the losses sustained in this action against the Venetian galleon, the overall result of the Battle of Preveza was a conclusive victory for Barbarossa. To be charitable to Andrea Doria, he was hampered by the fact that he was commanding a mixed fleet of oar-propelled galleys and wind-driven galleons. This meant that, when the wind fell light, his galleons dropped back and became a burden, whereas, when the wind piped up, the galleys could not keep pace with the sailing ships.

During the night of September 29, 1538, Andrea Doria withdrew his fleet from action and ordered them north to Corfu. When dawn broke next morning the Turks were astounded to find that this considerably larger and theoretically superior fleet had left them alone on the sun-burnished field of battle. Barbarossa, one commentator relates, used to tell the story of Preveza in later years and maintain, amid gales of laughter, that Andrea Doria had even extinguished his admiral's lantern on the poop so that he would not be detected as he slipped away under cover of darkness.

The Ottoman fleet moved calmly back to Preveza, prepared to sally out again if it should prove that Doria's withdrawal was no more than a ruse. As soon as it became clear that the combined allied force was splitting up in Corfu and making its way homewards, Barbarossa sent his dispatch recording the battle to the Sultan, who was at that time in Bulgaria. Relays of horsemen swept through the Grecian territories of the Ottoman Empire and on to the Bulgarian town of Yambol. Suleiman the Magnificent ordered the city to be illuminated as a mark of triumph and sent a personal dispatch to Constantinople. He ordered a special procession to be made in thanksgiving to Santa Sophia and to all the other mosques in the city to give thanks to Allah for so great a victory.

Barbarossa now acquired another title of acclamation. He would be known henceforth throughout the Sultan's lands as the "King of the Sea". He had made the Turks masters of a large part of North Africa; he had established their dominance in the central and western Mediterranean; and now, by defeating a combination of the principal European navies, he had secured Suleiman's position in Greece and the Levant. If the peak years of the Ottoman Empire may be said to lie between 1538 and the death of Suleiman in 1566, no small part of the credit must be given to this Turkish pirate turned admiral, a man who did indeed deserve his new sobriquet. Loaded with fame and honours, he died in his palace in Constantinople eight years after the victory of Preveza. The Turkish annals for the year 1546 record simply: "The King of the Sea is dead."

The meteorlike career of Barbarossa marks the beginning of the dominance of the Turks in the Mediterranean. This was, of course, constantly challenged by the Spaniards, but in the years immediately after Preveza they were destined to lose two whole fleets in their attempts to drive the Turks out of North Africa. If Preveza may be called the flood-tide of Ottoman naval expansion, then the next major event in the history of this sea was to prove its high-water mark.

Sixteen years before Barbarossa's great victory the Sultan Suleiman had achieved a resounding triumph in the island of Rhodes. He had long determined that he would no longer brook the insult to his power that the Knights of Saint John posed throughout the archipelago. His predecessor, Mohammed the Conqueror, had once publicly declared that he would take "Constantinople first, and then Rhodes". He achieved his first objective, but Rhodes eluded him, and he had to be content with capturing the far larger though strategically less important island of Euboea. It was left to Suleiman the Magnificent to remove the last of the Crusaders from the eastern seas. On June 26, 1522, he landed between 140,000 and 200,000 men on the island to attack less than 5000 men in the fortified walled city of Rhodes. Despite the discrepancy in numbers, the siege was very nearly a failure – not for nothing had the knights over their centuries in the Holy Land, Cyprus, and Rhodes perfected the art of defensive fortifications. Finally, however, after a siege lasting nearly six months, the seventy-year-old Grand Master, Villiers de l'Isle Adam, asked for and obtained an honourable capitulation. The Sultan had lost nearly half his men and there had been numerous occasions when the Turks had very nearly been forced to retire. He was willing, therefore, to allow the knights and such Rhodians as cared to accompany them to sail out unmolested from the island in their galleys. It was January 1, 1523, when the Grand Master and his knights left forever the gracious and fertile island that had been their home for two centuries. The Sultan is said to have remarked on seeing De l'Isle Adam board the Great Carrack, "It is not without some pain that I oblige this Christian at his age to leave his home."

For eight years the Order of Saint John had no permanent base, as the Grand Master and the other senior members of the Council canvassed the courts of Europe asking their rulers to provide them with another island, or a defensible promontory on a mainland coast, from which they could carry out their duty of eternal warfare against the Moslem. At that time, however, when Europe was increasingly conscious of its newly evolving nationalisms, this supranational body – owing allegiance to no one but the Pope – was viewed with some suspicion. The days of the Crusades were over, and the rulers of Europe were too much interested in the aggrandizement of their own countries to have much interest in this independent and militant band of nobles. Finally, it was Charles V – concerned more than any other sovereign of the time with the increasing power of the Turks – who ceded to the order the Maltese archipelago and the North African city of Tripoli in return for an annual token payment of one falcon. Charles saw clearly that the presence of the knights in Malta would provide a useful defensive outrider to his important possessions of Sicily and southern Italy.

The Knights of Saint John reached Malta in the autumn of 1530. They immediately began to erect defensive walls and towers and to organize their life upon the pattern that they had evolved in Rhodes. They were not particularly happy with Charles' gift, accepting it only because it was clear that they had no other option. For one thing, there were practically no defences in existence in Malta, which meant they had to start a very expensive building programme at a time when their treasury was badly depleted. For another thing, they found the islands barren and unattractive after Rhodes. Finally, they were unhappy at Charles' left-handed gift of Tripoli, which they had been obliged to accept in order to obtain this new island home. For Tripoli was a Christian enclave in the heart of the Moslem Barbary Coast, and they felt dubious about their ability to defend it successfully. It was, then, something of a relief when in 1551 Tripoli fell to a Turkish force led by the redoubtable Dragut.

All the knights' money and military abilities were now devoted to making Malta as strong and secure as Rhodes had once been. Meanwhile their galleys, ranging far and wide over the sea-lanes of the central and eastern Mediterranean, began to make their presence felt by Moslem shipowners. It gradually became clear that Malta was strategically a far better base from which to harass the enemy. In the past few decades of their residence in Rhodes the order's capacity to injure the Turk had been gravely hampered by the fact that Rhodes was almost encircled by Turkish-dominated islands, and Turkish shipping had long learned to give the area of Rhodes a wide berth. Malta, however, was admirably placed for raiding the North African territories, which, since the time of Barbarossa, had become largely Turkish controlled. The island was also, as Charles V had envisaged, an excellent advance post for protecting Sicily and Italy. The galleys of the knights were soon snapping up marauding corsairs and giving them a taste of what they had long been inflicting upon the Christians.

Forty-two years after he had driven the Order of Saint John from Rhodes, Suleiman, now aged seventy, decided that the time had come to expel them also from Malta. Their activities had recently become so damaging to the trade of his empire that his advisers, including Dragut, were constantly beseeching him to act against these Christian enemies. Dragut remarked: "Until you have smoked out this nest of vipers you can do no good anywhere." The Imam of the Great Mosque had reminded the Sultan that the dungeons of Malta were full of Turkish captives, and that true Sons of the Prophet were being lashed at the oars of the very galleys which were raiding the sea routes of his empire. "It is only thy invincible sword," the Imam cried to Suleiman, "that can shatter the chains of these unfortunates, whose cries are rising to heaven and afflicting the very ears of the Prophet of God. . . ."

Skilled in a lifetime of warfare against the Christians, Suleiman had early appreciated the geographic and strategic significance of the Maltese archipelago. Although some of his advisers proposed that he make a full-scale attack on Spain or Sicily, Suleiman pointed out that once he had his fleet based on Malta, he could, at his leisure, strike into Europe from the south, while his armies drove from the east hard into the heart of Hungary. He understood sea power as well as land warfare, and, as he remarked, he envisaged the day when "The Grand Seignior, or his deputies, master of the whole Mediterranean, may dictate laws, as universal lord, from that not unpleasant rock, and look down upon his shipping at anchor in its excellent harbour."

The siege of Malta took place in 1565, an army of some forty thousand men being transported across the Ionian in over two hundred ships. This armada consisted of one hundred and thirty galleys of the imperial fleet, together with a number of large sailing ships carrying stores and ammunition, and an unspecified number of private vessels that came along for whatever pickings they might find, once the lions had left the carcass. The whole army and fleet was later to be reinforced by a formidable squadron of galleys and fighting men under the command of Dragut, now Sultan of Tripoli. Dragut enjoyed the Sultan's favour to such an extent that the latter had ordered his general Mustapha and his Admiral Piali to accept any advice that Dragut might give them on the conduct of the siege. It was fortunate for the Knights of Saint John and for the inhabitants of Malta that Dragut was delayed and did not arrive until after the siege had begun. The tactics adopted by the commanders enabled the knights, led by their Grand Master, Jean Parisot de la Valette, to bleed the Turks against a single fortress commanding the entrance to Grand Harbour.

This fort, called after Saint Elmo, patron saint of Mediterranean sailors, stood at the tip of the peninsula on which Malta's capital, Valletta, now stands. Its heroic defence gave the knights, the Spanish soldiers who had been sent to reinforce them by Charles V, and the

The ruins of the Forum, painted by Pannini in the eighteenth century

The ruins of Diocletian's palace at Split, drawn by Robert Adam,
also in the eighteenth century

The Emperor Justinian,
shown on the Barberini ivory
from the sixth century

The mosaic of Christ Pantocrater in the cathedral at Cefalù

Maltese auxiliaries additional time to improve their positions on the other two main peninsulas in Grand Harbour. When Saint Elmo finally fell, and the Ottoman troops turned their attention to the real heart of the order's defences on these two points – Senglea and Birgu (which housed La Valette's fortress headquarters of Saint Angelo) – it was already late summer. The siege had begun in the spring, and the Turks had suffered from the fact that Malta, unlike Rhodes, could provide little sustenance for their troops, and they were far from their main sources of supply. It was partly their long lines of communications that bedevilled their attack on Malta and prevented its falling into their hands as the other island home of the knights had done.

A further misfortune befell the Turks during the siege of Fort Saint Elmo when Dragut was killed by a cannon shot. Dragut, who had driven the knights out of Tripoli, might, had he lived, have had a similar success in Malta. From the moment of his arrival, he had changed the whole pattern of the siege by his formidable talents. It was largely due to his distribution of troops and artillery that Saint Elmo was finally breached and overrun. Admiral Jurien de la Gravière wrote of him, in *Doria et Barberousse*: "Dragut was superior to Barbarossa. A living chart of the sea, he combined science with audacity. There was not a creek unknown to him, not a channel that he had not sailed. Ingenious in devising ways and means, when all round him despaired, he excelled above all in escaping by unexpected methods from situations of great peril. An incomparable pilot, he had no equal in sea-warfare except the Chevalier Romegas [one of the greatest seamen of the Order of Saint John, also present at the siege of Malta]. On land he was skilful enough to be compared with the finest generals of Charles V and Philip II. He had known the hardship of captivity and he showed himself humane to his own captives. Under every aspect he was a character. No one was more worthy than he, to bear the title of 'King'. . . ." Of Dragut the story is told that, several years before, he had had a premonition that he would die in the Maltese islands. He had been raiding the smaller island of Gozo, where his brother had been killed, and he is reported to have said: "I have felt in this island the shadow of the wing of death! One of these days it is written that I, too, shall die in the territory of the knights."

The death of Dragut, the hostility of the terrain, the incredible

417

valour of the defenders, sickness in the army – these were among the factors that defeated the immense Ottoman army and navy. The inspiring leadership and clever strategy of Grand Master La Valette also affected the outcome of the siege, enabling the defenders to hold on long enough for a relief force to reach them from Sicily, after a siege of nearly four months. "The arms of Soleyman the First," writes W. H. Prescott, in his *History of the Reign of Philip II*, "during his long and glorious reign, met with no reverse so humiliating as his failure in the siege of Malta. To say nothing of the cost of the maritime preparations, the waste of life was prodigious. . . ." Most of the accounts seem to agree that the Turks lost between twenty thousand and thirty thousand men – an immense figure for that period, and one which does not include the losses of the corsairs from the Barbary Coast. In the course of Suleiman's reign, one of the most glorious periods in Ottoman history, he met with only two reverses of any magnitude. One was his failure before the walls of Vienna in 1529, and the other – and by far the greater – was at Malta in 1565. The siege of Malta was the high-water mark of the expansion of the Ottoman Empire. It is significant that after this date the Turks made no real attempts to break into the western Mediterranean.

Queen Elizabeth I of England, no great lover of either Catholics or Spaniards, remarked during the course of the siege: "If the Turks should prevail against the Isle of Malta, it is uncertain what further peril might follow to the rest of Christendom." One of the main consequences of the siege was to focus the eyes of the European powers upon the unique strategic position of the Maltese archipelago. They became aware, as had the Romans and Carthaginians centuries before, that the low-lying limestone island of Malta was, because of its magnificent harbours, an essential acquisition for any power bent on ruling the Mediterranean. The island's heroic defence had aroused the admiration of the Christian powers, and the order soon found its finances significantly improved. The years of neglect were over, and the Knights of Saint John now found their image so indissolubly linked with the island that they became universally known as the "Knights of Malta". Within the lifetime of Grand Master La Valette the new fortified city that bears his name began to arise on the headland that terminates in Fort Saint Elmo and domi- nates the island's two main harbours. Malta itself passed into a fame and

legend that has subsequently rarely left it, and which was additionally
reinforced by an even longer siege in the Second World War. A Greek
folk song, sung all over the eastern Mediterranean, reminded the Turks
that they were not always invincible:

> Malta of gold, Malta of silver, Malta of precious metal,
> We shall never take you!
> No, not even if you were as soft as a gourd,
> Not even if you were only protected by an onion skin!
> And from her ramparts a voice replied:
> "I am she who has decimated the galleys of the Turk —
> And all the warriors of Constantinople and Galata!"

The siege of Malta in 1565 marked the moment that the seemingly
irresistible Ottoman tide was checked. Turkish and other Moslems
from the North African coast would continue to prey upon the sea-
lanes of the western Mediterranean basin for centuries to come, but the
main wave was spent. Of the Sultan Suleiman it can be said that, although little recognized in most histories of Europe, his achievements in
reorganizing the clerical class, in reforming and improving the administration of his country, and in his amelioration of the condition of the
Christian subjects of his immense empire entitle him to be considered
as the Turkish equivalent of Justinian. He and his great opponent,
Charles V, were men of similar calibre, although Suleiman was a far
more tolerant and broad-minded ruler — particularly when it came to
dealing with religious matters — than was Charles, the persecutor of
Moors and Lutherans alike. Unlike the empire of Charles V, however,
which broke up a generation after Charles' death, the empire of Suleiman
was to last for nearly three centuries. The repulse at Malta and the
Battle of Lepanto, the third great naval event of this period, were not
sufficient to shatter the Turkish grasp upon the eastern Mediterranean
and its lands.

The European forces which combined at Lepanto, under the supreme
command of Charles V's natural son, Don John of Austria, consisted of
a Genoese and Venetian squadron, the whole Mediterranean fleet of
Spain, and a squadron from the Papal States. The Knights of Malta also
dispatched all their galleys. It was the Pope himself, Pius V, who had
been largely responsible for forming the alliance in 1570, in response to

Venetian demands to secure help against the endless depredations of the Turks. The final blow had fallen when the Turks under Piali Pasha (who had so signally failed at Malta) began the conquest and occupation of Cyprus, the last important Venetian possession in the Levant. Eager to strike a major blow against these ruthless enemies of Christendom and at the same time reassert his authority over the European powers, the Pope exerted all his influence and managed by 1571 to get them to agree to a massive counter-attack upon the Turks. So, in the late summer of that year, the allied armada gathered at that eternal rendezvous of fleets throughout the ages – the ancient city of Messina – and set off across the Ionian Sea. The fleet consisted of over two hundred galleys, as well as eight large galliasses (oar and sail) and a number of smaller craft – about two hundred and fifty ships in all. The Turks meanwhile awaited them with two hundred and fifty galleys and a large number of smaller vessels. They had based themselves on the narrows of the Gulf of Patras, at the point where the small fortified town and harbour of Lepanto commands the northern shores of the strait.

The battle that took place between the allied forces and the Ottoman fleet on October 7, 1571, was very significant in the history of the Mediterranean. It was the last action in which the oared galley, for thousands of years the master of the sea, played the predominant part. Henceforth, as Condalmiero's Galleon of Venice had shown at Preveza, it was the heavily armed sailing ship that determined the outcome of naval battles. Shades from many nations must have been present on that day, bending over the narrow strait to watch the last great conflict between vessels that had changed little since Greek fought Phoenician and Carthaginian fought Roman.

Despite the fact that the Turks had a preponderance of ships, and that they had been able to take up a good defensive position – forcing the allies to deploy round the northern headland at the mouth of the narrows – they failed to exploit their advantages. Although Ochiali Pasha, another survivor from the siege of Malta, managed to out-manoeuvre Giovanni Andrea Doria (great-nephew of Andrea), the main action was conclusive. The Turkish fleet was completely broken in the centre, and the great galley of Ali Pasha, commander of the Ottomans, was captured. Don John of Austria's report on the action records how "The fighting on the galley [Ali Pasha's] went on for a whole hour. Twice our forces reached the mainmast of the Turkish ship, only to be forced back again by Moslem charges which drove our men back to the forepart of our own vessel. . . . But after an hour and a half, God granted us the victory and the Pasha together with five hundred Turks was captured. His flags and his standards were taken, and the Cross was hoisted to the mainmast. Don John caused the cry of victory to be raised." Serving aboard the Spanish vessel *Marquesa* in this action was the future author of *Don Quixote*, Miguel de Cervantes. Apart from two gunshot wounds in the chest, he was also maimed in the left hand, "for the greater glory of the right", as he later remarked.

Fifty Turkish ships were either sunk or burnt in the Battle of Lepanto, while their losses in man power were immense — as many as twenty thousand were killed or captured. The allies lost eight thousand dead, and twice that number wounded. One further outcome of the battle was that tens of thousands of Christians were released from the oar-benches of the defeated Ottoman fleet. It was a signal victory, the greatest that had ever been achieved over the Ottomans. There was rejoicing all over Europe, for suddenly it seemed as if the power of her most implacable enemy had been broken — perhaps for ever. It was indeed a great reverse for the Turks, and it is true that, after the Battle of Lepanto and the siege of Malta, they seem to have abandoned any idea of using their navy for an invasion of Europe. On the other hand, as Moritz Brosch points out in *The Cambridge Modern History*, "The Battle of Lepanto proved the superiority of Christians arms, its results that of Turkish diplomacy. . . . The maintenance of this position was facilitated by the divisions, nay hostility, which broke out not only between the cabinets of the three allies, but between the crews of the different nationalities, which had united to win the victory but went asunder over the distribution of the spoil."

Even at this moment, when the Turkish fleet lay broken before them, the Europeans were unable to forget their internecine feuds and hatreds. Marcantonio Colonna, the commander of the papal squadron, went so far as to write: "Only by a miracle and the great goodness of God was it possible for us to fight such a battle. But it is just as great a miracle that the prevailing greed and covetousness have not flung us one against the other in a second battle."

The Battle of Lepanto, the triumph of Don John of Austria, the massive success of Christian arms – these have often enough been celebrated in European history and verse. The fact remains that the victory was never followed up, and the humiliation of the Turks never exploited. It was a temporary humiliation only, and within a year the Grand Vizier in Constantinople had caused a hundred and fifty new galleys to be built. Three years after Lepanto, in 1574, Tunis, which had fallen into Spanish hands, was recaptured by the Turks. They sailed down unopposed to Barbarossa's old naval base, in a fleet that numbered two hundred and fifty brand-new ships, commanded by the same Ochiali Pasha who had extricated his squadron so skilfully at Lepanto. The recuperative powers of the Ottoman Empire astounded all Europe. As the French ambassador at Constantinople wrote in a dispatch: "I could never have believed that this monarchy was so great, if I had not seen it with my own eyes." The victory of Lepanto proved a hollow one for Venice: she never regained Cyprus, and the whole island ultimately became yet another part of the Ottoman Empire.

The millennium between the extinction of the Roman Empire of the West and the fall of Constantinople to the Turks in 1453 was one of the most disturbed in history. The impoverished centuries in which the "wandering of the Nations" had devastated all of western Europe contributed little or nothing except to mingle the blood of many nations. Had it not been for the Byzantine Empire exercising its civilizing influence over the eastern portion and holding back the streams of invaders from north and east, the whole period might have seemed sunk in barbarism. Yet the great Arab conquests, much though they were bewailed in Europe, were nevertheless part of a revitalizing process. They brought out of the East a considerable amount of new or forgotten knowledge (some of it of Greek inheritance) which enriched Sicily and Spain and, ultimately, all the countries bordering upon the sea.

Miscegenation has always been part of the Mediterranean inheritance, and the extraordinary vitality of the basin over thousands of years may be ascribed in no small degree to this mingling of the races. Europeans, Africans, Asiatics, Persians, and Arabs have all contributed their genetic structures, as well as their cultural inheritance, to the vast pool of human knowledge that is Mediterranean civilization. To call the twentieth-century product of all these cultures and comminglings "Western

European", as is sometimes done, is to insult the immense contribution of the East. After the opening of the Atlantic sea-lanes by the Portuguese – to be followed by the great age of discovery, which does, indeed, belong to western Europe – it was not uncommon to ignore the origins of so much of the knowledge that the new explorers and settlers took with them. The wars fought by Europeans over thousands of years, against Persians, Carthaginians, Arabs, and Turks had produced among their historians an understandable bias against the East. But it was the accumulated wisdom of the whole Mediterranean – and not just of one part – that was now to permeate the entire world.

BOOK IV

Dorthin – *will* ich; und ich traue
Mir fortan und meinem Griff.
Offen leigt das Meer, ins Blaue
Treibt mein Genueser Schiff.

Alles glänzt mir neu und neuer,
Mittag schläft auf Raum und Zeit –;
Nur *dein* Auge – ungeheuer
Blickt michs an, Unendlichkeit!

I *will* away – and henceforth I trust in myself and in my own hands.
Open lies the sea, my Genoese ship surges onward into the blue. Every-
thing glitters new and newer, noontide sleeps on space and time: *your*
eye alone – dreadfully it gazes upon me, infinity!
– Friedrich Nietzsche, *The Gay Science*, 1882.
Translated by R. J. Hollingdale in *Nietzsche:*
The Man and His Philosophy

ONE

Islands under the Sun

From the close of the sixteenth century onwards something of a slumber fell over the sea for nearly two hundred years. The Mediterranean had become of secondary importance in world economy. Expansion was elsewhere, and the whole basin, divided uneasily between the powers of Spain and the Ottoman Empire, drifted from the central stage of human affairs for the first time in its history. It was as if, exhausted by the events of the past three thousand years, the sea, like an overtaxed field, needed to lie fallow.

A glance at a manual of dates quickly shows the disparity between events in the inland sea and those in the new-found worlds beyond the Atlantic. In 1512, for instance, the French were expelled from Milan by the Swiss; in the same year Portuguese traders who had reached Malacca and the Spice Islands brought back the first consignments of spices to Europe by the ocean route. In 1524 Marseilles was besieged by the French and the Germans; in the same year Pizarro sailed from Panama, explored the South American coast, and landed in modern Ecuador. In 1612 the Turks regained Moldavia from Poland; at the same time the East India Company introduced the Joint Stock principle for a series of voyages. In 1624 the Spaniards captured Breda from the Dutch; in that year Virginia became a crown colony, and the Dutch, far from their home scene of conflict with the Spaniards, began to colonize Formosa. On the other hand, in literature, the pictorial arts, architecture, and mathematics the rich inheritance of the Italian Renaissance was being diffused throughout Europe. Spain, France, and Italy were making outstanding contributions to the civilization of the world, which Holland and Great Britain and other northern countries were quick to adopt. But the fact remains that the real balance of power and of interest in human affairs had moved from the mother sea into the oceans and distant continents of the world.

It has been said that "Happy is the country that has no history"; and if history, to some extent at least, had deserted the Mediterranean it might perhaps have been expected that similar words could be applied to the countries around it during this period of time. Unfortunately, it was largely a tale of stagnation and erosion; and of subsidence into low levels of peasant life for most of the inhabitants of once great and famous countries. Italian cities, even those in decline like Genoa and Venice, continued to present a lively surface picture, but the lives of most Mediterranean-dwellers had received a check, like a tree that has been over-pruned or blasted by frost.

Spain in the West looked mainly outwards towards her empire, where she carried on a running battle with the newcomers from France, Holland, and England. On the southern border of the sea, the Moslem kingdoms, largely Turkish dominated, maintained their rapacious inroads into the traffic of the Atlantic and of the western Mediterranean. Over all the East, the vast shadow of the Ottoman Empire hung like a upas tree, smothering life. The great city of Alexandria, for instance (which the Turks had occupied during their conquest of Egypt in 1517), is described in the following terms by an English traveller, John Sandys, writing in 1610: "Such was this Queen of Cities and Metropolis of Africa: who now hath nothing left her but ruins; and those ill witnesses of his perished beauties: declaring rather that towns as well as men have their ages and destinies. . . . Sundry Mountains were raised of the ruins, by Christians not to be mounted; lest they should take too exact a survey of the city; in which are often found (especially after a shower) rich stones and medals engraven with the figures of their Gods and men with such perfection of Art as these now cut seeme lame to those and unlively counterfeits." It is significant that the great Italian sculptor and goldsmith Benvenuto Cellini, writing his memoirs some years earlier, describes how he and others would dig in Italy for such treasures from the ancient world, and would pay large sums for them. But, unlike the citizens of Turkish Alexandria, the Italians were then fired to emulate them, and, although often confessing that the taste and craft of their predecessors exceeded their own, they produced, in their rivalry with the dead, many of the great art treasures of the sixteenth century.

The condition of the sea can be gauged by a glance at some of the more important islands lying within the basin. In the west, the Balearic Islands, the haunt of merchant seamen since Phoenician times, while enjoying some prosperity (when not suffering from corsair raids from the Barbary Coast), were in an intellectual sleep. Yet it was here that, in the thirteenth century, the mystic, philosopher, and poet Ramón Lull had renewed the Platonic tradition in his prose work *Blanquerna*, and had combined sincerity with springlike beauty in poems such as *El Desconort*. Lull had also founded the first European school of Oriental languages at Valldemosa in the thirteenth century. During the fourteenth century the Catalan Jews of Mallorca had been famous for their scientific knowledge and for their ability as cartographers, and it was from among them that Henry the Navigator had culled several of the experts and advisers for his court at Sagres. Outstanding among these mathematicians and cartographers were Abraham Cresques, also of Mallorca, and his son Jaime. The astrolabe, used for determining sun and star altitudes, most probably reached the Portuguese navigators from Mallorca. But this rich island culture, which had flourished during the Arabic conquest and the first century of Aragonese rule, had now fallen into sterility. It was not until the eighteenth century, when the warring British and French were to dispute over possession of the islands, that they emerged from their semi-obscurity once more.

Some two hundred miles east of the Balearic Islands, Corsica and Sardinia hang suspended like an elaborate pendant earring beneath the Gulf of Genoa. East of them is the Tyrrhenian Sea, that ancient domain of the Etruscans. The condition of both islands was miserable in the extreme, exploited by the powers that occupied them, and reduced to such extremities by taxation and oppression that banditry and the vendetta had become endemic. Throughout all their history, through classical, mediaeval, and now Renaissance times, they had been signally ignored by their rulers except in so far as their man power, their forests, and their metal mines could be exploited for the benefit of whoever happened to be their current occupier.

Corsica was administered, in theory at least, by the Republic of Genoa, but in practice by a powerful commercial corporation called the Banco di San Giorgio. The bank maintained its power by extreme cruelty, and exercised it with a selfishness so short-sighted that insurrections were constantly provoked – which then had to be suppressed with further cruelty. Even the defences of the coast were neglected to such an extent that the Barbary corsairs regarded the island as their own province, to be entered freely and looted at will. Villages and coastal towns were largely abandoned, the inhabitants withdrawing into the mountainous interior; with the result that the most fertile parts of the coastal belt deteriorated into malarial wastes. In the history of the Italian maritime republics, the Genoese showed themselves cupidinous and short-sighted to a degree that made the Venetians seem almost like benefactors to the islands in their possession. The condition of the Corsicans remained desperate and was almost unchanged until the middle of the eighteenth century, when James Boswell, biographer of Samuel Johnson, was so moved by their revolt under the patriot Pasquale di Paoli that he attempted to persuade William Pitt, the British Prime Minister, to intervene on their behalf against Genoa. (This prompted the remark of Lord Holland, "We cannot be so foolish as to go to war because Mr. Boswell has been to Corsica.") In 1769 the unhappy island fell to France, and in the same year Napoleon Bonaparte was born in the coastal town of Ajaccio.

Sardinia, second largest island in the sea, rivalled Corsica in its obscure misery. Outside the mainstream of history, Sardinia had been practically unaffected by the Renaissance. Sardinia, indeed, even more than Corsica, had hardly ever benefited by any of the great cultural changes of the centuries. The Phoenicians had annexed whatever areas of coastline they needed, pushing back the native Sards into the mountains. The Roman occupation had been on similar lines. As T. and B. Holme and B. Ghirardelli write in *Sardinia*: "The [Roman] occupation was a savage one, and it lasted for nearly seven centuries – centuries of persecution and extortion, and of guerrilla warfare launched by the Sards from their mountain hide-outs." Thus the pattern of Sardinian life was early established, and so it remained throughout the sixteenth, seventeenth, and eighteenth centuries. The island was now a subject state of Spain, and the Spanish viceroys regarded their appointment to the island with distaste, alleviating their dissatisfaction by exploiting it as thoroughly as they could during their three-year terms of office. As in Corsica, the coast was always subject to the raids of the Barbary pirates, with the result that the Sards withdrew even further into their mountains – to escape not only the pirates, but also the Spanish tax-collectors. Vast areas of potentially fine agricultural land became swampland, and malaria was persistent in the island until the twentieth century, when it was stamped out by D.D.T. at the close of the Second World War.

This island, so beautiful with its silvery mountains, its tangled maquis, and its strange fauna, has suffered the harshest fate of any in the Mediterranean. Not even Sicily, although constantly torn apart by warring nations, has tasted the bitterness of Sardinia. Sicily, at least, received the benefit of the cultures of the nations that occupied it. Sardinia, on the other hand, was mined for its antimony, coal, lead, silver, and zinc (which enriched Spain just as they had all the island's previous owners), while the miners themselves were treated almost like slaves. It was little wonder that the tactics of guerrilla warfare were as familiar here as in Corsica, and that the blood feud was, if anything, even more violent and long-lasting.

Italian ethnologists, investigating the perpetuity of brigandage and the vendetta in the mountain areas of Barbagia in the 1950s, made the amazing discovery that these Sardinians have been in continuous revolt against the state for over two thousand years. Despite all efforts, even the Romans never managed to bring the Barbagians within the framework of the state. No other power, out of the many who occupied the island in the succeeding centuries, ever made domesticated, tax-paying citizens out of them. (After the Second World War, within a decade the Italian Republic lost thirty-two *carabinieri* in attempts to discipline the Barbagians.) The inhabitants of this remote mountain region were no more than extreme examples of the Sardinian national character. Courageous, proud, and independent, they detested, despised, and fought against the rule of Spain, just as they had against all others.

Sicily, while it enjoyed through its natural resources and agriculture a happier state than forlorn Sardinia, was nevertheless under a similar Spanish yoke. The chief difference was that the viceroys of Sicily found in the capital of Palermo, and in the cultivated circles of the island, a world that was as pleasant as any to be found in Spain. Their rule, therefore, may be said to have been more indulgent – though this hardly applied to the condition of the peasantry, who remained, as they had been for millennia, little more than beasts of burden. Disorders and civil strife were not uncommon, for the Sicilians were as loath to pay taxes to the Spaniards as they had been to the Byzantines.

There was a difference, however, between the Sicilians and the Sardinians. Whereas the Sardinians were sturdy and independent, they were nevertheless a primitive and largely uncivilized people. The Sicilians, on the other hand, with their amazing mixture of blood and cultures, were a sophisticated and "old" people. They had known conquest, but they had absorbed it, whereas the Sardinians had merely retreated to their mountains. The peasant inhabitants of Sicily had known so many foreign overlords and conquering races that they had developed a cynical attitude and an unspoken resistance to all of them.

This attitude found its ultimate form in the organization known as the Mafia. Whatever the Mafia may have become in later centuries, it originated as a self-help organization designed to protect the Sicilians against foreign rulers, corrupt police, and the callous attitudes of absentee landlords. *Omertà* (Sicilian *omu*, man), the "Code of Manliness", engendered the obligation never to apply to the legally constituted authorities for justice. No doubt it existed long before the Mafia came into being. Under the rule of peculant Spanish governors and administrators, the Sicilians learned to administer their own "private" justice. As in Sardinia, the tradition of banditry and the vendetta was long established; the high, lonely mountains of the Madonie Range teemed with refugees from Spanish law, as well as with organized bands of robbers. Neither in Sicily nor in Sardinia was the bandit regarded by most inhabitants as a criminal, for as often as not he was the victim of some injustice inflicted upon him by the foreign occupying power. Spanish colonies, whether in the New World or the Old, were only too often distinguished by their cruelty and corruption. Sicily was no exception.

South of Sicily, on the dividing line between the two halves of the Mediterranean, the Maltese archipelago presented a marked contrast to most of the other islands in the sea. To the west lay the indifferently or badly administered islands that owed their allegiance to Spain; to the east lay the islands of the Aegean where, darker far than Spanish colonialism, the rule of the Ottomans brought nothing but desolation and despair. In Malta, however, the rule of the Order of Saint John, after the siege of 1565, created conditions of almost unprecedented prosperity. Robin Blouet writes in *The Story of Malta*: "During the next two and a half centuries the knights of St. John spent lavishly on fortifications, ordnance establishments, new towns, palaces and villas. The Maltese prospered on this spending and on the spending necessary to maintain the high standard of living which the knights enjoyed. During the Order's rule the number of Maltese increased fivefold, new trades and industries were developed and the islands became the home of one of the most prosperous communities in Europe." The galleys of the order went out regularly every year on their "caravans", or offensive patrols, into Moslem areas; they destroyed any corsairs that they came across and returned laden with booty, often towing captured Turkish merchantmen behind them. The defences erected around Grand Harbour and the other salient points of the islands during these centuries were so immense in scope and so daunting in their prospect that the Turks never again attempted to besiege Malta. Valletta, the fortified capital, which had been called after Grand Master La Valette *Humillima Civitas Valettae*, "The Most Humble City of Valette", became known throughout Europe for its richness and aristocratic dignity as *Superbissima*, "The Most Proud".

The last of the Crusaders, the militant and nursing brotherhood of Saint John, were also famous throughout Europe for their skills in navigation and shipbuilding, as well as for their advances in medical science and surgery. The cotton which the Arabs had introduced into the island made excellent sailcloth, and Maltese sails were renowned as being the finest in the Mediterranean. A major source of the island's wealth was the slave market, for, in their unending war with the Moslem enemy, the knights had adopted the tactics of the Algerians and Turks. Slaves were sold to traders from Genoa and Venice, and much of the island's own prosperity was based upon slave labour. It has been estimated that, even as late as the eighteenth century, there were always about two thousand slaves employed in Malta. All this was made possible by the use of sea power, and the Maltese galleys and sailing ships of the seventeenth century were probably the most efficient on the sea. A report on the knights' galleys and fighting qualities made to one of the Turkish Sultans concluded: "Their vessels are not like others. They have always aboard them great numbers of arquebusiers and of knights who are dedicated to fight to the death. There has never been an occasion when they have attacked one of our ships that they have not either sunk it or captured it."

It was in the management of their great hospital in Valletta, in their approach towards hygiene, improved surgical methods, and the general treatment of the sick, that the order made another significant contribution to Mediterranean history. Not only navigators and sea-captains came to the island for training in cartography, in the seaman's arts, and in tactics of naval warfare; the hospital was also a source of attraction for doctors and would-be doctors from all over Europe. All this depended on the fleet, and, as Paul Cassar comments in his *Medical History of Malta*, "Only on very rare occasions did the navy have respite from warfare. These short and infrequent lulls, however, were no periods of idle rest for the naval medical and surgical personnel, for at such times the navy might be summoned to render medical assistance to some neighbouring country stricken by sudden catastrophe. One of these major missions of mercy occurred in January 1693 when an earthquake destroyed the city of Augusta in Sicily. Although considerable damage was also caused in Malta by the earthquake, the Order's Government immediately dispatched five galleys to succour the inhabitants of the Sicilian town. When, in 1783, Messina and Reggio with the entire coast of Calabria suffered a similar fate, the Order's galleys were quickly on the spot laden with every article needed for the relief of the survivors. The best surgeons of the Holy Infirmary embarked on the galleys taking with them twenty chests filled with medicines, two hundred beds and a great number of tents. While the knights distributed food for some 1,200 to 1,500 persons on the verge of famine, the medical teams toiled with the sick and wounded." Such episodes are worth recording, for, although best remembered in European history for their endless warfare against the Turks, the knights never forgot their original vocation. It is evidence also of the prosperity of this small archipelago that it could afford to send relief ships, supplies, and medicine to its much larger neighbours, Sicily and Italy.

Five hundred miles east, across one of the most desolate and dangerous stretches of the Mediterranean, the island of Crete breaks from the waves like a dolphin. After Sicily, Sardinia, and Cyprus, this long fish-shaped island is the largest in the sea and, next to Sicily, its cultural contribution has been the greatest. The Minoan or Cretan civilization was the first to exercise a true thalassocracy. Even before the Phoenicians had begun their long voyages to the western end of the sea, the Cretans had been trading as far afield as the Balearic Islands and Spain. Their culture, unknown, forgotten for centuries (until Sir Arthur Evans began his excavations in 1893), had influenced the whole Aegean and had laid a substratum upon which the Greeks were later to build so successfully. In classical times its role had been negligible. In the sixteenth century Crete was one of the few Venetian possessions in the eastern part of the sea, and – after the capture of Cyprus by the Turks – by far the most important to their economy.

Kandia, a fortress originally built by the island's Saracen occupiers, had become the administrative centre and capital of the island. Under the Venetians, Crete was probably more prosperous than at any time in its recorded history. In Crete and in the Ionian islands of Corfu, Cephalonia, and Zante the Venetians had encouraged agriculture; and the local inhabitants had prospered through the activities of their traders and shippers. The Venetians had been reasonably efficient administrators, and they had built strong defences, as well as many attractive private homes and public offices in the great tradition of their city. Crete's tragedy during this period was that it lay east of the dividing line between the Spanish and Turkish spheres of influence. The Turks may have resigned themselves to the fact that Malta was unassailable, but they were certainly not prepared to accept that this was true of Crete.

The Cretans themselves, although enjoying a level of prosperity higher than that of the other Aegean islanders, did not take kindly to Venetian overlordship. The Cretans had always been a difficult people to rule. Like the Sardinians, they were a hardy race of mountaineers, and they had an impassioned love of freedom. It was perhaps for this intransigence, as much as anything else, that they had acquired so ill a reputation in classical times. It is difficult to find a single flattering reference to them. In the Epistle of Paul to Titus they are described as "always liars, evil beasts, slow bellies". Suidas remarks, "The three accursed K's, the Kretans, the Kappadocians, and the Kilikians", while both Horace and Plutarch quote the same Greek proverb: "When dealing with Cretans you must be Cretans" (that is, liars). Like the inhabitants of the other great Mediterranean islands frequently occupied by foreign powers, the Cretans had no doubt become masters of dissimulation. But it was their fiery and irrepressible temperament that made them the bane of their rulers. Like the Sicilians, they, too, had a healthy dislike of paying taxes to a foreign power.

Revolts were frequent, and the mountainous hinterland seethed with untameable robber bands. Between the years 1207 and 1365, one authority records that there were fourteen major insurrections. The last of these was in the nature of a large-scale revolt lasting three years, in which many of the Venetian colonists also rose against the Republic. The Cretans, for their part, tried to enlist the aid of Genoa against her rival. Finally – and it is an indication of their hatred of Venice – the Cretans even tried to secure Turkish help against their rulers.

But it was not until 1645 that the Turks seriously turned their attention to Crete, when they landed an army of fifty thousand men and quickly reduced Khania at the north-western corner of the island. But their siege of Kandia, the capital, was unsuccessful; the stout walls built by the Venetians proved too strong even for the weight of armament that the Turks brought against them. The city was besieged by the Turks off and on for over twenty years – the longest recorded siege in history. Finally, in spite of a magnificently heroic defence in which the Venetians lost some thirty thousand men, the city fell to the Turkish Vizier Achmet in 1669. Venice was allowed to retain three relatively unimportant trading stations along the northern coast of the island. These, too, were captured some years later, and the whole of Crete became a Turkish province. Those Cretans who had looked for Ottoman aid to rid themselves of the Venetians were now saddled with the dead administrative weight and the merciless military power of the Sublime Porte. Although a great many Cretans "turned Turk" and embraced the Moslem faith (thus securing for themselves a large part in the government of the island), it cannot be said that most of the inhabitants were any happier under the Turks than they had been under their previous masters. The Cretans were born to despise foreigners, to fight, and to live a type of existence that recalls the Homeric period of Greece.

The influence of environment upon human beings is nowhere more clearly illustrated than in the history of these Mediterranean islands; for the inhabitants of Corsica, Sardinia, the mountainous area of Sicily, and Crete display very similar traits. They confirm the words of Cyrus, spoken many centuries before: "'It is not the property of any one soil to produce fine fruits and good soldiers too.'" The mountain regions were prolific of great warriors, but the overlordship of the islands was always determined by the fact that he who rules the sea rules the coast-line. Since, in the mountainous limestone Mediterranean islands, the most fertile land is usually to be found on the coastal plains, this has also meant that a dominant naval power will not only enjoy the ports and harbours that it requires but also the best agricultural areas.

At the eastern end of the Mediterranean, Cyprus, which had been lost to the Venetians (and for which the Battle of Lepanto had largely been fought), remained under the firm control of the Turks. Sir James Frazer, in *The Golden Bough*, has described the home of the goddess of love, the descendant of the great Earth Mother, as follows: "The sanctuary of Aphrodite at Old Paphos (the modern Kuklia) was one of the most celebrated shrines in the ancient world. According to Hero-dotus, it was founded by Phoenician colonists from Ascalon; but it is possible that a native goddess of fertility was worshipped on the spot before the arrival of the Phoenicians, and that the newcomers identified her with their own Baalath or Astarte, whom she may have closely resembled. If two deities were thus fused in one, we may suppose that they were both varieties of that great goddess of motherhood and fertility whose worship appears to have been spread all over Western Asia from a very early time. The supposition is confirmed as well by the archaic shape of her image as by the licentious character of her rites; for both that shape and those rites were shared by her with other Asiatic deities. . . ."

This goddess had long since faded from the temples of the island. Her place, and that of her lover Tammuz, or Adonis, had been taken by the Orthodox Church, with the Virgin Mary and Her Divine Son. Now, however, the Ottomans imposed an all-male concept of religion upon the fertile island. The names of Allah and Mohammed resounded upon the resin-scented air of Paphos, Famagusta, and other centres of island life. Where once women had prostituted themselves to strangers at the sanctuary of the Mother Goddess, and where subsequently the obser-vances of the Greek Church had been celebrated, the voice of the Imam, winding among the phallic minarets, now enjoined the faithful that "There is no God but Allah, and Mohammed is his Prophet."

TWO

Dutch, English, and Corsairs

Vessels like the Galleon of Venice and the Great Carrack of Rhodes had pointed the way, and now the sea was increasingly dominated by large sailing ships, heavily built and heavily armed. For certain purposes the galley and the xebec never entirely lost their place; indeed, the galley was still in somewhat limited use in the nineteenth century, and the xebec remained the favourite vessel of the Barbary corsairs throughout the seventeenth and eighteenth centuries. Of galley form, and stepping three lateen-sailed masts, the xebec had only nine oar-ports aside. It was a fast sailing vessel that could be rowed in calms. For a vessel of this type a fairly heavy armament was carried: often as many as four 12-pounder, sixteen 6-pounder, and eight 3-pounder guns. Both the Spaniards and the French used xebecs in the Mediterranean as patrol craft and scouts – somewhat similar to the frigates or light destroyers of the twentieth century.

The death of the galley was unmistakably signalled in the year 1587, when Sir Francis Drake sailed into the harbour of Cadiz and, in thirty-six hours, destroyed thousands of tons of enemy shipping and captured six large merchantmen, then sailed out again without any loss to his own force. He had done all this in the face of a protective force of galleys that should, according to previous theory, have been able to cut a sailing vessel to pieces within the confined waters of a harbour. Drake proved finally what had been hinted at Preveza: a heavily armed sailing ship was a match for several galleys. Time and time again, when the galleys of Spain stood in against Drake's vessels, they were repulsed or blown out of the water before they could ever get near enough to ram or to board. This famous episode, which Drake laughingly referred to as "singeing the King of Spain's beard", was the moment that the pattern of sea warfare changed for ever.

In the following year, 1588, the failure of the Armada against England proved an immense check to Spanish sea power. Although it would be a long time before the might of Spain was appreciably humbled, it was again significant that the English successes were based entirely upon the use of sailing ships. The Armada, although it had no Mediterranean galleys in its composition, did have a number of galliasses in addition to its sailing galleons. The mixed nature of his fleet undoubtedly hampered the Duke of Medina-Sidonia, just as it had Andrea Doria at Preveza fifty years before. Spanish conservatism is not entirely to be blamed for the fact that both the Dutch and the English had somewhat overtaken the Spanish in ship design and naval tactics. The fact was that, whereas the two northern nations were able to concentrate their efforts on building ships suitable for the Atlantic and the North Sea, Spain was in the unhappy position of conducting a war upon two fronts. She not only had to safeguard her immense overseas empire against the constant depredations of Dutch, French, and English, but, being also a Mediterranean power, she had to build ships specifically for Mediterranean use. Whereas the thinking of her adversaries was entirely directed to one aim, Spain had to consider the Barbary corsairs and the Ottomans.

The historian Pietro Ubaldini, who, as a Florentine, could readily grasp the importance of sea power, commented in his history of the Armada campaign: "All the weight of defending the coast of England from the hostile invasion, and all the work of impeaching the Spanish Armada from joining hands with the Duke of Parma, and finally of not permitting it to take a moment's rest at anchor in any part of these seas, rested upon the sagacity and technical grasp of the naval art possessed by the English officers, who had command in the Royal Navy according to their ranks, and by those who under them commanded their particular vessels. These men making good use of the trustworthy quality of their excellent and fast sailing vessels, which were not encumbered with useless soldiers but free for the guns, so that at any moment they could play without fail upon the enemy, knew ever from moment to moment what was best for them to do."

The key phrases here are "excellent and fast sailing vessels", and "not encumbered with useless soldiers but free for the guns". The Spaniards and other Mediterranean naval powers carried into the late sixteenth century the concepts of sea warfare that had first been formulated by the Romans. That is to say, they concentrated on vessels containing a large number of soldiers, with the aim of fighting a land battle at sea. The Romans had triumphed over the Carthaginians by the use of the raven-bridge. The Spaniards, too, endeavoured to lay their vessels alongside the enemy, holding the ships together with grapnels while their own soldiers rushed aboard. It is significant that both the Roman and the Spanish empires were above all land empires; and that the Spaniards, although fine fighting men, had no real inclination towards the sea. It was left to the English and the Dutch to restore the ancient predominance of the mariner and well-handled ship over the soldier and the boarding party.

One of the reasons why the English, who were so soon to make their mark upon the trade of the inland sea, had concentrated on the "round ship", or sailing vessel, was of course climatic. Whereas a galley stood up well to the short seas of the Mediterranean, it did not have a suitable hull shape for the long ocean swells of the Atlantic. In the Mediterranean – largely on account of the summer calms – a big trading galley of the Venetian type was an economic proposition. But the number of days in which the weather would have been suitable for a galley in the North Sea, the English Channel, or the North Atlantic would not have made her economically viable. The difficulty of manning a galley in northern seas was another important factor in the English, Dutch, and Scandinavian preference for the sailing ship. Unlike the Mediterranean powers, they were not in daily conflict with the Moslems, who used slave labour to drive their galleys – and from whom slave labour could be recruited. All the countries bordering upon the Mediterranean had long grown used to the practice of slavery, but this was not true of the North. The few galleys which were used at one time and another by the English were manned by free men and by criminals. Even so, there was not a sufficient supply of volunteers, or of criminals, for the northern countries to have built up large galley fleets in the Mediterranean fashion.

Michael Lewis, in *The Navy of Britain*, makes a further point why the "round ship", rather than the galley, became the warship of the North as well as its cargo-carrier: "The Galley was, economically speaking, an unproductive thing. She could not be made to pay – between-whiles, when not required for war – as a cargo-carrier could. She was bound to be always on the debit side of the Crown's account sheet: she was essentially a revenue-spender. Now all the kings of England were expected to 'live of their own'; to carry on the government, that is, in ordinary times, out of their own revenues [quite unlike the rulers of the Mediterranean]. Only, normally, in times of crises could they call upon their subjects to help them, and even then the help, when it came, was usually in kind, not in cash. . . . This is significant, for it meant that, on occasions when ships were really necessary to them, they could acquire them from only one source – from their own ship-owning subjects, who were of course men who had built, or who owned, ships wherewith to make their living – that is, merchants. And the ships of such men were not, naturally, Galleys, but Round Ships; for no merchant in his senses would build a galley with which to trade."

It was for these varied reasons that the sailing ship saw its major evolution in the North, while its transformation into the most efficient fighting ship of its day was made possible by the discovery of gun-powder by the Europeans and the new skills of the cannon-founders. The sailing "ship-of-the-line", although destined to rule the waves for no more than three centuries – compared to the galley's two millennia – was, until the advent of the steam-propelled ship in the nineteenth century, the dominant vessel in the Mediterranean. Even the fast North African xebecs soon learned that these new traders from the North, Dutch, Scandinavian, and English, were more than a match for them. As Drake had shown in Cadiz harbour – even when becalmed and, therefore, by old concepts theoretically an easy prey – they carried such a weight of metal that no xebecs or galleys could stand up to them. Mediterranean craft, whether sail- or oar-propelled, had to be built to fairly light specifications. Whether under sail in the breezes of mid-summer or driven by their oarsmen, they necessarily had to be of slighter construction than sailing ships designed for the heavy seas and harsh winds of the North. An oak-built English ship-of-the-line might take half a gale to drive her, but she was so strong that she could with-stand a considerable amount of shot and shell.

With the arrival of the large sailing ship in Mediterranean waters, an age-old problem immediately declared itself. In the cold waters of the North, barnacles and weed on a ship's hull had not constituted too grave a threat, and a vessel had only needed to be slipped and hauled ashore about once a year. But the deadly teredo worm, that enemy of wood, flourished in the Mediterranean's warm waters. As early as Homer's days, ships had been regularly painted with pitch below water to protect them. But pitch was only a temporary protective – good enough in the days when vessels were light and easy to beach and clean. The Knights of Saint John had protected the Great Carrack of Rhodes by sheathing her with lead. This was a method that the Spaniards adopted for their more important vessels. Lead, however, was vastly expensive, and such sheathing could not be contemplated for ordinary warships, let alone trading vessels.

The early voyagers in the warm waters of the Caribbean had also encountered the problem of the teredo worm, and one of the first to propose a solution to it had been Sir John Hawkins, that great Elizabethan seaman, explorer, and Treasurer of the Royal Navy. Knowing that elm was one wood which was little to the taste of the voracious worm, Hawkins sheathed the Queen's ships with elm boards, which were nailed to the underwater planking through an inner covering of felt and tar. His methods proved successful against the teredo, although the problems of barnacles and weed growth were not solved for a long time to come.

In the second half of the eighteenth century, improving upon Hawkins' technique, the English began to sheathe their ships with thin plates of copper laid over felt. Not only was copper impervious to worm, but it was less easy for the persistent barnacle and underwater weed to affix themselves to the metal. Until the advent of chemical paints in the twentieth century (which discharge a substance poisonous to worm, weed, and barnacle alike), copper sheathing proved the answer to the problems of underwater timbers, which necessarily had to remain a long time in the sea between one docking and another. These improvements in protecting a wooden vessel were all-important in the warfare that later devastated the Mediterranean, as well as in providing better protection for the English, Scandinavian, and Dutch merchantmen who soon took over much of the trade in this sea.

Admiral Jurien de la Gravière, in his *Origins of the Modern Navy*, writes that there were three distinctive phases in its history: "The first of these periods was made up of the successive wars that Spain conducted against the Netherlands, England, and, finally, France. Most of the fleets engaged in these were composed of ships of about a hundred tons, or from three to four hundred more or less. . . . In the second period, it was England and Holland that disputed the supremacy of the seas. . . . The third period begins with the appearance of the navy of Louis XIV. Tactics now become more regular and disciplined. Guns are far more efficient. True naval gunnery begins, of the type still familiar in our days [1879]. The Navy of Sail, has, as it were, now found itself. From now on it will hardly change, except in almost insignificant details." The sailing ship, once its main problems had been solved, altered very little between the seventeenth and the nineteenth centuries. Vessels grew larger, so did guns, and navigational methods improved. Other than that, a sea-captain of Drake's age would not have found much to disconcert him aboard Nelson's flagship, the *Victory*.

The English connection with the Mediterranean had begun during the Crusades, but it was trade more than anything else that now drew this latest of the northern nations down into the landlocked sea. The Vandals had come as a barbaric nomadic tribe; the Vikings as organized sea-rovers; and the Normans as an expanding nation who wanted new territories in which to settle. The motives that impelled the English and their rivals, the Dutch, were quite different. They resembled the Phoenicians and the Carthaginians in that they did not expand – at least into the Mediterranean – in search of colonies, but in order to exchange their own manufactured goods for the goods and raw materials of other nations.

Since most of these traders were unarmed, or at the most only carried a few light cannon, they found it difficult to resist the determined onslaught of Algerian corsairs in xebecs and galleys. Rather than go to the expense of converting their ships into "armed merchantmen", which would, in any case, have greatly reduced their carrying capacity, it became a normal practice to pay tribute money to the raiders. This practice persisted into the nineteenth century, and the city of Algiers derived a large part of its revenue from such extortion. Shipping companies made their own private arrangements with the corsairs, and carried special passes to indicate that they had paid their tribute. There was hardly one of the seafaring nations trading in the Mediterranean that did not pay some form of protection money to these descendants of Barbarossa and Dragut. Where sufficient money was not available, gifts, including war materials, were often considered acceptable. This situation provoked one American consul to write that there was no chance of eradicating the mischief so long as the two principal naval powers, Britain and France, encouraged it by turning a blind eye to the money that their merchant companies paid the Sultan. As Augustin Bernard writes in the *Encyclopaedia Britannica*: "For 300 years Algiers was the headquarters of piracy, the meeting-place of sea-robbers, and the terror of all civilized countries, which it defied with audacity born of long impunity. The punitive expeditions of the European Powers against the Algerians were generally undertaken haphazard and after insufficient preparation. Bombardments and blockades produced no lasting result."

The convoy system, in which merchant ships were accompanied by men-of-war, was evolved in the Mediterranean as a protection against piracy, and was in use for well over a century. During the Napoleonic Wars the English adopted it on all their trade routes, to safeguard their shipping from the French. The maritime supremacy of the Royal Navy in the Mediterranean heralded a new era, and in the early nineteenth century British and American successes against the two main bases of the pirates, Algiers and Tripoli, paved the way for the French conquest of the whole area. Norman Douglas, in *Old Calabria*, drily, and accurately, commented: "It is all very well for Admiral de la Gravière to speak of 'Gallia Victrix' – the Americans, too, might have something to say on that point. The fact is that neither European nor American arms crushed the pest. But for the invention of steam, the Barbary corsairs might still be with us."

The shade of Barbarossa, which haunted the North African coast for three centuries after his death, was one reason why the Mediterranean remained in a state of decline. The other was that the great trade routes of the world and the riches of new continents and immense overseas territories engaged the attentions of kings and merchants alike. The course of history, for so long shaped within the Mediterranean basin, was now determined either upon the battlefields of France and Germany or on distant oceans and seas. Although trade in wine, sugar, silk, and spices still continued between the Mediterranean and northern Europe, it was a mere trickle compared with the volume of riches that now passed upon the "trade-wind" routes of the Atlantic. The Mediterranean, with one end partly sealed by the Algerians and the other inert under the weight of the Ottoman Empire, seemed to have become an appendix to history.

THREE

Gibraltar

Dominating the Mediterranean's entrance, the bald limestone head of Calpe, the Rock of Gibraltar, stands sentinel to the sea's approaches. Eight and a half miles away, on the African coast, its companion, the eminence near Ceuta known to the ancients as Abyla, forms the second of the Pillars of Hercules. The names Calpe and Abyla were both probably corruptions of Phoenician words whose origins have been lost. In the sixteenth and seventeenth centuries both Ceuta and Gibraltar belonged to the Spanish crown, which meant that the Spanish navy, in theory at least, should always have been able to close the whole sea to any hostile power that attempted to enter it from the Atlantic. Ceuta, which had been captured by Henry the Navigator in 1415, had become part of the Spanish crown after the subjugation of Portugal by Philip II in 1580. Gibraltar was formally incorporated in the Spanish kingdom in 1502, and had been turned into a formidable fortress during the sixteenth century.

Seen from the sea, the Rock rises like a lion's head to a height of nearly 1400 feet; unforgettable even to the most world-weary traveller. More often than not it trails from its grey crystalline peak a long streamer of "Levanter" cloud, so-called because when the wind comes out of the Levant, it strikes on the steep up-jutting eastern face and produces a grey, humid condition. In later centuries – since the British have owned the Rock – this cloud has caused the Spaniards to say, "They even bring their weather with them."

The winds in the strait are mainly westerly or easterly. Depressions from the Atlantic move in during the winter and bring grey heavy weather with them; in summer, on the other hand, the winds are generally easterly, and a warm airstream flows out of the Mediterranean.

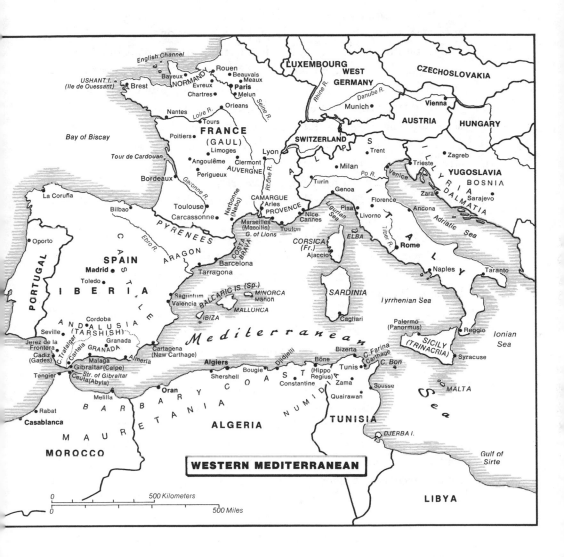

WESTERN MEDITERRANEAN

The Admiralty Pilot describes the weather: "In the strait, the easterly wind is known as the 'Levanter.' Outside the strait, the wind may be from between north-east and south-east, but inside it becomes easterly, and increases in strength towards the narrowest part of the strait. It has all the marked characteristics of the easterly wind, bringing excessive moisture, heavy dews, local cloud, a thick hazy or foggy atmosphere, and sometimes rain. . . . When it is fresh or strong, violent eddies are formed in the lee of the rock, the wind frequently blowing strong for some time from opposite directions at places only about 50 yards apart. These eddies, with their up and down, and cross currents, are troublesome and dangerous to sailing craft. In winds of about force 3 or 4 a banner cloud, known locally as the 'Levanter cloud,' or 'Levante,' usually stretches out from the summit of the rock for distances of a mile or more to leeward." The easterly wind is as irritating in its excessive humidity to the inhabitants of Gibraltar as is the southerly sirocco to the Maltese and the Sicilians.

The Rock's name, Gibraltar, derives from the name of its Arab conqueror, Tariq ibn Ziyad, who crossed the strait with a small force in the early eighth century and defeated the Goths after a three-day battle in Andalusia, near the town of Jerez de la Frontera (famous in later centuries as the home of sherry). *Jebel* is Arabic for mountain, and Gibraltar became known as *Jebel al Tariq*, "Tariq's mountain," because the conqueror, realizing the importance of its position, built himself a fortress there. It took thirty-one years to complete the work, the remains of which are still standing. A massive square tower, the keep of his castle, is commonly known as the "Moorish castle".

Captured by Spain some six hundred years later, then recaptured by the Moors, Gibraltar finally passed into Spanish hands in the fifteenth century. Except for Tariq's tower, nothing remains to show the centuries of Moorish occupation. But nothing remains either of the long centuries when the Rock was a regular calling place for Phoenician merchants, bound out on the grey Atlantic for trade with the tin miners of Cornwall. It was somewhere near here, on "the banks of the River of Ocean", that Ulysses dug a trench, poured libations, and sacrificed an all-black sheep – "and the souls of the dead came swarming up from Erebus all about him."

The geography of this strange natural fortress has been described by

The interior of the Capella Palatina at Palermo, in the Norman kingdom of Sicily

Venetian coin portrait of
Doge Dandolo

The walls of the city during the nineteenth century

A. C. Ramsay and Archibald Geikie in the *Quarterly Journal of the Geological Society*, 1878: "The extreme length of the Rock from the base of the cliff at the north front to Europa Point is only a little over 2½ m., and the promontory tapers somewhat gradually away from a breadth of 1,550 yds. between Gibraltar and Catalan Bay to a width of 550 yds. at Europa. The Rock shoots abruptly upwards from the low flat ground at the north front in a fine mural precipice, the basal portion of which is partly concealed by a sloping curtain of debris and breccia. This precipitous wall culminates . . . at the Rock Gun (1,349 ft.) from which point the dividing ridge or backbone of the promontory extends southward in a sharp jagged arch, the dominant points of which are Middle hill (1,195 ft.), Signal station (1,294 ft.), heights above Monkey's Alameda (1,396 ft.) and O'Hara's tower (1,370 ft.). At the latter the ridge is sharply truncated, and succeeded to the south by the well-marked plateau of Windmill hill and Europa. From the Rock Gun to O'Hara's tower the dividing ridge presents to the east a bold escarpment, which is for the most part inaccessible, and in places almost vertical. . . . A low sandy plain, that does not average more than 10 ft. in height above the sea, connects the Rock with the mainland."

It was little wonder that the Spaniards, once the Rock was in their hands, decided that so formidable a natural obstacle, and one already enriched by Tariq's castle, should be turned into an important strongpoint of their kingdom. Certainly, after the lavish fortifications designed by the military engineer Daniel Speckle had been added in the sixteenth century, the Rock was able to resist most assaults by its enemies.

It was not until 1704 that the Rock fell to the British, when Admiral Sir George Rooke, during the War of the Spanish Succession, captured Gibraltar by sea-borne assault. Since Rooke was, in theory at any rate, acting on behalf of the interests of the Archduke of Austria, he should have run up the Hapsburg flag on the conquered fortress. But, with admirable prescience and initiative, he hoisted the British flag and presented the Rock to his sovereign, Queen Anne; whose government with equal astuteness accepted the unexpected gift. Gibraltar has remained in British hands ever since.

Within a year of losing the great fortress, the Spaniards in alliance with the French made a determined attempt to recapture it. As with so many other sieges throughout Mediterranean history, it was soon shown that, provided the besieged retained mastery of the sea, they could endure almost indefinitely. Since the loss of the initiative by Spain, the British were the most formidable naval power, and the retention of the Rock confirmed that henceforth they would largely determine the course of history in this sea. Despite numerous other efforts to wrest Gibraltar from British control, the Spaniards were compelled to accept the presence of these northerners on the southern tip of their native peninsula.

The greatest and longest of all Gibraltar's sieges – one that in its own way rivals the Turkish siege of Malta – took place in 1779 and dragged on for over three years. For students of warfare its interest lies in the use made by both sides of artillery experiments, which heralded the modern age of gunnery and ballistics studies. The opportunity for the Spanish attack on the fortress was provided by the fact that England was at this time preoccupied with the American Revolution. It seemed unlikely, therefore, that she would be able to spare the ships or the men to maintain a steady reinforcement of the garrison. In the event, it turned out to be one of those classic sieges in which the besieged held on by courage, high morale, and inventive genius against a theoretically far superior foe. Some dramatic incidents starred the course of the siege: the privateer *Buck*, under her commander, Captain Fagg, fought her way into the harbour through lines of Spanish warships; and Admiral Sir George Rodney defeated the Spanish fleet and brought relief and supplies into the harbour at a moment when all seemed lost. (Among his midshipmen was Prince William, the future King William IV of England.) The siege continued in 1780, with attacks by Spanish fireships, numerous engagements at sea, the arrival of another British relieving squadron, and a successful sortie by the garrison in which most of the Spanish siege-works on the landward side of the Rock were destroyed.

An interesting feature of the siege, and one which showed that the modern age of "total" warfare was still far distant, lay in the correspondence which regularly passed between the British Governor, General Sir George Eliott, and his adversary, the Duke de Crillon. In the third year of the siege De Crillon wrote to Eliott: "Your Excellency will permit me to offer you a few trifles for your table, which you no doubt need, as I know that you live entirely on vegetables. I should be glad to learn what kind you prefer; I would also add a few partridges for the gentlemen of your entourage, and some ice. . . ."

In reply to this – and the tone is somewhat reminiscent of correspondence that had taken place between Saladin and his European enemies centuries before – General Eliott wrote: "A thousand thanks to Your Excellency for the handsome present of fruit and poultry. I must confess that it led me to violate a resolution formed at the beginning of the war, namely to eat nothing different from my comrades. Everything is publicly sold here. Anyone may have it who can afford it. Therefore I take the liberty of asking you no longer to load me with favours whose benefits I cannot enjoy. We have quite enough vegetables. The Englishman is accustomed to agriculture, with which he passes his spare time even here."

Despite these old-fashioned courtesies, the siege was a grim one; scurvy was rife among the garrison, and casualties from gunfire were heavy on both sides. The British had made two major technical advances. One was in the invention of a gun-carriage which allowed a large angle of depression. This enabled the gunners to fire at the besieging ships with, it is reported, an accuracy of 93 per cent at 1400 yards range. The second was an improved method of heating shot over iron grilles and loading them in such a way that they did not prematurely set off the charge. The idea of using heated cannon balls against wooden ships was nothing new in itself, but it had never been so efficiently applied before. In the siege of Gibraltar it played an important part, for it succeeded in defeating a major sea-borne attack launched against the garrison in 1782.

The Duke de Crillon had made all his preparations for what he, and the rest of his staff, were convinced would be the last action in the siege. They had specially built and prepared ten ships which were reckoned to be practically unsinkable, their intention being to anchor them off the fortress rock and blow the defences to pieces. The ships are described by John Drinkwater, in his *History of the Late Siege of Gibraltar*, as "fortified 6 or 7 ft. thick . . . with green timber bolted with iron, cork and raw hides; which were to carry guns of heavy metal and be bombproof on the top with a descent for the shells to slide off. . . ." They were to be moored "within half gunshot of the walls". At a later date, of course, such vessels would have been sitting targets and totally useless against explosive shell, but it must be remembered that both sides at this time were using solid shot. It was reckoned that the bombarding ships were strong enough not to be pierced by cannon balls fired from the Rock. The attack began on September 13, and at first it seemed as if the floating gun platforms were going to succeed where all the other attacks of the past three years had failed. But then the cannon on the Rock began to open a careful, slow fire with their red-hot shot. By nightfall the bombarding ships were beginning to suffer severe damage as the hot cannon balls caused their protective coverings to catch alight. The duel continued right through the night, and by noon next day the whole of the bombarding fleet had either been sunk or burned to the waterline. The records show that during this action one hundred guns on the Rock fired over 8300 rounds.

The siege continued for several months more, but the heart had gone out of the attackers, and in February of the following year peace preliminaries were signed, the Duke de Crillon confessing that his adversary was too much for him. The fifteenth siege of Gibraltar was over. The Rock's subsequent history was uneventful. There were rumours at various times of impending Spanish and French attacks, but these came to nothing. The British had established their presence at the Pillars of Hercules, and the fact that they now dominated the entrance to the Mediterranean was proof in itself that their fleet had the mastery of the seas. For the first time in its history the fate of the Mediterranean had been largely determined not by some great sea battle fought upon its waters but by a siege.

British supremacy was shortly to be challenged during the Napoleonic Wars, a period in which the Mediterranean was once again to witness ship-to-ship battles, the engagements of great fleets, and the destruction of a vast armada. During the giant struggle between France and England and her allies, the importance of Gibraltar became increasingly evident. England had good cause to bless the memory of Sir George Rooke, for the Rock's role in the Napoleonic Wars was all-important. By their possession of this base, the Royal Navy was largely able to seal the mouth of the Mediterranean.

During the eighteenth, nineteenth, and twentieth centuries, the fortifications and tunnelled galleries of Gibraltar were enormously extended, so that the Rock did finally become an almost impregnable fortress. As H. M. Field, a nineteenth-century American visitor, describes it in his *Gibraltar*: "Every spot from which a gun can be brought to bear is occupied by cannon, which oftentimes quaintly peep out of the most secluded nooks, among geraniums and flowering plants, while huge piles of shot and shell, some of enormous size, are stowed away in convenient places, screened from an enemy's fire, but all ready for use."

Gibraltar's Barbary Apes are not, as was once thought, descendants of apes left behind in Europe when the sea gates broke and the ocean rushed into the Mediterranean basin. No fossil remains of apes have been found anywhere on the Rock, and it is now presumed that they were imported either by the Romans or the Moors. One cave, however, near the northern end of the Rock has yielded evidence of two African mammals, the elephant and the rhinoceros. Apart from the imported flora – for the British remain as fond of gardening as they were in General Eliott's day – the isolation and barren character of this strange mountain has restricted Mediterranean growths to little save the stone pine and the wild olive. Both of these have probably grown here since the first navigators rested at the Rock, to gaze out with apprehension at the tremendous "Stream of Ocean" as it flowed on to the world's end.

FOUR

A Ship-of-the-Line

The sea's long period of inanition was drawing to a close. The storm that broke over Europe did not leave the waters of the Mediterranean unruffled. Once more the future of the world was, to a great extent, determined in this ancient cockpit of the nations. The word "cockpit", in nautical terminology, means the after part of the orlop deck of a man-of-war – that area which in action was set aside for the wounded. And it was the man-of-war, the sailing ship-of-the-line, that now swept the Mediterranean from the Strait of Gibraltar to Egypt and the Levant.

The French Revolutionary and Napoleonic wars, lasting from 1792 to 1815, were fought on the battlefields of Europe, on the great oceans of the world, and finally on the Mediterranean itself. It was here that disaster overtook the great Corsican when his expedition to Egypt was shattered by the loss of his whole fleet at the Battle of the Nile. Whereas on land the revolutionary ardour of the French was at one time or another turned against almost every nation in Europe, at sea the conflict was largely resolved between the British and the French. In the end, although Napoleon's ambitions were terminated on the field of Waterloo, it was the struggle between these two nations at sea which decided the issue and determined the course of the century that was to follow. Once again, as in the long-drawn struggle between Carthage and Rome, it was a battle between Leviathan and Behemoth; a sea empire confronting a land empire; a nation of merchants and traders fighting against a nation of hardy peasant farmers. In this case – and only because the British, unlike the Carthaginians, did not forget that their existence depended upon the mastery of the sea – the issue was differently resolved. Napoleon, war-lord, lawgiver, and statesman, had as great a dislike of the sea as any ancient Roman. Nelson, on the other hand, only faltered when he stepped ashore.

The ship comes proudly driving forwards, as she soars, lifts, and falters over the uneasy swell in the Bay of Biscay. Bound for the Mediterranean theatre of war, she looks as beautiful and assured as any sea-bird. Whether French or English, her composition differed only in minor points – often, when it came to design and manning, to the advantage of the French. Good though the English naval architects were, the French were frequently their superiors; when it came to the methods of manning their vessels, the French were certainly more intelligent. It was the French who gave special pay to their fishermen to induce them to train in the equivalent to a "naval reserve". The English, on the other hand, still largely depended upon "pressed", or forcibly conscripted, men to man what Admiral Mahan describes as "those far-distant, storm-beaten ships, upon which the Grand Army never looked, but which for ever stood between it and the dominion of the World."

Associated with the Mediterranean in the relief of Gibraltar, as well as in the sieges of Corsican Bastia and Calvi, was the most famous war-ship in history, the *Victory*. Since she was in many respects typical of the great ships-of-the-line that dominated the sea until the advent of steam, some description of her and of life aboard her may help to set the picture for the historical events of the late eighteenth and early nine-teenth centuries. Launched at old Single Dock, Chatham, Kent, in 1765, the *Victory* was the fifth ship of the Royal Navy to bear this name. The first had been the flagship of Sir John Hawkins during the Armada campaign of 1588 which had seen the ruin of Spanish hopes in the treacherous cold waters around the British Isles. The Elizabethan galleon had been only eight hundred tons, but the new *Victory*, fairly typical of other large ships-of-the-line, was designed at two thousand tons – although it has been estimated that she displaced nearer three thousand five hundred tons.

This ship, of which Thackeray was later to write that "the bones of the *Victory* ought to be sacred relics for Englishmen to worship", was built of English oak and elm. Her oak hull was over two feet thick; her stern post was made of one huge oak tree, and much of the oak used in her construction came from trees that were over one hundred years old. Her keel – over 150 feet long – was made of teak, one of the hardest and most worm-resistant woods in the world; and this again was protected by a false keel of elm. Her fastening consisted of oak pins, known as trenails, as well as copper bolts, six feet long and two inches in diameter. Both in her materials and in her weight of construction she was a vessel that no Mediterranean shipbuilder of the past could ever have conceived.

Her complement was upwards of 850 men. She carried sufficient water and provisions to stay at sea for four months, and enough powder and shot to last her – short of some major action – for three years. Even the Great Carrack of Rhodes dwindles into insignificance compared with these giants of the Age of Sail. Their most remarkable feature was the enormous weight of metal that they carried, for the lessons of those earlier gun battles had now been absorbed, and it was well understood that it was the broadside which determined battles and, consequently, the fate of empires. A ship like the *Victory* was known as a "three-decker", after her three gun decks, although there were, in fact, seven different levels to such a vessel. The lower gun deck carried the heaviest guns, 32-pounders; the middle, 24-pounders; and the upper, 12-pounders. Such ships were floating gun platforms, able not only to engage others of their own calibre, but also to blow land-based forts to pieces.

The famous broadside, of which so much has been written in both history and fiction, did not mean that all the guns on one side were fired at the same moment. Strong though these ships were, they could never have withstood such a concussion. "Ripple firing", whereby the guns fired consecutively from forward to aft, was what took place in a broadside action. This technique also implied that by the time the after guns were firing, the forward guns were all reloaded, ready to repeat the fire. The upper gun deck aimed at the enemy's masts and rigging, while the two lower decks sought to blow her sides to pieces. Such actions, sometimes lasting for a number of hours (as at the Battle of the Nile), were the bloodiest and most murderous in the whole history of man's warfare at sea.

Although launched in 1765, the *Victory* was held in reserve and not completed until 1778, when she became the flagship of Admiral Augustus Keppel in the battle near Ushant that sparked off the war with France. In 1771, Horatio Nelson, then a twelve-year-old boy, had joined his uncle's ship, the *Raisonnable*, at Chatham; at that time he probably saw an uncompleted first rate on whose stern, in yellow letters, was inscribed the name *Victory*. Thirty-four years later he was to bring her into the harbour of eternal fame when he destroyed the combined fleets of France and Spain on October 21, 1805, at Cape Trafalgar. This battle, although taking place just outside the Mediterranean – in the approaches to its sea gates – determined the whole area's history, and imposed upon it for over a century the first real peace since the *Pax Romana*. It was, in its different way, as momentous as the Battle of Salamis.

Much has been said about the condition of the men who manned the galleys of the Mediterranean during this and earlier periods. The expression "like a galley slave" has passed into the English language, to indicate an almost insupportable human existence, but the fact remains that the life of sailors aboard these great ships-of-the-line called for an almost equal degree of endurance. The expressions "Wooden ships need iron men" or, of an old-time sailor, "Every finger a marlinspike and every hair a bunch of spunyarn" were hardly exaggerations.

A large number of the seamen who manned and fought in the *Victory* and in her sister ships of the Royal Navy were "pressed" into the fleet. The Vagrancy Act laid down that "all disreputable persons" (which might mean anyone found in a tavern, let alone a bawdy house, or even walking peaceably down the streets of a fishing port) were liable for impressment. Fishermen, merchant seamen, and canal or inland watermen were also immediately subject to the act if they were unfortunate enough to be caught by the press-gang. The fact that so large a percentage of a ship's company was forcibly conscripted meant, inevitably, that discipline aboard had to be of an iron-bound severity. The oarsmen of Salamis had been free Greek citizens who, although poorer than the armoured "knights", were nevertheless volunteers. The citizens of England who manned her ships during the Napoleonic Wars were, by and large, ill-clad, ill-used, and, to a large extent, unwilling seamen. It is some evidence of the hardihood of the many northern seafaring races who had contributed to the complex genetic structure of the British that these "pressed men" proved themselves to be among the toughest who ever fought upon the battle-scarred waters of the Mediterranean.

Some indication of the sailor's lot can be gauged from a book published during this period called *Nautical Economy, or Forecastle Recollec-*

tions of Events during the last War. Dedicated to the Tars of Old England by a Sailor, politely called by the officers of the Navy Jack Nasty-Face. Even allowing for the fact that "Jack" was a deeply embittered man, there can be little denying the truth of his account, for it is substantiated by a number of others. "Out of the fleet of nine sail of the line I was with," he wrote, "there were only two Captains thus distinguished [for their humanity]. They kept order on board without resorting to the frequent and unnecessary call upon the Boatswain and his cat, adopted by the other seven: and what was the consequences? Those two ships beat us in reefing and furling; for they were not in fear and dread, well knowing that they would not be punished without a real and just cause. . . ."

"Jack" goes on to describe the discipline that prevailed aboard those "storm-beaten ships": "The cat-o'-nine tails is applied to the bare back, and at about every six lashes a fresh Boatswain's Mate is ordered to relieve the executioner of this duty, until the prisoner has received, perhaps, 25 lashes. . . . [He is then] conveyed from ship to ship, receiving alongside of each a similar number of stripes with the cat until his sentence is complete. . . . His back resembles so much putrified liver, and every stroke of the cat brings away the congealed blood; and the Boatswain's Mates are looked at with the eye of a hawk to see that they do their duty, and clear the cat's tails after every stroke, the blood at the same time streaming through their fingers: and in this manner are men in the Navy punished for different offences, more particularly impressed men who attempt to make their escape." This was the world of the human machinery that fought the *Victory's* canvas in a gale, or fired her guns in action – this ship so beautiful to the outward eye as she buried the green rollers of the sea beneath her "dolphin-striker" and stumbled towards Cape Trafalgar over the awkward Biscay swell.

Of Nelson himself it must be said that he was one of the principal commanders of his time who tried to improve the condition of his sailors. He might well have been one of those two captains whom "Jack" describes as keeping order on board without resorting to "the Boatswain and his cat". Apart from being a genius as a sailor, Nelson was a sensitive man. He knew, as Drake had known before him, that the seaman is every whit as entitled to fair and reasonable conditions as any other man. Since his captains, whom he called his "Band of

Brothers", always sought to emulate him, it is fair to say that he played a large part in improving the lot of the British seaman.

The food of these men was simple enough: "Breakfast usually consists of burgoo, made of coarse oatmeal and water; others will have Scotch coffee, which is burnt bread boiled in some water, and sweetened with sugar." At noon, "the pleasantest part of the day . . . every man and boy is allowed a pint, that is, one gill of rum and water, to which is added lemon acid, sweetened with sugar." The main dish consisted of salt beef or pork with pease pudding, and for supper "half a pint of wine, or a pint of grog, to each man, with biscuit, and cheese or butter." Life aboard may have been hard, the discipline harsh, but the food in general compared favourably with that of the country labourer at the time. The sailor, also, always had a chance of winning some prize-money.

The whole ship existed to serve the guns. It was in the sight, smell, service, and thunder of them that the sailor lived and died. The *Victory*'s true and indomitable face was revealed as soon as she stripped for action. Even the comparatively elegant quarters of the admiral were denuded of their furniture and gear, which was sent down to the main hold below the waterline. From the lower deck, where most of the seamen slept and fed, the men's hammocks were taken up and lashed along the bulwarks to serve as protection against flying splinters and the bullets of enemy marksmen. (Many of the casualties suffered in action were caused by splinters of wood gouged out of ships' decks and sides by cannon balls.)

The men fought the guns stripped to the waist, with handkerchiefs tied round their foreheads and ears to keep the sweat out of their eyes and to protect their ears against the deafening noise. They worked bare-footed, and the decks were swilled with sea-water to reduce fire risk and sprinkled with sand to prevent the sailors slipping. The mortally wounded and the dead were thrown overboard without ceremony. Those whose wounds were within the limited capacity of the surgeons were taken down to the cockpit. This area was painted red, so that the wounded would not notice how much of that red was their own blood. There were no anaesthetics, and major operations were undertaken either by stunning the patient or, if time permitted, by getting him blind drunk on brandy or rum. As often as not, the strong arms of the surgeon's mates were used to hold the wounded. The same hot pitch that served to caulk the ship's seams was used to seal amputations; while gunpowder, sea-salt, and brandy or rum were used as primitive antiseptics.

The officers could expect no better than the men if they had the misfortune to be wounded. Nelson himself, who in a lifetime of action lost both an arm and an eye, received no different medical attention from that given to the humblest ordinary seaman. It was a hard life and it bred hard men, but that they were not necessarily insensitive is proved by Nelson and many others. The sea life has always had its compensations, and there remained a vein of poetry in many sailors that their rough exteriors might have seemed to belie. As Admiral Edward Boscawen wrote in a letter to his wife: "To be sure I lose the fruits of the earth, but then I am gathering the flowers of the sea."

FIVE

French and English

The dynamism engendered by the French Revolution – that extraordinary impetus which extended France's power far beyond the dreams of any of even her most ambitious monarchs – was destined to make itself felt upon almost all the countries of the Mediterranean basin. France herself, because of her geographical situation, was a Janus country: one face turned to the north and west; the other looking south and east, from her long Mediterranean coastline. In some respects, in the struggle that took place between France and England, one may find a comparison with that earlier struggle between England and Spain. Both France and Spain had two seaboards. While England could concentrate mainly upon her northern waters and the long reaches of the Atlantic, France and Spain always had a Mediterranean fleet and Mediterranean preoccupations. The great difference in this Anglo-French conflict was that the sea warfare which raged throughout the Mediterranean was conducted by the British, and not by another Mediterranean power – as had been the case when the Ottoman Turks had been engaged against Spain in earlier centuries. The British, therefore, now found themselves in much the same position as their enemies: they had to maintain a Mediterranean fleet in order to attack and contain the French upon this southern front. At a later date, after the war had ended in Britain's favour, this remote northern island was to find itself in the strange position of having become a Mediterranean power.

The war with Revolutionary France dragged on for many years, because Britain, while strong at sea, was militarily weak. The focus sharpens upon the Mediterranean theatre in 1793, the second year of the war, when a young British naval captain, Horatio Nelson, who had "been on the beach" for five years, received a new sea-going appointment. As he wrote to his wife: "The Admiralty so smile upon me, that really I am as much surprised as when they frowned. Lord Chatham yesterday made many apologies for not having given me a Ship before this time, and said, that if I chose to take a Sixty-four to begin with, I should be appointed to one as soon as she was ready; and whenever it was in his power, I should be removed into a Seventy-four. Everything indicates War. One of our ships, looking into Brest, has been fired into. . . ."

The sixty-four-gun ship-of-the-line to which Nelson was appointed as captain was the *Agamemnon* – a name appropriate enough to the Mediterranean, whither she was immediately dispatched under the command of Lord Hood. Aided by French royalists, the British fleet enjoyed an immediate success by capturing the great port and naval base of Toulon. The British and their allies, however, soon found that it was impossible to maintain their hold on Toulon, which was retaken by the French Revolutionary forces – prominent among whose officers was a young commander of the artillery, Napoleon Bonaparte. In the same year, during the siege of Calvi in Corsica, Nelson lost the sight of his right eye when a shot from the French garrison landed near the battery where he was engaged, throwing up a mass of sand and splinters which struck him in the face. There is an erroneous belief that he always wore a patch over this damaged eye, but in fact the eye looked perfectly normal. Nelson did indeed sometimes wear a green eye shade which he had had specially made for him – but this was to shield his good left eye from the glare and dazzle of the Mediterranean.

During these years when he was learning to become, as he later put it, "an old Mediterranean man", his duties were similar to those of dozens of other sea-captains engaged around the French coast, or off Corsica and Sardinia, or in the long stretches of sea west of Sicily. British convoys had to be protected, contraband runners had to be intercepted, and there was sometimes an occasional brush with the enemy. But mainly the sailor's time was spent in long frustrating days at sea, with the ship's bottoms growing foul in the warm water, and the sun-baked ropes and canvas chafing and fraying in idle weather or blowing away in one of the sudden and fierce storms typical of the area. After one engagement, when Nelson had distinguished himself by capturing the huge French eighty-four-gun *Ça Ira* with his sixty-four-gun *Agamemnon*, he confessed in a letter to his wife: "I wish to be an admiral, and in command of the English fleet; I should very soon either do much, or be ruined: my disposition cannot bear tame and slow measures." Referring to the recent action, he went on: "Sure I am, had I commanded on the 14th that either the whole French fleet would have graced my triumph, or I should have been in a confounded scrape."

Another whose disposition could not bear "tame and slow measures" was the great Corsican who soon took the arms and the aims of the French Revolution all over Europe and the East. At the age of twenty-seven, Bonaparte, now a general, entered Italy with an army of thirty thousand half-starving soldiers, who were in want of everything except the fire and spirit that their revolutionary fervour had lit within them. In words that might have been spoken long centuries before by Hannibal, Napoleon addressed his troops: "You are badly fed and all but naked. . . . I am about to lead you into the most fertile plains in the world. Before you are great cities and rich provinces; there we shall find honour, glory, and riches." His promises were soon fulfilled, and the Italian people hailed him as a liberator from their Austrian masters.

All over Europe the nations were welcoming the new ideas of Revolutionary France. Tsarist Russia, for obvious reasons, was hostile; while England was concerned not only by the threat to her own security that a united Europe might pose, but also by the threat to her overseas empire. After the loss of her American colonies, England's great concern was India, and Napoleon was already looking in that direction. Beyond Italy lay the Mediterranean, the route to Egypt, and beyond Egypt lay all the wealth of the East.

Napoleon embodied, in his mission, all the dreams of his great predecessors. He had, first of all, a vision of restoring the ancient Roman Empire. The whole of the Mediterranean area, Italy, Spain, Egypt, and the adjacent countries of the Levant should be united within one framework, which would come under the dominance of France. It was not an ignoble dream, nor one incapable of fulfilment. The British, who more than any other prevented its becoming reality, prevented also the first union that the Mediterranean might have enjoyed since the fall of Rome. But Napoleon looked even further than the sea basin. He saw himself as the Caesar of this new empire, but he also dreamed of being an Alexander. Beyond a united Mediterranean he looked east, as had the great Macedonian; and it was this aspect of his nature that alarmed the English more than anything else. Had Napoleon confined his actions to Europe, it is possible that in the end the English would, however unwillingly, have accepted the imperial *fait accompli*. But the threat to their great eastern empire was not to be tolerated.

While Italy was being turned into a block of republics on the French model – even the Pope had to relinquish the Papal States and permit a republic to be set up in Rome – Napoleon's eyes were fixed upon the islands lying south of him. He saw them (as they had been in the days of ancient Rome) as stepping-stones to the East. A. T. Mahan, in his *Influence of Sea Power upon the French Revolution and Empire*, designates the political distribution of the islands of the Mediterranean at this period: "The most eastern, known as the Ionian islands, extending southward from the entrance of the Adriatic along the coast of Greece, from Corfu to Cerigo, were in the possession of Venice. When the ancient republic fell before the policy of Bonaparte, in 1797, the islands passed to France and began that circulation from owner to owner which ended in 1863 with their union to Greece. Sicily formed part of the kingdom of the Two Sicilies. It became the refuge of that monarchy from the arms of France, and, by its fertility and the use of its ports, was a resource to Great Britain throughout the Napoleonic period. Malta was still in the hands of the Knights of Saint John. . . . Sardinia gave its name to the kingdom of which Piedmont, forming the Italian frontier of France, was the actual seat, and Turin the capital. Amid the convulsions of the period, the royal family, driven from the mainland, found an obscure refuge in this large but backward island. . . . The Balearic islands were in the hands of Spain. . . . Of the greater islands there remains to give account only of Corsica. This was a recent acquisition of France, received from Genoa in 1769, somewhat contrary to the wish of the people, who would have preferred independence."

It became an obvious part of British policy throughout this period to see that Sicily remained under Bourbon control and free from the French. Not only did the island provide a number of excellent harbours for the Royal Navy, but also it was, as it had always been, an important supplier of fruit and cereals. The British needed it above all to provision their navy in an otherwise hostile sea. Two minor but not insignificant results of the Anglo-Sicilian connection during this period

The bronze horses
outside St. Mark's,
loot from
Constantinople

The Venetian castle
guarding the harbour
at Rhodes,
surmounted by a
modern lighthouse

Sultan Mohammed II, by Bellini

Aruj and
Kheir-ed-Din Barbarossa

An admiral's galley

THE ENGLISH
IN THE MEDITERRANEAN

Admiral Lord Nelson,
victor of the Battle of the Nile,
by Beechey

Gibraltar in the early nineteenth century

were the evolution of a new wine and the introduction of an important antiscorbutic drink for sailors. Cut off more often than not during these years from their wine-suppliers on the continent, and – worst of all for port-drinking Englishmen – from their favourite wine from Oporto, a number of astute wine merchants settled themselves in the western districts of Sicily. The local grapes from the Marsala region, when suitably fortified, were found to make an excellent drink which, although hardly resembling port, satisfied the after-dinner palates of the English. (A number of these families were totally assimilated, and still remain in the area.) Marsala, the ancient Lilybaeum and principal port of the Carthaginians, now witnessed a greater flow of naval and merchant shipping than it had since the third century B.C.

Scurvy, that deficiency disease common among sailors unable to obtain sufficient vitamin C from vegetables and fruit, had been little known in the Mediterranean in the past. The reason for this was that the galleys and other local vessels were rarely on long passages, and were accustomed to stop at regular ports of call to obtain bread, fruit, wine, and other fresh stores. The long sea-keeping qualities (sometimes amounting to many months) that were demanded from the great ships-of-the-line meant that scurvy soon became a major problem. It was known that it was the absence of fruit and vegetables from the diet that caused the disease, and the English soon found that the Sicilian lemon contained all the necessary qualities for preventing it. The *spadaforese*, the thick-skinned lemon of Sicily, as well as the smaller thin-skinned varieties, were pressed, and 10 per cent of alcohol (without which it would not keep) was added to the juice. At a later date, in 1867, the British Merchant Shipping Act decreed that every member of the crew, when at sea or in countries where fruit or vegetables could not be obtained, was to be issued with one ounce a head per day. By this time, however, most of the juice was provided by West Indian limes; a fact which led the seamen of the United States to refer to the lime-drinking English as "Limeys". But in the period of the Napoleonic Wars, the health of the British seamen, at sea for weeks or months on end, was largely safeguarded by the Sicilian lemon. This happy legacy of the Arabic occupation of the island served to preserve the English in their battle against the people of France – the country from which the

Normans had descended to capture Sicily from the Arabs seven centuries before.

If fertile and fruitful Sicily was barred to Napoleon by the sunbleached canvas, the oak hulls, and the 32-pounders of the Royal Navy, he looked further southwards and saw in Malta, as so many had seen before him, the perfect harbour from which to dominate the Mediterranean. It was some years, however, before he made a move in that direction – years in which the French were everywhere successful on land, and in which the British tried as far as they could to contain them by sea. By 1797 it was clear that the British position in the Mediterranean had become untenable – at any rate for the moment. The strain of keeping three fleets in being – one in the Mediterranean, the second based on Gibraltar and Portugal (England's only ally at this time), and the third at the western approaches to the Channel – was proving beyond the island's resources in men, money, and materials.

Admiral John Jervis (later Earl of St. Vincent) set in motion the withdrawal to Gibraltar, Britain's one secure fortress, and the one which above all must be held in order to keep control of the sea gates. It was not long after this withdrawal that, in an unsuccessful attack on Teneriffe in the Canary Islands, Nelson (by now an admiral) lost his right arm, which was taken off at the elbow by a grapeshot. He felt convinced that his career was over, that only retirement lay ahead, and that he would never again command the ships of England against the French, for whom he felt a passionate hatred. Curiously enough, Nelson does not seem to have disliked his Spanish opponents; indeed, he often expressed admiration for them. But he hated the French and everything they stood for, which, to his conservative nature, seemed to be the destruction of all law, order, and decency.

He wrote at this time to his commander-in-chief, Earl St. Vincent: "I am become a burthen to my friends, and useless to my Country. . . . When I leave your command, I become dead to the World; I go hence, and am no more seen." To this St. Vincent replied: "Mortals cannot command success. You and your companions have certainly deserved it, by the greatest degree of heroism and perseverance that ever was exhibited." At that moment in time, neither man could have envisaged that within a year the British would be back in force in the Mediterranean; let alone that within a year Nelson would have gained one of the most outstanding victories ever to take place in this sea.

Napoleon in the meantime had come to realize that the French fleet was in no state to cover the great invasion of England which had been planned. Large-scale invasion of the arrogant island was still the dream of the French Republic, but Napoleon was wise enough to see that it must be deferred. The immediate aim must be to strike in the East, and threaten India. To achieve this objective, an immense fleet and army must be assembled as quickly as possible in the Mediterranean. He explained to the Directory in Paris that his aims were "to go to Egypt, to establish myself there and found a French Colony [which] will require several months. Then, as soon as I have made England tremble for the safety of India, I shall return to Paris, and give the enemy his death-blow. There is nothing to fear in the meantime. Europe is calm. Austria cannot attack. England is occupied with preparing her defences against invasion, and Turkey will welcome the expulsion of the Mameluke. . . ."

At the time there seemed good grounds for Napoleon's optimism. The English had already withdrawn from the Mediterranean theatre, and he clearly did not consider that they could return even more swiftly than they had left. But this was the key that Gibraltar gave them, and Napoleon, although one of the greatest commanders in history, showed time and again that he did not understand the uses of sea power. Although an islander by birth, he had always been a landsman and a soldier. It is significant that even his birthplace, Ajaccio, turns its back upon the sea in true Latin fashion, and looks inland to the maquis and the mountains.

The aims of the great expedition of 1798 were nothing if not grandiose. Napoleon was empowered by his government to occupy Egypt, exclude the English from their possessions in the East, and seize Malta on his way through the Mediterranean. Finally, he was to have a canal cut through the isthmus of Suez, so that France might have access to the Red Sea and, of course, to India beyond it. Napoleon's own ambitions went even further than this. He foresaw the day when, having conquered all the East, he would sweep back through Turkey (calling upon Turkey's subject Christians to rise with him), smash the Ottoman Empire, and complete the encirclement of Europe. The great and revived "Roman Empire", led by France, would now encompass not only all the Mediterranean areas that had once belonged to ancient Rome, but also the territories that had fallen before Alexander the Great, as well as the immense British Empire of India. Whatever might be said about Napoleon, he certainly did not lack ambition; even the dreams of the world conquerors of the past pale into insignificance compared with his.

The fleet and the men were gradually assembled at Marseilles and Toulon, as well as in Genoa, Civita Vecchia, and the ports of his native Corsica. Thirty thousand infantry were to be embarked for the great adventure, together with specialized companies of sappers and miners, and over one hundred field- and siege-guns. Napoleon advised his admiral, François Paul Brueys, that he would join him at Toulon on May 1. He requested Brueys to provide him with a good berth aboard, since he expected to be seasick throughout the voyage. He had the honesty to admit to his weakness. Curiously enough, his great opponent, Nelson, was another sufferer – somewhat unusual in a sailor who had spent most of his life at sea.

The fleet that assembled consisted of thirteen ships-of-the-line, some gunboats for bombardment, seven frigates, and about three hundred transports. Although this was a formidable armada, the number of its transports was out of all proportion to the fighting ships designed to protect it. If Nelson or any other British admiral had come up with it at sea, there can be little doubt that it would have been annihilated. What distinguished this fleet from any other that had ever crossed the Mediterranean was that it carried aboard it not only the soldiers to execute the invader's designs, but also a whole team of *savants* – nearly two hundred of the finest intellects in France, together with their books and scientific instruments. Their purpose was to bring French culture to the East, and to bring back whatever knowledge unknown in Europe lay locked in the valley of the Nile. Not even Alexander had set out with the intention of deliberately cross-fertilizing the Mediterranean basin. Credit must be given to Napoleon for being the first man in history to perceive that what is done with plants in a garden may also be done with the cultures of the human race.

The expedition finally sailed from Toulon on May 19, escaping the vigilant British by sheer good fortune. "That devil," as Nelson remarked, "has the devil's luck." On June 9 Malta was in sight, and Napoleon at once sent a message ashore requesting permission for his fleet to enter Grand Harbour. The Order of Saint John, that last surviving link with the Crusades, had long been in a state of decline, and many of the French knights were actively in league with France. Despite the fact that Malta's superb defences, if properly manned, would have been capable of resisting any siege almost indefinitely, the island capitulated within three days. Thus "Malta of gold" with its curtain walls, bastions, ravelins, cavaliers, ramparts, parapets, scarps and counterscarps, ditches, glacis, and salients, all designed to repel the weight of the Ottoman Empire, fell without a struggle to the all-conquering French. The order, which had so honourably left Rhodes, and which had secured Europe's southern flank for two and a half centuries, was unceremoniously bundled out of its ancient home.

Napoleon stayed in Malta for a week, busy reorganizing the life of the islanders in accordance with the concepts of the Revolution. (These were not to local taste, as later events would show.) When he left for Egypt on June 19, Napoleon also took with him aboard the flagship *L'Orient* nearly a million pounds' worth of loot – the treasure of centuries that had been amassed in Malta's palaces and churches. With characteristic revolutionary fervour, as Thackeray writes, in his *A Journey from Cornhill to Cairo*, the French also "effaced armorial bearings . . . and a few years after they had torn down the coats-of-arms of the gentry, the heroes of Malta and Egypt were busy devising heraldry for themselves and were wild to be barons and counts of the Empire."

Napoleon, as he sat in his cabin, reading, among other things, the Koran, and an account of the voyages of Captain Cook, had every reason to be pleased with the progress of his expedition. Nelson, meanwhile, had arrived at Naples, where he heard of the French landing at Malta. Pressing on furiously in pursuit, he and his ships-of-the-line came surging down the east coast of Sicily, only to hear from a passing merchantman that Napoleon had already left the island for an unknown destination. Nelson, presuming quite correctly that the destination of the armada could only be Egypt, directed his course for Alexandria. The north-westerly winds which prevail over this part of the Mediterranean in midsummer served him well as he drove his ships southeastwards. He reached the port on June 28, six days after leaving Sicily.

There he learned, to his dismay, that no French ships had been sighted. A. T. Mahan writes, in his *Influence of Sea Power upon the French Revolution and Empire*, "This remarkable miscarriage, happening to a man of so much energy and intuition, was due primarily to his want of small lookout ships; and secondly, to Bonaparte's using the simple, yet at sea sufficient, ruse, of taking an indirect instead of a direct course to his object."

The French fleet, in fact, had taken a dog's leg route, and headed east from Malta for Crete, with the result that, just as Nelson was turning back from Alexandria, Napoleon was about three hundred miles north-west of him off Crete. Nelson, who sometimes remarked that, if he died, "lack of frigates" would be found written on his heart, now made a mistake. His judgement that the enemy was headed for Egypt had been sound, but he sailed off to the coast of Asia Minor, then back south of Crete, and so again to Sicily. Like a seine-net fisherman he had spread his net right round the eastern basin of the Mediterranean, but, in the course of doing so, he had allowed the enemy to escape clean through the head of it. Napoleon had slipped down from the north, and was in Alexandria.

The city which he entered – putting his army ashore immediately he heard that the English had preceded him – bore little resemblance to that proud capital where Antony and Cleopatra had loved and died. As Oliver Warner writes in *Nelson's Battles*: "The country which Bonaparte had entered so unceremoniously presented a picture of decay surpassing that of Malta of the Knights. The principal reason for this state of affairs was the same as had caused the decline of Venice. The flow of trade from the Far East had long ceased to pass through Egypt and the Mediterranean to the Adriatic and so into the heart of Europe. Decline, which had begun when the Portuguese discovered the sea route to India and China via the Cape of Good Hope at the end of the fifteenth century, had been gradual. It could perhaps have been arrested but for the greed of those who ruled the country. They inflicted so punishing a tax on the transit of goods (even after an alternative route had been shown to be practical), that no merchant would willingly face it.

"Nominally subject to the Sultan of Turkey, Egypt was in fact governed by the Mamelukes, a military order who were as picturesque a survival from the time of the Crusades as the Knights of Malta. The word signified in Arabic chattel or male slave, and the Mamelukes were indeed recruited as slaves from their homes in the Caucasus, their future loyalty being to their own Order [rather like the Janissaries]. They did not mix with or marry Egyptians, and the real slaves of the country were the patient fellahin, the peasants, poor and exploited, on whom the whole economy depended. . . ."

Within three weeks of reaching Alexandria Napoleon had met and defeated the Mamelukes in the celebrated Battle of the Pyramids. "Soldiers, from the summit of these pyramids, forty centuries look down upon you," he reminded his men. The remark is famous, so too his victory: both were hollow. As had been proved so often in the past, in the conduct of war in the countries surrounding the Mediterranean it is essential to have command of the sea.

On reaching Sicily, Nelson realized that his first surmise had been correct, that Napoleon was indeed in Egypt, and that his being there "will put our possessions in India in a very perilous situation." The fleet stayed three days in the famous old harbour of Syracuse, familiar to so many fleets throughout the ages, and the scene of so many desperate conflicts. Just before they left, Nelson wrote to the British Minister in Naples, Sir William Hamilton: "Thanks to your exertions, we have victualled and watered; and surely, watering at the Fountain of Arethusa, we must have victory. We shall sail with the first breeze, and be assured I will return either crowned with laurel, or covered with cypress."

On August 1, the English fleet was once more off Alexandria. They found it full of French transports, although there were no large warships to be seen. Admiral Brueys had mistrusted the entrance to the port and had sailed twelve miles further down the coast to drop anchor at Aboukir Bay. This was an immense, sand-rimmed bay, stretching over fifteen miles from Aboukir Point in the west to the Rosetta mouth of the Nile in the east. The French men-of-war were anchored in a wide V-shaped formation at the western end of the bay, in the lee of Aboukir Island, which lay just off the point. Admiral Brueys no doubt thought that he had made his dispositions very skilfully, but had in fact been somewhat negligent. The intervals between his ships were too large – about 160 yards – and the ships were only anchored by the bows. The fact, therefore, that they swung to the wind meant that the effectiveness of his V formation was very much reduced, unless the wind blew constantly from west-south-west. As it turned out, when Nelson arrived upon the scene the wind was from north-north-west, and the ships, having swung to it, had opened great gaps in their lines. Perhaps Brueys' casual placement of his fleet had been occasioned by the same over-confidence that had made Napoleon write only two days before: "All the conduct of the English indicates that they are inferior in number, and content themselves with blockading Malta and intercepting its supplies."

At about two o'clock on the afternoon of August 1, 1798, the English sighted the French fleet snug in its haven at Aboukir Bay. This was the moment for which Nelson had been waiting, and he at once steered to close them. Brueys could not believe that the English would attack that day; for the French practice would have been to make a careful reconnaissance, decide on a plan of action, and wait for the following day. This was not Nelson's way, for he reckoned that he and his "Band of Brothers" would have ample time to survey the French dispositions and prepare their plan of action as they drove in to attack them. During the long chase round the eastern Mediterranean, Nelson had been possessed of such anxiety that he had scarcely slept, nor had he taken any food other than a quick snack. Now, seeing the object of his ambition placidly awaiting him, and aware that it would be several hours before his ships could round the point to commence action, he ordered dinner to be served.

Shortly after six o'clock in the evening the action began. Captain Thomas Foley in the *Goliath*, the leading English ship, rounded into the bay and arrived off the first ship of the French line. Foley's trained eye had quickly observed that, through the failure to moor the ships both fore and aft, they had swung to the wind. This enabled him to pass between them and the land; a manoeuvre that would have been impossible if Brueys had made his dispositions correctly. The next four ships also passed to the landward side of the French, some of whom were so taken aback by this unexpected move that they had not even got their broadsides unencumbered on this side. Nelson in the *Vanguard* came up just as night was falling and launched an attack from the seaward side; his next two ships followed shortly with their attacks. The result was that the ships in the French van now found themselves engaged upon both sides.

Captain Samuel Hood of the *Zealous*, in his account of his action against the French *Le Guerrier*, gives an idea of what must have happened up and down the line, as more and more English ships sailed up and engaged their opponents: "I commenced such a well-directed fire into her bow within pistol shot a little after six that her fore-mast went by the board in about seven minutes, just as the sun was closing the horizon; on which the whole squadron gave three cheers, it happening before the next ship astern of me had fired a shot and only the *Goliath* and *Zealous* engaged. And in ten minutes more her main and mizzen masts went; at this time also went the main mast of the second ship, engaged closely by the *Goliath* and *Audacious*, but I could not get *Le Guerrier*'s commander to strike for three hours, though I hailed him twenty times, and seeing he was totally cut up and only firing a stern gun now and then at the *Goliath* and *Audacious*.

"At last being tired of firing and killing people in that way, I sent my boat on board her, and the lieutenant was allowed . . . to hoist a light and haul it down to show his submission."

The battle raged on throughout the night. Nelson, who had come prepared for a night action, had given orders for his ships to show a horizontal group of lanterns so that they could easily recognize one another. The French admiral, however, not having expected an engagement after dark, had made no such preparations. He seems to have had little knowledge of exactly what was happening as the English slowly and methodically moved down his ships, often on both sides of them, destroying them with their concentrated fire. Brueys himself, although he had lost both legs from a cannon shot, had tourniquets applied to the stumps and continued to direct the fire from his flagship *L'Orient* until another ball cut him in two. Meanwhile, a fire began to spread aboard the doomed flagship, and many of the crew, to save their lives, jumped into the sea. *L'Orient*'s captain, Louis de Casabianca, whose son had been wounded, is said to have refused to desert the ship without him – an incident which gave rise to Mrs. Felicia Hemans' popular poem "Casabianca", *The boy stood on the burning deck*. . . . An English midshipman, John Lee, who wrote his recollections of the action many years later, recorded: "The son of Casabianca had lost a leg, and was below with the surgeon, but the father could not be prevailed upon to quit the ship even to save his own life, preferring to die beside his son rather than leave him wounded, and a prey to the flames. . . ."

Soon after ten o'clock the fire reached the French flagship's main magazine, and *L'Orient* went up with a shattering crash that was heard as far away as Alexandria. The noise was so devastating that, as if by common consent, all ships stopped firing; for a brief period, the action came to a halt. When the battle started again, it was clear that by now it was no more than a tidying-up action. The French fleet had, to all intents and purposes, ceased to exist.

By daylight on August 2, apart from a few small vessels that had made their escape under cover of darkness, only three French men-of-war remained afloat. One of these ran aground and was set on fire by her own crew; the other two managed to escape – only to be captured during the next two years. Many years later, when Napoleon, a prisoner aboard the *Bellerophon*, sailed for his ultimate island-prison of Saint Helena, he remarked to her captain, "In all my plans I have always been thwarted by the British Fleet." He had a life of Nelson (possibly Southey's) read to him by his secretary. He clearly recognized that this was the man who had done more than any other to thwart his ambitions.

The Battle of the Nile was, in a sense, more important even than Trafalgar. It was Napoleon's first major reverse, and it put new heart into the whole of Europe. In a way it resembled the Battle of El Alamein in the Second World War. It showed that the apparently invincible conquerors were as subject to defeat as any other mortals.

"My Lord," Nelson wrote to the Earl of St. Vincent, "Almighty God has blessed His Majesty's Arms in the late Battle, by a great victory over the Fleet of the enemy, who I attacked at sunset on the 1st of August, off the mouth of the Nile. The enemy were moored in a strong line of Battle for defending the entrance of the Bay (of Shoals), flanked by numerous gunboats, four frigates, and a battery of guns and mortars on an Island in their van; but nothing could withstand the Squadron your Lordship did me the honour to place under my command. Their high state of discipline is well known to you, and with the judgment of the captains, together with their valour, and that of the officers and men of every description, it was absolutely irresistible."

The news of the victory swept through Europe like a forest fire. Its effect upon individuals, in that age when emotions were less restrained than now, was almost to deprive them of their senses. Sir William Hamilton's wife, Emma (soon to become deeply involved with Nelson), fell to the ground so overcome that, as Nelson wrote some days later, "she . . . is not yet properly recovered from severe bruises." Even back in London, within the austere walls of the Admiralty, Lord Spencer, on hearing the news, dropped to the floor in a dead faint. Politically, the principal result of the Battle of the Nile was to bring into being the Second Coalition against Revolutionary France. Nearly all that Napoleon had gained in Italy was swept away in one brief campaign, while Turkey now came into the war on the side of the Allies. Its greatest significance was, however, that although the war against France dragged on for many years, the English had now secured the dominion of the Mediterranean. It was a dominion which, though often challenged and sometimes imperilled, they never lost – until they vacated it of their own accord in the second half of the twentieth century.

SIX

Napoleon and Nelson

Napoleon ashore in Egypt, master of Cairo, and with his eyes turned towards the East, does not seem to have fully appreciated the consequences of the Battle of the Nile. His genius lay on the land, and the loss of a battle fleet – one that had already justified its existence by securing the safe transport of his army – may have seemed a small price for the conquest of a country. France had more sailors, and plenty of timber; another dozen or more men-of-war could be built. Meanwhile there was Egypt to be occupied and reorganized – and beyond Egypt, India. Some among his retinue, however, took a more gloomy view of things. M. Poussielgue, Controller-General of the Finances of the Army of Egypt, in a letter to his wife (it was intercepted by a British warship), expressed his fears: "The fatal engagement [of the Nile] ruined all our hopes; it prevented us from receiving the remainder of the forces which were destined for us; it left the field free for the English to persuade the Porte to declare war against us; it rekindled that which was barely extinguished in the heart of the Austrian Emperor; it opened the Mediterranean to the Russians, and planted them on our frontiers; it occasioned the loss of Italy and the invaluable possessions in the Adriatic which we owed to the successful campaigns of Bonaparte, and finally it at once rendered abortive all our projects, since it was no longer possible for us to dream of giving the English any uneasiness in India. Added to this was the effect on the people of Egypt, whom we wished to consider as friends and allies. They became our enemies, and, entirely surrounded as we were by the Turks, we found ourselves engaged in a most difficult defensive war, without a glimpse of the slightest advantage to be obtained from it."

Napoleon, however, was too occupied with immediate matters, and of far too sanguine a character to indulge in retrospection. His first preoccupation, since Turkey was now at war with France, was to strike north into Syria. If, for the moment at any rate, he must put the thought of India behind him, he reverted to his other dream – that of smashing the Ottoman Empire and coming round into Europe on its eastern flank. At first all went well, and Jaffa fell to the French on March 7, 1799. Napoleon promptly pushed on north to Acre.

This famous old city, situated on a rocky promontory overlooking the bay to which it gives its name, embodied much of the history of the eastern Mediterranean. Known in biblical times as Akko, it had been prominent as a source of the murex from which the famous Tyrian purple was extracted. Standing on the military highway of the coast, and being at the same time the natural port for Galilee and Damascus, it was inevitable that Acre should have been the scene of many sieges. The city enters history as one of the conquests of the Egyptian monarch Thutmose III about 1500 B.C. Afterwards it was subordinate to Tyre, and then became part of the Persian Empire. In the Hellenistic period its name was changed to Ptolemais. G. A. Smith writes, in the *Encyclopaedia Biblica*, "For Egypt, for Asia Minor, for the Greek isles and mainland, and for Italy its harbour was the most convenient on the Syrian coast, and its history till the end of the New Testament period is that of the arrival of great men from these shores, of the muster of large armies, of the winter camps of the invaders of the Syrian hinterland, and of bitter conflicts between Greeks and Jews." It became an Arab city, and was then captured by the soldiers of the First Crusade, only to be recaptured by Saladin. After its fall to the Turks, it had languished in a deathlike slumber, as did most of the once famous cities that had come within the shadow of the Ottoman Empire.

Its condition, at the time that Napoleon laid siege to it, was described as ruinous by Captain Ralph Miller, who had been sent to Acre to supervise the defences: "I found almost every embrasure empty except those towards the sea. Many years' collection of the dirt of the town had been thrown in such a situation as to cover completely the approach to the gate from the only guns that could flank it. . . ." Nevertheless, Acre was to prove a turning point in Napoleon's career, and in that of Sir Sidney Smith, who defended it. Napoleon was later to say of him: "That man made me miss my destiny."

Sir Sidney Smith, in command of Turkish troops reinforced by

British sailors, was to show, as Nelson had already done at sea, that the French were not invincible. His conduct of the defence of Acre, which cost Napoleon a large part of his army, was prophetic of later feats of British arms. The Turks and British were also aided by disease, which devastated the French army, encamped in the heat of summer in the marshy, malaria-ridden Plain of Acre.

Napoleon's failure in front of these old, sun-beaten walls was re-deemed to some extent by a decisive victory over a large Turkish force near the scene of his recent disaster, Aboukir Bay. Shortly after this, recalled by the Directory to France to take charge of an increasingly desperate situation at home, Napoleon slipped back via his native Corsica with the two remaining frigates of his fleet. It might be con-sidered that to have lost a fleet, to have failed at Acre, and to abandon an army were hardly the qualifications that would win a man a hero's reception in his native country. But the fact was that Napoleon himself still shone with an unquenchable glamour. Furthermore, there seemed every likelihood of the monarchy being restored – unless by some miracle a military leader could preserve the Republic. "I seek a sword," remarked Emmanuel Sieyès, one of the five Directors, and, as if conjured up by his words like a genie out of the East, Bonaparte re-turned.

Throughout the winter of 1799, Nelson was mainly in Palermo, where he was making an unenviable spectacle of himself in his slavish attachment to Lady Hamilton. The easy indulgent life of the ancient Sicilian capital and the atmosphere of adulation in which the "Victor of the Nile" now lived combined to sap his moral fibre. Fortunately, it was no more than temporary; Nelson only needed to get to sea again to become transformed by its clean air into the greatest sailor of his time. But the months in Palermo must be counted among the least attractive of his career, for he was politically ingenuous, and the devious and flattering entourage of the Court confused his judge-ment.

The Hamiltons spent much of their time in a villa just outside the city, now known as La Favorita. One relic of Nelson's Sicilian days still remains. On the walls of what was Emma Hamilton's bedroom there hangs a faded copy of the fleet flag signals in operation at that time. One group among them indicated that the admiral (Nelson) was in sight. From her bedroom window Lady Hamilton could look up at the Royal Navy signal station on nearby Monte Pellegrino and see, long before the saluting guns crashed out from the harbour, if her lover was homeward bound. Being, as Lord Spencer described him, "inactive at a foreign court" suited Nelson no more than the sea suited Napoleon.

The new century began well for France. On June 14, 1800, Napoleon, by the victory of Marengo, made himself once more master of Italy. In the same year (in which little else went right for them) the British achieved a minor success in the capture of the last two ships-of-the-line that had survived the Battle of the Nile, *Le Guillaume Tell* and *Le Généreux*. The former was taken shortly after leaving Malta, and the latter while on her way there. The capture of *Le Généreux* is of particular interest, for she was taken by Nelson himself, flying his flag aboard the *Foudroyant*. A midshipman who was aboard at the time recorded a vivid impression of the great admiral in action. Oliver Warner, in *Nelson's Battles*, retells the story from Midshipman G. S. Parsons' account: "After some days of groping about in a heavy sea, interspersed with fog, Nelson heard the sound of firing, and ordered Sir Edward Berry, who had by now resumed his old place as flag-captain, to steer towards it. Soon the admiral grew impatient, and took personal charge of affairs.

" 'Make the *Foudroyant* fly!' he said to Berry. 'This will not do, Sir Ed'ard, it is certainly *Le Généreux*, and to my flagship she can alone surrender! Sir Ed'ard, we must and shall beat the *Northumberland*!' [Another English ship in the chase.]

" 'I will do my utmost, my lord,' said Berry. '... Hand butts of water to the stays – pipe the hammocks down, and each man place shot in them – slack the stays, knock up the wedges, and give the masts play. Start off the water, and pump the ship.'

"The *Foudroyant* began to draw ahead, and slowly took the lead. 'The admiral is working his fin (the stump of his arm),' noted Parsons. 'Do not cross hawse, I advise you.' He was right, for Nelson suddenly burst out to the petty officer who was conning the ship:

" 'I'll knock you off your perch, you rascal, if you are so inattentive! Sir Ed'ard, send your best quartermaster to the weather-wheel.'

" 'A strange sail ahead of the chase,' called the look-out man.

" 'Youngster,' said Nelson to Parsons, 'to the mast-head! What – going without your glass and be damned to you! Let me know what she is immediately.'

" 'A sloop of war or frigate, my lord.'

" 'Demand her number.'

" 'The *Success*.'

" 'Signal her to cut off the flying enemy. Great odds though. Thirty-two small guns to eighty large ones.'

" 'The *Success*, my lord, has hove-to athwart-hawse of *Le Généreux* and is firing her larboard broadside. The Frenchman has hoisted the tricolour with a Rear-Admiral's flag.'

" 'Bravo, *Success*, at her again.'

" 'She has wore, my lord, and is firing her starboard broadside. It has winged the chase, my lord.'

"*Le Généreux* then opened fire on the frigate, and 'everyone stood aghast,' said Parsons, 'fearing the consequences. But when the smoke cleared, there was the *Success*, crippled it is true, but bulldog-like, bearing up for the enemy.'

" 'Signal the *Success* to discontinue the action and come under my stern,' said Nelson. 'She has done well for her size. Try a shot from the lower deck at her, Sir Ed'ard.'

" 'It goes over her.'

" 'Beat to quarters and fire coolly and deliberately at her masts and yards.'

" '*Le Généreux* at this moment opened her fire on us,' continued Parsons, 'and, as a shot passed through the mizzen stay-sail, Lord Nelson, patting one of the youngsters on the head, asked him jocularly how he relished the music: and observing something like alarm depicted on his countenance, consoled him with the information that Charles XII of Sweden ran away from the first shot he heard, though afterwards he was called "the Great" and deservedly, from his bravery. "I therefore," said Nelson, "hope much from you in the future." '

"At this point the *Northumberland* joined in. 'Down came the tri-coloured ensign,' said Parsons, 'amid the thunders of our united cannon.' Berry boarded the prize, and received Perrée's sword, but the admiral himself was dying of his wounds. . . ."

Many actions somewhat similar to this were to scar the waters of the

Mediterranean throughout the next decade – the cannon balls flying, the masts and yards falling, the men fighting and dying – as two nations once more battled for control of the inland sea. As always, when there is conflict for control of this area, certain ports, places, and islands recur, century after century. These are the Mediterranean's focal points, and once again it was the turn of Malta to witness the battle of giants for the control of its harbours.

The island had fallen, with scarcely a shot fired, when Napoleon had passed through on his way to Egypt. Some four thousand troops under the command of General Claude Vaubois had been left to garrison it and to make sure, from behind the magnificent defences of Valletta, that the Royal Navy never entered the waters. But the French, with their revolutionary fervour and in the arrogance of their new imperial aspirations, were not the easiest of taskmasters. At first, the Maltese had been eager to welcome the French as liberators from the rule of the knights, which had become not only oppressive, but in-efficient, in recent years.

"Liberty, Equality, Fraternity" are words that appeal to men the world over, and if the French had really brought these ideals to the island and transformed them into fact, then the Maltese would very probably have remained happy with their new rulers. Such was not the case. Apart from their initial looting of the order's treasury and the churches in the island (all the loot disappeared in Aboukir Bay when the flagship *L'Orient* blew up), the French also introduced heavy taxation. They refused to honour pensions and other commitments; increased interest rates in the official pawnshop; and, far from improving the islanders' lot, made it a great deal worse. The islanders had exchanged King Log for King Stork. As usual, however, the Maltese realized that they had another option – in this case the British. The inhabitants of small islands, ports, or bases that are constantly coveted by superior powers must necessarily learn to weigh the odds and judge accordingly. It was hardly surprising that a Maltese rebellion against the French occurred a little over a week after news reached them of Nelson's victory at Aboukir Bay.

Quite apart from material considerations, the people of this small archipelago were deeply affronted by the French revolutionary atheism and the cynical despoiling of the islands' churches – churches which were the centre of their lives. As a French consul in Malta remarked: "The Maltese is religious from the depths of his soul. His religion, whose duties he fulfils without ostentation, he loves the more because it has its origin not only in genuine faith, but indeed in habit dating from childhood. He finds in the heart of religious ceremonies a relaxation that other people do in public spectacles and festivities."

It would seem that the inhabitants of Malta and Gozo, cut off in the middle of the sea, have always had a deep need for the reassurances that religion can give. They were conscious all the time of their isolation; Homer had depicted this when he described Odysseus sitting on the rocky shore of Calypso's island, "looking out across the barren sea with streaming eyes". The Maltese devotion to a somewhat baroque form of Roman Catholicism was as strong in the nineteenth century as that of their predecessors had been to the Mother Goddess four thousand years before. The French treatment of Malta's churches and their assault upon the place that the Roman Catholic Church occupied in the island's society were major factors in provoking the revolt.

General Vaubois and his troops were now forced to concentrate within Valletta and the area around Grand Harbour, for the whole countryside was up in arms, and the French garrison in the old capital, Mdina, had been massacred. The British blockade of Malta should in theory have starved out the French in a few months, but at one moment – when the French fleet from Brest had managed to get into the Mediterranean – the blockading ships had to be withdrawn. This enabled the French to run in a considerable quantity of food and supplies. In the end, however, after a long hot summer during which the besieged French were reduced to eating dogs, cats, and even rats in Valletta, General Vaubois capitulated. He and his men were permitted to leave the island for France, and Malta to all intents and purposes became a British base. Although it was not until the Treaty of Paris in 1814 that the island was officially declared as belonging "in full right and sovereignty to his Britannic Majesty", the Royal Navy now had sole use of the island's harbours.

The Anglo-Napoleonic War, which lasted twelve years, was largely resumed on Malta's account. The English, who at first had been somewhat sceptical of the island's value, soon came to realize its supreme strategic importance. This was a factor that Napoleon had never had any doubts about, for, just prior to the final breach with England, he had remarked to the British Ambassador in Paris: "Peace or war depends on Malta. It is vain to speak of the Netherlands and Switzerland; they are mere trifles. For myself, my part is taken. I would put you in possession of the Faubourg Saint Antoine rather than of Malta." His reference to the Netherlands and Switzerland was occasioned by the fact that Great Britain had agreed to leave Malta within ten years if the French would evacuate these two countries. This small island, then, was an important cause of the resumption of the war; that war which after many years would end with the defeat of Napoleon.

Nelson, for his part, declared that he considered Malta "as a most important outwork to India, that it will give us great influence in the Levant and indeed all the southern parts of Italy. In this view I hope we shall never give it up." Lord Keith, another English admiral, asked for his views on the relative importance of the many islands and bases in the Mediterranean, declared: "Malta has this advantage over all the other ports that I have mentioned [Mahon, Elba, Sardinia], that the whole harbour is covered by its wonderful fortifications, and that in the hands of Great Britain no enemy would presume to land upon it, because the number of men required to besiege it could not be maintained by the island, and on the appearance of a superior fleet, that besieging army would find itself obliged to surrender . . . or starve. At Malta all the arsenals, hospitals, storehouses etc. are on a great scale. The harbour has more room than Mahon and the entrance is considerably wider."

Another island that figured briefly in the history of these extraordinary years was mountainous, maquis-scented Elba. In May 1814, the dethroned Emperor of the French entered Elba's principal port and harbour, Portoferraio, in the English frigate *Undaunted*. Not far across the water glimmered his native Corsica. It was significant that, even at this time, Napoleon had requested that he should travel in a warship or at least that one should accompany him. He was, he said, worried about the activities of the Algerian pirates. Centuries after his death, the shadow of Barbarossa still lingered over this sea – to fall upon the dejected shoulders of the most extraordinary soldier since Alexander the Great. Perhaps, in retrospect, Napoleon is nearer to Hannibal than to any of the other great captains. Nelson, like Alexander, died when his life was still borne forward on the shining wave of success. Napoleon, like Hannibal, survived to escape from his enemies; to try conclusions with them once again; to fail; and to die in exile. Both men were great administrators as well generals, and both, in the final analysis, were failures.

SEVEN

After the War

Nelson had been dead since 1805. The battle that was largely responsible for securing peace in the Mediterranean had been fought not in the sea itself, but in the approaches. Cape Trafalgar, indeed, was not so far removed from Cape Sagres; whence Henry the Navigator had dispatched the first ships to break the spell of the Atlantic. Napoleon had been in exile in the island of Saint Helena, thousands of miles from the sea where he had been born, ever since 1815.

When he had surrendered, after the disastrous "One Hundred Days", he had written to the Prince Regent of England: "Your Royal Highness, exposed to the factions which distract my country and to the enmity of the greatest powers of Europe, I have ended my political career, and I come, like Themistocles, to appeal to the hospitality of the British people. I put myself under the protection of their laws, and beg your Royal Highness, as the most powerful, the most determined and the most generous of my enemies, to grant me this protection."

It was an extraordinary request, coming as it did from one who had been universally declared, in the Latin phrase, *hostis generis humani*, "the enemy of the human race". Napoleon's comparison of himself with Themistocles was reasonable enough for a Mediterranean man to make, but it was far from accurate. Themistocles at Salamis had saved Greece from the invasion of the Persians; whereas Napoleon was responsible for the deaths of more Europeans than any other individual in history until the rulers of Germany in the twentieth century.

If there is an immense debit side to the Napoleonic contribution, it must be conceded that there is a credit side, too. When Napoleon became First Consul, France had fallen into a state of anarchy, and it was he who restored law and order in the country. He also placed the finances of the Republic on a sound basis, while his work in reforming the *Code Civil* is perhaps his greatest achievement. By combining Roman law and what was best of traditional law in France, he and the trained lawyers working under his direction produced a legal codification which combined good sense with logic, as well as with a sense of history. It was a system to be followed and adapted by many Mediterranean countries. The *savants* whom he had taken to Egypt did much to make the civilization of that ancient land known to Europe. Egypt, which had made so great a contribution to the Mediterranean world, but which had been almost forgotten by the West during its long centuries of Turkish rule, was now seen in its true perspective as one of the cradles of civilization. The Institute of Egyptology and the diffusion of the French language in Egypt and the Levant were two further contributions which France made to the East in return for what she took. Egyptian themes in furniture, jewellery, and many of the arts and crafts were to become prominent throughout Europe in the first half of the nineteenth century.

Another significant by-product of the Napoleonic era was the transformation of archaeology from a dilettante study into a serious branch of science. In the years 1806–1814, during the period of French rule in Naples, the remains of Pompeii were systematically excavated, and this evidence of the world of ancient Rome – so vivid with its suddenly extinguished life – had a revolutionary effect upon the arts and crafts of the period, as well as upon scholars' conceptions of the past. It was as if a breath from the ancient world was suddenly exhaled from the bars and brothels, the villas, shops, and cobbled streets of the buried city. Men read again Pliny's description of how it had been overwhelmed, and Pompeii and its sister-city, Herculaneum, were now visible to remind them of how life had once been in the days of imperial Rome. The Mediterranean world, with its satyrs and centaurs, its dancing fauns and phallic Sileni, its wine, olives, and hawk-eyed galleys, advanced into a thousand drawing rooms and libraries.

Now that the great conqueror had left, and the disturbance occasioned by his passing had subsided in East and West, the sea began to assume a new aspect. In the western basin, Great Britain, now the dominant power, from its bases in Gibraltar and Malta controlled all the main shipping routes. In the eastern basin, the dead hand of the Ottomans still lay upon cities, ports, and islands, but even here there were to be great changes as subject peoples – inspired largely by that dream of liberty which had been evoked by Revolutionary France – took up arms against their oppressors. It was still the great Age of Sail, but the Age of Steam was just on the horizon, and soon the sea would be transformed by vast iron ships, both steam- and sail-propelled, bringing with them the products of the industrial North.

The immediate consequence of peace in Europe was an immense expansion of trade, in which the Mediterranean region benefited considerably. For years the British blockade of France had strangled the free passage of goods and men between one country and another, while the constant warfare on the continent had equally hindered commercial and cultural exchanges. But now, with peace on the continent, and with the Royal Navy in command of the sea, the Mediterranean entered an era of prosperity such as it had not known for centuries.

One of the prime causes of the former ill-health of the trade routes was soon to be eradicated. The kingdom of Algiers, which had plagued European traffic in the Mediterranean ever since the sixteenth century, fell to the French in 1830. That this was so was due not only to French exertions but also to those of the English and even more of the Americans. This new power which now entered the Mediterranean – a power which owed its origin to that Mediterranean seaman, Christopher Columbus – had grown tired of paying tribute to the corsairs of the Barbary Coast.

Throughout the centuries, the Algerian pirates had always been able to play off one warring European power against another, and this had been equally true during the Napoleonic Wars. Although the Royal Navy, at least after the Battle of the Nile, had established its pre-eminence in the sea, it had been to its convenience to come to terms with the pirates. It had saved a lot of trouble for frigates and blockading ships-of-the-line to pay dues to Algiers, but always on condition that the French were not spared from constant harassment. The Americans felt very differently about the whole situation, and, since they were now doing a considerable volume of trade with Mediterranean countries, they bitterly resented having their ships seized or having to pay for a safe passage. In 1803 a squadron under Commodore Edward Preble was dispatched against Tripoli, that ancient fortress city which had once belonged to the Knights of Saint John, and which had been taken from them by Dragut. This first expedition was something of a failure, for a thirty-six-gun frigate, the *Philadelphia*, ran aground and was captured. Its loss, however, was redeemed when Lieutenant Stephen Decatur managed to sail into Tripoli harbour under the guns of the fortress, burn the frigate, and sail out again without the loss of a single man. Two years later, an American squadron attacked the seaport of Derna, in ancient Cyrenaica, another haunt of the pirates, and forced its ruler to waive any further claims for tribute from ships under the American flag.

The end of the Barbary pirates and the establishment of French colonial rule in North Africa came in 1830, when a French army was landed and Algiers swiftly capitulated. But it was still some years before the whole of the area was pacified and before the menace of the Barbary Coast passed into legend. There is, indeed, much truth in Norman Douglas's already quoted remark: "But for the invention of steam, the Barbary corsairs might still be with us." For three hundred years they had levied tribute from all the maritime powers, and Algiers had become one of the richest cities in the world on the products of piracy and the "gifts" which European nations presented to the city's rulers in return for the safe conduct of their merchant vessels.

It cannot be said that the English were particularly happy at seeing their recent enemy, France, established along the North African coast, and only fifteen years after finally eliminating the French challenge to their interests on the battlefield of Waterloo. But the eyes of this northern country were turned to India and the East, to her colonies on the far side of the world, and across the Atlantic to Canada. To the English of this period the Mediterranean appeared mainly as the repository of their culture, the source of classical knowledge, and an area to which young gentlemen of fortune went on that "Grand Tour" which was designed to complete their education. A knowledge of Horace, an acquaintance with the architecture of Italy, a taste for wine, and a certain grace of manner that was considered aristocratic – these were what the nobility expected their sons to bring back from the southern sea. But the English had absorbed so much of the Mediterranean culture over the centuries – in the design of their houses and furniture, in their poetry, their science, and their political thinking – that they had inevitably become deeply involved with this "Mother Goddess" of civilization. They might be resigned to seeing France established on the coastline of North Africa (so petty an area, it seemed, compared with their own vast overseas territories), but there was an emotional charge in the words "Greece" and "Hellas" that they could not resist.

The English involvement in the Greek War of Independence might be described as the first time in history that any country went to war solely for an ideal. The Crusades, it is true, had been triggered by idealism – and many of the men who went on them had undoubtedly desired no material gain – but these had not been "national" wars. They had been international, and the men from all the nations of Europe who took part in them had seen themselves as Christians engaged in a war against the infidel Moslem. All ancient wars and all wars subsequent to the growth of European nationalism had been based solely on motives of gain and material enrichment. But the English who became involved in the Greek revolt against the Ottomans were certainly not motivated by any desire to possess the land of Greece. In their case, certainly, it was poetry that inspired them as much as anything else. This was fitting, perhaps, for a people so largely descended from Scandinavian seafarers, whose bards (somewhat like Homer) had sung them into battle or recounted the fighting deeds of their ancestors over the long oak tables of northern nights.

The climate of the Romantic Revolution – itself so largely derived from the French Revolution – made the prose writers, poets, and painters of England, whose education was largely based on Greek and Latin literature, turn back to its origins. The Mediterranean beckoned them. The titles of some of Byron's works are indicative of the Mediterranean bias in English literature during this period: *The Corsair, The Siege of Corinth, Sardanapalus, The Bride of Abydos*, and even *Don Juan* itself; that poem so redolent of the middle sea, with its portrait of the young lovers "half naked, loving, natural, and Greek". Over and over again the English poets of the nineteenth century evoke the Mediterranean, and in particular the land of Greece.

> The Isles of Greece, the Isles of Greece!
>   Where burning Sappho loved and sung,
> Where grew the arts of war and peace,
>   Where Delos rose, and Phoebus sprung!

Eternal summer gilds them yet,
But all, except their sun, is set . . .
The mountains look on Marathon –
And Marathon looks on the sea. . . .

Keats, in almost all his poems, echoed Byron's preoccupation with the ancient Greeks and with their land which he, unlike Byron, had never seen. Thinking of Homer, he wrote:

Standing aloof in giant ignorance,
   Of thee I hear and of the Cyclades,
As one who sits ashore and longs perchance
   To visit dolphin-coral in deep seas.

Shelley, too, dreamed of a renaissance that would come out of the country that had given more than any other to European civilization:

The world's great age begins anew,
   The golden years return,
The earth doth like a snake renew
   Her winter weeds outworn. . . .
A loftier Argo cleaves the main,
   Fraught with a later prize;
Another Orpheus sings again,
   And loves, and weeps, and dies.
A new Ulysses leaves once more
Calypso for his native shore.

The reality, of course, was quite different from the dream. As H. A. L. Fisher puts it: "The Greeks . . . descended for the most part from unlettered Slavs and Albanians. . . . They spoke Romaic, a form of Greek fashioned by the lips of goatherds and seamen, drawing freely from the vocabulary of the Turk, the Latin, and the Slav, and racy with all the mariner's slang of the Aegean. They used the Greek characters; but as an influence on the education of the liberators the poems of Homer and the tragedies of Aeschylus might almost as well have been written in Chinese." One characteristic, however, which these modern Greeks possessed in common with the Greeks of antiquity was a passionate inability to act in concert with one another. Byron's letters

from Greece make sad reading, for they deal in the main with the endless bickering of the Greeks, with their deviousness, and with their
blatant dishonesty over money matters. He was almost totally disillusioned with them when his death from fever in marshy Missolonghi
did them the greatest service that any man could ever have done.
Byron, a martyr for the liberty of Hellas, provoked an international
wave of enthusiasm for the Greeks and their cause. His death in 1824
was the most crucial event in the whole of the Greek War of Independence until the allies, in particular the Royal Navy, took a hand in the
events.

Three years later, a sea battle was fought off the west coast of Greece
that had almost as much effect upon life in this area as the Battle of
Preveza had done. With it, some three hundred years after Barbarossa
had established the power of the Ottoman navy, there disappeared at
last that threat to the communications and the trade of the sea which
had existed ever since the fall of Constantinople in 1453. On October
20, 1827, the Battle of Navarino, fought by a combined fleet of English,
French, and Russians against a Turko-Egyptian force, was largely responsible for the creation of the new and independent kingdom of
Greece. It was here, too, that the moribund Ottoman Empire received
a wound from which it never wholly recovered. C. M. Woodhouse, in
The Battle of Navarino, gives the following picture of the historical
background: "The great powers had not wanted the Greek revolution
to succeed. After the convulsions of the Napoleonic Wars, the aim of
the peace settlement had been to restore the *status quo ante bellum*, and
the Ottoman Empire was part of that *status quo*. What all of them,
particularly the Austrian and Russian Emperors, feared most was that
the Sultan's dominions would break up and someone other than themselves would inherit the major share of the remnants. The Sultan, already known before the end of the 1820s as the 'sick man of Europe',
was kept alive by that fear. The Greeks counted upon the great powers,
as fellow-Christians, to help them against their Muhammadan oppressors, but largely in vain. Only the Russians, who shared with them the
Orthodox faith, gave some encouragement, but they did so chiefly in
order to gain control of Greece themselves as a foothold in the Mediterranean. The Austrians were openly hostile to Greek independence; so
were the Prussians; the French and British were indifferent except for

private groups of philhellenes. . . ." Nevertheless, for a complicated variety of reasons – one of the major being the prevalent philhellenism of many educated Englishmen, among them George Canning, the Foreign Secretary – the Battle of Navarino was fought, and the Turkish fleet practically annihilated.

With the exceptions of Trafalgar and the Nile, this was the most decisive sea battle to take place in the nineteenth century. It firmly established the British presence in the Mediterranean, for the major part of the ships engaged were of the Royal Navy. Furthermore, the admiral-in-command, Sir Edward Codrington, was a naval officer of the same style and distinction as his former commander-in-chief, Lord Nelson, with whom he had served at Trafalgar. The Turkish fleet, for its part, fought with immense courage and gallantry. From the accounts of the battle, it seems – as so often when reading of old wars – that if only the energy and the endurance of the human race had been directed into constructive co-operation, not just the Mediterranean, but the whole world, might long ago have resembled the Garden of Eden.

It was the last great battle of the Age of Sail to take place in this sea, and the memoirs of an anonymous British sailor (*Life on Board a Man-of-War*, 1829) give a vivid picture of an action that may well serve as an epitaph to Nelson's Mediterranean. "Lieutenant Broke drew his sword and told us not to fire till ordered. 'Point your guns sure, men,' said he, 'and make every shot tell – that's the way to show them British play!' He now threw away his hat on the deck, and told us to give the Turks three cheers, which we did with all our heart. Then crying out, 'Stand clear of the guns,' he gave the word 'FIRE'! and immediately the whole tier of guns was discharged, with terrific effect, into the side of the Turkish Admiral's ship that lay abreast of us. . . . The first man that I saw killed in our vessel was a marine, and it was not till we had received five or six rounds from the enemy. He was close beside me. I had taken the sponge out of his hand, and on turning round saw him at my feet with his head fairly severed from his body, as if it had been done with a knife. My messmate Lee drew the corpse out from the trucks of the guns, and hauled it into midships, under the after ladder. . . . As there is always a cask of water lashed to the stanchion on the deck in midships, called 'fighting water', one of the officers of the fore part of the deck, on his way to the cockpit, came aft, begging to get a drink. He had been wounded severely in the right arm with a piece of langridge shot, and the left was so bruised that he could not lift the jug to his head. De Squaw, who had been working the gun with an activity and smartness that surprised me for a man of his age, took he jug, and after skimming back the blood and dirt from the top of the cask, filled it, and offered it to the officer; but just as he was in the act of holding it to the wounded man's mouth, he dropt a mangled corpse, being cut nearly in pieces with grape-shot. . . . Cool, however, as a British sailor is in danger, nothing can approach the Turk in this respect. George Finney had hauled one into the boat, a fine-looking fellow, and elegantly dressed. He was no sooner seated in the bow of the boat, than taking out a portable apparatus, he began to fill his pipe, which having done, he struck a light from the same conveniency, and commenced sending forth, with inconceivable apathy, volumes of smoke from his mouth . . . Another instance of Turkish coolness I may mention, which, although it did not happen in our ship, was told me under well authenticated circumstances. Some of the crew of the French frigate *Alcyone* had picked up a Turk, who by his dress appeared to be a person of rank in their navy. When he was brought aboard, he found his arm so shattered that it would need to undergo amputation; so he made his way down the cockpit ladder with as much ease as if he had not been hurt, and as much dignity as if he had made a prize of the frigate. He pointed to his shattered arm, and made signs to the surgeon that he wanted it off. The surgeon obliged him so far, and having bound up the stump and bandaged it properly, the Turk made his way to the deck, and plunging into the water, swam to his own vessel that was opposed along with another to the very frigate he had been aboard of. He was seen climbing the side with his one arm, but had not been aboard many minutes, when it blew up. . . ."

The author concludes one section of his account with a description of the cockpit where the wounded were attended to: "The stifled groans, the figures of the surgeon and his mates, their bare arms and faces smeared with blood, the dead and dying all round, some in the last agonies of death, and others screaming under the amputating knife, formed a horrid scene of misery, and made a hideous contrast to the 'pomp, pride, and circumstance of glorious war.'"

In one way or another, the Mediterranean, so gracious and so graceful a sea, had been disfigured by such scenes ever since the first war galley had crept out upon its surface. The Battle of Navarino, which so largely helped to restore Greece to independence, was but one in the long succession of battles over who was to be master of these ancient lands and these "fish-infested" waters. It was not to be the last. But now, for nearly a century, the sea enjoyed comparative tranquillity. The *Pax Britannica* imposed by the distant island gave the Mediterranean a peace such as it had not known since the days of the *Pax Romana*.

EIGHT

Islands and English

The English appearance in the Mediterranean was somewhat dissimilar from that of the other powers who had been dominant in this sea. Like many others, the English had come there originally for trade. But it was the exigencies of the wars with France that had driven them to become a Mediterranean power. In this respect they resembled the Carthaginians, who had also been forced into imperial responsibilities against their inclination, but as their only means of maintaining their shipping routes. The English, it is true, had a world-wide empire by this period in their history, but they did not deliberately seek an extension of it in the Mediterranean. Their initial reluctance to become involved with Malta is an indication of their general approach. Somewhat similar was their attitude towards the Ionian Islands.

Corfu, Cephalonia, Zante, Ithaca, Kythera, Levkas, and Paxos, together with their many small dependencies, formed the group called the Ionian Islands, or, to give them their Greek name, the Heptanesoi, the "Seven Islands". Ever since the conquest of Constantinople by the Crusaders in 1204, these islands had been administered by Venice, and the influence of the great Adriatic city is still evident throughout them. The ruling classes spoke Italian, the Roman Catholic Church was established, and Greek ceased to be spoken except among the peasant classes, who clung to their ancient ways and cultures with the innate conservatism of all Mediterranean farmers and fishermen. Under the rule of Venice the islands prospered, and the centuries-old olives and fertile valleys of Corfu still bear witness to the intelligent husbandry inculcated by the Venetians. (In Corfu they had encouraged the planting of trees by giving special prizes to those who did so.)

After the fall of the Venetian Republic in 1797, the islands were annexed to France, but this situation did not last for long. During the next tumultuous twenty years, they were disputed over by Russians, Turks, British, and French. Then, in 1815, by the Treaty of Paris, they became known as "The United States of the Ionian Islands" and were placed under the executive protection of Great Britain. This protectorate remained in existence for nearly fifty years, until, in 1864, they were handed over to the kingdom of Greece. The years in which British governors exercised their rule over antique Corcyra, land of the Phaeacians, and Odysseus' kingdom of Ithaca are not without interest. They are typical of much that was happening at that time throughout the Mediterranean.

The German philosopher Hegel wrote of the English that their "material existence is based on commerce and industry, and the English have undertaken the weight and responsibility of being the missionaries of civilization to the world; for their commercial spirit urges them to traverse every sea and land, to create wants and to stimulate enterprise, and first and foremost to establish among them the conditions necessary to commerce – viz., the relinquishment of a life of lawless violence, respect for property, and civility to strangers." This attitude was foreign to the Greeks, who had grown resentful of foreign rule, had little respect for property (except their own), and were inspired by their new-found freedom to desire complete independence. The English protectorate of the Ionian Islands was not always a happy one. Anglo-Saxon and Levantine natures, though they had their points in common, did not sit too happily together.

Viscount Kirkwall, describing a visit to the islands during this period, writes of how a certain Colonel Napier, then stationed in Corfu, "On one occasion, hearing screams, and learning that a titled Ionian was beating his wife, rushed into the house, and inflicted on the spot, with his riding-whip, a severe personal chastisement on the astonished husband. To be sure, he immediately afterwards sent to offer to the sufferer complete personal satisfaction. But the Ionian, ignorant of Western refinements in such matters, and unused to the pistol, refused to understand how the being shot at could fully atone for the disgrace of being flogged."

The Viscount himself commented on the local cuisine: "Oil and garlic usually permeate all native cookery. The garlic grown in the island is insufficient for home consumption; and I was assured that, to supply the deficiency, 2,500 lb. worth of the unsavoury comestible is annually imported. The constant use of garlic, and the rare use of soap, impress an Englishman very disagreeably." In 1858, William Gladstone, then High Commissioner Extraordinary to the Ionian Islands, made a tour of this curious and somewhat troublesome asset to the British crown. "At Paxos, as everywhere else, he showed the most unbounded veneration for the dignitaries of the Greek Church. In Corfu, he had excited the, perhaps illiberal, disgust of the English by publicly kissing the hand of the Archbishop and dutifully receiving his blessing. . . . The simple Bishop of Paxos appears, also, to have been ignorant of the etiquette which the High Commissioner Extraordinary practised with ecclesiastical dignitaries. Mr. Gladstone, having taken and respectfully kissed the Bishop's hand, leaned forward to receive the orthodox blessing. The Bishop hesitated, not knowing what was expected of him; and not imagining, perhaps, that a member of the Anglican Church could require his benediction. At last, however, he perceived the truth, and, bending forward, he hastened to comply with the flattering desire of the representative of the British Crown. But at this moment, unfortunately, Mr. Gladstone, imagining that the deferred blessing was not forthcoming, suddenly raised his head, and struck the episcopal chin. The Resident and other spectators of the scene had considerable difficulty in maintaining the gravity befitting so solemn an occasion. . . ."

Thus, throughout the nineteenth century, these frock-coated English dignitaries flit incongruously across the Mediterranean scene, followed by their wives and children and by servants carrying picnic hampers and parasols. They were to be seen at, among many other places, the strange new court of Athens. Here King Otho, son of the King of Bavaria, was attended by blue-chinned Greek evzones bearing names like Agamemnon and Odysseus; while German advisers grumbled constantly about the dishonesty and tergiversation of the King's new subjects. They were to be seen admiring the ruins of Tiberius' villa on Capri (which for a brief time during the Napoleonic Wars had also come under the British flag). Palermo, Taormina, and Syracuse knew them well; and it is from this period that in many cities of the ancient world hotels began to be erected called the Bristol or the Splendid, the Grande Bretagne or the Albion.

Apart from their language, which now, at least for commerce, began to supersede French as the *lingua franca* of the sea, they brought other benefits. The amazing impetus of their Industrial Revolution began to make itself universally felt, and to be emulated throughout these southern lands. There had long been stagnation, but a fresh current was driving across the sea, impelled by this wind from the North. Improvements in plumbing, water supplies, and road-building followed the newcomers wherever they went. In minute Paxos, for instance, where Mr. Gladstone became for a moment such an unlikely figure of fun, the iron pipe that still brings the water supply into the port is stamped V.R.: Victoria Regina. In most of the older hotels and private houses throughout the sea, from Gibraltar and Sicily to Greece, Cyprus, and Egypt, the cast-iron lavatory cisterns still bear trade names from London and Birmingham, and inscriptions such as "The Great Niagara". Thus the English brought back into the Mediterranean (which had largely forgotten such things) improvements in sanitation and communications that Rome had first given to the world.

However, there was constant trouble in these islands, particularly in mountainous Cephalonia. Agitation for union with Greece began quite soon after the British protectorate was established. It was in Cephalonia that Byron had written in his journal: "Standing at the window of my apartment in this beautiful village, the calm though cool serenity of a beautiful and transparent Moonlight showing the Islands, the Mountains, the Sea, with a distant outline of the Morea traced between the double Azure of the waves and skies, has quieted me enough to be able to write." But there was another side to the picture and Byron knew it well, for it was in this same island that he also wrote: "The worst of them [the Greeks] is that (to use a coarse but the only expression that will not fall short of the truth) they are such damned liars; there never was such an incapacity for veracity since Eve lived in Paradise." It was with something like relief that the British handed back the islands in 1864 – though not to King Otho. He had already been deposed, after a turbulent reign during which it is difficult to know whether his subjects disliked their new monarch more than he disliked them. The new King, George I, a German from Schleswig–Holstein, was also to find out that the Greeks, although their blood might have changed over the centuries, were still the most factious people in the Mediterranean.

The island that more than any other epitomized this era of the *Pax Britannica* was Malta. It had become once more, as it had been in the heyday of the Knights of Saint John, the focal point of the whole sea. Here the great British Mediterranean fleet, soon to change from sail to steam, lay at anchor beneath the frowning fortifications of La Valette's city. Here the marines marched and countermarched, and giant new defence guns from the arsenals of England began to replace the out-moded, but more decorative, cannon of their predecessors. Admirals and generals, poets and painters, travellers and society ladies, all came here – some to escape the grey rigours of the English winter, some on duty, some bound east for Egypt and India, and others bringing eligible daughters, the "fishing fleet", to catch the eyes of young naval and military officers. The English involvement with the Mediterranean centred in this small limestone island, and, since nearly "anybody who was anybody" came here at one time or another, it is interesting to note some of the comments they made about the island and the sea around it.

Rear-Admiral Sir Alexander Ball, who had played a prominent part in the delivery of the island from the French and who had become its Civil Commissioner, found himself in the summer of 1804 with a new Private Secretary, Samuel Taylor Coleridge. Already an addict to opium, Coleridge was seeking in this island in the sun a cure for both his health and his addiction – neither of which he ever found. He did, however, strike up a close friendship with Alexander Ball, who was a man of intelligence, and who could appreciate Coleridge's charm and remarkable powers of conversation. The months that the poet spent in Malta, and later in Naples and Rome, undoubtedly had a con-siderable effect upon his nature and his work. It is perhaps significant that it was shortly after his stay in Malta that Coleridge made his re-turn to the Christian faith.

It was inevitable that Lord Byron, that lover of the Mediterranean above all else, should have called at the island during one of his many travels through the sea. Here, true to his nature, he immediately fell in love with a young married woman whom he later enjoined not to for-get him, but to

> . . . think upon Calypso's isles,
> Endeared by days gone by.

But the satirist in Byron was ever present, and it is amusing to see that the "noble lord" was not impressed by the garrison atmosphere his countrymen had imparted to Malta – as they did to all their other Mediterranean possessions. As he wrote in his farewell to the island, which he called a "little military hot-house":

> Adieu, ye females fraught with graces!
> Adieu red coats, and redder faces!
> Adieu the supercilious air
> Of all that strut *en militaire*!

Some twenty years later, a man who was to make an even greater mark upon the history of the Mediterranean arrived in the island. Benjamin Disraeli was at this time a young man of twenty-six, vain, impetuous, and brilliant. It was this particular Mediterranean tour, in which he visited Spain, Malta, Albania, Athens, Constantinople, Egypt, and Palestine, which largely contributed to his permanent interest in the area and particularly in its eastern basin. This was to lead in 1878 to his skilfully negotiated treaty with the Ottomans, whereby Britain took over the occupation and administration of Cyprus. Disraeli's Jewish blood drew him towards the East, and he felt relaxed and at home among Semitic peoples. The stiff upper lip and the cold blue eye of the Anglo-Saxon were not part of his nature, and it is hardly surprising that he found a congenial climate in Semitic Malta. Like Byron, he did not find its British defenders *simpatico*. That his feelings were equally returned is made clear by a description of his appearance and behaviour while in Valletta written by William Meredith, a friend who accompanied him on the tour: "He paid a round of visits in his *majo* [Spanish for "dandy"] jacket, with trousers and a sash of all the colours of the rainbow; in this wonderful costume he paraded all round Valetta, followed by one half the population of the place and, as he said, putting complete stop to all business. . . . His appearance was certainly against him: long hyacinthine curls, rings on his fingers, gold chains, and velvet dresses of the most gorgeous description. His conversation, too, was of a most offensive nature, calling in question every preconceived and revered opinion, together with flights of sarcasm, against all accepted maxims of the British Army. What rendered matters worse was his great knowledge and memory, which enabled him to make short work of any bold soldier who encountered his argument."

It can be imagined how those red faces got even redder when they saw Disraeli, as he described himself in a letter to his father, "in the costume of a Greek pirate. A blood-red shirt with silver studs as big as shillings, an immense scarf for girdle, full of pistols and daggers, red cap, red slippers, broad blue striped jacket and trousers...." Yet, even at this most flamboyant phase of his youth, Disraeli was a perspicacious observer. In *Henrietta Temple* he writes, "Malta is certainly a delightful station. Its city, Valetta, equals in its noble architecture, if it even does not excel, any capital in Europe; and although it must be confessed that the surrounding region is little better than a rock, the vicinity, nevertheless, of Barbary, of Italy and of Sicily, present exhaustless resources to the lovers of the highest order of natural beauty."

Other visitors to the island were Sir Walter Scott and William Makepeace Thackeray. Scott was a very sick man when he reached the island in 1831 (he died the following year). It is significant of the feeling the English had at this time not just for Scott, but for literature itself, that they placed a frigate at his disposal for his Mediterranean cruise. Not unnaturally, Scott, that lover of the Crusades and of the old days of chivalry, was inspired by the whole atmosphere of this island where the last of the Crusaders had had their abode. He contemplated, and indeed started, a new novel – designed to be the last of the Waverley series – entitled *The Siege of Malta*, but he died before its completion. Of Valletta he remarked: "This town is really a dream," and as he walked through it on the last day of his visit, "It will be hard if I cannot make something of this!" Among the friends whom he found settled in the island was that outstanding antiquarian and man of letters, John Hookham Frere, whose translation of the comedies of Aristophanes has never been surpassed.

Some years later, Thackeray, who had been given a complimentary ticket by the directors of the Pacific and Orient Line, also arrived in Malta. In his *Sketch Books*, his evocation of the island is of interest, for it shows how much the expenditure of the Royal Navy and the new trade with the North had already increased its prosperity.

"We reached Valetta, the entrance to the harbour of which is one of the most stately and agreeable scenes ever admired by sea-sick traveller. The small basin was busy with a hundred ships, from the huge guard-ship, which lies there a city in itself; – merchantmen loading and crews cheering, under all the flags of the world flaunting in the sunshine; a half-score of busy black steamers perpetually coming and going, coal-ing and painting, and puffing and hissing in and out of the harbour; slim men-of-war's barges shooting to and fro, with long shining oars flashing like wings over the water; hundreds of painted town-boats, with high heads and white awnings. . . . Round this busy blue water rise rocks, blazing in sunshine, and covered with every imaginable device of fortification; to the right, St. Elmo, with flag and light-house; and opposite, the Military Hospital, looking like a palace; and all round, the houses of the city, for its size the handsomest and most stately in the world.

"Nor does it disappoint you on a closer inspection, as many a foreign town does. The streets are thronged with a lively comfortable-looking population; the poor seem to inhabit handsome stone palaces, with balconies and projecting windows of heavy carved stone. The lights and shadows, the cries and stenches, the fruit-shops and fish-stalls, the dresses and chatter of all nations; the soldiers in scarlet, and women in black mantillas; the beggars, boatmen, barrels of pickled herrings and macaroni; the shovel-hatted priests and bearded capuchins; the tobacco, grapes, onions, and sunshine; the signboards, bottled-porter stores, the statues of saints and little chapels which jostle the stranger's eyes as he goes up the famous stairs from the Water-gate, make a scene of such pleasant confusion and liveliness as I have never witnessed before."

Edward Lear, landscape artist, author of the famous "Nonsense" rhymes, and teacher of the art of water-colour to Queen Victoria her-self, was yet another of these travelling Britons who brought to the Mediterranean quite as much as they took. Greece, and in particular the Ionian Islands, were other regions that he knew well. During a visit to the islands in 1863, he wrote in a letter that "there was no winter, but *en revanche* 43 small earthquakes." His *Views in the Seven Ionian Islands* is a work that more accurately reflects their quality than any other. Some years before this he, too, had come to Malta – an island which he revisited several times, and whose austere landscape he depicted with insight and sympathy. As he wrote on one occasion to a friend: "I draw constantly on the Baracca point – meaning to paint a picture thereof one day; and I wander up and down the beautiful streets of Valetta and Senglea; and rejoice in the delightful heat and the blue sky; and watch the thousand little boats skimming across the harbour at sunset, and admire the activity and industry of the Maltese; and am amazed that their priests should consider that a constant ringing of bells should be any sort of pleasure to the Deity; and I drink very admirable small beer plenteously from pewter pipkinious pots. . . ."

Victorian England, which dominated so much of the affairs of the world in the nineteenth century, cannot be understood unless the contribution of the Mediterranean to its culture is appreciated. The Royal Navy brought peace to this sea, and the merchants and others who followed after it brought trade and prosperity. The southern lands, and the British bases in them, returned the compliment by introducing these new visitors to the olives and the lizards and the heat. There had been "tourists" in the days of ancient Rome who had made the "Grand Tour" of Greece, but the British were the first tourists in the modern sense of the word. Impelled for a hundred and one reasons, but largely because of their classical education, they came to the ancient mother sea and invigorated their works from it, leaving behind them a fair return in cash and culture. There are only a few of the great Victorian writers who did not, in one way or another, acknowledge a debt to this southern world. Tennyson, Arnold, Browning, Ruskin, even Oscar Wilde and Ernest Dowson – their works are suffused with memories of Homer, Vergil, Dante, and Catullus. They are suffused also with images derived from Mediterranean lands.

> All round the coast the languid air did swoon,
> Breathing like one that hath a weary dream.
> Full-faced above the valley stood the moon. . . .
> Then some one said, "We will return no more;"
> And all at once they sang, "Our island home
> Is far beyond the wave; we will no longer roam."

Tennyson's poem "The Lotus-Eaters" was only one work among thousands that expressed the nostalgia induced among this northern people for the salty, tideless basin, where "everything had happened before".

NINE

Mid-Victorian

The long periods of summer calm in the Mediterranean had always proved frustrating for the masters and crews of sailing ships. There are many references in log-books and letters written during the Napoleonic Wars which tell of the irritation felt by blockading squadrons off Toulon, watching their yards swinging idle, while the sun-bleached canvas slatted to shreds as the ship rolled in a swell, and the ropes chafed and frayed in the blocks. Except for the transport of bulk cargoes such as wheat, the sailing vessel, as the Romans had long ago found out, was not really suitable for this sea. The galley, with its auxiliary sail when the wind blew fair, was really more efficient for war, as well as for the transport of small or perishable cargoes.

The ships-of-the-line and their merchant-marine equivalents, the great sail-driven cargo-carriers, were efficient enough on the ocean trade routes of the world where they could use wind systems – the monsoon winds of the Indian Ocean or the prevailing trade winds of the Atlantic. In the Mediterranean, however, with the limited exception of the Aegean in summer, there were no such regular winds. A ship dependent upon sail might sit absolutely motionless for over a week in the smoky Ionian or in the steamy sea west of Sicily, picking up no more than a faint whisper in her upper canvas. What was needed – and it was a problem that had taxed men's minds for centuries – was some efficient form of mechanical propulsion. At last, in the nineteenth century, with the invention of the marine steam engine, man was on the verge of changing the whole pattern of sea travel.

The French, the Americans, and the English made an almost equal contribution to solving the problem of how to adapt the steam engine for marine use. As early as 1788, William Symington had built a small steam-driven paddle-boat, and had navigated it on a lake in Dumbartonshire. But it was the American Robert Fulton who first made a commercial success of a steamboat with his famous *Clermont* launched in 1807. She was followed in the first three decades of the century by numerous others. These included the *Great Western*, a vessel considered to be the first Atlantic liner, since she was large (over 1300 tons) and able to do the crossing in fourteen days.

Both the British and French admiralties were seriously troubled by the fear that the other might be the first to put a fleet of steam warships into action. At first, however, the cumbersome machinery of the early steam engines and the fact that the paddles and paddle-boxes took up so much of the ship's sides, thus limiting her number of guns, ensured the survival of sail, at least for warships. It was not until the invention of the screw, or, more accurately, its practical application for marine work (Archimedes of Syracuse had invented a water-screw as early as the third century B.C.), that steam propulsion really became efficient. In 1845 the British Admiralty fitted a screw to the steam-sloop *Rattler*, and conducted a series of trials which proved its efficiency and its superiority over paddle-wheels. The scene was now set for the greatest transformation of the seas and oceans of the world since man had first ventured upon them. The invention of the screw, as applied to a marine steam engine, was one of the peak points in the history of Man the Navigator. From now on, both warships and merchant ships were to change utterly, and the Mediterranean would benefit by this invention relatively more than any other sea area in the world. The tideless calms of summer would be conquered, and sea-captains would be able to give their times of arrival with a confidence that had never previously existed.

However, in the next war that involved the Mediterranean theatre, the vast majority of the ships were still sailing vessels. This was because of the innate conservatism of the British Admiralty, which could never forget that the Nile and Trafalgar had been won by sail. Naval officers regarded machinery and all that it entailed (such as stokers and engineers) with some distaste. They had brought the ship-of-the-line to the peak of perfection, and they were loath to see it go.

Michael Lewis, in *The Navy of Britain*, writes: "The Crimean War found us with our main fleet still composed of full-rigged sailing ships. Of the British 'line' ships, for instance, engaged in the bombardment of

Sevastopol on 17th October, 1854, only two were fitted with screws. The action brought little credit to anyone. The sailing ships, having taken an unconscionable time in being pushed and prodded into position by the exertions of small paddle- and screw-vessels, engaged the enemy batteries at too long a range, and inflicted very little damage while receiving much. But the two screw-ships steamed into action much more briskly, with much greater dignity, and opened fire at shorter range. . . . Elsewhere the smaller ships fitted with steam did rather well. At Odessa in April 1854, for instance, five paddle-ships, steaming as they fought, contrived to escape any serious punishment from the enemy's shell-guns, and did a great deal of damage to the port installations. None of our ships, perhaps, achieved outstanding success, for War had reached one of those moments in its history when Offence (as represented by the new shell-guns) was temporarily forging ahead of Defence. Yet it is safe to affirm that, by the end of the conflict, the steam-engine had established its claims to be installed in all ships as a matter of course."

The Crimean War, in which Britain and France found themselves as unlikely allies, although arising from a number of involved causes, was basically connected with the determination of the western European powers to keep the Russians out of the Mediterranean. Although occurring in that distant appendix of the Mediterranean the Black Sea, it focused attention on, indeed, largely started from, the necessity of keeping the Dardanelles, the Bosporus, and Constantinople itself in friendly hands. Russian interest in the Mediterranean went back as far as the reign of Peter the Great (1672–1725), the creator of the Russian navy, who had first laid down a policy of expansion in the direction of Constantinople. The Tsar Nicholas I had also had his eye on Malta, while his predecessor, Paul I, had helped the finances of the Order of Saint John before its defeat by Napoleon, and had then become Grand Master of the order after it went into exile.

This distant conflict in the Crimea with its terrible losses on both sides caused by inefficiency, disease, and the rigours of the Russian winter was remote in all senses of the word from life in the Mediterranean basin. It did prove yet again, however, the importance of sea power. E. W. Sheppard and F. J. Hudleston, in the *Encyclopaedia Britannica*, sum it up as follows: "As far as concerns the military art, the Crimean War is usually regarded as worthy of remembrance only as perhaps the most ill-managed campaign in English history, and a standing example of the difficulties and dangers of a coalition war. Yet from a broad point of view it may well be regarded as a highly creditable feat of arms on the part of the Allies. An expeditionary force of never more than 200,000 men, composed of troops of different nationalities and under divided and incompetent leadership, was yet able to set foot on the territory of an enemy immeasurably superior in every resource of war; to rend from his grasp a strong fortress, the possession of which was vital to the pursuit of his chosen policy; and to inflict on him during the struggle losses amounting to more than double its own strength. History affords no more striking demonstration of the range and potency of armies based on sea power. . . ."

One benefit which accrued from the war was the hospital reform initiated by Florence Nightingale. This did not affect England alone, for her improvements and suggestions were copied by many other countries throughout Europe. Another major advance resulting from the Crimean War was the introduction of the electric cable. This was first used for the transmission of messages from the field headquarters of the English and French to their capitals. This new invention cut down the time of transit of correspondence from ten days to twenty-four hours. Later, when commercially developed, the electric cable ended the isolation of many a lonely island, and until it was superseded by the radio, it was all-important in linking one end of the sea with the other.

The Crimean War heralded the end of the ship-of-the-line, which, although it lingered on to the end of the century, was steadily replaced by the steam-and-screw-propelled warship. Oars had yielded to canvas, canvas had yielded to steam, and, by the 1870s, wood itself was being replaced by iron. Yet many of the small trading vessels of the Mediterranean were to remain wooden-built sailing ships until the second half of the twentieth century. It was not until the advent of efficient small diesel engines after the Second World War that sail at last disappeared commercially from the sea. But it reappeared immediately in the guise of tens of thousands of pleasure yachts, whose owners found that in the combination of sail and diesel engine they had found an ideal solution to the problems of Mediterranean navigation.

Another major change in warship design during this century was from the smooth-fired cannon firing solid shot to the rifled gun firing an explosive shell. This revolutionized later sea battles, for the object was no longer – as it had been in Nelson's day – to "lay your ship alongside the enemy", but to engage him at long range. In 1855 Sir William Armstrong produced a revolutionary and extremely efficient gun: the father of all subsequent naval guns. It had polygroove rifling and fired an elongated projectile, while the gun jacket was reinforced by an ingenious technique which gave it immense strength. Another major step forward was that the gun was breech-loading, and thus the rate of fire could be immensely increased. Although the Armstrong gun was not adapted for naval warfare until the 1880s, it was the ancestor of all the many guns that were to be used in the Mediterranean in the course of the world wars of the twentieth century.

While these developments were taking place at sea, the pattern of events on the lands surrounding it was undergoing a kaleidoscopic change. The surge and swell left behind by the great storm emanating from Revolutionary France affected not only the mountainous, olive-silvery land of Greece. Even before the fall of the restored monarchy in France, Italy was crackling with the flames of revolt against its foreign occupiers. In the north, the Hapsburgs ruled most of the land, while in the south the Bourbons exercised a corrupt and inefficient government over the kingdoms of Naples and Sicily. Napoleon might have failed, but in the years in which he and his appointees had ruled Italy, he had given the people a glimpse of stability and enlightenment such as the country had not known since the fall of Rome.

West, in the Spanish peninsula, another Bourbon had returned after the defeat of Napoleon. Both the Spanish and Portuguese overseas empires were doomed in the long run, and with their collapse the life of their home countries was further enfeebled. Stagnation, bankruptcy or semi-bankruptcy, revolutions and abortive revolutions, the return of tyrannies, and all the unhappy and ineffectual strivings to redeem themselves and to revive their famous past – these formed the pattern for the inhabitants of the Iberian peninsula for the next century.

It was as if this western land-mass of the Mediterranean had caught some infection from beyond the seas, a disease for which there was no local cure. Portugal, which had first opened the doorways of the Atlantic, and Spain, which had capitalized upon this original "invention", were countries that through inefficient government and the repressive nature of their Church (and therefore of their education) were unable to meet the demands of an age in which change was so rapid. England had lost her American colonies, but she had found others, and she had also benefited immensely by being the creator of the Industrial Revolution. Portugal and Spain had neither the means nor the methods, the coal nor the iron, nor indeed the scientific drive, to compete efficiently in this new industrial age. It was as if, having breached the Pillars of Hercules and having established vast empires overseas, their strength was now exhausted.

The Mediterranean is undoubtedly the sea which taught Nietzsche the doctrine of the "eternal recurrence": "that all things recur eternally, and we ourselves with them, and that we have already existed an infinite number of times before and all things with us." The unknown author of Ecclesiastes, a Mediterranean man to his finger-tips, had long ago anticipated this knowledge: "One generation passeth away, and another generation cometh: but the earth abideth for ever. The sun also ariseth, and the sun goeth down, and hasteth to his place where he arose. The wind goeth toward the south, and turneth about unto the north; it whirleth about continually, and the wind returneth again according to his circuits. All the rivers run into the sea; yet the sea is not full: unto the place from whence the rivers come, thither they return again. . . . The thing that hath been, it is that which shall be; and that which is done is that which shall be done: and there is no new thing under the sun."

In Egypt, the inescapable revolution of the wheel had already seen the weakening of the Turkish control of that important province by an Albanian, Mehemet Ali. Having overthrown the Mamelukes, he had shown himself a reasonably enlightened despot. He had started the country's cotton industry, had embarked on the conquest of the Sudan, and had begun to draw his ancient country into the pattern of the new century. The dream of Mehemet Ali and his son Ibrahim of seizing Greece was finally shattered at the Battle of Navarino. His even more ambitious scheme of smashing the Ottoman Empire and remoulding it, with Egypt as its core, could not be tolerated by the Great Powers.

The condition of Turkey, the "sick man of Europe", gave them cause enough for alarm, but they had no intention of allowing a powerful new empire to arise in the East. England, most of all, could not brook the idea of a strong Moslem power achieving what Napoleon had failed to do, and posing a threat to India. What was to transform Egypt, however, during the reign of Mehemet Ali's other son, Said Pasha, was the successful conclusion of that enterprise of which Napoleon had dreamed – the construction of a canal linking the Mediterranean with the Red Sea. Once this had been opened, the English were quick to realize that their ultimate aim must be to control Egypt, since there could be no security for this new "Gateway to the East" unless they themselves had the key to it. Once again India, invisible beyond the horizon, determined actions and policies within the Mediterranean.

There had been in the past a waterway system connecting the Mediterranean with the Red Sea via the Nile. Aristotle, Strabo, and Pliny all attribute the building of the first canal to the Pharaoh Sesostris, but it seems clear from an inscription on a pillar at Karnak that there was indeed a canal by the reign of Seti I (1313–1292 B.C.). This connected the Red Sea with the Nile, not with the Mediterranean direct. This canal became gradually silted up, until it was reopened by Darius I of Persia in 520 B.C. Nothing very much appears to have been done during Roman times, except to maintain and repair this early excavation. 'Amr, the great Arab conqueror of Egypt, had a new canal built, which linked Cairo with the Red Sea near the modern town of Suez. None of these early ventures attempted to cut right through the isthmus itself, although it is possible that the slave-labour force available to the ancient Pharaohs would have been capable of cutting such a canal. But in the days of the Egyptian Empire, and later of the Arabs, a ruler's concern was for communication between Egypt itself (the Nile and Cairo) and the Red Sea. There would have been no advantage, indeed, positive danger, in opening a direct connection through their own land between the Mediterranean and the Red Sea. The first man on record to have projected a canal through the isthmus, the famous Harun-al-Rashid, is said to have been deterred from the project by the thought that the Byzantine fleet might storm through it and attack Arabia. Napoleon, apart from his other troubles and concerns, was mainly deterred from embarking upon the construction by his engineer, J. M.

Lepère, who had come to the erroneous conclusion that there was a difference of nearly thirty feet between the levels of the Mediterranean and the Red Sea.

It was after reading the memoirs of Lepère that Ferdinand de Lesseps, a member of the French consular service, decided that the plan was practicable. More advanced scientific knowledge backed his conclusions, and in 1854 the Compagnie Universelle du Canal Maritime de Suez was constituted, with the avowed aim of constructing a ship canal through the isthmus. It was inevitable that the British should be against the idea from the start. Here, yet again, was a threat to India – a new line of communications being opened, and the whole operation in the hands of their old enemies, the French. Lord Palmerston, who was then Prime Minister, did all he could to prevent De Lesseps from securing any support. He maintained that it was an impossibility, in any case; that it would injure British maritime supremacy; and that he had no intention of having any French interference in the East. De Lesseps, however, had a close friend in Said Pasha, who in 1886 formally gave the concession to the Frenchman. Subscription lists for the company were opened; the capital was to be 200 million francs in 400,000 shares. In less than a month over 300,000 shares had been applied for. France asked for the bulk of these shares – 200,000 – and the Ottoman Empire for 96,000. England, together with Austria, the United States, and Russia, held resolutely aloof from the whole concern. The residue of the shares was taken up by Said Pasha. It was this Egyptian holding which was later to prove the Achilles' heel to any French dream of becoming the dominant partner in the canal company.

On April 25, 1859, the first spadeful of sand was turned near the site of what was to become the port and city called after Said Pasha. This was as momentous an event in the history of the Mediterranean as any of the great battles that had been fought upon its waters. It was to give the whole sea a new lease of life, and to determine its future for the next century. Under the Ottomans, the eastern end of the basin had relapsed into a stagnant lake, an area that the great maritime powers could afford to avoid – and did. But the construction of the Suez Canal, against which the British had fought so hard, was in the end to give them a new and speedy route to India, as well as enlivening the whole trade of the inland sea.

Another thing that the construction of the canal brought about – and this was a further reason why Lord Palmerston had mistrusted the idea from the start – was to involve Britain in the affairs of Egypt. No foreign power throughout history seems to have been able to cope with Egypt without burning its fingers. Gibbon's description of "the super-stition and obstinacy of the Egyptians", although applied to the period in which Alexander had founded his great city, still remained true. As the British found out in due course, the modern Egyptians were just as inclined to "abandon themselves to the ungoverned rage of their passions". However much the genetic structure of the inhabitants of a country may be changed by centuries of conquest, reconquest, and inter-marriage with many nations, it seems that climatic and geographic conditions reshape the inhabitants into something like the original pattern. Faction had been, was, and remained as much a part of the Egyptian nature as of the Greek.

Meanwhile, despite the complex international web of rivalry and intrigue, the canal slowly advanced. By early 1862, the sweet-water canal, designed to connect Cairo with Suez, had reached Lake Timsah, and by the end of the same year the first channel of the ship canal proper had reached the same point. Britain, together with other countries, now protested loudly against the system of forced labour which was employed; but not, it seems, because they cared overmuch about the *fellahin*, who, in any case, were living better than they normally did. After much argument, this international protest led to the abolition of such labour: a fact which was probably the salvation of the whole enter-prise, for it entailed the introduction of modern machinery and engin-eering methods. At times near-bankruptcy threatened the whole project, and in 1866 the company had to sell to the Egyptian govern-ment a large estate which De Lesseps had purchased from his friend Said Pasha. In the end, the total expenditure proved to be over four hundred million francs – more than double the original estimate. Nevertheless, by November 1869 the canal was finished. After a formal opening ceremony, the wife of Napoleon III, Eugénie, Empress of France, steamed down the canal in the royal yacht, followed by the vessels of sixty-seven other nations. From Port Said to Suez the total length of the canal was one hundred miles, but it had shortened the passage to India and the Far East by thousands of miles. Ironically

Napoleon at the Battle of
the Pyramids, 1798

Nelson's flagship, H.M.S. *Victory*

THE SUEZ CANAL

Tenniel's famous comment
on Disraeli's coup

The opening of the Canal in 1869

enough, the first merchantman to proceed down the canal and pay her dues was British-owned.

It very soon became evident to the British that, despite their earlier hostility to the project, they would benefit from it more than anyone else. In the first year of operation 486 vessels with a gross tonnage of 654,915 had used the canal, and the receipts were £206,373. This figure trebled within five years, and it was plain that before long millions of tons of shipping would be using the canal annually. It was at this moment that Benjamin Disraeli, now Prime Minister of Britain, pulled off the most brilliant stroke of his career. The new ruler of Egypt, Ismail Pasha, had an Oriental streak of extravagance (far greater than Disraeli's own), and within a comparatively few years had reduced his country to a state of bankruptcy. Ismail, however, now owned some 177,000 shares in the canal. Disraeli, who was well aware of all this, borrowed four million pounds on his own account from the Rothschilds, in the name of the cabinet, and bought Ismail's shares. Parliament's approval for his audacious (and totally unparliamentary) action was not slow in forthcoming. Disraeli had made Britain the owner of nearly 50 per cent of the company.

Three years later, with the aims of curtailing Russian ambitions in the Mediterranean and preserving the security of the canal, Disraeli (by now Lord Beaconsfield) came to his agreement with Turkey whereby Cyprus became to all intents and purposes a British possession. "The Old Jew", as some of his opponents called him, had secured a life-line through the Mediterranean that stretched from Gibraltar at the western gate to the new eastern gate at Port Said. Bismarck was quick to perceive what the canal meant to Britain, and could mean to her enemies. "It is," he said, "the cord in the neck of the British Empire that connects the spine with the brain."

As bastions and outriders to this channel of sea-communications and commerce the British now had Malta and Cyprus. The man whose imagination had been touched by the East in those early days when, with "long hyacinthine curls", he had appalled the garrison in Malta, had made Byron's "red coats and redder faces" the masters of the ancient sea. Cyprus, which he had once called "the rosy realm of Venus", and "the romantic kingdom of the Crusaders", he now handed to his Queen and her people. It is an interesting fact that this great statesman was descended on his father's side from an Italian Jewish family, and on his mother's side from distinguished Spanish and Portuguese Jewish stock. He thus united in his blood the western, central, and eastern basins of the sea. One of the greatest Prime Ministers in Britain's history, Disraeli was a complete Mediterranean man.

TEN

The Great Transformation

The harbours, cities, and even the small fishing ports of the sea were now ineradicably changed by the industrial age and the advent of the steamship. Old methods of ship construction and repair that had hardly altered in thousands of years were adapted from canvas and wood to coal-fired boilers and iron. Great coaling stations like Gibraltar, Malta, and Port Said adapted themselves from sail to steam without much difficulty, because the presence of the Royal Navy and British capital made such changes not only necessary, but also comparatively easy to effect. Venice languished upon its lagoons – delighting foreign travellers and aesthetes – but the real movement of life was elsewhere. Toulon, main port for the French fleet; Genoa, recapturing some of its ancient pride through the commercial abilities of its citizens; mercantile Marseilles; earthquake-shaken Messina; Algiers under its new French rulers: these cities and a number of others like them managed to adapt to the requirements of the new age. The nineteenth century was a curious patchwork era, in which certain sections of the sea became reflections of the industrial North, while others were only partly affected, and yet others remained almost totally unchanged, breathing the same atmosphere and the same climate of opinion that they had breathed for centuries. It was, after all, hardly to be expected that the French and the Industrial revolutions should completely shatter the habits of ages, in an area which had known so many marchings and countermarchings of races, religions, and cultures.

In Italy itself, once the heart of this sea, and for so many centuries either under foreign occupation or a network of divided minor principalities, the leaven of France – the memory of those principles which the great conqueror had preached (even if he had not always practised them) – was quick to swell the Republican cause. Giuseppe

Mazzini, the idealist, was inspired by the classical ideas of Republican Rome, and he has rightly been described as the "saint of the Italian republican movement". Camillo Benso di Cavour, whose first venture into journalism, *Il Risorgimento* (The Revival), gave its name to the movement that ultimately unified Italy, was an intellectual liberal. Giuseppe Garibaldi was a Byronic romantic, whose landing with the "Thousand" in Sicily resulted in the return of this eternally disputed island, as well as the kingdom of Naples, to the new King of Italy. These three men, together with Pope Pius IX, were the principal figures in the long struggle that convulsed Italy for many years – from 1820 until 1870 – when the expulsion of its foreign rulers was at last achieved, and the long peninsula possessed its own identity for the first time in many centuries. It is perhaps not without some significance that these four men were all northern Italians by birth. The only other people who had ever made a cohesion out of Italy, the Romans, had also been northerners.

The enthusiasm that the cause of liberty in Europe evoked during this period can be gauged by the innumerable political speeches, books, tracts, and poems composed by the committed and the uncommitted. In England, where the memory of Byron's involvement with Greece would never be forgotten, another romantic poet, Algernon Swinburne, hailed the pattern of events on the continent in verse which, though far from his best, conveys the feelings of the time:

The heart of the rulers is sick, and the high-priest covers his head:
For this is the song of the quick that is heard in the ears of the dead. . . .
The wind has the sound of a laugh in the clamour of days and of deeds:
The priests are scattered like chaff, and the rulers broken like reeds.

Revolutions unfortunately are only made by fallible men, and, though they may improve the lot of the peoples involved, they inevitably produce another set of problems which are often as difficult to solve as the previous ones. The coalescence of peoples in Europe during the second half of the nineteenth century, resulting in the emergence of new nation states – Italy and Germany, for example – did not necessarily herald an era of sweetness and light. The old Roman instinct of "divide and rule" (which Britain had to some extent inherited) had been a sound one, even if cynical. But this word may be used in more than one way; for the original cynic philosophers had merely disapproved of wealth, ease, and luxury. In its generally accepted modern sense, "cynical" has become applied to those who deny the sincerity of human motives and actions. There are, indeed, "sincere" men – with all their faults, Mazzini, Cavour, and Garibaldi were examples of such. But the trouble with such men is that their activities are often exploited by the less sincere. In the history of the Mediterranean, it sometimes seems that less harm has been done by realists ("cynics", as some would call them) than by idealists. This is not to say that the unification of Italy was, in any sense, something that should not have happened; but merely that the fact of its happening produced a further set of problems which have hardly been resolved by the seventh decade of the twentieth century.

The settlement of Algeria by the French was another major event of this period. Like the transformation of Italy, it was an operation that took many years to effect. Although Algiers was firmly in French hands from 1830 onwards, and Turkish rule had been ended, the French found that this in no way meant that the country itself was theirs. Every yard of territory was disputed by the native population; and for some time the French were forced to confine their occupation to the principal ports along the coast – Algiers itself, Oran, Bougie, and Bône. Their conquest of the country started, in fact, in exactly the same way as Barbarossa's had done. Only gradually was the area brought under control. The important rich province of Constantine was organized under a French commandant in 1838, but it was a further twenty years before the whole of Algeria was securely in French hands. Even after this, there were constant revolts among the wild tribes of the hinterland; revolts that were still occurring right into the twentieth century. The Algerian hill tribes, rather like the bandits of Barbagia in Sardinia, had never really acknowledged any of the imperial powers which had occupied their country. Romans, Arabs, and Turks had found that it was often wisest to leave these freedom-loving horsemen alone in their gloomy mountains rather than to attempt to subjugate them. Frenchmen were recruited for resettlement in North Africa from among the poor and the unemployed of Paris and other major cities, and thus large areas of Algeria were slowly transformed into an echo of the mother country. Finally the colony was declared a French territory, and was divided into departments somewhat similar to those of France. At long last the scourge of the Algerian pirates had been laid, and a revived Algeria once more made its contribution to the trade and stability of the Mediterranean.

The kingdom of Tunisia went bankrupt in 1869, and the French (on a secret understanding with the British) moved into the ancient homeland of Carthage. The conquest of the country was not effected without a struggle, but by the 1880s nearly all Tunisia was under French control – not as a colony, but as a French protectorate. Industrialization and French culture, as in Algeria, rapidly restored this famous territory to the community of Mediterranean nations.

Not since the second century A.D. had the Mediterranean basin known such peace and prosperity as it did by the second half of the nineteenth century. It had taken 1700 years of barbarism, warfare, stagnation, and torpor for human affairs to return to something that approximated to the genial climate of the sea itself.

At the eastern end of the sea, where lines of shipping now steamed slowly through the desert – their funnels, masts, and superstructures rearing up incongruously against a foreground of sand, camels, long-robed *fellahin*, and ancient squalor – another struggle was taking place. This time it was for the control of Egypt. The bankrupt condition of the country (which had led to Ismail selling his canal shares to Disraeli) had inevitably brought a series of international inquiries; each one of which caused Egypt to come more and more under European control. British and French bondholders now had a very large stake in the political and economic stability of this country through which ran a large source of their incomes. By 1879, Egypt was virtually governed by a dual control system set up by the British and the French, the one country being concerned with finance and the other with public works. Ismail had been forced into retirement and his son appointed his successor. For two years the system worked smoothly enough, although it was inevitable that it should antagonize the upper classes who had for so long misgoverned Egypt for their own benefit. A social conscience or a humane concern for one's less fortunate fellows had not at any time played a part in Egyptian philosophy.

A movement of revolt gradually matured throughout the country, and it was ably led by an Egyptian army officer, Ahmed Arabi. As so often happens, the leader was an honest and devoted idealist who had grown tired of seeing his country either mismanaged by Turks or managed for their own convenience by "Franks" – the English and the French. Again, the leader was no more than the tool of others considerably more powerful, who used him solely with a view to promoting their own interests. Their scheme succeeded for a time, and Arabi managed to wring a number of concessions from the government. But this state of affairs did not last long. In June 1882, a riot developed in Alexandria in which a considerable number of Europeans were killed. A month later, a British admiral, in command of a squadron of eight ironclads, requested that Arabi should cease adding further guns to the city's forts; when he received no satisfactory reply the squadron opened fire on them, destroying two and damaging the others. The city itself, however, was almost untouched, for naval gunnery had reached a point where a shore bombardment could be rigidly selective. Since it was now clear that the only way to settle the trouble in Egypt was by landing armed forces, the British invited the French to co-operate with them. The French declined, as did the Italians, who were the next to be invited. Neither country was willing to involve itself too deeply; possibly both hoped, if the British were successful, to benefit materially while at the same time maintaining in Egyptian eyes the benevolent aspect of neutrality.

In September 1882, therefore, a British force was landed; Arabi was defeated and exiled; and the British found themselves governors of the country. They had little real wish to be so, and, as they explained in a missive to the governments of Europe, they felt that their position required of them "the duty of giving advice with the object of securing that the order of things to be established shall be of a satisfactory character and possess the elements of stability and progress."

From now on, for a further fifty years and more, the British were entangled in the affairs of Egypt – a thankless task, and one necessitated only by their concern about the canal that led to their Indian Empire. Their subsequent involvement in the Sudanese War, the eternal problems of maintaining law and order in the Nile Delta, the complexities of reorganization and policy: all these belong to the history of Egypt rather than to that of the Mediterranean. In 1960, writing of Alexandria itself, E. M. Forster concluded: "Her future like that of other great commercial cities is dubious. Except in the cases of Public Gardens and the Museum, the Municipality has scarcely risen to its historic responsibilities. The Library is starved for want of funds, the Art Gallery cannot be alluded to, and links with the past have been wantonly broken. . . . Material prosperity based on cotton, onions, and eggs, seems assured, but little progress can be discerned in other directions, and neither the Pharos of Sostratus nor the Idylls of Theocritus nor the Enneads of Plotinus are likely to be rivalled in the future. Only the climate, only the north wind and the sea remain as pure as when Menelaus, the first visitor, landed upon Ras-el-Tin, three thousand years ago; and at night the constellation of Berenice's Hair still shines as brightly as when it caught the attention of Conon the astronomer."

Except for its reappearance as an important naval base in the world wars of the twentieth century, Alexandria once again fades from the story of this sea. Its own history during the past fifty years and more reflects that of Egypt and of much of that area which is (inaccurately) known as the Middle East.

The psychology of the peoples in this part of the Mediterranean is best indicated by a story couched in fable form – and attributed to an Alexandrian Greek, possibly one of Aesop's descendants. "A frog was crouched on the sandy banks of the sweet-water canal near Ismailia in Egypt, just preparing to swim across, when he heard a voice behind him. He turned round and saw to his alarm that he was being addressed by a scorpion. 'Don't be frightened,' said the latter, 'I was only about to ask a favour of you. Would you be so kind as to ferry me across to the other side where my wife and family are waiting for me?' 'I should think not,' said the frog, preparing to jump in at once. 'No sooner had you got on my back than you would sting me to death!' 'Now wouldn't that be absurd,' said the scorpion smoothly, 'for, if I did, I should drown with you. Scorpions can't swim, you know.' 'You have a point there,' said the frog thoughtfully, and – for he was a good-hearted fellow – 'All right, jump aboard!' The scorpion embarked, and the frog struck out for the far bank. Half-way across he was horrified to find that the scorpion had stung him. The venom acted swiftly. As he began to sink, he looked up at his passenger and cried, 'You've killed me! Now we shall both drown! What did you do that for? It doesn't make sense!' 'Of course it doesn't,' said the scorpion as the water closed over both of them, 'but we are in the Middle East, you know!'"

The Suez Canal had transformed the Mediterranean, and was undoubtedly the most significant event in the sea's history during this century. Of far less importance, but interesting since it solved an age-old problem, was the opening of the Corinth Canal in 1893. The narrow rocky isthmus of Corinth, less than four miles wide at its narrowest point, divides the Gulf of Corinth, which leads into the Ionian, from the Aegean Sea. In classical times it had been one of the most disputed areas in the world, and it was the existence of this barrier between one sea and another that had given the ancient city of Corinth its maritime importance. Ships wishing to avoid the long and often stormy route round Cape Matapan, the southern tip of Greece, off-loaded at Corinth and were dragged across the isthmus on rollers. Corinth collected trans-shipment dues, and became an important centre of the entrepôt trade, as well as evolving into a great manufacturing city in its own right.

In A.D. 66, when the Emperor Nero was making his triumphant cultural tour of Greece, he had projected cutting a canal through the isthmus, and work was actually begun in the following year. But Nero died soon afterwards, and his death, combined with the material difficulties encountered, led to this first attempt being abandoned. Nearly two millennia passed before the canal was finally made. Even with the machinery available in the late nineteenth century, it took twelve years to cut the canal, which is a little over three miles long, approximately sixty-nine feet wide at the base, and affords passage for ships of no more than twenty-two-feet draught. For small passenger and cargo ships, as well as for fishing and coastal vessels, it still serves a useful purpose. But, even when it was first opened, it was not deep enough for the larger tonnages, and with the steady increase in the size of ships, it has become somewhat outmoded. The saving of distance by using the canal is considerable for vessels bound from the Adriatic and the western coast of Greece for ports in the Aegean and Black seas. From Sicily, the west coast of Italy, and southern France the saving is of little consequence; from Messina, for instance, to Piraeus and Istanbul the distance saved is about fifty and eighty miles respectively. Those who have benefited most by the canal are the fishermen, caique skippers, and coastal sailors of Greece, who can now move from the brisk, island-studded waters of the Aegean to the soft, hazy Ionian within a matter of hours. If the canal had been cut in classical times, it would have made an immense difference to maritime affairs. Galleys would have been able to pass swiftly from one sea to another, and the whole course of history might have been altered.

ELEVEN

Another Century

Apart from the change to steam-driven ships fired by coal – so soon after the First World War to be superseded by oil fuel – there was another major revolution in the appearance of the Mediterranean during the nineteenth century. From cape and headland, from the steep sides of islands like the Liparis or lonely promontories like Cape Matapan, the lights began to stammer out their warnings. All over this sea, as in all the other areas of the world where the major shipping routes passed, the new lighthouses, products of nineteenth-century technology, began to flash their messages of rock, shoal, or headland.

A new safety at sea, complementing the advances that had been made in cartography and navigational methods and instruments, was introduced when the great builders and technicians of the Victorian era turned their attention to lighthouse construction and design. The immense increase in shipping during the nineteenth century (when world trade developed beyond all measure) coupled with the new speeds attainable by modern vessels made an improvement in lighthouse methods essential. In the past, when galley or galleon, galliass or ship-of-the-line, had a rate of advance of only a few knots, it had been less necessary for the land to send out a long-range warning of its presence. All was now changed. Even where it was sail that still drove the merchantmen – such as the great clipper ships which were cleaving the Atlantic and the Pacific – the rate of approach might be as much as fourteen knots. At these speeds it was essential that the dangers which haunt all coastlines should be signalled long in advance.

Even in the past, the necessity of indicating an important headland or port had led to the construction of lighthouses. The first of any note, perhaps the first real lighthouse in the world, had been the great Pharos of Alexandria. Subsequently the Romans, with their usual thoroughness, had constructed lighthouses at all their major Mediterranean ports. Ostia, the port of Rome; Ravenna, the western empire's second capital; Puteoli, just north of Naples and commanding the trade route between Rome and the great southern city; and Messina, that embattled harbour dominating the famous strait: these were but a few of the places where the Romans had built lighthouses. Outside the sea itself they had erected them at the mouth of the Garonne, and far north in the English Channel, at Dover and Boulogne. At La Coruña, departure point across the Bay of Biscay for the distant "Tin Islands", the Phoenicians had built a lighthouse that was later restored in the reign of the Emperor Trajan. There must have been hundreds of others of which there is no record, for the sea had been so thoroughly tamed during the golden age of the Roman Empire that merchant ships constantly made landfalls at night. The real darkness had fallen in succeeding centuries; centuries in which men were not eager to advertise the presence of their cities to the innumerable pirates who, generation after generation, haunted the waterways.

George R. Putnam, in the *Encyclopaedia Britannica*, comments on some of the later buildings: "The light of Cordouan, on a rock in the sea at the mouth of the Gironde, provides the first example now existing of a wave-swept tower. Two earlier towers on the same rock are supposed to have been built, the first by Louis le Debonnaire (c. A.D. 805) and the second by Edward the Black Prince. The existing structure was begun in 1584 during the reign of Henry II of France, and completed in 1611. The upper part of the beautiful Renaissance building was removed towards the end of the 18th century. . . . [Until then] the light was exhibited by means of an oak-log fire, and subsequently a coal fire was in use for many years. The ancient tower at Corunna, known as the Pillar of Hercules, is supposed to have been a Roman Pharos. The Torre del Capo at Genoa . . . was built in 1139 and first used as a lighthouse in 1326. . . . The Pharos of Meloria was constructed by the Pisans in 1154 and was several times rebuilt until it was finally destroyed in 1290."

All of these early lighthouses suffered from the grave disadvantage that they were dependent upon wood for their fuel and, at a later date, upon coal. Neither of these were satisfactory, particularly in the winter months when rain fell and high winds blew. Some of them were particularly expensive to maintain, one being quoted as using as much as four hundred tons of coal a year (no small amount in those days of difficult transportation). The light in all these early structures was provided by a fire burning on grates or chauffers at the top of the structure. No efficient forms of mirror were then available, and it was not until the sixteenth century that reflectors were used behind lamps lit by oil or large candles. (One lighthouse was powered by twenty-four candles, five of which weighed two pounds.) The placing of a parabolic mirror behind the source of light meant that all the rays of light which fell upon its surface were reflected parallel to the axis, emerging as a beam of light. This was the beginning of the lighthouse proper, which transformed the Mediterranean from the nineteenth century onwards.

Olive oil was often used to fuel the cotton skeins that formed the wicks of the lamp, as well as whale oil and animal fat. In the nineteenth century these were slowly superseded by paraffin, while later, in areas adjacent to big cities, coal gas was used. The greatest transformation of all came when electricity took over the task of illumination, although this again was limited to large ports until small efficient generators were devised. Acetylene supplied the light for many of the small or un-attended stations throughout the sea.

There are, to quote George R. Putnam again, "three lines of defence [to the coasts of a country]. There are first great sea lights which indicate important 'landfalls', and require the most powerful apparatus; secondary lights which, though not requiring to be so powerful as these of the first order, are of great importance, as indicating turning-points in navigation; and, lastly, harbour lights to guide ships into havens of safety. . . ." All of these were being erected throughout the Mediterranean during the late nineteenth and early twentieth centuries. The new security that they offered the mariner was without parallel in history. From Alexandria to the Piraeus, from the Gulf of Patras to Trieste, southwards via Cape Spartivento at the toe of Italy, round Sicily's southern cape of Passero, westwards past Cape Bon and Tunis to the distant, cloud-broomed Rock of Gibraltar, a necklace of lights was laid upon the sea. Along the southern coast of France, with its many ports and harbours, they sparkled like a *rivière* of diamonds, while in western Italy, Corsica, and Sardinia the lights were individual brilliants set in a velvet ribbon of darkness. It was several decades before the coasts themselves, with their towns, hill villages, roads, and houses, spread a banner of light all round the sea. When that happened, the navigator nearing a port would once more have to strain his eyes – this time not so much to descry the loom of a light or the dark shoulders of the land, but to distinguish between the guidelights for which he was searching and the innumerable conflicting signs of cafés, restaurants, hotels, and advertisements.

In this transition period, there had ensued a period of comparative peace for almost one hundred years. During this time, with the exception of the areas under Ottoman control, the Mediterranean benefited immensely from the ideas liberated by the French Revolution and those other, and more pragmatic, ideas generated by the Industrial Revolution.

Although the First World War did not directly stem from the Mediterranean, did not see the major part of its action in this area, and was not resolved there either, the basin and the lands around it were indeed at the heart of the matter. The troubled state of the Balkans, the steady degeneration of the Ottoman Empire, the ambition of the Germans towards overseas empire (inevitably their eye fell upon Egypt, just as Napoleon's had done), all these were contributory factors to a war that was to be waged all over the world. Just as Corcyra had been the apple of discord that had led to the Peloponnesian War, so it was a comparatively minor issue that was largely responsible for the explosion which was to blow the continent to pieces.

Helen, an adulterous queen, had been made the scapegoat for the Trojan War – which was really caused by the far more important issue of the control of the Dardanelles and the Russian grain trade. Similarly, the relatively unimportant area of the Balkans triggered the worst war in the history of mankind. The assassination of Francis Ferdinand, Archduke of Austria, on June 28, 1914, in Sarajevo, the obscure capital of Bosnia, was similar in effect to the rape of Helen. The event, except to the individuals concerned, was not important in itself, but it provided the lever which set immense forces in motion.

It is not within the framework of this history to chronicle in any detail the two world wars that were to change the face of Europe and the Mediterranean, and to alter the whole pattern of life in almost every country in the world. It is still too early to see the twentieth century in perspective. The modern historian inevitably labours under the disadvantage of being too close to his subject. Events, names, and reputations which bulk large to a contemporary historian are often seen, from the standpoint of later centuries, to fall into quite different categories from those into which he assigns them. To gain any real objectivity, at least a century must separate the historian from his subject. In the overall history of the Mediterranean Sea, for instance, it may well be found that Gaiseric the Vandal, or 'Amr, conqueror of Egypt, are of more significance than Kitchener of Khartoum or Mussolini.

Everything flows, and nations, cities, and the deeds of individual men are often transmuted or drowned entirely under the silt of the ages. It is possible that poets greater than Homer have existed, but we do not know their works. It may be that Diogenes was a more considerable philosopher than Socrates, but he had no Plato to immortalize him. In the day of Magna Graecia, the greatest city of all the Greek foundations was Sybaris. It has given us no more than a word in the English language. The site of Sybaris has been found, but it is twenty feet beneath the soil, and it is possible that it will never be excavated. On the other hand, Pompeii, that relatively unimportant Roman seaside resort, is a household name, and the works excavated from it have left a permanent mark upon the furniture and taste of Europe. Our knowledge of the past is conditioned by fate and fortune. But our knowledge of recent events is inevitably conditioned by the circumstances of our personal lives or by inherited prejudices. What Englishman, Frenchman, German, or American can discuss the events of the last two world wars as dispassionately as if he were talking about some reaction taking place in a chemical experiment in a test-tube? History, whatever some may pretend, is not an exact science. It is dependent upon limited, and often biased, evidence, and the elements that might correct the bias are only too frequently not available. (It would have been a valuable corrective to have a history of the Romans written by a Carthaginian.) Clio, the Muse of History, has more in common with her poetic sisters than she has with Urania, the Muse of Astronomy and the exact sciences.

At the turn of the century, in 1899, the British Colonial Secretary, Joseph Chamberlain, remarked: "The most natural alliance is that between us and the German Empire." There was some substance for his statement – a basic bond of blood and language, and some similarity of temperament. The newly united German people, however, did not reciprocate these sentiments. They suspected them as evidence of that liberalizing English corruption against which Bismarck had warned them. They saw in them, too, and in other similar expressions, an attempt by a decadent power to shore up its imperial gains by recourse to a new and virile race.

Edward VII, for his part, was enamoured of France, and it was not unnatural therefore that he should try – as far as was possible within the framework of British constitutional monarchy – to impel his country towards the *Entente Cordiale* with her ancient enemy. The German Kaiser, William II, while admiring certain aspects of aristocratic England, had little or no use for the country's other traits. He disliked his corpulent uncle and was consumed with envy for the vast British possessions overseas. Even in the extraordinary complex of human affairs in the twentieth century – so much more involved than those seemingly simple webs which had impelled ancient empires or city-states to join battle with one another – there was still a personal element involved. If the English King and the German Emperor had been on friendly terms with one another, it is just possible that the First World War might have been avoided.

As far as the Mediterranean was concerned, all the actions in this theatre were but side-shows to the main horrific drama that was taking place on the continent. Nevertheless, the expeditions to the Dardanelles, Salonika, and Mesopotamia all involved the transport of tens of thousands of men across this sea. Once again, despite the new menace of submarine warfare, the British and their French allies accomplished these immense movements of men and material more successfully even than they had done in the Crimean War.

The objective of the Dardanelles expedition as laid down by the War Council in January 1915 was "to take the Gallipoli peninsula, with Constantinople as its objective." It was rightly seen that Germany's Turkish allies were the potential Achilles' heel of the Central Powers. The Allied effort, however, was not made with sufficient decisiveness and fully adequate forces to achieve what was a strategically sound objective. By the time reinforcements had been sent to back up the initial force which had landed at Cape Hellas, the Turks, with the advantage of their interior lines of communication, had brought up more than enough divisions to keep the Allies pinned down on their beachheads. When in January 1916 the decision to withdraw was made, the whole operation could be seen as a costly failure. It was, nevertheless, an operation which might have drastically curtailed the war had the initial blow been struck with sufficient strength. Once again Allied sea power proved itself superbly efficient. All the troops were withdrawn from the embattled peninsula without the loss of a single man. The campaign itself, however, had cost the British alone 120,000 casualties.

The Salonika campaign, which was principally undertaken with the objectives of checking German influence in the Balkans and taking some of the pressure off Serbia, lasted from 1915 to 1918. In the end, it was crowned with success – the first decisive Allied military success of the war – but against this must be laid the fact that for three years it kept a large part of the Allied forces bottled up within the chain of mountain ridges that protect the Balkans. The German remark that Salonika was their "largest internment camp" contained an element of truth. Even so, the overthrow of Germany's ally Bulgaria in 1918 began a series of capitulations which ended with that of Germany itself on November 11 of that year.

It was in the eastern basin of the sea, and centring inevitably around Egypt and the Suez Canal, that the major events in the Mediterranean theatre took place. The Turks had made an abortive attempt to invade Egypt in 1915, but the British, only too well aware of the value of that narrow neck of water connecting the Mediterranean to the Red Sea, had more than sufficient troops to counter any threat in this direction. In 1916 they themselves took the offensive, and advanced north into Palestine. Despite some initial setbacks, the Palestine expedition ended in success with the capture of Jerusalem by General Edmund Allenby in 1917. Since this was the only triumph of that year for the Allies, the importance of the city's capture has sometimes been exaggerated. But Jerusalem, as so often in the past, was more than just a city – it was a symbol to Moslem and Christian alike. And whatever power held it, seemed to have acquired the virtue of victory. On the other hand, as Sir Basil Liddell Hart observes: "As a moral success the feat was valuable, yet viewed strategically, it seemed a long way round to the goal. If Turkey be pictured as a bent old man, the British, after missing their blow at his head – Constantinople – and omitting to strike at his heart – Alexandretta – had now resigned themselves to swallowing him from the feet upwards, like a python dragging its endless length across the desert."

Throughout the long years of war, while millions of men were dying on the continent, and while the oceans of the world were devastated by the thunder of depth charges, the hiss of torpedoes, and the up-ended stems and sterns of merchant ships as they prepared for their death-dive, the Mediterranean was mainly unruffled. The immense superiority that their fleets and their dominant bases gave the British and the French in this sea made it one of the most peaceful areas in the world. Large islands like Cyprus and Sicily and Sardinia lived through these years as if there was no more than a summer storm flickering far away on the horizon. The shores of North Africa slumbered peacefully under French rule. All around the basin to north and east the tides of men swayed back and forth; but in the sea itself the fishermen of a myriad islands and ports put out with nets and lines in a security very similar to that which they had known for a century.

The final offensive in Palestine, which had been delayed for nearly six months because of the withdrawal to the Western Front of most of General Allenby's British troops, was finally resumed in the autumn of 1918. The conduct of his offensive was carefully planned. The mass of infantry and the cavalry were concentrated against the Turkish front on the Mediterranean coast in such a way that although the Turks had a numerical superiority of two to one, at the point where Allenby struck, his troops achieved a superiority of four to one. The Turks and the Germans were rolled back to the north-east in the direction of the hilly interior. Meanwhile, the Allied cavalry thundered north up the coastal corridor, finally swinging east to cut the Turks' communications and to deprive them of an escape route. It was one of the most brilliant actions involving the use of cavalry that had ever been seen in this area of the world, recalling in its dash and decision the exploits of Alexander the Great. It was, also, possibly the last major cavalry action in history.

The Turkish forces, trapped and encircled, were swiftly rounded up, and Allenby's men moved on to capture Damascus and Aleppo. On October 30, 1918, little more than a month after the offensive had started,

Turkey capitulated. It was the end of the Ottoman Empire. The Turks, who had been the dominant power in the eastern Mediterranean for five centuries, were henceforth to be confined to their territories in Asia Minor, together with the relatively small hinterland north of the Sea of Marmora known as Turkey-in-Europe. In the history of the Mediterranean there had been no upheaval of so great a consequence since the fall of Constantinople in 1453. It was true that, in the nineteenth century, Greece and Egypt had splintered away from Turkish control, but the Ottomans had, during their long period of empire, at one time or another terrorized all Europe, and later they had lain like a huge shadow over the once brilliant countries of the East. The passing of this empire could hardly be lamented, but, as always when any central authority collapses, its place would soon be taken by the violence of newly emergent nationalisms.

The defeat of Turkey may have solved some of the problems of the Levant and the Near East, but others would swiftly take shape. The British, in their anxiety to defeat Germany's ally and to make quite sure of the security of their lifeline to India, had enlisted the aid of the Arabs and had promised them much in return for it. As T. E. Lawrence, who played so large a part in this eastern campaign, wrote in his *Seven Pillars of Wisdom*: "Next in force [to personal ambition] had been a pugnacious wish to win the war: yoked to the conviction that without Arab help England could not pay the price of winning its Turkish sector. When Damascus fell, the Eastern war – probably the whole war – drew to an end." Lawrence was soon totally disillusioned with the subsequent policies of British governments towards the Arabs. The Arab lands, which, in the past, had been geographically important because of their trade routes, were now to assume an even greater significance. The oil which lay beneath their barren territories was to bring them once again into the forefront of history.

In the tumult of collapsing empires, the establishment of new nationalisms, the rejoicing of the victors, and the counting of the cost, one small factor might have gone unremarked by the historian. In November 1917, just one year before the war ended, Arthur James Balfour, the British Foreign Secretary, had made a solemn promise and had thus committed his country to fulfilling it. This, subsequently to be known as the "Balfour Declaration", was to the effect that, "His

531

Majesty's Government view with favour the establishment in Palestine of a national home for the Jewish people, and will use their best endeavours to facilitate the achievement of this object, it being clearly understood that nothing shall be done which may prejudice the civil and religious rights of existing non-Jewish communities in Palestine. . . ."

Thus Britain, in order to win the favour of world Jewry at a difficult moment in the war, undertook to reverse the Diaspora. The decree of the Roman Empire that the Jews should be dispersed was to be annulled by the decree of the British Empire. Whatever the merits or demerits of this policy, the British would find, as the Romans had done before them, that to meddle in the affairs of this corner of the Mediterranean was as dangerous as playing with a desert scorpion.

TWELVE

Peace – and War Again

Once more, when the dust and confusion had subsided, it became possible to see, through the slowly clarifying waters, what alterations had taken place in this eternally earthquake-ridden area of the world. In the West, Spain, which had remained neutral (though pro the Allies) throughout the war, tottered from one internal crisis to another. To the south, most of North Africa lay tranquil under the colonial hand of France. The British were still astride Egypt and the Suez Canal – their objectives apparently attained. But they now became involved in the affairs of Palestine. Under a mandate from the newly formed League of Nations, Palestine had become a territory officially appointed for British administration. At the same time, Arab nationalism, which had been asleep for centuries, became an increasing source of ferment. The British, who had (along with others) an expanding economic interest in the oil resources of the Arab countries, became even more involved in this explosive area, where, as in the fable of the frog and the scorpion, a nation would happily drown, provided that it could see its neighbour drowning with it.

But it was in the Aegean that the final act took place in a drama that had been playing for centuries. The "Asia Minor problem" – the problem of those hundreds of thousands of Greeks who lived outside their homeland in what had been ancient Ionia – had never been solved. They had lived there in the days when all Ionia was Greek; they had lived there under Persian occupation; liberated by the conquests of Alexander, they had created some of the greatest cities in the Greek world; they had been there throughout the Roman and Byzantine empires; and, finally, hundreds of years later, they had remained as subjects of the Ottomans. It was not until 1922 that this ancient problem was at long last brutally solved.

In 1919, Eleutherios Venizelos, the Greek Prime Minister, obtained leave from the British and French governments to land troops at Smyrna. The result was a disaster. The Turks had lost the war, but they were inspired and led by the greatest Turkish soldier of his time, Kemal Ataturk, the "Saviour of the Dardanelles". This iron man, who came of hardy Anatolian peasant stock, had all the will to victory as well as the diplomatic subtlety of some of the earlier Sultans. He was determined not only to expel the Greeks from the heartland of his race, but also to transform his own people. Turkey, he believed, had suffered because she had allowed herself to become enmeshed in the hatreds and rivalries of Europe. He would disentangle his country from European commitments; after which, he would reform it and make it a revived modern power. But his first problem was to deliver Anatolia from the Greeks.

In the war that followed, the Greeks, after some initial success, went from one misfortune to another – everything, as usual, being aggravated by political instability and chicanery. Venizelos was expelled, and the pro-German King Constantine returned to Greece. He promptly spurred his army on to a further rash adventure in Anatolia, where it suffered a major defeat. Worse was to follow. On August 26, 1922, the Greeks were totally routed and fell back in panic flight towards the coast. The Turks followed hard on their heels, and entered Smyrna in a manner reminiscent of their terrible advances in the fifteenth and six-teenth centuries.

The Greeks themselves had behaved in an atrocious manner during their occupation of the city, but they were now to learn that the old fury of the Ottoman Turk had not abated over the ages. Smyrna was devastated. A fire which broke out in the Armenian quarter burnt most of the city to the ground; in the words of a contemporary dispatch, "the loss of life is impossible to compute." Over a million Christians fleeing for their lives were rescued by Allied ships and transported across the Aegean to Greece and the islands. The dream of Ionia was extinguished, and in its place, dominant over the smoking battlefield, stood Kemal Ataturk, the man who was to fashion out of his backward country and illiterate people a twentieth-century state. As he himself said, when arguing with members of his new National Assembly who were doubtful of some of his reforms: "Sovereignty is acquired by force, by power, by violence. It was by violence that the sons of Othman acquired the power to rule over the Turkish nation and to maintain their rule for more than six centuries."

Meanwhile an immense problem confronted the Greeks and their friends in Europe: how to absorb and resettle well over a million immigrants. A young reporter, Ernest Hemingway, describes in the Toronto *Daily Star*, October 20, 1922, the flight of the Greeks from Thrace: "In a never-ending, staggering march the Christian population of Eastern Thrace is jamming the roads towards Macedonia. The main column crossing the Maritza River at Adrianople is twenty miles long. Twenty miles of carts drawn by cows, bullocks and muddy-flanked water buffalo, with exhausted, staggering men, women and children, blankets over their heads, walking blindly along in the rain. . . . It is all they can do to keep moving. Their brilliant peasant costumes are soaked and draggled. Chickens dangle by their feet from the carts. Calves nuzzle at the draught cattle wherever a jam halts the stream. An old man marches bent under a young pig, a scythe and a gun, with a chicken tied to his scythe. A husband spreads a blanket over a woman in labor in one of the carts to keep off the driving rain. She is the only person making a sound. Her little daughter looks at her in horror and begins to cry. And the procession keeps moving."

It is sad to reflect that such a report might have been duplicated thousands of times over in the long history of this sea. The immediate impact of such an event is to leave the observer stunned. Yet only thirteen years later, in 1935, H. A. L. Fisher, in *A History of Europe*, could write dispassionately: "Out of the burning wreck of Smyrna there arose an unfamiliar and more hopeful East. Two monarchies disappeared, the Greek and the Turkish, the one an alien institution of some ninety years, the other rooted in the immemorial traditions of the race of Othman. Greece became, by reason of its industrious Asiatic immigrants, richer, stronger, more populous than before. A like concentration of national power marked the new Turkish Republic of Mustapha Kemal." Turkey is still a republic, but the Greek monarchy was restored; although at present it is once again in exile, and the country is ruled by a military oligarchy.

In the years preceding the Second World War, while Spain on the sea's western flank presented a pitiable picture as the country slid towards one of the most bitter civil wars since that of nineteenth-century America, Italy began to rattle her ancient armour. The first of the new-style dictators emerged upon the European scene. Benito Mussolini, who did much for his country (and then lost all by becoming subservient to Germany's Adolf Hitler) was a demagogue of a type that had been seen often before in his own land and throughout the Mediterranean. He and Hitler were products of the chaotic political and economic circumstances which arose throughout Europe as the consequence of the war. But, although no more than Cleons of the marketplace, they were backed by the weight of modern industry and armaments.

Mussolini's involvement in Abyssinia was a folly; but his attempt to re-establish the Italian colonies that the Romans had once maintained in North Africa was not without its merits. It was a step towards solving Italy's over-population problem, and – if the war had not come – the hardy peasantry of southern Italy and Sicily might have pushed back the desert even further than they did manage to do. His rebuilding of ports (designed mainly for the new Italian fleet) and his road- and municipal-building schemes in derelict southern Italy and Sicily were, even if designed largely for self-aggrandizement, of considerable benefit to the people of these areas. Mussolini's impact upon the Mediterranean, although in many ways disastrous, was not entirely without value. His recognition of the problems of that large section of Italy which lies south of Naples was intelligent. In subsequent years it has inspired the first reasonable approach to all that area of their country which so many northern Italians have always dismissed as barbarous, adding patronizingly, "Africa begins at Naples."

As early as 1923, however, Ernest Hemingway had divined that Mussolini was not really *Il Duce*, who would restore his people and bring back Roman power to the Mediterranean. He writes in the Toronto *Daily Star* of January 27, 1923, "And then look at his black shirt and his white spats. There is something wrong, even histrionically, with a man who wears white spats with a black shirt." He continues, "The Fascist dictator had announced he would receive the press. Everybody came. We all crowded into the room. Mussolini sat at his desk reading a book. His face was contorted into the famous frown. He was registering Dictator. . . . I tip-toed over behind him to see what the book was he was reading with such avid interest. It was a French–English dictionary – held upside down."

The Fascist party, called after the Roman *fasces*, or rods that were carried in front of the chief magistrate as emblems of the authority of the state, was authoritarian in the extreme. Italian liberalism, the product of those nineteenth-century heroes of the *Risorgimento*, was swiftly strangled. As evidence of the new pretensions to represent "Rome Revived", Mussolini expanded the Italian navy. On the surface, at least, he created a formidable fleet of new battleships, cruisers, destroyers, and submarines. Faster and more modern than most of the British ships lying in the harbours of Malta, Gibraltar, and Alexandria, they constituted the first real challenge to British naval supremacy in the Mediterranean since the Napoleonic Wars. Italy's great weakness, however, and one which Mussolini might be able to disguise from the mass of his countrymen but not from clear-sighted observers outside, was the fact that the country had no native sources of fuel. To start with, she had no coal; and the fact that ships were now oil-fueled did not help, for Italy had no oil either. In the event of war with Britain, her imports from the East would automatically cease. If "lack of frigates" was written on Nelson's heart, "lack of oil fuel" was soon to be written on the hearts of the Italian admirals.

During the troubled twenty years between the two world wars – that period which Robert Graves has aptly called the "Long Weekend" – the sea was stirring uneasily. The French fleet was constantly on manoeuvres out of Toulon and its bases in North Africa; the Italian battle fleet paraded its new might over all the central area south as far as Tripoli; while the British Mediterranean fleet prowled between Alexandria, Malta, and Gibraltar. During this period there were more warships, and of greater capacity for destruction, active upon the surface of the Mediterranean than at any time in its previous history.

Mare Nostrum Mussolini had proudly called it, reminding his listeners that the whole sea was once again under Roman control, and that it was the intention of Fascism to reassert another ancient authority, the *Imperium Romanum*. As his ally, Adolf Hitler, pointed out, just prior to Italy's entry into the war in 1940: "The outcome of this war will also decide the future of Italy. If this future is considered in your country in terms of merely perpetuating the existence of a European state of modest pretensions, then I am wrong. But if this future is considered in terms of a guarantee of the Italian people from a historical, geopolitical and moral point of view, or according to the rights of your people, those who are fighting Germany today will be your enemies too."

Italy, in any case, could only be hoisted to victory on the back of Germany. To quote from A. J. P. Taylor's essay "The Supermen": "Italy . . . is dependent for her power on others, condemned to jackal diplomacy. The hesitations and manoeuvres of Mussolini were not . . . the results of doubt so much as a hero's resentment against the limit-ations of real life – truly, Mussolini was a hero of the suburbs. Vain and arrogant as he was, he yet had the sense to see that Italy could simulate greatness only by hunting with Hitler: he never suffered the futile misjudgement of those western diplomats who thought that Italy could take the place of Russia in an anti-Hitler coalition (a favourite idea of the British Foreign Office), and he never accepted for a moment the ambition of Italian diplomats, from Ciano downwards, to play fast-and-loose with Germany and yet swagger among the great." Mussolini, in fact, was a typical Latin bourgeois, imbued – but not to a sufficient extent – with Mediterranean pragmatism. His disaster, and Italy's, was to become involved in the Wagnerian dreams of Hitler. Once fastened to the wheel of the Juggernaut's car, he was unable to cut himself and his country free.

While the diseased condition of Europe – soon to be speeded by the economic plague of the American Depression – was hastening the fever crisis, the sea itself, its islands and coastlines, was being changed by a new, comparatively agreeable, phenomenon. This was the advent of tourism. Middle-class citizens (largely from Britain, the United States, and other prosperous countries) had now discovered the delights of the Mediterranean climate – its sun and sea, its wine and food, and its fabulous legacy of art and archaeology. Upon the Balearic Islands in the west, upon Crete, Cyprus, Egypt, and the Levant (particularly the Holy Land), there descended a new form of invader – one who paid money for his acquisitions.

The new visitors were a logical extension of the "Grand Tourists" of the eighteenth century, who had been followed in their turn by the Victorian *haute bourgeoisie*. Apart from the great cultural centres of Florence, Venice, Athens, and Rome, which had their own special attractions, there were many places where those who could afford it built summer villas for themselves, rented houses, or stayed in the new hotels which had been rising in ever-increasing frequency since the nineteenth century. A favourite of the Edwardian rich, for instance, had been Taormina (where a pæderastic German baron had taken many photographs of local youths in the nude – prints of which still hang in tobacconists' shops). Capri, with its erotic miasma supposedly left behind by Tiberius (but really the product of the gossip Suetonius) had long had its devotees. The whole of the south of France, spiced with wine and pine, was to become a haunt as frequented as it was fragrant.

European painters and writers, who had long ago found out for themselves the stimulating, yet comparatively cheap, delights of this sea that had mothered so many of their pictures and books, found themselves in economic competition with richer and less aesthetically minded visitors. The Mediterranean of Byron, Keats, and Shelley, of the French Impressionists, and of moderns like Matisse and Picasso was now to lure businessmen from all over the world. At the same time, since air travel was expensive and only in its infancy, this invasion was still largely undertaken only by those rich enough to be able to afford long summer holidays, hotels, villas, and private motor cars. The American Scott Fitzgerald, in his novel *Tender Is the Night*, has possibly caught the flavour of this period better than anyone else. This is a Mediterranean that has become a playground; where many of those who seek its shores for pleasure have little knowledge that it has ever been anything other than a midsummer play-pen for adults. Another novel, *The Rock Pool*, by the British writer Cyril Connolly, captures the feeling of this aspect of the inter-war Mediterranean – so remote from the harsh reality that was being evolved for it in the political power houses of the world.

"Naylor woke late, with a hang-over. . . . The sun streamed in over the purple bougainvillaea. He tottered down to the sea. . . . Opening his eyes, the sky and sand were grey as a photograph, his antennae played over the tiny crystals, women's brown legs passed him on the board-walk, but he could not look up. 'You see in me a creature in the most refined state of intoxication,' he thought, and waves of sensual and lotophagous reminiscence swept over him. He pushed his inert body slowly into the sea, till his back, his legs, and at last his bottom floated clear. There were no waves. The whole of the Juan-les-Pins shallows consisted of scent and oil, to where began, a hundred feet beyond them, the authentic brine."

A reminder that beneath the outwardly smiling, peaceful face of this Janus sea, there lay another visage – the cold mask of war – is to be found in innumerable books published in Italy and Germany during this period. One of them, *Il Mediterraneo*, by Hummel E. Siewert (its place and date are significant – Milan, 1938) is an exposition of the theory, common at that time, that it was Italy's destiny to rule the Mediterranean. "By the will of the Mediterranean people, by the affirmation of their national independence, the 'British Episode' in this sea is finished – that period during which, for some length of time, they included the basin of this sea in the security system of their imperial communication routes." Time was to show that, so long as the British retained their interest in India, so long would they have to concern themselves with their Mediterranean bases. Siewert queried whether Malta, in the new age of the aeroplane, could be said to have any further value, pointing out by means of a diagram that the island was within easy bombing-range of the Italian air force operating out of its bases in Sicily. Yet Malta was to survive; indeed, it was largely from her shores that the invasion was to be launched which would bring Italy to her knees.

Unlike the First World War, the Second World War, in the European theatre, was very largely fought out in the Mediterranean basin. This was because, with the fall of France in 1940, it was the only area in which the British and the Germans could get to grips with one another. It was also the area in which Italy was directly involved, and – once he had decided to throw in his lot with Hitler – it was here that Mussolini hoped for easy pickings. The battle for the control of the Mediterranean lasted for almost three years – from Italy's entry into the war in June 1940 to the final surrender of the Axis forces in Tunisia in May 1943. After that date, although there were to be land campaigns in Sicily and Italy, the control of the sea was never in doubt. Despite losses still occasioned by German submarines, the British and their American allies were able to transport great armadas of men and material with relative impunity.

One action which will long be famous in the history of Mediterranean warfare was the attack by Royal Naval aeroplanes, operating from the aircraft carrier *Illustrious*, on the Italian battle fleet in its southern base at Taranto. It was delivered after dark by twenty-one torpedo-carrying aircraft upon a concentration of five battleships, nine cruisers, and a number of destroyers and auxiliaries. The operation was an astounding success. The aircraft skimmed in low over the ships and dropped their torpedoes; despite an intense anti-aircraft barrage, the British lost only two aeroplanes. The Italians, in those brief blinding minutes, had their naval superiority destroyed and their morale shaken beyond measure. Two of their battleships were put out of action for months, while a third was a total loss. Captain Donald Macintyre comments in *The Battle for the Mediterranean*: "The scene in Taranto harbour which greeted the eye at dawn on the 12th November 1940 marked, for those who had eyes to see, the end of the battleship era in naval warfare. For five months two opposing battle-fleets had faced each other in the restricted waters of the Mediterranean, one unwilling to risk an action though superior in strength, the other unable to force one. Neither had been able to wield sea power over the other in the fullest sense. The Italians had been unable to prevent supplies being sent to Malta by sea. The British had been unable to cut the Italian supply line to North Africa.

"The relative strength of the two battle-fleets had now been reversed in favour of the British. Only two battleships remained available to the Italians against five in Cunningham's fleet."

Taranto was an action as significant in its way as Drake's at Cadiz in 1587. Although battleships would continue to be used in the Mediterranean and in the Pacific Ocean for the rest of the war, their passing was heralded that night when the torpedo-carrying aircraft altered the balance of power at sea in a few minutes. (Taranto served as the model for the Japanese attack upon Pearl Harbor, which later brought the United States into the war.) The huge armoured battleship, which had dominated the sea with its fifteen-inch guns since the turn of the century, now went to join the ship-of-the-line, the galleon, the galliass, and the galley in the museum of naval history.

Never before had so many areas of the Mediterranean been involved in war at the same time as during the years 1940 to 1944. After Mussolini's inefficient invasion of Greece and failure in Africa had involved the Germans in this theatre of war, there was hardly a cove, island, or port that did not at one time or another feel its effects. Italian-occupied Rhodes, for instance, was shelled by the British navy, while even obscure islands like Cos and Leros were later to become familiar with the headlong dash of destroyers, the whine of German dive-bombers, the thunder of depth charges, and the death-sigh of escaping air as ships rolled over and sank. From the Levant to Algeria, the battle rolled back and forth. Derna, Mersa Matruh, and Tobruk, places hitherto unknown except to coastal traders, featured in the headlines of the world. Crete witnessed a massive air-borne invasion, in which the Germans, although successful in capturing the island, lost the flower of their paratroops. In succouring Greece and Crete, the British themselves lost so many of their ships to air attack that they once again found themselves heavily on the defensive. Alexandria figured constantly in the news, for it had become the main British base – Malta for a time being untenable except by submarines. It was in Alexandria, too, that the Italians, in an action involving the use of miniature submarines, crippled two British battleships and to a great extent redeemed Taranto. Air power, although it showed that it more than had the edge over the defensive fire power of warships, was yet to prove insufficient to win a Mediterranean war. In the final analysis, it was still seen that invading armies, as well as their weapons, stores, and military material, must be carried by sea.

Although there were times when the British were very nearly excluded from the Mediterranean, they managed to hang on – though by a narrow margin – during the worst months of 1941–1942. Important to their plans, to their very existence even, was the retention of Malta, which once again, as it had done in 1565, achieved an importance in world affairs quite out of proportion to its size. It was from Malta alone that the British could most successfully strike at the enemy shipping route as it wound south between Italy and the main theatre of war in North Africa. British submarines accounted for hundreds of thousands of tons of German and Italian shipping bound for North Africa. If Malta had fallen there can be no doubt that, with his supply line intact, the German general Erwin Rommel would have successfully captured Cairo, Egypt, and the Suez Canal. If the small limestone island had been the hinge upon which Europe's fate had turned in the sixteenth century, it was equally so in the Second World War.

The story of the convoys that fought their way through to the beleaguered island from Gibraltar and Alexandria has been often told – and will continue to be, as long as men recall the memories of ancient wars. Less well known, however, is the pattern of life as it was lived by the Maltese people and the garrison of soldiers, sailors, and marines during those months when the German Luftwaffe and the Italian Regia Aeronautica hurled everything that they could at La Valette's impregnable fortress. In the middle of the nineteenth century, a British general, Whitworth Porter, in his *History of the Knights of Malta*, had said with prophetic insight: "English hearts and English swords now protect those ramparts which formerly glistened with the ensigns of the Order of St. John; and should occasion ever demand the sacrifice, the world will find that British blood can be poured forth like water in defence of that rock which the common consent of Europe has entrusted to her hands."

The following excerpts are from a letter written by a former Royal Marine who was present in the cruiser *Aurora* during the second siege of Malta. It gives something of the flavour of those times. "I first went to Malta beginning of October 1941 and was with the Royal Marines aboard H.M.S. Aurora. We were with our sister ship the 'Penelope', sunk later by U-boat off Anzio, and the two big destroyers 'Lively' and 'Lance' (both sunk). These 4 ships formed Force 'K', and for the first three Saturdays we went out at night after Italian convoys and returned unsuccessfully on Sundays. The third Saturday night was a different story, however. We sailed in a hurry, in fact, some men were still ashore and the captain of 'Penelope' went aboard in a launch just as his ship was going through the boom [the anti-submarine and torpedo net laid across the mouth of the harbour]. We sailed until about one a.m. and were on the point of turning back empty-handed when one of our bridge look-outs spotted ships – two Italian convoys on the point of joining together. We crept round to silhouette them against the moon and opened fire at 4,000 yards. From then on until 2.30 a.m. it was like a shooting gallery. We sank 10 merchant ships, 3 destroyers, and left another destroyer burning, which one of our submarines polished off next day. Arrival back in Malta was pretty exciting because those Maltese knew just about before anyone that we had been in a successful action, and they used to line the front and all viewpoints waving and cheering. . . . [Later, on a patrol off Tripoli, his ship ran into a minefield.] We ourselves in 'Aurora' hit a mine with our port paravane which exploded and blew a huge hole in the bottom of the ship. We struggled back to Malta and drydock at about 4 knots and with a 40 degree list, so Christmas Day saw us in dock. . . . The Russian front was dead for the winter and the German air force withdrew large numbers of its Stukas and Junkers 88 and fighters from there and based them in Sicily, so from then on until we left early in April 1942 they never left that dockyard alone. The place was like a battlefield, and in those 4½ months we had nearly 540 air-raid warnings. My own action station was on the Royal Marine twin 4-inch gun, and I just about saw all that happened. I rarely talk about it now, of course, but in my opinion some things you *never* forget. We were one of the only ships to have to fire and join in the barrage in dry-dock – the whistle of bombs and the thunder of the explosions, and the dust across Valetta, Sliema, Floriana, and Corradino, it was absolutely hell itself and I often think our lucky stars must have been shining as we had bombs all round the dock-caissons. . . . One day I had to go for dental treatment ashore and the dentist had just put the needle in my mouth to freeze my jaw when the siren went. We got down to the shelter, gunfire, thunder of bombs, dust and terrific concussion from a close one. What do you know? – no dental surgery. Bomb in the courtyard outside and the building wrecked, so that tooth was another 3 months till I got it taken out in England. . . ."

Every major episode in the war might have provoked a myriad such letters reflecting the madness of war and the courage of man. The Mediterranean had never in its entire history been shaken by such an earthquake, and Poseidon – as if remembering his other ancient duties – later stirred up Mount Vesuvius into a major eruption, shortly after the Allied landings in Naples in 1944. A classic *pino* plume opened above the mountain, in whose ashy umbrella static lightning flickered and thunder rolled. It was more impressive even than the man-made violence of the war. At the mountain's feet, the bombed and typhus-ridden city of Naples steamed and sweltered – a far call from the gracious city of Neapolis which had once gleamed like a pearl on the brow of this bay.

Throughout these years the British were admirably served at sea by one of their finest sailors since Nelson, Admiral Andrew Browne Cunningham. It was he who, early in the war, in a successful night

The Gallipoli campaign: landing at Suvla Bay, 1915,
by Norman Wilkinson

TWO WORLD WARS

The convoy system: the tanker *Ohio* in a Malta convoy, 1942,
by Norman Wilkinson

The Mediterranean as a twentieth-century playground: a cruise ship anchored off Patmos

engagement off the southern tip of Greece (the Battle of Cape Matapan) had sunk three Italian heavy cruisers with no loss to his own side. Later, it was he who, with a badly depleted fleet, still managed from his base in Alexandria to keep the sea-lanes open, despite all that the enemy air force and submarines did to close them. Here, in his own words, from *A Sailor's Odyssey*, is how it all ended: "On September 11th [1943], I flew into Malta to meet the Italian Admiral da Zara, in charge of the Taranto detachment, to give him instructions for the disarmament and the disposal of the Italian fleet. Malta was *en fête*, with the people wild with jubilation and many of the streets draped in flags. Among others, the parish priest of shattered Senglea, contiguous to the dockyard and therefore one of the main targets for air attacks, announced the Italian surrender from his pulpit. He was the undaunted man who calmly walked up and down the main street reciting his office during the worst air raids to give courage and comfort to his people. . . . That day, September 11th, I made a signal to the Admiralty: 'Be pleased to inform their Lordships that the Italian Battle fleet now lies at anchor under the guns of the fortress of Malta.' "

Although the war in Europe was to drag on for many months, the battle was over as far as the Mediterranean theatre was concerned. The shattered cities of North Africa, the ruined villages of Greece and Crete, of Sicily and Italy, the tortured lands through which the tanks had passed, all testified to a devastation without parallel. From one end of the sea to the other, at all the approaches to the land, the waters were as dense with mines as with their native sea-urchins. Rusting off every cape and headland, and disintegrating fathoms deep beneath the blue acres of the sea, lay millions of tons of merchant and naval shipping, together with the whitening bones of men from almost every race under the sun. On May 8, 1945, the Germans surrendered uncon- ditionally. Somewhere, in that eternal Rome which transcends the noisy city apparent to the eye, the doors creaked close; concealing the bearded double face of Janus. The sea was at peace again.

THIRTEEN

Time and the Ocean

The sails are almost gone now from the sea. Even off the coast of western Sicily there are few to be seen, except for those of visiting yachtsmen who are wandering round the island (paying a Mafia-sponsored night watchman in harbour, if they are wise) and exploring the ruined temples that are adjacent to the shore. Between Trapani and Marsala, those former haunts of the Phoenicians, the coastal traders and fishing boats chug out under their heavy diesel engines, no longer confined to the ancient sailing season of May to September. Only in the west and the east of the Mediterranean does one find the sail being used commercially. A few Spanish schooners still carry canvas, though it is no more than auxiliary to their engine. In the Aegean, some of the caiques do indeed use their sails to drive between one island and another whenever the meltemi blow.

Within two decades of the devastation of war, the sea, the islands, and the adjacent coastlines show a welcome return of prosperity. Although parts of North Africa, Spain, Sicily, southern Italy, Greece, and Turkey are still numbered among the economically depressed areas of the world, much of the Mediterranean is enjoying a higher standard of living than it has ever known before. Cities and ports that were bombed, shelled, and smouldering in the 1940s have risen from their ashes to glitter with new buildings; between which the new roads are clogged with millions of motor cars. Unfortunately, most of the modern flats, hotels, and villas are often of that international substandard architecture that might well be called "Cosmo-Cola". New cargo vessels and cruise liners cleave the old trade routes, and the strait where Scylla and Charybdis made the heroes pale with fear is breached hourly by the thunder of high-speed hydrofoil craft, carrying passengers and cargo between Sicily and Italy.

Even the remote Aegadian Islands, whose insignificance and isolation make them symbolic of so many other islands and little-known coastal areas of the sea, are linked by hydrofoils cutting a white swathe across the strait where Odysseus once mocked the blinded Polyphemus. On Favignana there are taxis, an aqualung sports club, and, on Faraglione Point – to accommodate the summer visitors who have been so largely responsible for the revived prosperity of this sea – there stands a modern hotel. At night, in the cafés which less than twenty years ago were lit by oil lamps, brown faces are illuminated by the sepulchral glow of the television screen as they watch the doings of that curious world beyond the water. Motor scooters buzz round the island's miniature road system, driving out of their way with impatient horns the shaggy goats and sheep. Yet still the fishermen are preparing the tunny nets in the old way, and making cane lobster-pots and fish-traps in the dusty stretches around the harbour walls.

Marettimo broods in something like its antique isolation, although even here the ferry calls regularly at the small pier run out from an inhospitable beach. In rock-cut tombs on the sacred mountain, funerary urns guard the remains of Phoenician mariners who failed to reach the tin-mines in the West. At nightfall, the sun dips into a horizon that is usually void of traffic. There is little to indicate that anything has changed since Hannibal's father, Hasdrubal, founded New Carthage, 680 miles due west of here, in 243 B.C. The mountain keeps many of its secrets. Secretive, too, is the dialect of the islanders, and almost incomprehensible to a visiting northern Italian.

Little has changed at Levanzo, except that a concrete quay now accommodates the hydrofoil, and that a few villas have cropped up behind the village (where holiday-makers from the North come to affront local susceptibilities with their brief bathing costumes). The secret of the painted cave has been noised abroad, and the village postmaster is often asked to act as guide for visitors with a taste for prehistoric art.

Another cave, Cyclopean-style, has been claimed as a rival to Erice's Cave of Polyphemus, and its validity has been established in the eyes of the villagers by the fact that a film company used it as such in a documentary on the voyage of Odysseus. At sunrise, when the sparse, sweet-scented scrub gleams with dew, or at moonrise, when the limestone crags shine silver, the island returns to a nameless period before Man the Boatbuilder ventured upon these waters.

"Night and silence! who is here?"

If many things have remained unchanged, the political systems of the sea have altered almost beyond recognition since the end of the Second World War. Spain remains tranquil under one of the most successful dictatorships of the twentieth century. Whatever the future course of the peninsula's history, it will be seen that General Francisco Franco, the victor of the country's bitter civil war, was one of the most astute politicians of his time. Having been helped into office by Hitler and Mussolini, he yet managed to avoid involving his country in the world war that followed. Capitalizing subsequently on American aid (for the Americans were fearful that Spain might join the Communist camp), he also enjoyed that new fruit of the Mediterranean, international tourism. Spain's sunshine, wine, long sand beaches, historical backwardness, and relatively cheap prices invited millions of visitors a year from the newly economically enfranchised citizens of Britain, the Scandinavian countries, Germany, and France. General Franco had been the third potential partner in the Axis; he had carefully avoided many promising offers made to him by the Axis; and he had watched from the sidelines as the two other dictators went down in flames and desolation. Whatever he has failed to do in ameliorating the condition of his people, he still deserves well of his country.

In North Africa the situation has changed beyond all measure. British and French power was almost completely broken by the 1960s, for the French lost all real influence after their ignominious defeat during the Second World War, while the British were so economically crippled in achieving victory that they were now a second-rate power. Britain, having given independence to the subcontinent of India, no longer had any use for the garrison stations that had been so important during the nineteenth and early twentieth centuries. Once India was gone, of what interest to this northern island were fleet bases in the Mediterranean? Quite apart from this, as had happened with so many other dominant powers, the British in the course of the recent exhausting struggle had lost their will to power.

Their attitude at the end of the Second World War is summed up by Sir Osbert Sitwell in *Laughter in the Next Room*. Describing the emotional climate at that time, he writes: "At this hour, in every Western country, national character, though in process of dissolution, became for the instant emphasized. The English celebrated the world's end with neither a bang nor a whimper, but with their old traditional booby trap, a general election. Nevertheless, a change in them was evident. Their former vigour and robustness had succumbed before a cult of timid, pallid suffering, alternating with paltry rewards. Issuing victorious from a long war waged with stubborn heroism by the whole people, they now dingily begged, out of an Empire which their buccaneering forefathers had smashed entire nations to build, salvaging it from the ensuing chaos, only to retain a few dehydrated or reconstituted eggs, a once-a-week dusting of tea, and a banana for the children. . . ." Clear or prophetic sight became, in the new code, a treachery to patriotism. A novel democratic folly possessed the educated, making them praise virtues that did not exist: the very faces of the former rulers had altered, softened, lost force, while a creeping wave of envy about small things seeped into the homes of the people. ("She has a quarter of an ounce of marge more than I have; I don't mind how little I have, but no one must have more!") Britain now joined Scandinavia in the ranks of the socialist countries. The ancient vigour of these Nordic peoples was now transmitted into a care and consideration for their own – which had never been very evident when they were young and aggressive nations. Their wave, which had once beat upon these ancient shores, was spent. Other waves would take its place.

The weakness of the old colonial powers induced, inevitably, a rising tide of nationalism. The Arab states, many of which were now rich through oil, were no longer willing to submit to the old process of "divide and rule" which both Britain and France had practised in the Near East. Egypt was taken over by a military dictatorship and the Suez Canal was nationalized. After a fatal and frustrated intervention by Britain and France in the affairs of Egypt in 1956, the influence of these two countries declined even further. Everything that Disraeli and others had schemed and fought for was lost almost overnight. Symbolically, the statue of Ferdinand de Lesseps at Port Said was hurled to the ground by an Egyptian mob. Cyprus, after a bloody struggle with the British, broke away and achieved an independence that was almost immediately bedevilled by a civil war between its Greek and Turkish citizens. This beautiful island, with its long beaches, its resin-scented mountains, its fertile plains and gracious old cities, seems to have been destined by implacable fate to a condition always either miserable or obscure.

The whole of the North African coastline had split into independent Moslem states by 1960; states which, though often at variance with one another, were united in their dislike of their former masters. Algeria, which the French had thought tamed and pacified in the years preceding the war, broke away after a murderous conflict that was only resolved by the statesmanlike decision of the French President, Charles de Gaulle, to leave the country. With Morocco, Algeria, Tunisia, Libya, and Egypt independent Moslem states, there was much talk of a revival of Pan-Arabism. It seemed just possible that the current in this sea was about to reverse itself once again; and that the influence of the Arabs, which had been negligible since the conquest of their countries by the Turks, might once again make itself felt on the Mediterranean world.

The most significant event of this post-war period was the establishment of the new state of Israel on May 14, 1948. The British, whose will had become feeble and whose hand nerveless in these years, relinquished their mandate, and – stemming from Lord Balfour's declaration made thirty-one years previously – the Jews had a homeland for the first time since the Diaspora. In the years that followed, their hold upon it was maintained only by successive wars against the surrounding Arab states, a climax of which was reached in June 1967 when they soundly defeated the Egyptians in a lightning campaign that was almost without parallel even in the much-embattled history of this part of the Mediterranean.

On the very day that this war broke out, the last British Commander-in-Chief of the Mediterranean left Malta. The long involvement of Britain in the affairs of the Mediterranean was at an end. With the decline of her power and influence throughout the world, with the loss – whether by *force majeure* or by deliberate relinquishment – of all her colonies, the British joined the long list of nations which at one time or another had dominated this sea. They did have one major claim upon its history, however. For a century they had imposed upon it, by the weight of their naval and financial power, a peace such as it had not known since the days of the Roman Empire.

The future of the new nation of Israel, despite its successes against the Arabs, still remained very much in the balance. The Arabs, although much at variance with one another, were united in their detestation of Israel. Furthermore, they were far from being little more than poor and backward nomads, as so many of them had been during their centuries of Ottoman rule. Because of their oil revenues, a number of them had become extremely wealthy; and (always allowing for the extortion and chicanery endemic in the East) a certain amount of this wealth had been channelled into medical and educational improvements. These would one day lift their peoples above the primitive and illiterate level which was all that they had hitherto known.

It would be fair to say that the "Six-Day War", as the 1967 Arab–Israeli conflict became known (for this was all the time it took for the Jews to drive the Egyptians back to the Suez Canal), was destined to have a greater impact upon Mediterranean history than even the Second World War. It led to two startling – and at the time unforeseen – events; the long-term closure of the Suez Canal; and the entry of Russia as a major naval power into the area. In both world wars Britain had closed the canal to enemy vessels, and had exercised a close control over such neutrals as sought to use it, but it had never before been completely blocked as it now was by the Egyptians. They refused to reopen it until the Israelis withdrew to their former boundaries. But, since the latter were unwilling to give up what they had gained without an assurance of territorial recognition, it seemed likely that the canal would remain closed for many years. Egypt thus deprived itself of one of its most important sources of revenue – a loss that could only be sustained because some of Egypt's oil-rich neighbours were, temporarily, prepared to make good the deficit. The closure of the Suez Canal was a bad blow to the whole Mediterranean, since it once again became an appendix to the trade of the world, and no longer a main artery.

The oil-tanker owners of the world, incensed at this second closure (the first had been during the Anglo-French intervention in Egypt in 1956), were determined not to be held to ransom any more, and began the construction of immense "super tankers". These could take hundreds of thousands of gallons of crude oil direct from the Persian Gulf round the Cape of Good Hope to Europe and America. Since these vessels were much too large for the canal in any case, it was doubtful

whether, even were it reopened, it would ever regain anything approaching its former importance. This was economically distressing
for many of the ports and dockyards of the Mediterranean, which had
relied for a considerable part of their income upon the repair and
maintenance of the "passing-through" traffic. Although independent
India was now of no immediate concern to the British, what they had
long feared had finally happened – a hostile power lay across this shipping route to the East. But the new tankers and the increased speed and
greater carrying capacity of modern merchant ships meant that the
disruption of world trade was far less than might have been expected.
The irresponsibility of the Egyptians and the insecure state of the whole
area meant moreover that shipowners came to the conclusion, whatever
might happen in the future, that they would organize their trading as if
the Suez Canal no longer existed. In this respect, then, the sea returned to
its *status quo* before De Lesseps achieved his dream.

The entry of the Russian fleet into the Mediterranean began almost
immediately after the Arab–Israeli war of 1967. Russian interest in the
area was nothing new in itself. As long ago as the seventeenth century,
Peter the Great announced, "I am not looking for land, I am looking
for water." Now that the British had all but vanished from the sea, the
dominant naval power was that of the United States, and it was their
supremacy that the Russians set out to challenge. At the same time,
since they were actively intriguing in the affairs of the Near East
(underwriting the Egyptians, for instance, against the American-
sponsored Israelis), they needed bases for their activities. The condition
of the eastern basin of the sea, therefore, in the second half of the
twentieth century, was as uneasy as it had ever been. Two great powers
were playing the usual dangerous game upon its chequered waters.

While the warships and submarines spied upon one another, or
conducted their practice war-games out of sight of the land, the inhabitants of the coasts were undergoing a type of invasion quite different
from any in their long history. Whereas, in the inter-war period,
certain favoured areas had witnessed the annual visitation of rich
aristocrats or prosperous middle-class visitors from foreign countries,
the new age of cheap air travel brought mass tourism to almost every
corner of the sea. From the coastline of Spain to Sardinia, Sicily, Crete,
and Cyprus, even to the remote Greek islands like Mykonos, there

spread a summer wave of millions of visitors. No longer "travellers", as they had once been known, they were designated "tourists" – to indicate that it was no more than a brief tour, or holiday, that they were making in these southern lands. Spain, for instance, received well over a million tourists annually from Britain alone, and tourism rapidly became a major asset to the Spanish economy. France, Italy, and Greece benefited equally from the spending power of these holiday-making workers from industrial northern Europe and the United States. Prominent among the sun-seekers were the inhabitants of West Germany. They had lost the war, but – economically, at least – had won the peace. They now found, somewhat to their surprise, that they could occupy the Mediterranean without having to fight for it; and villas bearing remote German names blossomed along the coasts of Italy and Greece.

The influence of mass tourism upon the pattern of life in the inland sea was considerable. Although the money brought a new prosperity to many hitherto depressed areas, the touch of Midas was not without its usual contagion. Customs, manners, and mores which had survived intact over the centuries, furnishing the fabric of many an island or country life, tended to wither under the impact of these new visitors. Their holiday mood, coupled with the morals of the so-called "permissive" societies, often led them into a pattern of behaviour which they themselves would not have tolerated in their own home towns. (A fisherman in Rhodes, opening a platinum cigarette case, remarked: "I go fishing no more in the summer, now that all these rich Swedish ladies are around!" In Sicily, the slang description for a woman of loose morals is *una Inglesa*.) Jet planes, newspapers, television, juke-boxes, and transistor radios changed old patterns of life almost as much as the impact of a conquering race or the raids of pirates had done in the past. The sea was rapidly becoming internationalized; in the process, it was losing much of its individuality.

The North African countries remained, as yet, little affected by the impact of tourism, for their political instability coupled with their anti-Europeanism, stemming from their colonial pasts, made them unattractive to foreign visitors. Alexandria, to take but one instance, which during the years of British rule in Egypt had become once again one of the most cosmopolitan and stimulating cities in the sea, had declined – as it had done previously under the Arabs and the Turks – into a shabby port where the bones of ancient poverty showed only too clearly through the skin of modernity. In its harbour, in place of the British or French fleets, the Russian ships turned idly at their buoys. The new protecting power was in the process of finding out that he who meddles in the affairs of Egypt and the Near East inevitably burns his fingers. At the other end of the sea, Algiers, once so prosperous through its piracy, and then prosperous again through its relationship with France, slumbered in dusty dejection – independent but intransigent. Many of the "emergent nations", as the new states were called, were in fact *submerging* nations. Only financial handouts or favourably rigged trade agreements from their former masters prevented many of them from collapsing into anarchy – or into the bearlike embrace of the Russians. The latter sought them not out of love, nor even out of simple acquisitiveness, but because they might be useful for the encirclement of Europe.

At the gateway of the sea, Gibraltar alone remained faithful to Britain. The inhabitants of the Rock had no wish to cast in their lot with the Spaniards, for they could clearly see that they enjoyed a far higher standard of living than did their next-door neighbours. The ageing Spanish dictator, General Franco, cajoled and bribed, and finally brought harsh economic pressure to bear upon the Gibraltarians, but they remained reluctant to yield either their prosperity or their liberty. Britain had, indeed, no longer any real interest, other than emotional, in her old colony; but justice compelled the British to support Gibraltar in her demands. Meanwhile, at the headquarters of the United Nations in New York, Britain was urged by numerous emergent nations to restore the Gibraltarians to a union with Spain – an idea that the inhabitants of the Rock had firmly rejected. Thus were perpetuated in the second half of the twentieth century stupidities similar to those which had characterized the League of Nations. Even Cleon of Athens might have smiled wryly at the kind of democratic forum that gave the minute independent state of Malta (population 330,000) an equal vote with Italy, Spain, or France.

> Time, and the ocean, and some fostering star,
> In high cabal have made us what we are.

These words of the Victorian poet William Watson might well have applied to the inhabitants of the Mediterranean zone. Eternal conflict had shaped them, and had patterned their fiery spirits; as well as inducing that fatalism, or sense of resignation, which often provoked the irritation of visitors from other lands. It was as if they had learned over the long tumult of the centuries that, whatever happened, the wheel would always turn again. "The thing that hath been, it is that which shall be; and that which is done is that which shall be done: and there is no new thing under the sun."

As T. S. Eliot wrote, echoing a shadowy host of Mediterranean poets from the past:

> Phlebas the Phoenician, a fortnight dead,
> Forgot the cry of gulls, and the deep sea swell
> And the profit and loss.
>   A current under sea
> Picked his bones in whispers. As he rose and fell
> He passed the stages of his age and youth
> Entering the whirlpool.
>   Gentile or Jew
> O you who turn the wheel and look to windward,
> Consider Phlebas, who was once handsome and tall as you.

No one can forecast the future; the present is unreadable because it is still being written; only the past, within the limits of our information, is knowable. Even when dealing with the past, one intuition is sometimes worth a hundred facts. As Keats wrote, "The Imagination may be compared to Adam's dream – he awoke and found it truth." The X-ray of imagination can still occasionally reveal, through the centuries of "overpainting", and the millennia of old varnish, and the hands of so many indifferent restorers, something of the Mediterranean as once it was. The real difficulty is that there have been many masterpieces here; not just one. Baroque is laid over classic, Christian themes upon pagan, philosophical subjects over erotic, and massive battle scenes over delicate pastoral miniatures. But as well as the successes, there have been many failures. Indifferent painters have daubed over works that one would long to see, but it is no longer possible to decipher them.

Occasionally the sea and the lands around it do reveal themselves. It is easiest perhaps to read them, when alone and aboard a sailing boat, for the silence that is in the wind and the wave makes its own contribution towards a heightened sensibility. One becomes then like a medium who has achieved the desired suspension of body-awareness, and is tuned in to a wave-length that can never normally be heard above the roar or rumour of the world. A face perhaps, the fragment of an empire, a drowned ship, or the aspect of an island in its youth – these swim to the surface. They move there like golden carp, instinct with life, visible down to the smallest gleaming scale – until suddenly a wind or a wave stirs the pool, and all becomes opaque again. At such a moment, if one listens carefully, it is possible to hear the voice of this sea. On the long sand beaches of North Africa, in abandoned and forgotten coves of the Adriatic, against the ruins of ancient cities, or in idle inlets where pines scent the air, all the waves of the sea are saying Yes.

Bibliography

Admiralty Pilot (Mediterranean), Volumes I–IV. London, Her Majesty's Stationery Office, 1953.

Aeschylus, *The Persians*. Quoted passage translated by Ernle Bradford.

Arbman, Holger, *The Vikings*. New York, Frederick A. Praeger, 1961.

Aristophanes, *Knights*, translated by John Hookham Frere. London, 1840.

Arnold, Matthew, *The Portable Matthew Arnold*. New York, The Viking Press, 1949.

Arrian, *The Life of Alexander the Great*, translated by Aubrey de Sélincourt. Harmondsworth, Middlesex, Penguin Books, 1958.

Barrow, R. H., *The Romans*. London, Cassell, 1949.

Bathe, B. W., *Ship Models*. London, Her Majesty's Stationery Office (Science Museum Booklet), 1963.

Baynes, N. H., and Moss, H. St. L. B., *Byzantium*. Oxford, Clarendon Press (paperback edition), 1961.

Blakeney, E. H., *A Smaller Classical Dictionary*. London, J. M. Dent (Everyman's Library), 1916.

Blouet, Brian, *The Story of Malta*. London, Faber & Faber, 1967.

Boardman, John, *The Greeks Overseas*. Harmondsworth, Middlesex, Penguin Books, 1964.

Bradford, Ernle, *Companion Guide to the Greek Islands*. London, Collins, 1963.

———— *The Great Siege*. New York, Harcourt, Brace & World, 1961.

———— *The Journeying Moon*. London, Jarrolds, 1958.

———— *The Sultan's Admiral*. New York, Harcourt, Brace & World, 1968.

———— *Ulysses Found*. New York, Harcourt, Brace & World, 1963.

———— *The Wind Commands Me*. New York, Harcourt, Brace & World, 1965.

———— *A Wind from the North*. New York, Harcourt, Brace & World, 1960.

Browning, Robert, *The Ring and the Book*. New York, W. W. Norton (The Norton Library), 1961.

Burn, A. R., *Alexander the Great and the Hellenistic Empire*. London, Hodder & Stoughton for English Universities Press, 1947.

———— *History of Greece*. Harmondsworth, Middlesex, Penguin Books, 1966.

———— *Persia and the Greeks*. New York, St. Martin's Press, 1962.

Byron, Lord, *Selected Poetry*. New York, Random House (Modern Library), 1954.

The Cambridge Ancient History. London, Cambridge University Press, 1923–1939.

The Cambridge Medieval History. London, Cambridge University Press, 1911–1936.

The Cambridge Modern History. London, Cambridge University Press, 1934.

Camoens, Luis de, *Lusiads,* translated by William Julius Mickle. London, 1775.

Cassar, Paul, *Medical History of Malta.* London, Wellcome Historical Medical Library, 1964.

Cavafy, C. P., "The God Abandons Antony," translated by George Valassopoulo, in E. M. Forster, *Alexandria.* New York, Doubleday (Anchor Books), 1961.

Cavaliero, R., *The Last of the Crusaders.* London, Hollis and Carter, 1960.

Cheyne, Thomas K. (editor), *Encyclopedia Biblica.* London, A. and C. Black, 1899–1903.

Childe, Gordon, *What Happened in History.* Harmondsworth, Middlesex, Penguin Books, 1942.

Connolly, Cyril, *The Rock Pool.* New York, Charles Scribner's, 1936.

Cunningham of Hyndhope, Viscount, *A Sailor's Odyssey.* New York, E. P. Dutton, 1951.

Currey, Edward Hamilton, *Sea Wolves of the Mediterranean.* London, 1910.

Demosthenes, *The Olynthiacs,* Book III. Quoted passage translated by Ernle Bradford.

Dickinson, G. Lowes, *The Greek View of Life.* New York, Collier, 1961.

Douglas, Norman, *Old Calabria.* New York, Dodd Mead, 1928.

Drinkwater, John, *A History of the Late Siege of Gibraltar,* London, 1785.

Eliot, Sir Charles, *Turkey in Europe.* New York, Barnes & Noble, 1965 (first published in 1900).

Eliot, T. S., "The Waste Land" in *Collected Poems 1909–1962.* New York, Harcourt, Brace & World, 1963.

Encyclopaedia Britannica, eleventh and fourteenth editions.

Evans, J. D., *Malta.* New York, Frederick A. Praeger, 1959.

Field, H. M., *Gibraltar.* New York, Charles Scribner's, 1889.

Finley, M. I., *The Ancient Greeks.* Harmondsworth, Middlesex, Penguin Books, 1963.

Fisher, H. A. L., *A History of Europe.* Boston, Houghton Mifflin, 1935.

Flaubert, Gustave, *Salammbô.* London, J. M. Dent (Everyman's Library), 1931.

Forster, E. M., *Alexandria.* New York, Doubleday (Anchor Books), 1961.

Frazer, Sir James, *The Golden Bough.* New York, Macmillan, 1922.

Freeman, Edward A., *The History and Conquests of the Saracens.* London, Macmillan, 1877.

Gardiner, Dorothy, *The Great Betrayal.* New York, Doubleday, 1949.

Gibbon, Edward, *Decline and Fall of the Roman Empire.* London, J. M. Dent (Everyman's Library), 1910.

Glubb, Sir John, *The Course of Empire: The Arabs and Their Successors.* London, Hodder & Stoughton, 1965.

—— *The Empire of the Arabs.* London, Hodder & Stoughton, 1963.

—— *The Great Arab Conquests.* London, Hodder & Stoughton, 1963.

Gordon, R. K., *Anglo-Saxon Poetry.* London, J. M. Dent (Everyman's Library), 1926.

Grant, Michael, *Ancient History.* London, Methuen, 1952.

Graves, Robert, *Collected Poems.* New York, Doubleday, 1955.

Gravière, Jurien de la, *Origins of the Modern Navy.* Quoted passage translated by Ernle Bradford.

Harden, Donald, *The Phoenicians.* New York, Frederick A. Praeger, 1962.

Hemingway, Ernest, *By-Line.* New York, Charles Scribner's, 1967.

Herodotus, *The Histories*, translated by Aubrey de Sélincourt. Harmondsworth, Middlesex, Penguin Books, 1954.

Hollingdale, R. J., *Nietzsche: The Man and His Philosophy.* Baton Rouge, Louisiana State University Press, 1965.

Holme, T. & B., and Ghirardelli, B., *Sardinia.* London, Jonathan Cape, 1967.

Homer, *The Odyssey*, translated by E. V. Rieu. Harmondsworth, Middlesex, Penguin Books, 1946.

Housman, A. E., *Collected Poems.* New York, Holt, Rinehart & Winston, 1965.

Hughes, Quentin, *Fortress.* London, Lund Humphries, 1969.

"Jack Nasty-Face," *Nautical Economy, or Forecastle Recollections of Events during the last War. Dedicated to the Tars of Old England by a Sailor, politely called by the officers of the Navy Jack Nasty-Face.* London, 1815 (?).

Juvenal, *Sixteen Satires*, translated by Peter Green. Harmondsworth, Middlesex, Penguin Books, 1967.

Keats, John, *The Selected Poetry of Keats.* New York, The New American Library (Signet Classics), 1966.

The Koran, various translations.

Lampedusa, Guiseppe di, *The Leopard.* New York, Pantheon Books, 1960.

Lane-Poole, Stanley, *The Story of the Barbary Corsairs.* New York, G. P. Putnam's, 1890.

Lawrence, D. H., *Etruscan Places.* New York, The Viking Press (Compass Books), 1957.

Lawrence, T. E., *Seven Pillars of Wisdom.* Harmondsworth, Middlesex, Penguin Books, 1962.

Lewis, Michael, *The Navy of Britain.* London, George Allen & Unwin, 1948.

Lieder, P. R., Lovett, R. M., and Root, R. K., *British Poetry and Prose.* Boston, Houghton Mifflin, 1950.

Lucan, *Pharsalia.* Quoted passage translated by Ernle Bradford.

Luke, Sir Harry, *Malta.* London, George G. Harrap, 1949.

McGuffie, T. H., *The Siege of Gibraltar.* London, Batsford, 1965.

Macintyre, Donald, *The Battle for the Mediterranean*. New York, W. W. Norton, 1965.

Mahan, Captain A. T., *Influence of Sea Power upon the French Revolution and Empire*. London, Sampson Low, Marston, 1892.

Newbigin, Marion I., *The Mediterranean Lands*. London, Christophers, 1924.

Ovid, *Fasti*, Book III. Quoted passage translated by Ernle Bradford.

Parkes, James, *A History of the Jewish People*. London, Weidenfeld and Nicolson, 1962.

Pears, Sir E., *The Fall of Constantinople, Being the Story of the Fourth Crusade*. London, Longmans Green, 1885.

Petronius, *Satyricon*, translated by Jack Lindsay. London, Paul Elek, 1960.

Pliny, *Natural History*, translated by H. Rackham. Cambridge, Massachusetts, Harvard University Press (Loeb Classical Library), 1938.

—— *Works*, translated by William Melmoth. London, 1746.

Plutarch, *Lives*. New York, Random House (Modern Library), 1932.

—— *Opera Moralia*. Quoted passage translated by Ernle Bradford.

Polunin, Oleg, and Huxley, Anthony, *Flowers of the Mediterranean*. Boston, Houghton Mifflin, 1966.

Pomponius Mela, *De Situ Orbis*. Quoted passage translated by Ernle Bradford.

Prescott, W. H., *History of the Reign of Philip II*. Boston, Phillips Sampson, 1855.

Ramsay, A. C., and Geikie, Sir Archibald, "Gibraltar", in *Quarterly Journal of the Geological Society*, London, 1878 (p. 505).

Rawson, Geoffrey (editor), *Letters from Lord Nelson*. London, Staples Press, 1949.

Rice, David Talbot, *Art of the Byzantine Era*. New York, Frederick A. Praeger, 1963.

—— (editor), *The Dark Ages*. London, Thames & Hudson, 1965.

Runciman, Sir Steven, *The Fall of Constantinople*. London, Cambridge University Press, 1965.

—— *A History of the Crusades*. London, Cambridge University Press, 1951.

Sherrard, Philip, *Constantinople*. London, Oxford University Press, 1965.

Siewert, Hummel E., *Il Mediterraneo*. Milan, 1938. Quoted passage translated by Ernle Bradford.

Singer, C. J., *et al.* (editors), *A History of Technology*, Volume I. London, Oxford University Press, 1954.

Sitwell, Sir Osbert, *Laughter in the Next Room*. Boston, Little Brown, 1948.

Smollett, Tobias, *Travels through France and Italy*. London, John Lehmann, 1949.

Smyth, Captain William Henry, *Sicily and Its Islands*. London, John Murray, 1824.

Swinburne, Algernon Charles, *Poems*. New York, Harper, 1904.

Taafe, J., *History of the Holy, Military, Sovereign Order of St. John of Jerusalem*. London, 1852.

Tacitus, *Annals*, Book III. Quoted passage translated by Ernle Bradford.

Tarn, Sir William, *Hellenistic Civilisation*. London, Edward Arnold, 1952.

Taylor, E. G. R., *The Haven-Finding Art*. London, Hollis and Carter, 1956.

Thackeray, William Makepeace, *Sketch Books: Notes of a Journey from Cornhill to Grand Cairo*. New York, Harper, 1898.

Thiel, Johannes Hendrik, *Studies on the History of Roman Sea-Power in Republican Times*. New York, Hafner, 1946.

Thucydides, *History of the Peloponnesian War*, translated by Benjamin Jowett. London, Oxford University Press.

Torr, Cecil, *Ancient Ships*. London, Cambridge University Press, 1894.

Trump, D. H., *Malta's Archaeology*. (In preparation.)

Vergil, *Aeneid*. Quoted passage translated by Ernle Bradford.

——— *Georgics*, Book I. Quoted passage translated by Ernle Bradford.

Villehardouin, Comte de, *La Conquête de Constantinople*. Quoted passage translated by Ernle Bradford.

Warner, Oliver, *Nelson's Battles*. New York, Macmillan, 1965.

Wilde, Oscar, "Theocritus", in *Selected Poems of Oscar Wilde*. London, Methuen, 1911.

Williams, Oscar (editor), *Mentor Book of Major British Poets*. New York, New American Library, 1963.

Woodhouse, C. M., *The Battle of Navarino*. London, Hodder and Stoughton, 1965.

Zahl, Paul, "Fishing in the Whirlpool of Charybdis", in *National Geographic Magazine*, Washington D.C., November 1953, pp. 579–618.

Index